# African-British Writings
# in the Eighteenth Century

**Recent Titles in**
**Contributions to the Study of World Literature**

# African-British Writings in the Eighteenth Century

## The Politics of Race and Reason

### HELENA WOODARD

Contributions to the Study of World Literature,
Number 94

**GREENWOOD PRESS**
Westport, Connecticut • London

**Library of Congress Cataloging-in-Publication Data**

Woodard, Helena, 1953–
    African-British writings in the eighteenth century : the politics
of race and reason / Helena Woodard.
        p.    cm. — (Contributions to the study of world literature,
ISSN 0738–9345 ; no. 94)
    Includes bibliographical references and index.
    ISBN 0–313–30680–X (alk. paper)
    1. English literature—African influences.   2. African literature
(English)—Black authors—History and criticism.   3. Politics and
literature—Great Britain—History—18th century.   4. English
literature—18th century—History and criticism.   5. Africans—Great
Britain—History—18th century.   6. Africans in literature.
7. Africa—In literature.   8. Blacks in literature.   9. Reason in
literature.   10. Race in literature.     I. Title.   II. Series.
PR129.A35W66      1999
820.9′358—dc21          98–6758

British Library Cataloguing in Publication Data is available.

Library of Congress Catalog Card Number: 98–6758
ISBN: 0–313–30680–X
ISSN: 0738–9345

First published in 1999

Greenwood Press, 88 Post Road West, Westport, CT 06881
An imprint of Greenwood Publishing Group, Inc.

Printed in the United States of America

The paper used in this book complies with the
Permanent Paper Standard issued by the National
Information Standards Organization (Z39.48–1984).

10 9 8 7 6 5 4 3 2

Dedicated to the memory of Lovenia Cooper Woodard
and Jeannie Woodard Shade.
*Thanks for believing.*

# Contents

# Acknowledgments

I wish to acknowledge a University Cooperative Society Subvention Grant awarded by the University Co-op at The University of Texas at Austin for the generous support of this book. I am also deeply indebted to the University for the following additional grant support: the University Research Institute Faculty Research Fellowship, the Center for African and African-American Studies Fellowship, and the Katherine Ross Richards Centennial Teaching Fellowship. The unstinting editorial support and advice of numerous colleagues have made this publication possible. I gratefully acknowledge Janice Rossen, Beth Hedrick, Dolora Wojciehowski, Bill Scheick, Ben Lindfors, Leah Marcus, Lisa Moore, Lance Bertelsen, Adam Newton, Brian Bremen, Judith Rosenberg, and James Garrison.

# Introduction

What I propose here is to examine the impact of notions of racial hierarchy, racial exclusion, and racial vulnerability and availability on
nonblacks who held, resisted, explored, or altered those notions.[1]
                                                    —Toni Morrison
                                                 *Playing in the Dark*

I begin this book with a passage from Sir Richard Steele's *The Spectator*
#215, or "The Barbados Negroes," 1710, which provides a striking example
of how the category of race can disrupt the rhetoric of Enlightenment
humanism. The passage is also ironic because it represents literature as a
tool for moral instruction. Through the voice of Mr. Spectator as eidolon,
Steele laments the contemptible treatment of enslaved blacks in the British
West Indies, though at the same time he maneuvers around the issues of
both slavery and the abuse of women:

> And what Colour of Excuse can there be for the Contempt with which
> we treat this Part of our Species; That we should not put them upon the
> common foot of Humanity, that we should only set an insignificant Fine
> upon the Man who murders them; nay, that we should, as much as in us
> lies, cut them off from the Prospects of Happiness in another World as
> well as in this, and deny them that which we look upon as the proper
> Means for attaining it?[2]

In the story to which he refers, two blacks enslaved to an Englishman
at St. Christophers fall in love with the same woman, who is also enslaved
on the plantation. Unable to resolve conflicts inherent in their love for her
and their deep friendship for one another, the enslaved pair stab the woman

to death. After much despairing and weeping over the corpse, they both commit suicide. Mr. Spectator concludes that proper education might have allowed the two friends to temper their passion with reason: "We see, in this amazing instance of Barbarity, what strange Disorders are bred in the Minds of those Men whose Passions are not regulated by Vertue, and disciplined by Reason" (340). He further allows that individuals born "in those parts of the world where wisdom and knowledge flourish" should be grateful, for they might claim essential differences from, and superiority over, those "barbarians" born in remote, non-European countries (340).

Through the *Spectator* account, murder-suicide is condemned, but slavery is displaced as an irrelevant issue through the metaphor in "what colour of excuse," which at once elides and joins the abuse of slavery and the abuse of women. Steele may well have expected that as a subtext for "The Barbados Negroes," readers would instinctively abhor slavery. Or perhaps, more typically of this time, he attempted to maintain moral integrity without offending some *Spectator* subscribers in England who (like himself) might have maintained slave plantations in the West Indies. Steele's anecdote falsely imagines that it presents race within a depoliticized humanist rhetoric. But the exclusionary discourses that it provides through intellect and education "appeal either to inherent superiority or to differences,"[3] and thus promote racism. Steele's dramatization of the literary didactic function in an imaginative fictional framework metaphorizes how certain writers in the Enlightenment[4] incorporate into theory and practice a universalist, humanist rhetoric that distorts or misrepresents the idea of race as a mitigating factor in that universality.

I am especially interested in those Enlightenment humanists who vacillated between incorporating social and historical events into didactic messages and denying the relevance of social conditions as informing such events and as being vital to spiritual and intellectual growth.[5] I refer particularly (though not exclusively), to a cluster of "canonical" writers who sought to inculcate morality in the literate populace. While noting the perils of defining humanism too narrowly, Walter Jackson Bate and Paul Fussel have long acknowledged its "collective system of values"[6] and its "uniformity" and "orthodoxy" of human nature.[7] Yet it is just such a universality that poststructuralists investigating race in a theoretical framework—Paul Gilroy, Etienne Balibar, and Howard Winant among them—have found inconsistent and exclusive.[8] The aspect of humanism that unites neoclassicists like John Dryden, Jonathan Swift, and Alexander Pope; Whig modernists like Addison and Steele; and Christian humanists like Samuel Johnson is a fervent belief in art as the postlapsarian response to disharmony.[9]

Given the aforementioned framework, Steele could cite the lack of civility and education, without ever mentioning the role and/or conditions of slavery, as the culprit in *Spectator* #215, the story described before. In

*Gulliver's Travels,* Swift could portray a race of Yahoos in a manner uncannily like that used to describe the South African Hottentot of the Cape of Good Hope in eighteenth-century travelogues, but only as a moral standard for English behavior. And waxing philosophical in the moral treatises, David Hume could equate respect and honor from child to parent with that of slave to master and proclaim both as comprising naturally inherent inclinations rather than cultivated ones.

In the chapters that follow, aspects of the Enlightenment period, circa 1660 to 1833, are explored that roughly parallel both Britain's participation in slavery and the concept of "social anthropology's historicized version of the Great Chain of Being."[10] (Though England ended the slave trade in 1807, Parliament did not outlaw slavery itself until the Emancipation Act of 1834.) Enlightenment humanists like Addison and Steele, Dryden, Swift, and Pope participated in discussions that, in effect, connected literary didacticism with issues like the Great Chain of Being, slavery, and exploratory ventures. One such example is the debate in the early phase of the Enlightenment that pitted ancients against moderns on the value of navigational discoveries like the compass and lodestone over the writings of Homer, Virgil, and other classicists. The compass and loadstone made possible the introduction of Europeans to such ethnic groups as the Khoikhoin or Hottentot. The Hottentot was the subject of an enduring but unflattering legacy in mass culture as well as in travel and other imaginative fiction. Collectively, ancients and moderns, humanists, and intellectual movers and shakers like Hume, Immanuel Kant, Voltaire, and Montesquieu span the Enlightenment and foreground the appearance of African-British writings in the late eighteenth century. In turn, African-British writings inhabit (and alter) the universalizing, rationalist, and racialist discourse[11] of the Enlightenment.

This study, therefore, has a dual purpose: it explores how the Enlightenment reasons race both through a complex, aesthetic language—typically didactic instructions about the function of literature and moral assertions about the human condition—and through concepts that obscure, displace, or absent race precisely where social practice dictates that it figures most prominently. The study further examines eighteenth-century African-British writings that uniquely underscore the mediative function of race between literature's historical role as a tool for moral instruction and certain social conditions that profoundly complicate that role.

In referencing race, I address a prevailing black/white racial paradigm in the European Enlightenment, or what Robert J. C. Young refers to as a racial difference "constructed by a fundamental binary division between black and white"[12] and underpinned by a system of hierarchies. I also refer to blacks who were primarily of African descent,[13] as they overwhelmingly reflected the British chattel slave population in the eighteenth century. In the

Enlightenment, race was not just a method of classifying humanity into categories by phenotype or like characteristics, as it was practiced by French naturalist Francois Bernier, Swedish botanist Carl Linne (Linnaeus), Swiss naturalist Charles Bonnet, Manchester physician Charles Whites, and German craniologist Johann Fredrich Blumenbach; rather, the very concept inferred differences among individuals.[14]

Literary works that diminish certain complications of race or "other" in perpetuating universalist principles extend well beyond the domain of some traditional neoclassicists, however. Additional works include abolitionist and/or sentimental writings, contemporaneous with the actual publication of African-British writings, dating from the 1770s. Indeed, eighteenth-century writers as diverse as Daniel Defoe, Laurence Sterne, Sarah Scott, and Maria Edgeworth share with Addison and Steele, Swift, and Pope a consistently problematical and ambivalent literary treatment of race or "other," particularly regarding blacks and slavery. For example, as we can see in Defoe's *Colonel Jack* (1722), Scott's *History of Sir George Ellison* (1766), and Edgeworth's "The Grateful Negro" (1802), from her *Popular Tales* (Philadelphia: C. G. Henderson, 1854), concepts like the "principle of gratitude," although they may seem to advocate the humane treatment of slaves, actually act not only as a disguise but even as a support for the owners' concern with the productive return on capital. These writers issued a moral code that prescribed a potently biased agenda, tainted by presuppositions about who or what is worthy of moral consideration.

With seminal links to historical events like the growing black presence in England, dating from the sixteenth century to Parliament's outlawing of slavery, African-British writings destabilize the rhetoric of Enlightenment humanism. By African-British writings, I mean those published works written or "related" by Africans formerly enslaved in England or the British West Indies in the late eighteenth century. The published works of James Albert Ukawsaw Gronniosaw, A *Narrative of the Most Remarkable Particulars in the Life of James Albert Ukawsaw Gronniosaw, an African Prince. Related By Himself* (1770), and Quobna Ottobah Cugoano, *Thoughts and Sentiments on the Evil of Slavery* (1787), specifically thematize inconsistencies in the most sacred of didactic spaces—where theological assertions sanction collective, universal belief systems while effectively removing blacks from certain moral equations. Ignatius Sancho's published epistolary collection, *Letters of the Late Ignatius Sancho* (1782), illustrates how even humanitarian efforts (or concepts like the principle of gratitude in antislavery writings) can inadvertently reinforce racial inferiority in the native "other" while offering itself up as the most humane solution to inequality. Olaudah Equiano's published work, *The Interesting Narrative of the Life of Olaudah Equiano, or Gustavus Vassa, the African. Written By Himself* (1789), and Mary Prince's ghost-written narrative, *The History of Mary*

*Prince* (1831), expose the constant, albeit often hidden, presence of race, gender, and hierarchy in travel and other imaginative fiction in the English literary tradition.

Collectively, these writings perform a key epistemological task, notably in the contexts of religion (Gronniosaw and Cugoano), society (Ignatius Sancho), literature (Equiano), and gender (Prince). Consequently, my exploration extends well beyond their rearticulation as biographical studies or as protest literature (which are sufficiently covered in pioneering studies by Keith Sandiford, *Measuring the Moment* (1988), and David Dabydeen and Paul Edwards, *Black Writers in Britain, 1760–1890* (1991) to show how they measure "the impact of notions of racial hierarchy, racial exclusion, and racial vulnerability and availability on *nonblacks*" (to return to my introductory quotation from Toni Morrison).

Because of its penchant for imposing order on creation and humanity, its Great Chain of Being, the eighteenth century is a pivotal period in which to explore the genealogies of rank and racial hierarchies. I point to a largely Eurocentric, interdisciplinary coalition among philosophers and scientists who proclaimed the racial inferiority of blacks to whites in order to rationalize slavery. These include the now lesser-known figures (Henry Home, Lord Kames; Sir William Petty; Samuel Estwick; Edward Long), as well as the renowned sages of the time (Hume, Kant, Voltaire, and Thomas Jefferson). However, I do not wish merely to dredge up antiquated eighteenth-century pseudo-science about racial differences, which has been long since deconstructed, though similar scientific data continually reappear in various forms. As Steele's *Spectator* #215 illustrates, the aesthetic principles that claimed to neutralize race in Enlightenment humanism were as acutely vulnerable to certain misinformation about race as the perhaps more easily assailable claims of the pseudo-scientific community. Literature may well function to instruct and entertain the masses, but the same hierarchical constructs that inform the ordering of society and the ranking of humanity ultimately inform the canonization of curriculum studies.

Chapter 1 therefore begins by examining the discursive legacy of the Chain of Being—not to be confused with Arthur O. Lovejoy's philosophical investigation or simply with pseudo-scientific racialist data—but what I regard as an Enlightenment discourse that allowed diverse writers to foreground and maintain a constancy of racial exclusion and racial hierarchy. For example, along with literary links to the Chain of Being and with measurable influence on interdisciplinary writers also connected with the Chain's legacy—Estwick, Long, Kant, Jefferson, and Voltaire among them— Alexander Pope perhaps best represents such a discourse. In his magnum opus, *Essay on Man* (1733–1734), for example, Pope argues for the universal, unbiased ranking of humanity but advocates a concept that has far-reaching racial implications. And in "Windsor Forest" (1713), when Pope

pronounces England's slavery and colonialist Treaty of Utrecht as the
civilizing force for a disorderly world, he operates around the unstable
boundaries where literary didacticism intersects with racial hierarchies and
the ordering of society. Because Pope's ideas provide a crucial historical
context both to Enlightenment humanism and to the Chain's discursive
legacy, he is the dominant focus of chapter 1. As Robert Markley observes,
"I suspect, Pope—as poet, critic, translator of Homer, and editor of Shakespeare—embodies the values we have been taught to associate with the study
of literature."[15]

Although Pope critically upholds the Chain's discursive center in the
time-honored tradition of Enlightenment humanism, other eighteenth-century
writers who address race and slavery in some ethical context—from Defoe,
Addison and Steele, and Swift to Sterne, Scott, and Edgeworth—also produce and maintain this legacy of racial hierarchy and racial exclusion. As
Paul Fussel observes, humanism has long employed a "'vertical' cast of
mind [that] seems impelled to order everything in rank, whether the elements of animated nature which it delights to contemplate as a vertical scale
of being, or the social stations in a society, or the various studies in a
curriculum."[16] I am especially interested in the enduring capacity of a
discourse that—whether marked by humanism or humanitarianism, whether
fashioned in the political economy of slavery or through religious conviction—systematically alters and transforms itself in matters of race.

The past and present implications of such a discourse—a literary whiteness—can best be ascertained from within its excluded ranks.[17] Therefore,
in subsequent chapters the alternative perspectives on race that African-
British writings provide, are contextualized with those exclusionary discourses that certain English writings produce. For example, in published
works that appeared seventeen years apart, James Ukawsaw Gronniosaw and
Ottobah Cugoano expose similar exclusionary practices among some theologians who represented the subordination of blacks as an element of natural
order, regardless of their Christian status. In a ghost written narrative,
Gronniosaw relates his struggle to maintain Christian faith and personal
dignity in the face of enslavement, poverty, and betrayal. Those personal
struggles connect with inconsistencies in ecclesiastical and common-law
discourse on the legality of slavery, thus binding the private and the public
arenas. What Gronniosaw's life experiences say about social practice,
Cugoano's philosophical essay reveals about social policy, particularly in the
religious community.[18] For example, citing gross misinterpretations of the
Book of Genesis, Cugoano refutes the Hamitic hypothesis, i.e., the concept
crediting the accursed son of Noah with darkening the faces of humankind.
Though it was publicly dismissed by abolitionist clergy like Thomas Clarkson, the Hamitic hypothesis remained a widely disseminated idea that sanctioned racial hierarchies for some in both the religious establishment and in

social practice. Through contrasting contemplative and polemical styles, respectively, both Gronniosaw and Cugoano deconstruct the very moral foundations of Judeo-Christian doctrine.

In chapter 3, a reading of Ignatius Sancho's *Letters* shows how slaves' capacity for gratitude is exhibited in order to make slavery more efficient, not to put an end to it. But any slaves who do not exhibit the "principle of gratitude" common to all humanity of course prove themselves inhuman and thus worthy of the lowest place on the Chain of Being. The principle of gratitude historicizes a fictional benevolence, extending from Defoe's *Colonel Jack* to Scott's *History of Sir George Ellison* and Edgeworth's "The Grateful Negro."[19] But even in the so-called age of sentimentality, where sensibility in literary representation would seem to lead logically to an anti-slavery position, we find no formulation of it that urges any kind of action. In Sterne's *Tristram Shandy*, for instance, sensibility certainly features, and we can even find a provisional anti-slavery passage, but its didacticism shields inaction and calls the reader's attention and admiration to an inert benevolence.

In chapter 4, I historicize Olaudah Equiano's entry into a colonial discursive arena that projects negative images of blacks and that demonstrates how racial hierarchies function repetitively as a literary trope, especially in travel and other imaginative fiction. Consider the indelible image of blacks portrayed through the South-African Hottentot in seventeenth-century travelogues by William Dampier (*A New Voyage Round the World*, 1697), Sir Thomas Herbert ("Description of the Cape of Good Hope in Aethiopia," 1634), and John Ovington (*A Voyage to Surat in the Year 1689*) that influences readers' conceptions about third-world indigenous cultural groups. In popular culture these images become transformative discourse in fiction by writers such as Defoe (*Robinson Crusoe*, 1719), Aphra Behn (*Oroonoko*, 1688), Addison and Steele ("Inkle and Yarico," in *The Spectator* #11), and Swift (*Gulliver's Travels*, 1726). When Swift transfers the Yahoo (the Hottentot equivalent to racial degeneracy) to a universal symbol of human degradation in order to satirize certain behaviors in English society, he fulfills an essential moral objective that is part of a humanist philosophy. A West-African Ibo who published his narrative in a European literary market, Equiano destabilizes Enlightenment ideas about race, literacy, and morality and exposes his own perplexed position as an African within a hierarchical space.

Although my examinations of works by Gronniosaw, Cugoano, Sancho, and Equiano expose the displacement of race in the Enlightenment (e.g., didacticism, humanism, general truths) and social practice, my analysis of the work of Mary Prince further reveals similar displacements in the context of gender. Scholarship about eighteenth- and nineteenth-century pseudo-science tends to mask an all-too-common practice that overlooks the social and cultural space that women of color occupied in racial studies.[20] In other words, studies that linked race to gender have typically marginalized the black female or omitted her altogether from racial consideration, thereby making race and gender mutually exclusive. Prince's narrative shows how moral perceptions and expectations about women as individuals and as artists cohere around both race and gender.

Until recently, the limited amount of scholarship on Gronniosaw, Sancho, Cugoano, Equiano, and Prince typically tended to legitimize them by placing them within Western literary traditions. But these and other literary publications by blacks in England actually uncovered an elusive racialist presence in Western literary tradition. The African-British writer does not provide, however, by some specific or willed design, a corrective reading to English and other European texts on the subject of race and reason. Rather, the dialectic between the conditions of production for African-British writings (to prove the authors' literacy, but not the literary quality of their works) and literary and racial practices among some Enlightenment humanists poses a challenge to traditional readings of canonical English works that (mis)appropriate race.

The politics of race and reason in Enlightenment English literature and its impact on colonial African-British writings have scarcely been examined.[21] In *The Black Atlantic: Modernity and Double Consciousness* (1993), Paul Gilroy encourages a diasporic black Atlantic in the aftermath of an eighteenth- and nineteenth-century Enlightenment, filling the discursive space between nationalist and culturalist identities. Keith Sandiford's *Measuring the Moment* (1988) and Henry Louis Gates, Jr.'s *Figures in Black: Words, Signs and the "Racial" Self* (1987) and *The Signifying Monkey: A Theory of African-American Literary Criticism* (1988) remain indispensable foundations to any epistemological study that examines African-British writings in the context of the European Enlightenment. (Edward Said, especially his observations on Dickens in *Culture and Imperialism*, even preserves a humanistic strain—an enjoyment of literary aesthetics amid a recovery of social conditions that inform literary production.)

It seems ironic that the period most recognizable as the age of reason (a misnomer since both the distrust of the imaginative faculty and the unreliability of reason were proclaimed by these writers), has escaped scrutiny in specific racial contexts in literary investigations.[22] But a poststructuralist analysis of what Cornel West identifies as the relationship of "extradiscursive formations to discursive operations," coupled with specifically identifiable racial events, especially those associated with slavery, uncovers interesting developments where race and reason intersect with Enlightenment principles about morality and the role of literature in society.[23] As Lucius Outlaw observes, "'Race' continues to function as a critical yardstick for the rank-ordering of racial groups both 'scientifically' and socio-politically, the latter with support from the former" and remains a major point of contentious relations for power and dominance.[24]

To date, no book-length epistemological study has mapped the intense racial scrutiny that African-British writings bring to Enlightenment humanism, literary didacticism, and natural hierarchies in social practice. But recent new editions of African-British publications have laid a foundation for such a study. Through numerous publications, the late Paul Edwards, renowned scholar of African-British writers, made available the necessary tools—letters, diaries, and subscription lists available for research. Edwards's 1969 publication of the *Interesting Narrative of Life of Olaudah Equiano, or Gustavus Vassa, the African* remains the standard edition of Equiano's work. The two-volume publication is based on Equiano's own first edition of the narrative, published in 1789. With the publication of *Olaudah Equiano: The Interesting Narrative and Other Writings* (1996), Vincent Carretta has made accessible the ninth and final edition of the narrative, published in Equiano's lifetime, which contains his most extensive alterations. Moreover, Carretta has edited a comprehensive anthology, entitled *Unchained Voices: An Anthology of Black Authors in the English-Speaking World of the Eighteenth Century* (1996), along with a new edition of *Letters of the Late Ignatius Sancho*. Paul Edwards and David Dabydeen coedited an anthology, *Black Writers in Britain, 1760–1890*, published in 1991. Adam Potkay and Sandra Burr have edited an anthology, *Black Atlantic Writers of the 18th Century* (1995), which includes Ottobah Cugoano's *Thoughts and Sentiments on the Evil of Slavery* (1787). Paul Edwards and Polly Rewt have coedited *Letters of the Late Ignatius Sancho* (1994).

Peter Fryer's *Staying Power: The History of Black People in Britain* (1984) is perhaps the most comprehensive study of social, political, scientific, and philosophical data on the history of black people in Britain. Fryer's work includes brief biocritical segments on Sancho, Cugoano, Equiano, and others. Scholars still owe a huge debt to Folarin Shyllon's 1977 publication, entitled *Black People in Britain*, for his exhaustive and meticulous examination of data on those who touched the lives of Sancho, Cugoano, and Equiano.

Fortunately, the future of scholarship on African-British writings has been greatly enhanced by recent events. For example, the life, music, and writings of Ignatius Sancho were celebrated at an exhibition, held in London at the National Portrait Gallery 24 January to 11 May 1997. To commemorate this exhibition, Reyahn King, Sukhdev Sandhu, James Walvin, and Jane Girdham published a collection of essays in *Ignatius Sancho: An African Man of Letters* (London: National Portrait Gallery, 1997).

## NOTES

1. See Toni Morrison, *Playing in the Dark: Whiteness and the Literary Imagination* (New York: Vintage Books, 1990), 11. Writing about race and the American literary tradition, Morrison argues that the issue of race has never been separate from mainstream American literature. Some, like Edgar Allan Poe, Willa Cather, and Henry James have employed subtle, indirect means by which to incorporate racial issues into their writings (9).

2. Joseph Addison and Sir Richard Steele, *The Spectator*, 5 vols., ed. Donald F. Bond (Oxford, England: Clarendon Press, 1965), 2: 339. Joseph Addison was a commissioner of trade and plantations, and Sir Richard Steele owned a slave plantation in the West Indies. According to David Dabydeen, Jonathan Swift and Alexander Pope are named on the South Sea Company's subscription books, which are stored in the House of Lords Records Office. See David Dabydeen, ed., *The Black Presence in English Literature* (Manchester: Manchester University Press, 1985), 28–29.

3. David T. Goldberg, *Anatomy of Racism* (Minneapolis: University of Minnesota Press, 1990), 308.

4. The Enlightenment period is sometimes referred to as "the long eighteenth century." Walter Jackson Bate dates the European Enlightenment from the mid-seventeenth to the eighteenth century. Other scholars set the period of the European Enlightenment as a self-conscious movement-in-earnest from around the mid-eighteenth to the end of the century. See Walter Jackson Bate in *From Classic to Romantic: Premises of Taste in Eighteenth-Century England* (Cambridge, MA: Harvard University Press, 1946; rpt. 1961).

5. Bate writes that humanism "viewed man's intellectual and moral nature as ideally the same, and it assumed as its goal the evolution of the total man in accordance with that view" (Bate, *From Classic to Romantic*, 2). Fussel finds "a marvellous concurrence of imagination, design, and method" in six eighteenth-century writers: Swift, Pope, Johnson, Reynolds, Gibbon, and Burke (Preface, vii). See Paul Fussel in *The Rhetorical World of Augustan Humanism: Ethics and Imagery from Swift To Burke* (London: Oxford University Press, 1965).

6. Bate, 2.

7. Fussel, 4.

8. See Paul Gilroy, "One Nation under a Groove: The Cultural Politics of "Race" and Racism in Britain," in *Anatomy of Racism*, ed. David Theo Goldberg (Minneapolis: University of Minnesota Press, 1990), 263–82. Gilroy's essay originates from observations that he made in *There Ain't No Black in the Union Jack: The Cultural Politics of Race and Nation* (London: Hutchinson, 1987). See also Etienne Balibar, "Parodoxes of Universality," in *Anatomy of Racism*, 283–94, and Etienne Balibar and Immanuel Wallerstein, *Race, Nation, Class: Ambiguous Identities*, Trans. of Etienne Balibar by Chris Turner (London: Verso, 1991). See Howard Winant, *Racial Conditions: Politics, Theory, Comparisons* (Minneapolis: University of Minnesota Press, 1994).

9. Dryden, in "An Essay of Dramatic Poesy," Addison and Steele, in *Spectator* #409, and Pope, in "Essay on Criticism," meticulously outline a literary didacticism as the most appropriate function of the artist in society. They assert that the

component qualities of human nature (e.g., humanity, compassion, contempt) are universal and therefore racially, socially, and nationally transcendent and that moral suasion is equally accessible and applicable to the masses.

10. Robert J. C. Young, *Colonial Desire: Hybridity in Theory, Culture and Race* (London: Routledge, 1995), 180. Young also writes, "Thus racialism operated both according to the same—Other model and through the 'computation of normalities' and 'degrees of deviance' from the white norm, by means of which racial difference became identified with other forms of sexual and social perversity as degeneracy, deformation or arrested embryological development" (180).

11. Anthony Appiah provides a useful definition of the term "racialism" as an expressible theory of the content of racism. Racialism refers to "a sort of racial essence" that accounts for more than phenotype, or like physical characteristics among individuals. (See Anthony Appiah's article, entitled "Racisms," in *Anatomy of Racism*, 5). Appiah writes, "Racialism is at the heart of nineteenth-century Western attempts to develop a science of racial difference; but it appears to have been believed by others . . . who have had no interest in developing scientific theories" (5).

12. Young, 180.

13. South Asians were frequently identified in print as Negro or black. For a discussion of Asian servants in Britain, see Peter Fryer, *Staying Power: The History of Black People in Britain* (London: Pluto Press, 1984), 77–78. See also Winthrop Jordan, *Black over White: American Attitudes Toward the Negro, 1550–1812* (Baltimore: Penguin Books, 1969; first published by the University of Chapel Hill Press, 1968), 95–96. Jordan writes that a scrutiny of racial terminology for those who were enslaved by the English "affords the best single means of probing the content of their sense of difference" (95). The term "Negro" has a Spanish derivative related to color or complexion.

14. Goldberg, ed., *Anatomy of Racism*, writes that race as biology is consigned to cultural, political, and social readings. Howard Winant writes, "There is no biological basis for distinguishing human groups along the lines of 'race,' and the sociohistorical categories employed to differentiate among these groups reveal themselves, upon serious examination, to be imprecise if not completely arbitrary" (115).

15. Robert Markley, "Beyond Consensus: The Rape of the Lock and the Fate of Reading Eighteenth-Century Literature," *New Orleans Review* 15 (Winter 1988): 68. Although some scholars record Pope's elevation to Olympian canonical status as taking place in the nineteenth century, others insist that Pope was denigrated, hotly contested, or out of fashion from around 1750 onward, though Maynard Mack convincingly disputes the latter idea. However, I regard the Chain's discursive legacy—and Pope's central role in it—as integral parts of the ethnographic components of "reason," especially as their function in establishing past, present, and future hierarchies is more significant than scholarship has previously revealed. Furthermore, Pope remains a central figure in the academic canon.

16. Paul Fussel, *The Rhetorical World of Augustan Humanism: Ethics and Imagery from Swift to Burke* (London: Oxford University Press, 1965), 4. Fussel may not have had race in mind here, but how ironic that these writers seemed to share an ambivalent literary treatment of race or "other" in spite of differences on other leading issues of the day.

17. Both the literary and philosophical pervasiveness of racial hierarchies and the recognition that those who presumably ranked lowest among racial hierarchies could most effectively dismantle such hierarchies led British abolitionists like William Dickson to call for "specimens of African literature" in the late 1770s to counter charges of racial inferiority made against blacks. Believing (as does E. P. Thompson, in *Whigs and Hunters*) that historical, sociopolitical, even literary subjects are most revealing when uncovered in the inverted pyramid form—from the bottom up—I locate in African-British writings perceptions among blacks and whites alike about racial differences. Thompson's pyramid model seemingly privileges the individual and the text, albeit in a material context, but I explore ideological complications of that model brought by class, race and gender, and slavery. Studies by Stuart Hall, Paul Gilroy (*The Black Atlantic: Modernity and Double Consciousness*, 1993), and Raymond Williams (*Problems in Materialism and Culture*, 1980, and *Culture and Society*, 1983) are especially pertinent to my interest in the relationships among neo-Marxist materialism, the didactic literary function, and Enlightenment humanism.

18. Some have attributed the text of Cugoano's theological argument against the Hamitic hypothesis to Thomas Clarkson, whose *Essay on the Slavery and Commerce of the Human Species* (1786) was published a year earlier than *Thoughts and Sentiments*. Clarkson, whom Cugoano acknowledges in the essay, may well have constructed his own theological premises from Granville Sharp. Such is the nature of period practices in editing and revision. In *The Origins of Modern African Thought* (Faber and Faber, 1968), Robert July notes that the intricate argument requires extensive knowledge of "the legalistic complexities of biblical exegesis" (40; also quoted by Paul Edwards in the introduction to *Thoughts and Sentiments on the Evil of Slavery*, vii). In his introduction to Cugoano's essay, Paul Edwards doubts (though he has not proven to the contrary) that the hand of a single author composed an essay that exhibits, as he sees it, at least two distinctly different literary styles. Edwards further believes that if indeed there was a collaborator for the essay, the likely hand belongs to none other than Olaudah Equiano. A friend and fellow member (with Cugoano) of an abolitionist group known as the Sons of Africa, Equiano demonstrates in his own narrative a discursive craftiness. See the introduction to *Thoughts and Sentiments on the Evil of Slavery* (London: Dawsons of Pall Mall, 1969), v–xvii.

19. See Anthony Ashley Cooper, 3rd Earl of Shaftesbury, *Characteristics of Men, Manners, Opinions, Times*, ed. John M. Robertson (Gloucester, MA: P. Smith, 1963); see Francis Hutcheson, *A System of Moral Philosophy*. 2 vols. Rpt. of the 1755 London edition (New York: A. M. Kelley, 1968). See also Adam Smith, *Theory of Moral Sentiments*, ed. D. D. Raphael and A. L. Macfie (Oxford: Clarendon Press, 1976). These philosophers would have laws return to an impartial truth as lofty perspective, a function long claimed by the legal community. I discuss Ottobah Cugoano's use of these ideas more fully in chapter 3.

20. See Nancy Leys Stepan, "Race and Gender: The Role of Analogy in Science," in Goldberg, ed., *Anatomy of Racism*, 38–57.

21. In terms of literature, Henry Louis Gates, Jr., traces "an ironic circular thread of interpretation that commences in the eighteenth century but does not reach its fullest philosophical form until the decade between 1965 and 1975: the movement

from blackness as a physical concept to blackness as a metaphysical concept" (*Figures in Black: Words, Signs, and the 'Racial' Self*, New York: Oxford, 1987), 28. See also David Dabydeen's *Hogarth's Blacks* and *The Black Presence in English Literature*. Paul Gilroy sets a hybrid modernity in the context of an Enlightenment project; see chapter 1, "The Black Atlantic as a Counterculture of Modernity," in *The Black Atlantic*.

22. J. W. Johnson, in *The Formation of English Neo-Classical Thought* (Princeton, NJ: Princeton University Press, 1967), 4; and Donald Greene, in "Augustanism and Empiricism," *Eighteenth-Century Studies* 1 (1967–68), 38, are among those who deconstruct the Age of Reason as a conceptual category for the eighteenth century. In *Figures in Black*, Gates contextualizes colonial black writers with certain aspects of the European Enlightenment. He focuses on literary theory and the black tradition in a neo-Marxist reading of the impact of race on a materialist culture, and he examines the ambiguous validation of colonial black writers within a Western literary and literacy tradition.

23. See Cornel West, *Keeping Faith: Philosophy and Race in America* (New York: Routledge, 1993). West believes that an analysis of the relationship between extra-discursive and discursive operations, particularly in racial matters, can reveal the structural bases for racial dominance in European societies.

24. See Lucius Outlaw, in *Race, Nation, Class: Ambiguous Identities*, ed. Etienne Balibar and Immanuel Wallerstein, trans. of Balibar by Chris Turner (London: Verso, 1991).

# Reading Pope/Reasoning Race: Enlightenment Humanism and the Chain's Discursive Legacy

Though traceable to Plato and others in classical antiquity largely as an abstract philosophical and theological principle, the concept of the Great Chain of Being rarely appeared in print as a construct for dividing humanity by race before the late eighteenth century, when proslavery factions used it to justify and to protect a lucrative slave trade. But encounters between Europeans and so-called third-world indigenous cultural groups that took place much earlier helped alter the Chain's course from a placement of humanity with respect to a deity to a placement of individuals based on racial hierarchies.

One curious example of this effect is Sir William Petty, who completed four chapters of an intended project titled "The Scale of Creatures" (1675) that attempted to establish gradations among humankind.[1] An original member of the Royal Society, a member of Parliament, and a follower of Bacon's New Philosophy,[2] Petty wrote about the project in a letter to Sir Robert Southwell, also a member of Parliament. Though the four chapters that Petty completed have not survived, a synopsis of the intended project is included in *The Petty Papers: Some Unpublished Writings of Sir William Petty* (1927), a two-volume work.

In "The Scale of Creatures," Petty cites the "eyewitness" accounts of travelers to support claims that Africans who inhabited the Cape of Good Hope, the so-called Hottentots, were the most bestial of the human species. Possibly referring to Thomas Herbert, whose "Description of the Cape of Good Hope in Aethiopia" (1634) was among the first travel accounts to describe the Hottentots in this manner, Petty expresses ethnocentric views toward Africans who differed from Europeans on the basis of skin color, hair texture, facial features, physiognomy, and general body shape and size.

But he adds a detail that goes beyond simple ethnocentric notions about racial differences. Alluding to the intellectual capacity of the Hottentots, Petty writes that "they differ also in their Naturall Manners, & in the internall Qualities of their Minds."[3] In advancing the idea of gradations—ranking individuals by race rather than en masse—Petty prided himself on having made a distinct contribution to the concept of the Chain of Being that supplemented previous religious and philosophical conceptions of it by Platonists like Sir Matthew Hale.[4]

Though the ideological distance may seem slight, Petty equates difference with inferiority, a judgment not commonly found in print until much later in the eighteenth century, when debate on the legality of slavery helped spawn the appearance of pseudo-scientific racialist data. To elaborate further, Petty discusses race in *The Scale of Creatures* but does not mention slavery, which was not yet fully profitable for England. In fact, in early English common-law cases like *Butts v. Penny*, 1557, and *Gelly v. Cleve*, 1694 (which I examine in chapter 2), the very legality of slavery was still being tested, but mostly it remained based on the slave's Christian or non-Christian status. And as I shall discuss more fully later in this chapter, slave profits would soar after 1713, when the Treaty of Utrecht gave England the slave trade monopoly for the next thirty years.[5] Even when Petty's ideas drew objections—Southwell reportedly burned all letters from him about the project—they were regarded as possible heresy because of Petty's lofty religious assumptions rather than because of his placement of blacks at the bottom of the scale of humanity.

In a matter of greater significance, however, Sir William Petty's *The Scale of Creatures* is an early illustration of a major discursive transformation in the Chain's legacy—an abstract, philosophical idea's unveiling as a hidden social agenda. In other words, a concept identifying humanity's position within universal creation in an era when explorers ventured to remote places and encountered foreign cultures, became grist for the pulp fiction mill in the travelogue industry. In relegating a specific racial group (gleaned from eye witness accounts, no less), to the Chain's lowest regions, Petty demonstrates travel fiction's exploitive potential as discursive propaganda to readers who sought exotic tales about indigenous cultural groups from well beyond England's borders.

Though Petty eventually abandoned composition of "The Scale of Creatures," he joined an international, interdisciplinary coalition of intellectuals in the seventeenth century, known as Ancients and Moderns, who emerged as early but decisive players in the Chain's discursive legacy on race. While the debate between Ancients and Moderns centered primarily on contributions to learning made by intellectuals through the ages, a major point of contention among the members was the value to the advancement of civilization of engineering feats such as the printing press, the air pump, gunpowder, and the discovery of blood circulation. For example, the very inventions that made travel and trade possible—the discovery of the lodestone and magnetic force—fueled a propaganda war on the value of Europe's introduction to indigenous cultural groups outside the Continent. In England, Moderns like William Wotton (*Reflections Upon Ancient and Modern Learning*, 1694) thought that explorations permitted enlightened European cultures to disseminate knowledge to unenlightened ones. On the other hand, Ancients like Sir William Temple ("An Essay Upon the Ancient and Modern Learning," 1690) quipped that such travel promoted greed and merely led to the discovery of the barbarism of indigenous groups and was hardly a contribution to humanity.[6]

Much earlier, in *The Advancement of Learning* (1605), Francis Bacon had already set the tone for a merger to take place between the regard for invention as economic advancement and the regard for invention as art or aesthetics. He wrote, for instance, that "it cannot be found strange if no further progress has been made in the discovery and advancement of the arts, when the art itself of discovery and invention has as yet been passed over."[7] Bacon's insistence on the need for a philosophy of invention corresponded with his belief in the vital role of inventions in changing the appearance and state of the whole world for the better. He wrote, "Let men be assured that the solid and true arts of invention grow and increase as inventions themselves increase" (87). Bacon's allusions to the art of invention included those instruments of trade that ultimately made slavery and conquest possible. For example, he also wrote that were it not for the mariner's needle the West Indies might not have been discovered.

While the Ancients versus Moderns debate is seemingly out of fashion for discussion in contemporary scholarship, certain discursive transformations (e.g., in aesthetics, art, and science) produced by this debate are well worth examination. For one thing, the recognition of the aesthetics of science and the quest for an empirical, rationalistic basis for art in an age of racial discovery marks yet another dimension to the Chain's discursive legacy. In other words, with an expanding trade in tea in the West Indies and tobacco in the North American Colonies that increasingly relied upon slave labor, concerns about the method and means of social and economic advancement would soon give way to a greater concern for the moral benefits of such advancements.[8]

Concern with improving the morals of humankind is often reflected in major writings in the Enlightenment period, especially in the literature of new or *neo*classicists in England. Seeking to emulate, even to imitate, Greek and Roman classicists like Homer, Virgil, Aristotle, and Plato, John Dryden, Sir William Temple, Jonathan Swift, Alexander Pope, and others advanced the Ancients' suggestion to utilize art as the postlapsarian response to disharmony in the universe. These writers' objectives to determine the appropriate function of art are fundamentally known. But their mission to appropriate universal, uniform standards for art in connection with a changing social climate in England (e.g., foreign expeditions and participation in the slave trade) needs further exploration, especially in light of inconsistencies in the application of those standards in subsequent writings.[9]

As contributors to the Chain's discursive legacy on race, Sir William Petty, other members of the Royal Society, and participants in the Ancients versus Moderns debate connect with the Chain's most powerful champion—Alexander Pope, whose poem on the subject appeared in 1733–34. As a quintessential Enlightenment humanist, however, Pope claims an even higher calling as a basis for the Chain's legacy than the likes of Sir William Petty et al. If Petty unveils the Chain's hidden social agenda in order to divide humanity into racial hierarchies, then Pope subordinates the concept's racialist implications to a more lofty, aesthetic objective—the advancement of an Enlightenment humanism. Pope was thus spokesperson for a combined ancients versus moderns debate, literary didacticism, aesthetics, and humanism.

An examination of the Chain's discursive legacy in the context of Enlightenment humanism, selected writings of Alexander Pope, and numerous interdisciplinary writings achieves two primary objectives for our understanding of these interconnections. This concept rekindles a massive dialogue on the subject of learning, which also coincides with explorers' encounters with indigenous cultural groups in England and on the Continent.[10] Most significantly, an examination of the Chain's discursive legacy from among the coalition above demonstrates the process by which "collective belief systems [are] shaped, moved from one medium to another, concentrated in manageable aesthetic form, [and] offered for consumption."[11] As I have stated, a discursive forum that debated the value of art and a social arena that grappled with a growing black population and the legality of slavery foreground the appearance of African-British writings that I examine in subsequent chapters.

In reflecting the humanist mission to represent art as an instructive, guiding force, Pope seeks to rehabilitate the masses from vice, ignorance, and the sin of pride. Still, in promoting a literary didacticism in the socioeconomic environment of slavery, Pope conceives of a language of commerce as the civilizing mechanism for a disorderly world.[12] Pope's epistemology is far too complex, however, to be reduced simply to a presentation of negative racial politics, but inconsistencies in the ideas that he puts forth are worth mentioning. For example, Pope expresses anti-slavery sentiments in "Windsor Forest," antipathy toward wealthy excesses in "Epistle to Bathurst," and, at the same time, support for imperialist pro-slavery interests in England's Treaty of Utrecht. Pope heavily influenced the writings of Philis[13] Wheatley and Ignatius Sancho, black writers whom I examine in the course of this study. And yet, in justifying the ways of God to humanity in the *Essay on Man*, Pope betrays an epistemological investment in ideas which are historically steeped in racial mythology: the missing links idea, the ennobled or so-called primitive being myth, and the individual's intellectual capacity with particular allusions to the Native American.

In a letter to Swift, Pope describes the *Essay on Man* as a project designed "to make mankind look upon this life with comfort and pleasure, and put morality in good humour."[14] Further describing the planning of his magnum opus in a letter to the Earl of Oxford, dated 2 December 1730, Pope writes that the poem "will consist of nothing but such Doctrines as are inoffensive, & consistent with the Truest Divinity and Morality" (IV. 153). In poems like *Essay on Man*, "The Rape of the Lock," and "Windsor Forest" Pope particularly grapples with individual conflict in ways that acknowledge his concession to a social agenda's functioning in the service of art.

The commodious trade that Pope scorns in "The Rape of the Lock" quickly becomes part of England's destiny in "Windsor Forest." After implicitly criticizing England's colonial exploits (and explicitly satirizing women's vanity) in the boudoir scene in "The Rape of the Lock," Pope unabashedly celebrates the Treaty of Utrecht in "Windsor Forest," in part as the reconciliation between England's imperialist ventures and its moral destiny. In "Windsor Forest," Pope acknowledges the loss of these trees in the service of British domination: "Let *India* boast her Plants, nor envy we / The weeping Amber or the balmy Tree, / While by our Oaks the precious Loads are born, / And Realms commanded which those Trees adorn" (29–31).[15] Pope catalogues the Normans' tyrannies in royal forestation, on the one hand. But he then heralds the ending of slavery, while proclaiming English imperialism in trade, though he never connects the Treaty's bountiful Asiento Pact with the enormous slave profits it produced for the English. Pertaining to similar inconsistencies, Maynard Mack suggests that "Windsor Forest" shows that Pope "was haunted throughout his life . . . by a vision of England as the ideal commonwealth to be realized on earth—a Prospero's island, House of Temperance, Garden of Alcinous, and demi-Eden, all rolled in one."[16]

After the Civil War ended in 1660, the Earl of Clarendon issued a slave-trading monopoly to the Company of Royal Adventurers Trading to Africa in 1663 for one thousand years. The earl voiced hopes that in the company would "be found a model equally to advance the trade of England with that of any other company, even that of the East Indies."[17] The Royal African Company was formed in 1672, after the Company of Royal Adventurers had suffered huge losses. The company lost its monopoly in 1698, and with the advent of free trade and of course the thirty-year monopoly on the slave trade, which was granted to England by the Asiento Pact of 1713, slave profits soared.

The trade that gluts Belinda's vanity table with useless trifles in "The Rape of the Lock" gains sanctity in "Windsor Forest" in the form of oak trees that were felled to support Britain's shipping industry—ships that transported enslaved Africans across the Atlantic. Apparently, garters, billets-doux, and French romances were no match for the economic importance of the trade in human cargo in which Pope and many others invested through the East India Company. I am reminded here of Dryden's tongue-in-cheek compensatory defense of King Charles's adultery in "Absalom and Achitophel" as the King's fulfillment of a divinely ordained role as England's patriarch. Under the guise of universal order, *Essay on Man* thus devises a manifesto by which a theory of subordination masks a system of dominance and control that approves just such an institution as slavery. Pope shifts attacks away from the greed and tyranny of trade and instead focuses on the benefits of trade.

I believe it to be misleading to divorce literature from socioeconomic and political contexts, especially in light of the fallacies inherent in a so-called universalist, didactic language, to which Enlightenment humanists subscribed. A universal didacticism denies its exclusivity, such that it matters racially, as when blacks are discounted as being deserving moral people in the first place.[18] The coming together of universal didactic literary principles in eighteenth-century English, when set against a backdrop of nationalist politics (e.g., who is English versus who is not, exemplified in Queen Elizabeth's 1596 decree to deport England's black population)[19] enabled the formation of racialist politics.

England agreed to supply its colonies (in the West Indies and in the colonies of the New World) with 4,800 slaves, annually, for a total of around 104,000. Between 1680 and 1686, the Royal African Company transported around 5,000 slaves annually. In 1760, 146 ships with a holding capacity of 36,000 slaves sailed from British ports to Africa; in 1771, 190 ships had transported some 47,000 slaves. Between 1680 and 1786, Britain transported an estimated two million slaves into all its colonies.[20] As Basil Davidson observes, by around 1700, English citizens who had been exposed to blacks either from travel accounts or as domestic slaves in English society likely saw them as shackled and powerless.

Interestingly, the strategic appearance of an anonymous poem in Samuel Richardson's *Pamela* (1740) several years after Pope's *Essay on Man* appeared in print further underscores the complexities that the political economy of slavery produces for self-proclaimed humanist literature. The poem's references to the sinfulness of pride and to universal order share similarities in theme with *Essay on Man*. Pope proclaims in *Essay on Man* that the union of disparate states among individuals requires the cooperation of all: "From Order, Union, full Consent of things! / Where small and great, where weak and mighty, made / To serve, not suffer, strengthen, not invade, More pow'rful each as needful to the rest, / And, in proportion as it blesses, blest" (297–300). But in referencing slaves and gradations among individuals, the poem in Richardson's novel invokes a hierarchical reading of the Chain that tacitly acknowledge race, but which privileges class.

Quoting from the poem in Richardson's novel, Pamela acknowledges an enslaved population's support of that universal order. Furthermore, Pamela's status as a servant girl who retains her virtue (and as a result is able to marry her wealthy boss) explicitly subjects the Chain of Being to overtones of class and gender: "The meanest slaves, or those who hedge and ditch, / Are useful, by their sweat, to feed the rich. / The rich, in due return, impart their store; / Which comfortably feeds the lab'ring poor. / Nor let the rich the lowest slave disdain: / He's equally a link of Nature's chain." The poem concludes by observing that death equalizes all individuals, without making distinctions either for kings or for the enslaved.[21] The poem is highly allusive, conveying a *memento mori* theme that was part of numerous sermons and other moral literature from the seventeenth and eighteenth centuries. For example, in *Cooper's Hill* (1755) Sir John Denham suggests that tyrant and slave, king and subject are happiest in a state of interdependency. In Richardson's novel, the poem features an individual's subordination, attended by subservience—that is, until death levels all.

In an enormously popular fictional work, displayed in the new novel form, Richardson places a minor poem of immeasurable socioeconomic proportions in the ideological domain of his heroine. As a white female servant, Pamela represents Britain's majority, an indentured servant population. Ironically, however, the poem hearkens to a brutal chattel slavocracy that is more consistent with the Euro-African trade than with Pamela's indentured servant status. The enslaved population is perceived as comprising an equal link with others in Nature's chain, but only by virtue of their support of the wealthy. The poem thus approves an equality for slaves that is reminiscent of Pope's concept of equitable distribution in *Essay on Man*. The poem's "lab'ring poor," whom the wealthy in turn subsidize, may well stand for the indentured servant. In accounting for historical veracity, however, the poem demonstrates that, based on scientific perception at least, enslaved blacks indeed occupied the Chain's lowest links with their only *real equality* occurring in death.

In proclaiming a universal theodicy in his *Essay on Man*, Pope recognizes humanity as forming one vast collective or chain, subordinate only to an impartial deity. While Pope acknowledges vast social disparities in different contexts throughout the poem, he cloaks them within this universal theodicy and does not attribute them to specific racial, social, or economic issues: "Vast chain of being, which from God began, / Nature's Aethereal, human, angel, man / Beast, bird, fish, insect! what no eye can see, / No glass can reach! from Infinite to thee, / From thee to Nothing!—On superior pow'rs / Were we to press, inferior might on ours: / Or in the full creation leave a void" (I. 237–43).[22] In denying that happiness derives from wealth, rank, or social status, Pope is able to justify inequities under the guise of universal order: the sacrifice of some (the part) promotes the good of all (the whole) in a system that finite human intelligence cannot comprehend. He concludes that "ORDER is Heav'n's first law; and this confest, / Some are, and must be, greater than the rest, / More rich, more wise; but who infers from hence / That such are happier, shocks all common sense" (IV. 49–52).

Though Pope makes no claims for hierarchical divisions among individuals, he makes an implicit reference to one's position with respect to others on the Chain as a whole. Pope's emphasis on passivity, acquiescence, and docility locks humanity into a deterministic framework that may well thwart individual human endeavor. "And who but wishes to invert the laws / Of ORDER, sins against th'Eternal Cause," Pope affirms (I. 129–30). This idea may well encourage individuals to accept certain social conditions as immutable. Since the wish for self-efficacy implicitly questions one's position in the Chain as a whole, the threat offered by individual mobility to that stable order is great.

The ability of vested interests to maintain order through a Great Chain of Being cautions the masses to silence, and lends support to the notion that "Whatever IS, is RIGHT" (I. 294). Pope acknowledges "that the Pow'rful still the Weak controul, / Be Man the Wit and Tyrant of the Whole: / Nature that Tyrant checks; he only knows, / And helps, another creature's wants and woes" (III. 49–52). The pernicious manner in which this doctrine can serve the interests of the powerful at the expense of the dispossessed is keenly apparent. Though Pope does not directly approve of racial subordination in the poem, he sanctions certain beliefs that allow such an interpretation to be easily formed among those who reverenced his intellectual, literary stature.

When Pope warns of the perils of breaking rank, not only does he refer to humanity's penchant for proclaiming the quality of angels or even gods, but he also refers to desire for change in status or condition in contrast with others. Another implication here is that Fortune—or some external hand—determines the disparities among individuals, acting as a sort of predestination that locks individuals into one state or another, regardless of their daily hopes and fears. Such a deterministic philosophy proves beneficial to the support of legalized slavery because it naturalizes dominance and makes slavery acceptable on religious grounds because a Supreme Being would presumably approve of it.

The humanist quest for an essentialist, universal literary didacticism is admirable for its seeming equality, but it distorts reality by framing sameness in exclusivity and by negating difference and otherness in contexts where they figure most prominently.[23] In eighteenth-century England, surplus (i.e., unpaid) workers, which included an enslaved population that was overwhelmingly black and/or African, had to be maintained as peripheral insiders in order to uphold a burgeoning capitalism or face expulsion from a nationalist community. But they also had to be portrayed as outsiders— nonpersons or heathens—to a universalist moral doctrine that would otherwise exclude them from slavery on religious and ethical grounds.

Intellectually, Alexander Pope serves as a historical and literary center in a discursive Chain of Being that evolved from abstract philosophy to the concrete historical, political, and economical trappings of slavery to its transformation in a humanist framework. Discursive markers associated with humanism—for example, universality, uniformity, and orthodoxy—disregard certain historical particularities. In a revealing observation of Thomas Gray's "Elegy Written in a Country Churchyard" that could also apply to Pope's *Essay on Man* and the slavery question, Richard Sha observes that "historical particularities demand that we look beyond a poem's universalizing rhetoric."[24] As Sha further says about Gray (and we might add Pope here), in "displacing material economics by a spiritual one [he] makes poverty a theological rather than political or economic issue" (342).

A deterministic interpretation of Pope's *Essay on Man* might regard slavery as necessarily sacrificing the lives of some individuals for the general good of all under the guise of universal order. Some scholarly observers have disparaged what they believe to be misrepresentations of Pope's Chain of Being (*Essay on Man*, 1733) as a metaphor for socioeconomic inequities. But complaints about *Essay on Man* by Pope's contemporaries centered on the Poet's lofty Olympian stance and heavy-handed theodicy, not on the poem's ranking of humanity and implications for slavery.[25]

David Fairer strikes an appealing kind of middle ground in acknowledging the importance of newer, politicized readings such as *Pope: New Contexts* (1990), edited by David Fairer, alongside *The Enduring Legacy: Alexander Pope tercentenary essays* (1988), edited by G. S. Rousseau and Pat Rogers, in an effort to broaden knowledge about Pope and the principle debates of the period. Citing opposition to Pope by some contemporaries, Fairer argues with some validity that the epistemological arena in the eighteenth century was just as divided, perhaps, as it is today. Fairer's work challenges "both the cultural stability of the eighteenth century and Pope's centrality or representativeness within it . . . by locating the power of his work in its resistance to discourses of coherence and stability."[26]

Ironically, it seems that Pope was unable finally to divorce himself from the very (mis)application of rationalism that he typically deplored. The notion that literacy was itself an essential measure of intellectual enlightenment would soon give way to an added requirement. The truly literate had to acquire an exquisite taste for belle lettres.[27] Race complicates such distinctions by means of exclusivity and negation. In other words, conventional wisdom asserted that Blacks could not be literate, and hence they could not acquire the essential attributes of learnedness; concomitantly, blacks were deemed immoral, and moral consideration was denied them.

The split persona of the (ig)noble savage is well documented as either a Virgilian hearkening to the Golden Age (the *Georgics*) or to a Hobbesian postlapsarian state of brutishness (*Leviathan*, 1651).[28] For example, the ennobling qualities of "primitive beings" included their isolation from the trappings of civilization. Montaigne, and later Jean-Jacques Rousseau, were part of a long-standing Renaissance and Enlightenment debate about racial hierarchies. But when embodied in the South African Hottentot as the European's opposite, the twin portraits above represent contrasting depictions of innocence as a classical paradigm. The Virgilian persona featured a childlike being in need of patronage, while the Georgian persona revealed a bestial, uncivilized Other in need of containment.

Pope's brief tributary passage in *Essay on Man*, featuring the Native-American, is rather revealing for the ironic ways that it fits unobtrusively into an internal ranking of humanity that Pope's own construction intrinsically denies. For example, in *Essay on Man*, Pope's reference to a "scale of sense" in the limitations of human wisdom metaphorizes the Enlightenment's literary treatment of Africans as the "missing link," or lowest member of the human species.

Significantly, Pope's own allusions to the Golden Age, separate from his Native American passage, do not so much depict humanity as bestial so much as they equate it with the beastly kingdom. As Pope sees it, in the postlapsarian state, the animal's instinct is a direct expression of divine will, far superior to the individual's capacity to act on the basis of free will, since the latter admits room for tremendous error. In *Essay on Man*, Pope allows that the untutored mind of the Native American, like Science, is incapable of understanding God's ways—and that others must learn from the Native American's simple nature, which is regarded as happier, more trusting, and more humble than Science: "Lo! the poor Indian, whose untutor'd mind / Sees God in clouds, or hears him in the wind; / His Soul, proud Science never taught to stray" (I. 101–103). The Native American seeks merely to exist securely in a humble abode—away from a technological world "where slaves once more their native land behold" and where "no fiends torment, no Christians thirst for gold" (I. 107–08). Pope cannot apply the hierarchical Chain to a concept with the social and historical implications befitting the primitive being without implicating the cultural politics of such a portrait.

The myth of the ennobled being is a corollary to the theory of plenitude—a teleological notion also described by Arthur O. Lovejoy—that connects individuals both below and above certain other species on the Chain. The idea that a primitive being is ennobled by virtue of ignorance and simplicity is patronizing because of what it professes to admire. For Pope urges unidentified others (nonprimitives?) to "Go, wiser thou! and in thy *scale of sense* [my italics] / Weigh thy Opinion against Providence" (I. 113–14). In an adverbial usage, "wiser" means that Pope urges others to choose a more instructive course than the one based on the Native American's example. On the other hand, positioned adjectivally in relation to the pronoun "thou," *wiser* means that Pope assigns superior wisdom to the intended audience beyond the capacity of the "primitive." F.E.L. Priestley reads the phrase ironically, as an indication that individuals are not so wise as they may believe themselves to be (226), while A.D. Nutall advances the idea that it is an expression of condescension toward the unlearned (69–70).

The Native American's alleged humility and simplicity (i.e., perceived acquiescence to subordination) is held up as the admirable, or at least acceptable, trait here.[29] This doublespeak is further evident when Pope debunks, in Epistle 4, the same ennobling traits that he seems to admire in the Native American in Epistle 1 of the poem. Pope mocks the Native American's burial custom of taking those goods, which he deems the improper rewards of virtue, into the next life: "Go, like the Indian, in another life / Expect thy dog, thy bottle, and thy wife: / As well as dream such trifles are assign'd, / As toys and empires, for a god-like mind" (IV. 177–180).[30]

Laura Brown highlights Pope's contradictions even further. She locates the Native American as a model of submission for others squarely in the social realm, where such submission meant enslavement and the loss of freedom and power. Brown interprets this passage historically and politically as comprising the story of the Native American's treatment by England and Spain up to the dating of Pope's poem. She writes that in *Essay on Man*, the Native American "enacts a fantasy of power, but one located in the present rather than the future—a fantasy of the quiescence and collaboration of the oppressed."[31] Brown's refusal to deny the poem the benefit of its historical "lineage" draws ire from some critics. But Louis A. Montrose's cultural poetics, when used as a theoretical interpretive tool, refuses "unproblematized distinctions between literature and history, between text and context."[32]

Donald Greene takes Brown (and particularly Terry Eagleton, who provides a preface for Brown's *Alexander Pope*) to task for what he describes as "a mish-mash of long-exploded errors about the eighteenth century," and by extension, about Pope.[33] In an article with an intriguing title, "An Anatomy of Pope-Bashing," published in G. S. Rousseau and Pat Rogers' tercentenary collection of essays on Pope, Donald Greene deplores what he terms as misreadings of Pope, eighteenth-century literature, and the nineteenth century's preservation of neoclassical texts. Among other things, Greene points out that Pope was far from privileged as a member of his own society; he endured discrimination in education and law as a Roman Catholic, bore a physical handicap, and cultivated an aversion toward hack writing in order to curry favors among patrons—none of which, of course, makes the Poet impervious to complex culturalist readings.[34] And yet, to choose "the poor Indian" as a model of simplicity and humility while urging others to "Go wiser, Thou"—without a hint of irony for the socioeconomic and political historical model that the Indian presented to England at the time invites criticism of the work itself (if not the poet).

I am interested specifically in the ways in which Enlightenment principles about morality and the role of literature in society intersect with concepts of race and reason. Not only do these ideas recover a genealogical mapping of past racial directives or unveil what Paul Gilroy calls "the changing contours of racial ideologies," but they are relevant to the academic roots of a literary tradition as we know it.[35] These ideas inform my analysis of the Chain's discursive legacy on race in this chapter, and I connect them with key aspects of colonial African-British writings in what follows.

Pope's theological interest essentially lies in identifying the individual's inferior relationship to an impartial deity: "To him no high, no low, no great, no small; / He fills, he bounds, connects, and equals all" (I. 279–80). Pope's backhanded claims of impartiality translate into a kind of interdependence, based on an equitable distribution of value in the duties of master and servant—an ironic twist on the notion of equality. "And who but wishes to invert the laws / OF ORDER, sins against th' Eternal Cause" (I. 129–30). In this conception, "Heav'n forming each on other to depend, / A master, or a servant, or a friend, / Bids each on other for assistance call, / 'Til one Man's weakness grows the strength of all" (II. 249–52). A case for mutual dependency among disparate social groups dictates that each remain at a fixed position in an effort to preserve the total social structure. Pope's concept of impartiality reveals inherent ambiguities about individuals' abilities to act justly, but he dismisses such inequities as part of the Divine Plan.

He rationalizes that happiness is equally bestowed to all, as Hope for a better state and Fear or lack of knowledge of future events. Such a stoical, paralytic determinacy thwarts individuals' motivation and efforts toward change.

Priestley sees Pope's concept of impartiality in *Essay on Man* as promoting organic unity rather than supporting inequality or hierarchies. Priestley's metaphysical reading of Pope infers an ontological conception of being as a state of existence, rather than as individual entities. Pope goes on to ask, "What if the foot, ordained the dust to tread, / Or hand to toil, aspired to be the head" (I. 259–60)? He adds, "Just as absurd for any part to claim / To be another, in this gen'ral frame: / Just as absurd, to mourn the tasks or pains, / The great directing MIND of ALL ordains (I. 263–66). While acknowledging Pope's seemingly organic social meaning, Priestley concludes that the lines represent a nonhierarchical extended analogy of function, an organic unity in the service of the divine Will. In other words, like fingers on the hand or limbs to the body, individuals function equally in tasks for society's benefit, regardless of their social stations.

A further illustration might be Pope's assertion: "Where, one step broken, the great Scale's destroy'd: / From Nature's chain whatever link you strike, / Tenth or ten thousandth, breaks the chain alike" (I. 244–46). The many interpretations of Pope's poem may actually further the aims of metaphor, or metaphorize the metaphor, especially since his actual words seem to favor any number of readings at any given time. By formulating a theory of subordination, though, and affirming a fixed scale of beings as a necessary component of cosmic unity or universal order, Pope contributed to an ideological climate in which racial hierarchies would be an integral part of the Chain's discursive legacy. A number of interdisciplinary writers who acknowledged the Chain of Being drew intellectual influence and inspiration from Pope.

Pope's urging his readers to make personal sacrifices for the benefit of the public good seems to complement certain aspects of Bernard Mandeville's philosophy in *The Fable of the Bees; or, Private Vices, Publick Benefits* (1714).[36] Mandeville warned against the paradox inherent in a moral system that was consistent with church doctrine but conflicted with the avarice associated with trade and commercialism. The conflicting issues that Mandeville raises in the public and private sector reflect those inconsistencies between literary discourse and the social realm. Mandeville would resolve the contradiction by openly acknowledging the benefits of certain vices and by advocating indulgence in those vices that economically secured the nation's infrastructure.

Mandeville's private vices and Pope's personal sacrifices, though appearing in different contexts, both support universal order. The former might include anything from thinning gin to engaging in prostitution, while the latter—broadly interpreted—might include one individual's enslavement to another who enjoys the right to life, liberty, and the pursuit of happiness. The clear distinctions begin with the personal choices that some might have made to indulge in certain vices in the first place, as opposed to the enforcement of slave labor with which others had to contend in support of the public good.

In the "Epistle to Bathurst" (1733) from the Moral Essay collection, Pope's portrait of Cotta undermines Mandeville's promotion of private vices as public benefits, and it compromises a philosophical solution such as *Essay on Man* might propose. For example, in a seeming reversal of principles espoused in *Essay on Man*, Pope suggests through profiles of the Man of Ross and the Cutler that reconciliation, a kind of concordia discors, is unworkable in the face of human frailties.[37] In the view of the miserly Cotta, individual moral agency is irreducible. The greed that engulfs Cotta's son, who becomes bankrupt over Hanoverian politics, establishes no public beneficence for a thankless government. The disparity between the public and the private here exposes inherent flaws in a theory that purports to divorce one from the other. In other words, Cotta reveals what happens to theory when it is applied to real social models. Pope's claims that individual personal sacrifices work for the good of the whole and that evil misunderstood by humanity can translate into universal good clash with specific situations as complex and tragic as slavery.

When racial identity is itself considered a precondition to an individual's qualifications for moral consideration, a crisis of interpretation develops. Two vastly contrasting causes—moral and physical—are given in order to explain the differences in individuals' behavior. In "Of National Characters," perhaps the best documented pronouncement on race to have been published in the Enlightenment, Hume illuminates these complexities. In the essay, Hume writes that differences among diverse racial groups are attributed to both moral and physical causes. Not surprisingly, he assigns blacks the lowest position on the scale of humanity. But Hume does not chronicle the effects of sub-Saharan slavery on what he regards as the lack of liberal arts among African nations:

> I am apt to suspect the Negroes, and in general all other species of men (for there are four or five different kinds) to be naturally inferior to the Whites. There never was a civilized nation of any other complexion than white, nor even any individual eminent either in action or speculation. No ingenious manufactures amongst them, no arts, no sciences.[38]

And yet, if Hume's essay is easily dismissed because its scientific racism is so apparent, then the essay seems less inflammatory for its aesthetics, which are rooted in moral claims. Hume's observations amount to a Chain of Being cloaked in an aesthetic language that is far more subtle, though no less problematical, than his pseudo-biogenetics.

Hume attempts to devise an empirical basis for determining appropriate expressions of sentiment, which connects him with a popular literary movement late in the eighteenth century. For example, Hume suggests that individuals have a natural propensity to recognize hierarchy when choosing to empathize with others or to express sentiment toward others. He contradicts this, however, by attributing the ability to express sentiment appropriately to instruction, cultivation, and learning. The natural supremacy of the father over the son and the master over the slave are esteemed by natural selection on the part of individuals. Still, Hume does not explain how it is natural to hierarchize individuals, based on race. Nor does he explain how to determine, objectively, who is most deserving of goodwill.

In claiming that the regulation of sentiment is governed by education and training, Hume comes close to subscribing to Locke's theory of the association of ideas. Experience may lead one to generate sorrow, joy, pathos, and exuberance for a suffering child, a literary document, or a landscape. But Hume would have readers believe that this innately endowed ability is accessed through a faculty that is divinely connected at levels deemed appropriate for maintaining social order. Though he acknowledges contradictions in this philosophy, Hume ignores the slippage between the intuitive and the instructive, especially how the latter may reinforce power disparities among individuals in society. Hume's observations amount to a Chain of Being cloaked in an aesthetic language that is far more subtle, though no less problematical, than his pseudo-biogenetics.

When a hierarchical theory of humanity accompanies the identification of a specific indigenous racial group (deemed repugnant), it requires only a small nudge to shift discussion from an abstract idea to specific theories about racial hierarchies. I have noted that racial implications of the Chain of Being were documented and intensely debated by interdisciplinary writers in the face of a burgeoning anti-slavery consensus late in the eighteenth century. In the decades after Pope's *Essay on Man* appeared in print, the perception of the Chain of Being as a specifically racial phenomenon solidified. Some observers attribute this trend to powerful proslavery Whig planters and do not implicate Pope's Chain of Being as part of the cause.

Historically situated around the primitive being mythology, mass cultural representations of the Hottentot in travel literature, and slavery, the Chain's discursive legacy on race easily extends from Petty to Pope, to Voltaire, Kant, Hume, and Estwick. The concept's discursive transformation particularly implicates Sir William Petty's *The Scale of Creatures*, Pope's *Essay on Man*, and Enlightenment humanism. In the context of Enlightenment humanism and literary didacticism, Pope's Chain of Being fuses with naturalists' penchant for imposing order upon creation.

Examples of this fusion abound. For instance, in an article entitled "Variety of the Human Species: Tartars, Hottentots, Negroes, Americans, etc." that appeared in the *London Magazine* in 1750, the anonymous author claims "a gradation from the most perfect and rational of the human to the most perfect, and . . . the most sensible of the brute creation."[39] The author, who abstracted the article from Georges [Louis Leclerc, comte de] Buffon's *Natural History, General and Particular . . .* (1781–85), moreover asserted that while climate accounted for differences in color and lifestyle, religion might support differences in features and intellectual capacity.

Similarly, in Voltaire's "Of the Antiquity of Nations," published in *The Philosophy of History*, the inhabitants of the Cape of Good Hope are identified among those who were unable to formulate "a regular language and a distinct punctuation."[40] In "Disquisitions on Several Subjects: Disquisition I: On the Chain of Universal Being," Soame Jenyns writes that "in the brutal Hottentot, reason, with the assistance of learning and science, advances, through the various stages of human understanding, which rise above each other, till in a Bacon or a Newton it attains the summit."[41]

In a further example of the fusion between the Chain of Being and the effort to impose order upon creation, Immanuel Kant (a fervent devotee of Pope) constructs a variation of Pope's ennobled being in the guise of the Hottentot. The passage from Pope reads as follows: "Superior beings, when of late they saw / A mortal Man unfold all Nature's law, / Admir'd such wisdom in an earthly shape, / And shew'd a Newton as we shew an Ape" (II. 31–34). Kant writes that other planets may harbor human life superior to human life on earth. Kant inserts Hottentot for Ape as a model of degeneracy to suggest that there are gradations of humankind below and above others (the Hottentot below the European), an idea that supports gradations among individuals, based on race:

> If we limit ourselves to the solar system, in our speculative imaginings regarding the spiritual world, we may suppose that the perfection of the inhabitants of the planets constantly increases from Mercury to Saturn, so that perhaps on Mercury a Greenlander or a Hottentot would be considered a Newton, while on Saturn a Newton would be wondered at as an ape.[42]

Kant's example shows that racial ideologies are at least detectable in the primitive being motif, while racial hierarchies are located in travelers' identification of the indigenous South African Hottentots of the Cape of Good Hope.

But scientific data relegating the Hottentot to subhuman status cannot be dismissed as being either archaic or insignificant. For one thing, the very scientific data that replaced naturalists' findings by those who purported to be more egalitarian is no less ideological. For example, Linnaeus, who advanced the theory that humanity was actually part of the animal kingdom, first completed the nonhierarchical classification of racial groups. But even though Linnaeus's classifications did not include gradations among humanity, he still favored a hierarchical arrangement. In characterizing ethnic groups, Linnaeus concluded that Europeans were "gentle, acute, inventive"; Asians were "melancholy" and "rigid"; and Africans were "crafty, indolent, negligent."[43]

The work of Johann Friedrich Blumenbach, a German physiologist, is another interesting case in point. Blumenbach (*De Generis Humani Varietate Nativa*, 1775) revised Linnaeus' four-race geographical model of humanity and eliminated a hierarchical arrangement. In the 1781 edition of his treatise, Blumenbach constructed a five-race model of humanity that is actually more lineal—hence more prone to hierarchical interpretation than was his predecessor's model. Furthermore, in the 1795 edition of his treatise (*On the Natural Variety of Mankind*, translated from the Latin by Thomas Bendyshe) Blumenbach constructed humanity in groups of descending order. For the first time, he identified these groups as Caucasian, Asiatic, American, Ethiopian, and Malay, and held the Caucasian to be the ideal race. He also accepted the widespread notion that the Ethiopian's color resulted from the biblical curse that was placed upon Ham, and he compared the physiognomy of certain species of apes with people of color.

Indeed, abolitionists disseminated the work of Blumenbach as a corrective to publications by Dr. Charles White (*An Account of the Regular Gradation in Man, and in Different Animals and Vegetables; and from the Former to the Latter*, 1799), an English physician and member of the Royal Society, and Edward Tyson, who dispensed such information as the orangutan's alleged preference for the African female to female members of its own species. But in subscribing to a belief in climatology, which held that those born in torrid zones were lascivious, lazy, and immoral, Blumenbach further suggests inherent degeneracy among racial groups who purportedly had their brains cooked by the sun.[44]

Ironically, Blumenbach actually set out to dispute any racist notions that blacks were inferior to whites. Yet Blumenbach believed that his own revisions of outmoded data were more advanced than those of his predecessors. While he recognized no intellectual differences among categories of individuals of varying races, Blumenbach still argued that Europeans were the original divine creations. In observations on the genealogical impact of theories of racial hierarchies, Stephen Gould posits that the shift from a geographic to a hierarchical ordering of human diversity must stand as one of the most fateful transitions in the history of Western science—for what, short of railroads and nuclear bombs, has had more practical impact, in this case almost entirely negative, upon our collective lives? Indeed, these writers seemed "unaware of their own mental impositions upon the world's messy and ambiguous factuality."[45]

By the mid- to late eighteenth century, the concept of the Chain had undergone a discursive transformation from abstract Platonic theory to hierarchical construction of humanity to co-optation in an Enlightenment humanism. While numerous Enlightenment figures were involved in this transformation, Pope particularly operates around the unstable boundaries where literary didacticism intersects with racial hierarchies and the ordering of society. As an Enlightenment humanist, he provides a crucial historical context both to Enlightenment humanism and to the Chain's discursive legacy. Perhaps Pope's mediative function in the Chain's transformation is best illustrated in the placement of *Essay on Man* between Petty's *The Scale of Creatures* (1676) and Samuel Estwick's relatively obscure *Considerations on the Negroe Cause* (1788). Framing Pope's poem by some fifty years, these works excite curiosity primarily because, unlike *Essay on Man*, they posit the Chain quite literally as a device for ranking humanity by race.

Samuel Estwick, an assistant agent in London for Barbados, a paymaster-general, and the son-in-law of a governor of Barbados, held large possessions in the West Indies. In *Considerations on the Negro Cause* (1772; 1788), Estwick wonders (rhetorically) why the human kingdom, unlike the animal world, should not have been subjected to hierarchical construction. To order gradations among humanity would unlock Heaven's great chain. Estwick questions whether "it not be more perfective of the system to say, that human nature is a class, comprehending an *order* of beings, of which man is the *genus*, divided into distinct and separate *species* of men" (74). In proposing such an idea, Estwick directly implicates Pope, by interpreting the Chain and the *Essay on Man* as being highly racial in structure. He goes on to observe: "All other species of the animal kingdom have their marks of distinction: why should man be universally indiscriminate one to the other?"[46] While Petty lacked the political economy of slavery or a powerful proslavery planters' lobby to advance his ideas about blacks' inferior position on the Chain of Being back in 1675, Estwick suffered no such impediments in 1774. At this point in the evolution of this cultural idea, he argues boldly that the Chain of Being should be used outright as a formula for constructing racial hierarchies. Estwick infers

> that the measure of these beings may be as compleat, as that of any other race of mortals; filling up that space in life beyond the bounds of which they are not capable of passing; differing from other men, not in kind, but in species; and verifying that unerring truth of Mr. Pope (82).

Estwick uses Pope's own words to legitimize racial hierarchies, asserting that "'Order is Heaven's first law; and this confest, / Some are, and must be, greater than the rest'" (Pope, IV. 49–50; Estwick, 82).

Estwick quotes Pope on the subject of universal order to substantiate the former's claims of blacks' inferiority to whites, and to support his call for verifiable scientific and anthropological data. In standing upon Pope's "unerring truth," Estwick thus performs the sordid task of making the impolitic connections between theory and practice. In other words, he posits the Chain as a racial paradigm outright, rather than as an abstract universal principle—something that Pope does in his poetry only implicitly. Estwick's linking of the Poet's theological Chain with racial hierarchies is ironic, especially in light of Pope's tendency to elide those ideological leanings—or to pretend that they don't exist.

Estwick's abstraction of Pope is particularly noteworthy, because the former closes the divide between popular culture or nonliterary discourse and traditional literature in the Chain's legacy. For instance, he was already the most vocal among West Indian planters who defended slavery before Parliament. Estwick reveled in citing other noted Enlightenment intellectuals like Pope, Hume, Locke, Montesquieu, and others in a publication in order to support his belief in the inferiority of blacks to whites. Claiming to have read Hume's "Of National Characters" only after his own essay had been completed, Estwick expresses delight in observing "the ideas of so ingenious a writer corresponding with my own" (77). Edward Long, who comments on Estwick's views, claimed to provide such data in *History of Jamaica* (1774). Like Estwick, Long, the son of a Jamaican planter, would enjoy prosperity in the Caribbean. Surely a matter of no coincidence, Long's *History of Jamaica* contains lengthy quotations from Estwick's *The Negroe Cause*.

Estwick fervently believed in the inferiority of blacks so that he might justify a defense of slavery against a powerful abolitionist movement. While he argued that England's prosperity and independence might be maintained if the House of Lords permitted slavery to be confined to America, Estwick also urged the House of Lords to prohibit the importation of blacks into England in order to "preserve the race of Britons from stain and contamination" (94–95).

Though his essay lacks artistic merit, Estwick, who served for sixteen years in the House of Commons, was taken seriously enough to be permitted to address Britain's parliamentary bodies. Ultimately Estwick may seem easy to dismiss because of his relative obscurity and embarrassing candor. Still his confrontational reading of racial hierarchies in the Chain's construction has an important bearing on the work of Pope, even though Pope's essentialist theories can escape the perhaps lesser regard for a writer such as Samuel

Estwick. As a minor public figure, he nonetheless spoke for his time; and the debasement of Pope's lofty ideals does not render them the less culpable.

As Henry Louis Gates, Jr., observes in *Figures in Black*, Estwick devises moral boundaries for humanity, since blacks who could read and write debunked the notion exercised by Locke and Hume that "the exercise of reason" was "a privileged category" (63). Estwick fashions a highly rhetorical argument from Pope's aesthetic poem about the Chain and then enters it in a nonliterary, discursive domain—a parliamentary body that enacts laws shaping social policy. Consequently, Estwick's publication, like Petty's *Scale of Creatures* nearly a century earlier, is neither an insignificant nor minor a part of the Chain's discursive legacy.

Ultimately Pope mediates the ideological space between the Chain as a placement of individuals in universal creation and as a hierarchical arrangement of individuals, by proclaiming a universal positionality in the former and racial transcendence in the latter. A representative, recurrent Enlightenment figure, Pope is nominally sympathetic but resolutely hierarchical. Indeed, Pope seems quick to argue on behalf of the noble savage that innocence and simplicity are superior virtues, yet quickest to argue this to the extent that innocence and simplicity uphold the status quo, the belief that "whatever is, is right." In other words, Pope works poetically and rhetorically out of a theological and philosophical background with which Equiano, Cugoano, Sancho, and Prince all must grapple. Pope's Chain of Being can hardly be assessed so straightforwardly as a universal, theological system for organizing humanity without accounting for the complications brought on by slavery.

The Chain's legacy on race is, at once, most scripted and elusive. In other words, in antiquated scientific studies proclaiming the racial inferiority of blacks to whites, the Chain's existence has been well documented—but without its full aesthetic and literary implications. In this chapter, I have sought to examine its subtle transformation from abstract philosophy to hierarchical formula for humanity to aesthetic form. As an aesthetic, the Chain was fitted into an Enlightenment humanist framework in a manner that has been largely ignored in contemporary scholarship. An interdisciplinary, chain-linked crew, including Petty, Ancients and Moderns, Pope, Kant, Voltaire, Hume, and Estwick, connect with both an Enlightenment construct for learning and with a philosophical formula for ordering the universe. Collectively, these writers offer a revealing look at how a concept like the Chain of Being can traverse the boundaries of science and can be made (to paraphrase Stephen Greenblatt) manageable, aesthetic, and consumable when it disseminates into popular culture.

An irreconcilable, strange tension exists in writings that at once assert a uniformity of human nature in all times and all places while they simultaneously insist upon the determining influence of geography, climate, and historical events in the development of culture. It is within a discursive environment where art functioned as a postlapsarian response to disharmony and in a social environment, grappling with slavery, that African-British writings appeared in late eighteenth-century England. We can see how a discourse that professes a universality through its moral teaching gets tested by the very social changes that it must account for in order to maintain credibility. In what follows I will show how African-British writings provide a context for the movement between literature and the social strata, where readings deemed natural, timeless, and universal converge with distinct historical circumstances such as slavery.

## NOTES

1. See Sir William Petty, *The Petty Papers: Some Unpublished Writings of Sir William Petty*, ed. Marquis of Lansdowne, vol. 2 of 2 (London: Constable, 1927), 31. Petty was an important figure in the promotion of the new science. A professor of anatomy, he was among those who approved of eliminating theology from university curricula after Puritan complaints about the mixing of Christianity with heathen philosophy. Petty also surveyed Ireland for the Commonwealth.

2. For a thorough treatment of Bacon and the New or Experimental Philosophy, along with the debate between Ancients and Moderns, see Richard Foster Jones, *Ancients and Moderns: A Study of the Rise of the Scientific Movement in Seventeenth-Century England* (New York: Dover, 1961), 89. The New or Experimental Philosophy referred to discoveries in anatomy, astronomy, and navigation that ushered in modern science. Bacon was seen as a modern who freed philosophy from the shackles of the past.

3. See Marquis of Lansdowne, ed., *The Petty-Southwell Correspondence* (London: Constable, 1928).

4. Sir Matthew Hale's *Primitive Origination of Mankind* was published in 1677.

5. G. F. Zook, *The Company of Royal Adventurers Trading into Africa* (Lancaster, PA: Press of the New Era Printing, 1919), 9, 16. See also Eric Williams, *Capitalism and Slavery* (New York: G. P. Putnam's Sons, 1966), 30, 31. As a result of the War of the Spanish Succession, the English received a monopoly of the slave trade from the Spanish as part of the Asiento Pact.

6. Sir William Temple, Jonathan Swift's boss at Moor Park, negotiated the Triple Alliance with England, France, and Holland. See Temple's "An Essay on the Ancient and Modern Learning," in *Five Miscellaneous Essays*, 3rd ed. (Ann Arbor: University of Michigan Press, 1963), 58. Ancients included Sir William Temple, Nicolas Boileau-Despreaux, and Jean de la Fontaine. Moderns included William Wotton, Charles Perrault, and Bernard le Bovier de Fontenelle. Discoveries in the sciences, especially inventions by members of the Royal Society, were chronicled in Thomas Sprat's *History of the Royal Society*, (1667).

7. See Francis Bacon, *The Advancement of Learning*, vol. 9 of 13 vols. in *The Works of Francis Bacon*, ed. James Spedding et al. (Boston: Taggard and Thomp-

son, 1864), book 5. ch. 2, 64; republished by Scholarly Press, St. Clair Shores, MI. The World's Great Classics Colonial Press version of Bacon's famous observation reads, "It is no wonder that the discovery and advancement of arts hath made no greater progress, when the art of inventing and discovering the sciences remains hitherto unknown" (Book 5. ch. 2, 135). Bacon's claims that certain inventions made possible new geographical discoveries and his elevation of certain inventions to the status of "art" are mediated by the political economies of conquest and slavery. For Bacon, invention as art is metaphorical; it includes the arts and sciences, even speech or rhetoric. See Sahiko Kusukawa, "Bacon's Classification of Knowledge" in *The Cambridge Companion to Bacon*, ed. Markku Peltonen (Cambridge: Cambridge University Press, 1996), 62–63.

In the earliest documented example of an English slave-raiding expedition (1562), John Hawkins describes Africans as "a Species almost distinct from the rest of human Kind, hardy, miserable, and in continual Servitude to one another." Hawkins obtained over three hundred Africans, whom he sold to Spaniards in the West Indies. Like many others in the sixteenth century, John Hawkins's Elizabethan buccaneering expedition was an encroachment on the Portuguese monopoly of the slave trade. The earliest documented evidence of the buying and selling of African slaves in England is the "Petition of William Bragge to the Honorable Sir Thomas Smith, Knight, and all the Company of the East India and Sommer Islands," which claims 6,875 pounds from the East India Company and offers thirteen "Negroes or Indian people" as items. The English joined in on an already-thriving business in slave trading by the Spanish and Portuguese. (Richard Hakluyt, *Hakluyt's voyages; the principal navigations, voyages, traffiques and discoveries of the English nation*, ed. Irwin R. Blacker, vol. 6 [New York: Viking Press, 1965], 258–61. Text from the Glasgow ed., 1903–1905. See also C. M. MacInnes, *England and Slavery* [Bristol: Arrowsmith, 1934], 18, Zook, 4, 11–12, 19, and Eric Williams, 30).

8. A neo-Marxist culturalist, Raymond Williams unites social conditions with cultural influences. He historicizes culture as a reaction to changes in perceptions about art and class, though not as the embodiment of a way of life that these terms came to mean in the nineteenth century. For Williams, it is not so much that economics predetermine culture, but that culture is appropriated to economics in a way that maintains social order and stability. See Raymond Williams, *Culture and Society, 1780–1950* (New York: Columbia University Press, 1983), xiii–xx.

9. In the earliest documented example of an English slave-raiding expedition (1562), John Hawkins justifies encroaching on the Portuguese monopoly on the slave trade by referring to Africans as different than any other species of humankind and perpetually enslaved to one another. Backed by London merchants and a crew of one hundred, Hawkins sailed the *Swallow*, the *Solomon*, and the *Jonas* from England in 1562 to the Guinea coast. Through a combination of piracy, trading with African merchants, and kidnapping, Hawkins obtained over three hundred Africans whom he sold to Spaniards in the West Indies.

The earliest documented evidence of the buying and selling of "Negroes or Indian people" as slaves in England is the "Petition of William Bragge to the Honorable Sir Thomas Smith, Knight, and all the Company of the East India and Sommer Islands," which claims 6,875 pounds from the East India Company and offers thirteen blacks as items. With the entry of Hawkins and other sixteenth-century merchants into the slave trade, the English moved in on an already-thriving business conducted by the Spanish and Portuguese. Revealingly, the William Bragge petition recognizes South Asians or Indians as indistinguishable from "Negroes" or blacks as slaves. The recognition of Indians as blacks was widespread in the sixteenth century before the trade was almost exclusively a trade in blacks or Africans. W. Pinkerton, "Cats, Dogs, and Negroes as Articles of Commerce," *Notes and Queries*, 3rd series 2 (1862), 345–46. See Peter Fryer, *Staying Power: The History of Black People in Britain* (London: Pluto Press, 1984), 9. The first case in English common law case, *Butts v. Penny* (1557), to test the legality of slavery involved Indians. In a chapter entitled "Battle for the Coast," Basil Davidson (*The African Slave Trade: Precolonial History, 1450–1850* [Boston: Little, Brown, 1961]) chronicles the commercial shipping companies trading in the West Indies as follows: Portugal, Holland (1611–12), and England (1618; James I charters the Company of Adventurers of London Trading into Parts of Africa). Strongholds were established by English settlements in the Bermudas (1609), St. Christopher (1623), and Barbados (1625). The French settled in Guadaloupe and Martinique (1626); and the Dutch settled in the Southern Caribbean in the 1630s (Davidson, 55, 58. Davidson's book, *The African Slave Trade*, was originally published in hardcover as *Black Mother* (New York: Penguin Books, 1961).

Although the British did not seek an aggressive stronghold in the slave trade until sugar-producing colonies in the West Indies and tobacco-producing colonies in the New World profited heavily by the 1700s, evidence suggests the existence of British slave-trading expeditions in the late 1500s. In 1555, after an expedition to Africa, John Lok returned to England with five Africans who apparently were not slaves but students. Lok's intentions were to train the students to be interpreters for English slave traders in West Africa (Davidson, 41–43; C. M. MacInnes, *England and Slavery*, [Bristol: Arrowsmith, 1934], 18). See also Peter Fryer, 6.

10. Captain George Berkley, *The Naval History of Britain, from the Earliest Periods of Which there are Accounts in History, to the conclusion of the Year MDCCLVI*, ed. John Hill (T. Osborne and J. Shipton, etc., 1756), 292. See Fryer, *Staying Power*, 12. See also Davidson, *The African Slave Trade*, 50–51.

11. See Stephen Greenblatt, introduction to *Shakespearean Negotiations: The Circulation of Social Energy in Renaissance England* (Berkeley: University of California Press, 1988); also quoted by Louis Montrose in *The New Historicism*, ed. H. Aram Veeser (New York: Routledge, 1989), 32. The coalescence of a literary aesthetics and a social agenda is a revised facet of Stephen Greenblatt's much maligned New Historicism that reconfigures the dialogical nature of language around the diachronic structuring of history. I find Greenblatt's theoretical construction of a cultural poetics, however, a particularly invaluable aspect of a revised, neohistoricist concept. New Historicists are, at present, charged with becoming the thing that they assail—quasi humanists, determinists, unable to produce an objective history—all the while occupying a relative, interpretive space in a discontinuous history. Yet, this point is open to debate. In an essay in *The New Historicism*, Hayden White claims that some new historicists are led by their own inconsistencies to create formalist, poststructuralist, and culturalist fallacies in both literary and historical studies (293).

But in the introduction, H. Aram Veeser acknowledges "the heterogeneity and contention" of a volume that "has given scholars new opportunities to cross the boundaries separating history, anthropology, art, politics, literature, and economics" (ix).

12. As David Dabydeen puts it, Pope's age had to "reconcile their belief in the civilising effects of commerce to the barbaric realities of the slave trade." See David Dabydeen, "Eighteenth-Century English Literature on Commerce and Slavery," in *The Black Presence in English Literature*, ed. David Dabydeen (Manchester: Manchester University Press, 1985), 32. Like others who invested in the slave trade, Pope suffered heavy losses in the East India Company.

13. The Poet's first name, Philis, was correctly spelled with one "l." Most writers opt for the double "l." She was named for the schooner that brought her to the New World as a slave.

14. George Sherburn, ed., *The Correspondence of Alexander Pope*, vol. 3 of 4 (Oxford: Clarendon Press, 1956), 117, 163. Letters dated 1 January 1730–31 and 19 June 1730. Pope first published *Essay on Man* anonymously in order to ensure objective critical readings of the poem. Indeed, early responses to the poem by William Somervile, Leonard Welsted (whom Pope parodied in the *Dunciad*), and the Abbe du Resnel and others were highly favorable. See Spence, *Anecdotes* #308 and #454 in *Observations, Anecdotes, and Characters of Books and Men*, ed. James M. Osborn, vol. 1 of 2. (Oxford: Clarendon Press), 1966. Pope's most notable critic for the *Essay on Man*, Swiss professor Jean-Pierre de Crousaz, relied on an erroneous, poorly made French translation of the *Essay on Man* from which to base his attacks on the poem. Crousaz came dangerously close to accusing Pope of heresy and misread the *Essay on Man* as supporting a Deistic, pro-Spinoza philosophy. See J. P. de Crousaz, *Examen de l'Essai sur l'Homme* and *Commentarie*. See Spence, *Anecdotes* #306 and #308, vol. 1. Samuel Johnson declared the *Essay on Man* "not the happiest of Pope's performances" and further noted that "never were penury of knowledge and vulgarity of sentiment so happily disguised," in *Lives of The English Poets*, ed. George Birkbeck Hill, vol. 3 (Oxford: Clarendon Press, 1905), 242, 243. Praising Pope and Swift as moral writers, Bolingbroke writes: "I have sometimes thought that if preachers, hangmen, and moral-writers keep vice at a stand, or so much as retard the progress of it, they do as much as human nature admits." Upon learning Pope's true identity as author of *Essay on Man*, Swift writes, "I confess I did never imagine you were so deep in Morals, or that so many new & excellent Rules could be produced so advantageously & agreeable" (Sherburn, *Correspondence*, vol. 3, 439).

15. Alexander Pope, *Pastoral Poetry and An Essay on Criticism*, in *The Poems of Alexander Pope*, vol. 1, ed. E. Audra and Aubrey Williams (London: Methuen, 1961), 148–94. Subsequent references to "Windsor Forest" and "Epistle to Bathurst" are taken from the Twickenham edition of Pope's poems. See also Alexander Pope, "Windsor Forest," in *The Poems of Alexander Pope*, ed. John Butt (New Haven, CT: Yale University Press, 1963), 195–210. [References to *Essay on Man* are taken from Alexander Pope, *An essay on Man*, ed. Maynard Mack (London: Methuen, 1950); these citations appear in this book by line and page number. See notes 22 and 30.] As David Gross observes, "a moral critique of the dominant economic order combined with the evident willingness to share in the benefits of it—can be seen in

Pope and in the residual values of Neo-Classicism generally" (David S. Gross, "The Conqu'ing Force of Unresisted Steel: Pope and Power in *The Rape of the Lock*," *New Orleans Review* 15 [Winter 1988]: 23–30).

16. Maynard Mack, *Collected in Himself: Essays Critical, Biographical, and Bibliographical on Pope and Some of His Contemporaries* (Newark: University of Delaware Press, 1982), 74.

17. Zook, 9, 16.

18. As Etienne Balibar writes, "Nationalism aspires to uniformity and rationality . . . and yet it cultivates the symbols, the fetishes of an autochthonous national character, which must be preserved against dissipation." See Etienne Balibar in *Anatomy of Racism*, ed. David Theo Goldberg (Minneapolis: University of Minnesota Press, 1990), 283. Though addressing issues in the twentieth-century arena, Balibar affirms just as validly for the eighteenth century that racism's excesses both universalize nationalism (almost subversively) by "correcting in sum its lack of universality," and particularize it, "correcting its lack of specificity" (283).

19. Queen Elizabeth herself ordered the deportation of blacks from England on 11 July 1596 in an open letter to the Lord Mayor of London and the mayors of other cities. The Queen wrote that "there are of late divers [*sic*] blackmoores brought into this realme, of which kind of people there are allready here to manie [sic]." Queen Elizabeth's suggestion stemmed from widespread paranoia. See Great Britain, *Acts of the Privy Council of England: New Series*, 1542–1631, vol. 26 (London: H. M. Stationery Office, 1890–1940), 20–21. For an excellent study on black people in Britain, see Peter Fryer, *Staying Power*.

20. Eric Williams, *Capitalism and Slavery*, 32–33. See also J. Latimer, *Annals of Bristol in the Eighteenth Century* (Bristol, 1893), 271.

21. See Samuel Richardson, *Pamela*, vol. 1 of 2 vols. (London: J. M. Dent and Sons; New York: E. P. Dutton, 1950), 6; first published 1914, 230. See also Arthur O. Lovejoy, who cites the poem in *The Great Chain of Being: A Study of the History of an Idea* (Cambridge, MA: Harvard University Press, 1936), 207. Lovejoy duly notes that the poem represents a subordination that was "more gratifying to the higher than consoling to the lower ranks" (207). The poem from *Pamela* closely resembles part of a sermon written by John Fell 22 December 1680, who cites St. Paul in the twelfth chapter of the *First Book of Corinthians*: "We are all born naked and unarmed, needing the assistance of each other; but wanting strength or weapons to enforce it; but the divine Wisdom has so suited things, that the strong depends upon the weak, as much as the weak do's on the stong: the rich is assisted by the poor, as the poor is by the rich . . ." (2–3). In the *First Book of Corinthians*, St. Paul addresses the diversity of gifts among individuals, such as wisdom, knowledge, and faith that serve a greater humanity. John Hawkesworth also wrote a poem, "The Death of Arachne, an Heroi-Comi-Tragic Poem," that thematized the Chain as a concept. Literary uses of non race-specific hierarchical contexts also appear in Addison and Steele's *Spectators* #518, #519, and #621. See Joseph Addison and Richard Steele, The *Spectator*, ed. Donald F. Bond, 5 vols. (Oxford: Clarendon Press, 1965). Addison and Steele acknowledge a Chain of Being in ascending order below and above the individual but do not differentiate among individuals by race.

22. Alexander Pope, *An Essay on Man*, in *Reproductions of the Manuscripts in the Pierpont Morgan Library and Houghton Library*, ed. Maynard Mack (Oxford: 1962).

23. See Immanuel Wallerstein, "The Ideological Tensions of Capitalism: Universalism versus Racism and Sexism," in *Race, Nation, Class: Ambiguous Identities*, ed. Etienne Balibar and Immanuel Wallerstein (London: Verso, 1991), 29.

24. Richard C. Sha, "Gray's Political 'Elegy': Poetry as the Burial of History," *Philological Quarterly* 69 (Summer 1990): 337.

25. In "Reading Philosophical Poetry: A Hermeneutics of Metaphor for Pope's *Essay on Man*," in *The Philosopher as Writer: The Eighteenth Century*, ed. Robert Ginsberg (London: Associated University Presss, 1987, 130), for example, Harry M. Solomon argues that misreadings have charged Pope with "Cosmic Toryism," accusing him of extolling the Chain in order "to keep people within their social class" and to "sanction submission to one's social superiors." Yet F.E.L. Priestley, who, according to Solomon, authored "the only first-rate essay on Pope's use of the great chain metaphor," acknowledges the poem's relationship with the empirical Chain's history of ideas—a link that Solomon denies having sanctioned. (See Priestly, "Pope and the Great Chain of Being," in *Essays in English Literature from the Renaissance to the Victorian Age*, ed., Millar MacLure and F.W. Watt [Toronto: University of Toronto Press, 1964], 226). It seems ironic for Solomon to charge others with metaphorical misrepresentations of Pope's poetry while ascribing oxymoronic terms like "regulative metaphor," even to a regulated Olympian figure like Pope. As to Pope's belief in impartiality, social inequities, and hierarchies, in *Alexander Pope* (Cambridge: Cambridge University Press, 1976), 107, Yasmine Gooneratne sees submission to one's station in life as "social and political propaganda . . . designed to keep thrones safe for Tudor, and later for Stuart and Hanoverian monarchies." But rather than view Pope's depicting social subordination negatively, she considers it as a timely, appropriate brand of Augustan democracy.

26. David Fairer, *Pope: New Contexts* (New York: Harvester Wheatsheaf, 1990), 1.

27. Henry Louis Gates, Jr., makes this observation in *Figures in Black: Words, Signs, and the 'Racial' Self* (New York: Oxford University Press, 1989).

28. See Malvaern Van Wyk Smith, "'The Most Wretched of the Human Race': The Iconography of the Khoikhoin (Hottentots) 1500–1800," *History and Anthropology* 5 (1992): 285; see also J. Robert Constantine, "The Ignoble Savage, An Eighteenth-Century Literary Stereotype," *Phylon* 27 (Summer 1966): 171–179.

29. Pope accesses Locke's empirical method for apprehending a Deity by hierarchical reasoning, *Essay Concerning Human Understanding*, 61–63. See James Sambrook, *The Eighteenth Century: The Intellectual and Cultural Context of English Literature, 1700–1789* (London: Longman, 1986). See also A. D. Nutall, *Pope's 'Essay on Man'* (London: George Allen & Unwin, 1984).

30. In the Pierpont Morgan Library Manuscript (MLM), Pope's working draft of *Essay on Man*, the passage is extensively altered from the way it appears in the Twickenham edition. In MLM, Pope merely disapproves of idolizing the improper rewards of virtue and softens the portrait of the ignorant, albeit ennobled, native: "[the Indian] thinks, admitted to that equal sky / His faithful Dog shall bear him

company" (I. 117–18). As Maynard Mack notes, Pope's *Essay on Man* received a popularity in Europe for more than one-hundred years after publication that "can hardly be exaggerated" (243). Translations included Czech, Danish, Dutch, French, German, Italian, Latin, Portugeuse, Russian, Swedish, and so on. In America alone, Pope's *Essay on Man* appeared in print at least "sixty-eight times between 1747 and 1809," according to Agnes Marie Sibley, Alexander Pope's *Prestige in America, 1725–1835* (New York, 1949) 23; quoted in Winthrop Jordan, *White over Black: American Attitudes Toward the Negro, 1550–1812* (Baltimore: Penguin Books, 1969), 483.

31. Laura Brown, *Alexander Pope* (Oxford: Basil Blackwell, 1985), 70. See also Joseph Spence, *Anecdotes*, vol. 1 #575, 240. Spence records Pope's explication of the Indian Passage in *Essay on Man* as follows: "Our flattering ourselves with the thoughts of enjoying the company of our friends here when in the other world, may be but too like the Indians thinking that they shall have their dogs and their horses there" (240).

32. Louis Montrose, "Professing the Renaissance: The Poetics and Politics of Culture," in *The New Historicism*, ed. Veeser, 18.

33. Donald Greene, "An Anatomy of Pope-bashing," in *The Enduring Legacy: Alexander Pope Tercentenary Essays*, ed. G. S. Rousseau and Pat Rogers (Cambridge: Cambridge University Press, 1988), 241–281.

34. Ibid., 246.

35. See Paul Gilroy, "One Nation Under a Groove: The Cultural Politics of 'Race' and Racism in Britain," in *Anatomy of Racism*, ed. David T. Goldberg (Minneapolis: University of Minnesota Press, 1990), 263.

36. Bernard Mandeville, *The Fable of the Bees: or, Private Vices, Public Benefits* (Oxford: At the Clarendon Press, 1924).

37. Alexander Pope, "Moral Essays: Epistle to Bathurst," *The Poems of Alexander Pope*, ed., John Butt (New Haven, CT: Yale University Press, 1963), 570–586.

38. The remainder of the essay reads, "On the other hand, the most rude and barbarous of the whites, such as the ancient *Germans*, the present *Tartars*, have still something eminent about them, in their valour, form of government, or some other particular. Such a uniform and constant difference could not happen, in so many countries and ages, if nature had not made an original distinction between these breeds of men. Not to mention our colonies, there are *Negroe* slaves dispersed all over *Europe*, of whom none ever discovered any symptoms of ingenuity; tho' low people, without education, will start up amongst us, and distinguish themselves in every profession. In Jamaica, indeed, they talk of one negro, as a man of parts and learning; but 'tis likely he is admir'd for slender accomplishments, like a parrot who speaks a few words plainly" (David Hume, "Of National Characters," in *Essays and Treatises on Several Subjects*, 4th ed., vol. 1 of 4, [London, A. Millar, 1753]), 277–300. See the revised essay in David Hume, *Essays: Moral, Political and Literary* (Oxford: Oxford University Press, 1963), 202–203.

39. "Variety of the Human Species: Tartars, Hottentots, Negroes, Americans, etc." in *London Magazine*, 16 July 1750, 318. Anthony Barker identifies only three printed, fleeting references to the Chain of Being as a racial phenomenon that appear before the 1770s (often cited as the onset of the abolitionist movement); these

specifically connect the Chain with racial hierarchies rather than define it as a general prescription for universal order. The articles include the unsigned article named above, an article in a minor geographical work, 1766; and a publication on unbaptized blacks in the West Indies, 1768. Barker, along with Basil Davidson, regards ideological notions about racial differences between blacks and whites as appearing in print only late in the eighteenth-century. See Anthony Barker, *The African Link: British Attitudes to the Negro in the Era of the Atlantic Slave Trade, 1550–1807* (London: Frank Cass, 1978). But bearing Sir William Petty, Sir Thomas Herbert, and others firmly in mind, I believe that formulations about black inferiority as truth attend Europeans' early encounters with blacks and with Africa. As M. Van Wyk Smith writes, the negative implication of blacks, especially in seventeenth- and eighteenth-century travelogues, was not merely "purblind ethnocentricity," but "the imprint of an anxious contemporary European polemic surrounding the European transition from absolutist to constitutional monarchies."

40. Voltaire, "On the Antiquity of Nations," in *The Best Known Works of Voltaire* (1940), 365. See also Soame Jenyns, "Disquisitions on Several Subjects, on the Chain of Universal Being," in *The Works of Soame Jenyns*, vol. 2 of 2 vols. (Philadelphia: Printed by Thomas Dobson, 1790). Samuel Johnson thoroughly debunks Jenyns's theory of subordination but does not discuss the idea's racial implications. See Johnson's "Review of [Soame Jenyns], *A Free Inquiry into the Nature and Origin of Evil*" (1757), published in Donald Greene, ed., *Samuel Johnson* (New York: Oxford University Press, 1984), 522–543. For an interesting study of Soame Jenyns's controversial position in the History of Ideas debate, see Bertram H. David, ed. *Soame Jenyns* (Boston: Twayne, 1984).

41. Jenyns, 133. In 1799, Dr. Charles White, an English physician and member of the Royal Society, wrote that species exist in hierarchical arrangement with one another, and that differences were based on race, intelligence, and biosexual factors. Using an analysis of a friend's collection of human skulls, White ranked humanity in descending order from Europeans to Africans: "Nature exhibits to our view an immense chain of beings, endued with various degrees of intelligence and active powers, suited to their stations in the general system." See Charles White, *An Account of the Regular gradation in man, and in different animals and vegetables; and from the former to the Latter* (C. Dilly, 1799), 41, 66–67. White also interpolated bio-sexual differences between blacks and whites into his equation in a perverted "reverse hierarchy" of sexual endowment and prowess. Placing blacks below Europeans on the Chain, White added differences in sexual capacity and size of genitalia between black and white men and women.

42. See Dr. Konrad Dieterich's "Summary of Kant's Theory of the Heavens," Appendix A, Immanuel Kant, "Natural History and Theory of the Heavens," in *Kant's Cosmogony*, trans. W. Hastie, D.D. (New York: Johnson Reprint Corporation, 1970), 177. See also W. H. Werkmeister, "Kant, Nicolai Hartmann, and the Great Chain of Being," *The Great Chain of Being and Italian Phenomenology*, ed. Angela Ales Bello (Boston, MA: D. Reidel, 1981), 71. Werkmeister (whose translation of Kant's passage on Pope differs from W. Hastie's version above) cites Immanuel Kant, *Allgemeine Naturgeschichte und Theorie des Himmels*, 1755, Akademie-Ausgabe, I, 359f.

43. Thomas Bendyshe, "The History of Anthropology," Anthropological Society of London, *Memoirs* 1 (1863–64), 424–26. See also Winthrop Jordan, *White Over Black: American Attitudes Toward the Negro, 1550-1812* (Baltimore: Penguin Books, Inc., 1969), 216–268; first published by the University of North Carolina Press, Chapel Hill, 1968. Works by naturalists like Linneaus (*Systema Naturae*, 1758), Charles Bonnet, Swiss naturalist, 1763, François Bernier, 1684; and Dutch anatomist Peter Camper, 1770s, classified the human species into racial groups by using a nonhierarchical method. But though not divisible by racial hierarchies, the method by which they classified racial groups, nonetheless, did the pernicious work of reinforcing racist ideologies. François Bernier, a student of Linneaus, generally based his classifications of humanity on physiognomy: facial features, hair texture, and color. He divided humanity roughly into four categories—Europeans, Africans, Orientals, and Lapps. Edward Long, who was influenced by Samuel Estwick, wrote *History of Jamaica* (1774) which identified blacks as lowest on the Chain of Being. James Burnett, Lord Monboddo, a Scottish philosopher, was so preoccupied with the Chain of Being as ethnography that he wrote six volumes over twenty years, beginning with 1773. And in 1774, Henry Home, Lord Kames published *Sketches of the History of Man*.

44. Bendyshe, 106. Sir William Temple, who actually opposed slavery, nevertheless believed that Africans were physiologically suited to it, because of the intense heat of the sun on the African continent.

45. Stephen Jay Gould, "The Geometer of Race," *Discover* 15 (November 1994), 67. Blumenbach's findings were reprinted in the preface to the *Letters of the Late Ignatius Sancho* in order to show that blacks could be as learned as whites (see chapter 3).

46. See Samuel Estwick, *Considerations on the Negroe Cause Commonly so called, addressed to The Right Honourable Lord Mansfield, Lord Chief Justice of the Court of King's Bench* (London: J. Dodsley in Pall-Mall, 1788), 82. Estwick published this pamphlet in order to challenging the Mansfield Decision of 1772. See also Peter Fryer, *Staying Power*, 156–57; James Burnet, *Lord Monboddo, Of the Origin and Progress of Language*, Vol. I (Edinburgh: J. Balfour, 1774), 239; and Arthur O. Lovejoy, 'Monboddo and Rousseau', *Modern Philology*, 30 (1932–33), 283ff.

# 2

# Ukawsaw Gronniosaw and Ottobah Cugoano: Perspectives on a Theological Chain

Sir—I am a six year-old blackmoor boy, and have, by my lady's order, been christened by the chaplain. The good man has gone further with me, and told me a great deal of news; as that I am as good as my lady herself, as I am a Christian, and many other things; but for all this, the parrot who came over with me from our country is as much esteemed by her as I am. Besides this, the shock dog has a collar that cost as much as mine. I desire also to know whether, now I am Christian, I am obliged to dress like a Turk and wear a turban. I am, sir, your most obedient servant, Pompey.
—Sir Richard Steele
*The Tatler*, #245, 31 October–2 November 1710

In the preface to *A Narrative of the Most Remarkable Particulars in the Life of James Albert Ukawsaw Gronniosaw, an African Prince. Related by Himself*, 1770, the Reverend Walter Shirley, cousin to the Countess of Huntingdon, interprets Gronniosaw's journey from Bornu in West Africa (modern-day Bornu in Nigeria) to Christian conversion in New York City as a fitting response to the question put by skeptics who rejected the Calvinist doctrine known as predestination and election.[1] Treating the journey as a kind of foreordained pilgrimage inspired by Gronniosaw's own intellectual curiosity rather than by missionary efforts, Reverend Shirley writes: "In what manner will God deal with those benighted parts of the world where the gospel of Jesus Christ hath never reached" (27)?

As a young boy growing up in Bornu, West Africa, James Albert Ukawsaw Gronniosaw had yearned for an adventure. He had also sought answers to questions about the existence of the "GREAT MAN OF POWER," maker of all things. Frustrated family members, who rejected the idea of a single omnipotent being,[2] believed that all power beyond humanity was vested in the celestial bodies, the sun, moon, and the stars. A Gold Coast merchant had finally lured the despairing Gronniosaw away from his family by promising to show him "houses with wings to them walk upon the water," white folks, companions his own age, and a safe and early return to Bornu (31). Prophetically, the merchant assured Gronniosaw that a trip across the Atlantic would be of "more service" than anything that his parents could do for him. But what the Gold Coast merchant did not tell Gronniosaw, and what Reverend Shirley does not divulge in the narrative's preface to the reader, is that the journey "out of darkness into . . . marvelous light" was not intended for spiritual enlightenment, but for a period of enslavement and a life of poverty and suffering in a faraway land. Ottobah Cugoano (who later read Gronniosaw's narrative), aptly noted that enslavers do not bring away Africans in order to improve them, but so that "they may serve them as . . . beasts of burden" and in order to advance their own profit.[3] As an adult, Gronniosaw would later recall, "Indeed if I could have known when I left my friends and country that I should never return to them again my misery on that occasion would have been inexpressible" (31).

Both James Albert Ukawsaw Gronniosaw and Quobna Ottobah Cugoano (*Thoughts and Sentiments on the Evil of Slavery*, 1787), convey the difficulty of erasing social conditions from certain universalist moral equations. As I noted in chapter 1, Pope unveils a theory of subordination, rooted in a theological Chain of Being, which he intends as neither overtly hierarchical nor racial; and in the *Essay on Man*, he pointedly boasts of the existence of an impartial God. But viewed in a broader historical context, the Chain's discursive legacy relays a more complex philosophical message: the sacred realm was no more excluded from the politicization of race than were the scientific, philosophical, and literary communities. Through personal beliefs and experiences reflected in religious-centered publications, Gronniosaw and Cugoano mediate the dialectic between a universalist, moral theodicy and a hierarchical, racialist theodicy that was evident in social practice. Addressing a theological theory of subordination from the bottom up (E. P. Thompson's so-called inverted pyramid in *Whigs and Hunters*, 1975), Gronniosaw and Cugoano expose the Chain to a far different kind of scrutiny than do the Platonists of antiquity who originated the idea. As formerly enslaved Africans, they demonstrate that the fundamental bases of certain religious principles, which were taught to them by European theologians, represented black subordination as an element of natural order and accordingly supported a discursive ideology proclaiming the racial inferiority of blacks to whites. Hence, the publications of Gronniosaw and Cugoano require close analysis so that the Chain of Being might be revised as relevant historical, literary, and theological metaphor.

The idea of racial subordination as an element of natural order saturates eighteenth-century philosophical and theological discourse. Slaves who had been baptized were often referred to as both black *and* Christian, as though race and reverence were mutually exclusive. (Olaudah Equiano proudly records that he himself was frequently identified as the "black Christian.") Long after converting to Christianity, Gronniosaw still regarded himself as a "poor heathen" who sometimes felt unworthy among Christian ranks. He also gives conflicting messages throughout the narrative, alternately expressing both deep regret for ever having been removed from family and homeland and gratitude for a fate of captivity, poverty, and suffering as a prelude to a Christian conversion.

When he arrived in Amsterdam as a free man in 1762, Gronniosaw was considered to be so phenomenal as a reformed Christian specimen of a so-called ennobled being that he was obliged to relate the story of his conversion before forty-eight Calvinist ministers each Thursday for seven weeks. He must have been an imposing figure; standing before an all-white ministerial congregation, telling the story of an odyssey that led from his self-described pampered surroundings in Bornu to enslavement in Barbados and New England, followed by betrayal and poverty in England. But to the congregation, he most likely expressed the religious philosophy that he relates in the narrative: that he desired "to be counted as nothing, a stranger in the world, and a pilgrim here." He might have added, as his written narrative affirms, "'I know that my REDEEMER liveth,' and I'm thankful for every trial and trouble that I've met with, as I am not without hope that they have been all sanctified to me" (46). And yet the actual circumstances of Gronniosaw's life, along with the reality of the social world that he inhabited, severely undercut the ruminations he frequently made to the contrary.

Born between 1710 and 1714, Gronniosaw was kidnapped from Bornu along the Guinea Coast as a young boy and enslaved briefly in Barbados; then he was transported to the New York City and New Jersey areas. Perhaps as a consequence of his close brushes with death early in captivity, Gronniosaw acquired the essential skills that shaped a Christian philosophy (grafted onto a Muslim upbringing). He also learned to assume a posture of subordination toward enslavers that helped to ensure his long-term survival. For example, when he was first taken by the merchant from Bornu to the Gold Coast, more than a thousand miles away, Gronniosaw was brought before a king who, according to custom, prepared to behead him. However, impressed with Gronniosaw's "undaunted courage" in the face of death, and discovering that he was a king's offspring, the Gold Coast King spared his life and put him up for sale instead. A French brig captain rejected the fifteen-year-old Gronniosaw because of his slight build. After additional failed attempts to sell him, merchants finally approached a Dutch sea captain and trader whose vessel had just sailed into harbor.

Upon discovering that he would be thrown overboard if the purchase fell through, Gronniosaw soon found himself in the peculiar position of seeking protection while in captivity. Clutching the Dutch sea captain, Gronniosaw exclaimed, "Father save me" and was purchased by the Captain for two yards of cloth (33). In the ensuing confusion, Gronniosaw blurs the distinction among the Father figure as Saviour, the Father figure as enslaver, and the Father figure as patriarch. For example, with immediate death as the alternative to enslavement, Gronniosaw understandably gushes that "it pleased the Almighty to influence [the Captain] in my behalf" (34). On a later occasion around 1730, when enslaved to "Mr. Freelandhouse" (identified as Dutch Reformed minister Theodorus Jacobus Frelignhuysen), in New England, Gronniosaw asked him the meaning of prayer. Freelandhouse replied that "God who liv'd in Heaven" was "[Gronniosaw's] father and best friend" (35). But Gronniosaw protested that *his* father lived in Bornu and added that there must have been some mistake. He further expressed a strong desire to return to Bornu and to see his father, mother, and sister and asked that Freelandhouse would be so kind as to return him to his family. When Freelandhouse tearfully informed him that "God was a great and good Spirit" who created everyone in "Ethiopia, Africa and America," Gronniosaw responded, "I always thought so when I lived at home! Now, if I had wings like an eagle, I would fly to tell my dear mother that God is greater than the sun, moon and stars; and that they were made by him" (36). The incident is the first of many throughout the narrative in which he continually questions his captors and/or local clergy about the true meaning of God and asks their guidance in interpreting the Scriptures.[4]

When en route to Barbados from the Guinea coast, Gronniosaw listens to prayers each Sunday that the ship's Captain reads from a biblical text. The ritual is a significant prelude to what Henry Louis Gates, Jr., calls the trope of the talking book, described in five slave narratives that were published in the eighteenth century.[5] Gronniosaw was the first of three narrators to utilize the literal version of the trope of the talking book, however. He recalls that "the master" moves his lips as he reads from the book, giving the impression that the book is actually speaking to him. When he puts the book down, Gronniosaw picks it up and presses it against his ear. When the book does not speak to him, he interprets its silence as evidence "that everybody and everything despised me because I was black" (34). While Gates's brilliant analysis of the passage as an early indication of the formation of a black literary tradition need not be repeated here, I want to point to the trope's pertinence in a different context related to my theological discussion of the narrative.

The book that does not speak to Gronniosaw is a biblical text, perhaps symbolizing the Christian doctrines by which Gronniosaw must abide, but whose enforcement with respect to his equality is seriously compromised. This passage is the only one in the narrative in which the usually unperturbed Gronniosaw refers directly to race or color as the specific reason that "everybody and everything despised" him. Not only does he reveal an awareness of racial prejudice in this scene, but he also acknowledges its direct impact on him. His otherwise subdued treatment of incidents which can be attributed to racial prejudice may have stemmed both from an amanuensis discretely honoring written decorum and from Gronniosaw's escaping the severest brutalities of slavery that others suffered.

In a paradoxical twist on the trope of the talking book (which is, of course, a silent book) and on language as power, Gronniosaw later describes a Calibanesque scene in which he says that learning how to curse and swear "'twas almost the first English I could speak" (34). After being sold in Barbados by the Dutch sea captain to one Mr. Vanhorn for fifty dollars, Gronniosaw was dressed in serving livery, according to custom, and taken to New England where he waited tables and cleaned utensils as a domestic servant.[6] Gronniosaw does not direct this hostile, newly acquired English language toward his enslavers, but rather to his fellow domestic servants. The envy and rivalry that he cites among servants is all too common in an environment in which individuals sometimes competed for—and were singled out by enslavers for—favored servant status as a reward for obedience and docility. Gronniosaw is surprised to witness the other servants using foul language among themselves. Heavily favored by Vanhorn and later by the Freelandhouses, he drew resentment from other servants, and if anyone dared to cross him, he "was sure to call upon God to damn them immediately" (34).

Listening to the sermons of Freelandhouse, Gronniosaw thought it comical but in the end agreeable when instructed to kneel down and put his hands together in prayer, and he eventually converted to Christianity. Though the conversion seemingly resolved differences he had with his Muslim upbringing, which included conflicts such as the practice of idolatry, it raised a multitude of questions about the new religious principles that he was taught to embrace. For instance, Gronniosaw was pleased when Freelandhouse informed him that God made beings of all races and all other living things as well. But embracing perhaps the only view that could make sense of his present situation, he regarded himself as a most abominable, vile sinner who, above all others, deserved a fate of enslavement and poverty. On yet another occasion, when Freelandhouse cited the Book of *Revelations* and said that when God comes, every eye shall see him, Gronniosaw imagined that he alone was singled out for God's condemnation because the minister directed a piercing gaze at him as he spoke. He avoided Freeland-house for some time afterward, believing that the minister-enslaver disliked him intensely.

Interpreting such guideposts as God on high unleashing his wrath, Gron-niosaw believed that he had created his own predicament as a consequence of his own sins and personal behavior and that he therefore deserved any cruelty that befell him. In an effort to console him, Mrs. Freelandhouse gave Gronniosaw Richard Baxter's *Call to the Unconverted* (1658) and John Bunyan's *The Holy War* (1682). But he believed these writers to be as tor-mented as he and remained confused about the nature of God's punishment for the wicked and his regard for the just.

Not surprisingly Gronniosaw could only blame himself personally if he could not criticize a society that regarded him as one who was well suited to a fate of enslavement and poverty. Numerous inconsistencies in religious, as well as legal, practice—had he been more knowledgeable of them—might have explained that at least some of his personal dissatisfaction was not so personal after all but amounted to the protection of profits from slavery. Some religious figures struggled with the unsavory, immoral practices of those planters who attempted to prevent the baptism of their slaves for fear that they might then have legal grounds to go free. In *A Christian Directory: Or, A Summ of Practical Theologie, and Cases of Conscience* (Nevell Sim-mons, 1673), ii. 557–58, Richard Baxter excoriated planters for preventing their slaves from being baptized as Christians. A Presbyterian himself, Baxter chastised these planters for putting profit ahead of morality, con-cluding that they desisted from this practice since christianizing blacks could in some instances make their (re)enslavement more difficult. Though heavily influenced by Baxter, Morgan Godwyn, in *The Negro's and Indians' Advo-cate . . . in our Plantations*, went even further in exposing avarice in the exploitation of slaves. Godwyn wrote that the West Indian planter lobby knew "no other God but money, nor Religion but Profit."[7] He was threat-ened with charges of slander by representatives of the planters' lobby, who claimed that to christianize slaves did not serve the planters' best interests. Like Morgan Godwyn before him, the Methodist founder, Reverend George Whitefield, echoes Richard Baxter's complaints of hypocrisy among Chris-tian planters. But in 1751, Whitefield paradoxically affirmed slavery to John Wesley, even as he welcomed Georgia's growing black population "for breeding up their posterity in the nurture and admonition of the Lord."[8]

Gronniosaw, whose own enslavement was not affected by his religious beliefs, chose to make himself responsible for his own contentment. After undergoing great emotional turmoil, Gronniosaw meditated alone in a clear-ing in a nearby wood and experienced a religious awakening: "The peace and serenity which filled my mind after this was wonderful, and cannot be told. I would not have changed situations, or been any one but myself for the whole world" (39). Gronniosaw also emerged from deep meditation with an anti-materialist philosophy that would forever haunt him. "I blest God for my poverty, that I had no worldly riches or grandeur to draw my heart from him," he confessed (39).

Throughout the course of the narrative, even after he is free, Gronniosaw is continually cheated of large quantities of money, perhaps enough to have relieved his near-constant poverty and suffering by people whom he identifies as Christians. In each instance, he discovers that he has no legal recourse by which to recover these financial losses. Cugoano would later complain in a philosophical essay that slave holders would "rob men of some of their property" and would keep any property that belonged to the slave (113). Gronniosaw gives the first evidence of suffering from a lifelong difficulty in earning and maintaining a living wage when the Dutch sea captain in Bornu takes from him large quantities of gold that he wore in huge ringlets according to his country's customs: "I found all this [gold] troublesome, and was glad when my new master took it from me.—I was now washed, & clothed in the Dutch or English manner" (34). In a series of observations, he registers further confusion about the incompatibility between having money and keeping his commitment as a Christian. First he says that he "never regarded money in the least" (43). But later he admits: "I had always a propensity to relieve every object in distress as far as I was able, I used to give to all that complained to me; sometimes half a guinea at a time, *as I did not understand the real value of it*" (45; my italics). Such conflicting views are natural to Gronniosaw's state; indeed they are encouraged by the way in which the outside world treats him. We see in this instance Gronniosaw's struggle to make sense of his impoverishment.

Freelandhouse stipulated that upon his death, which occurred in 1747/48(?), his faithful servant was to be set free. Gronniosaw remained first with Mrs. Freelandhouse, who died two years later, then with the five Freelandhouse sons, one after the other, until they also died about four years later. A family acquaintance, whom Gronniosaw identifies only as a principal merchant in New York, paid the three-pound debt that Gronniosaw had accumulated after the Freelandhouse deaths and vowed never to expect repayment. Within a month, however, the merchant reneged and threatened to reenslave Gronniosaw, who was unable to pay off the debt. In order to expunge the debt, Gronniosaw agreed to go privateering with a sea captain to Santo Domingo in Britain's war with France. But upon the crew's return to New York, the merchant "swept . . . into his handkerchief" Gronniosaw's entire 135-pound share of the profits and refused to pay him any of it (42). Frightened of retaliation and leaving matters to "Providence," Gronniosaw refused to press for the money or to allow a Mr. Dunscum, who took him under protection, to do so on his behalf. He concludes, "I believed that it would not prosper with him, and so it happened, for by a series of losses and misfortunes he became poor, and was soon after drowned, as he was on a party of pleasure" (42).

Gronniosaw referred, of course, to the Calvinist belief in predestination and election, which stipulates that one cannot alter fate. In another example, he reveals that in battle near Saint Domingo, his enemies were not all on the other side of the battle; some fellow sailors were particularly cruel to him. "I can't help mentioning one circumstance that hurt me more than all the rest, which was, that he snatched a book out of my hand, that I was very fond of, and used frequently to amuse myself with, & threw it into the sea" (41). Gronniosaw goes on to say that the sailor later became the first member of the engagement to lose his life. "I don't pretend to say that this happened because he was not my friend," Gronniosaw professes, "but I thought 'twas a very awful providence, to see how the enemies of the LORD are cut off" (41).

But Gronniosaw is unable to reconcile the contradiction between his belief in predestination or divine providence and his belief in personal responsibility. Similarly, he is unable to recognize the contradiction between his own denial of worldly treasures while his enslavers and Christian advisors reap great wealth from him and others, all of which occurs compliments of the slave trade. At the same time, accepting personal responsibility for his predicament gave Gronniosaw the impetus to mend his character as the key to freedom and salvation. A part of him, perhaps subconsciously, believed his blackness to be a factor in a foreordained punishment from God. Gronniosaw's self-perception is thus a critical factor in the way in which he regards his Christian conversion.

Like the fictional Pompey in *Tatler* #245 (quoted in my introductory headnote to this chapter), Gronniosaw struggles with the dehumanizing conditions of slavery and poverty in tandem with trying to understand Christian principles conveyed to him by various religious figures. In addition, while Reverend George Whitefield and John Wesley became sources of inspiration for him, others, like the beloved Vanhorn and Freelandhouse, are participants in the slave trade and thus are major forces in Gronniosaw's enslavement and continued poverty. Innocent and naive, Gronniosaw is not unlike the ornamented youth[9] whose commentary Steele entered in the *Tatler* as a parody of contradictory Christian practices (which I shall discuss shortly) on the legality of enslaving baptized blacks or the ethics of baptizing enslaved blacks. Gronniosaw believes that his personal sins and shortcomings have imposed poverty and enslavement upon him, but the reader can immediately see his dilemma in a far different context: a greater, more broadly encompassing social order was able to preserve its dominance by altering the conditions of inclusion by disenfranchised groups or individuals like Gronniosaw.[10]

Ironically, Gronniosaw's inability to reconcile messages of faith with the deceitful practices of the messengers who preached it reveals to readers the very religious hypocrisy that seems to elude him. While Gronniosaw's dilemma reflects similar conflicts fought out in the arena of social practice, terms of his presentation mirror certain contradictions in ecclesiastical and common law discourse on slavery in eighteenth-century England. The narrative itself is a window into the heart and soul of a flawed theological concept, through which an entire debate on race and religion can be viewed.

In 1762, Gronniosaw went to Portsmouth, England, where he sought membership in the church of Dr. Andrew Gifford, a Baptist theologian, but was told that he first had to be baptized. The Yorke and Talbot Joint Opinion of 1729 rendered by Attorney General, Sir Philip Yorke, and Solicitor General, Charles Talbot, had eliminated baptism as a mitigating factor in the legal status of blacks. Technically, it had an impact on Gronniosaw's legal status in England in the 1760s and 1770s. But long after the Yorke and Talbot Joint Opinion, the still-popular practice of baptizing enslaved blacks could possibly have aided their quest for freedom. Furthermore, for the sake of Gronniosaw's future in Kidderminster, baptism stood to lessen his chances of being reenslaved. Yet it had immediate consequences as well. When Gronniosaw's small daughter died from fever (he had married Betty, an English weaver), a Baptist minister refused to bury her because Gronniosaw's family were not members of that church. In addition, the parish parson also denied the child a burial because "she had never been baptized" (52). Gronniosaw next asked a Quaker pastor to bury her but was once again rejected. Just as he resolved "to dig a grave in the garden behind the house, and bury her there," the parson offered to bury the child, though he refused to read a eulogy for her. "I told him I did not mind whether he would or not, as the child could not hear it," Gronniosaw replied (52).

From the first legal test case on slavery in 1557 until Parliament outlawed the practice in 1834, Britain's legal experts failed to define clearly the status of blacks in England as domestic servants or as slaves, even though many were bought and sold as slaves on British soil.[11] At the very least, baptism could make them appear more presentable and potentially docile as slaves and domestic servants. But their individual Christian status bore little relevance to the legal or social perception of blacks as inferior beings. For example, in *Butts v. Penny* (1557), the first case brought before English courts to test the legality of slavery, a judge pronounced that English law recognized the enslavement of blacks as merchandise and as infidels.[12] Another ruling, in *Gelly v. Cleve* (1694), pronounced that "the court, without averment made, will take notice that [blacks] are heathens" and resolved that "a man may have property in them." Furthermore, the Court ruled that blacks might be construed as property, since by custom and practice, they were usually bought and sold as merchandise by merchants. Legal definitions of blacks as heathens and infidels in British common law—*Butts v. Penny* and *Gelly v. Cleve*—actually removed them from moral consideration and thus made their enslavement more acceptable. However, both rulings left open a loophole whereby baptism might be construed by law as a means of protecting blacks from being enslaved. In other words, non-Christian slaves might obtain freedom through baptism. Through *Butts v. Penny* and *Gelly v. Cleve*, English law could live up to its professed functions to uphold truth and morality. But because legal experts did not intend to set national precedent by any single case, these decisions promoted confusion.[13] Ultimately, because Britain had no constitutional basis or preexisting statutes as guidelines for slavery, its legality was decided on a case by case basis until the outlawing of the practice by Parliament in 1834.

Ironically, a slave who sought to be baptized in England was sometimes viewed as more threatening than one who sought to become literate, because baptism was thought to encourage enslaved blacks to seek freedom and to prevent free blacks from being reenslaved.[14] For example, in 1773 Ottobah Cugoano was advised to seek baptism as protection from enslavement or reenslavement even though the Mansfield Decision, passed in 1772, should have granted him that protection. Cugoano, who was baptized at Saint James's Church by a Dr. Skinner, noted that a number of friends and fellow servants "got themselves turned away" for assisting in his baptism. And Olaudah Equiano also related some difficulty in getting approval to be baptized, although his enslaver did not object to his being sent to school to learn how to read and write.

A law that recognized the enslavement of blacks as infidels and merchandise may well have left open a loophole for freedom for Christianized blacks, but it nonetheless endorsed a social order that granted social and economic superiority for well-to-do whites, while denying legal protection for blacks. The African as Other in legal discourse was, by definition, chattel—a nonperson. By protecting slave traders, judges could maintain the economic stability of society. By failing to extend the right of liberty to "heathens," they could uphold morality. A law that linked enslavement to heathenism could be unhinged by the simple act of baptism. Thus, the true test of the law was whether its perception of blacks as heathens, who stood to gain plaudits by Christian instruction, was sincere. Both ecclesiastical law and common law refused to recognize baptism as a route to freedom from slavery. Granville Sharp maintained that "the Crown and the nobles—and the monied interests—and the church and the bench and the bar" consolidated to preserve an ideology of racial inferiority to protect slavery.[15]

Slave proponents conflated theology and ethnography to produce a biblically based hierarchy for identifying individuals as good and evil. The religious community, like proslavery planters, philosophers, and scientists, conflated theology and ethnography to produce a biblically based hierarchy for identifying individuals as good and evil. When enslaved to Vanhorn back in New England, Gronniosaw was admonished by an old slave for swearing. "Old Ned" told him that "there was a wicked man called the Devil, who lived in hell, and would take all who said these words, and put them in the fire and burn them" (18). But when Gronniosaw repeats the admonition to Mrs. Vanhorn, after she swears at a servant, he alters the story: the Devil has become "a black man call'd the Devil, that lives in hell."[16] While Old Ned was whipped for his offense, Gronniosaw was elevated to favored-slave status for his effort to save Mrs. Vanhorn from a fate in hell's fire. (It was upon hearing this story that the greatly moved Freelandhouse had first purchased Gronniosaw from the Vanhorns for the sum of fifty pounds.)

There is a further connection here. John Bunyan's *The Holy War* (1682) and Francis Bacon's *New Atlantis* (1624) are among the many works that identified the Devil or evil spirit as black or African. In the *New Atlantis*, Bacon's unfinished fable, fornication and debauchery took the shape and form of "a little foul ugly Aethiop."[17] In this work, a Spanish sailor whose crew was blown off course by a storm is given escort throughout parts of the Island of Bensalem. Joabin, the sailor's merchant host, tells how the Island retained its utopian identity by alone surviving a flood that destroyed all other ancient civilizations. Consequently, the Island of Bensalem escaped much of the debauchery present in Europe:

> I remember I have read in one of your European books, of an holy hermit amongst you that desired to see the Spirit of Fornication; and there appeared to him a little foul ugly Aethiop. But if he had desired to see the Spirit of Chastity of Bensalem, it would have appeared to him in the likeness of a fair beautiful Cherubim. For there is nothing amongst mortal men more fair and admirable, than the chaste minds of this people (392).

Bacon's work, published posthumously, was designed to showcase an idyllic environment in which he could explore ideas on science, religion, learning, and invention. The merchant's anecdote dichotomizes good and evil in a religious allegory that seeks to encourage purity in its readers by vilifying a convenient scapegoat.

By virtue of its largely indeterminate origins, theological racism is even more puzzling than that produced in the eighteenth-century scientific community.[18] Alleged differences between blacks and whites were couched in the belief that not all members of the human race descended from a single act of creation—the biblical Adam and Eve. In the theory of single origins, arguments that portray a deity who presides over a hierarchically arranged scale of humanity, posed problems in Judeo-Christian doctrine. For instance, in affirming a separate or multiple-origins theory, Voltaire and the Scottish jurist Henry Home, Lord Kames (*Sketches of the History of Man*, 1774) risked being charged with atheism and blasphemy for disputing the sacred text. On the other hand, Thomas Jefferson (*Notes on the State of Virginia*, 1781–82), who seemingly endorsed a single-origins theory of creation, had problems claiming vast intellectual differences among diverse racial groups.[19]

Judging physiology, as well as lack of intelligence and civilization, to be the determining factors in separate or multiple origins, Voltaire declared blacks to be "a species of men different from ours [Europeans]."[20] Meanwhile, faced with charges of blasphemy for refuting biblical evidence of a single origins theory, Kames finally concluded that the separation of the races occurred when the Tower of Babel was built and when scrambling the languages meant reducing individuals to savages: "With an immediate change of bodily constitutions, the builders of Babel could not possibly have subsisted in the burning region of Guinea, or in the frozen region of Lapland; especially without houses, or any other convenience to protect them against a destructive climate."[21] Like the Hamitic hypothesis, the theory of separate or multiple origins still excluded certain individuals from moral consideration on the basis of race.

Though he does not mention Jefferson or Lord Kames in *Thoughts and Sentiments on the Evil of Slavery*, Ottobah Cugoano was certainly familiar with debate on the theory of origins, for he asserts "that all mankind did spring from one original, and that there are no different species among men" (30). He further notes that since God made all inhabitants of all nations of one blood, "we may justly infer, as there are no inferior species" (31). And since "colour, features or form" does not determine intelligence, "it never could be lawful and just for any nation, or people, to oppress and enslave another" (31). For those who made "inconsistent and diabolical use of the sacred writings" in order to justify slavery, Cugoano warns that it is better to be an infidel than to pervert the scriptures to deal "unjustly with their fellow men" (31).

From the time of his years in New York after the death of Freelandhouse, Gronniosaw "had a vast inclination to visit England" because he believed that Reverend Whitefield and all other inhabitants of England were holy and, accordingly, superior to such negative thinking. Gronniosaw fondly recalled that Reverend Whitefield had visited the Freelandhouses in New England and that Baxter and Bunyan, whose works he had read, were both English (41). He also desired to go to England for humanitarian reasons: "I entertained a notion that if I could get to England I should never more experience either cruelty or ingratitude, so that I was very desirous to get among Christians" (43). In an ironic repetition of his experience among fellow servants in New England, Gronniosaw was astonished when he first landed in Portsmouth, Old England, "to hear the inhabitants of that place curse and swear, and otherwise profane. I expected to find nothing but goodness, gentleness and meekness in this Christian land" (43). Instead, he suffered "great perplexities of mind," especially after he was later robbed of nineteen guineas and a watch by the very first Christian inhabitant that he met in the place (43).

When Gronniosaw traveled by stagecoach to London for the first time, a "creditable tradesman" offered to direct him to Reverend Whitefield's New Tabernacle. At first, Gronniosaw thought it kind of the gentleman to escort "a perfect stranger" to Whitefield, "but he obliged me to give him half-a-crown for going with me, and likewise insisted on my giving him five shillings more for conducting me to Dr. Gifford's meeting" (44). At this point, a frustrated Gronniosaw writes, "I soon perceived that I was got among bad people [and] could scarcely believe it possible that the place where so many eminent Christians had lived and preached could abound with so much wickedness and deceit" (44). He concludes with a kind of pathetic but endearing recognition: "I began now to entertain a very different idea of the inhabitants of England than what I had figured to myself before I came among them" (44).

In a scene that shows the depth of poverty to which Gronniosaw's family was reduced in their final years in Kidderminster, he describes efforts to find work with a local gentleman's gardener. Gronniosaw's Portsmouth friends opposed his proposed marriage to a poor widow who was left with a child and with a huge debt by her deceased husband and even asked the woman's minister to persuade her to refuse marriage to him. But a determined Gronniosaw sold everything that he owned and raised enough additional money to clear Betty's debts, because he believed the marriage to be foreordained and divinely sanctioned (47). Though unable to offer him a job, the gardener gave Gronniosaw four large carrots, on which the family survived for four days. Mrs. Gronniosaw chewed them into small pieces in order to feed their infant daughter. Although the family survived in this manner until the carrots were gone, Gronniosaw refused any food at all so that his wife and children might survive (49).

Gronniosaw takes leave of his readers in Kidderminster (the birthplace of Richard Baxter), where his family lived in extreme poverty as he suffered declining health. During this time, Gronniosaw recounted his life and spiritual experiences to "a young Lady of the town of Leominster" who recorded his story but initially had no intention of making it public. Gronniosaw's impoverished circumstances soon led his patron to publish the narrative with "sole profits arising from the sale of it" intended to relieve the family's suffering. The outcome of these plans, along with Gronniosaw's subsequent fate, is apparently lost to history. But the reader is left with the striking image of a remarkable, highly-principled man; albeit with an unfortunate streak of gullibility. At the narrative's close, he continues to lean heavily on religious faith: "As pilgrims, and very poor pilgrims we are traveling through many difficulties towards our heavenly home, and waiting patiently for his glorious call, when the Lord shall deliver us out of the evils of this present world, and bring us to the everlasting glories of the world to come.—To HIM be praise for evr [*sic*] and ever. AMEN" (53; Galatians 1:4.).

In 1770, the year listed as publication date for Gronniosaw's narrative, thirteen-year-old Ottobah Cugoano was brought from Africa and enslaved briefly in the West Indies. Although the two are not known to have met, Cugoano later read Gronniosaw's narrative and was enormously impressed by his staunch Christian faith. In *Thoughts and Sentiments on the Evil of Slavery* (1787), a philosophical essay, Cugoano credits divine intervention with granting Gronniosaw liberty, knowledge, and grace in spite of the contrary intentions of enslavers. In citing him as an exemplary Christian model, Cugoano carefully treads the divide between his own belief in divine intervention and claims by others that enslavement in Britain was superior to the barbarous conditions that blacks had endured in Africa. For example, while Reverend Walter Shirley praises Providence for Gronniosaw's delivery from heathenism in Africa, Cugoano charges the hand of Providence with Gronniosaw's delivery from slavery in New England. Both clearly share the Calvinist tenet of divine intervention, though with a subtle, yet significant semantical distinction.

In an observation that suggests a spiritual camaraderie with Gronniosaw and a shared affinity for the solid Christian faith that he exhibited, Cugoano writes, "[Gronniosaw] would not have given his faith in the Christian religion, in exchange for all the kingdoms of Africa, if they could have been given to him, in place of his poverty, for it" (22). But in acknowledging the beneficence of "a charitable attorney" who had helped Gronniosaw after he was free from slavery, Cugoano also asserts that most slaves who become free do so "by their own industry and ingenuity" (22). Like Gronniosaw, Cugoano harbors a characteristic Calvinist conflict, suggesting that individual responsibility was ultimately the catalyst for the faith and liberty that Gronniosaw and other blacks gained. Cugoano confesses his shame "that I was first kidnapped and betrayed by some of my own complexion, who were the first cause of my exile and slavery," but he makes it clear that "if there were no buyers there would be no sellers."[22] He adds that most blacks enslaved in Britain "are generally more corrupt in their morals, than they possibly could have been amongst their own people in Africa" (22).

Similarities between the experiences of Gronniosaw and Cugoano generally end with a shared, abiding Christian faith and do not extend to their publications or individual styles of expression. Gronniosaw seeks to relate his life, consciously, in order to instruct his readers. Inconsistencies in Gronniosaw's narrative can only be inferred, subtly, from the experiences that he relates. While Gronniosaw's narrative was ghostwritten, evidently by patron Hannah More, Cugoano wrote an essay that was probably edited and corrected by Olaudah Equiano, his acquaintance and coactivist.[23] Surviving letters between Cugoano and Equiano attest to their friendship and collaboration in various anti-slavery activities, including protest letters written to newspapers, British royalty, and Parliament. While Gronniosaw presents a docile, humble, even naive persona, Cugoano assumes a radical position, constructing an anti-slavery polemic that seeks to reveal the hypocrisy of proslavery Christian supporters. The resulting publication, atypical of writings by blacks in England at that time, is among the earliest specimens of protest literature.

Launching a counter argument against slavery, grounded largely in established theological precepts, Cugoano outlines the inconsistencies inherent in some Judeo-Christian beliefs. At the request of his supporters, Cugoano first wrote a brief autobiographical sketch of his early years in Africa.[24] He was born Quobna Ottobah Cugoano circa 1757 in Ajumako on the coast of Fantyn (modern-day Ghana). Reared among the children and relatives of the king of Fante, Cugoano lived for several years in relative tranquility. While visiting an Uncle who lived a good distance away from Ajumako, Cugoano ventured into the woods on a dare from a playmate, though against his own better judgment. Within a couple of hours, he was seized by ruffians who pretended that he had committed a fault against their leader— the one who had captured him in the first place. When Cugoano later encountered white people for the first time, he feared that he would be eaten, echoing the later sentiments of Equiano. He spent just under a year as a slave in Grenada, followed by a year in other West Indian locations. One Alexander Campbell brought Cugoano to England in 1772 where, under obscure circumstances, he obtained the surname Stuart from a "Master John Stuart." He received spiritual instruction from a Dr. Skinner, who also baptized him.

In a letter to Edmund Burke, Cugoano tacitly solicits funds from the conservative English writer toward the publication costs of an essay that outlines a pointed attack on Christian hypocrisy toward both enslaved and free blacks. Edmund Burke was among hundreds of mostly aristocratic British patrons who subscribed to Cugoano's philosophical essay. "I hope the Arguments therein will meet your approbation, and all good Christians, if I should be so happy as to have your approbation of my small undertaking, a trifle towards the printing will be acceptable," Cugoano wrote. As a formerly enslaved African, soliciting support from a prominent, white fellow Christian in the uncertain environment of slavery, he proves himself a skillful negotiator. Recognizing the radical nature of his arguments, Cugoano writes to Burke, "Permit me to lay my thoughts and sentiments before you, the production of a young man a native of Africa, in a domestic employment wherein it may appear rather harsh against the carriers on of such abandoned wickedness, as the African slave trade and West India Slavery" (xx).

Burke's stance on the slavery issue ultimately strengthened regulations for slavery's continuance rather than its total destruction, though this view contradicts his efforts in the 1780s to fight for slavery's abolishment. Burke's views on slavery are somewhat consistent with the concept of patriarchy—modeling government after a patriarchal divinity, a father and son relationship, and correcting systemic flaws on a gradual basis—rather than completely dismantling or overthrowing a government. It is a view that Burke espouses in *Reflections on the Revolution of France*, that Pope outlines in Epistle III in *Essay on Man*, and that Dryden expresses in *Absalom and Achitophel*.

Anticipating a hostile reception from readers, Cugoano prepares a similar, preemptive rejoinder in the essay's opening: "I must say, I can find no other way of expressing my Thoughts and Sentiments, without making use of some harsh words" against supporters of slavery (4). He suggests that future detractors, whom he identifies as those "who can lay their cruel lash upon the backs of thousands," will be held less accountable for their crimes against humanity than will he for criticizing their practices (5). And he hopes that "in this little undertaking . . . the impartial reader will excuse such defects as may arise from want of better education" (5). With these words, he deftly deconstructs theodicy as a context for the universal, unbiased ranking of humanity.

Cugoano begins the essay proper by paying homage to those "learned gentlemen of distinguished abilities" who have written articles against the slave trade (1). Abolitionists like Thomas Clarkson, Granville Sharp, and William Wilberforce published anti-slavery works and labored indefatigably to end slavery. In *Thoughts and Sentiments*, Cugoano particularly numbers Clarkson and Sharp, along with writers like Thomas Day, Edward Young, and Anthony Benezet, among his most ardent supporters. In referring to these writers by name, Cugoano evokes an illusion of unanimity among the truly faithful. Cugoano even echoes Clarkson's own words on the cruel and inhumane treatment of slaves. In *An Essay on the Slavery and Commerce of the Human Species*, Clarkson argued that slave labor and the cruel treatment of slaves suppressed the development of genius.[25] Cugoano further adds that "the robbers of men, the kidnappers, ensnarers and slave-holders" behave contrarily to "every precept and injunction of the Divine Law" (22). Anyone laying claim to the title of Christian would have to agree that the trafficking of African slaves must end, he adds.

Unlike his Anglican counterparts who condemned slavery, however, Cugoano seems keenly aware that such religious debate, already caught up in complex issues about race and science, could not be separated from epistemological discussions on morality, literary didacticism, and humanism. For instance, Cugoano regards the Chain of Being outright, as a system of racial hierarchies, as though the idea had had no prior existence as an abstract theological concept free of racial overtones. Moreover, he directly connects the Chain of Being with the so-called missing-links idea.

Cugoano expresses disappointment toward those who believe "that nature designed [the African] for some inferior 'link in the chain, fitted only to be a slave'" (5). Extending the argument a step further, he singles out the concept known as the Hamitic hypothesis or the theory of Canaan as precisely the kind of venomous idea that can derive from such connections. Indeed, he quickly cites the concept, which identified blacks as the accursed descendants of Ham, as both brainchild and driving force behind the missing links idea and the Chain of Being.[26] As Cugoano puts it, the story of Ham "affords a grand pretence for the supporters of the African slavery to build a false notion upon, as it is found by history that Africa, in general, was peopled by the descendants of Ham" (34).

According to the account in *Genesis*, Ham was cursed for looking upon his father's nakedness. As a result, when Noah discovered what Ham had done, he said, "Cursed be Canaan; the lowest of slaves shall he be to his brothers" (*Genesis* 9:24). But while the account in *Genesis* mentions nothing about color or race, the Hamitic hypothesis took on a life of its own in racialist discourse, and the descendents of Ham have been identified repeatedly in literary and nonliterary discourse as black or African. Although the Hamitic hypothesis was widely disseminated as justification for the enslavement of blacks, especially after the sixteenth century, its identification with color, specifically "blackness," appeared in sacred texts and commentaries much earlier than the start of Britain's participation in the slave trade.

A brief examination of racist origins of the Hamitic hypothesis exposes a concept whose historical direction and duration have been so insidious. Some English and other European travelers, along with a number of theologians, particularly promoted and disseminated a racialist Hamitic hypothesis by demonizing race through sacred readings. For example, in the *Midrash Rabbah*, Noah's curse to Ham is interpreted as follows: "You have prevented me from doing something in the dark [cohabitation], therefore your seed will be ugly and dark-skinned."[27] In *The Sanhedrin*, from *The Babylonian Talmud*, an interpretation of Ham's punishment for sinning against Noah reads, "Ham was smitten in his skin," while an explanatory footnote adds that "from him descended Cush (the negro) who is black-skinned."[28] *The Sanhedrin* refers to Ham as "the notorious world-darkener" and as the father of Canaan "who darkened the faces of mankind."[29] *The Encyclopedia Judeica* identifies Egyptians and Ethiopians as the nucleus of the Hamite genealogy. *The Midrash*, commentaries on the Hebrew Scriptures, was written down well after 200 *B.C.*, after the expulsion of Jews from the Roman Empire. *The Sanhedrin* is "the highest judicial and ecclesiastical council of the ancient Jewish nation."[30] A central, authoritative text for traditional Judaism, *The Babylonian Talmud* is a commentary on *The Midrash* but does not issue folklore or demonology. Nonetheless, the race or color of Ham, father of Canaan, is not yet presented as an ideological reading of racial inferiority.

Interpretations of Ham's sin against Noah range from castration to sodomy; *The Sanhedrin*, for instance, alleges that Ham committed bestiality. Winthrop Jordan writes that Ham's descendents in the *Talmud* included Canaanites who were driven from the promised land and committed sexual offenses over a period of two thousand years before Europeans reinterpreted the story to refer to blacks of African descent. The story of Ham further united with pseudo-scientific observations about alleged black sexual prowess and size of genitalia in the era of slavery, and the curse of Ham was popularized as justification for slavery.

In 1578, an Elizabethan voyager, George Best, published his own version of the Scripture's story of Noah. Best's book was the result of his search (with Martin Frobisher in 1577) for the Northwest Passage. In this version, "Cham" (variant of Ham) disobeyed Noah's decree that in reverence to God, the three sons abstain from sexual relations with their wives. Cham, mindful that the first-born child would inherit the earth, had sex with his wife and bore a son, Chus. As punishment for this sinful deed, God willed that Chus and "all his posteritie after him should bee so blacke and lothesome" that they might remain a symbol for disobedience to God for all the world to see. The story concludes that black Africans descended from the accursed son, Chus.[31] Interestingly, both Best's version and the Judeo-Christian version of Ham conflate color or blackness with illicit sex, size of genitalia, and a pronounced lack of discipline in the refusal to obey paternal authority.

Traveling in West Africa, Richard Jobson recorded some observations of the Mandingos. Though Jobson acknowledged that schoolmen had refuted the Hamitic hypothesis, he wrote that "undoubtedly these people originally sprung from the race of Canaan, the sonne of Ham, who discovered his father Noah's secrets, for which Noah awakening cursed Canaan as our holy Scripture testifieth."[32] But Jobson does not identify the sacred text that serves as his source.

In *Chronographiae Libri Quatuor* (1609), Gilbert Genebrard, a six-teenth-century Benedictine monk and archbishop of Aix, held that Chus, the son of Ham, was the ancestor of all Africans, having been allegedly made black as fulfillment of the curse of Ham. But Guillaume Postel (*De Orinini-bus*, 1553, and *Cosmographicae Disciplinae Compendium*, 1561) preceded Genebrard in perpetuating the myth, and the originator of the tale is probably impossible to identify. A "scholar-monk," Agostino Tornielli (*Annales sacri and Profani*, 1611), identifies both Chus and his wife as white but claims (without explanation) that they produced both black and white children—the blacks being the accursed offspring who were relegated to the earth's "hotter" regions, or Africa. Yet another Englishman, his-torian-theologian Peter Heylyn, in *Microcosmus, or A Little Description of the Great World* (1621), first affirmed, then later recanted, then conceded again the Hamitic hypothesis. Heylyn's book appeared in numerous editions throughout the seventeenth century.[33]

In his essay, Cugoano searches out enthymemes, or implied premises, in certain religious doctrines that demonize blacks and refutes them in classic rhetorical style. Liberally sprinkling biblical quotations throughout the essay, Cugoano discredits the belief by some that the mark placed upon Cain as a token of his crime against Abel was an assignation of blackness. He notes that Cain's entire posterity was destroyed in the flood and that only Noah and his family survived. Cugoano further deconstructs the Hamitic hypothesis as justification for the enslavement of Africans. Relying on recent biblical exegeses, he reconstructs the biblical story, initially designed apparently by a biblical scribe to explain the subjugation of the people identified as "Canaan" by the people known as "Shem" and "Japheth." He identifies Ham's youngest son, Canaan, as responsible for uncovering his grandfather, and Ham as the one who ridiculed the sight to his brothers. The curse of servitude thus fell upon the descendents of Canaan, though Ham was equally guilty of his son's offense. The Canaanites were later destroyed for their wickedness by fire and by the Hebrews. It was Cush, Ham's oldest son, whom Scripture placed in Arabia and whose descendents (from Cush's son Nimrod) migrated to Ethiopia and throughout Africa (36). According to this reading, Africans more than likely descended from Cush rather than from Ham.[34]

While Cugoano is by no means alone in disputing the Hamitic hypoth-esis, he effectively demonstrates how the theory of Canaan serves as an idea that could be plugged, conveniently, into a theological formula that hier-achized all of humanity in universal creation. Both Cugoano and Clarkson (his mentor on the treatment of the subject) argue that the scripture, if true, had already been fulfilled on two counts: Cain's posterity perished in the flood and that all of humanity descended from the first act of creation, known as the single origins theory. Like Clarkson, Cugoano regards the Hamitic hypothesis as a fallacious argument, drawn in order to justify the enslavement of blacks.[35] Unlike Clarkson, in conflating racialist discourse, such as the Chain of Being and the missing links idea *with* the Hamitic hypothesis, Cugoano affirms that the debate on race pointed in a decidedly theological as well as scientific direction.

In diminishing the significance of the Hamitic hypothesis, David Brion Davis argues that "the influence of the Biblical account cannot be measured by the relatively few eighteenth-century apologists for Negro slavery who appealed to the curse of Canaan."[36] He further claims that "early abolitionists felt it necessary to refute both the theory of a Biblical curse and the theory that blacks were a separate and inferior species" (540). Davis also notes that medieval England utilized the theory of Canaan in order to rationalize serfdom, a form of indentured white servitude. Winthrop Jordan goes on to cite anti-slavery advocates like William Edmundson who, in 1676, refuted the Hamitic hypothesis as a curse on black servitude.[37] Winthrop Jordan observes that the "old idea of Ham's curse floated ethereally about the [American] colonies without anyone's seeming to attach great importance to it" and adds that the "Christian tradition demanded the acceptance of Negroes in the community of men" (201). Jordan also admits, however, that "the curse upon Ham's posterity took on for Christian Englishmen a potential immediacy and relevance which it could never have had if Englishmen had not as a people been undergoing an experience which they half sensed was in some measure analogous to that of the ancient special people of God's word" (36). Consequently, Jordan points up the inherent problems in too easily dismissing the impact of the curse of Ham theory, particularly for enslaved blacks. First, there is some irony in the fact that a concept of "no great importance" remained so widely in circulation down through the ages. In addition, the faint cries of denial apparently had little impact on social practice and the behavior of numerous individuals in the treatment of enslaved blacks.

In attempting to discount the curse of Canaan's measurability in mass culture, scholars like Davis actually demonstrate further evidence of its broad dissemination. For example, Davis observes that Morgan Godwyn "accepted the possibility that black skin was a mark of the original curse," yet Godwyn "denied any sanction for enslavement" (540)! To add to confusion, Godwyn still believed in slavery. Davis further claims that "even in eighteenth-century Brazil many whites assumed that Negroes were the children of Cain—if not of Canaan—and thus deserved to be slaves" (540).

Davis might have added the American colonies to this list; he does not cite Thomas Jefferson among those who believed in the theory of separate origins, an equally racist idea.

The Hamitic hypothesis or theory of Canaan had an active and lengthy shelf life, well beyond the period of slavery. For example, as late as 1850, African-American Episcopalian priest Alexander Crummell, who was educated at Cambridge by British abolitionists, evidently felt compelled to refute the Hamitic Hypothesis in "Africa not Under a Curse," in the *Christian Observer*.

In his extensive treatment of the theory of Canaan in *Thoughts and Sentiments*, Cugoano turns the tables on the debate by charging that when the Canaanites "fled away in Time of Joshua," they intermingled with other nations and that some of them ended up in England and settled around Cornwall (36). Consequently, the descendents of Ham may well have sired some of the West Indian enslavers, rather than the slaves themselves (35–36). Ignatius Sancho also reveals an astuteness for analyzing the political implications of the Hamitic hypothesis. In a letter to a Mr. Meheux, dated 5 October 1779, he chides his acquaintance for making false assumptions about Sancho's failure to write more promptly: [People like you] should make election of wide different beings than Blackamoors for their friends.— The reason is obvious—from Othello to Sancho the big—we are either foolish—or mulish—all—all without a single exception."[38] In mocking the perception that blacks descended from Ham, the accursed son of Noah, Sancho continues, "Tell me, I pray you—and tell me truly—were there any Blackamoors in the Ark?—Pooh" (191)!

Interpretations of the Book of *Genesis* that construed Ham's descendents to be black or African imposed a racial hierarchy upon the sacred text and on humanity itself in a manner that equates evil with blackness.[39] The story of Ham thus ensures that a ranking of sorts exists—but on the basis of good and evil behavior rather than race. The concept embarked upon a strange odyssey and has maintained an extraordinary life span and a powerful psychical survival. Efforts to deny the impact of the Hamitic Hypothesis on some whites' negative attitudes toward blacks, especially slaves, did little to inhibit the fact that theology was widely used, discursively, to justify unequal treatment for Britain's black slave population. Hence, the Hamitic hypothesis or theory of Canaan remains what Cornel West calls the most pervasive scriptural misreading in the history of biblical discourse.[40] Too often, even when refuting the theory of Canaan, writers still expressed a vague belief in the inferiority of blacks, a fundamental belief in the immorality of blacks, and a belief in inequality and slavery for blacks as biblically or God-ordained.

In his attack, Cugoano challenges planter and enslaver James Tobin (*An Apology for Slavery*, 1786), whose defense of slavery amounted to a "brutish philosophy."[41] Identifying Hume as a friend of Tobin, Cugoano writes that "the poor negroes in the West-Indies have suffered enough" of the religion that "philosophers of the North" have produced (146). In a reference, perhaps, to Hume's Scottish lineage, he writes that "protestants, as they are called, are the most barbarous slave-holders, and there are none can equal the Scotch floggers and negroe-drivers, and the barbarous Dutch" (146). Cugoano does not hesitate to chronicle the parade of nations involved in the scramble for African slaves: "The base traffic of kidnapping and stealing men [that] was begun by the Portuguese on the coast of Africa" was soon followed by the Spanish, he begins (93). The French, English, and other European nations formed settlements in the West Indies and in the North American colonies. But Cugoano reserves his most scathing attack for "European depredators and pirates," because not only have they "robbed and pillaged the people of Africa," but they have also "infested the inhabitants with some of the vilest combinations of fraudulent people" (93).

Much of Cugoano's essay specifically refutes comments made by Hume in his moral essays. For example, Hume writes that poverty, an oppressive government, and intensive labor "debase the minds of the common people, and render them unfit for any science and ingenious profession."[42] He adds that these impediments would ultimately "banish all the liberal arts from among [the oppressed]" (225). But Hume does not reconcile the effects of oppression on learning and achievement with his belief in the inferiority of blacks to whites and other racial groups. Nor does he chronicle the effects of sub-Sahara slavery on so-called liberal arts development among blacks. While Hume's essay "Of National Characters" (like Jefferson's racial observations in *Notes on the State of Virginia*) may, by many, be relegated to the margins of their more important contributions, I want to emphasize the extent to which he, along with others, relies upon racial identity as first and foremost a precondition to the crafting of an intellectual and moral aesthetic. In other words, blacks were considered incapable of intelligence; hence, any works produced by them must be substandard.

For Cugoano, removing Africans from the center of debate effectively removes the burden of proof for him to argue, defensively, in order to prove their competence. Furthermore, this strategy would, by design, displace Africans as the "accursed race" in the minds of whites. Cugoano argues offensively, exposing the moral and ethical vulnerability of proslavery arguments produced in numerous publications and disseminated among a vast readership.

In yet another avenue of criticism, Cugoano chides Europeans for building settlements among diverse cultures in different parts of the world:

"None but men of the most brutish and depraved nature, led on by the invidious influence of internal wickedness, could have made their settlements in the different parts of the world discovered by them, and have treated the various Indian nations, in the manner that the barbarous inhuman Europeans have done" (77). On the role of African chieftains procuring slaves for Europeans, Cugoano wrote that if these chieftains knew what they were sending fellow Africans into, they would not persist in doing so. He added that they had been deceived by European traders who dressed servants in "gaudy cloaths, in a gay manner, as decoy ducks to deceive others" whom they enticed to travel to England to live as slaves (27). To those who argued that slavery was an ancient custom that had always been a part of civilization, Cugoano responded that historical precedence did not make slavery just. As I pointed out in chapter 1, such arguments had appeared also in the writings of David Hume, Immanuel Kant, Voltaire, Thomas Jefferson, and others. Refuting their views, Cugoano exposes several fallacies inherent in both ecclesiastical and common-law support of slavery.

Calling for a valid religious doctrine that would accept blacks as partners in faith with whites, he wrote, "It is my highest wish and earnest prayer to God, that some encouragement could be given to send able school masters, and intelligent ministers, who would be faithful and able to teach the Christian religion" (126). Cugoano thought that missionaries might utilize the Christian religion as "a Kind restitution for the great injuries that [blacks had] suffered." He envisioned that partnership taking place through well-educated English missionaries, who would be dispatched to Africa to teach the gospel and to undertake an alternative system of religious instruction for Africans.[43] But in proposing that well-educated English missionaries be dispatched to Africa to undertake an alternative system of religious instruction for Africans, Cugoano risked endorsing the spread of unsettling information in the missionary program. In everything that he wrote, Cugoano urged that blacks be respected as equals with whites, especially by the religious teaching that inherently claimed to uphold this belief.

Ottobah Cugoano's outspokenness against slavery and inequality extended well beyond the publication of his essay. Cugoano, Olaudah Equiano, and others who called themselves the Sons of Africa had forged alliances with Wilberforce, Granville Sharp, and other abolitionists to intervene in local cases in which black domestic servants in England found themselves about to be deported as slaves to the West Indies. An entry from Granville Sharp's journal reveals Cugoano's activism on behalf of the black poor in London, and letters, such as the one to Edmund Burke at the beginning of this chapter, attest to his efforts to publish *Thoughts and Sentiments*. In addition, Cugoano, in league with Equiano and others, protested several atrocities associated with slavery by writing letters to the media, to British aristocrats, and to members of the British Parliament.

Perhaps the most notorious such atrocity, the *Zong* case (formally known as *Gregson v. Gilbert*),[44] drew the angriest comments found anywhere in Cugoano's essay. A slave merchant bound for the West Indies threw 132 Africans overboard and tried to recover their value from insurers. Because many of the slaves had fallen ill, the merchant reasoned that recovering their value in insurance would greatly exceed their price in the marketplace. "The vast carnage and murders committed by the British instigator of slavery, is attended with a very shocking, peculiar, and almost unheard of conception," he wrote (111). Further, Cugoano challenged the merchant's claims in court that he had committed no murders, because slaves were considered to be property: "Our lives are accounted of no value, we are hunted after as the prey in the desert, and doomed to destruction as the beasts that perish" (112).

When Cugoano sought support from numerous British aristocrats—both for the publication costs of *Thoughts and Sentiments on the Evil of Slavery* and for the ending of slavery—he appealed to the humanitarian arguments, which had been outlined by Shaftesbury, Hutcheson, and Smith. To the Prince of Wales, Cugoano urged that those in power put a stop to the trading of African slaves sanctioned by the British government, for they were treated more inhumanely than in any so-called uncivilized country. In a letter appended to his published essay, Cugoano shrewdly pointed out to the Prince of Wales the emotional and psychological benefits that an anti-slavery position would bring:

> Should your Highness endeavour to release the oppressed and put a stop to that iniquitous traffic of buying and selling Men you would not equal the Virtuous Queen of Portugal in this respect but it would add Lustre and Greatness to your aspiring Years all generous minds would admire you the wise and virtuous would praise you The prayer of the oppressed would ascend to pour down those Blessings upon you and your Name would resound with applause from Shore to Shore and in all the records of Fame be held in the highest Esteem throughout the Annals of time. (xix)

Appealing to vanity as well as to justice, Cugoano assured the Prince that if he advocated the abolitionist cause, he would achieve fame and recognition, internationally. And in a letter to King George III, he asserted that "the cause of justice and humanity are the only motives which induced me to collect those thoughts and sentiments on the evil of slavery with a view to the natural liberties of Men which your Majesty as a Sovereign will be pleased to support" (xxi).

Cugoano was also practical. He offered several proposals toward the means of ending slavery.[45] First, he called for atonement, "days of mourning and fasting appointed" to study the formation of such an evil practice. Second, slavery should be totally abolished through a proclamation issued by the British legislature and "published throughout all the British empire, to hinder and prohibit all men under their government to traffic either in buying or selling men" and to prevent it under the threat of monetary penalty (130). Finally, Cugoano proposes that warships be sent immediately to Africa, along the trading coast "with faithful men to direct that none should be brought from the African coast without their own consent and the approbation of their friends, and to intercept all merchant ships that were bringing them away, until such a scrutiny was made, whatever nation they belonged to" (132).

In letters to the Prince of Wales, King George III, and Edmund Burke, Cugoano enlisted support for *Thoughts and Sentiments* and for the ending of slavery. Though the work had broad appeal, as evidenced by its publication in at least three editions, including a French translation, the battery of patrons who flanked Sancho and Equiano evidently did not materialize for Cugoano. The essay was less successful in either book sales or size of readership than Sancho's *Letters* or Equiano's *Narrative*. The relative silence of the British media in its treatment of Cugoano's work can be attributed to any number of causes.[46] For instance, its prolonged arguments against slavery (the essay is not divided into chapters or sections) may have seemed tedious to readers who were too impatient, uneasy, or defensive to wish to see proslavery Christians come under such attack. Ironically, the sharp, biting attacks that Cugoano levels at proslavers may have resulted in some discomfort among readers who were sensitive to such attacks, though a discomfort that more readily led to denial than to consideration of Cugoano's claims.[47]

All the same, Cugoano's life story as an African who was sold into slavery in the West Indies, along with abolitionist activities associated with membership in the Sons of Africa, proved to be a critical component in the fight to end slavery. For British abolitionists who sought to disseminate stories of blacks like Gronniosaw, Cugoano, and others, their publications refuted charges of intellectual inferiority among blacks. But more significantly, Cugoano's religious and literary identification with Ukawsaw Gronniosaw (and his similar links with Equiano) made a more distinct impact on eighteenth-century racialist discourse itself. In other words, through their lives and experiences, Gronniosaw and Cugoano forced the spotlight on the contradictions between certain Christian doctrines and their embodiment in social practice in the eighteenth century. Their writings show that complex race and science issues, including debate about the inferiority of blacks to whites, could not be separated from epistemological discussions on literary didacticism and moral instruction. We see how some religious figures and organizations (even those who accepted slavery as an ancient, biblically sanctioned practice) genuinely struggled with the moral implications of an institution that yielded profits from their investments. We also learn how some missionaries rationalized the "rescue" of Africans from heathenism in their own countries to enslavement in the "civilized" world. And from legal rulings in England on the status of infidels as slaves and the identification of Africans as infidels to the persistent presence of the curse of Ham idea, we learn that the construction of the Great Chain of Being, even in the most sacred of spaces, was never really free of racial overtones.

## NOTES

1. Selina Hastings, the Countess of Huntingdon, was a patron for numerous Black Methodists. Those who followed the teachings of John Calvin believed that only the elect, a small number of individuals, would gain eternal salvation and that all others would be condemned to eternal damnation. (See *Romans* 8:28–9:18.) Methodism, led by Reverend George Whitefield and John Wesley and known for its fierce opposition to slavery, was adopted by many blacks during slavery. Ukawsaw Gronniosaw (anglicized James Albert), Ignatius Sancho, Quobna Ottobah Cugoano (anglicized John Stuart), and Olaudah Equiano (anglicized Gustavus Vassa) all subscribed to Calvinism and other Methodist tenets.

See also Adam Potkay and Sandra Burr, eds., *Black Atlantic Writers of the Eighteenth Century: Living the New Exodus in England and the Americas* (New York: St. Martin's Press, 1995), 1–20. (All subsequent references to the narrative of James Ukawsaw Gronniosaw are made to Potkay and Burr's edition of the 1774 imprint of the narrative in *Black Atlantic Writers* and will be cited in the manuscript by page number.) The date 1770 appears on imprint lists as the original publication date for Gronniosaw's narrative in the British Museum (see Jahn Janheinz's *Neo-African Literature; a History of Black Writing*, Trans. from German by Oliver Coburn and Ursula Lehrburger [New York: Grove Press, 1968]; see also Dorothy Porter, *Early Negro Writing, 1760–1837* [Boston, MA: Beacon Press, 1971]). However, Potkay and Burr make a convincing case that the publication date is closer to 1774. For example, Hannah More, English author and abolitionist, is identified as Gronniosaw's amanuensis only in the 1774 imprint of the narrative. Interestingly the 1774 imprint is the only one in which "Written by Himself" rather than "Related or Dictated by Himself" appears (26). For this study I follow Potkay and Burr's lead in using the 1774 imprint, the most complete of the four major versions of the narrative.

2. Ottobah Cugoano's Fante cultural roots probably exposed him to both practices: a belief in one supreme being and a belief in personal tribal gods as deities. Olaudah Equiano recalls many similarities between the Igbos' belief in a single, omnipotent being. See Brodie Cruickshank, *Eighteen Years on the Gold Coast of Africa including an account of the native tribes, and their intercourse with the Europeans*, 1853, 2nd ed., 2 vols. rpt. New York: Barnes & Noble, 1966), vol. 1,

p. 19; vol. 2, pp. 127–29. For an account of similarities between the concept of divine providence and Igbo religious beliefs, see Paul Edwards and Rosalind Shaw, "The Invisible Chi in Equiano's Interesting Narrative," *Journal of Religion in Africa* 19 (1989): 146–56. Citations in Potkay and Burr.

3. See Ottobah Cugoano, *Thoughts and Sentiments on the Evil of Slavery* (London: Dawsons of Pall Mall, 1969), 22. While Potkay and Burr provide much needed documentation on Cugoano's work and include the full text of his brief, sketchy autobiography, they have only published excerpts from the essay itself in *Black Atlantic Writers*. Consequently, in further references to Cugoano's text, I cite Paul Edwards's complete 1969 reprint of the London, 1787, imprint of Cugoano's essay. (See Ottobah Cugoano, *Thoughts and Sentiments on the Evil of Slavery*, 1787, ed. and introduction by Paul Edwards. Rpt. of 1787 ed. [London: Dawsons of Pall Mall], 1969).

4. See Seymour Drescher, *Capitalism and Antislavery: British Mobilization in Comparative Perspective* (New York: Oxford University Press, 1987), 111–34. Drescher writes, "The clergy emulated the social and economic behaviour of their secular co-religionists as individual and corporate owners of slaves, as sexual exploiters, and as defenders of the legitimacy, if not the glory, of the slave system to the very end" (112).

5. Henry Louis Gates, Jr., writes that the five black narrators who are "linked by a revision into the very first black chain of signifiers, implicitly signify upon another chain, the metaphorical Great Chain of Being." See chapter 4, "The Trope of the Talking Book," Henry Louis Gates, Jr., *The Signifying Monkey: A Theory of African-American Literary Criticism* (New York: Oxford University Press, 1988), 167. Gates uses the Kraus reprint of the 1840 edition of Gronniosaw's narrative in his critique. While Gronniosaw, Cugoano, and Equiano utilize the "talking book" or literal version of the trope, John Marrant's Indian captivity narrative (*The Narrative of Lord's Wonderful Dealings with John Marrant, a Black*, 1785) and John Jea's narrative (*The Life, History, and Unparalled Sufferings of John Jea*), offer revised versions.

6. Many household domestic servants included poor whites who fit the status of the indentured servant and whose servitude was usually limited to seven years. Indentured servants, particularly women, hardly escaped abuse, however, often including rape. Though Gronniosaw is often referred to as a domestic servant, he clearly fits the legal status of a slave and could become free only by stipulations set by his enslaver.

Besides instances of subjugation chronicled in the Old Testament, a classical, Aristotelian view of slavery held that natural inferiority and conquest in war were adequate justification for the enslavement of an individual (*The Politics*, I, v–vi). In addition, the classical definition of slavery received support in Thomas Hobbes's social contract and in John Locke's belief that slavery was "the state of war continued between a lawful conquerour, and a captive." See John Locke, *Two Treatises on Government*, ed. Peter Laslett (Cambridge: Cambridge University Press, 1988), 285. But Locke, exhibiting trademark inconsistency, also believed that since individuals did not have power over their lives, they could not subject themselves as slaves "under the absolute, arbitrary power of another" (284). Locke had to reconcile the individual's right to freedom from enslavement through natural law with the selective application of slavery to individuals, based on race.

Around the sixteenth century, English legal authorities made clear efforts to keep black enslavement under the narrow confines of the classical definition of slavery. Queen Elizabeth, on behalf of the British government, allowed traders to buy and sell slaves by any means other than force. In other words, traders would procure slaves, presumably from African chieftains who had captured them in tribal warfare, thus allowing the English to comply with Aristotle's definition of slavery. In the early voyages, the Queen sought assurances from government-sponsored English explorers that Africans who were captured as slaves meet two criteria: that they not be taken by force and that they be sold to English colonies in the West Indies or in the New World rather than domestically, on English soil. Though there is indeed evidence that some blacks initially carried the same status as white indentured servants, accounts by members of slaving expeditions indicate that numerous explorers ignored the Queen's stipulations. (See Peter Fryer, *Staying Power: The History of Black People in Britain* (London: Pluto Press, 1984), 2–12.

7. See Morgan Godwyn, *The Negro's and Indians' Advocate . . . in our Plantations*, London, the author, 1680.

8. Seymour Drescher calls Methodism "the most centralized of all the new revivalist sects" and the best barometer for grasping the social dimension of large-scale abilitionism (117). John Wesley's impulse to support abolitionism only after 1787 when popular religious sentiment in Manchester favored it "may provide the best proxy indicator for the general relationship between the Anglo-evangelical religious and antislavery mobilizations" (*Capitalism and Antislavery*, 117). George Whitefield had supported slavery in Georgia, though trustees had first prohibited the practice. See Reverend George Whitefield, Letter III, "To the Inhabitants of Maryland, Virginia, North and South-Carolina, Concerning Their Negroes" in *Three Letters From the Reverend Mr. G. Whitefield* (Philadelphia, 1740), 15; cited by Winthrop Jordan, 214. Whitefield was the subject of a memorial poem by Philis Wheatley.

9. In the eighteenth century, a popular and rather fashionable custom existed, especially among English royalty, who viewed blacks paternalistically, as cute domesticated pets. A black, domestic enslaved population was often outfitted in ornate, exotic costumes, compelled to wear identification collars and other slave paraphernalia, and forced to bear the pompous-sounding names of noted historical figures. Cementing the image of the slave as a liveried, showy possession was an ever-present religious script; it depicts the black domestic slave, tempered by baptism but not freed as a result of it. See Folarin O. Shyllon, *Black People in Britain, 1555–1833* (London: Oxford University Press, 1977).

For example, the Right Honourable Earl of Suffolk and Brandon named his servant Scipio Africanus. (See Kenneth Little, *Negroes in Britain: A Study of Racial Relations in English Society*. 2nd ed. [London: Routledge and Kegan Paul, 1972], 190). Clearly, the pompous-sounding names given to these slaves contrasted with their social positions. The classical names may well have given enslavers an appearance of status and gentility even as the slaves' position in society undercut the names' meaning, a point that Little makes in *Negroes in Britain* (190). The attitude resulting from blacks being represented in this manner could hardly be perceived as anything less than patronizing and nothing greater than the affection one might have for a favored pet.

In a curious aside (and related custom), the French horn, brass symbol of European musical culture, casts a veneer of cultural exoticism over human oppression for those slaves who mastered the instrument. Note Matthew Bramble's disgust with upstart classes in *Humphrey Clinker* when he complains about being kept awake during the night by a black practicing to blow the French horn. In addition, while on a visit to England, Benjamin Franklin's brother had "lost" his enslaved companion to abolitionists, who had actually hidden him. After futile efforts to retrieve the slave, Franklin records that his brother had given up because some anti-slavery activists had taken him over and had taught him to play the French horn. Olaudah Equiano is offered an opportunity to learn to play the instrument as well.

10. Numerous enslavers tried to prevent their slaves from being baptized and Christianized, sometimes by elaborate means. For example, Morgan Godwyn, author of *The Negro's and Indians' Advocate* (1680), writes that when an enslaver discovered that his slave had petitioned a local minister to baptize him, the enslaver produced a gun and informed the minister that he would carry out the baptism only at his own peril. Besides revealing slaves' expectations about the benefits of baptism, the passage also describes the customary attire often worn by black house slaves in well-to-do English homes.

The Society for the Propagation of the Gospel, which dealt in the trading of slaves, forbade teaching Christianity to its slaves in Barbados. See Eric Williams, *Capitalism and Slavery* (New York: G. P. Putnam's Sons, 1966), 42. As Drescher notes, the Anglican Society for the Propagation of the Gospel (SPG) operated a plantation endowment much like other "well-run plantations" in Barbados (*Capitalism and Antislavery*, 112). The SPG declined to support "a motion that would have declared West Indian incompatible with Christianity" (see C. F. Pascoe, The Record, 21 October 1830, in *Two Hundred Years of the S.P.G.: An Historical Account of the Society for the Propagation of the Gospel in Foreign Parts*, London: n.p., 1901, 822–32; cited in Drescher, 232.

A letter written to the lord bishop of London in 1730 stresses the economic losses slave owners would endure if slaves were Christianized. The writer noted that slaves would have to be given time off to attend Bible classes, which would mean a sixpence loss of profit to the owner per slave for a total of 65 pounds loss annually per hundred slaves. See David Dabydeen, ed., *The Black Presence in English Literature* (Manchester: Manchester University Press, 1985), 46.

11. A 1569 judicial decision declared English air "too pure . . . for slaves to breathe in," according to John Rushworth in *Historical Collections of Private Passages of State, Weighty Matters in Law, Remarkable Proceedings in Five Parliaments*. vol. 2 of 8 (London: D. Browne, 1721–22), 468. The William Bragge Petition, 1621, implies that because the blacks whom he offered for purchase were not Christians ("in time the Lord may call them to be true Christians"), the East India Company could dispose of them commercially.

12. *Butts v. Penny*, the first in a series of cases on slavery, involved slaves living in India. Discursive similarities between definitions of heathenism and slavery

and descriptive references to the racial identification of Africans and East Indians as blacks, appear in British common law and in social practice. These events took place just after the trading of slaves on English soil had been documented in the sixteenth century but before England officially took over the slave trade from Portugal in the seventeenth century. See Edward Fiddes, "Lord Mansfield and the Somersett Case," *Law Quarterly Review* 50 (1934): 501. See 3 Keble 785; 2 Levinz 201; Trin. 1677, and *Gelly v. Cleve*, 1 Ld. Raym. 147; Hill. 5 Will. and Mar. in *The English Reports*. In *Smith v. Browne & Cooper* (1701), Holt wrote that "as soon as a Negro comes into England, he becomes free; one may be a villein in England but not a slave" (Smith v. Brown and Cooper, 2 Salk, 666, *The English Reports*, 1701). In *Smith v. Gould* (1706), Holt declared that "by the common law no man can have a property in another" (Smith v. Gould, 2 Salk, 667, *The English Reports*, XCI, 567).

A closer analysis of judicial decisions made under English common law, up to the 1729 Yorke and Talbot Joint Opinion, reveals a series of inconsistences rooted in perspectives on truth, economics, popular concerns, and ideological representations of blacks. For example, until 1729, blacks were represented contradictorily in ecclesiastical and common law and in social practice in England regarding their legal status as slave or free. In 1729, when a West Indian deputation asked the Lord High Chancellor of Great Britain, law official of the Crown, whether a slave could become free by the above-named acts, the result was the Yorke and Talbot Joint Opinion. In Lincoln's Inn Hall, Attorney General Yorke and Solicitor-General Talbot issued the Yorke and Talbot Joint Opinion, which stated that slaves were not made free by baptism nor by being brought to England. See Helen T. Catterall, ed., *Judicial Cases Concerning American Slavery and the Negro* (Washington, DC: Carnegie Institution of Washington, 1926), 12. Furthermore, Yorke and Talbot compelled slaves to return with their masters to plantations. When West Indian planters transported servants to England, they sought assurance that these slaves not be allowed to obtain freedom through baptism or by simply being on English soil. Though not decided in a court, the Yorke and Talbot opinion, in effect, provided British enslavers with a legal sanction to buy and sell slaves.

13. In *Chamberlain v. Harvey* (1697), Chief Justice Sir John Holt, who represented the Court of King's Bench, avoided the issue of baptism in writing that "trespass does not lie for a black" (1 L. Raym, 146–47, *English Reports*). Chamberlain claimed ownership of a slave that Harvey had befriended and employed. Attorneys for Harvey claimed that by the laws of nature, no man could claim ownership of another. Furthermore, lawyers for Harvey contended that since the slave had been baptized, he could not be made a slave. Attorneys for Chamberlain pointed out that if baptism freed a slave, the Trade itself would be threatened. Though the jury was inclined to convict Harvey of trespass, the judge ruled that "no man can have property in the person of another while in England" (see *Chamberlain v. Harvey*, 1 Ld. Raym. 146, *The English Reports*, XCII, 605). Holt overruled (without reference) *Butts v. Penny* and *Gelly v. Cleve* but limited his ruling to domestic slavery (slavery on English soil). Holt's decision did not resolve the defendant's claims that slavery was constitutional law rather than natural law and that English laws made all individuals free. This case sustained a challenge to the rights, by natural law, of all

individuals to be free. The jury was unable to reach a verdict, and by limiting the jurisdiction of his ruling, the judge sidestepped more issues than he resolved.

In fact, with debates challenging blacks' very qualifications for personhood—not to mention pressure from a West Indian plantocracy to preserve slavery's legality—the Yorke and Talbot Joint Opinion (1729) definitively removed baptism altogether from consideration as protection against enslavement. For a study of Britain's common law practices on slavery, see Edward Fiddes, 499–511.

14. Two years after arriving in England, Equiano sought permission from his enslaver, Captain Michael Henry Pascal, to be baptized after being warned by a servant that he would not otherwise go to heaven. Pascal had reluctantly agreed only after Miss Guerins, Equiano's London patron, had insisted upon it (52).

15. See Charles Stuart, *A Memoir of Granville Sharp* (New York: American Anti-Slavery Society, 1836), 6–7.

16. See Potkay and Burr, eds., 35, and citation 19 (55). In John Bunyan's *The Holy War* (London: Printed for Dorman Newman and Benjamin Alsop, 1682), Diabolus, the aggressor in the battle over the city of Mansoul, is identified as "king of the blacks, or negroes."

17. Francis Bacon, *New Atlantis*, ca. 1624 in *The Works of Francis Bacon*, ed. James Spedding et al. Vol. 5 (Boston: Brown and Taggard, 1864), 347–413. King Solamona, the lawgiver of Bensalem, shielded his subjects from foreign colonization, though Bensalemites had knowledge of the manners, customs, and languages of Europe. The *New Atlantis* formed a model for England's Royal Society.

18. Drescher notes that "what was true of Christianity in general for more than a millennium and a half was true of British Christianity in the slave colonies for a century and a half after the settlement of Barbados" (112). He points out the "co-existence of Christianity with ancient and medieval Mediterranean slavery, with Eastern Christian slavery and with Atlantic slavery" (111).

19. Reflecting classic ambivalence on the subject, Jefferson initially cited the dilemma of "degrad[ing] a whole race of men from the work in the scale of beings which their creator may perhaps have given them." But he then expressed strong suspicions that whether or not racial differences were due to creation or "time and circumstance," blacks were intellectually inferior to whites in any case. Jefferson extricates himself by concluding that it really did not matter anyway whether nature or nurture determined the status of blacks in society. By performing semantical acrobatics on the word "originally" to the notion that blacks might have been a distinct race, he opens the door to Kames' idea of a separate creation: "I advance it therefore as a suspicion only, that the blacks, whether originally a distinct race, or made distinct by time and circumstances, are inferior to the whites in the endowments both of body and mind" (155).

20. See Voltaire, "On the Antiquity of Nations," in *The Best Known Works of Voltaire* (New York: Blue Ribbon Books, 1940), 240–41.

21. See Henry Home, Lord Kames, *Sketches of the History of Man* (Edinburgh, 1788), 78.

22. When comparing slavery in Africa and Europe, Cugoano approximates the classical definition of slavery: "So far as I can remember, some of the Africans in my country keep slaves, which they take in war, or for debt; but those which they

keep are well fed, and good care taken of them, and treated well" (12). (Equiano would later make similar observations.) Cugoano also claims that Africans suffered far less poverty in their own country than in the "inhospitable regions of misery which they meet with in the West Indies" (12).

23. In his introduction to *Thoughts and Sentiments*, Paul Edwards doubts that the hand of a single author composed an essay that exhibits, as he sees it, at least two distinctly different literary styles. *Thoughts and Sentiments* does contain sharp variations in style, tone, and grammatical construction, indicating that more than one writer might have had a hand in its composition. If there was a collaborator for the essay, Edwards argues convincingly for the hand of Olaudah Equiano, who in league with Cugoano as one of the Sons of Africa, demonstrates in his own narrative a clear knowledge of discursive craftiness (v–xvii). Potkay and Burr uncover additional, striking similarities between phraseology in letters known to be written by Equiano and similar expressions in *Thoughts and Sentiments on the Evil of Slavery*. I accept speculation that the philosophical essay may have been edited or corrected by Equiano or even that it may have been a collaborative effort between Equiano and Cugoano. But until some definitive answers are provided, I regard Cugoano as the primary author in producing this essay.

24. Cugoano's autobiographical sketch was later published separately in Thomas Fisher's *The Negro's Memorial, or Abolitionist's Catechism: By an Abolitionist* (London: Printed by Hatchard, 1825).

25. Cornel West, "Marxist Theory and the Specificity of Afro-American Oppression," in *Marxism and the Interpretation of Culture*, ed. Cary Nelson and Lawrence Grossberg (Urbana: University of Illinois Press, 1988), 17–29. Cornel West identifies the Hamitic hypothesis as one of three "discursive logics (the others being scientific and psychosexual) that inform principal modes of European domination of blacks." Because the conditions of publication for Cugoano's essay include a fermenting climate in common and ecclesiastical law, I also examine here an interpretive shift in the discourse surrounding the Hamitic hypothesis, concurrent with the vagaries of common and ecclesiastical laws on the baptism and legalized enslavement of blacks in England. Therefore, implicit in this chapter is the notion that an embellished Hamitic hypothesis, demonizing blacks in the sacred text, would further complicate an already-divisive issue in English ecclesiastical and common law. As I have already discussed, by the late 1770s, England's laws against slavery were hardly enforceable, and an act of Parliament was eventually required to outlaw the practice. The baptism of free and enslaved blacks, a key issue in the debate on the slavery question in the eighteenth century, induced some to embellish the biblical story of Ham, which proclaimed blacks to be an accursed heathen race.

26. Some skeptics have attributed the entire text of Cugoano's theological argument to Thomas Clarkson, whom Cugoano acknowledges in the essay. See part 3, chapters 7, and 8 in Clarkson's *An Essay on the Slavery and Commerce of the Human Species, Particularly the African* (Miami, FL: Mnemosyne Publishing Co., 1969; first published in Philadelphia, 1786).

In *The Origins of Modern African Thought* (London: Faber & Faber, 1968), Robert July notes that the intricate argument requires extensive knowledge of "the legalistic complexities of biblical exegesis" (40; also quoted by Paul Edwards in the introduction to *Thoughts and Sentiments* (Dawsons of Pall Mall, 1969), vii.

Cugoano followed his 1787 edition with an abbreviated version in 1791 that included a proposal to found a school for fellow Africans. In the 1787 edition, Cugoano lists over a hundred names of subscribers in addition to the names of booksellers who sold copies of the essay. A French edition of Cugoano's work, *Reflexions sur la traite et l'esclavage des Negres*, appeared in 1788, but I am unable to locate it.

Blacks' efforts to meet those standards set for freedom, equality, and morality were mostly futile, a fact that makes the publication of African-British writer Ottobah Cugoano (*Thoughts and Sentiments on the Evil of Slavery*, 1787) all the more interesting and unusual.

27. H. Freedman and Maurice Simon, trans. *Midrash Rabbah*, 6–7 (London: 1939), 293.

28. *The Sanhedrin*, VIII, in Seder Nezikin, *The Babylonian Talmud* (London: Soncino Press, 1935), 745.

29. *The Zohar*, I, trans. Harry Sperling and Maurice Simon (London: Soncino Press, 1935), 246–47.

30. *The American Heritage Dictionary of the English Language*, ed., William Morris (Boston, MA: Houghton Mifflin, 1981), 1150.

31. George Best, *A True Discourse of the Later Voyages of Discoverie, for the Finding of a Passage to Cathaga, by the Northwest*, vol. 7 (Henry Bynnyman, 1578), 263–64.

32. Richard Jobson, *Golden Trade: Or, a Discovery of the River Gambra, and the Golden Trade of the Aethiopians*, 1623, ed., Charles G. Kingsley (Teignmouth: Devonshire, 1904), 65–66; see Jordan, 19 and 35.

33. See Don Cameron Allen, *The Legend of Noah: Renaissance Rationalism in Art, Science, and Letters* (Urbana: University of Illinois Press, 1949), 119. Gilbert Genebrard, *Chronographiae Libri Quatuor* (Leyden: Sumptibus Ioannis Pillehotte, 1609), 26–27. See Guillaume Postel, *De Originibus* (Basle: Per Ioannem Oporinum, [1553]), 96ff, and Guillaume Postel, *Cosmographicae disciplinae compendium* (Basle: per Ioannem Oporinum, 1561), 37ff. See also Agostino Tornielli, *Annales sacri and Profani* (Frankfurt: Apud Ioannem Theobaldum Schon Wetteum, 1611), I. 133ff. Cited in Peter Fryer, *Staying Power: The History of Black People in Britain* (London: Pluto Press, 1984), 142–43.

34. Cugoano and Equiano were also frequent cosigners of letters against slavery, written to various influential or aristocratic white abolitionist patrons like Granville Sharp and Thomas Clarkson. An entry from Granville Sharp's *Journal*, quoted by Prince Hoare in *Memoirs of Granville Sharp* (London: Printed for Henry Colburn, 1820), reveals Cugoano's activism on behalf of the black poor in London, and letters such as the one that he wrote to Edmund Burke, quoted at the beginning of this chapter, do attest to his efforts to publish *Thoughts and Sentiments*. Passages on Cugoano's theological argument historicizing Africans as descendants of the sons of Noah probably derived from Thomas Clarkson's *Essay on the Slavery and Commerce of the Human Species*, 178–186. But Clarkson himself may have borrowed material from a letter written to Granville Sharp (Introduction, vii, *Thoughts and*

*Sentiments*, 1787). Clarkson's work had originated as a Latin essay for which he won an award when a student at Cambridge University. In 1785, Peter Peckard, the vice chancellor, master of Magdalene College, and dean of Peterborough, based the contest on the following question: "Anne liceat invitos in servitutem dare" [Is it right to make slaves of others against their will?]

35. West, 22. See the *Narrative of Frederick Douglass*, 1845; he writes that "if the lineal descendants of Ham are alone to be scripturally enslaved, it is certain that slavery at the south must soon become unscriptural; for thousands are ushered into the world, annually, who, like myself, owe their existence to white fathers, and those fathers most frequently their own masters" (257). Numerous slave narratives, including those of Frederick Douglass and Harriet Jacobs (*Incidents in the Life of a Slave Girl*, 1861) make caustic remarks about the concept that indicate its unfortunate durability, though they do not all accept the story's veracity. Douglass writes, for example, that the growing biracial population, the offspring of enslavers and slaves, would some day eliminate the argument that justified slavery on the basis of God's curse against Ham (257). Nella Larsen's *Passing*, 192? and Toni Morrison's *Sula*, 197? contain references to the curse of Ham in the context of blacks. Their references to the Hamitic hypothesis uphold Cornel West's essential reading of how localized analyses of white supremacy are assiduously inscribed, psychically, in the daily lives, culture, language, and identities of blacks.

36. See David Brion Davis, *The Problem of Slavery in the Age of Revolution, 1770–1823* (Ithaca, NY: Cornell University Press, 1975), 540.

37. See Jordan, citation 48 (201). These include Colonel William Byrd's letter to the Earl of Egmont, Virginia, 1736; William Edmundson's undated letter, "For Friends in Maryland, Virginia, and other parts of America"; and Jacob Bryant to Granville Sharp. See Granville Sharp, *Extract of a letter to a gentleman in Maryland wherein is demonstrated the wickedness of tolerating the slave trade*, 3rd ed., 1st pub. in London in 1793 (London: J. Phillips, 1797).

38. (Also reprinted as "The Negro Race not under a Curse," in *The Future of Africa*, 2nd edition (New York: Charles Scribner, 1862), 325–354). See also Ignatius Sancho, *The Letters of Ignatius Sancho*, ed., Paul Edwards and Polly Rewt (Edinburgh: University of Edinburgh Press, 1994), 191.

39. Sources for the Hamitic hypothesis include Don Cameron Allen, *The Legend of Noah*; Winthrop Jordan, *White Over Black: American Attitudes Toward the Negro, 1550–1812* (Baltimore: Penguin Books, 1969); Anthony Barker, *The African Link: British Attitudes to the Negro in the Era of the Atlantic Slave Trade, 1550–1807* (London: Frank Cass, 1978); Thomas Clarkson, *The History of the Rise, Progress, and Accomplishment of the Abolition of the African Slave Trade by the British Parliament*. 2 vols. (Philadelphia: James P. Parke, 1808); and Cugoano's *Thoughts and Sentiments on the Evil of Slavery*.

40. West, 17.

41. Cugoano, 145–46. In a letter to Gordon Turnbull ("Apology for Negro Slavery"), Olaudah Equiano criticizes both Turnbull and Tobin for sacrificing "your fellow-creatures on the altar of avarice." (Letter reprinted in Vincent Carretta, ed., *Olaudah Equiano: The Interesting Narrative and Other Writings* (New York: Penguin Books, 1996), 330–31.

42. See David Hume, *Essays: Moral, Political, and Literary* (London: Longmans, Green, 1898), 236.

43. Cugoano not only read Gronniosaw's narrative and shared the sentiments of faith, but he also signified upon Gronniosaw's trope of the talking book. Cugoano borrows a key concept from Gronniosaw—the trope of the talking book—which Henry Louis Gates, Jr., discusses at length in chapter 4 of *The Signifying Monkey*. At least six black writers, including Olaudah Equiano, utilize the trope in their publications.

44. For a thorough treatment of the Zong case, see *The English Reports*, 83 (London: William Green & Sons, 1908), 518; see also Catterall, ed., I. 1, 9. Prince Hoare, *Memoirs of Granville Sharp* (1820) also contains an account of this case, 236–47. Peter Fryer details the *Zong* case in *Staying Power*, 108, 127–29.

45. By the mid-eighteenth century, the third Earl of Shaftesbury, Francis Hutcheson, Adam Smith, and others advanced alternatives to legalized slavery. They offered a humanitarian perspective to legal issues. In effect, they would have law "return" to an impartial truth as lofty perspective, a function that law has long claimed. Shaftesbury wrote, "If the Love of doing Good, be not, of it-self, a good and right inclination; I know not how there can possibly be such a thing as Goodness or Virtue" (Anthony Ashley Cooper, 3rd Earl of Shaftesbury, *Characteristics of Men, Manners, Opinions, Times*, ed. John M. Robertson [Gloucester, MA: P. Smith, 1963], vol. 1, 98). Hutcheson wrote, "As to the notions of slavery which obtained among the Grecians and Romans, and other nations of old, they are horridly unjust. No damage done or crime committed can change a rational creature into a piece of goods void of all right" (*A System of Moral Philosophy* [New York: P. M. Kelley, 1968], vol. 2, 202–203). And Adam Smith wrote, "there is not a negro from the coast of Africa who does not . . . possess a degree of magnanimity, which the soul of his sordid master is too often scarce capable of conceiving (*Theory of Moral Sentiments*, ed. D. D. Raphael and A. L. Macfie [Oxford: Clarendon Press, 1956], vol. 2, 37).

46. Henri Grégoire reviewed Cugoano's *Thoughts and Sentiments* in *An Enquiry Concerning the Intellectual and Moral Faculties, and Literature of Negroes*, trans. D. B. Warden (Brooklyn: Printed by Thomas Kirk, 1810). Grégoire revealed some of the problems that other reviewers may have had with the essay (192).

47. Keith Sandiford takes this viewpoint in *Measuring the Moment: Strategies of Protest in Eighteenth-Century Afro-English Writing* (London: Associated University Presses, 1988).

# 3

# Ignatius Sancho and Laurence Sterne: The Measure of Benevolence and the "Cult of Sensibility"

> I have observed a dog will love those who use him kindly—and surely, if
> so, negroes, in their state of ignorance and bondage, will not act less
> generously, if I may judge them by meself—I suppose kindness would do
> anything with them;—my soul melts at kindness—but the contrary—I own
> with shame—makes me almost a savage.
>
> —Ignatius Sancho
> *Letters*

In an anonymous novel entitled *Memoirs and Opinions of Mr. Blenfield*,
1790, one chapter features a character who is reportedly inspired by the life
of African-British writer Ignatius Sancho (*Letters of the Late Ignatius
Sancho*, 1782).[1] Introducing "Shirna Cambo" to a gathering of acquaintances as "my worthy African friend," the narrator in this sentimental fiction
describes someone whose opinions and personage would be recognizable to
even the most casual reader of Sancho's epistolary collection as Sancho
himself, thinly disguised. Sancho shared with his character prototype in
*Memoirs of Mr. Blenfield* a particular proclivity for long discussions with his
acquaintances on sensibility.

Like Sancho, the character Shirna Cambo believes sensibility to be the
link in the chain of humanity that promotes justice, devotion, and human
bonding. "'Teach this doctrine among your women,'" Cambo says, and
"'you will do a service to the cause of humanity, for which they will esteem
you, and every transplanted African will pour forth all his sighs and tears
in your behalf.'"[2] Cambo thus declares women to be the purveyors, and
transplanted or enslaved Africans to be the ideal beneficiaries, of sensibility
as practice. To teach this concept would be to earn their gratitude and thus

ultimately to benefit humanity and promote universal order. After passionately venting his views on this subject, the character from *Memoirs of Mr. Blenfield* then narrates a story that replicates the early years of Ignatius Sancho's own bondage to a Greenwich family:

> If a native of a free country, stolen from the embrace of paternal fondness; conveyed through dangers, and over seas, to be made the victim of rapacious commerce and ungoverned cruelty, because God has chosen to habit him in a different colour—if he can dream of sensibility, and not feel for his fellow countrymen hourly bending under ignominious bondage, he must deserve a far worse lot than has fallen to him. (152)

By identifying women and slaves with the concept of sensibility, Cambo singles out two dispossessed groups in eighteenth-century English society as key players in the formation of a "cult" of sensibility. Furthermore, he refers to a massive abolitionist movement in the late eighteenth century whose organizers included large numbers of English women who wrote and published numerous anti-slavery poems, stories, and essays. Writers such as Janet Todd (*Sensibility: An Introduction*, 1986), C. J. Barker-Benfield (*The Culture of Sensibility: Sex and Society in Eighteenth-Century Britain* 1992), and Patricia Meyer Spacks have all commented on the fostering of sensibility in women in eighteenth-century society.[3] Paradoxically, women were appropriated as the bearers of sensibility by what was perceived as their delicate constitutions, emotionalism, and innate virtue; but they were also viewed as the endangered beneficiaries of a seductive fictional sensibility that was disruptive to their traditional roles as wives and mothers. In other words, it was good to feel and to love; but not too much, or in the wrong way. The regulative properties of sensibility for British women and their anti-slavery involvement are connected with benevolence and sensibility as humanitarian gestures for enslaved blacks.[4]

The unique subject of British women's role in colonial slavery is explored in Moira Ferguson's study, *Subject to Others: British Women Writers and Colonial Slavery, 1670–1834*, which critiques anti-slavery writings by Hannah More, Sarah Scott, and others. I am not altogether convinced, though, by Ferguson's argument that Anglican women's participation in the anti-slavery effort "displaced anxieties about their own assumed powerlessness and inferiority onto their representations of slaves."[5] I believe that British women's abolitionism more likely resulted from a dual, paradoxical identification with enslaved blacks because of shared forms of oppression. But because of racial acculturation, Anglican women also identified, in part, with a white, male patriarchy. Later in this chapter, I shall discuss Maria Edgeworth's story, "The Grateful Negro," as one case in point. In an interesting contrast, Mary Wollstonecraft seems aware of this dilemma in *A Vin-*

*dication of the Rights of Men* (1790), in which she writes, "Where is the dignity, the infallibility of sensibility, in the fair ladies, whom, if the voice of rumour is to be credited, the captive negroes curse in all the agony of bodily pain, for the unheard of tortures they invent" (111)? In a written review, Wollstonecraft had expressed mixed feelings about Olaudah Equiano's narrative for *Analytical Review* in May 1789. In it, she had expressed lukewarm sentiments toward the work and referred to it as a curiosity, "as it has been a favourite philosophic whim to degrade the numerous nations, on whom the sun-beams more directly dart, below the common level of humanity, and hastily to conclude that nature, by making them inferior to the rest of the human race, designed to stamp them with a mark of slavery."[6]

Wollstonecraft's *Vindication* is intended foremost as an attack on Edmund Burke's *Reflections on the Revolution in France* (1790). For example, she charges Burke with characterizing sensibility as "a kind of mysterious instinct" that "is supposed to reside in the Soul, that instantaneously discerns truth."[7] Furthermore, she believes that were sensibility inbred rather than acquired, as Burke infers, atrocities such as slavery would not exist. Declaring that "such misery demands more than tears," Wollstonecraft thus joins with British abolitionist William Wilberforce and others in acknowledging that sensibility produced mostly sheer emotionalism attended by inaction.

In rare instances when contemporary scholarship has identified slavery as a dominant driving force in much of the popular sentimental literature published in the late eighteenth century, it has concurred with and even reinforced Wilberforce's and Wollestonecraft's earlier findings on the value of those contributions.[8] Wilberforce suggests that as a literary contribution to abolitionism and to the plight of blacks in England, sentimentality as rhetoric concealed deeply rooted, complex problems confronting England's black population. Wilberforce acknowledges that sensibility is highly useful, but only when offered in the service of religion. He believes that most individuals err by replacing religion with an egalitarianism and a positive temperament.[9] Distinguishing sensibility from benevolence, which he regards as a more favorable attribute, Wilberforce suggests that those who possess the former "can solace themselves with their imaginary exertions in behalf of ideal misery, and yet shrink from the labours of active benevolence" (202). As it is presented in numerous literary contexts throughout the eighteenth century, sensibility as a literary trend leaves in place a tacit approval of, and an assumption of, intellectual inferiority in blacks.

Unlike Wollestoncraft and Wilberforce, Ignatius Sancho follows Burke on the idea of sensibility. As Sancho regards it, sensibility in tandem with benevolence, is a link in the chain of human existence. For Sancho, benevolence offers itself up as a naturalist antidote to despair because it fosters empathy and urges the bestowal of goodwill toward those of lesser social rank and economic status. True to form, Sancho's character likeness in *Memoirs of Mr. Blenfield* defends Burke against the criticism that he has advocated a selfish sensibility in which individuals gratified their own vanity by relieving others. In the novel, Cambo argues that the gesture to benefit others is an instinctive one and that spontaneity renders the deed a selfless act. Citing Burke's *Philosophical Inquiry into the Origin of Our Ideas on the Sublime and Beautiful* (1756), Cambo, the fictive voice of Sancho, goes on to observe that

> Even when we are most affected with another's distress, we feel a kind of delight that hinders us from shunning scenes of misery; and the degree of pain we feel prompts us to relieve ourselves, in relieving those who really suffer; and this, merely by an instinct that works us to its own purposes without our concurrence. (152–53)

The dialogue that engages Cambo in *Memoirs of Mr. Blenfield* accurately registers Sancho's point of view on benevolence as a remedy designed to relieve human suffering, but it is not known whether or not the author ever witnessed or participated in such a conversation with Ignatius Sancho. Though the novel achieved little literary acclaim, Ignatius Sancho's simulated role in a published work indicates both the extent of his popularity to eighteenth-century English readers *and* the impact of sensibility on Sancho's literary and social reputation.

A formerly enslaved African, and the first to publish an epistolary collection in England, Ignatius Sancho uniquely problematizes sensibility and benevolence as philanthropic discourse and philosophical gesture, respectively, as they relate to slavery and abolitionism. In addition, he codifies some of the unique ways in which patronage and benevolence were administered in relations between blacks and whites. As a social leveller and as an antidote to despair, benevolence promised to cement the unequal parts of the Great Chain of Being, an idea that simulates Pope's theories in the third book of *Essay on Man* on the concept of happiness as a humanitarian philosophy. In other words, on a humanitarian level, benevolence achieves universal order and fulfills Pope's conception of happiness as service to others.

In wresting a form of sensibility from authors like Pope and Burke whose ideas did not overtly include race, Sancho's readaptation of sensibility as a seemingly custom-made philosophy for the debate on race and slavery proved clever and unabashedly opportunistic. For instance, whereas Burke saw sensibility universally as a form of benevolence, Sancho viewed it as a theory, especially designed to promote interracial bonding, and used his own rescue from bondage as an example. If Pope's idea of happiness was service to others, then Sancho translated that service as abolitionism, designed to free those who remained in bondage in the West Indies. And when Sancho believed Laurence Sterne to be the only major literary figure who agreed with him—who openly urged an end to slavery because it was incompatible with the philosophy of sensibility—Sancho quickly adopted him as a role model, philosopher, and friend. (I will examine the exchange of letters between Sancho and Sterne later in the chapter.)

Accordingly, as indicated through his letters, Sancho devised an aesthetic "chain of love" as a more exacting philosophy of benevolence that individuals could express toward the downtrodden. Like the idea of sensibility, Sancho's chain of love had an Anglican, though metaphysical, base, which can be found in writings by Boethius, such as his *Consolation of Philosophy*, (*A.D.* 524), in John Dryden's *Palamon and Arcite* and imitation of the *Tenth Satire of Juvenal*, and, of course, in Pope's *Essay on Man*. For example, Boethius espoused a medieval concept of happiness that offered love as the conduit that transports harmony in the universe. A staple of medieval humanism, *The Consolation* demonstrates the possibility of achieving human happiness amid great suffering and tragedy. Boethius wrote *The Consolation* from prison while awaiting execution from seeming trumped-up charges of sacrilege and treason for allegedly invoking evil spirits against the Roman ruler, Theodoric. Rather than analyze the Chain as a platonic, theological hierarchy, Boethius links its disparate parts with love, a highly accessible attribute for all of humanity. He sees humanity as a microcosm for a greater divine love that heals discord in the universe and observes that love "commands the heavens" and "rules the earth and the seas" (41). In *The Consolation of Philosophy*, Boethius notes that "the universe carries out its changing process in concord and with stable faith, [and] that the conflicting seeds of things are held by everlasting law" (41). Without the benefit of a universal love that achieves a harmonious order of things, war and strife would be waged continually, and the world would be split asunder. Boethius observes that the human race would be happiest if that love which rules the heavens also ruled all souls (41).

But in calling directly for racial and multiethnic unity, Sancho (who certainly knew major writings by Pope, probably knew some by Dryden, and might have known Boethius' *Consolation*) redirects this metaphysical chain from the universal or the general to the particular and the practical. In other words, in an observation that brings to mind Dryden's *Palamon and Arcite* and imitation of Juvenal's *Tenth Satire*, Sancho imaginatively envisions a new world order[10] in which Africans would mix with all nations, races, and religions: "See the countless multitudes of the first world—the myriads descended from the Ark—the Patriarchs—Sages—Prophets—and Heroes" (Letter 44, 23 July 1777). In his imitation of Juvenal's *Tenth Satire*, Dryden notes, "In youth, distinctions infinite abound; / No Shape, or Feature, just alike are found; / The Fair, the Black, the Feeble, and the Strong; / But the same foulness does to Age belong, / The self same palsie, both in Limbs, and Tongue" (lines 313–17). Dryden uses the term "Black" in a nonracial context but deconstructs a prevalent Renaissance standard of beauty that favors fair skin over dark skin. Like Samuel Johnson in *Vanity of Human Wishes*, Dryden exposes the follies of those who seek happiness in wealth, fame, longevity, and beauty. And in *Palamon and Arcite, or The Knight's Tale*, he thematizes the transitoriness of life and paints death as the great equalizer of all. Dryden observes that all humanity, however, is cemented by a chain of love: "The Cause and Spring of motion, from above, / Hung down on earth the golden chain of love. Great was th' effect, and high was his intent, / When peace among the jarring seeds he sent. / Fire, flood, and earth, and air by this were bound, / And love, the common link, the new creation crown'd" (1024–33).[11]

In contrast with Dryden's observations, Sancho enthusiastically fancies a consolidation between Africans and those in the first world: "My head turns round at the vast idea," he gushes to an acquaintance; "We will mingle with them and untwist the vast chain of blessed Providence!"[12] If Dryden expresses a chain of love as a way to equalize both fair and black alike, Sancho uses it to urge equality for blacks and to unify blacks and whites as racial groups. As a specific pronouncement on racial unity and harmony then, Sancho's "vast Chain" pointedly usurps, and even subverts, previous conceptions of the idea in most Anglican philosophical writings.

Sancho falls somewhere between abstract philosophies that absent or displace race and stinging observations, such as Hester Thrale Piozzi's, that divide race. Piozzi, an acquaintance of Dr. Samuel Johnson, described the following "apocalypse," with which I suspect a consensus of the English population might have identified:

> Well! I am really haunted by black shadows. Men of colour in the rank of gentlemen; a black lady covered with finery, in the Pit at the Opera, and tawny children playing in the Squares,—in the gardens of the Squares I mean,—with their Nurses, afford ample proofs of Hannah More and Mr. Wilberforce's success in breaking down the wall of separation. Oh! how it falls on every side! and spreads its tumbling ruins on the world! leaving all ranks, all custom, all colours, all religions, jumbled together.[13]

Fortunately for Sancho, acquaintances like Laurence Sterne expressed a different viewpoint from Piozzi's. In a letter dated 27 July 1766, Sterne commends Sancho for escaping the "Chains of Misery" and for "falling into the hands of so good and merciful a family." Still, when commenting on the changing "insensible gradations" at St. James, Sterne alludes to the Chain of Being in a manner that seems problematical:

It is by the finest tints, and most insensible gradations, that nature descends from the fairest face about St. James's, to the sootiest complexion in Africa: at which tint of these, is it, that the ties of blood are to cease? *and how many shades must we descend lower still in the scale*, 'ere Mercy is to vanish with them? (Curtis, 286; italics are mine)

Sancho would ideally mingle with, rather than hierarchize, individuals of different races, nationalities, ethnicities, and religions, countering the Chain's discursive legacy on race in science and theology. It is a unification that might have proved more difficult for his English compatriots, however. I am reminded here of an anecdote recorded in Aleyn Reade's *Johnsonian Gleanings*; a visiting clergyman by the name of Noel Turner was greeted at the door by Johnson's servant, Francis Barber, who was entertaining his own friends inside. Turner recounts that when Barber opened the door to say that Johnson was not at home, "a group of his African countrymen were sitting round a fire in the gloomy ante-room, and on their all turning their sooty faces at once to stare at me, they presented a curious spectacle."[14] The "curious spectacle" of blacks, gathered simply to interact with one another, as observed by the clergyman and Hester Thrale Piozzi, is akin to a dominant cultural group's inability to see what constitutes a different cultural or racial group as normal individuals in normal settings. In the eighteenth century, England's steadily increasing black population was mostly centered in and around London and was becoming more visible, though not necessarily more welcome.

A similar anecdote is recorded in the *Diary of Katherine Plymly*, who records a visit to her home by Olaudah Equiano. In order to raise enough subscription money to pay for the printing of his narrative, Equiano had launched a solo journey throughout England and Scotland. Plymly commented that Equiano's efforts to promote his own narrative might backfire and make getting subscriptions for its publication even more difficult. She echoed her brother, who was away at the time of Equiano's visit, but who had initially invited Equiano to come to his home, in hinting, perhaps, that white abolitionists should do this work: "The luke-warm would be too apt to think if this be the case, & weare [*sic*] to have Negroes come about in this way, it will be very troublesome" (Plymley's *Diary*). Both Turner and Plymley express their musings in the private format of a diary or journal, and this raises questions about their views and the mixed motives demonstrated by even the most ardent supporters of positive race relations. Meanwhile, Equiano's perception of his efforts differed dramatically from that reported by Katherine Plymley. In a letter to a Reverend G. Walker (27 February 1792), he reported having sold 1,900 copies of his narrative in England and Scotland and expressed hope that his efforts would aid the abolitionist cause.

Similarly, Sancho's relationship with the British aristocracy, who made up the bulk of subscribers to *Letters of the Late Ignatius Sancho*, was attended by social constraints. In spite of Sancho's admiration for Sterne (shown in his copious imitation of the Sternian style), and for Pope, Fielding, Swift, Edward Young, Sarah Scott, and other literary figures, Sancho was well aware of his marginality in English society. Tensions inevitably erupted from Sancho's identity as an African on the one hand, and his assimilation into English society, on the other. Sancho thus poses as a paradoxical social and cultural phenomenon, born of British aristocratic and abolitionist fervor. He is both an individual, independently establishing an identity as an author and a person, and a product of the rhetoric of sensibility. The strain takes its toll, however, both on the objects of its projections—members of a minority culture—and those in the dominant culture who project such feelings.

As my opening headnote suggests, Sancho demonstrates the uniqueness of the relationship that typically existed between the white benefactor and those blacks who were served by beneficence. Philosophizing about the benefits of kindness to those of the "Negro" persuasion in a letter to Mr. Brown, Sancho threatens to meet its opposite—malevolence—with savagery, then casually expresses good wishes, requesting to be sent a dozen cocoa nuts. Sancho knowingly allows a highly offensive term like "savagery," typically bestowed upon blacks, to linger inhospitably and subversively in the letter. Such observations clearly complicate the notion that a requisite docility is the most appropriate expression of gratitude for the beneficiary. Here, Sancho all but demands that patronage be granted for blacks who exhibit appropriate humility.

Sancho's own words of advice, supplied wittily and affectionately to friends, attest to his own benevolence, dignity, and general social condition as an African living in a largely white population. For example, in a letter to Jack Wingrave, Sancho implores him to "eat moderately, drink temperately, and laugh heartily, sleep soundly, converse carefully with one eye to pleasure, the other fixed upon improvement." He further advises Wingrave that "peace of mind" brings about a dignity that even kings have no power to bestow. Expressing a consistent philosophy of temperance, benevolence, humility, and gratitude, Sancho advises a young Mr. Brown to be thankful for "the noble and generous benefactors [God's] providence has so kindly moved in your behalf" (Letter 13, 18 July 1772). In one letter after another, he never lost an opportunity to remind friends and acquaintances of the benefits that Providence had bestowed upon him.

Highly erudite, Sancho had a particular affinity for the work of Alexander Pope and was fond of quoting or paraphrasing his poetry. Sancho's reverent attention to aphorisms from the poet may seem ironic, but it actually illuminates, rather than undermines, the mediative function that he serves in the debate about racial hierarchies and in his own rank and social status. Sancho's admiration for the poet and his apparent fondness for the *Essay on Man* are highly relevant in light of the two men's different interpretations of the Great Chain of Being. In a letter addressed to John Meheux, a clerk in the Board of Controls, Sancho begins with a quote from *Essay on Man*. In it, Sancho expresses gratitude and humility for God's mercy, even as he ponders the insignificance of the individual in universal creation: "Know your own self, presume not God to scan; / 'The only science[15] of mankind, is man.'" In another quotation from Pope, Sancho writes: "One self-approving hour whole years outweighs / Of idle starers, or of loud huzzas; / What can ennoble sot, or slaves or cowards?" And to Miss Lydia Leach (his daughter's namesake), Sancho points out the importance of sincere praise as opposed to flattery: "I protest that you have something very like flattery; . . . Vanity is a shoot from self-love—and self-love, Pope declares to be the spring of motion in the human breast."[16]

Born in 1729, Ignatius Sancho was given the name Ignatius from the bishop who baptized him. Both Sancho's parents, also enslaved, died soon after their arrival in the West Indies. After Sancho's mother died, in an illness likely related to complications of his birth, his father committed suicide. At the age of two, Sancho was given to three sisters, who lived at Greenwich, England. He acquired his surname from the sisters, who imagined that he might resemble Don Quixote's squire.[17] Rescued from domestic enslavement by the Duke and Duchess of Montagu, Sancho saw his apportioned lot in society as serving some abstract divine plan, albeit one that required compliance and docility in order to support the concept of universal order.

Benevolent patrons provided Sancho with freedom and education, allowing him to choose contentment with his lot, as a formerly enslaved African whose good fortune was divinely ordained. He could certainly regard his fate much more comfortably than those blacks who remained in captivity in the West Indies and the North American colonies. The instinctive, spontaneous outpouring of feeling, along with specific acts of kindness and goodwill toward others, governed both Sancho's philosophy of life and his epistolary method and were shared with numerous English writers of his age. Mindful, perhaps, of the seeming futility of efforts toward a total and meaningful racial equality, Sancho quickly embraced benevolence as an acceptable alternative, realizing a measure of his own power to persuade, cajole, or even slyly embarrass those who might otherwise pay lip service to abolitionism in order to be held accountable for their (in)action.

The representation of blacks in fictional works throughout the eighteenth century (linked at least philosophically with Sancho and the idea of benevolence) bear out this conflict. These include Aphra Behn's *Oroonoko*, Maria Edgeworth's "The Grateful Negro," and Sarah Scott's two-volume *History of Sir George Ellison*. Not coincidentally, a trendy humanitarian movement that arose at this time is a haunting resurrection of the principle of gratitude, interspersed throughout England's literary history. It appears in works as diverse as Defoe's *Robinson Crusoe* and *Colonel Jack* and Maria Edgeworth's "The Grateful Negro" and Sarah Scott's *History of Sir George Ellison*. For example, Defoe's *Colonel Jack* utilizes the transported felon concept, whereby undesirable felons are transported from England to America and later to Australia—on continents well away from British soil.[18] *Colonel Jack* preaches benevolence as a philosophy for delusionary youths who are not privy to aristocracy. The concepts of criminal transportation and benevolence link *Colonel Jack* to Britain's slavery and colonialist history in the eighteenth and nineteenth centuries.

In considering Defoe's fictional impoverished orphan turned thief, who was later sold into indentured servitude in America and aided by a benefactor, what has gone unchallenged, even by scholars who are particularly critical of Defoe's ambivalent moral suasion, is the notion that such "opportunism" as Jack achieves was never meant to apply to the blacks whom he enslaved. C. Duncan Rice, in "Literary Sources and the Revolution in British Attitudes To Slavery," asserts that Defoe takes great pains to stress that labor relationships with black slaves should be governed by the same humane principles as those with free and half-free whites. What this amounts to is an attempt to bring slavery into consistency with eighteenth-century assumptions about social justice and the work ethic (325). Having sought absolution for career thievery, Colonel Jack could flaunt his loot—perhaps quadrupled on slave trade investments—and he could live out his prosperity literally on the backs of Others. He offers no remorse for enslaving other human beings in order to obtain wealth. And it seems to escape his notice that the blacks whom he enslaves are unable to share similarly even in his lowly status as an indentured servant who could transcend his station on an economic and social scale.[19]

In fact, Colonel Jack explains the reason for his upward mobility from an impoverished, orphaned birth to single parents to ill-gotten prosperity as motivation for other reform-minded felons: "and thus I was set up in the world, and in short, removed by the degrees that you have heard from a pick-pocket, to a kidnapp'd miserable slave in Virginia; . . . then from a slave to a head officer, and overseer of slaves, and from thence to a master planter" (152). Furthermore, he delivers a prelude to the future Horatio Alger concept of upward mobility, proclaiming that any "Newgate wretch, every desperate forlorn creature; the most despicable ruin'd man in the world" can end up in America, and by his own example, make it in the world—well, *almost* anyone (153). Theft is a crime, but perpetual enslavement is perfectly legal, and indentured servitude for Colonel Jack provides an opportunity.

Yet another factor problematizes the roots of Colonel Jack's prosperity. While benevolence spelled untold wealth and prosperity for Colonel Jack, it magically transformed into the "principle of gratitude" for enslaved blacks. To use "those miserable creatures" with humanity, claims Colonel Jack, would ensure that they do their work faithfully, cheerfully, and thankfully. As it turns out, showing benevolence toward the enslaved meant first conflating morality with economic necessity while normalizing the process by engaging in psychological terrorism rather than by beating slaves into submission. Jack's encoded "principle of gratitude," as a prelude to a complex literary, humanitarian, and abolitionist agenda later in the century, has mostly escaped interrogation by scholars. In a rare exception, C. Duncan Rice notes that Defoe's work is clearly not a criticism of slavery; rather, it is a model of an ideal social order (324).

Other authors in the eighteenth century thematize the concept, known as the principle of gratitude, as well. For instance, Maria Edgeworth's short story "The Grateful Negro" (1802) and Sarah Scott's *History of Sir George Ellison* address the popular concept that Defoe employed in *Colonel Jack*. Edgeworth's "The Grateful Negro," which appeared in a collection of moral tales that she wrote, particularly resembles *Colonel Jack* in its depiction of a planter in the West Indies. In opposition to a neighboring planter, Jefferies maximizes profits from his own plantation after applying the principle of gratitude, bestowing kindness and humane treatment upon slaves. Jefferies even allows slaves to cultivate their own land and trusts them to carry weapons. He argues that incentive rather than tyranny would produce far more labor, not to mention loyalty, from the enslaved. Humbled by this treatment, Jefferies' loyal slave Caesar vows never to betray his enslaver. When Caesar discovers a plot by other slaves to kill whites, he informs Jefferies, who foils the plot. Voicing her own approval of this outcome, Edgeworth writes that "the principle of gratitude conquered every other sensation."[20] More revealingly, she allows that as to "the treachery of the whole race of slaves," the reader might make "at least one exception . . . in favour of the Grateful Negro" (326).

Interestingly, Maria Edgeworth's planter-character delivers lines possibly taken from "The Task," William Cowper's well-known poem. At one point in the story, Jefferies defends slavery in the West Indies by announcing: "for indigo, and rum, and sugar we must have."[21] The planter's allusion to the profit margin, which offers a far more credible motive than goodwill or gratitude, also connects Edgeworth's story with Sarah Scott's two-volume novel. Perks that Sir George Ellison give to his slaves include training in education and religion. But he adds an ironic twist to the principle of gratitude. To treat slaves humanely also meant to protect them from one another, as they were considered to be a lawless bunch when provoked. Africans were largely depicted as a childlike people, for whom slavery in the West offered protection from almost certain death in Africa. Sir George Ellison opines that "Negroes are naturally faithful and affectionate, though on great provocation, their resentment is unbounded, and they will indulge their revenge through their own certain destruction."[22] Needless to say, the characters, Ellison and Jefferies, seemed not to notice these inherent contradictions.

Until recently, works like Sterne's *A Sentimental Journey* and *Tristram Shandy*, along with Henry MacKenzie's *The Man of Feeling*, have dominated the era of sentimentality in traditional scholarship. Addressing the neglect of slavery as an issue in MacKenzie's *Man of Feeling*, C. Duncan Rice quips that the Negro must be the only victim of oppression who "does not plead explicitly for sentimental tears" (321). As for Sterne's *Tristram Shandy*, Rice notes that even in the "infatuated world" that Uncle Toby and Corporal Trim occupy, "there is no cavil about black humanity, no question about extending the balm of Shandean sentiment to black people" (325).

Without a doubt, it was the cultivation of the friendship between Ignatius Sancho and Laurence Sterne, culminating with an obscure passage in *Tristram Shandy*, that most fully enabled Sancho to gain literary notice in England in the 1780s. The relationship between Laurence Sterne and Ignatius Sancho is among the first of many such pairings of the usually well-placed white benefactor or patron and the black charge.[23] Sancho and Sterne's mutually beneficial friendship is acted out on the literary page, where it actually becomes scripted in Sterne's *Tristram Shandy*. Curiously, however, serious issues like slavery threatened to become trivialized by the results of the passage, which included a demeaning fad (which I will explain shortly), and Sancho's relegation—at least until recently—to a canonical footnote. Even Sancho's obituary is appositioned by a reminder that he was "immortalized by his correspondence with Sterne."

But little social interaction took place between the two acquaintances that would adequately explain the historical immortalization of the relationship.[24] Rather, it seems to be based on the exchange of a few surviving letters between Sancho and Sterne, the most famous being the exchange of letters between the two of them regarding Sterne's obliging passage in *Tristram Shandy*. Sancho had apparently enlisted the Duke of Montagu's support of Sterne's work by selling advanced subscriptions to the Montagu family. Sterne thanks Sancho in a letter (16 May 1767) for his subscription and for securing the Montagus' support as well, then asks that they all send in their subscription money.[25]

When Sancho asked Sterne to help the cause of blacks enslaved in Britain and in British colonies, their friendship connected with the sentimental literary movement. In his reply to Sancho, Sterne claims to have already composed just such a passage about "a friendless Negro girl" whom the character, Uncle Toby, encounters in a local shop. Sterne promises to incorporate the passage into *Tristram Shandy*, which he was in the process of writing and indeed so does.[26] Sancho's letter of request for Sterne's support arrived at a depressing time for Sterne, whose health and finances were both in decline, partly as a result of the huge expenses associated with his ailing wife's medical condition. Mrs. Sterne frequently traveled in search of a good climate. The arrival of Sancho's letter in July lifted Sterne's spirits considerably, as Sterne's comments in another letter indicates: "Tis affectation to say a man is not gratified with being praised—we only want it to be sincere—and then it will be taken, Sancho, as kindly as yours."[27]

Though Sancho initially appeals to Sterne's humanity in the letter, he also uses subtle pressure to urge Sterne's complicity: "Reverend Sir, it would be an insult on your humanity (or perhaps look like it) to apologize for the liberty I am taking," Sancho begins. Lacing bravura with deference, he both anticipates a positive response from Sterne and defuses what might be construed in epistolary etiquette as "upstart" behavior from one whose rank and social station were perceived as inferior to Sterne. The actual request for Sterne's assistance is deeply layered in diplomacy:

> I think you will forgive me;—I am sure you will applaud me for beseeching you to give one half-hour's attention to slavery, as it is at this day practised in our West Indies.—That subject, handled in your striking manner, would ease the yoke (perhaps) of many—but if only of one—Gracious God!—what a feast to a benevolent heart!—and, sure I am, you are an epicurean in acts of charity.—You, who are universally read, and as universally admired—you could not fail—Dear Sir, think in me you behold the uplifted hands of thousands of my brother Moors.—Grief you pathetically observe is eloquent;—figure to yourself their attitudes;—hear their supplicating addresses!—alas!—you cannot refuse.—Humanity must comply—in which hope I beg permission to subscribe myself, Reverend Sir, &c. Ign. Sancho! (Letter 36, 27 July 1766)

In a reproduction of Sancho's letter, which Sterne evidently edited with an eye toward its publication among his own collection of letters, his syntactical polishing effectively formalizes relations between himself and Sancho, as well as tones down Sancho's effusive praise, passion, and emotionalism. For example, he writes that "It would be an insult, (or perhaps look like one), on your Humanity, to apologize for the Liberty *of this address—unknowing and unknown*" [italics added to emphasize Sterne's changes]. In another sentence, Sterne removes "and only" from Sancho's version: "I was placed in a family who judged ignorance the best and only security for obedience." He also replaces Sancho's "what a feast to a benevolent heart" with simply, "what a feast."[28]

Next to Sancho's hopes that Sterne's actions "would ease the Yoke of many," Sterne inserts in his edited version, "perhaps occasion a reformation throughout our Islands" (283). In addition, Sterne substitutes "Yorick" for Sancho's use of Sterne's own name as "an Epicurean in [acts of] Charity" who is "universally read and admired"; (Sancho's words are in brackets). Sancho had cited an anti-slavery passage in Sterne's "Sermons of Mr. Yorick," Tenth Discourse, Volume 2. Oddly Sterne's sermon has the same ebullient sentimental style as Sancho's letter to Sterne, perhaps an indication that Sancho wrote letters as Sterne drafted sermons. The oratorical, emotional sermon like quality of Sancho's epistolary style contrasts with Sterne's more muted, formal epistolary style—though both convey a strong, sentimental message. Sancho urges Sterne to

> Consider how great a part of our species in all ages down to this, have been trod under the feet of cruel and capricious Tyrants who would neither hear their cries, nor pity their distresses—Consider Slavery—what it is,— how bitter a draught! and how many millions have been made to drink of it. (Letter 36, 27 July 1766)

Sterne's edited version removes the phrase, "alas!—you cannot refuse" while it retains the words, "Humanity must comply" (283). Amid the letter's expressed urgency, Sancho, who had initiated the correspondence with Sterne regarding the passage, is careful to preserve the social status and power differential between himself and Sterne.

In the passage itself, printed in *Tristram Shandy*, Uncle Toby gives an emotional account of the actions of a young black girl in a sausage shop who shows mercy for small creatures. She holds a long stick fastened with white feathers. Uncle Toby notices that she slowly waves the stick back and forth, gently "flapping away flies, not killing them," and he marvels at the "pretty picture" struck by her act of charity (vol. 9, chap. 6, 466). Toby speculates that "she had suffered persecution . . . and had learnt mercy." As though mindful of naturalists' ideas about the alleged genetic inferiority of blacks, Trim says that "she was good, an' please your honour, from nature as well as from hardships." Further implicating pseudo-science data, Uncle Toby and Corporal Trim ponder whether or not a black person is born with a soul.

"A Negro has a soul?" says Trim, "doubtingly." "I am not much versed, Corporal," Toby replies, "in things of that kind; but I suppose, God would not leave him without one, any more than thee or me" (466). Trim wonders aloud, "Why then, an' please your honour, is a black wench to be used worse than a white one?" Toby responds that it is only "because she has no one to stand up for her" (466). The sentiments of the entire exchange are contained in Toby's stirring, though ambiguous conclusion: "Tis that very thing . . . which recommends her to protection—and her brethren with her; 'tis the fortune of war which has put the whip into our hands now—where it may be hereafter, heaven knows!—but be it where it will, the brave, Trim! will not use it unkindly" (466).

Sterne's passage does not mention slavery, though eighteenth-century readers most likely would have understood its racial overtones. But Toby's comments on the ill usage of black females harbors sexual overtones, focusing attention on the sexual abuse of countless enslaved black women. (I examine this issue more closely in chapter 5 in discussing *The History of Mary Prince*, which subtly exposes sexual and other forms of abuse.) Popular opinion held that black females were inherently lewd and lascivious, a perception that covered for, and denied responsibility to, white male planters in the West Indies who sexually abused them. The "Negro girl" in the sausage shop never speaks aloud in the scene with Toby and Trim, perhaps symbolizing the fact that only a white person could represent or validate the black woman, whether as narrative voice or as an individual. Toby's observation that the black woman "has no one to stand up for her" shows sterility in the English legal system, since black women were rarely able to obtain redress and could not testify on their own behalf in court. He speculates that "there are circumstances in the story of that poor friendless *slut* that would melt a heart of stone."[29] The term "slut" was nonpejorative and was indeed a term of affection in this context. Nevertheless the complex troping on the use of a pejorative (non)pejorative word in the anecdote is highly ironic.

In the passage, Toby becomes a mouthpiece for Sterne, though his antislavery beliefs are actually expressed more vehemently through Yorick in the tenth sermon. In challenging those who held the reins of power—the "whip" of authority—to exercise the spirit of benevolence, Toby echoes rhetorically a principal credo of sensibility as humanitarianism, but he pronounces no direct call to action. By including the passage in *Tristram Shandy*, Sterne preserves the principles of sentimentality and his friendship with Sancho, with little chance of offending readers or distracting them from the primary story line.

Singling out Laurence Sterne as a principal architect of sentimentality as rhetoric, Wilberforce writes, "Never was delicate sensibility proved to be more distinct from plain practical benevolence, than in the writings of [Sterne]" (202). Ironically, without any specific references to the "Negro girl in a sausage shop passage" in *Tristram Shandy*, Wilberforce makes this scathing observation about Sterne: "Instead of employing his talents for the benefit of his fellow-creatures, they were applied to the pernicious purposes of corrupting the national taste, and of lowering the standard of manners and morals" (203).

Sterne's literary response to Sancho's request for some small contribution to abolitionism provoked public responses to Sancho and called attention to the passage in *Tristram Shandy*. It is credited with bringing public notice to Sancho before the polite world as a formerly enslaved African who, remarkably, had mastered the feat of becoming literate. The resulting publicity also led to a portrait being made of Sancho, painted by the notable Thomas Gainsborough as a true mark of Sancho's notice among the British aristocracy. Sancho's *Letters*, published posthumously in 1782, would provoke yet additional responses from the literary community.

But perhaps most stunningly, Sterne's anti-slavery contribution in *Tristram Shandy*, which made no mention of slavery, produced a curious fad. Wilbur Cross notes that "in the years that followed, it became the fashion among the tender-hearted to rid themselves of flies, not by torturing or killing them, but by gently brushing them aside or spouting cold water upon them."[30] Still, the fad to imitate the black girl's act of charity was undertaken by British aristocrats who most likely purchased the huge, feathered fans in order that their servants might more humanely chase away house flies. In *The Politics of Sensibility*, Markman Ellis interprets the feathered fan as a "'white' version of the cat-of-nine-tails, such as was used on Oroonoko to such terrible effect" as a metaphor for the whips and chains of slavery. Ellis observes

> There is a witty, though perilously risky, irony to Sterne's metonymic invocation of the violence congenital to the slave system of coerced labour, figured in the play of whips and swats: the whip of the slave owners has been translated into the fly swat of the woman slave, and is mimetically echoed again by the flourish of Trim's stick, which even looks like a whip on the page. (70)

Regardless of charges of patronizing in the sentimental movement, Sancho firmly believed that his entire experience led him to grasp firmly the reins of a benevolent philosophy over an overt, anti-slavery activism. Spared from a potentially worse fate, Sancho understandably chose benevolence as antidote to a nihilism that might otherwise have overtaken him. He was fully aware of the rarity of his case as compared with those of blacks enslaved in the West Indies. Not surprisingly Sancho found Laurence Sterne, whose Uncle Toby exhibited a hearty benevolence, highly appealing as an author and as an individual. In a letter dated 10 June 1778, Sancho compares Sterne first with Fielding and then with Swift, with the judgment heavily favoring Sterne. "Fielding and Sterne both copied nature," and their characters, Allworthy and Toby, respectively, shared a hearty benevolence. After applauding Fielding for wit, humor, and morality, Sancho adds that Sterne equals Fielding in all things but the one in which he excels all—"the distribution of his lights, which he has so artfully varied throughout his work, that the oftener they are examined the more beautiful they appear." Further comparing Sterne's wit with Swift's "grave-faced irony," Sancho writes that Sterne's philanthropy contrasted with Swift's cynicism. He added that Sterne employed humor in place of Swift's bitterness. "I know you will laugh at me—Do—I am content: if I am an enthusiast in any thing, it is in favor of my Sterne," Sancho concludes.

The relationship between Sancho and Sterne surely provided both with more than a measure of gratification; it combatted Sterne's growing despondency and bolstered Sancho's recognition. Sterne later wrote, "I shall live this year at least, I hope, be it but to give the world, before I quit it, as good impressions of me, as you have, Sancho."[31] He vowed to remain temperate and to bear his afflictions "just as it pleases God to send them." He believed that the truest philosophy was to be "indebted to ourselves, but not to our fortunes" (370). This was Sterne's great appeal and, perhaps, his greatest legacy to Sancho—a temperate spirit, tinged with optimism and flavored with colorful humor.

In the style, form, and content of his epistolary collection, Sancho proudly cast himself as a Sternian imitator, characterized by scattering his letters with Sterne's trademark dashes, by inconsistent use of capital letters, by bursts of exuberance, and so on. Still, others would cast him as a "Shandean fabricator of words." The label of Sternian imitator was applied, derisively, by Thomas Jefferson, who wrote that although Sancho may have rated highly among his fellow Africans, he was no comparison with European writers. Jefferson further claimed that Sancho's letters "do more honor to the heart than the head" and that "his imagination is wild and extravagant, [and] escapes incessantly from every restraint of reason and taste" (152). Henri de Grégoire (*An Enquiry Concerning the Intellectual and Moral Faculties, and Literature of Negroes*, Trans. D. B. Warden [Brooklyn: Printed by Thomas Kirk, 1810]), in turn, criticizes Thomas Jefferson for his negative assessment of Sancho's literary talents. "The more respectful the authority of Jefferson is, the more important is it to combat his judgment, which seems too severe," wrote Grégoire (234). He added that Sancho "has the grace and lightness of the fancy style," calling him, by turns, clever, grave, and pompous (232).

Certainly Sancho was appreciated by patrons who worked to get his letters into print. In a letter dated 20 April 1779, from Bath, Edmund Rack asked Sancho for permission to publish two letters that had fallen into his hands in a collection, entitled *Letters of Friendship*, that is no longer available. Similarly, Frances Crewe, Sancho's literary patron and editor, thought that his letters would show that "an untutored African may possess abilities" equal to those of Europeans. She professed a desire to serve Sancho's family by publishing the letters that she had collected from his correspondents in a two-volume set two years after his death. The letters that Edmund Rack wished to publish in the autumn of 1779 were from Sancho to acquaintances in the East Indies and in Philadelphia. Thinking that the letters showed "humanity and strong sense," Rack informed Sancho that

> the sentiments they contain do thee great honour; and, if published, may convince some proud Europeans, that the noblest gifts of God, those of the mind, are not confined to any nation or people, but extended to the scorching deserts of Guinea, as well as the temperate and propitious climes in which we are favoured to dwell. (Letter 83, 20 April 1779)

Rack added that were he so empowered, he would put an end to slavery or "lessen the misery" of one countryman (Letter 83, 20 April 1779). He noted that though not personally acquainted with Sancho, he admired good character wherever and among whomever he observed it. He believed that the equality of all individuals, regardless of place of origin, was divinely ordained. Responding with characteristic modesty, Sancho wrote that if Rack found "the simple effusions of a poor Negro's heart worth mixing with better things," then he could do as he wished with the letters (Letter 83a; undated).

According to Frances Crewe, designated "Miss F. Crewe" in the preface to the first edition of *Letters* (1782), Sancho had no desire to publish his letters in the first place. Crewe's insistence that Sancho never expressed to her a desire to have the letters published was likely designed to remove the impression that he had dared to seek recognition in this manner, as records indicate that no blacks had previously published writings done in their own hand, and such publication efforts were usually reserved for white aristocrats. In addition, Crewe had collected Sancho's letters from acquaintances to whom he had written in order to convince readers further of the letters' authenticity and to show that she had not altered or heavily edited them. After publishing the *Letters* in 1782, Crewe expressed delight in the early public response: "The world [has not been] inattentive to the voice of obscure merit," she wrote with understandable pride.[32]

Meanwhile, Joseph Jekyll, who wrote a brief biographical sketch of Sancho in the introduction to Crewe's edition of the *Letters*, represents a familiar paradox: the benefactor whose beneficence is predicated—perhaps inadvertently—on maintaining racial disparity. The ambiguities of racial patronage and racial bias address themselves in Sancho's dependence upon the efforts of Crewe and Jekyll and his earlier dependence upon the three

Greenwich sisters who enslaved him as a domestic. In the biography Jekyll cites racial prejudice as the reason behind the sisters' refusal to educate the precocious Sancho or to allow for his education to be undertaken by the neighboring Duke and Duchess of Montagu. Jekyll notes that racism had taught the sisters that "African ignorance was the only security for [Sancho's] obedience" (*Letters*, ii). He also cites the intellectual benefits of the education that Sancho eventually acquired from the Montagus.

To further support his own claims of Sancho's intellectual abilities, Jekyll included an essay in the *Letters'* introduction by Johann Blumenbach that disputes the belief that an African lacked the intellectual capacity of a European. But Jekyll also informs readers that "a disposition of African texture" led Sancho to gamble away money left to him by the Duchess of Montagu: "A French writer relates, that in the kingdoms of Ardrah, Whydah, and Benin, a Negro will stake at play his fortune, his children, and his liberty" (iv). Unlike the Greenwich sisters, Jekyll stands in a position that is neither premeditated nor consciously constructed, especially since he buries it beneath an expressed humanitarian fervor and the fact that he worked to help publish Sancho's *Letters*. But it demonstrates, nonetheless, that he internalizes the philosophy of racial subordination embedded in the Chain of Being.

Ironically, one small detail buried in Jekyll's description of Sancho's gambling habits nearly escapes notice; yet it makes negligible the differences in beliefs held by Joseph Jekyll and the Greenwich sisters. Jekyll writes that Sancho was so smitten with the theater (he attempted acting but was rejected because of obesity) that he once spent his last shilling to see David Garrick perform as Shakespeare's King Richard at Drury Lane. Jekyll commits a paradoxical oversight here: the fact that Sancho's "innately inscribed" gambling leads him to see a theatrical performance seriously undercuts a propensity to ignorance (if not prudence) in the whole theory of racial subordination. The professed fears of the Greenwich sisters that an educated Sancho would subsequently be unfit for slavery undermines the notion that an African could not exhibit a capacity for learning in the first place. The Greenwich sisters, like Frederick Douglass's enslaver, Captain Hugh Auld, may have unconsciously harbored fears that Sancho actually did have an intellectual capacity, while Joseph Jekyll, the professed humanitarian, may have feared that he did not have such a capacity.

The extent to which sensibility contributed simplistic solutions to complex racial problems is particularly illuminated in the relationship among Ignatius Sancho, members of the English aristocracy, and the literary patronage system. Those writers who responded to calls for literary contributions for the abolishment of slavery played a unique role in promoting a humanitarian agenda. In other words, they helped to create a discursive benevolence whereby the expression of good feelings was allowed to cover for inaction. In this fashion, benefactors could showcase the few successful products of remediation without having to address gross racial inequities that existed for the masses.

The letters that Ignatius Sancho addresses to acquaintances present a stunning example of his predicament as a racial outsider in a culture that he comes to know very well, but of which he can never truly be a part. Eruptions of suppressed rage, which are also present in some of his letters, underscore an alienation from whites and bears witness to the suffering of blacks. In these letters, he expresses fierce opposition to the slavery question. One can argue—as does Paul Edwards—that Sancho's letters reveal a deferential, accommodating side to his character, seasoned in the school of sensibility, while the angry, activist side shows in the one subject for which he admitted no compromises—slavery. The intimate nature of the epistolary form, however, potentially allows the author more self-revelation than other genres while at the same time it is also more susceptible to manipulation, for better or worse, by the author.

It is by no means surprising that Sancho would offer an angle of himself in conflict with the society in which he lived and wrote. In a letter written to an acquaintance on the merits of Philis Wheatley's poetry, suppressed rage got the better of Sancho's usually effervescent disposition. He praises Wheatley, whose poems are a "credit to nature." But on the subject of her benefactor, he writes that Wheatley "reflects nothing either to the glory or generosity of her master . . . except that he glories in the *low vanity* of having in his wanton power a mind animated by Heaven—a genius superior to himself" (Letter 58, 27 January 1778). A few lines later, though, he notes that the "splendid—titled—learned" Englishmen whose signatures affirmed Wheatley's authorship and authorized her humanity "show how very poor the acquisition of wealth and knowledge is—without generosity—feeling— and humanity." Contradictions between Sancho's acknowledgment of both the critical need for white patronage and frustration from blacks having to utilize such patronage, is a principal characteristic of his letters.[33]

In a related instance, Sancho scolds Julius Soubise, a young African in the service of the Duchess of Queensberry, who had gone into exile rather than face accusations of raping a maid of the duchess.[34] Sancho writes that Soubise's letter "gave me more pleasure than in truth I ever expected from your hands" (Letter 14, 11 October 1772). Declaring that Soubise did not recognize good fortune when it was at hand, Sancho praised the divine qualities of his benefactors as "more than parents." And he challenged Soubise to

> look up to thy almost divine benefactors—search into the motive of every
> glorious action—retrace thine own history—and when you are convinced

that they (like the All-gracious Power they serve) go about in mercy doing good—retire abashed at the number of their virtues—and humbly beg the Almighty to inspire and give you strength to imitate them. . . . (Letter 14, 11 October 1772)

In thus advising Soubise, Sancho passes on Sterne's reminder, much earlier, that Sancho's own rescue had taken place because of the benevolence of an English family. Furthermore, Sancho's words to Soubise hearken to both Dryden's translation of Juvenal's *Tenth Satire* and Johnson's *Vanity of Human Wishes*. For example, Dryden writes, "Look round the Habitable World, how few / Know their own Good; or knowing it, pursue / How void of Reason are our Hopes and Fears" (lines 1–3). Sancho urges Soubise to count his blessings for avoiding the fate of blacks enslaved in the West Indies: "Look round upon the miserable fate of almost all of our unfortunate colour—superadded to ignorance,—see slavery, and the contempt of those very wretches who roll in affluence from our labours" (Letter 14, 11 October 1772). He advised Soubise to "tread as cautiously as the strictest rectitude can guide ye" and to arm himself with honesty and integrity in order to invite "the plaudit and countenance of the good" (11 October 1772). In short, Sancho wished that Soubise would adopt his own formula for surviving in a hostile society. In other words, he advises him to count on—even to court—the benevolence of those most empowered to give it; it will take you far; it may even be the only way. Sancho clearly felt that his advice was valuable and that the choice for virtue rested with Soubise alone.

There is a certain irony here, however, in that the very first letter in Sancho's published collection warns Jack Wingrave, a white acquaintance, against lending money to, or trusting, Soubise. Sancho claims: "There is sent out in the Besborough, along with fresh governors, and other strange commodities, a little Blacky, whom you must either have seen or heard of; his name is Soubise" (Letter 1, 14 February 1768). Sancho then tells Wingrave of Soubise's plans to move to Madras or Benegal to teach fencing and riding. The Duchess of Queensberry had paid for Soubise's expert training in both. Sancho urges Wingrave (who is in India) to pass on some wholesome advice to Soubise should they meet. Later, he enlisted John Meheux, an acquaintance to monitor Soubise's behavior to see if he truly meant to reform his character.[35] Sancho wrote that if Soubise would dedicate as much energy and effort to virtue in the future as he had previously devoted to error, then he would recover the good graces of his "noble patrons," and he would glorify himself in the bargain.

In the figure of Soubise, Sancho likely saw a former, younger version of himself before he mended his own ways. Having been rescued from domestic enslavement by the Montagus, Sancho was well schooled in the patronage system. They, in turn, showed him virtues that he now attributed to Soubise's benefactress—the Duchess of Queensberry. Sancho believed that to be brave is to be good and to show mercy, which blends public and private virtues in the name of survival. In the private sphere, Soubise confronts feelings of envy, revenge, goodness, and sin. On a larger scale, however, it is impossible to disengage those feelings from the obligation to win the good graces of the rich and powerful patron.

When the duchess died, reportedly two days after Soubise had fled to India in exile, Sancho wrote again to Meheux, confiding that the death of the duchess might be the catalyst that would bring about Soubise's reform. He added as well that Soubise would probably not be too wounded by the news (Letter 44, 23 July 1777). And when Sancho caught up with Soubise and reported the death of his "noble, friendly benefactress, and patroness, the good duchess of Queensberry," he noted, "Thus it has pleased God to take your props to himself—teaching you a lesson at the same time, to depend upon an honest exertion of your own industry—and humbly to trust in the Almighty" (Letter 80, 29 November 1778). Simply put, Sancho demands accountability from British patrons and benefactors in exchange for the docility that recipients must display in order to obtain the support of the patron. He is willing to participate in the patronage system, to comply with "the principle of gratitude," but only at a price.

Sancho's tone of address to most acquaintances was usually deferential and accommodating—even gently self-deprecating. Sancho addresses Jack Wingrave, a young Englishman who lived in Bombay, more gingerly than he does Soubise, albeit under different circumstances. Sancho warns Wingrave about the dangers of unkindness. In a letter to yet another acquaintance (identified only as Mr. Browne), Sancho urges that he behave deservedly toward Garrick, his benefactor and patron, and that he prove himself worthy of Garrick's generosity. At the same time, the letter is ingratiating: "I thank you for your kindness to my poor black brethren—I flatter myself you will find them not ungrateful—they act commonly from their feelings"— an echo of Thomas Jefferson (Letter 13, 18 July 1772).

In a separate incident, Sancho learned that Jack Wingrave had snubbed blacks whom he encountered while in India. Wingrave wrote that the mostly black inhabitants of Bombay were "canting" and "deceitful," with no such word as "gratitude" in their language. Angrily reminding Wingrave to remember from whom the native Indians had learned such vices, Sancho sought an explanation for Wingrave's racist behavior toward the blacks. Wingrave wrote that he was compelled to comply with a custom while in India that prevented him from associating with blacks. He further explained that Europeans who defied such custom faced ostracism and impediments to achieving success in business and career ventures. Wingrave asked Sancho's understanding for his predicament and expressed hope that his compliance with custom would not destroy their friendship. Sancho replied, "I praise thee sincerely, for the whole and every part of thy conduct, in regard to my two sable brethren." Sancho then apologized for "the impropriety" of his demand that the young man explain his conduct toward the two blacks (Letter 127, 5 January 1786).

English patrons sought to present a whole new breed of African—literate, molded in the image of whites, and amenable to social and spiritual adaptation.[36] On the other hand, black writers also bore the heavy burden of proof for their own certification as intelligent beings. The scrutiny of a pathological "gaze" that Sancho endured occasionally forced him to adopt a defensive posture in some letters. "Hearty wishes . . . to all who have charity enough to admit dark faces into the fellowship of Christians," reads one letter (Letter 66, 31 May 1778). To a Mrs. Cocksedge, he writes, "Pray be so Kind to make our best respects to Miss A—s, and to everyone who delighteth in Blackamoor greetings" (Letter 70, 23 July 1778). And he writes to yet another acquaintance, "Figure to yourself, my dear Sir, a man of a convexity of belly exceeding Falstaff (he was quite corpulent)—and a black face into the bargain—waddling in the van of poor thieves and penniless prostitutes" (Letter 118, 17 December 1779).

Describing the Gordon Riots, in which anti-Catholics protested Parliament's proposed anti-discriminatory, pro-Catholic measures, Sancho decried "the worse than Negro barbarity of the populace" that burned and rioted in the streets (Letter 134, 6 June 1780). While Sancho, who witnessed part of the disturbance, does not necessarily charge blacks with barbarity, he clearly absorbs the ideological association of the term "savage" with black behavior. In other words, Sancho illustrates that whites are behaving in a manner that they themselves associate exclusively with blacks. When the *European Magazine and London Review* later reviewed Sancho's accounting of the Gordon Riots in June 1780, editors credited his "strength of reasoning" and "facility of expression" in writing, though they tacitly ignored his perplexed leanings. Though well-intentioned, the magazine painted a benevolent but condescending portrait of Sancho in an effort to counter those "philosophers and anatomists" who disparaged the accomplishments of Africans. The magazine failed to note the irony that the author himself recognized—being acculturated to, yet racially separated from, English culture. To the editor, Sancho is either a symbolic spectacle or a cause, but never an individual capable of personal turmoil and conflict. The magazine sums up its review of Sancho's person by calling attention to its own ambivalent position: "God's image, though cut in ebony" (201).

Sancho's reveals a persistent awareness of his liminal status in society in a nationalist context. In a letter discussing England's war with France,

Sancho begins, "We are all in the wrong—a little" and goes on to catalogue Britain's numerous quarrels with the American colonies, Ireland, and of course, France (Letter 105, 7 September 1779). He continues: "The British empire mouldering away in the West—annihilated in the North—Gibraltar going—and England fast asleep." Still, as though pondering the absurdity of the situation, he adds that "for my part, it's nothing to me—as I am only a lodger—and hardly that." After extolling England as "Europe's fairest example" of liberty, truth, and loyalty in one letter, Sancho addresses his own paradoxical citizenship in another letter: "For God's sake! What has a poor starving Negroe, with six children, to do with kings and heroes, armies and politics?—aye, or poets and painters?—or artists—of any sort?"[37]

Sancho embraces the doctrine of an exploitative Christian commerce between Europe and Africa while he attacks the greed of Christian navigators. Sancho expresses love for his own adopted country while assailing English navigators' greed for "money—money—money," without "strict honesty" and "religion" as companions. These had produced corruption and wickedness "in the East—West Indies—and even on the coast of Guinea" (Letter 68, 1778; exact date unknown). "I mentioned these only to guard my friend against being too hasty in condemning the knavery of a people who, bad as they may be—possibly—were made worse by their Christian visitors," Sancho added (Letter 68, 1778). Reserving his most scathing attack on slavery and on the greed of "Christian Navigators," he wrote that

> the first Christian visitors found them a simple, harmless people—but the cursed avidity for wealth urged these first visitors (and all succeeding ones) to such acts of deception—and even wanton cruelty—that the poor ignorant Natives soon learnt to turn the knavish and diabolical arts—which they too soon imbibed—upon their teachers (Letter 68, 1778).

In the eighteenth century, patrons who sought out black publications had the opportunity to transform the African's image from so-called primitive beings into Western civilization's finest specimens, thus securing them within its own social order. Clearly printers and booksellers served an overwhelmingly white male reading audience. To encourage support and acceptance among readers, many abolitionists likely felt the need to publicize blacks, whose writings would appeal to that audience. Rather than forge a bond of solidarity with blacks, some of these measures would perpetuate subordination and thus reinforce an ideology of racial inferiority or what Pierre Bourdieu explains as the spatial boundaries between objective structures in literary and social practice that account for benevolence and sensibility. When used in the historical context of abolitionism and the sentimental movement in late-eighteenth-century England, what Bourdieu terms the symbolic violence of economy versus the actual or overt forms of violence exists in just such a concept as literary patronage: "it is present both in the debt and in the gift, which, in spite of their apparent opposition, have in common the power of founding either dependence (and even slavery) or solidarity, depending on the strategies within which they are deployed."[38]

For Sancho, there was nothing worse than to be a pretender to benevolence and an ungrateful charge who failed to reward the benefactor with appropriate behavior. A strict adherence to moral and ethical principles (he was Methodist by faith) undergirded Sancho's beliefs. Sancho saves his most scathing attacks for two groups of individuals: duplicitous Christian navigators and supporters of slavery who engaged in deceptive practices and the ungrateful recipients of benevolence. Consequently in the process of showcasing benevolence as moral principle, the letters occasionally reinforce its limitations. The measure of beneficence and the cult of sensibility in humanitarian efforts ultimately urged no racial parity for blacks.

It is nevertheless from Sancho's unique vantage point as an author and formerly enslaved African that we are able to see the entire sentimental movement (e.g., sensibility, benevolence, humanitarianism) differently than in most traditional Anglican writings in the eighteenth century. Sancho struggled with the philosophical and literary principle of expressing good feelings amid a legal climate that still permitted slavery. Unlike Gronniosaw, however, Sancho seemed fully aware of some of the inconsistencies between theory and practice. Also unlike Gronniosaw, Sancho commented on his still marginalized social position, in spite of living in London as a free black. Consequently his letters to acquaintances reveal a carefully crafted, somewhat Afrocentric version of such prevailing ideas as sensibility, benevolence, and even the Chain of Being. For instance, Sancho fashioned for himself a chain of love that urged racial unification and equality for blacks, a sensibility that defined happiness as service on behalf of blacks enslaved in the West Indies, and a benevolence commensurate with abolitionism. He posited that well-to-do whites might rescue and educate other enslaved Africans, just as his own benefactors had done.

On a more personal level, Sancho's relationships with Julius Soubise and Laurence Sterne perhaps sum up Sancho's own philosophical and literary contributions. Sancho could ill afford a friend like Soubise, who proved to be an ungrateful recipient of beneficence and a potential spoiler for other blacks who might stand to gain patronage from other whites. On the other hand, Sancho desperately needed the support of Laurence Sterne, whose literary stature could lend credibility to Sancho's own ideas about the treatment of blacks in England and in the West Indies. Laurence Sterne proved to be Sancho's ultimate benefactor—his entry into the white world of belles lettres or some close proximity to it.

## NOTES

1. See *Memoirs of Mr. Blenfield* (London: Printed for W. Lane, 1790), 2 vols. The popular circulating libraries of the late eighteenth century included sentimental fiction, much of it published by Minerva Press. The Minerva Press lists *Memoirs* as a book written by an unnamed attorney who also authored another sentimental work called *Tales of Sympathy*, 1789 (no longer available). The book, *Memoirs of Mr. Blenfield* survives in two volumes at Harvard Library and is available on microfilm. At least two writers, Wylie Sypher (*Guinea's Captive Kings: British Anti-Slavery Literature of the XVIIIth Century* [Chapel Hill: University of North Carolina Press, 1942]) and O. R. Dathorne ("African Writers of the Eighteenth Century," *London Magazine*, 5 [September, 1965]: 51–58) have identified *Memoirs and Opinions of Mr. Blenfield* as a work believed to have been based on the life of Ignatius Sancho, who was known to Britain's abolitionist community. Wylie Sypher identifies Shirna Cambo as a fictional tribute to Ignatius Sancho but does not cite his sources.

Pierre Bourdieu states the following: "Symbolic violence, the gentle, invisible form of violence, which is never recognized as such, and is not so much undergone as chosen, the violence of credit, confidence, obligation, personal loyalty, hospitality, gifts, gratitude, piety . . . cannot fail to be seen as the most economical mode of domination" (Pierre Bourdieu, *Outline of a Theory of Practice*, trans. Richard Nice [New York: Cambridge, 1992, 192]).

2. *Memoirs of Mr. Blenfield*, 152.

3. See Patricia Meyer Spacks, "Ev'ry Woman Is at Heart a Rake," *Eighteenth-Century Studies* 8 (1974): 31. Spacks further notes that women's awakening to their oppression and mistreatment by patriarchal powers in the eighteenth century is caught up in the cultural epistemology of sensibility.

4. Ann Cvetkovich explores a related concept, the politics of "affect" or sensation in selected Victorian novels in the 1860s and 1870s. Cvetkovich notably observes that in this period, the middle class woman was particularly "constructed as a feeling subject," and that "mass and popular culture" were instrumental in the formation of affect as discourse. See Cvetkovich, *Mixed Feelings: Feminism, Mass Culture, and Victorian Sensationalism* (New Brunswick, NJ: Rutgers University Press, 1992), 6–7. While analyses of gender and mass and popular culture strikingly separate Cvetkovich's study from those of Todd, Spacks, and others who write about women and sensibility, it is Cvetkovich's emphasis on the "regulative" aspects of affect that is most beneficial for my objectives for this chapter.

5. Moira Ferguson, *Subject to Others: British Women Writers and Colonial Slavery, 1670–1834* (New York: Routledge, 1992), 3.

6. See Mary Wollstonecraft's review of Olaudah Equiano's narrative in *Analytical Review*, May 1789. Wollstonecraft also writes the following: "How they are shaded down, from the fresh colour of northern rustics, to the sable hue seen on the African sands, is not our task to inquire, nor do we intend to draw a parallel between the abilities of a negro and European mechanic; we shall only observe, that if these volumes do not exhibit extraordinary intellectual powers, sufficient to wipe off the stigma, yet the activity and ingenuity, which conspicuously appear in the character of Gustavus, place him on a par with the general mass of men, who fill

the subordinate stations in a more civilized society than that which he was thrown into at his birth" (Quoted in Carretta, *Olaudah Equiano: The Interesting Narrative and Other Writings*, xxvi).

7. See Mary Wollstonecraft, *A Vindication of the Rights of Men, in a Letter To the Honourable Edmund Burke; occasioned By His Reflections on the Revolution in France* (London: J. Johnson, 1790; 2nd ed.), 68–69. See also Janet Todd, *Sensibility: An Introduction*, (London: Methuen, 1986), 132–33.

8. One such example is Markman Ellis, who in *The Politics of Sensibility: Race, Gender and Commerce in the Sentimental Novel* [Cambridge: Cambridge University Press, 1996] devotes two of six chapters to slavery's connection with sentimentalism and the late eighteenth-century novel. Ellis identifies "anti-slavery and slavery-reform" as significant tropes in the sentimental novel in the late eighteenth century (4).

While he does not discuss blacks or slavery in his book, Chris Jones addresses the illusive properties of sensibility as "a Janus-faced concept" that "translated prevailing power-based relationships into loyalties upheld by 'natural' feelings" (*Radical Sensibility: Literature and Ideas in the 1790s* [London: Routledge, 1993]), 7.

Sensibility, alternately described as sentimentality, benevolence, and humanitarianism, governed the sentiments of an era, though these sentiments mostly appeared in a cluster of writings late in the eighteenth century. Though some called for an end to slavery while others simply urged reform in the treatment of the enslaved by the enslaver, few sought equality for the slave on a par with free whites. Scholars, including Markman Ellis, agree only that the period usually identified as existing loosely between neoclassicism and romanticism is problematical, difficult to define, and inadequately expressed through scholarship. I contend that any difficulties largely stem from the neglect or misidentification of the anti-slavery movement as the period's central driving force. Sensibility (like such rigid concepts as neoclassicism or romanticism), yields greater clarity when connected with specific social conditions or issues, such as abolitionism and child labor reform, rather than when artificially or abstractly applied.

C. Duncan Rice ("Literary Sources and the Revolution In British Attitudes To Slavery," in *Anti-Slavery, Religion, and Reform: Essays in Memory of Roger Anstey*, ed., Christine Bolt and Seymour Drescher [Kent, England: William Dawson & Sons, 1980]), writes that "compassion for the slave would certainly have been articulated more slowly without the cult of humane sensibility, which so dominated polite eighteenth-century letters" (320–21). Rice concedes, however, that "anti-slavery literature in itself reveals nothing more than the standpoint of the pressure group that produced it" (320).

9. See William Wilberforce, *A Practical View of the Prevailing Religious System of Professed Christians in the Higher and Middle Classes of Society, Contrasted with Real Christianity* (Philadelphia: Printed by John Ormond, 1798; 1st American edition).

10. Lloyd Brown refashions Sancho's "vast chain of blessed Providence" as "the blessed chains of brotherly love." But the reference is more likely—as Edwards and Rewt find it—to the Great Chain of Being. Brown sees Sancho's comments as a strategic subversion of eighteenth-century satire, but I believe Paul Edwards more accurately reads those comments as an ironic, but not strategic, feature of Sancho's

"divided self." See Lloyd Brown's review of Sancho's *Letters* in *Eighteenth-Century Studies* 3 (Spring 1970), 415-19. Edwards and Rewt point out differences between their interpretations of Sancho's tone in the *Letters* and Brown's views. See the introduction to *The Letters of Ignatius Sancho*, ed., Paul Edwards and Polly Rewt (Edinburgh: Edinburgh University Press, 1994), 1-21.

11. See John Dryden, *Palamon and Arcite, or the Knight's Tale*, ed., George E. Eliot (Boston: Ginn, 1899), Book 3, lines 1030-1037).

12. Letter 44, 23 July, 1777, 15. See also Maynard Mack's (Twickenham) edition of Pope's *Essay on Man* (London: Methuen, 1950), 92, for the references to Boethius and Dryden.

13. See Oswald G. Knapp, ed., *The Intimate Letters of Hester Piozzi and Penelope Pennington 1788-1822* (London: n.p., 1914), 243. Samuel Johnson employed a black servant, Francis Barber, who had been freed from slavery in Jamaica in the will of Colonel Bathurst, the father of Johnson's acquaintance, Dr. Bathurst. Johnson sent "Frank" to Bishops Stortford Grammar School in 1767 and spent 300 pounds on a Latin and Greek tutor for him. Though strains in the relationship led Barber to run away from Johnson on two occasions, he returned both times, and Boswell reported that the improvement of Barber's education "[did] Johnson's heart much honor." In a letter to Francis Barber, Johnson made his famous observation: "Let me know what English books you read for your entertainment. You can never be wise unless you love reading" (20). Sir John Hawkins, Johnson's acquaintance, who regarded Barber with a jaundiced eye, remarked that Johnson had spent a huge sum of money educating Francis Barber "for no assignable reason, nay, rather in despight of nature, and to unfit him for being useful according to his capacity determined to make him a scholar" (in Aleyn Lyell Reade, *Johnsonian Gleanings*, vol. 2 of 11 vols. [London: Arden Press, 1912]), 17-23). In spite of Johnson's efforts, even his undertaking of Barber's education itself uncovers an established social order that Sir John Hawkins's observation exemplifies. Johnson left Barber a seventy pound annuity, plus all household goods, much to the chagrin of his executors (37). Hester Thrale wrote that "when he spoke of negroes, he always appeared to think them of a race naturally inferior, and made few exceptions in favour of his own" (quoted in Reade, *Johnsonnian Gleanings*, 30). Thrale thought that Barber was such an exception.

Other benefactors purchased enslaved blacks in order to engage them in educational experiments. In an effort to counter the ideology that represents the African as innately inferior, a number of European patrons financed the education of certain blacks at elite institutions or sanctioned the writings of a small number of select blacks, including Philis Wheatley. Problems attended efforts to accord self-recognition to those individuals, independently of white sponsorship. One such prodigy, Francis Williams, a native Jamaican and Latin scholar, who was sent to Cambridge University by a benefactor, the second Duke of Montagu.

14. Albert Memmi addresses this idea in *The Colonizer and Colonized*, (New York: Orion Press, 1965). Noel Turner's anecdote is quoted in Reade, 2: 15.

15. Letter 10, 31 August 1770, 50; see Pope, *Essay on Man*, ["The proper study of mankind is man]; Epistle 2, 1-2; quoted in Sancho as "the [only science of mankind] is man."

16. Letter 46, 8 August 1777, 97, and Letter 141, 23 June 1780, 242; Sancho quotes from *Essay on Man*, Epistle 4, 215-16.

17. See Edwards and Rewt. All subsequent references to Sancho's *Letters* will be cited in the manuscript by page number. The Edwards and Rewt Edinburgh edition of Sancho's letters identifies, by name, most of Sancho's correspondents. In previous editions, those individuals have remained anonymous. The late Paul Edwards, along with Polly Rewt, also corrected numerous dating errors from earlier editions and provided invaluable details about Sancho's relationship with correspondents and other acquaintances. I also examined a facsimile reprint of the fifth edition of Sancho's letters issued in the Black Heritage Library Collection, but this collection has no introduction and does not include notes. See *Letters of the Late Ignatius Sancho, An African* (Freeport, NY: Books for Libraries Press, 1971). Vincent Carretta's Penguin edition of Sancho's letters makes the collection readily available in the United States; it includes an introduction and notes (*Letters of the Late Ignatius Sancho, An African* (New York: Penguin Books, 1998).

18. After the Revolutionary War, Australia was used to placate Britain for its loss of America as a colony for undesirables. These colonialist and imperialist aspects of British history get played out as normative discourse on the pages of Defoe, whose convicts (Colonel Jack and Moll Flanders) end up in America, and of Dickens in *Great Expectations*, whose Magwitch goes to Australia. While these textual details have been acknowledged in the general, albeit contextual footnotes in literary history, traditional readings have typically depicted *Great Expectations* as a didactical model for a delusionary, idealistic Pip who reconciles with his embarrassingly scraggly, felonious benefactor, Magwitch. Until recently, literary pundits have not tended to exploit the colonialist aspects of the text. Edward Said points out this tendency among some humanists to disassociate oppressive practices like slavery and colonialism in the "real" world from their representation in literary forums and practices (*Culture and Imperialism*, [New York: Alfred A. Knopf, 1993], xiv). But rather than see Magwitch and Dickens as incidentals in Australia's history as England's white, colonized criminal dumping ground, Said locates them "as participants in it, through the novel and through a much older and wider experience between England and its overseas territories" (xiv).

Connecting these works with historical models that are not altogether attractive need not diminish them as entertaining fictions, Said rightly observes. It is a bit like resurrecting Charlotte Brontë's enslaved, mad West Indian woman in *Jane Eyre*'s attic as a silenced aspect of feminism or culling the South African Hottentots from Swift's Yahoos as a distinct cultural group. In *Great Expectations*, Dickens's convicts could succeed in Australia but could hardly return to England. The social space that Australia authorizes has gone largely unrecognized (see Said, xv).

19. Daniel Defoe, *Colonel Jack*, ed. Samuel Holt Monk (Oxford: Oxford University Press, 1989).

20. Maria Edgeworth, "The Grateful Negro," in *Popular Tales* (New York: D. Appleton, 1854), 289-326.

21. A striking example of the rhetoric of sensibility at work is William Cowper, who was apparently commissioned—perhaps under pressure—to contribute a poem in support of abolitionism. As is typical among numerous writers of abolitionist

literature, Cowper seemingly produced sentimentality as rhetoric, born of popular consensus and enacted from experiments in new verse trends. But the poet reveals ambivalences about the abolitionist cause that his poems supported. Perhaps Cowper best sums up the dilemma in the poem "Pity for Poor Africans": "I own I am shock'd at the purchase of slaves, / And fear those who buy them and sell them are knaves." A few lines later, Cowper adds, "I pity them greatly, but I must be mum, / For how could we do without sugar and rum" (Cowper, "Pity for Poor Africans," lines 1–2, 5–6, The *Poems of William Cowper*, ed., J. C. Baily [London: Methuen, 1905]). Cowper, who was initially persuaded by abolitionists to write an anti-slavery poem, requested a waiver of his agreement. (Sypher, 186). He had apparently made the agreement with a Mr. Phillips but soon asked John Newton in a letter (5 June 1788) to intercede on his behalf. Nevertheless, in "The Task" (1785), Cowper argues that individual liberty is sanctioned by nature: "I would not have a slave to till my ground, / To carry me, to fan me while I sleep, / And tremble while I wake, for all the wealth / That sinews bought and sold have ever earned (2: 29–32, 40–44).

22. Sarah Scott, *The History of Sir George Ellison* (London: A. Millar, 1766), 41. See also Sarah Scott, *The History of Sir George Ellison*, ed. Betty Rizzo (Lexington, KY: University Press of Kentucky, 1996).

23. Others include William Lloyd Garrison and Frederick Douglass, Lydia Maria Childs, and Harriet Jacobs, Charlotte Osgood Mason, and both Langston Hughes and Zora Neale Hurston. In *My Bondage and My Freedom* (1855), for example, Douglass discussed his break with Garrison when the latter asked him to restrict his lectures to factual narrations about his slave experiences. Douglass, whose *Narrative of the Life of Frederick Douglass* (1845) was heavily influenced by Garrison, wanted to transcend the liminal stage of his struggle after freedom from slavery in order to work for the equality of blacks in America.

24. Ellis examines the relationship between Laurence Sterne and Ignatius Sancho in connection with slavery and sentimentalism. He also critiques Sterne's treatment of slavery both in *The Sermons of Mr. Yorick* and in a passage from *Tristram Shandy*. While viewing the Sancho/Sterne relationship as a positive one, Ellis does point out complications in Sterne's views on race as follows: "Sterne's argument is a powerful denial of racial difference, but embedded within it are the still more powerful remnants of the language of racial difference, observable when he writes of the descent down the 'scale' of 'shades' from the white metropolis to the black colony" (65).

25. Lewis Perry Curtis, ed., *Letters of Laurence Sterne* (Oxford: Clarendon Press, 1935), 340.

26. See Book 9, chapter 6, in Laurence Sterne's *The Life and Opinions of Tristram Shandy*, ed. Ian Watt (Boston: Houghton Mifflin Company, 1965).

27. Sterne, *Letters*, 30 June 1767, 370.

28. Sterne, *Letters*, 283.

29. See Sterne, *Tristram Shandy*, 466.

30. Wilbur Cross, *The Life and Times of Laurence Sterne* (New York: Macmillan, 1909), 390. See also Mark Lovridge, "'Liberty and *Tristram Shandy*,'" in *Laurence Sterne: Riddles and Mysteries*, ed. Valerie Grosvenor Myers (London: Vision and Barnes & Noble, 1984), 140.

31. Sterne, *Letters*, 30 June, 1767, 370.

32. *Letters*, 1st ed., vol. 1, London, 1782, i–ii. The *Letters of the Late Ignatius Sancho* went through five editions by 1783. The names of over 600 subscribers, largely members of the British aristocracy, printed in that first edition (and reprinted in Carretta's Penguin edition), point to a hearty reception. Beeton's *Dictionary of Universal Information* (London: n.p., 1877) records that "from the profits of the first edition, and a sum paid by the booksellers for liberty to print a second edition, Mrs. Sancho, we are well assured, received more than [500 pounds]" (97n). And *Monthly Review* reported that the first edition of Letters "sold with such rapidity that we could not procure a copy" (119, [1783], 492n). Sancho's marginal position in relation to England's nationalist identity raises the spectre of his reception among critics and reviewers in the eighteenth-century literary establishment. Ironically, those who were bent on using Sancho as a model of rare spark and genius, and as a literate, fully assimilated African in England, e.g., Francis Crewe and Joseph Jekyll, among them, neglected the seriousness of his writings. Meanwhile, those journal and magazine reviewers who examined Sancho's collective correspondence never focused on his personal thoughts, torn allegiances, and ambivalent feelings about his treatment as an African in English society.

Responding to doubts about the authenticity of Sancho's letters, editors for *Monthly Review* wrote that the collection was "the genuine productions of [Sancho's] private correspondence" (119 [1783]: 492n). The *European Magazine and London Review* responded favorably to Sancho's letters in its September, 1782, review. The reviewer noted that the collection would be read "with avidity and pleasure by those who desire to promote the common elevation of the human race" and that "those who wish to degrade the species" would be shown "the error of that wild opinion" (199). After further emphasizing the unrestored quality of Sancho's Letters, the *European Magazine and London Review* warned that they should be viewed for their warmth and feeling rather than for "elegance of diction" and "correctness." The publication then went on to print Sancho's memorial tribute to Laurence Sterne and to affix selections from Jekyll's biographical sketch of Sancho. The *Gentleman's Magazine* wrote that most of Sancho's letters are "little more than common-place effusions, such as many other Negroes, we suppose, could, with the same advantages, have written, and which there needed "no ghost to come from the grave," or a black from Guinea, "to have told us" (1782).

However, not all reviewers responded so begrudgingly. I have already discussed how Henri de Grégoire challenged Thomas Jefferson's negative reading of Sancho's letters. On the basis of having read Sancho's letters, some abolitionists called for more publications by African writers. Peter Peckard, who had evidently reviewed some letters that were still in manuscript form, wrote that Sancho "had done honor to himself and to Human Nature" with his moral and epistolary writing. Peckard added that Sancho's "epistles in general breathe the purest and most genuine Spirit of Universal Benevolence." In addition, Peckard acknowledged Sancho's interest in the rights of the individual and cited his mentoring of a young Cambridge student in a liberal education, roles rarely cited by others. See Peter Peckard, *Am I Not A Man? And A Brother? With All Humility Addressed to the British Legislature* (Cambridge, 1788); quoted in Shyllon, 197).

33. Besides Philis Wheatley and Julius Soubise, few blacks have been identified as correspondents in Sancho's letters. Details from the collection show evidence of social interaction between Sancho and others in the African-British community and reveal tidbits about Sancho's West Indian wife, Anne Osborne, and family. The collection includes a letter to Sancho's brother-in-law, John Osborne, and to black musician Charles Lincoln. Sancho also composed a large number of musical pieces, several of which are in the British Library. According to Josephine Wright, at least "sixty-two compositions" were published by Sancho from around 1767 to 1779. See Josephine Wright, *Ignatius Sancho (1729-1780): An Early African Composer in England: the Collected Editions of His Music in Facsimile* (New York: Garland, 1981). See the introduction to Edwards and Rewt's *Letters of Ignatius Sancho*. The Sanchos, who had seven children, lived in Mayfair and operated a grocery store on Charles Street, Westminster. George Cumberland, one of many visitors from the London literary establishment, wrote this account: "I must tell you (because it pleases my vanity so to do) that a Black Man, Ignatius Sancho, has lately put me into an unbounded conceit with myself—he is said to be a great judge of literary performances (God send it may be true!) and has praised my Tale of Cambambo and Journal wh. I read to him, so highly, that I shall like him as long as I live" (quoted in Edwards and Rewt, *The Letters of Ignatius Sancho*, 3). Sancho died from complications of gout and obesity 14 December 1780, and he was buried at Westminster Broadway.

34. See the following works: Folarin Shyllon, *Black People in Britain, 1555-1833* (London: Oxford University Press, 1977), 41-43, James Walvin, *Black and White: The Negro and English Society, 1555-1945* (London: Penguin, 1973), and Paul Edwards and Walvin, eds., *Black Personalities in the Era of the Slave Trade* (London: Macmillan, 1983), 223-37. Julius Soubise, who was pampered by the duchess of Queensberry, was trained in fencing and horseback riding and other recreations. The duchess, who paid for these lessons, apparently held deep sentiments for Soubise, and Sancho scorned his reckless behavior and poor morals. To Sancho, his young friend was spoiled, immoral, and inappreciative of his great fortune, especially in light of the plight of blacks enslaved in the West Indies and in the North American colonies. Sancho regarded him as a pariah to the race and with the aid of friends sought to reform Soubise before his antics got out of hand. When Soubise was charged with raping a maid in the Duchess of Queensberry's household, she reportedly paid his fare to India to avoid trial.

35. Letter 15, 8 November 1772, 58.

36. In *Lenin and Philosophy and Other Essays*, Louis Althusser demonstrates the ways in which power apparatuses, like literary patrons within a dominant culture, adopt writings and/or writers from a culture or group alien to their own as ideological model (trans. Ben Brewster [New York: Monthly Review Press, 1971]). The dominant culture must then integrate the other into the natural order of things, neutralize the other under the guise of exotica or spectacle, or deny the other's existence altogether.

37. Sancho, Letter 139, 16 June 1780, 240; and Letter 56, 20 December 1777, 117.

38. Bourdieu, 192.

# 4

# Dampier's Hottentots, Swift's Yahoos, and Equiano's Ibos: Imaging Blackness in a Colonialist Discourse

> There are no Books which I more delight in than travels, especially those that describe remote countries, and give the Writer an Opportunity of sharing his Parts without incurring any Danger of being examined or contradicted.
>
> —Sir Richard Steele
> *Tatler*, #254, 1710

> Send those on land that will show themselves diligent writers.
>
> —Henry Hudson
> sailing directions

Sir Richard Steele's admission in the headnote to this chapter invites a conspiratorial coalition among author, and/or eidolon, reader, and text. But his revealing comment shows how wish fulfillment in the reader, coupled with the problems of veracity inherent in narrative, offers the potential for exploitation by the author of travel literature. To subject the traveler's discourse to examination or contradiction is to endanger its ideological domain. In the remote and alien communities where Africans and other so-called third-world figures are represented in early eighteenth-century European travel literature, they are seldom speaking bodies. Instead, European spectators observe and classify them as spectacles. While both reader and "Other" are passive in these accounts, those writers sent on land to observe the Other are diligent, as Henry Hudson's comment, also cited in my headnote, indicates. Somewhere between the reader's desire for exoticism and the diligence of those writers who obliged them, the earliest images of blacks as uncivilized, sordid, and bestial were formed in eighteenth-century thought and letters.

The comprehensive role played by travel literature both in the concept of the African as Other in English thought and letters and in the British involvement in the slave trade remains insufficiently explored.[1] Readers of the time clearly delighted in, and readily absorbed, popular accounts of remote and exotic places like Africa and Asia, collectively known as travel literature. Percy Adams claims that "as propaganda for international trade and for colonization, travel accounts had no equal."[2] He might have added that Africans were without a doubt among the most clear and direct targets of the propagandistic motives of Spanish, English, and other European explorers, dating from the sixteenth century. In fact, indicating the importance and demand for these texts, the British Admiralty sanctioned official, carefully edited accounts of government-sponsored explorations, while confiscating all the rest (Adams, 42).

The *Interesting Narrative of the Life of Olaudah Equiano* (1789) intersects with this body of explorational writings—not only through the mutual handling of history, travel, and narration—but especially in an epistemological framework measuring the impact of race and slavery on certain universalist equations such as the function of literature as a didactic tool. In a complex narrative, Equiano necessarily posits humanist, didactic tenets as being progressive, even desirable, while concomitantly he destabilizes Enlightenment ideas about race, literacy, and morality. Enslaved first in a self-described familial environment in Africa and later bound to British merchants before eventually purchasing his freedom, Equiano published the narrative in a European literary market.[3] A first-generation African, he thus entered the discursive arena that had invalidated the very conditions that informed his existence.

Travel literature utilizes geographical remoteness and manipulates the foreign-observer motif in a manner that authorizes sameness between the "author-spectator" and reader.[4] But as both foreign observer and the foreigner being observed, Equiano had to realign a semantic field, pitting the author and reader coalition against a native Other. In effect, his entry into a colonial discursive arena that projects images of blackness historicizes the ways in which racial hierarchies function repetitively as a literary trope. As I have noted, James Albert Ukawsaw Gronniosaw and Ottobah Cugoano expose a similar hierarchical function in religious practice, and Ignatius Sancho reflects it in a socially constructed sensibility.

In examining composite ethnic characters that influenced conceptions about third-world indigenous cultural groups, this chapter critiques the process by which they converge ideologically to represent Otherness in both popular culture and canonical contexts. Like Gronniosaw, Sancho, and Cugoano before him, Equiano had to reconstitute himself on the Chain of Being, though always against hierarchical structures of dominance that are consistently European; further, he had to assert an identity independently of an ideological Chain. Equiano's position on the hierarchical Chain threatens to compromise his credibility as an author in a European literary marketplace. In other words, before he could authorize his commentary to (re)shape readers' conceptions about Africans, he first had to establish self-authorization.

In an apologia, a narrative convention included in most slave autobiographies, Equiano writes, "I am not so foolishly vain as to expect from [my narrative] either immortality or literary reputation" (I. 3). He points out that the narrative is the product of requests from numerous friends to promote the interests of humanity: "Let it therefore be remembered, that, in wishing to avoid censure, I do not aspire to praise" (I. 3). Simply, he could not inculcate morality nor sanction his story's credibility without acquiring the powers of authorial agency. Consequently, in addition to historicizing the ethnic character as a literary trope, this chapter also examines Equiano's own perplexed position within that hierarchical space.

Providing a rare glimpse into his early life in Benin in West Africa, where he was born in 1745, Equiano begins his account by portraying an Edenic, revisionist Africa that was unlike most European representations of that continent at that time.[5] For example, he writes that before his encounter with Europeans he had been "totally unacquainted with swearing, and all those terms of abuse and reproach which find their way so readily and copiously into the language of more civilized people" (I. 31).

Equiano describes an orderly tribal-governed society, with his own father presiding as judge, where he lived harmoniously before falling into the hands of the "bad spirits" with the "long hair" who changed his very universe. By featuring an African society as having a juridical system, complete with an arbiter administering justice in cases involving Ibo citizens, Equiano likens Benin to a judiciary that is probably familiar to English readers. In order to alter white perceptions about blacks and slavery, Equiano thus contests those prevailing representations of Africans as Other that accompany a long history of European travel writings.[6]

Utilizing the political economy of defamiliarization as an offensive strategy[7] in the narrative's opening, Equiano momentarily loses the "burden" of self-authorization and focuses on discomforting readers who would perceive him as the native Other. By discursive means, Equiano opens up the possibility of agency, but only by subversion, since agency outright is problematical for a mere pupil of reform.

After his removal from African soil as a slave captive at around the age of ten, but before completing the dreaded Middle Passage across the Atlantic, Equiano feared for his life, because "the white people looked and acted, as I thought, in so savage a manner; for I had never seen among any people such instances of brutal cruelty; and this not only shown towards us blacks, but also to some of the whites themselves" (I. 75). Equiano was taken first to Barbados, then to the North American colonies, where he was sold to a Mr. Campbell. After working briefly on a Virginia plantation, he was sold to Michael Henry Paschal, a British naval lieutenant who soon set sail for England.

Equiano thus provides the apparatus by which readers can gauge their own discomfort as members of an enslaving society, and he highlights their roles in perpetuating negative racial stereotypes. Most significantly, the narrative provokes newer readings of those imaginative fiction writers who have omitted the impact that race and slavery had on certain interpretive, universalist equations.

Other travelogues give similar accounts. For instance, in the mid-to late seventeenth century, Sir Thomas Herbert ("A Description of the Cape of Good Hope in Aethiopia," 1634), John Ovington (*Voyage to Suratt*, 1689), and William Dampier (*A New Voyage Round the World*, 2nd ed., 1697) wrote travel accounts of the Khoikhoin, or the Hottentots, indigenous black inhabitants of the Cape of Good Hope whom I described in chapter 1. Aphra Behn, Daniel Defoe, Addison and Steele, and others initiated a small industry of turning Elizabethan and seventeenth-century accounts of actual voyages into exotic tales for eighteenth-century audiences. There is a direct line from these more or less "official" travelogues to representations of Africans to which English readers of corresponding imaginative fiction were exposed. For example, the most recognizable such fictional model of the Hottentot by far is the Yahoo, produced by Swift in the final and most notable book in *Gulliver's Travels*. Swift reproduces the Yahoo as a probable fictional counterpart of Dampier's popular culture symbol of human depravity.[8] Then, in keeping with a neoclassical, humanist literary tradition, Swift features the Yahoo as a satirical model for moral reform for the English reader. Casual references to the pervasive, bestial image of the Hottentot have appeared in works from David Garrick and Tobias Smollet to William Makepeace Thackeray and many others. For example, David Garrick's play, *High Life Below the Stairs* (1759), features servants who imitate the aristocratic behavior of their employers and refer to "low bred fellows" as "Hottenpots" [*sic*]. William Thackeray also pejoratively features the Hottentot in *Vanity Fair*.[9]

Some travel writers were sensitive to frequent accusations of falsehood in their reports, though few readers challenged the presentation of the Hottentot as a construct, which was manufactured by travelers like William Dampier, Sir Thomas Herbert, and John Ovington.[10] In fact, Swift's parodic references to the credulity of travel writers at the beginning of *Gulliver's Travels* do not preclude him from resuscitating the Hottentot, albeit for aesthetic purposes, even as he mocks the eyewitness account of Lemuel

Gulliver as narrative voice. Swift adheres to didactic, neoclassical tenets in order to instruct the masses, a calling that purportedly places him, along with other neoclassicists, a cut above the sensationalist travel writer.

Even as he gently satirizes the tedious prose style and dubious veracity of travel writers in general, Swift both mimics and mocks William Dampier, in particular. For example, in an exchange of letters between Gulliver and his cousin, Richard Sympson, placed in the *Travels* between the publisher's address to the reader and book 1, eighteenth-century readers recognize the name of another "cousin" by the name of Dampier. Gulliver chides Sympson for persuading him to publish the travels in the manner of Dampier—uncorrected and loosely thrown together—with the idea that some university fellow would be hired to edit them. According to William Bonner, Dampier's biographer, it was commonly known that someone else either edited or perhaps ghosted Dampier's books from his own dictation. In the preface to the *Voyage to New Holland*, Dampier, the dashing buccaneer turned travel writer, had answered similar charges lodged against him by pointing out that even the best authors hired others to edit their writings (Bonner, 158).

Among those travelogues who portrayed the Hottentots as racially inferior beings, comprising the opposite to all European manners and customs, Dampier's *New Voyage* is by far the most popular and the most emulated by imaginative fiction writers.[11] Because of the discursive implications of Swift and others' co-optation of Dampier, I cite him as most representative of those travel writers who ventured to the Cape of Good Hope. Dampier's description of the Hottentot, appearing in *New Voyage* in five editions and at least three foreign languages by the time he died in 1715, helped to foster anti-black sentiment that in turn allowed an ideology of Otherness to form among those who encountered this image in popular culture. Dampier's image of the Hottentot was also internalized by judicial experts who reproduced them in legal discourse, by clergy who perpetuated the Hamitic hypothesis, and of course by imaginative fiction writers who transported the image on into perpetuity.

The most ardent claims of Dampier, Herbert, and Ovington, explorers to the Cape of Good Hope, were for faithfully registering what they witnessed on their journeys. But they seemed oblivious to the politics of perspective—to the notion that what they referred to as mirrored reproductions were ideological readings of bodies and landscape as textual terrain.[12] As is typical of many exploration accounts, what Dampier wrote about the Hottentots' tribal life was based on observations he made from a distance, not from having lived among them. In the final chapter of *A New Voyage Round the World*, Dampier wrote this: "As for these Hottantots [*sic*], they are a very lazy sort of people, and tho they live in a delicate country, very fit to be manured, and where there is Land enough for them, yet they choose rather to live as their fore-fathers, poor and miserable, than be at pains for plenty."[13]

Dampier's readings of an indigenous cultural group's activities, manners, and customs are necessarily suspect because these readings are bound by his cultural, spatial, and temporal limitations. In other words, Dampier bases his account on detached observations of the Hottentots—not from prolonged interaction with them. In examining the ideological nature of temporality in *Time and the Other*, Johannes Fabian writes that travel accounts tend to characterize the explorers' observations of manners and customs of the Other as the timeless embodiment of a predetermined behavior.[14] In other passages in Dampier's *New Voyage* select descriptions are meant to acquaint readers with the manners and customs of the Hottentots in their entirety. Hence, what readers see inhabitants doing at their moment of encounter with the English explorer is also the way in which we are meant to view them perennially, as if (to apply a contemporary analogy) centered in a *National Geographics* glossy print or a Polaroid snapshot. Not only do readers not see the explorers interacting with members of these cultural groups; we also do not see interaction of any kind among tribal members in any sustained way.

As Mary Louise Pratt observes in "Scratches on the Face of the Country," such writing "textually produces the Other without an explicit anchoring either in an observing self or in a particular encounter in which contact with the Other takes place."[15] Pratt writes that the discursive formation of much travel writing tends to "center landscape" and to bracket the "indigenous people" (142–43). In other words, in descriptive portraits, such writing represents inhabitants separately from the land on which they live: "Signs of human presence, when they occur, are . . . expressed as marks upon the face; the human agents responsible for those signs are themselves rarely seen" (142). And when they do appear, these individuals are decidedly discounted, as explorer William Smith observes: "Before I describe the vegetables, I shall take notice of the animals of this country; beginning with the natives, who are generally speaking a lusty strong-bodied people, but are mostly of a lazy, idle disposition."[16] Since the ultimate purpose of such accounts is to showcase territory that might be ripe for future trade by Europeans or sponsors of such explorations, the narrating "I"/eye typically adopts a seemingly passive posture as an observer that allows the "scene/ seen" (to borrow from Pratt) to speak for itself. Dampier follows this pattern in his references to the Hottentots: "The warmer Climates being generally very productive of delicate Fruits, etc. and these uncivilized people caring for little else than what is barely necessary, they spend the greatest part of their time in diverting themselves, after their several fashions" (542).

Dampier portrays the Hottentots as being disconnected from the land they inhabit because they do not exploit its wealth, the same argument used later to disfranchise Native Americans. He thus makes no allowances for the ecological advantages that the Hottentot's frugality might have brought both to their own lifestyle and to the land which they inhabit. Ironically depletions of the sort Dampier prescribes would, over time, destroy the land's wealth and diminish its natural beauty much more readily than the Hottentot's way of living. A native inhabitant who is incidental, who lives in some kind of symbolic balance with the land is perceived as undeserving of the land. Therefore, the land is there for plundering and pillaging with minimal conscience lost for its displaced inhabitants, who do not know what to do with the land's wealth in the first place.[17]

Not surprisingly, with more than a century of similarly damaging portraits of the African before him in popular culture and European travel writings, Equiano devotes the opening segment of his own account to a staunch defense of Africa. And though focusing on the Ibo, his own cultural group, he writes that "the history of what passes in one family or village may serve as a specimen of the whole nation" (I. 5). In fact, as I shall discuss later in this chapter, Equiano's account of the manners and customs of Benin is so uncompromising and utopian that an ideological chasm separates it from the remainder of the narrative, which fully embraces Eurocentric customs and practices. Acting as a foreign observer of English culture—though an insider geographically—Equiano undertakes an ideological journey that both vilifies and esteems the European, ultimately challenging readers to view themselves as the objectified Other. Only Ukawsaw Gronniosaw and Ottobah Cugoano, also first-generation Africans enslaved in Europe, set the beginning of their publications in Africa.

Equiano reverses the claims of Dampier, Herbert, Ovington and other travel writers, whose descriptions of Africa privilege the landscape and bracket the indigenous people. "[The Ibos] are all habituated to labour from our earliest years. Every one contributes something to the common stock; and as we are unacquainted with idleness, we have no beggars," he notes (I. 20–21). The image of the Ibo as an active, vibrant fixture on the land known as Benin is antithetical to the image of the Hottentot in travel narratives by Dampier, Herbert, and Ovington. He thus rejects Africa as being a primitive, disorderly society devoid of intellectual sophistication. And although Equiano's African setting embodies the Edenic myth, or a primitive societal ideal, the narrative demythologizes the concept of the Other as untutored and uncivilized. He connects the land with its inhabitants, describing both as strong and powerful, especially as they interact with one another. Using the collective pronoun "we," Equiano solidifies his personal ties to his homeland. By telling his story retrospectively, after he has purchased his freedom from slavery, he acts as both detached observer and as an active participant in Ibo tribal life. He thus eliminates the problems of physical and emotional detachment that plague most European travelogues and introduces scenes based on boyhood memories of sustained interactions among Ibo citizens that invite the reader to take part.

As Lennard Davis describes this dynamic in *Resisting Novels: Ideology and Fiction*, "The refashioning of the terrain through language and extended description is a development in political control and the rise of the modern state, with its concomitant reliance on covert rather than overt compulsion."[18] Dampier attempts to construct a scene for the reader in a manner that—at first glance—seems unaffected by political concerns. But in addition to the cultural, temporal, and spatial mapping of an indigenous cultural group, the colonialist dialogue of the "passive" observer clearly allows for the maximum possible political and ideological shaping to take place.

In constructing the Ibo as a counter representation of the Hottentot, Olaudah Equiano reveals an awareness of the latter's pervasive, symbolic implications for blacks and slavery. For example, at one point in the narrative, an outraged Equiano wrote that the Barbados Assembly's proslavery laws "would shock the morality and common sense of a Samaide or Hottentot" (I. 219). Equiano notes that the 329th Act of the Assembly of Barbados states that no person shall be held liable for the murder of a slave who had attempted to escape from or had committed some offense against, his enslaver. But if someone willfully murdered a slave in the heat of passion or out of just plain wantonness, then that person would be forced to pay fifteen pounds sterling to the public treasury.

Equiano blamed such cruelties on absentee planters who often resided in England and left their plantations in the hands of overseers, "persons of the worst character of any denomination of men in the West Indies" (I. 207). He cited instances of benevolent, humane planters who managed their own estates and increased their own profit, since "the negroes are treated with lenity and proper care, by which their lives are prolonged" (I. 209). This was, moreover profitable; because fewer slaves died, fewer new slaves were needed to replace them. Coincidentally, some fifty years later Mary Prince offered a different perspective on the subject of the absentee landlord. "Since I have been here [in England] I have often wondered how English people can go out into the West Indies and act in such a beastly manner. But when they go the West Indies, they forget God and all feeling of shame, I think, since they can see and do such things," she wrote.[19]

In revising the image of the ethnic Other, Equiano addresses a more complicated history than that provided by the popular travelogue industry. Indeed, the narrative also speaks to ethnic characters drawn in other fictional writings, usually held in greater scholarly esteem than the travelogue from which they originated. For example, Aphra Behn's *Oroonoko*, Defoe's *Robinson Crusoe*, and Addison and Steele's "Inkle and Yarico" portrayed blacks either as ennobled beings, by virtue of their unacculturation to certain Eurocentric standards or, by virtue of their assimilative value as admirable characters. Even when imaginative-fiction writers (some of whom were also influenced by early travel narratives) produced sympathetic portraits of blacks and other people of color antithetical to travelers' accounts, these images of blackness were distinctly sanitized. Adorned with European like physiognomy, hair texture, and color, this so-called "primitive being," this professed ideal, was barely recognizable as African at all.[20] In other words, the standard of measure for the upper and lower echelons in these stories is always based on Eurocentric measures of superiority. In *Oroonoko, Robinson Crusoe*, and "Inkle and Yarico," it is not so much that the African as character was positivized but that the positive standard for humanity was purged of a so-called African likeness. These stories have long been examined by scholars who charge that they reinforce racism through cultural relativism.

However, in revising the consensus viewpoint on the subject, I would like to argue that this something-other-than-African character who occupied the middle ground between the bestial and the benevolent, the illiterate and the authorial may have inadvertently prepared European readers for the moral and intellectual exploration of Gronniosaw, Cugoano, Sancho, Equiano, and Prince, who entered the literary stage late in the century.[21] In other words, the African's bestial and uncivilized literary representation in early English travelogues was so repugnant that sympathetic writers were either unable or unwilling to portray such a character as the object of sentimentality. They wrote, in some sense, as though they had to present an object of sentimentality that was first appropriated to certain European standards.

Aphra Behn's Oroonoko, Defoe's Friday, and Addison and Steele's Yarico are among just such enormously popular early eighteenth-century ethnic characters that advance my premise about the neo-African character as part of a remediation process. For example, Behn chastises Europeans for failing to reward Oroonoko's civility or his acculturation from African to European. In effect, in distinguishing Oroonoko from his comrades, Behn cites his nobility and social rank as a prince in African society. Even beneath his royal garb, she writes, "the Royal Youth appear'd in spite of the Slave," and other people treated him accordingly (137). In *Robinson Crusoe*, Friday's keen observations often displace Crusoe as the superior intellect. For example, Crusoe is at a loss to explain to Friday why God does not simply destroy the devil as an evil creature. And he expresses regret at his nation's mistreatment of others like Friday. But Friday is still identified as remaining hopelessly ignorant and barbaric. In spite of Crusoe's effusive observations about Friday's goodness and honesty, he must accept Crusoe's religious doctrines and deny his own in order to be morally acceptable. And he must recognize his subordinate place in Crusoe's world.

Like Behn and Defoe, Steele offers a complex commentary that utilizes racial exoticism and slavery as popular fictional motifs, although he appropriates them to a neoclassical, humanist literary didacticism.[22] Reminiscent of Pope's literary didactic role, discussed in chapter 1, Addison and Steele similarly function as architects who craft a uniformity of ideas in the *Spectator* essays and stories that they impose upon a national readerly coalition. Unlike Pope, however, Addison and Steele further dramatize these ideas in popular imaginative fiction in stories that contain racial content, such as "Inkle and Yarico" and "The Barbados Negroes."

In "Inkle and Yarico" a young Indian maid rescues a young London man, Thomas Inkle, who is shipwrecked on a West Indian island. Inkle has been taught by his father to love riches above all else. Most of the crew is slain by Indians when they dock in search of provisions, but Inkle escapes and is saved by Yarico. In appreciation for the rescue, Inkle promises Yarico marriage and a privileged lifestyle back in England. But months later, after they are rescued and taken to Barbados, he sells Yarico—now pregnant with his child—into slavery. Steele writes, "If the European was highly charmed with the limbs, features, and wild graces of the naked American; the American was no less taken with the Dress, Complexion and shape of an European, covered from head to foot" (50). Steele's "Inkle and Yarico," a more inventive version than the original story written by Richard Ligon,[23] emphasizes Inkle's commercial greed and his inconstancy to Yarico. However, Steele concurs with Ligon's observation of Yarico's "excellent shape and colour," suggesting an adherence to a stereotyped, erotic Other.

I would submit that, as part of a conscious remediation process, Behn's Oroonoko is a noble or ennobled character, while Trefry, the white male colonialist who brutalizes him, is reprehensible. Defoe's Friday has "all the sweetness and softness of an European," [because] his nose was small, "not flat like the Negroes," and he had "a very good mouth, thin lips" (160). And Addison and Steele's Yarico is a "wildly graceful" ennobled being who does not bear the attributes of her predominantly African counterparts enslaved in the West Indies. Like numerous other writers, poets, and dramatists, most of whom wrote far less popular spin-offs of an enduring colonial narrative, Steele chose not to portray Yarico as an African woman. As Wylie Sypher poignantly observes:

> The noble Negress, like the noble Negro, became all things to all poets. Anti-slavery found ready for its purposes a symbol, the African who united the traits of the white man, so that he might not be repulsive; the

traits of the Indian, so that the might not seem base; and the traits of the Negro, so that he might rouse pity.[24]

To many eighteenth-century readers, these sanitized images of blackness may well have complicated efforts by African-British writers to break free of the reinforced binaries of racial hierarchies and to control their own representations.

In the midst of this complex phenomenon, Equiano measures up with mixed results. His knowledge of European culture certainly acquaints him with discursive counterstrategies against negative stereotyping but also cloaks him within a nationalist hegemony in alignment with these writers. Keenly sensitive to the political economy of racial and ethnic hierarchies, Equiano attempts to distinguish the Ibos from other Africans, a move that ironically intersects with proslavery interests in the slave's body as product.[25] For example, espousing the work ethic of the Ibo, he notes: "The West Indies planters prefer the slaves of Benin or Eboe to those of any part of Guinea, for their hardiness, intelligence, integrity and zeal" (I. 21). Dutch settlers on the Cape of Good Hope were largely unsuccessful in their efforts to enslave the Hottentots because of what the Dutch perceived as their inability to follow instructions. To compensate, they also imported and enslaved numerous West Africans. Perhaps mindful of such accusations of slothfulness in some travel accounts, Equiano expresses an appreciation for Europeans' preference for enslaving the Ibo. But such an observation is complicitous with a materialist culture.

Equiano's observations are somewhat mediated by his ability to process the very theory-of-travel language that Dampier, Herbert, Ovington, and others utilize in order to reconstruct the historically unflattering Hottentot as a positivized West African Ibo. Consequently, in depicting the Ibo, he validates claims that the "native other" can possess discursive power, however tenuously, in the space where ambivalences about self and other reside.[26] He simultaneously reconstructs the Ibo in the subjective posture that European readers likely imagine themselves to occupy and dislocates readers from a lofty position of superiority. In other words, he centralizes readers, but only as "deposed" Ibos. In asserting power, discursively, Equiano's narrative disrupts a shared vision between himself and the reader in opposition with the Other.

The movement between images of blackness from Dampier to Swift to Equiano dramatizes the means by which they become recognizable and consumable as universalized apparatuses of truth. While travel books enjoyed unrivaled success among the general reading populace, the intellectual or cultivated reader tended to dismiss them. (Bonner notes that for all of Dampier's notoriety, Pope mentions him only once.) According to James Boswell in the *Life of Samuel Johnson*, the author of *Rasselas* thought that "a man had better work his way before the mast, than read [travel books] through; they will be eaten by rats and mice, before they are read through. There can be little entertainment in such books; one set of Savages is like another."[27] Yet the moral teachings that Johnson infused in *Rasselas*—itself a work of travel—and that Swift formulated in *Gulliver's Travels* allowed them to appropriate a popular culture form to a didactic literary objective.

It is hardly surprising that we can trace the African as Other in English thought to explorational accounts. If the works of Dampier, Herbert, and Ovington are generally unfamiliar to readers today, they are nonetheless a prominent influence on well-known eighteenth-century English imaginative fiction. It is from writers like Behn, Defoe, Addison and Steele, and Swift that we can look back to find the African as an indelible fixture in English writings. A popular culture symbol of human depravity serves a polite readership and a cultivated intellectual establishment more purposefully when turned to didactic ends.

Swift, whose Yahoo is probably the most recognizable literary symbol of human depravity, transforms the raw, artless data of Dampier's text into artful instruction designed to rehabilitate the masses from vice and ignorance. Swift's portrait of the Yahoos as being physically and morally repugnant, as well as devoid of intelligence, is analogous to images of blacks, especially the Hottentots, in most turn-of-the-eighteenth-century travelogues. Amid a shifty, complex narrative structure, he provides an eerily uncomplicated model.[28] But he still leaves intact the problematical emblematic representation of depravity as black, female, and African.

Clearly sensitive to the political economy of the ennobled-being concept, the astute Equiano retains the primitive idyllic likened to Virgil's *Georgics*, though he sheds the mythological primitive. For example, he depicts the Ibos as members of a self-contained, well-ordered civil community: "As our manners are simple, our luxuries are few" (I. 11). In a possible allusion to trade among nations—particularly, the slave trade—Equiano writes, "As we live in a country where nature is prodigal of her favours, our wants are few, and easily supplied" (I. 17–18). He similarly praises the simplicity and innocence of the Woolwow, Miskito Indian inhabitants in South America who had not been colonized by the Spanish: "Upon the whole, I never met any nation that were so simple in their manners as these people, or had so little ornament in their houses" (II. 182). Regarding their lack of worship, he wrote that they were "no worse than their European brethren or neighbours," going on to conclude: "I am sorry to say that there was not one white person in our dwelling, nor any where else that I saw in different places I was at on the shore, that was better or more pious than those unenlightened Indians . . ." (II. 182–83).

In *Gulliver's Travels*, Swift also blesses nature's bountiful store, though he offers a perspective that reveals the conflicting position held by some neoclassical, Tory skeptics on the political economy of international trade. For example, after ingratiating himself with the Houyhnhnm master in book 4, Gulliver settles contentedly into a home built entirely from materials, e.g., Yahoo skins, hemp, and feathers, found only in Houyhnhnmland. Gulliver remarks on his ability to fulfill all his essential needs on this island, *"No Man could more verify the Truth of these two Maxims, That, Nature is very easily satisfied; and, That, Necessity is the Mother of Invention"* (278). And yet, the quotations are complicated by the opposing logic that they represent. While Gulliver seemingly misses the ironic connection, Swift takes a swipe at international trade and/or product importation, a major point of disagreement between Ancients and Moderns. For example, housing at Houhynhnmland consisted of simple, unadorned huts from materials harvested in the nation's backyard. But the dwellings also symbolize exploitation domestically, since they are constructed from the hides and the labor of the Yahoos.

Following the practice of the typical foreign observer in the manners and customs section of most travel accounts, Gulliver bases his negative impressions of the Yahoos on their repulsive physical appearance. A foreign observer in the land of the horses, Gulliver bases his description of the Yahoos on the distinctiveness of their "singular and deformed" shape.[29] They were unclean, they fought among themselves, and males and females slept together, indiscriminately. The Yahoo female was especially depicted as degenerate and promiscuous. The female Yahoo who leers at a naked, disgusted Gulliver as he bathes in a stream brings to mind the Hottentot in the travel narratives or the female African whom Thomas Jefferson and Edward Long (among others) believe to have copulated with the orangutan. The aggressive, sexually perverse behavior of the female Yahoo's behavior toward Gulliver is likened to the perception that the female body is the site of sexual promiscuity and disease.[30]

Like Dampier, Herbert, and Ovington who observe the Hottentots from afar without interacting with them, Gulliver comments on the Yahoos' vulgar behavior. Clearly it is impossible to ignore the racist, colonialist implications that this scenario reveals for the Houyhnhnms, though obviously not for Swift, who increasingly caricatures Gulliver's infatuation with them. The Houyhnhnms reveal a caste system in which gradations of beasts, from sorrel nags and dapple greys to Yahoos, exhibit varying degrees of intelligence. The master Houyhnhnm informs Gulliver that

> The white, the sorrel, and the iron-grey were not so exactly shaped as
> the bay, the dapple-grey, and the black; nor born with equal talents of the
> mind, or a capacity to improve them; and therefore continued always in the

condition of servants, without ever aspiring to match out of their own race,
which in that country would be reckoned monstrous and unnatural (257).

Gulliver concludes that "all savage nations" share similar features with
the Yahoos, such as broad, flat faces, depressed noses, and large lips. These
features, he proclaims, are distorted by "the natives suffering their infants
to lie grovelling on the earth, or by carrying them on their backs, nuzzling
with their face against the mother's shoulders" (228). By equating the
female yahoos' nursing habits with the mothers of "all savage nations,"
Gulliver concurs with travel descriptions of the Hottentot female. Consider,
for instance, Sir Thomas Herbert's claim that female Hottentots nurse infants who hang at their backs by stretching their breasts over their shoulder[31]
with Gulliver's description of the "dugs" that hang to the feet of female
Yahoos. Furthermore, the Yahoo was portrayed as an uneducable lot, comparable to Dampier's description of the Hottentots.

In pronouncing the dehumanizing effects of slavery, Equiano exploits
the foreign-observer motif, popular in English writings, like Swift's
*Gulliver's Travels*, albeit as a natural consequence of the actual circumstances of his life.[32] By relating the story of his early years in Benin,
Equiano reveals much more than his ties to his homeland. He publishes an
anti-slavery narrative in a nation in which slavery was still a legal institution. Reflecting on his childhood in Benin, Equiano invokes a passage from
*Gulliver's Travels* that describes racial hierarchies in the Houyhnhnm
society: "I remember while in Africa to have seen three Negro children,
who were tawny, and another quite white, who were universally regarded
by myself, and the natives in general, as far as related to their complexions,
as deformed" (I. 21–22).

In effect, he reverses the Western concept of color that identifies white
as good and black as evil in a manner not likely encountered before by
European readers. As though mindful of connections frequently made
between physical shape and form and disease and promiscuity, Equiano
remarks on the absence of "deformity" among the Ibos. And when he falls
into the hands of European enslavers for the first time, Equiano likens them
to "bad spirits," because "their complexions, their long hair, and the
language they spoke" differed from that of the Africans. Equiano enables
English readers to see their flaws mirrored in the eyes of someone "outside"
their circle and to examine with renewed clarity.

Dismayed by the tribal group's use of "European cutlasses and cross-
bows, which were unknown to us," Equiano observed that they fought "with
their fists among themselves" (I. 67). In addition, he commented on the
immodesty of the women who "ate, and drank, and slept, with their men"
(I. 67), which is especially ironic for its resemblance to Swift's description

of Gulliver's initial encounter with the Yahoos. Equiano criticizes the customs practiced by these Africans, because his own English captors had practiced similar customs.

Ironically, it is Gulliver's uniqueness as a Yahoo possessed with reason that poses the greatest threat to the Houyhnhnms' survival, and that leads to his expulsion from Houyhnhnmland. They fear that Gulliver might some day use his reasoning skills to rally the debased Yahoo troops and to destroy the Houyhnhnms. Swift strategically positions Gulliver as an advanced Yahoo or, according to Clement Hawes, as both colonizer and the colonized Other. As a colonized Other, Gulliver is the medium between a rational animal (Houyhnhnm) and a brute (Yahoo), an identification that he presumably shares with the reader. Indeed, the Houyhnhnm master distinguishes Gulliver from the Yahoo only because of the former's teachableness, personable qualities, civility, and hygiene. Gulliver, then, is the educable Yahoo—the one whom Houyhnhnms can tolerate—at least temporarily.[33]

In fact, Gulliver, who initially avoids the loathsome Yahoos, soon finds himself inexplicably drawn to them. He is particularly mortified to discover that the Yahoos' physiognomy, which he at first attributes to "all savage nations," actually resembles his own. In addition, the Yahoos, like Gulliver, eat the flesh of dead animals. Meanwhile, Gulliver has to monitor his own behavior constantly for fear of descending into Yahooish behavior, which is a losing battle because, no matter what he does, he will never be seen by the Houyhnhnms as anything but a Yahoo.

How, then, does one reconcile that the model of all human depravity is consistently depicted in ethnic form that is not recognizably English, but English at its unrecognizable, worst state? The Yahoo, then, is merely an instrument of voyeuristic spectacle and exoticism like the London peep shows that secured the observers' sense of a moralistic, saner self by contrast. In the figure of the Yahoo, Swift provides an eerie though useful model that allows for a critique of colonialism by the perceptive reader. But Swift takes this critique only so far. Simply stated, Swift may have dismantled "the very identity of the colonizing subject," while he leaves unaltered an indelible image of the depths of human depravity in a highly charged ethnic portraiture that is black and Other.[34] Ultimately, Gulliver (and Swift's contemporaries?) fear that they may become—in a worst-possible case of human imbecility—European Yahoos/Hottentots. Like Hogarth's paintings of black domestic slaves, the satirical mirror poses blacks in order to expose the British aristocracy's depraved behavior—but only as "worse than Negro barbarity."[35]

This idea held true in graphic arts as well. According to David Dabydeen, Hogarth was England's "most prolific painter and engraver of blacks." Blacks appear in Hogarth's satirical series, including *The Harlot's Progress*.

These paintings depict blacks, often in diminution, as servants in various attitudes of deference toward white characters. In these paintings, blacks are often featured on equal footing with domestic pets, with both typically leaning on the knee of the owner or gazing fondly at a white child or adult also in the painting. Hogarth's *Taste in High Life* is believed to be a portrait of African-British writer Ignatius Sancho as a young boy.[36] In the painting, an English woman (possibly one of his enslavers) fondly strokes the child's chin. Dabydeen notes that while these paintings show blacks in isolation from their peers, English prints portray them in social settings that involve other black and white individuals from lower socioeconomic backgrounds. These portraits lend another dimension to images of blacks as the standard of measure for reprehensible behavior who can even be shocked by witnessing moral decadence among the British aristocracy.[37]

Therefore, in spite of Swift's shifting of subject-object relations in the narrative, I would argue that readers consistently fed a literary diet of Otherness in the form of indigenous third-world representations may well have viewed the Yahoo as the Not me, or, as the thing which the reader most assuredly was not.[38] The uneducable, sexually perverse Yahoo, like Dampier's Hottentot, is a quintessential identifiable barometer for readers' own normalcy, a postulate that history repeats, as I have illustrated with regard to Achebe's observations on Joseph Conrad's *Heart of Darkness*. And yet, in spite of the Houyhnhnms' unflattering attributes—caste, nobility, slavery, expulsion of the Other, even bad poetry—they would not have been shocking or unrecognizable to the English.

Consider, for instance, Swift's colonialist critique in his powerful, concluding denunciation of British colonization. Gulliver refuses to offer up the sites of his travels to the government for colonizing, claiming that an "Execrable Crew of Butchers employed in so pious an Expedition" would be "sent to convert and civilize an idolatrous and barbarous People."[39] But Gulliver's primary reasons for refusing to colonize the objects of his discovery for the British government may be viewed as Swift's anti-imperialist manifesto: the Lilliputians were not worth the bother; securing Brobdingnag might prove an unsafe venture; and the Houyhnhnms would be formidable foes for the British military. Gulliver's specious claim, however, that the Houyhnhnms might do well to civilize Europe in the virtues of humanity hardly militates against his remark that these foreign species are not worth the English undertaking the efforts needed to colonize them. In other words, Gulliver would harvest only those colonies that proved valuable for exploitation by his country, thus revealing a colonialist regime's true objectives.

Further irony exists in that the Houyhnhnm/horse is in actuality a fully domesticated animal in the European stable. In a colonialist reading, if Swift satirizes British colonization (through Gulliver and text), then the joke is on those whose greed is exposed. Gulliver's mixed motives, if indeed they represent Swift's own anti-imperialist/anti-colonialist position, are confounding at best. It is as though Swift's morally ambivalent critique of Britain's colonial abuses mirrors what Edward Said identifies as his perplexed Anglo-Irish Toryism, coupled with a feisty anarchical spirit.[40]

In the larger historical cycle of psychical imaging of blackness, Swift's text comes full circle. To say that the Yahoo is the Hottentot is to suggest, finally, that the Hottentot is forever lodged as an abominable symbol of human depravity in colonialist discourse. Gulliver's judgment that the Yahoos are physically and morally repugnant, as well as devoid of intelligence and reasoning powers, is analogous to most portraits of blacks, especially the Hottentots, who are depicted in travel accounts just at the turn of the century. The image of the Hottentot as the worst specimen of human nature has interesting implications for the way in which dominant cultures have formed conceptions about culturally diverse groups.

After more than a century of negative African images, frustrated British abolitionists like William Dickson called for specimens of black writings in the 1770s as the best final hope, perhaps, by which to counter a pervasive ideology of racial inferiority. And yet, by the time that Olaudah Equiano published his narrative in 1789, the Hottentot was a permanent fixture in the English cultural vocabulary, and the former slave from Benin, West Africa, was well aware of it. In order to alter the negative perceptions that whites had about blacks—which likely stemmed, in part, from the use of the Hottentots and the Yahoos as ethnic symbols—Equiano had to demythologize the primitive-being concept, to expose the dehumanizing effects of slavery, and to prove his membership in the very ranks of humanity.

Much has been written about the powers of surveillance and the pathological gaze that penetrates and punishes its object. Such powers necessarily have their effects when applied to a work like the narrative of Equiano. In it, Equiano removes himself from the viewfinder of the imperial lens and returns to the subject an oppositional "gaze." In other words, "the look of surveillance returns as the displacing gaze of the disciplined, where the observer becomes the observed and 'partial' representation rearticulates the whole notion of identity and alienates it from essence."[41] In fact, the Other's potential for displacing such powers mediates the totalizing effects of surveillance.[42] The reader stares into the text in order to observe the narrator, to watch for the qualities that will allow his fitness for personhood and for authorship, only to find that the narrator is simultaneously observing the reader for moral and ethical fitness. Equiano places the reader at the center of the text. Thus, readers glimpse their own moral inadequacies as individuals, particularly enslavers.

In reversing the emblematic representations of depravity from being

black and African to being white and European, Equiano speaks from the
margins as the embodiment of the Other. He deconstructs images of blackness in a colonialist paradigm,[43] projects a vehemently anti-slavery stance,
and criticizes capitalistic greed and pro-slavery politics. Ultimately, the
narrative itself provokes newer readings of certain canonical works. It is
thus tempting to view Equiano as a corrective visionary who completely un-
does those damaging stereotypes left by travelers and other imaginative
fiction writers with his descriptive composite of the West African Ibo. But
his achievement is risky.

In the first place, in order to lionize the Ibos as the group most favored
by West Indian enslavers, Equiano must imbue them with intellectual and
physical trappings that effectively create a hierarchy of Otherness among
Africans and increase slave procurers' desire for Ibos as slaves. Furthermore, in order to secure his own freedom, he must participate in and reap
profits from an industry that in some way touches every employment venue,
business venture, and trade—an industry that he deeply deplores. Finally,
in a discourse endemic to a Eurocentric, colonialist paradigm, Equiano poses
as a wannabe who cannot be a humanist without doing serious damage either
to the very ideas that he conveys or to his precarious position as Other in
the colonialist discursive equation. Consequently I explore in the final segment of this chapter the possibility that in the perhaps-elusive quest for an
identity—independent of the Chain—Equiano unwittingly writes directly to
the Chain as an overarching trope. He thus ascends from his lowly rank, but
inadvertently, reinforces the permanency of a measured hierarchized form.

I stated at the beginning of this chapter that Equiano's conflicting posture with regard to the European is most evident in the ideological separation between the African setting and the transatlantic segments. Ironically,
in order to establish credibility, not only as author but also as a human
being worthy of acceptance from an overwhelmingly white, male readership,
Equiano had to register anti-slavery sentiments, yet without revealing anti-
European feeling.

Within a few years of first arriving in England in the spring of 1757,
twelve-year-old Equiano lodged with families in Falmouth and Guernsey and
saw snow for the first time. Encouraged by kind treatment by the "Miss
Guerins," who sent him to school, Equiano worked to improve his English.
But he expressed horror at being unable to wash his face and acquire the
same rosy color as his little white playmate (I. 109). Indeed, he soon
fashioned himself to be "almost an Englishman," in that he no longer feared
them (I. 132). The "bad spirits with the long hair," whom he feared in the
Ibo manners and customs section of the narrative, are now replaced by an
image of the European as a superior being whose very spirit Equiano seeks
to imbibe (I. 132–33).

Paul Edwards attributes Equiano's conflicting narration to the polished words of an experienced free adult writer grafted onto the naive bewilderment and wonder of an enslaved youth.[44] Textual discrepancies that remain are treated as irreconcilable anomalies, attributed to a hopelessly conflicted narrator presiding over a seriously flawed narrative. For example, in order to prevent Equiano from seeking asylum while in England, Captain Henry Paschal offered him up for sale to Robert King, a Quaker merchant. Though slavery was legal in England until 1834, lawyers like Granville Sharp had successfully freed numerous domestic slaves on England's soil by manipulating legal loopholes. Though bitterly disappointed, Equiano was relieved upon being told that because of his good character King had purchased him in order to train him as a clerk. Instantly relieved, Equiano expressed thanks to both Captain Doran and to his former enslaver, Campbell, "for the character they had given me; a character which I afterwards found of infinite service to me" (I. 193).

Later, upon returning to the West Indies, Equiano defended King against criticism from other slave planters for providing his slaves with plenty of food. Yet, in the very next clause, Equiano complained that he "often went hungry" (I. 205). Similarly, he first noted, with pride, that he was fortunate enough to satisfy King, his enslaver, in every capacity in which King employed him. After boasting a savings of more than a hundred pounds a year to his enslaver, Equiano nevertheless quipped that clerks in the West Indies who performed similar tasks were usually paid "from sixty to a hundred pounds current a year" (I. 203). Paul Edwards calls Equiano's posture of benign benevolence toward those who mistreated him as muted anger, not unlike that which Sancho occasionally vents in his letters. Edwards drily observes that "as so often happens in the narrative, the 'kindness' of their Lordships is acknowledged in a process of ironic knee-bending that reveals a thinly concealed rage."[45]

In acquiring skills associated with entrepreneurship, Equiano buys and resells a number of products in a pyramid-style business arrangement. He first turns one half-bit or three-pence into one dollar within four to six weeks. He purchases a tumbler on a Dutch island, which he then sells in Montserrat for a full-bit or sixpence. He then purchases two additional tumblers, which he sells for two bits (a shilling). Again he doubles the purchase to four tumblers and resells them for four bits, as shown in this extraordinary account:

> I bought two glasses with one bit, and with the other three I bought a jug of Geneva, nearly about three pints in measure. When we came to Montserrat I sold the gin for eight bits, and the tumblers for two, so that my capital now amounted in all to a dollar, well husbanded and acquired

in the space of a month or six weeks, when I blessed the Lord that I was
so rich (I. 234–35).

Equiano put his efforts to excellent use. He doubles his diligence—
putting in one full day's work in order to prevent his being sold to a more
cruel enslaver and to lay money aside (from hiring himself out) in order to
purchase his freedom from Robert King, his third and final enslaver. "My
master was several times offered by different gentlemen one hundred
guineas for me; but he always told them he would not sell me, to my great
joy: and I used to double my diligence and care for fear of getting into the
hands of these men who did not allow a valuable slave the common support
of life," Equiano explained (I. 204–205). At one point, after complaining
that slaves were being sold "from three pence to six pence or nine pence a
pound," Equiano boasts that his own enslaver, whose "humanity was
shocked at this mode," sold slaves "by the lump" (I. 220).

Ironically, acquiring the many skills necessary in order to raise the
money for his freedom placed Equiano at great risk of being kidnapped by
traders and resold into slavery in the West Indies. At one point, a ship's
captain, whom Equiano paid for his voyage out of South America, kidnapped and threatened to sell him to Spanish captors in Cartagena. The
captain first tried to convince Equiano to work for sailor's wages, but
Equiano refused and demanded to go to Jamaica instead. He was accordingly hung up by the heels in the captain's attempt to force him to Cartagena
"without any crime committed, and without judge or jury; merely because
[he] was a free man, and could not by the law get any redress from a white
person in those parts of the world" (II. 196). Fortunately, a sympathetic
carpenter on board urged the captain to release Equiano, especially since he
was formerly the steward of Doctor Richard Irving, an important man in the
area. With the aid of others aboard the vessel, Equiano was able to escape
in a canoe while the two men argued. He was also denied the wages that he
had earned as a steward while on a voyage to Jamaica. Even the nine Kings-
ton magistrates refused to collect Equiano's eight pounds, five shillings
sterling, saying that a black man could not, by law, swear an oath against
a white man.

Equiano thus poses as a thorough assimilator to Western, European culture who approximates but cannot fully assume the role of the colonizer.
The colonizer's position exhibits the seductive power and exhilaration of
ownership. But to assume this position, Equiano must first purchase himself
in a necessary approval of the civilizing strategies of commercialism. The
more valuable his labor, the more expensive his purchase price. The high
cost of buying his own person (forty pounds sterling) demands skills in
lucrative jobs, some of which are directly and indirectly associated with

enslaving or colonizing others, for example, navigator, overseer, merchant, slave ship's captain, and overseer.

Indeed, when Equiano presented Robert King with the money for his freedom, the stunned merchant declared that had he known Equiano would raise the money so soon, he never would have promised him freedom in the first place. Equiano adopts a cultural mercantilism that poses few contradictions for him, perhaps because of his circuitous route to freedom in an eighteenth-century commercial environment. Consider Equiano's observations upon gaining his freedom on 11 July, 1766: "Accordingly [King] signed the manumission that day, so that, before night, I who had been a slave in the morning, trembling at the will of another, was become my own master, and completely free" (II. 16–17). Equiano also notes that his joy "was still heightened by the blessings and prayers of many of the sable race, particularly the aged, to whom [his] heart had ever been attached with reverence" (II. 17).

Equiano's endorsement of England's capitalistic ventures, including commerce between Britain and Africa as an alternative to slavery, is further symptomatic of the total human cost in maintaining a material economy for the Commonwealth even in lieu of slavery. Houston A. Baker suggests that Equiano "masters the rudiments of economics that condition his very life" and "creates a text which inscribes these economics as a sign of its 'social grounding.'"[46] Near the end of the narrative, Equiano argues: "As the inhuman traffic of slavery is to be taken into the consideration of the British legislature, I doubt not, if a system of commerce was established in Africa, the demand for manufactures will most rapidly augment" (II. 249). He believes that in exchange for ridding the continent of slavery, the British might reap untold wealth from resources from Africa and that native African inhabitants might "insensibly adopt the British fashions, manners, customs," and so on (II. 250). Both Sancho and Cugoano expressed similar beliefs in the merits of such trade if conducted in a responsible and ethical manner.

Equiano's acculturation to Western European society generally separated him from other enslaved comrades but still cast him in the pall of the European subject. A series of incidents that occurred after he had purchased his freedom on 11 July 1766 best illustrates this point. First, he became an aide to a slave ship's captain and thus performed the routine duties associated with colonization. Upon acquiring the job of overseer, Equiano noted that he "managed an estate, where, by those attentions, the negroes were uncommonly cheerful and healthy, and did more work by half than by the common mode of treatment they usually do" (I. 210). During a stopover in Jamaica, when asked by Doctor Irving to select slaves in order to start a plantation, Equiano boasted of having "[chosen] them all my countrymen" (II. 178).

Equiano's early exposure to literacy and Christianity bolstered his efforts to serve as missionary "interlocutor." As early as 1757, the Guerins had sought permission from Michael Henry Paschal to baptize Equiano. After being told by servants that he could not otherwise go to heaven without first being baptized, Equiano had pressed the Guerins to arrange this sacrament. Paschal first refused (possibly for fear that Equiano or others acting on his behalf might seek his freedom) but later granted permission for the baptism to take place. In February 1759, at St. Margaret's Church in Westminster, London, Equiano was finally baptized. The clergyman gave him a book written by the Bishop of Sodor and Man entitled *A Guide to the Indians*, which Equiano identified, along with the Bible, as his favorite book.

Displaying a missionary's zeal many years later, Equiano attempted moral instruction of the Miskito Indians, an indigenous group situated between Honduras and Nicaragua in Central America. Though the British never colonized the Indians (they reportedly requested protection in the hopes of warding off neighboring Spanish forces), the British operated a settlement near them in the seventeenth century.[47] Equiano wrote that in November 1775, he accompanied a British doctor to Jamaica and to the Miskito Shore where the doctor had intentions of founding a plantation. Equiano attempted to christianize a young Miskito Indian prince, and later, to quell a rebellion along the Miskito shore. In both instances, Equiano followed the instructions contained in *A Guide to the Indians*, along with another missionary manual entitled *The Conversion of an Indian*, which he had received after acquiring literacy skills and religious training.

When left to explain to a young Miskito Indian prince why the white men who abused the moral code that the prince was told to honor also held the reins of power and knowledge, Equiano uncovered some vulnerabilities in his role as mediator. The prince asked Equiano why "all the white men on board who can read and write, and observe the sun, and know all things, yet swear, lie and get drunk, only excepting yourself" (II. 176). Equiano answered that they did not fear God and would pay in hell for their sins. The prince responded that if the white sailors went to hell for their behavior, then he, too, would go to hell. The subject of God and religion had taken on racial overtones. After being ridiculed by companions who did not believe in the hereafter, and who chided him for listening to Equiano in the first place, the prince ceased further Bible studies, along with his friendship with Equiano.

Equiano might well have recalled his own similar experience with the religious double standards of which the prince spoke. At first, he notes that traders who had brought the four Miskito Indians to England for a year in order to learn English and to expedite trade between the English and the

Indians had done so for their own benefit and not for the benefit of the Indians. Further, he noted that in their lack of piety, the Indians were "not worse than their European brethren or neighbours" (II. 182). But when he discovered that the four Indians had not been baptized, nor undertaken any improvement of their morals, he pronounced them to be heathens.

This incident suggests that a neocolonial figure like Equiano must reformulate a human hierarchy where his own ascension can occur only upon the identification of, and replacement by, a new Other. For example, when a dispute later broke out between the Miskito Indians and the English party that included Equiano, he resorted to a strategy that he recalled from reading a book on the life of Columbus that detailed his use of superstition, fear, and the Bible to control the Indians whom he encountered. Equiano read from the Bible, then threatened the Indians that if they did not behave, God would "make them dead," a tactic that "succeeded beyond my most sanguine expectations" (II. 186). After quelling the rebellion, he rewarded the Indians with rum. Along the way, Irving located various sites along the Miskito shore wherein to establish a plantation, using slaves whom Equiano had selected.

Equiano reconfigures a hierarchical scale of difference and sameness that is part and parcel of the colonialist paradigmatic construction. Discrepancies are attributable to the colonialist paradigmatic function, which is so strong "that even a writer who is reluctant to acknowledge it and who may indeed be highly critical of imperialist exploitation is drawn into its vortex."[48] This may explain Equiano's occasional benevolent depiction of European enslavers in addition to his disparaging treatment of the Miskito Indians. In a colonialist paradigm, Equiano contains the narrative within a symbolic imaging of blackness that shares a structural alliance with Dampier and Swift but contests the racialist implications of the Hottentot and the Yahoo with a composite of the Ibo. He presents to the paradigmatic construction a (neo)colonial in the form of a strident capitalist, a caustic pragmatist, and an indefatigable anti-slavery activist who revitalizes textual readings with a vision of renewed clarity.

As a representation of this phenomenon, Equiano exploits the foreign-observer motif, popular in English writings, albeit as a natural consequence of the actual circumstances of his life. He is no tourist, no foreign visitor to the Western world. Equiano's function as author, like others, is "tied to the legal and institutional systems that circumscribe, determine, and articulate the realm of discourses.'"[49] And yet, as illustrated above, he is grounded in a liminal relationship, materially and discursively, within a paradigmatic colonialist construction. I noted at the beginning of this chapter that those who were impacted most by social conditions involving race and slavery later became contributors to the very literary environment that invalidated their existence in the first place. Unlike Dampier's Hottentots or Swift's Yahoos, images of blackness in Equiano's Ibos come to the reader unconventionally, penned by a black author.

To further clarify subject-object relations in a colonialist discourse, I return to my introductory examination of three ethnic models that shaped European readers' perceptions about blacks and other third-world cultural groups. Arguably, such an epistemological configuration depends upon the centrality of author, text, or reader. But it is precisely through outside intervention, via a conducive socioeconomical and political climate, that this community is shaped, whether by solidarity or disrupture. In other words, England's sociopolitical climate, perceptions about race, images of blackness, even Equiano's fractured position, determine the impact that literary and nonliterary discourse ultimately have in the social, literary, and academic environment.

In this chapter, I have explored how three compelling ethnic portraits particularly shaped European readers' perceptions about blacks and other third-world cultural groups at a time when a universalist literary, didactic language excluded race from consideration. Here, Equiano's contributions differ from those of his African-British contemporaries. Like Gronniosaw, Sancho, and Cugoano, Equiano could not automatically assume membership among that coalition of shared ideals among reader, author, and text, since he stood apart from many European readers' conception of themselves. And in like manner with them, Equiano approximates a "master narrative" that the Other is required to enact in order to achieve sameness within that discursive community. By narrative intervention, however, Equiano forces a realignment of the semantic field that enables readers to discern difference and sameness, albeit in a complex maneuver.[50]

## NOTES

1. The large readership for these accounts is discernible, in part, from the frequency of publication, the number of editions, and the size of collected volumes of travel literature. Over a hundred collections of travel accounts appeared in the eighteenth century; at least twenty-five of them were published in English. Samuel Johnson regularly published reviews of these accounts for Edward Cave (Walter Jackson Bate, *From Classic to Romantic: Premises of Taste in Eighteenth-Century England* [Cambridge, MA: Harvard University Press, 1946], 189–90). Countless additional volumes of travel literature appeared in England, including A. J. Churchill's *A Collection of Voyages and Travels* in six volumes (1732), Thomas Astley's *A New General Collection of Voyages and Travels* in four volumes (1745–47), and John Newberry's fourth edition of *The World Displayed: Or, A Curious Collection of Voyages and Travels* (1759–61), in twenty volumes.

2. See Percy G. Adams, *Travel Literature and Evolution of the Novel* (Lexington: University Press of Kentucky, 1983), 77.

3. Equiano carefully characterizes captivity in Africa as familial and humane as compared with enslavement in the West Indies, and he identifies enslavement in Africa primarily as a trade in prisoners of war: "How different was their condition from that of the slaves in the West Indies! With us they do no more work than other members of the community, than even their masters; their food, clothing, and lodging were nearly the same as theirs, (except that they were not permitted to eat with those who were free-born)." Olaudah Equiano, *The Interesting Narrative of the Life of Olaudah Equiano or Gustavus Vassa The African, 1789*, Vol. 1, Ed. Paul Edwards (London: Dawsons of Pall Mall, 1969), 26–27. (I will use the two-volume standard edition of Equiano's narrative, edited by Edwards, for all future quotations from the narrative itself; these are cited in the manuscript by page number.)

4. The shifting epistemological framework that is created by William Dampier, Swift, and Equiano hierarchizes positions of dominance that alternately favor author, reader, and/or textual subject. While Dampier and Swift attempt to form an alliance, a uniformity of ideas with their readers against an objectified Other, Equiano estranges the presumptuous reader from a position of dominance. He thus manipulates subject-object relations and semantically realigns a field that identifies author with reader against a native Other.

5. Equiano relies on Anthony Benezet's *Some Historical Account of Guinea* (1771) for geographical descriptions of Benin. But a comparison of the two texts reveals that Equiano utilizes Benezet for accuracy in the geographical placement of Benin, West Africa, but does not rely on Benezet's work for the representation of Ibo culture. See Benezet, *Some Historical Account of Guinea* (London: Frank Cass, 1968); reprint.

6. Defoe and Swift both utilized Dampier's *New Voyage*. Addison and Steele refer to Dampier in *Spectator #121* and in Sir Richard Steele's *Tatler #62*. Defoe's *Captain Singleton, Robinson Crusoe*, and numerous other works owe a debt to William Dampier's *New Voyage*.

7. Defamiliarization is, of course, a utilization of Russian formalism; it lacks the conviction of a poststructuralist analysis of the political economy of such language, however. Viktor Shklovsky writes that "the purpose of art is to impart the sensation of things as they are perceived and not as they are known. The technique of art is to make objects unfamiliar, to make forms difficult, to increase the difficulty and length of perception because the process of perception is an aesthetic end in itself and must be prolonged." See Shklovsky, "Art as Technique," in *Contemporary Literary Criticism: Modernism Through Poststructuralism*, ed., Robert Con Davis (New York: Longman, 1986), 55.

8. The argument that Swift's Yahoos uncannily resemble the Hottentots in travelogues by Dampier, Herbert, and others is not a new one. Scholars have speculated on the origin of Swift's Yahoos since the turn of this century. These speculations range from Churton Collins' belief that the Yahoos derive from the travel accounts of Sir Thomas Herbert, which Swift apparently read, to W. A. Eddy's opinion that they derive from the *Voyage of Gonzales* to Charles Firth's suggestion that the Yahoos typified the Irish. A list of books that Swift is believed to have read between

1697 and 1698 includes the *Histoire d'Aethiopie*, the *Voyage De Maroc*, and the *Voyage De Syam*, eds. A. C. Guthkelch and D. Nichol Smith. Furthermore, Swift's library, at least by 1715, contained travel accounts by Purchas, John Nieuhof, Le Blanc, Bernier, Wafer, Addison, and Dampier, and included a copy of *Voyage in South America*, 1698 (see T. P. Le Fanu, "Catalogue of Dean Swift's Library in 1715," Proceedings of the Royal Irish Academy 37 [1927]: 270–73). Swift also probably read Sir Thomas Herbert's account of the Hottentots; see R. W. Frantz, "Swift's Yahoos and the Voyagers," *Modern Philology* 29 (1931): 49–57. (See also note 28).

9. For further references on literary use of the Hottentot, see Garrick's *High Life Below Stairs: A Farce* (London: Printed for W. Cavell, 1797). 1st ed. pub. in London by J. Newberry, 1759. Though this play is officially ascribed to David Garrick, it was written by James Townley. See also Deborah A. Thomas, *Thackeray and Slavery* (Athens: Ohio University Press, 1993), 54–61. In explaining his rejection of Miss Rhoda Swartz as a marriage candidate, the protagonist, George Osborne, likens her to the Hottentot Venus. Because of her large buttocks and unusual body size and shape Sartje Bartmann was displayed in London in 1810 (see chapter 5). Furthermore, Osborne disdains Miss Swartz's "color" (she is identified as a mulatto). In spite of her wealth, George Osborne married Amelia, a woman deemed suitable for a proper English gentleman.

10. William Hallam Bonner, Dampier's biographer, writes that William Dampier's *New Voyage Round the World* and other books were viewed as the major authority "in many matters" (43). According to Bonner, some seventy years before Dampier's *New Voyage* appeared in 1697, only three collections of travel in English were notable. But some fourteen years after Dampier's work appeared, at least eight new collections of travel literature were published in London (53). "Other writers of voyages soon after Dampier . . . imitated his manner, digested his chapters, referred to him, or in other ways showed his influence upon them," Bonner adds. See William Hallam Bonner, *Captain William Dampier: Buccaneer-Author* (Stanford, CA: Stanford University Press, 1934), 38.

11. Bonner notes that Dampier wrote "the most influential [travel] books of their kind in England in the hundred years following 1631" (43). He further observes that "Dampier's Voyages are prominent among those travel works containing vivid descriptions of monkeys and primitive men in Central America, South Africa, Australia, and the East Indies who, like Swift's Yahoos, live nastily, cohabit bestially, and display no glimmer of reason, who smell foul and eat putrid flesh, who move with ape-like agility, chattering in the branches of trees and flinging down their excrement" (177). Other voyagers who wrote about the Hottentots of the Cape of Good Hope included Sir Thomas Herbert and John Ovington. Both Herbert and Ovington portray the Hottentots even more scathingly than does Dampier. Swift very likely knew all three texts; see note 5. See Herbert, "A Description of the Cape of Good Hope," in *A Relation of Some Yeares Travaile* (London: Printed by William Stansby and Jacob Bloome, 1634) and Ovington, *A Voyage to Surat in the Year 1689*, ed., H. G. Rawlinson (London: Oxford University Press, 1929).

12. Though scholars may disagree about the degree of actual power being wielded through the construction of any given colonial discourse, the dangers of denying

or minimizing conflict because its manifestations are unpleasant or discomforting are inestimable. See Abdul JanMohamed, "The Economy of Manichean Allegory: The Function of Racial Difference in Colonialist Literature," *Critical Inquiry* 12 (1985): 60. Mohamed complains that Homi Bhabha makes that very omission when he "[circumvents] entirely the dense history of the material conflict between Europeans and natives" and treats "colonial discourse as if it existed in a vacuum." Bhabha argues that "the point of intervention should shift from the identification of images as positive or negative, to an understanding of the processes of subjectification made possible (and plausible) through stereotypical discourse" (Bhabha, ed., *Nation and Narration* [London: Routledge, 1990], 18). Bhabha's formulation creates a way around the pitting of disparate powers between colonizer and colonized in a perpetual vise grip that reenforces the very inequities that it seeks to undo. But Bhabha's quest to transgress the spatial limitations of a stereotypical Otherness forces a recognition of ambivalences inherent in power relations—especially when that relationship has a fictive base.

13. William Dampier, *A New Voyage Round the World* (London: Printed for James Knapton, 1697), 342.

14. See Johannes Fabian, *Time and the Other: How Anthropology Makes Its Object* (New York: Columbia University Press, 1983).

15. See Mary Louise Pratt, "Scratches on the Face of the Country," in *"Race," Writing, and Difference*, ed. Henry Louis Gates, Jr. (Chicago: University of Chicago Press, 1986), 140. See also Pratt, *Imperial Eyes: Travel Writing and Transculturation* (London: Routledge, 1992).

16. William Smith, *A New Voyage to Guinea* (London: John Nourse, 1744), 142–43; also quoted in M. Van Wyk Smith, "The Most Wretched of the Human Race": The Iconography of the Khoikhoin (Hottentots), 1500–1800," *History and Anthropology* 5 (1992): 287.

17. Images of Africa grew more intimate in these accounts. Francis Moore (*Travels into the Inland Parts of Africa* [London: Printed by Edward Cave at St. John's Gate, 1738]) sought to systematize the slave trade; to remove interlopers and small-time profiteers; and to keep the trade in the hands of large companies such as the Royal African Company. Michael Adanson (*A Voyage to Senegal*, 1759) opposed removing Africans from their homelands for enslavement purposes but still viewed them as illiterate and inferior. Travel historian Anthony Benezet (*Some Historical Account of Guinea*, 1771) opposed slavery and actually challenged previous assumptions about cultural relativism and innate inferiority in Africans. Perhaps with the exception of Benezet, these works achieved two significant objectives: they portrayed intimate, detailed examples of life in African nations, and they exposed riveting and disturbing practices in the trading of slaves; they seldom, however, opposed the practice outright.

18. Lennard J. Davis, *Resisting Novels: Ideology and Fiction* (New York: Methuen, 1987), 73.

19. Mary Prince, *The History of Mary Prince, a West Indian Slave, Related by Herself*, ed. Moira Ferguson (Ann Arbor: The University of Michigan Press, 1993), 83.

20. Defoe's sources for *Robinson Crusoe* include William Dampier (*New Voyage Round the World*) and Woodes Rogers (*The Cruising Voyage Round the World*, 1712), and Steele drew upon Richard Ligon (*True and Exact History of the Island of Barbados*, 1657) for the Inkle and Yarico story. Scholars disagree on whether or not Aphra Behn drew upon her own experience in Surinam or whether she uses George Warren's *Histoire Generale des Antilles* (1667), as sources for *Oroonoko*; see Adams for a bibliographical citing of these sources.

21. Numerous writers have also discussed the European like physiognomy of Oroonoko, Robinson Crusoe, and Yarico as characters and have acknowledged the premium placed on their adaptability to Eurocentric cultural standards. For example, see Peter Hulme, *Colonial Encounters: Europe and the Native Caribbean, 1492–1797* (London: Routledge, 1986).

Aphra Behn's *Oroonoko: or, The Royal Slave* (1688), later adapted for the theater by Thomas Southerne in 1696, is one of the earliest English literary works to feature a leading black character. See Aphra Behn, *Oroonoko, or The Royal Slave*, ed. Montague Summers (New York: Blom, 1916). Oroonoko's appropriation to Eurocentric standards, partly by virtue of his classic heroism, fluency in English and Spanish, and European like physiognomy, have all been well documented. Behn writes that Oroonoko's "nose was rising and Roman, instead of African and flat," and his mouth was finely shaped; "far from those great turn'd Lips, which are so natural to the rest of the Negroes" (136). These physical distinctions anticipate Kant, Francis Hutcheson, and others later in the century who hierarchize physical appearance by applying culturally relativist techniques. Oroonoko trades slaves in the narrative and plans to present Imoinda (his betrothed) with slaves whom he had captured in battle. Later, when he himself is enslaved, Oroonoko offers an exchange of gold or slaves in return for the couple's freedom (174). The lower ranks find whites who behave barbarously; and, of course, enslaved blacks, especially the cast-off mistress in *Oroonoko*, who loses her favored status because of advanced age.

Defoe displaces force and economic materialism as visible controlling mechanisms and substitutes more subtle, ideological mechanisms of control as a civilizing force. Crusoe names Friday and instructs him to call him "Master." Friday's goodness, then, is a testament to European benevolence. See Daniel Defoe, *Robinson Crusoe*, ed. Michael Shinagel (New York: Norton, 1975). See Paula Backsheider, *Daniel Defoe: His Life* (Baltimore, MD: Johns Hopkins University Press, 1989). Defoe denounced slave traders, yet he defended slavery as an economic advantage to Britain's general commerce. See Defoe's *Reformation of Manners, a Satire* (N.p.: 1702), 17; and *A Brief Account of the Present State of the African Trade* (London, 1713), 55.

22. Readers of the the *Tatler*, the *Spectator*, and other eighteenth-century periodicals, most of whom seldom ventured far from their homes, clearly delighted in reading popular accounts of remote and exotic places like Africa and Asia, collectively known as travel literature. This "armchair spectator," or passive reader, readily absorbed whatever information Addison's and Steele's periodical essays delivered. Addison and Steele's *Spectator* community formulation, didactic credo, and affinity for exoticism as overarching tropes are useful here to explore how images of blackness uniformly converge as representations of Otherness in popular culture

as well as canonical contexts. The *Spectator* community, in other words, epitomizes a phenomenological process that frames my analysis of a colonialist discourse in Dampier, Swift, and Equiano. Addison and Steele's agenda in *Spectator* #409, "to banish vice and ignorance out of the territories of Great Britain [and] to establish . . . a taste of polite writings," authorizes a uniformity of ideas among readers. As eidolon, Mr. Spectator formulates an intellectual framework replete with language, stories, and a community of readers by which to achieve this task.

23. Richard Ligon, who wrote the original version of "Inkle and Yarico," also features an enslaved Indian woman who is betrayed by her European lover. Ligon's brief story concludes that "Yarico for her love, lost her liberty." See Richard Ligon, "Inkle and Yarico," in *A True and Exact History of the Island of Barbados* (London: n.p., 1657). Like other short fiction in the *Spectator*, Steele utilizes "Inkle and Yarico" in order to shape readers' moral, philosophical, and ethical standards in literature and in social practice. Steele's version is a story-within-a-story that moralizes on the constancy of women versus the inconstancy of men. Mr. Spectator listens as a woman, Arietta, tells the story. Arietta tells the story in order to counter one (told to her by a man) that illustrated the inconstancy of women. The end of the story-within-a-story told to Mr. Spectator prompted this response: "I was so touch'd with this story . . . that I left the Room with Tears in my Eyes which I'm sure Arietta admired far more than she would any complements I might have paid her." With all the scaffolding in the story-within-a-story framework, the dehumanization of slavery and its accompanying greed threaten to get lost in the mire. To complicate matters (and motives), Steele owned a plantation in the West Indies, where the story is set. In typical fashion, Mr. Spectator allows overwhelming sentimentality to cover for his failure to express a verbal position on the story's tragic overtones. Though several *Spectator* tales depict Indian and African slaves sympathetically (*Spectator* #11, #80, #215), none attacked slavery outright as practice or institution. See Sir Richard Steele, "Spectator #11" in Jospeh Addison and Sir Richard Steele, *The Spectator*, ed. Donald F. Bond, vol. 1 of 5 (Oxford: Clarendon Press, 1965), 47–51. For an excellent, critical discussion of "Inkle and Yarico," see Hulme, *Colonial Encounters*. See also Darnell Davis, *The Spectator's Essays Relating to the West Indies* (Demerara, British Guiana, 1885).

24. Wylie Sypher, *Guinea's Captive Kings: British Anti-Slavery Literature of the XVIIIth Century* (Chapel Hill: University of North Carolina Press, 1942), 31. Sir Richard Steele's "Inkle and Yarico" enjoyed a popularity among readers that never came to Richard Ligon. Steele's version stirred a sensation and led to a flood of spin-offs in poetry and drama that lasted well into the nineteenth century in both England and on the Continent. Lawrence M. Price catalogues some forty-five versions of the popular narrative in the *Inkle and Yarico Album* (Berkeley: 1937). A brief list of titles includes the following:

- "Yarico to Inkle. An Epistle" (1736), a sixteen-page Epistle.
- "The Story of Inkle and Yarrico" (1738), written by a countess. Ambiguous references to Yarrico as a Negro virgin in some stanzas and as an Indian maid in others.
- "Yarico to Inkle, An Epistle" (1766), written by Edward Jerningham, who features Yarico as a Nubian maid.

• 1742, one of three dramatic versions of Yarico, printed by Mrs. Weddell who gives the work an anti-slavery theme.

• "Inkle and Yarico" (1787), written by George Colman.

These do not include the various French and other foreign-language adaptations of Inkle and Yarico. Interestingly, the 1738 version of the story, entitled "Zamore et Mirza, ou l'heureux Naufrage," was amended in 1786 by Olympe de Gouges. The new version, entitled "L'Esclavage des noirs, ou l'heureux Naufrage," features Negro protagonists.

25. As Vincent Carretta notes in *Olaudah Equiano: The Interesting Narrative*, Equiano's flattering portrait of the Ibos was not necessarily supported in other published accounts. For example, James Grainger wrote that the *Ibbos* or *Ebboes* "make good slaves when bought young; but are, in general, foul feeders, many of them greedily devouring the raw guts of fowls" (*The Sugar-Cane. A Poem London*, 1764, 2: 75; quoted in Caretta, 243). Bryan Edwards observes, "'All the Negroes imported from these vast and unexplored regions [the Blight of Benin] . . . are called in the West Indies Eboes; and in general they appear to be the lowest and most wretched of all the nations of Africa'" (quoted in Carretta, 243). Contrary to Equiano's assertion of hardiness among the Ibos, Edwards writes that their "timidity," and "despondency of mind" make them objectionable as slaves (Caretta, 245; See also Bryan Edwards, *The History, Civil and Commercial, of the British Colonies in the West Indies*, vol. 2 of 2 [London, 1793], 69–71).

26. See Homi Bhabha, "The Other Question: Homi Bhabha Reconsiders the Stereotype and Colonial Discourse," *Screen* 24 (1983): 18.

27. James Boswell, *Life of Johnson* (Oxford: Oxford University Press, 1980), 1304. In an essay, *Taxation No Tyranny*, Samuel Johnson proclaimed his opposition to slavery, particularly as practiced in the American colonies; he charged enslavers there with hypocrisy for seeking independence from Britain while practicing slavery.

28. In this context, Dennis Todd, like numerous critics, cites Swift's ingenious satirical twist on sameness and difference in the portrayal of the Yahoos as potentially disconcerting but nonetheless instructional for the reader:

> Brought face to face with the monstrous, the viewer would see in it a grotesque likeness that would reveal uncomfortable but salutary truths about the self. The falsity of our quotidian identities would be revealed, and a a more disfigured but truer shape of the self—its identity with the monster—would be made manifest (260).

Dennis Todd traces the Yahoo to the Wild Monstrous Hairy Man exhibited in London in 1710. Although he does not identify the Monstrous Hairy Man's ethnic origins, evidence shows that Hottentots were removed from their habitats and displayed as exotica throughout Europe. Todd speculates that local London could have been the source of numerous spectacles, exotic menagerie, curiosities that Gulliver beheld in his travels, culminating with the Hairy Man, who spoke imperfect High Dutch, lacked education, and dined on "Roots, Herbs and fruit, very greedily, and also Raw flesh" (247). But Todd's Hairy Man does not account for the particularly striking portrait of the female Yahoo whose sexual aggression toward Gulliver mimics contemporary non-fictional renderings of black female sexual behavior. Interestingly enough, Dennis Todd's Hairy Man theory lacks the efficacy of a compelling ethnic model, and Laura Brown's view requires the full narrative context that Todd provides for Swift's treatment of the Other. I have already explained the importance of moving beyond mere representation or recovery of Otherness in colonialist discourse and examining its full capacities for knowledge and power. I contend that the Swiftian Yahoo is that fictional representation of the African that corresponds to the so-called nonfictional representation in explorational literature. See Dennis Todd, "The Hairy Maid at the Harpsichord: Some Speculations on the Meaning of *Gulliver's Travels*," *Texas Studies in Literature and Language* (Summer, 1992): 239-283.

29. Jonathan Swift, *Gulliver's Travels*, ed. Herbert Davis (New York: Oxford University Press, 1977); reprinted from *Prose Works of Jonathan Swift*, ed. Herbert Davis (London: Basil Blackwell, 1939-68). All subsequent references made to *Gulliver's Travels* will be taken from this text and cited in the manuscript by page number.

30. See Laura Brown, "Reading Race and Gender: Jonathan Swift," in *Eighteenth-Century Studies* 23 (Summer 1990): 425-443. Thomas Jefferson claimed that the orangutan preferred black women "over those of his own species" (see Thomas Jefferson, "Laws," in *Notes on the State of Virginia*, ed. William Peden (London: 1787. Reprint. Chapel Hill: University of North Carolina Press, 1955), 149.

31. Herbert, 17.

32. In *Gulliver's Travels*, Book 1, the Lilliputians thought that Gulliver's loud, ticking watch was the God that he worshipped since he hardly did anything without first consulting it. Expressing the foreign observer's innocence in similar fashion, Equiano described seeing a watch for the first time while in Virginia: "The first object that engaged my attention was a watch, which hung on the chimney, and was going. I was quite surprised at the noise it made, and was afraid it would tell the gentleman anything I might do amiss" (39). Later, upon first seeing a framed portrait of someone hanging on a wall, Equiano was certain that the Europeans had found some unique way to preserve their dead.

33. Albert Memmi (*The Colonizer and the Colonized*, trans. Howard Greenfield [New York: Orion Press, 1965]) and Frantz Fanon (*Black Skin/White Masks*, trans. Charles Lam Markmann [New York: Grove Weidenfeld, 1967]) are useful here in dissecting the psychological complexities of relations between a dominant culture and an objectified Other who is codified in opposition to that culture. Swift's vision of the Yahoos is not a singular or original portrait, but rather a composite and representative one where the African is concerned. I am not arguing that Swift set out in any conscious way to portray the African through the Yahoo. It is also important to note that while the composite is Swift's, the descriptive assessment of the Yahoos belongs to Gulliver as character. Swift's portrait of human nature, or at least of the individual's moral character at its worst, shares striking affinities with consistent representations of blacks in earlier examples of English fiction. As I have said, it is essential in analyzing a colonialist discourse to establish the currency of its representation of Otherness and to assess its manifestations in established literature.

34. See Clement Hawes, 189.

35. See David Dabydeen, *Hogarth's Blacks: Images of Blacks in Eighteenth Century English Art* (Athens, GA: University of Georgia Press, 1987). The phrase "worse than Negro Barbarity" was used by African-British author Ignatius Sancho

in letter 134 (6 June 1780) to describe whites' behavior during the Gordon Riots. See Ignatius Sancho, *Letters of the Late Ignatius Sancho*, ed. Paul Edwards and Polly Rewt (Edinburgh: Edinburgh University Press, 1994), 230.

36. Dabydeen, *Hogarth's Blacks*, 9. Hogarth's paintings and additional evidence support the notion that numerous blacks were domestic servants though they were not free to leave their "employers" (Dabydeen, 22–37). See also Ronald Paulson, *Hogarth's Graphic Works*, vol. 1 of 2. (New Haven, CT: Yale University Press, 1965), 25.

37. I am reminded here of Chinua Achebe's interpretation of Joseph Conrad's *Heart of Darkness*. Achebe contends that Western psychology sets up Africa "as a foil to Europe, as a place of negations at once remote and vaguely familiar, in comparison with which Europe's own state of spiritual grace will be manifest" ("An Image of Africa: Racism in Conrad's *Heart of Darkness*," *Hopes and Impediments: Selected Essays* [New York: Doubleday, 1989]), 3. Ardent literati see Conrad's use of Africa as a microcosmic function of psychological disintegration (for Kurtz as character) or of Europe's civilizing mission in third-world countries. Achebe writes that "*Heart of Darkness* projects the image of Africa as 'the other world,' the antithesis of Europe and therefore of civilization, a place where man's vaunted intelligence and refinement are finally mocked by triumphant bestiality" (3).

I find Achebe's complaint a valid one. Conrad's anti-imperialist sympathies notwithstanding, Achebe detests the consistency of Africa's representation as negative in the face of the potential moral evolution of Europe and/or Europeans. Having made a necessary, critical point about the dangers of "mere" representations, Achebe leaves to others the task of sifting through the cultural, psychological, and literary complexities of Joseph Conrad's paradoxical imperialist/anti-imperialist stance in *Heart of Darkness*. It is through this opening that Edward Said attempts to address Bhabha's challenge to break through the bind of reinforcing negative stereotypes simply by calling attention to their existence. Said writes that Conrad's narrative, like imperialism, monopolizes "the entire system of representation," which should then give the perceptive reader the opportunity to study the mechanisms of such monopolies (25). Said, who does not find Conrad's position paradoxical, further writes that from the ironically posed distance of an unacculturated Englishman, Conrad analogizes empire building with the narrative process. Conrad's stance, along with the work's multiple readings of a politicized, imperialist Africa, metaphorizes the interrelatedness of cultural narrative (67). Similarly, in spite of his depiction of the Yahoos, Swift's Anglo-Irish lineage and condemnations of Britain's treatment of the Irish problematize any singular conception of his imperialist leanings and expose complexities in European representations of Otherness similar to those frequently pointed out in Conrad's novel. But the perceptive reader in Said's (or any) equation is an essential, though ironic fixture, especially since colonialist readings like Achebe on *Heart of Darkness* and those linking *Gulliver's Travels* to Britain's slave history have only recently emerged.

38. See Edward W. Said, *The World, The Text, and The Critic* (Cambridge, MA: Harvard University Press, 1983). See also Fanon, *The Wretched of the Earth*, trans. Constance Farrington (New York: Grove Press, 1964), 31–32.

39. "But, I had another Reason which made me less forward to enlarge his Majesty's Dominions by my Discoveries: To say the Truth, I had conceived a few Scruples with relation to the distributive Justice of Princes upon those Occasions. For Instance, A Crew of Pyrates are driven by a Storm they know not whither; at length a Boy discovers Land from the Top-mast; they go on Shore to rob and plunder; they see an harmless People, are entertained with Kindness, they give the Country a new Name, they take formal Possession of it for the King, they set up a rotton Plank or a Stone for a memorial, they murder two or three dozen of the Natives, bring away a Couple more by Force for a Sample, return home, and get their Pardon. Here commences a new Dominion acquired with a Title by *Divine Right*. Ships are sent with the first Opportunity; the Natives driven out or destroyed, their Princes tortured to discover their Gold; a free Licence given to all Acts of Inhumanity and Lust; the Earth reeking with the Blood of its Inhabitants: And this execrable Crew of Butchers employed in so pious an Expedition, is a modern Colony sent to convert and civilize an idolatrous and barbarous People" (297–98).

40. Subramanian Shankar, "Colonialism, *Gulliver's Travels* and the Deconstruction of the Colonial Travel Narrative as a Genre" in "From Hearts of Darkness to Temples of Doom: The Discursive Economy of the Travel Narrative in the Colonial Context," Ph.D. diss. (University of Texas-Austin, 1993), 25. Shankar's work specifically critiques the colonial travel narrative as genre "that mediates between representations of the colonizer and the colonized through certain narrative strategies" (abstract). Shankar reads *Gulliver's Travels* as a "difference-in-sameness" text that purports to critique "real" travel narratives. As such, it metaphorizes British colonialism and other European nations under a rubric of divine right. For Shankar, it is "in the irony of this dislocation of the travel narrative, which typically participates in the economy of colonialism and insists on its legitimacy, [that] the violence of the colonial traveller (and colonial travel narrative as a genre) in particular and colonialism in general stands revealed" (25).

41. Homi K. Bhabha, "Of Mimicry and Man: The Ambivalence of Colonial Discourse," in *The Location of Culture*, ed., Bhabha (London: Routledge, 1994), 89.

42. In *Imperial Eyes: Travel Writing and Transculturation*, Pratt locates the imperial gaze in the contact zone, where the colonizer writes a geopolitical text onto the body and landscape of the colonized, as I have already noted. Michel Foucault sets it, controversially, in the panopticon, where even the knowledge of a trained surveillance is supposed to elicit desired behavior—a kind of self-policing—from those who are being monitored. Fanon historicizes it in a colonialist paradigm in specific power relations between whites and blacks, or a dominant subject and an objectified Other. (Foucault, of course, uses the architectural model of the penitentiary, whose interiors are visible from all angles to the guards in the tower). All identify the potential room for maneuver amid pockets of resistance to the powers of surveillance, though Foucault neglects to account for the specific nature of such resistance. See Michel Foucault, *Discipline & Punish: The Birth of the Prison*, trans. from the French by Alan Sheridan (New York: Vintage Books, 1979).

43. A colonialist discourse requires an Other to validate its own raison d'etre by fostering onto it assimilative strategies or imitative behaviors. The reformed, recognizable Other is what Bhabha sees as the "subject of a difference" that is

"almost the same but not quite" or, as he also phrases it, *"almost the same but not white."* The discourse of the Other is articulated through the very reform process that seeks to discipline it. See Bhabha, "Of Mimicry and Man," 89.

44. See Paul Edwards, Introduction, *The Life of Olaudah Equiano*, ed. Paul Edwards (London: Longman, 1988), 28.

45. Ibid., 18. In spite of being sold by Paschal and Doran, who had initially promised Equiano freedom, he praised them for their kindness and for complimenting his "good character" to the next buyers. Years later, Equiano expressed a strong desire to visit Paschal in England, writing that "I still loved him, notwithstanding his usage of me, and I pleased myself with thinking of what he would say when he saw what the Lord had done for me in so short a time, instead of being, as he might perhaps suppose, under the cruel yoke of some planter" (102).

46. See Houston Baker, who provides one of the earliest (and most capable) marxist readings to Equiano's narrative in *Blues, Ideology, and Afro-American Literature: A Vernacular Theory* (Chicago: University of Chicago Press, 1984), 33.

47. See Edwards's introduction, Equiano, *The Life of Olaudah Equiano*, vii–xxxviii.

48. JanMohamed, 63.

49. Ibid.

50. Robert Scholes, "Language, Narrative, and Anti-Narrative," in *On Narrative*, ed. W.J.T. Mitchell (Chicago: University of Chicago Press, 1981), 203. As Scholes writes, "the laws of the perception process bind together reader and author by a semantic field of potential meanings which is partly governed by a social code and partly individualized by the unique features of whoever utters or interprets the word" (203).

# Reading *The History of Mary Prince*: The Politics of Race and Gender

Slave narratives written or related by black women—unlike those of their male counterparts—did not appear in print until sixty years after the work of Ukawsaw Gronniosaw and forty years after the narrative of Olaudah Equiano were published. This is in part due to the double prejudice of race and gender endured by black women. The sponsorship of stories that often included revelations of sexual abuse toward enslaved females, as well as perceptions about black women as being immoral and sexually promiscuous, was a delicate issue.[1] While male writers such as Ukawsaw Gronniosaw, Ignatius Sancho, Ottobah Cugoano, and Olaudah Equiano expose inconsistencies in the treatment of enslaved blacks in ecclesiastical, legal, and literary discourse, as well as in social practice, Mary Prince, in *The History of Mary Prince* (1831), is an outsider in at least two dimensions. She uniquely demonstrates how black and white women in the eighteenth century are differently marginalized along both racial and gender lines. The intersections of race and gender in black and white female relations in that period are underrepresented in contemporary scholarship.[2]

The separation of these two issues—race and gender—made them conflict in different ways. Further, these two paradigms tended to intersect in odd ways. In this chapter, I focus on difference as well as sameness in the subordination of women, based on the defining parameter of race. I particularly explore how Prince's personal and artistic identity as a formerly enslaved black woman who broke into a traditionally male literary environment, is informed by consideration of the effects of race and gender. The literary value of Prince's work has precipitated a reexamination of outmoded assumptions and a textual recovery that now confront, rather than silence or bracket, discomforting perspectives on race, gender, and slavery.[3]

The politicization of race and reason in the eighteenth century necessarily engages the complex, mutually inclusive issues of race and gender in black and white female relations. While merely exploiting issues about black and white female subordination would be akin to battling for space among the assigned lower regions on the Chain of Being, there are significant differences in perceptions about gender that cluster around the boundaries of race. The scientific community that proclaimed the racial inferiority of blacks to whites in some eighteenth-century studies later focused more exclusively on the alleged inferiority of women to men. For example, Galenic theories that the female body was an imperfect version of the male body—claiming the physical inversion of sexual organs—gave way to claims that males and females were indeed distinct beings.[4] Both viewpoints, however, supported the hierarchical arrangement of men and women in a system of classification. These gender-based studies proliferated particularly in the nineteenth century.[5]

The story of Prince's enslavement came to be made public when she crossed paths with Thomas Pringle, secretary of the Anti-Slavery Society. While living in the Pringle household, Prince met Susannah Strickland, an English abolitionist, who transcribed the narrative before Pringle published it in 1831. Though Prince told her story in order to expose slavery as inhumane, the narrative required the authenticating hands of both Strickland and Pringle in order to bring about its publication—not just as ghostwriter and editor, respectively—but also as whites whose word counted for more and could verify Prince's account. In an attempt to encourage the impression of authenticity, Thomas Pringle poignantly reminds readers, through editorial notes in the preface and throughout the text, that the "strong expressions, and all of a similar character in this little narrative, are given verbatim as uttered by Mary Prince" to Susannah Strickland, who then allegedly entered the words "verbatim" in the narrative (54). In addition to the task of formulating a credible self-presentation and creating an acceptable feminine persona, Prince also had to transcend those liminalities imposed on the narrative's ghostwritten form, one steeped in orality but documented by another's hand.

Before she could tell her story to a credible English readership, that is, Prince first had to prove herself morally worthy as a woman and as an individual. Furthermore, in order for the narrative to be effective as an anti-slavery document, she had to engender sympathy for her inability to participate in the cult of womanhood. Ironically, Prince's compromised abilities to maintain sexual and reproductive control of her own body as a formerly enslaved woman disqualified her in others' eyes from moral consideration as a worthy witness to the horrors of slavery that she was forced to endure. Consequently she has been marginalized by some scholars in the literary establishment, and her narrative has been subjected to certain exclusionary canonical practices.

Prince's story is certainly poignant. Born around 1788, at Brackish-Pond, Devonshire parish, in Bermuda, which was then colonized by Britain, Prince was first enslaved, along with her mother, by the Darrell family. Prince was enslaved from birth. Her parents, though enslaved nearby, were virtually powerless to intercede for their daughter, who suffered numerous cruelties associated with slavery. Captain Richard Darrel had purchased Prince as a slave for his young granddaughter, Betsy Williams. Prince called the years she spent with Williams the happiest of her life, though she added that she was too young to understand her condition as a slave at that time. While in the Williams household, Prince remained under the care of her own mother, and her father was enslaved nearby as a sawyer to Mr. Trimmingham, a shipbuilder at Crow-Lane. Though Prince's parents had no legal authority over her, their geographic proximity surely provided some psychological if not physical stability for Prince. At around the age of twelve, she was sold, along with two sisters, to an enslaver from Spanish Point whom she identified only as Captain I. After five years, she was sold to "Mr. D" at Turk's Island, where she labored in the salt ponds. Prince's final purchaser was John Wood, who took her to Antigua. In December 1826, while enslaved to the Wood family, Prince married a free black carpenter, Daniel James. When the Woods went to England to put their son in school, they took Prince with them. While in England, Prince sought asylum with Moravian church missionaries who brought Prince before Thomas Pringle, a Methodist secretary for the British Anti-Slavery Society, in November 1828.[6]

Because of the publicity generated by Prince's story, the couple who had enslaved her, Mr. and Mrs. Woods, brought charges against the Anti-Slavery Society, Pringle, and Prince for libel and defamation of character. Ironically, the couple denied the accuracy of the publication, while at the same time they blamed Prince's "tart tongue" for abuses that they did admit to having inflicted upon her. The same voice that catalogued those abuses in a published work was forbidden by law to give court testimony in order to fend off the couple's charges of libel, though she could speak through her narrative. Hence, Prince's articulation of voice, presence, and experience in the narrative thus produced for her a measure of empowerment.

Early in the narrative, Prince forges a nationalist coalition composed of slaves and unsuspecting English readers, whom she then pits against enslavers in the West Indies. In addition, she chronicles events that are unique to her experiences as a black woman who was enslaved in the West Indies. Finally, she articulates words and expressions that specifically connote a Caribbean cultural environment, thus setting her story apart from slave narratives and other autobiographical accounts. In making pointed references to the heart when describing slave auctions,[7] Prince emphasizes humanity in the slave and distinctly points out its absence in the enslaver, an important step in building a coalition with "the good people in England" (64). For example, describing the scene at auction when her mother witnesses the selling of her three daughters, Prince observes that only God knows "the thoughts of a slave's heart" (3). Not only does Prince's "immorality equation" include the enslaver, but it also includes hard-hearted bystanders as well. She attributes this show of indifference for her mother's grief to proslavery sympathizers who surround the slave auction block where the Prince sisters are sold. "Did one of the many bystanders, who were looking at us so carelessly, think of the pain that wrung the hearts of the negro woman and her young ones?" she asks. "No, no! Oh those white people have small hearts who can only feel for themselves" (52).

Verification for these procedures was provided by Thomas Pringle, Prince's abolitionist editor. Pringle published a letter from an acquaintance who had witnessed a slave auction at the Cape of Good Hope that bore striking similarities to Prince's own description, emphasizing the different responses of slave versus bystander to the separation of families.[8] The letter notes that the grief and anguish of the mother who watched her children being sold away "contrasted with the marked insensibility and jocular countenances of the spectators and purchasers, [and] furnished a striking commentary on the miseries of slavery, and its debasing effects upon the hearts of its abettors" (52).

Upon arrival at Spanish Point, where Prince was taken after being sold in Antigua, she compared the hearts of the new enslavers, Captain and Mrs. I, with the stones and timber used to construct some homes in that part of the Caribbean. "The stones and the timber were the best things in it; they were not so hard as the hearts of the owners," she observes (54). Again, Pringle claims that these words were spoken, verbatim, by Prince to her amanuensis. As I discussed in chapter 3, the liberal use of sentimentality in the narrative is a well-established formulaic convention of eighteenth- and nineteenth-century slave narratives, but Prince subverts its use in Western, European form in order to foster anti-slavery sentiment.[9] The so-called sentimental literary tradition in eighteenth-century England has long been recognized as a transition between neoclassicism and romanticism, though more current studies point out artificialities in such chronological constructions. The artificiality is traceable to rigid dating patterns for such trends, however.

Perhaps the most horrendous portrait of Prince's enslavement in a Caribbean environment is her description of her labors in the salt ponds on Turk's Island. Salt was not only a substance that was mined by the slaves, but its bitter properties also metaphorize the suffering that Prince and others endured. Upon arriving on Turk's Island where she is sold to Mr. D for £100 currency, she carefully points out that he is paid a certain sum for every slave who works for him from profits made from the salt mines. First, Prince describes the emotional pain of being sold away from her family in bitter salt tears: "Oh, the trials! the trials! they make the salt water come into my eyes when I think of the days in which I was afflicted—the times that are gone; when I mourned and grieved with a young heart for those whom I loved" (54). She goes on to describe the painful marks of physical suffering. Those long hours standing in the salt water created huge boils, especially on the feet and legs, that ate "to the very bone, afflicting the sufferers with great torment" (62). Finally, the salt—that selfsame substance which helped to bring about these ills—is given to the workers as a medicinal for healing, so that they might be well enough to return to the mines and begin the process anew. Prince writes, "When we were ill, let our complaint be what it might, the only medicine given to us was a great bowl of hot salt water, with salt mixed with it, which made us very sick" (63).

Prince appeals to Britain's moralistic and legalistic sense of its nationalist identity, particularly as a purported slave-free land: "Oh that Turk's Island was a horrible place! The people in England, I am sure, have never found out what is carried on there. Cruel, horrible place!"[10] Her references to an English readership connect her with a moral hegemony and an English nationalism.[11] For example, she connects an abject materiality with those who own and sell human beings for economic profit; and she abjures any associations between feelings and profit. But by contrast, Prince and other fellow slaves, profitless individuals who cannot share in the economic gains of slavery demonstrate richly rewarding feelings in a collective and responsive grief over being separated from one another:

> They were not all bad, I dare say, but slavery hardens white people's hearts towards the blacks; and many of them were not slow to make their remarks upon us aloud, without regard to our grief—tho their light words fell like cayenne on the fresh wounds of our hearts (52).

Believing that few people in England knew what went on in the West Indies slave trade, Prince informed them in this manner: "I have felt what a slave feels, and I know what a slave knows; and I would have all the good people in England to know it too, that they may break our chains, and set us free" (64). Her personal story is revealed here for the benefit of others: "Oh the horrors of slavery!—How the thought of it pains my heart! But the truth ought to be told of it; and what my eyes have seen I think it is my duty to relate; for few people in England know what slavery is" (64). She goes on to conclude: "I tell [my story] to let English people know the truth; and I hope they will never leave off to pray God, and call loud to the great King of England, till all the poor blacks be given free, and slavery done up for evermore" (84).

Prince in her narrative mirrors Gronniosaw in his account, believing that all of the inhabitants of England were Christians who would never tolerate slavery and other abuses if only they knew of them. Like Gronniosaw, Prince was certain that English citizens were free of such malice and merely ignorant and uninformed about the atrocities committed against slaves in the West Indies. These beliefs probably stemmed from claims that slavery did not exist on English soil, and there was some justification for her view. Just a few years away from Parliament's outlawing of slavery and more than fifty years after the Mansfield Decision of 1772, Prince had little difficulty obtaining asylum in England after being turned out of doors by the Woods. But for slaves, freedom or rescue from slavery on English soil was not necessarily an automatic occurrence, and even a few years before 1834, asylum for slaves was not always possible.

Both Prince and her counterpart Gronniosaw may have been aware of the popular boasts of John Rushworth and William Cowper. Rushworth records a 1569 judicial decision that declared English air "too pure . . . for slaves to breathe in."[12] William Cowper echoes Rushworth's sentiments in "The Task": "Slaves cannot breathe in England; if their lungs Receive our air that moment they are free" (II. 40–41).[13] Writers and judicial officials could easily vent such rhetoric regarding domestic slavery without disturbing profitable West Indian and North American slave colonies that filled planters' coffers.

In relating the barbarities of slavery, Prince excludes from Britons' nationalist coalition those West Indian enslavers and overseers whom she refers to as "Buckras" and whom she depicts as calloused, immoral supporters of slavery. Prince sees this group as collective misfits whose verbal and physical abusiveness to slaves is offensive to England as a nation. For example, on more than one occasion, Prince says that after she had displeased her enslavers, they abused her with words that were so vile that they could not be spoken in England. When an earthen jar, already cracked along its center, broke completely while Prince attempted to empty it, Captain I abused her with words "too, too bad to speak in England" (58). She thus appeals particularly to English readers with whom she clearly seeks a moral alliance, recognizing fully the supportive strength of the anti-slavery climate in Britain at this time.

Unlike her black male counterparts, however, Prince had to prove her sexual purity as an added requirement in promoting a valid public self.[14] While Gronniosaw, Cugoano, Sancho, and Equiano wrote very little about enslaved black females in their accounts, both Cugoano and Equiano witnessed abuse against them, especially during the Middle Passage. Cugoano wrote that before leaving the Gold Coast, he and several enslaved comrades hatched a plan to burn the slave ship and to perish in the flames rather than live as slaves. "But we were betrayed by one of our own countrywomen, who slept with some of the head men of the ship, for it was common for the dirty filthy sailors to take the African women and lie upon their bodies," he observed (10). Equiano reported hearing the screams of very young girls who were sexually abused during the passage to the West Indies. When in Virginia, Equiano witnessed a black female slave "cruelly loaded with various kinds of iron machines; she had one particularly on her head, which locked her mouth so fast that she could scarcely speak, and could not eat nor drink" (I. 91). The iron muzzle was designed to prevent the woman from eating the food that she was required to cook. And in one instance, Equiano also commented on the double standard in punishment for black males who slept with white female prostitutes as opposed to white men who went unpunished for sexually abusing black women.

In relating her story, Prince widened the moral chasm between herself and the West Indian enslavers who exercised sexual control over slaves by detailing the sadistic, albeit sexually implicit, nature of beatings that she received from enslavers. Still, ever mindful of the need to present a credible public self that complied with abolitionists' dictates or with those of the amanuensis, Prince carefully encodes the language of sexual abuse amid other forms of physical abuse, such as beatings. Yet, although Prince's composite feminine persona in the narrative is devoid of overt sexual language, the subtext of such language is readily discernible. For example, she contrasted two methods of punishment by two enslavers, Captain I and Mr. D. Prince described a particular beating inflicted upon her first by the slave mistress and later the same day by Captain I after she had accidentally broken the earthen jar. Captain I's frenzied style was to inflict a rapid succession of strokes until exhaustion completely overtook him, followed by periods of rest, then more beatings. This sharply contrasts with Mr. D's more studied, ritualistic, brutal style. Prince's descriptive use of language suggests that the sadistic nature of the beatings—inflicting pain upon her naked flesh—elicited from both enslavers a perverted pleasure:

> There was this difference between them; my former master used to beat me while raging and foaming with passion; M. D—was usually quite calm. He would stand by and give orders for a slave to be cruelly whipped, and assist in the punishment, without moving a muscle of his face; walking about and taking snuff with the greatest composure (62).

Prince becomes, by her own account, the recipient of increasingly vicious beatings for the most innocuous infractions, such as letting the cow into the sweet potato slips. Contrary to popular-culture perception, then, Prince dispels the notion that as a black woman, she is responsible for the moral degradation of the white male enslaver. For example, Prince leaves enshrouded in obscurity the details of another ritual that Mr. D engaged in; he forced her to bathe his naked body. She does not discuss further improprieties that might have attended such a ritual. Yet Prince's rage is so great that she eventually asks to be transferred to the service of her eventual owner, John Wood. In a very revealing passage, Prince details the beatings that she received on her naked body by Mr. D and writes that these beatings were for her far more tolerable than the bathing ritual.

> He had an ugly fashion of stripping himself quite naked, and ordering me then to wash him in a tub of water. This was worse to me than all the licks. Sometimes when he called me to wash him I would not come, my eyes were so full of shame. He would then come to beat me. One time I had plates and knives in my hand, and I dropped both plates and knives, and some of the plates were broken. He struck me so severely for this, that at last I defended myself, for I thought it was high time to do so. I then told him I would not live longer with him, for he was a very indecent man—very spiteful, and too indecent; with no shame for his servants, no shame for his own flesh. So I went away to a neighbouring house and sat down and cried till the next morning, when I went home again, not knowing what else to do. (67–68)

Prince's words leave open speculation that other untold abuses may have occurred. But more revealingly, they show Prince's struggle to maintain personal dignity in opposition to the indecency of Mr. D and others.

As previously stated, Prince's struggle for moral propriety is an essential aspect of a credible self presentation. Prince is certainly not alone in engaging in the struggle for moral recognition.[15] But as a black female in an era when science increasingly turned to gender studies, she was forced to endure the negative politics centered on the black female body. "I was soon surrounded by strange men, who examined and handled me in the same manner that a butcher would a calf or a lamb he was about to purchase, and who talked about my shape and size in like words—as if I could no more understand their meaning than the dumb beasts," Prince writes (52). As I have already noted, the idea that the black female copulated with the orangutan was accepted wholesale by the likes of Thomas Jefferson who, based on comments that he made in *Notes on the State of Virginia*, believed that the black female actually preferred the orangutan to male members of her own human species.[16]

Prince's observations conjure up images of Sartje (original surname unknown, but later renamed Sarah Bartmann, the Hottentot Venus), a South

African Khoikhoin whose story is perhaps the most notorious example of the exploitation of the black female body. Like numerous misnomers of enslaved blacks—Pompey, Caesar—the Hottentot Venus was a derisive deviation from Venus, the goddess who exhibited a European standard of beauty that bore no resemblance to Sartje. Sartje (as I shall refer to her) was brought to Piccadilly from the Cape of Good Hope in 1810 and displayed in a variety of peep shows in London. Even as Prince suffered through enslavement in the West Indies, Sartje was being exploited as the physical embodiment of the "grotesque" female body.[17] Sartje stirred public fascination centered on her large buttocks and general body shape, treated as deformities.

Placed on exhibit at Piccadilly, Sartje was made to prance back and forth in a cage that was elevated several feet above the floor, displaying her unusual physique, while she endured prodding and occasional pinches from the hands or objects of gawkers who paid extra money for the "privilege." Robert D. Altick's description is uncannily like Prince's own description of being poked and prodded at auction. He writes that "the Hottentot Venus" was paraded like a wild beast and ordered to move backward and forward and come out and go into her cage, more like a bear in a chain than a human being.[18]

When complaints were sent to the *Morning Chronicle* and the *Morning Post* about the inhumanness of Sartje's ordeal, they were actually focused more directly on the display's indecency for public consumption rather than on Sartje's fate. The attorney-general, representing the African Association, declared before the Court of King's Bench that Sartje was compelled to come to England against her will, and complained that she had endured ill treatment and confinement. For example, the secretary of the African Association charged that her appearance was highly offensive to delicacy. The members of the African Association desired that she be placed under protection and returned to her country. A three-hour examination, including an interview of Sartje in Dutch, satisfied court officials that she came to England voluntarily and was happy and well treated. Given a thin flesh-toned garment to wear in order to further exaggerate her size, she asked for warmer clothes. She reportedly responded temperamentally to confinement and exhibition. Lord Ellenborough declined any further action but threatened prosecution for any known "offence to decency in the exhibition" (Altick, 270).

The daughter of a herder, Sartje had been persuaded to return to England with Hendrick Cezar, visiting brother of Peter Cezar, the Dutch farmer for whom she worked as a domestic. Hendrick Cezar promised Sartje large sums of money to return to England for the purpose of exhibition. It is not clear whether Sartje fully understood exactly how she would earn herself and Cezar the money, but she went willingly, agreeing to split the profits. Lord Caledon, governor of the Cape, is said to have later regretted granting permission for Sartje's departure. But Bartmann's consent to her own display is indeterminable at least, moot at best.

Ensconced in the twin discursive tropes of exhibition and containment, which translated in mass popular culture as desire and repulsion, Sartje metaphorizes the historical predicaments of black women generally and Mary Prince specifically. In the first place, few of her own words survive, and where they do, translations are made in Dutch, which she understood, but not in her own native language. In addition, the carnivalesque tradition that featured a "grotesque" black female body aided pseudo-scientific discourse around the boundaries of race and sexuality. The Hottentot Venus could then validate the findings of the pseudo-scientific community and could lend assurances to what England—as a civilized society—was not (Altick, 269).

Sartje was baptized in December 1811 at Manchester and was soon taken to Paris for continued exhibition. In 1815, she died from the ravages of alcoholism and smallpox in Paris after which the anatomist George Cuvier thoroughly dissected her cadaver, which was placed on display in the Musée de l'Homme, a Paris museum. Thus, even in death, as Bernth Lindfors notes, Sartje Bartmann "continued to influence the way Africans were perceived in Europe until ultimately she became reified as a biological concept, a scientifically sanctified racial cliché."[19]

Ironically, vague allusions to the eventual female European craze for the bustle as a hip enhancement are apparently connected with spectators' fascination with the size of Bartmann's buttocks. The bustle, typically made of whale bone, artificially enhanced the hip size of European women wearers. The contraption exaggerated the so-called hourglass look, which further emphasized the waist-to-hip ratio and presumably provided sex appeal to the wearer.

Significantly, a number of British women writers, especially those with religious affiliations, relied on their own recognizable moral grounding to argue that slave women were innocent victims of an unjust practice.[20] Though Prince's sexual persona in the narrative is consistent with the British women's objectives, the work's construction resists clear patronage. Prince utilizes voice and experience, defying efforts to restrict her to an objectified, victim's status. By way of self presentation, then, she achieves something, artistically. In *Reconstructing Womanhood: The Emergence of the Afro-American Woman Novelist*, Hazel Carby points out the ideological polarities between perceptions about black and white womanhood:

> Black women, in gaining their public presence as writers, would directly confront the political and economic dimensions of their subjugation. They

had to define a discourse of black womanhood which would not only address their exclusion from the ideology of true womanhood but, as a consequence of this exclusion, would also rescue their bodies from a persistent association with illicit sexuality (32).

As Ferguson writes in her introduction to Prince's narrative, the anti-slavery society that sponsored the publication of Prince's narrative had to present slave women as victims whose moral stature was beyond reproach in order to win public support for them and to turn sentiment against slavery. This stringent moral code was observed even when women were forced to comply with sexual demands against their will. "Christian purity, for those abolitionists, overrode regard for truth," Ferguson points out (4). Prince was trapped by the cult of true womanhood, but only because she faced societal expectations of chastity for women by a populace that saw the black woman as sexually promiscuous.

As I have illustrated through Prince's employment of sentimental and other language forms, she was unable to divorce her self-identity from artistry; on the contrary, her identity is rooted in the narrative's artistry. Prince's presentation thus fulfills the challenges stipulated by the cult of womanhood, and it reinforces her suitability for moral recognition by readers. For the slave woman as narrative voice this effort to gain recognition as credible and morally pure was doubly challenging.

Prince's quest for agency is shared in varying degrees by other slave narrators, especially James Ukawsaw Gronniosaw, whose narrative was also ghostwritten. Olaudah Equiano and Ottobah Cugoano were accorded greater recognition and visibility by patrons, in part to publicize their own authorship. Of course, Equiano's impressive command of story and presentation of self is filtered through his use of defamiliarization, signification, and other literary motifs.[21] Similar discursive beginnings characterize "resistance" literature and are commonly associated with oppressed and/or colonized groups. As long argued by observers from W.E.B. Du Bois to Henry Louis Gates, Frantz Fanon, Albert Memmi, and others, black literature commonly depicts individuals who are conflicted by living as blacks in a culturally alienating Western society.[22]

Thomas Pringle's appendix to Prince's narrative provides some clues to her complex sexual history, clues that she could not relate because of book marketing concerns at the time. These clues reveal that measured empowerment for Prince could likely be achieved through sexual means. John Wood, Prince's former enslaver, sued Thomas Pringle for publishing Prince's damaging accusations of brutality against him. Furthermore, Wood charged Prince with immorality. In defending Prince, Pringle reveals a relationship that she had with a white man that occurred prior to her marriage to a free black man. Pringle also charged Wood and enslavers, in general, with hypocrisy and sexual misconduct with slave women. In the narrative, Prince is preoccupied with cleansing her life of past indiscretions that she does not identify, and she later seeks moral healing by embracing Moravianism. "I never knew rightly that I had much sin till I went" to the Moravian church (73). "When I found out that I was a great sinner, I was very sorely grieved, and very much frightened" (73).

Though initially angered by Prince's marriage to a free black, Wood claims to have provided the couple with a domicile in order to encourage her faithfulness to her husband. Discrepancies and omissions in the narrative and in the appendix to it show that Prince's struggle to achieve recognition and respectability as a narrator and even as a victim of slave abuses were connected, inextricably, to her sexual persona. Prince's struggle to maintain sexual and reproductive control is similar to that of African-American slave narrator Harriet Jacobs, whose *Incidents in the Life of a Slave Girl* (1861) was published some thirty years later. Prince shares with Jacobs the complexities of formulating an acceptable self-presentation that included feminine purity. Both Prince and Jacobs relied on white feminist patrons to edit their narratives. Susannah Strickland and Lydia Maria Childs (Jacobs's editor), downplayed their roles as editors.[23] But the mere presence of an authenticating (white) voice in a slave's narrative was a critical publishing strategy. Indications are that English women found it easier and more empowering to make strides by engaging in strategic oppositional maneuvers for another's cause rather than in resistance outright on behalf of their own cause.[24] The feminists' fight for slave women was a plea for their right to function as wives and mothers in the domestic arena—a plea that was safe, of course, from white male opposition.

Mary Prince featured herself at the center of her narrative, though her self-conscious artistry is also rooted in the mechanics of productivity.[25] Prince's story filtered through a complex productive webbing that included the "authenticating" words of Thomas Pringle and Susannah Strickland. But Pringle and Strickland had to be effective and convincing in their representation of Mary Prince, while simultaneously downplaying their own roles in Prince's creation as character. Thus, Pringle provides a statement in the narrative that seeks to lend authority and credibility to Prince's own voice. "It [the narrative] is essentially her own, without any material alteration farther than was requisite to exclude redundancies and gross grammatical errors, so as to render it clearly intelligible" (Preface, 45).

Ironically the grammatical roughness of the narrative flaunted the bareness of Prince's literacy skills and actually served to authenticate her slave past. The production of the narrative would lend its voice to a growing number of voices set to expose cruelties to slaves in the hope that England would outlaw the practice. Thus, Mary Prince's individuality was secondary to the cause for which her story provided needed evidence. Prince's "devaluation" enhanced her usefulness for the Anti-Slavery Society, while it posed a liability in her struggle for identity beyond that of an ennobled, primitive, untutored being.

Both the presence of patrons and their simultaneous need to affirm and to deny the extent of their own function in Prince's presentation are familiar paradoxes in slave narrative methodology. Pringle's introduction, however well intentioned, and the growing anti-slavery climate attending the publication of the narrative diminish Prince as subject and threaten to privilege the conditions that portray her as slave rather than as enslaved. In addition, the shared roles between Prince and amanuensis, between oral artist and the guiding hand of written expression, place Prince in a liminal position as controlling artist and makes her struggle for self-identity and empowerment all the more challenging. Prince's narrative was never destined to find its place among the Bunyanesque spiritual autobiographies.

Its presentation to the reading public was self-consciously intended as a political act, a plea for Britain's complete outlawing of slavery. In addition, the very presence of a battery of authenticating voices and their ambivalent "affirming/denying" posture threatened to delimit the voice of the enslaved woman that patrons sought to empower. Simply stated, Prince's word was not her bond, but was, at least in part, her bondage. The irony, of course, is the nonfiction status of Prince's *History*—a story seemingly with questionable veracity for some eighteenth-century readers.

Mary Prince, Olaudah Equiano, and other former slaves saw their human worth commodified in the slave market. A widely perpetuated pro-slavery notion held that Africans enslaved in European colonies were merely "rescued" from a worse fate than awaited them in their homelands and that Europeans offered slaves "enlightenment" through Christianity and civilization, as is evident in Philis Wheatley's poem "On Being Brought from Africa to America." Wheatley's poem begins, "'Twas mercy brought me from my Pagan land, / Taught my benighted soul to understand / That there's a God, that there's a Saviour too / Once I redemption neither sought nor knew" (1–4).[26]

Prince's narrative acts as a gloss on Britain's slavocracy, and it forces a collective national (un)conscious to confront its sins. Prince readily indicts a systemic malignancy that, in the words of her editor, Thomas Pringle, dehumanized both oppressor and oppressed. A reading of Mary Prince's narrative mediates the dialectic between an unauthorized European slavocracy and an authorized literary didacticism. Such a reading meshes not only inside versus outside and fiction versus nonfiction, but it transgresses the boundaries of contemporary cultural experience.

## NOTES

1. In *Subject to Others: British Women Writers and Colonial Slavery, 1670–1834* (New York: 1992), Moira Ferguson speculates that black women's slave narratives appeared in print in England several decades after the publication of black male narratives because of the difficulties in sponsoring black women's narratives and the delicacy of recounting the sexual abuse of black women in captivity.

2. Mary Prince, *The History of Mary Prince, A West Indian Slave, Related by Herself* (London: Pandora, Reprint, 1987). This edition, no longer in print, contains Moira Ferguson's invaluable introduction to *The History of Mary Prince*. The introduction is also available in the 1993 edition of Mary Prince, edited by Moira Ferguson and published by the University of Michigan Press. All citations are from the 1993 edition and are hereafter noted by page numbers within the text. A convenient edition of Prince's narrative (without the Ferguson introduction) is, of course, *The Classic Slave Narratives*, ed. Henry Louis Gates, Jr. (New York: Mentor, 1987). See Carol Barash, "The Character of Difference: The Creole Woman as Cultural Mediator in Narratives about Jamaica," *Eighteenth-Century Studies*, 23 (Summer 1990): 407–423. In discussions pertaining to two anonymous Jamaican novels, *The Jamaica Lady* (1720) and *The Fortunate Transport* (1741–42)—which I have been unable to locate—Barash locates sexual, reproductive, and material power in the West Indian slave trade squarely at the site of the black female body, particularly the Creole woman, who was frequently used as plantation mistress.

3. Sandra Pouchet Paquet, "The Heartbeat of a West Indian Slave: *The History of Mary Prince*," *African American Review* 26 (Spring 1992): 131–46, has convincingly restored authorial agency to Prince as the primary voice and activist force in the narrative rather than assign that role to her British patrons, Susannah Strickland and Thomas Pringle, in spite of the narrative's ghosted form.

4. Nancy Leys Stepan, "Race and Gender: The Role of Analogy in Science," in *Anatomy of Racism*, ed., David Theo Goldberg (Minneapolis: University of Minnesota Press, 1990). Stepan writes that "gender was found to be remarkably analogous to race, such that the scientist could use racial difference to explain gender difference, and vice versa" (39).

5. As Felicity Nussbaum writes in "The Politics of Difference," queries "over the predominance of race or sex, centering as they did on the black male [as the inferior race] and the white woman [as the inferior sex], effectively erased the black woman from scientific consideration." See Felicity Nussbaum, "The Politics of Difference," *Eighteenth-Century Studies* 23 (Summer 1990): 375–86. The interrelations of race and gender are discussed in Londa Schiebinger, "The Anatomy of Difference: Race and Sex in Eighteenth-Century Science," *Eighteenth-Century Studies* 23 (Summer 1990): 387–404, and *The Mind Has No Sex? Women in the Origins of Modern Science* (Cambridge, MA: Harvard University Press, 1989); Nancy Leys Stepan, "Race and Gender: The Role of Analogy in Science," *Isis* 77 (June 1986): 261–77; and Sandra Harding, "Taking Responsibility for Our Own Gender, Race, Class: Transforming Science and Social Studies," *Rethinking Marxism* 2 (Fall 1989): 8–19. As I discussed in chapter 1, some of the racial data proclaiming the inferiority of blacks to whites cited alleged mating practices (copulating with the orangutan) of

black women like the South African Hottentot in order to document the inferiority of the racial group.

6. Thomas Pringle provides a continuation of the life of Mary Prince in a supplement to the first edition, reprinted in the 1993 edition published by the University of Michigan Press. The narrative went through three editions shortly after its initial publication in 1831.

7. Paquet aptly notes that Prince's emotive language of the heart is "an alternative to the material measure of the marketplace as a measure of the moral and ethical sensibility that governs the well-being of individuals in society" (142).

8. "Having heard that there was to be a sale of cattle, farm stock, etc. by auction, at a Veld-Cornet's in the vicinity, we halted our waggon one day for the purpose of procuring a fresh spann of oxen. While the sale was going on, the mother and her children were exhibited on a table, that they might be seen by the company which was very large. There could not have been a finer subject for an able painter than this unhappy group. The tears, the anxiety, the anguish of the mother, while she met the gaze of the multitude, eyed the different countenances of the bidders, or cast a heart-rending look upon the children; and the simplicity and touching sorrow of the young one, while they clung to their distracted parent, wiping their eyes, and half concealing their faces . . ." (53).

9. See John Sekora and Darwin T. Turner, eds. *The Art of Slave Narrative: Original Essays in Criticism and Theory*. (Macomb: University of Western Illinois Press, 1982).

10. "'Sir, this is not Turk's Island.' I can't repeat his answer, the words were too wicked—too bad to say. He wanted to treat me the same in Bermuda as he had done in Turk's Island" (Prince, 64; 67).

11. See Homi K. Bhabha's "Introduction: Narrating the Nation," in *Nation and Narration*, ed. Homi Bhabha (London: Routledge, 1990); for specific references to Britain's nationalism, see Linda Colley, "Britishness and Otherness: An Argument," *Journal of British Studies* 31 (October 1992): 309–29.

12. John Rushworth, *Historical Collections of Private Passages of State, Weighty Matters in Law, Remarkable Proceedings*, vol. 2 of 8 vols. (London: D. Browne, 1721–22): 468.

13. William Cowper, "The Task," in *The Poems of William Cowper*, ed. J. C. Baily (London: Methuen, 1905): 40–41.

14. In "The Anatomy of Difference: Race and Sex in Eighteenth-Century Science," Londa Schiebinger examines how classifiers of the human species formulated their views largely on the basis of racial and sexual social hierarchies (388). Indeed, Olaudah Equiano briefly alludes to the sexual abuse of enslaved black women in his 1789 narrative. Moira Ferguson speculates that the paucity of pre-nineteenth-century black women's narratives may result from abolitionists' reluctance to address in print the morally thorny issues of sexual abuse and reproductive control that enslavement raised for the enslaved black woman.

15. Elizabeth Ashbridge, a white female indentured servant, also writes, evasively, about an attempted rape in an eighteenth-century autobiography. "Among the stock of the farm sold, was a female slave and her three children" (Letter to Thomas Pringle, 1826, 53).

16. Jefferson, *Notes on the State of Virginia*, 149.

17. Spellings vary (depending upon the source) for Sartje's first name and surname. These include "Saartjee," "Sartjee," or "Sartje," and "Bartman" or "Baartmann." See Sander Gilman, "Black Bodies, White Bodies: Toward an Iconography of Female Sexuality in Late Nineteenth-Century Art, Medicine, and Literature," in *"Race," Writing, and Difference*, ed. Henry Louis Gates, Jr. (Chicago: University of Chicago Press, 1986), 223–61; see also Houston Baker's response to Gilman in "Caliban's Triple Play," from the same edited collection, 381–96. Baker is offended by what he believes is Gilman's reinforcement of the exploitation of Bartman, primarily because the article includes graphic (re)illustrations of her sexual organs.

18. Robert D. Altick, "The Noble Savage Reconsidered," *The Shows of London* (London: Belknap Press of Harvard University Press, 1978), 270.

19. Bernth Lindfors, "The Afterlife of the Hottentot Venus," in *Neohelicon*, XV1/2, Akademiai Kiado, Budapest and John Benjamins B. V., Amsterdam, 295. See also Lindfors, "The Bottom Line: African Caricature in Georgian England," in *World Literature Written in English* 24 (Summer 1984), 43–51. In May 1994, the Musée D'Orsay in Paris displayed photographs, charts, graphs, and other records on Sartje Bartmann, which were borrowed from the Musée de l'Homme. These artifacts, which included a life-sized statuette molded in Bartmann's likeness were part of a special ethnographic exhibit that the Musée d'Orsay displayed temporarily.

20. These British women writers include Ann Yearsley, Hannah More, Helen Maria Williams, Mary Scott, and Mary Wollstonecraft, Mary Shelley's mother.

21. Henry Louis Gates, Jr., *The Signifying Monkey: A Theory of Afro-American Literary Criticism*. New York: Oxford University Press, 1988).

22. W.E.B. Du Bois, *Writings* (New York: Library of America, 1986); Paulette Nardal, *La Revue du Monde Noir* (Paris, 1930); Frantz Fanon, *Black Skin, White Masks*, trans. Charles Lam Markmann (New York: Grove Weidenfeld, 1967); Albert Memmi, *The Colonizer and the Colonized*, trans. Howard Greenfeld (Boston: Beacon, 1965); Audre Lorde, *Sister Outsider* (Trumansburg, NY: Crossing Press, 19784); and Henry Louis Gates, ed., *"Race," Writing and Difference* (Chicago: University of Chicago Press, 1985). See also Eslanda Goode Robeson, "Black Paris," *New Challenge: A Literary Quarterly* (January and June 1936); Robert P. Smith, Jr., "Rereading *Banjo*: Claude McKay and the French Connection," *CLA* (September 1986): 46–58; and Janet G. Vaillant, *Black, French, and African: A Life of Leopold Sedar Senghor* (Cambridge, MA: Harvard University Press, 1990).

23. See Harriet Jacobs, *Incidents in Life of a Slave Girl*, ed. Jean Fagan Yellin.

24. Ferguson argues that white British feminists battled slavery (especially its impact on black women and family dissolution) even while showing remarkable restraint in fighting, simultaneously, for equal protection under the law for England's female population.

25. Introduction, *The History of Mary Prince*, ed. Ferguson. (Pandora reprint, 1987).

26. Phillis Wheatley, *The Poems of Phillis Wheatley*, ed. Julian D. Mason (Chapel Hill: University of North Carolina Press, 1966): 53.

# Conclusion

As numerous scholars have observed, the eighteenth century witnessed tremendous tensions in commercial, legal, theological, scientific, and philosophical thinking about race and slavery. Others have argued that stiff assertions about these ideas from David Hume, Voltaire, and Immanuel Kant stood alongside what we now call liberal assertions about the integrity and autonomy of every individual, regardless of race and sex, from Granville Sharpe and Thomas Clarkson to Laurence Sterne and Mary Wollestonecraft. But ideological persuasions in literary and nonliterary discourse designed to instruct, correct, and reform humanity bear some inescapable connection, however subtle, to a patently hierarchical system that continually renews itself in matters of race. Some sixty years after Arthur O. Lovejoy's study of the Great Chain of Being in the eighteenth century, many scholars perceive it as too antiquated and too easily refutable an idea to take seriously any longer or to require further analysis. As a system of racial hierarchies, the Chain was certainly viewed by some in the eighteenth century as distasteful but not so vitriolic as to do irreparable damage to major policies and ideas on race. But African-British writings in this book—which were quite good at detecting racial hierarchies wherever they existed—dispel such notions.

These writings show that the circuitous route and duration of the Chain's discursive legacy extend well beyond pseudo-scientific data to core principles about the value of literature, religion, and humanitarian efforts. In the hands of James Albert Ukawsaw Gronniosaw, Ottobah Cugoano, Ignatius Sancho, and Mary Prince, the Chain of Being broadly implicated race from the very beginning; nearly all mention it directly or allude to it repeatedly in their writings. Though these writings appear late in the eighteenth century in an alignment, historically, with an activist abolitionist and feisty sentimentalist spirit, they seem to endorse the moral imperative of earlier, more traditional neoclassicists, who crafted literature as an instructive, didactic tool designed to educate the reading populace. Gronniosaw, Cugoano, Sancho, Olaudah Equiano, and Prince shaped these tenets to their own life experiences and social predicament. But for them, the only moral imperative worth pursuing demanded the recognition and humane treatment of enslaved blacks. Such universalist concepts as humanism or general truths did not exist in the abstract for them. Rather, they connected these ideas with the plight of blacks enslaved in the West Indies. In so doing, they exposed exclusionary discursive practices, as illustrated in works like Sir Richard Steele's "The Barbados Negroes," Jonathan Swift's *Gulliver's Travels*, Hume, Kant, and Voltaire's philosophies of race, and Mariah Edgeworth's "The Grateful Negro."

Ukawsaw Gronniosaw's enslavement and Christian redemption forcibly juxtapose with conflicts and inconsistencies in certain religious principles and in social practice. Cugoano expresses no illusions about the Hamitic hypothesis as believable; its circulation as a dangerous doctrine in need of being revoked was not something that he took for granted in his essay. Sancho takes particular pleasure in his knowledge of Edmund Burke, Alexander Pope, John Milton, John Dryden, and other traditional Anglican writers. Rather than merely providing a contextual footnote to the patronage of Laurence Sterne, however, Sancho reappropriates an entire literary movement that was mostly mired in theatrics. In light of his new world order, an aesthetic, racially harmonious chain of love and mixed-race people from the first and third worlds, Sancho's citation of the writers above actually exaggerates, rather than diminishes, the racial divide that stood between them. Equiano forces a re-examination of those English writers who omitted a slave past from interpretive equations in their writings. Consequently, *Gulliver's Travels* cannot be read so expediently, nor is it even the same work without consideration of its connections to the Khoikhoin and other cultural groups. We are accustomed to searching for evidence of Paul Bunyan, Aphra Behn, Daniel Defoe, and Jonathan Swift in African-British publications, but we can also discover the African-British text in Joseph Addison and Sir Richard Steele, Pope, Sterne, Edgeworth, and Sir Walter Scott. Mary Prince, alone, wants no part of a British literary coalition. After freedom from slavery, she wants to be removed from England and to return to the West Indies and is an anti-assimilator in that sense of the word.

Collectively, Gronniosaw, Sancho, Cugoano, Equiano, and Prince illustrate that the triumph of the human spirit ultimately prevailed for them. But this book is not so much about an exaggerated ideal or elevation of the few, nor is it about the racial victimization of the many. Rather, the book has probed a lesser-demonstrated epistemological function of African-British writings, their ability to inhabit and alter the universalizing and rationalist discourse of the Enlightenment on race. Ultimately, they reflect those tensions inherent in literary, theological, social, and gender issues in the eighteenth century. African-British writings engaged in, broadened, and complicated debate that pertained to race in religious, social, literary, and gender contexts.

To explore the epistemological function of the African-British text in British studies necessarily means to deal with its capacity to reconstruct a revisionist Enlightenment. Cornel West writes about American literature what might also be said for British studies: "the mere addition of African American texts to the present canon without any explicit and persuasive account of how this addition leads us to see the canon anew reveals the worst of academic pluralist ideology" (34). West also argues that revisions of literary canons depends on "rendering a canonical historical reading of the crisis that in part authorizes literary canons."[1] African-British writings are not posed here as a corrective reading to English and other European texts on the subject of race and reason. But neither is Gronniosaw, Sancho, Cugoano, Equiano, and Prince the rear-guard auxiliary team or the familial black sheep in British studies.

Consequently I conclude by turning my attention to the status of African-British writings in academic, canonical ranks. The charted course of African-British writings in the academy parallels what Paul Gilroy writes about the history of the black Atlantic. Sancho, Cugoano, Equiano, and Prince "provide a means to reexamine the problems of nationality, location, identity, and historical memory" (16).[2] They each affirm as well as deny the controlling, socio-historical context of their textual production. But most significantly they extend a racial presence beyond the scope of their own existence and promote ethnographic readings of some traditional, canonical English texts.

## NOTES

1. Cornel West, *Keeping Faith: Philosophy and Race in America* (New York: Routledge, 1993), 34.

2. Paul Gilroy, *The Black Atlantic: Modernity and Double Consciousness* (Cambridge, MA: Harvard University Press, 1993), 16.

# Bibliography

Achebe, Chinua. "An Image of Africa: Racism in Conrad's *Heart of Darkness*." In *Hopes and Impediments: Selected Essays*. New York: Doubleday, 1989.

*Acts of the Privy Council of England: New Series*, 1542–1631. Vol. 26. London: H. M. Stationery Office, 1890–1940.

Adams, Percy G. *Travel Literature and Evolution of the Novel*. Lexington: University Press of Kentucky, 1983.

Adanson, Michael. *A Voyage to Senegal, the Isle of Goree and the River Gambia*, 1759. London: Printed for J. Nourse and W. Johnston, 1969.

Addison, Joseph, and Sir Richard Steele. *The Spectator*. Ed. Donald F. Bond. 5 vols. Oxford: Clarendon Press, 1965.

Allen, Don Cameron. *The Legend of Noah: Renaissance Rationalism in Art, Science, and Letters*. Urbana: University of Illinois Press, 1949.

Althusser, Louis. *Lenin and Philosophy and Other Essays*. Trans. Ben Brewster. New York: Monthly Review Press, 1971.

Altick, Robert D. "The Noble Savage Reconsidered." In *The Shows of London*. London: Belknap Press of Harvard University Press, 1978.

Alvarez, Francisco. *Histoire d'Aethiopie: Contenant Vraye Relations des Terres and Pais du Grand Roy and Emporeur Prete-Ian*. Amvers: J. Bellene, 1558.

Anonymous. *Memoirs and Opinions of Mr. Blenfield*. Vol. 1. London: W. Lane, 1790.

Appiah, Anthony. "Racisms." In *Anatomy of Racism*. Ed. David Theo Goldberg. Minneapolis: University of Minnesota Press, 1990.

Aristotle. *The Politics*. Ed. Stephen Everson. Cambridge: Cambridge University Press, 1988.

Ashbridge, Elizabeth. "Letter to Thomas Pringle, 1826." In *The History of Mary Prince, A West Indian Slave, Related by Herself*, 1831. Ed. Moira Ferguson. Ann Arbor: University of Michigan Press, 1993.

Astley, Thomas. *A New General Collection of Voyages and Travels in Four Volumes*, 1745–47. London: Cass Library of African Studies, Rpt., 1968.

Atkins, G. Douglas. *Quests of Difference: Reading Pope's Poems*. Lexington: University Press of Kentucky, 1986.

Audley, John. *The John Audley Papers*. Cambridgeshire Public Record Office. Cambridge, England.

Backsheider, Paula. *Daniel Defoe: His Life*. Baltimore, MD: Johns Hopkins University Press, 1989.

Bacon, Sir Francis. "The Advancement of Learning." In *The Works of Francis Bacon*. Ed. James Spedding et al. Boston: Taggard and Thompson, 1864. Republished by Scholarly Press, St. Clair Shores, MI.

Bacon, Francis. *New Atlantis*, 1624. *The Works of Francis Bacon*. Ed. James Spelling et al. Vol. 5. Boston: Brown and Taggard, 1862.

Baker, Houston. *Blues, Ideology, and Afro-American Literature: A Vernacular Theory*. Chicago: University of Chicago Press, 1984.

——. "Caliban's Triple Play." In *"Race," Writing, and Difference*. Ed. Henry Louis Gates, Jr. Chicago: University of Chicago Press, 1986.

Balibar, Etienne. "Parodoxes of Universality." In *Anatomy of Racism*. Ed. David Theo Goldberg. Minneapolis: University of Minnesota Press, 1990.

Balibar, Etienne, and Immanuel Wallerstein. *Race, Nation, Class: Ambiguous Identities*. Trans. of Etienne Balibar by Chris Turner. London: Verso, 1991.

Barash, Carol. "The Character of Difference: The Creole Woman as Cultural Mediator in Narratives about Jamaica." *Eighteenth-Century Studies* 23 (Summer 1990): 407–23.

Barker, Anthony J. *The African Link: British Attitudes to the Negro in the Era of the Atlantic Slave Trade, 1550–1807*. London: Frank Cass, 1978.

Barker-Benfield, C. J. *The Culture of Sensibility: Sex and Society in Eighteenth-Century Britain*. Chicago: University of Chicago Press, 1992.

Bate, Walter Jackson. *From Classic to Romantic: Premises of Taste in Eighteenth-Century England*. Cambridge, MA: Harvard University Press, 1946. Rpt., 1961.

——. *Samuel Johnson*. New York: Harcourt, Brace, Jovanovich, 1976.

Baxter, Richard. *Call to the Unconverted*. London: Printed by R. W. for Nevil Simmons and by Nathaniel Ekins, 1658.

——. *A Christian Directory: Or, A Summ of Practical Theologie, and Cases of Conscience*. London: Printed for Nevell Simmons by Robert White, 1678.

Beeton, Samuel Orchart. *Dictionary of Universal Information*. London: n.p., 1877.

Behn, Aphra. "Oroonoko, or The Royal Slave." In *Oroonoko and Other Prose Narratives*. Ed. Montague Summers. New York: Blom, 1916.

Bendyshe, Thomas. "The History of Anthropology." Anthropological Society of London. *Memoirs* 1 (1863–64), 424–26.

Benezet, Anthony. *Some Historical Account of Guinea*, 1771. Reprint. London: Frank Cass, 1968.

Berkley, George. *The Naval History of Britain, from the Earliest Periods of Which there are Accounts in History, to the Conclusion of the Year MDCCLVI*. Ed. John Hill. London: T. Osborne and J. Shipton, 1756.

Bernier, François. "Nouvelle Division de la Terre, par les Differentes Especes ou Races d'Hommes qui l'Habitent." *Journal des Scavans.* [Amsterdam] 12 (1684): 148–55. Trans. from French and published by Thomas Bendyshe in "History of Anthropology," Anthropological Society of London. *Memoirs* 1 (1863–64): 360–64.

Bernstein, John Andrew. *Shaftesbury, Rousseau, and Kant: An Introduction to the Conflict Between Aesthetic and Moral Values in Modern Thought.* Rutherford, NJ: Fairleigh-Dickinson University Press, 1980.

Bertram, David H., ed. *Soame Jenyns.* Boston: Twayne, 1984.

Best, George. *A True Discourse of the Later Voyages of Discoverie, for the Finding of a Passage to Cathaga, by the Northwest.* London: Henry Bynnyman, 1578.

Bhabha, Homi K., ed. *Nation and Narration.* London: Routledge, 1990.

——. "Of Mimicry and Man: The Ambivalence of Colonial Discourse" In *The Location of Culture.* Ed. Homi K. Bhabha. London: Routledge, 1994.

——. "The Other Question: Homi Bhabha Reconsiders the Stereotype and Colonial Discourse." *Screen* 24 (1983): 18–36.

"Biography and Memoirs." *Monthly Review* 80 (1789): 551.

Blumenbach, Johann Friedrich. *De Generis Humani Varietate Nativa,* 1775. Trans. and ed. by Thomas Bendyshe. Rept. of 1st ed. In *The Anthropological Treatises of Johann Friedrich Blumenbach.* London: Longman, 1865.

——. *On the Natural Varieties of Mankind,* 1795. Trans. and ed., Thomas Bendyshe. Rept. of 3rd ed. In *The Anthropological Treatises of Johann Friedrich Blumenbach.* London: Longman, 1865.

Boethius, *The Consolation of Philosophy.* Trans. Richard Green. Indianapolis: Bobbs-Merrill, 1962.

Bolt, Christine, and Seymour Drescher, ed. *Anti-Slavery, Religion, and Reform: Essays in Memory of Roger Anstey.* Kent, England: William Dawson and Sons, 1980.

Bonner, Willard Hallam. *Captain William Dampier: Buccaneer-Author.* Stanford, CA: Stanford University Press, 1934.

Bonnet, Charles. *Consideratum Sur les Corps Organises: Ou, l'on Traite de Leur Origine.* Amsterdam: M. M. Rey, 1762.

Bosman, William. *A New and Accurate Description of the Coast of Guinea.* London: Printed for Sir Alfred Jones by Ballantyne, 1907.

Boswell, James. *Life of Johnson.* Ed. R. W. Chapman. Oxford: Oxford University Press, 1980.

Bourdieu, Pierre. *Outline of a Theory of Practice.* Trans. Richard Nice. Cambridge: Cambridge University Press, 1992.

Brown, Laura. *Alexander Pope.* Oxford: Basil Blackwell, 1985.

——. "Reading Race and Gender: Jonathan Swift." *Eighteenth-Century Studies* 23 (Summer 1990): 425–43.

Brown, Lloyd. "Review of the *Letters of Ignatius Sancho, an African to which are Prefixed Memoirs of His Life by Joseph Jekyll,* introduced by Paul Edwards." *Eighteenth-Century Studies* 3 (Spring 1970): 415–19.

Browne, Alice. *The Eighteenth-Century Feminist Mind.* Sussex, England: Harvester Press, 1987.

Buffon, Georges [Louis Leclerc Compte de]. *Natural History, General and Particular*, 2nd ed. Trans. William Smellie. 9 vols. London: Printed for W. Strahan and T. Cadell, 1785.

Bunyan, John, *The Holy War*. London: Printed by Dorman Newman and Benjamin Alsop, 1682.

Burke, Edmund. *Philosophical Inquiry into the Origin of Our Ideas on the Sublime and Beautiful*. London: Printed for R. and J. Dodsley, 1757.

———. *Reflections on the Revolution in France*, 1790. New York: Doubleday, 1961.

Burnet, James, Lord Monboddo. *Lord Monboddo, Of the Origin and Progress of Language*, 1774. Vol. 1 of 16 vols. London: T. Cadell, 1792.

Burr, Sandra, and Adam Potkay, ed. *Black Atlantic Writers of the Eighteenth Century: Living the New Exodus in England and the Americas*. New York: St. Martin's Press, 1995.

Carby, Hazel. *Reconstructing Womanhood: The Emergence of the Afro-American Woman Novelist*. New York: Oxford University Press, 1987.

Carretta, Vincent, ed. *Ignatius Sancho: Letters of the Late Ignatius Sancho, An African*. New York: Penguin Books, 1998.

———, ed. *Olaudah Equiano: The Interesting Narrative and Other Writings*. New York: Penguin Books, 1996.

———, ed. *Unchained Voices: An Anthology of Black Authors in the English Speaking World of the Eighteenth Century*. Lexington: University of Kentucky Press, 1996.

*Catalogue of Dean Swift's Library in 1715. Proceedings of the Royal Irish Academy* 37 (1927): 270–73.

Catterall, Helen T., ed. *Judicial Cases Concerning American Slavery and the Negro*. Washington, DC: Carnegie Institution of Washington, 1926.

Certeau, Michel de. *The Writing of History*. Trans. Tom Conley. New York: Columbia University Press, 1988.

Césaire, Aimé. *Discourse on Colonialism*. Trans. Joan Pinkham. New York: Monthly Review Press, 1972.

Churchill, Awnsham and John. *A Collection of Voyages and Travels in Six Volumes*. London: Printed for John Walthoe et al., 1732.

Clarkson, Thomas. *An Essay on the Slavery and Commerce of the Human Species, Particularly The African*. Philadelphia: n.p., 1786. Reprint. Miami, FL: Mnemosyne, 1969.

———. *The History of the Rise, Progress, and Accomplishment of the Abolition of the African Slave Trade by the British Parliament*. 2 vols. Philadelphia: James P. Parke, 1808.

Clifford, James, and George E. Marcus, eds. *Writing Culture: The Poetics and Politics of Ethnography*. Berkeley: University of California Press, 1986.

Cogan, T., trans. *The Works of the Late Professor [Peter] Camper, on the Connexion Between the Science of Anatomy and the Arts of Drawing, Painting, Statuary*. London: n.p., 1794.

Colley, Linda. "Britishness and Otherness: An Argument." *Journal of British Studies* 31 (October 1992): 309–29.

Collins, Churton. *Jonathan Swift*. London, 1902.

Constantine, J. Robert. "The Ignoble Savage, An Eighteenth Century Literary Stereotype." *Phylon* 27 (Summer, 1966): 171–79.

Cooper, Anthony Ashley, 3rd Earl of Shaftesbury. *Characteristics of Men, Manners, Opinions, Times.* Ed. John M. Robertson. 2 vols. Gloucester, MA: P. Smith, 1963.

Costanza, Angelo. *Surprising Narrative: Olaudah Equiano and the Beginnings of Black Autobiography.* New York: Greenwood Press, 1987.

Cowper, William, "The Task." In *The Poems of William Cowper.* Ed. J. C. Baily. London: Methuen, 1905.

Cox, Stephen D. *"The Stranger Within Thee": Concepts of the Self in Late-Eighteenth-Century Literature.* Pittsburgh, PA: University of Pittsburgh Press, 1980.

Cross, Wilbur L. *The Life and Times of Laurence Sterne.* New York: Macmillan, 1909.

Crousaz, Jean-Pierre de. *Commentaire sur la Traduction en Vers de M. l'Abbe du Resnel, de l'Essai de M. Pope sur l'Homme.* Paris, n.p., 1738.

——, *A Commentary on Mr. Pope's Principles of Morality, or Essay on Man.* Trans. Samuel Johnson. London: Printed for E. Cave, 1742.

——. *Examen de l'Essai de M. Pope sur l'Homme and Commentarie.* Lausanne: n.p., 1737.

——. *An Examination of Mr. Pope's Essay on Man.* Trans. Eliz Carter. London: Printed for A. Dodd, 1739.

Cruickshank, Brodie. *Eighteen Years on the Gold Coast of Africa Including an Account of the Native Tribes, and Their Intercourse with the Europeans*, 1853. 2nd ed. 2 vols. rpt. New York: Barnes & Noble, 1966.

Crummell, Alexander. "Africa Not Under a Curse." *Christian Observer.* Reprinted as "The Negro Race Not Under a Curse." *The Future of Africa*, 2nd ed. New York: Charles Scribner, 1862.

Cugoano, Quobna Ottobah. *Thoughts and Sentiments on the Evil of Slavery*, 1787. Intro. Paul Edwards. 1787 reprint. London: Dawsons of Pall Mall, 1969.

Curtis, Lewis Perry, ed. *Letters of Laurence Sterne.* Oxford: Clarendon Press, 1935.

Cvetkovich, Ann. *Mixed Feelings: Feminism, Mass Culture, and Victorian Sensationalism.* New Brunswick, NJ: Rutgers University Press, 1992.

Dabydeen, David, ed. *The Black Presence in English Literature.* Manchester, England: Manchester University Press, 1985.

——. *Hogarth's Blacks: Images of Blacks in Eighteenth Century English Art.* Athens, GA: University of Georgia Press, 1987.

Dabydeen, David, and Paul Edwards, eds. *Black Writers in Britain, 1760–1890.* Edinburgh: Edinburgh University Press, 1991.

Dampier, William. *A New Voyage Round the World.* 2nd edition. London: Printed for James Knapton, 1697.

——. "A Voyage to New Holland, in the Year 1699." From *A New Voyage Round the World*, 5th ed. Vol. 3 of 3 vols. London: J. Knapton, 1703–1709.

Damrosch, Leopold, Jr. *The Imaginative World of Alexander Pope.* Berkeley: University of California Press, 1987.

Dathorne, O. R. "African Writers of the Eighteenth Century." *London Magazine* 5 (September 1965): 51–58.

David, Bertram H., ed. *Soame Jenyns*. Boston: Twayne, 1984.

Davidson, Basil. *The African Slave Trade: Precolonial History, 1405–1850*. Boston: Little, Brown, 1961. (Originally published in hardcover as *Black Mother: Africa and the Atlantic Slave Trade*, 1961.)

———. *Black Mother: Africa and the Atlantic Slave Trade*. New York: Penguin Books, 1961.

Davis, Darnell. *The Spectator's Essays Relating to the West Indies*. Demerara: British Guiana, 1885.

Davis, David Brion. *The Problem of Slavery in the Age of Revolution, 1770–1823*. Ithaca, NY: Cornell University Press, 1975.

Davis, Lennard J. *Resisting Novels: Ideology and Fiction*. New York: Methuen, 1987.

Defoe, Daniel. *A Brief Account of the Present State of the African Trade*. London: 1713.

———. *Captain Singleton*. London: Oxford University Press, 1969.

———. "Casio and His Brother; as Described in the Satyr, Call'd The Reformation of Manners." In *A True Collection of the Writings of the Author of the True Born English-Man*. London, 1703./*Reformation of Manners, a Satire*. N.p.: 1702.

———. *Colonel Jack*. Ed. Samuel Holt Monk. Oxford: Oxford University Press, 1989.

———. *Robinson Crusoe*. Ed. Michael Shinagel. New York: Norton, 1975.

Denham, John. *Cooper's Hill*. London: Printed for Humphrey Moseley, 1655.

Dickens, Charles, ed. *All the Year Round*. 13 (1875): London, 489–93.

———. *Great Expectations*. 2nd ed. New York: Heritage Press, 1939.

Dickson, William. *Letters on Slavery*. Westport, CT: Negro Universities Press, 1970.

Dieterich, Konrad. "Summary of Kant's Theory of the Heavens." Appendix A, Immanuel Kant, "Natural History and Theory of the Heavens." In *Kant's Cosmogony*. Trans. by W. Hastie, D. D. New York: Johnson Reprint Corporation, 1970.

Dodd, William. "The African Prince to Zara." *Gentleman's Magazine* 23 (July 1749): 323–24.

———. *Poems by Dr. Dodd*. London: Printed by Dryden Leach, 1767.

Donald, James, and Stuart Hall, eds. *Politics and Ideology*. Milton Keynes: Open University Press, 1986.

Douglass, Frederick. *My Bondage and My Freedom*, 1855. New York: Dover, 1969.

———. *Narrative of the Life of Frederick*. Boston: The Anti-Slavery Office, 1845.

Drawcansir, Alexander. *Covent-Garden Journal*, 1 February 1752, n.p.

Drescher, Seymour. *Capitalism and Antislavery: British Mobilization in Comparative Perspective*. New York: Oxford University Press, 1987.

———. *Econocide: British Slavery in the Era of Abolition*. Pittsburgh: University of Pittsburgh Press, 1977.

Dryden, John. *Absalom and Achitophel*. London: Printed for J. T.; first published 1681.

———. "Juvenal's Tenth Satire." In *The Satires of Decimus Junius Juvenalis*. Trans. into English verse by John Dryden et al. London: Jacob Tonson, 1693.

———. *Palamon and Arcite, or The Knight's Tale*. Book 3. Ed. George E. Eliot. Boston: Ginn, 1899.

Du Bois, W.E.B. *Writings*. New York: Library of America, 1986.

Duffield, Ian, and Paul Edwards. "Equiano's Turks and Christians: An Eighteenth Century View of Islam." *Journal of African Studies* 2 (Winter 1975–76): 433–44.

Eddy, W. A. *Gulliver's Travels: A Critical Study*. Princeton, 1923.

Edgeworth, Maria. "The Grateful Negro." In *Popular Tales*. New York: D. Appleton, 1854. 1st ed. London: Printed for J. Johnson, 1804.

Edwards, Bryan. *The History, Civil and Commercial, of the British Colonies in the West Indies*. Vol. 2 of 2 vols. London: J. Stockdale, 1793.

Edwards, Paul. "A Descriptive List of Manuscripts in the Cambridgeshire Record Office Relating to the Will of Gustavus Vassa (Olaudah Equiano)." *Research in African Literatures* 20 (Fall 1989): 473–80.

———. "'Written by Himself': A Manuscript Letter of Olaudah Equiano." *Notes and Queries* (June 1968): 222–25.

———, ed. *Equiano's Reizen: De Autobiografie van een Negerslaaf*. Trans. Claire-Lise Charbonnier. Paris: Editions Caribeennes, 1987.

———, ed. *The Interesting Narrative of the Life of Olaudah Equiano, or Gustavus Vassa, the African*, 1789. 2 vols. London: Dawsons of Pall Mall, 1969.

———, ed. *Letters of the Late Ignatius Sancho: An African*. Facsimile reprint of the 5th edition. London: Dawsons of Pall Mall, 1968.

———, ed. *The Life of Olaudah Equiano*. Essex, England: Longman, 1988.

Edwards, Paul, and Polly Rewt, eds. *The Letters of Ignatius Sancho*. Edinburgh: Edinburgh University Press, 1994.

Edwards, Paul, and James Walvin, ed. *Black Writers in Britain, 1760–1890*. Edinburgh: Edinburgh University Press, 1991.

Ellis, Markman. *The Politics of Sensibility: Race, Gender, and Commerce in the Sentimental Novel*. Cambridge: Cambridge University Press, 1996.

*Encyclopedia Judaica*. New York: McMillan, 1971–72.

*The English Reports*. King's Bench Division. London: William Green and Sons, 1908.

Equiano, Olaudah. *The Interesting Narrative of the Life of Olaudah Equiano or Gustavus Vassa The African, 1789*. Ed. Paul Edwards. Colonial History Series. 2 vols. London: Dawsons of Pall Mall, 1969.

———. Letter to Reverend G. Walker (27 February 1792). Cambridgeshire Record Office. Cambridge, England.

———. *The Life of Olaudah Equiano*. Ed. Paul Edwards. Essex, England: Longman, 1988.

Estwick, Samuel. *Considerations on the Negroe Cause*, 3rd ed. London: Dodsley, in Pall-Mall, 1788.

*The European Magazine and London Review* (September 1782).

Fabian, Johannes. *Time and the Other: How Anthropology Makes Its Object*. New York: Columbia University Press, 1983.

Fairer, David, ed. *Pope: New Contexts*. New York: Harvester Wheatsheaf, 1990.

Fanon, Frantz. *Black Skin, White Masks*. Trans. Charles Lam Markmann. New York: Grove Weidenfeld, 1967.

———. *The Wretched of the Earth*. Trans. Constance Farrington. New York: Grove Press, 1964.

Ferguson, Moira. *Subject to Others: British Women Writers and Colonial Slavery, 1670–1834*. New York: Routledge, 1992.

Fiddes, Edward. "Lord Mansfield and the Somersett Case." *Law Quarterly Review* 50 (1934): 499–511.

Firth, Charles. "The Political Significance of Gulliver's Travels." *Proceedings of the British Academy* (1919–1920).

Fish, Stanley. *Doing What Comes Naturally: Change, Rhetoric, and the Practice of Theory in Literary and Legal Studies*. Durham, NC: Duke University Press, 1989.

Fisher, Thomas. *The Negro's Memorial, or Abolitionist's Catechism: By an Abolitionist*. London: Printed by Hatchard, 1825.

Foucault, Michel. *Discipline and Punish: The Birth of the Prison*. Trans. Alan Sheridan. New York: Vintage Books, 1979.

———. *Power/Knowledge: Selected Interviews & Other Writings*. Ed. Colin Gordon. Trans. Colin Gordon et al. New York: Pantheon Books, 1977.

Frantz, R. W. "Swift's Yahoos and the Voyagers." *Modern Philology* 29 (1931): 49–57.

Freedman, and Simon, trans. *Midrash Rabbah*, I. London, 1939.

Fryer, Peter. *Staying Power: The History of Black People in Britain*. London: Pluto Press, 1984.

Fussel, Paul. *The Rhetorical World of Augustan Humanism: Ethics and Imagery from Swift to Burke*. London: Oxford University Press, 1965.

Garrick, David. *High Life Below Stairs: A Farce*. London: J. Newbury, 1759.

Gates, Henry Louis, Jr., ed. *The Classic Slave Narratives*. New York: Mentor, 1987.

———. *Figures in Black: Words, Signs, and the "Racial" Self*. New York: Oxford University Press, 1989.

———. *"Race," Writing, and Difference*. Chicago: University of Chicago Press, 1986.

———. *The Signifying Monkey: A Theory of African-American Literary Criticism*. New York: Oxford University Press, 1988.

Genebrard, Gilbert. *Chronographiae Libri Quatuor*. Leyden: Sumptibus Ioannis Pillehotte, 1609.

*Gentleman's Magazine*. 19 (1749): 89–90.

*Gentleman's Magazine*. 20 (1750), London: Printed for Edward Cave, 272.

*Gentleman's Magazine*. 52 (September 1782): 199.

George, Dorothy M. *London Life in the Eighteenth Century*. 1925 Reprint. London: Kegan Paul, 1951.

Gilman, Sander. "Black Bodies, White Bodies: Toward and Iconography of Female Sexuality in late Nineteenth-Century Art, Medicine, and Literature." In *"Race, " Writing, and Difference*. Ed. Henry Louis Gates, Jr. Chicago: University of Chicago Press, 1986.

Gilroy, Paul. *The Black Atlantic: Modernity and Double Consciousness*. Cambridge, MA: Harvard University Press, 1993.

———. "One Nation under a Groove: The Cultural Politics of 'Race' and Racism in Britain." In *Anatomy of Racism*. Ed. David Theo Goldberg. Minneapolis: University of Minnesota Press, 1990.

———. *There Ain't No Black in the Union Jack: The Cultural Politics of Race and Nation*. London: Hutchinson, 1987.

Godwyn, Morgan. *The Negro's and Indians' Advocate . . . in Our Plantations*. London: Printed for the author by J.D., 1680.

Goldberg, David Theo. *Anatomy of Racism*. Minneapolis: University of Minnesota Press, 1990.

Gooneratne, Yasmine. *Alexander Pope*. Cambridge: Cambridge University Press, 1976.

Gossett, Thomas F. *Race: The History of an Idea in America*. Dallas, TX: Southern Methodist University Press, 1963.

Gould, Stephen Jay. "The Geometer of Race." *Discover* 15 (November 1994): 67.

———. "The Hottentot Venus." *Natural History* 91 (1982): 20–28.

Grainger, James. *The Sugar-Cane. A Poem*. London: Printed for R. and J. Dodsley, 1764.

Grant, Douglas. *The Fortunate Slave: An Illustration of African Slavery in the Early Eighteenth Century*. London: Oxford University Press, 1968.

Great Britain. *Acts of the Privy Council of England*. New Series. 26 (1596–97). London: Printed for H. M. Stationery Office by L. D. Mackie & Co., 1902.

Greenblatt, Stephen. *Marvelous Possessions: The Wonder of the New World*. Chicago: University of Chicago Press, 1991.

———. *Shakespearean Negotiations: The Circulation of Social Energy in Renaissance England*. Berkeley: University of California Press, 1988.

Greene, Donald. "An Anatomy of Pope-bashing." In *The Enduring Legacy: Alexander Pope Tercentenary Essays*. Ed. G. S. Rousseau and Pat Rogers. Cambridge: Cambridge University Press, 1988.

———. "Augustanism and Empiricism." *Eighteenth-Century Studies* 1 (1967–68).

———, ed. *Samuel Johnson*. Oxford: Oxford University Press, 1984.

Grégoire, Henri. *An Enquiry Concerning the Intellectual and Moral Faculties, and Literature of Negroes*. Trans. D. B. Warden. Brooklyn: Printed by Thomas Kirk, 1810.

Gronniosaw, James Albert Ukawsaw. *A Narrative of the Most Remarkable Particulars in the Life of James Albert Ukawsaw Gronniosaw, an African Prince. Related by Himself*. London: R. GroomBridge, Panyer-Alley, Paternoster-Row. Manchester, England. Bath, 1770. Reprint, Kraus, 1972.

Gross, David S. "The Conqu'ring Force of Unresisted Steel: Pope and Power in *The Rape of the Lock*." *New Orleans Review* 15 (Winter 1988): 23–30.

Hakluyt, Richard. *Hakluyt's Voyages; The Principal Navigations, Voyages, Traffiques and Discoveries of the English Nation*. Ed. Irwin R. Blacker. New York: Viking Press, 1965. Text from the Glasgow edition, 1903–1905.

Hale, Matthew. *Primitive Origination of Mankind*. London: Printed for William Shrowsbery by William Godbid, 1677.

Hall, Stuart. "Gramsci's Relevance for the Study of Race and Ethnicity." *Journal of Communication Inquiry* 10 (Summer 1986): 5–27.

Harding, Sandra. "Taking Responsibility for Our Own Gender, Race, Class: Transforming Science and Social Studies." *Rethinking Marxism* 2 (Fall 1989): 8–19.

Hardy, William J. *Middlesex Country Records: Calendar of the Sessions Books 1689 to 1709*. London: n.p., 1905.

Hawes, Clement. "Three Times Round the Globe: Gulliver and Colonial Discourse." *Cultural Critique* 18 (Spring 1991): 187–214.

Hawkes, Terence. *Shakespeare's Talking Animals: Language and Drama in Society*. London: Edward Arnold, 1973.

Hawkins, Sir John. *The Life of Samuel Johnson*. London: 1786.

Herbert, Sir Thomas. "Description of the Cape of Good Hope in Aethiopia." In *A Relation of Some Yeares Travaile*. London: Printed by William Stansby and Jacob Bloome, 1634.

Heylyn, Peter. *Microcosmus, Or a Little Description of the Great World*. Oxford: John Lichfield and James Short, 1621.

Hoare, Prince. *Memoirs of Granville Sharp*, 2nd ed. London: Printed for Henry Colburn, 1820.

Hobbes, Thomas. *Leviathan*, 1651. Ed. Nichard Tuck. Cambridge, England: Cambridge University Press, 1991.

Hogue, W. Lawrence. *Discourse and the Other: The Production of the Afro-American Text*. Durham, NC: Duke University Press, 1986.

Home, Henry, Lord Kames. *Sketches of the History of Man*, 1774. Edinburgh: W. Creech, 1788.

Horton, James Africanus. *West African Countries and Peoples*. London: n.p., 1868.

Howes, Alan B. *Sterne: The Critical Heritage*. London: Routledge, 1974.

Hulme, Peter. *Colonial Encounters: Europe and the Native Caribbean, 1492–1797*. London: Routledge, 1986.

Hume, David. *Essays: Moral, Political, and Literary*. London: Longmans, Green, 1898.

———. "Of National Characters." In *Essays: Moral, Political, and Literary*. Revised essay. Oxford: Oxford University Press, 1963.

———. "Of National Characters." In *Essays and Treatises on Several Subjects*, 4th ed. Vol. 1 of 4 vols. London: A. Millar, 1753.

Hutcheson, Francis. *A System of Moral Philosophy*. 2 vols. Reprint of the 1755 London edition. New York: A. M. Kelley, 1968.

Jackson, Wallace, and R. Paul Yoder, eds. *Critical Essays on Alexander Pope*. New York: G. K. Hall, 1993.

Jacobs, Harriet. *Incidents in the Life of a Slave Girl*. Ed. Jean Fagan Yellin. Cambridge, MA: Harvard University Press, 1987.

Janheinz, Jahn. *Neo-African Literature; a History of Black Writing*. Trans. from German by Oliver Coburn and Ursula Lehrburger. New York: Grove Press, 1968.

JanMohamed, Abdul. "The Economy of Manichean Allegory: The Function of Racial Difference in Colonialist Literature." *Critical Inquiry* 12 (1985): 60.

Jefferson, Thomas. *Notes on the State of Virginia*, 1781–82. Ed. William Peden. London: Printed for John Stockdale, 1787. Reprint. Chapel Hill: University of North Carolina Press, 1955.

Jekyll, Joseph. "Biographical Introduction." In *Letters of the Late Ignatius Sancho: An African*. Ed. Paul Edwards. Facsimile reprint of the 5th ed. London: Dawsons of Pall Mall, 1968.

Jenyns, Soame. "Disquisitions on Several Subjects, on the Chain of Universal Being." In *The Works of Soame Jenyns*. Vol. 2 of 2 vols. Philadelphia, PA: Printed by Thomas Dobson, 1790.

Jobson, Richard. *The Golden Trade, or A Discovery of the River Gambra, and the Golden Trade of the Aethiopians*, 1623. Ed. Charles G. Kingsley. Teignmouth, Devonshire, 1904.

Johnson, Barbara. *A World of Difference*. Baltimore: Johns Hopkins University Press, 1987.

Johnson, J. W. *The Formation of English Neo-Classical Thought*. Princeton, NJ: Princeton University Press, 1967.

Johnson, Samuel. "Alexander Pope." In *Lives of The English Poets*. Ed. George Birbeck Hill. Oxford: Clarendon Press, 1905.

———. *Rasselas*, 7th ed. London: Printed for J. Dodsley et al., 1786.

———. "Review of [Soame Jenyns], *A Free Inquiry into the Nature and Origin of Evil*," 1757. In *Samuel Johnson*. Ed. Donald Greene. New York: Oxford University Press, 1984.

———. "Vanity of Human Wishes." In *Samuel Johnson*. Ed. Donald Greene. New York: Oxford University Press, 1984.

Jones, Chris. *Radical Sensibility: Literature and Ideas in the 1790s*. London: Routledge, 1993.

Jones, Richard Foster. *Ancients and Moderns: A Study of the Rise of the Scientific Movement in Seventeenth-Century England*. New York: Dover, 1961.

Jordan, Winthrop D. *White Over Black: American Attitudes Toward the Negro, 1550–1812*. Baltimore: Penguin Books, 1969. First published by the University of North Carolina Press, Chapel Hill, 1968.

July, Robert. *The Origins of Modern African Thought*. London: Faber and Faber, 1968.

Kant, Immanuel. *Allgemeine Naturgeschichte und Theorie des Himmels*, 1755, Akademie-Ausgabe, I, 359f.

———. *Foundations of the Metaphysics of Morals and What Is Enlightenment?* Trans. Lewis White Beck. Indianapolis: Bobbs-Merrill, 1959.

King, Reyahn et al. *Allgemeine Naturgeschichte und Theorie des Himmels*, 1755, Akademie-Ausgabe, 1, 359f.

———. *Ignatius Sancho: An African Man of Letters*. London: National Portrait Gallery, 1997.

Knapp, Oswald G., ed. *The Intimate Letters of Hester Piozzi and Penelope Pennington, 1788-1822*. London, 1914.

Kovel, Joel. *White Racism: A Psychohistory*. London: Free Association Books, 1988.

Kusukawa, Sahiko. "Bacon's Clssification of Knowledge." In *The Cambridge Companion to BACON*. Ed. Markku Peltonen. Cambridge: Cambridge University Press, 1996, 62–63.

Larsen, Nella. *Passing*. New York: Alfred A. Knopf, 1929.

Latimer, J. *Annals of Bristol in the Eighteenth Century*. Bristol, 1893.

Le Fanu, T. P. "Catalogue of Dean Swift's Library in 1715." *Proceedings of the Royal Irish Academy* 37 (1927): 270–73.

Leranbaum, Miriam. *Alexander Pope's "Opus Magnum," 1729-1744*. Oxford: Clarendon Press, 1977.

Ligon, Richard. *True and Exact History of the Island of Barbados*. London: Printed for Humphrey Moseley, 1657.

Lindfors, Bernth. "The Afterlife of the Hottentot Venus." *Neohelicon*. Ed. Miklos Szabolcsi and Gyorgy M. Vajda. Vol. 16, no. 2. Budapest, Hungary: Akademiai Kiado, 1989: 293–301.

———. "The Bottom Line: African Caricature in Georgian England." *World Literature Written in English* 24 (Summer 1984): 43–51.

Linne, Carl (Linneaus). *Systema Naturae*. Weinheim: J. Kramer, 1759. Reproduced from the 10th edition.

Little, Kenneth. *Negroes in Britain: A Study of Racial Relations in English Society*. 2nd ed. London: Routledge and Kegan Paul, 1972.

Locke, John. *Two Treatises on Government*. Ed. Peter Laslett. Cambridge: Cambridge University Press, 1988.

*London Magazine*. 18 (1749): 522.

Long, Edward. *History of Jamaica*. 3 vols. New York: Arno Press, 1972.

Lorde, Audre. *Sister Outsider*. Trumansburg, NY: Crossing Press, 1984.

Lovejoy, Arthur O. *The Great Chain of Being: A Study of the History of an Idea*. Cambridge, MA: Harvard University Press, 1936.

———. "Monboddo and Rousseau." *Modern Philology* 30 (1932–33): 283ff.

Lovridge, Mark. "'Liberty and Tristram Shandy.'" In *Laurence Sterne: Riddles and Mysteries*. Ed. Valerie Grosvenor Myers. London: Vision and Barnes & Noble, 1984.

Macherey, Pierre. *A Theory of Literary Production*. Trans. Geoffrey Wall. London: Routledge and Kegan Paul, 1978.

MacInnes, Charles M. *England and Slavery*. Bristol: Arrowsmith, 1934.

MacKenzie, Henry. *The Man of Feeling*. New York: W. W. Norton, 1958.

McKeon, Michael. *The Origins of the English Novel, 1600-1740*. Baltimore: Johns Hopkins University Press, 1987.

Mack, Maynard. *Collected in Himself: Essays Critical, Biographical, and Bibliographical on Pope and Some of His Contemporaries*. Newark: University of Delaware Press, 1982.

———, ed. *Alexander Pope: An Essay on Man*. London: Methuen, 1950.

Mandeville, Bernard. *The Fable of the Bees: Or, Private Vices, Public Benefits*. Oxford: At the Clarendon Press, 1924.

Markley, Robert. "Beyond Consensus: *The Rape of the Lock* and the Fate of Reading Eighteenth-Century Literature." *New Orleans Review* (Winter 1988): 68–77.

Marquis of Lansdowne, ed. *The Petty-Southwell Correspondence*. London: Constable, 1928.

Maurice, Henry William Edmund Petty Fitz, 6th Marquis of Lansdowne, ed. *The Petty-Southwell Correspondence*. London: Constable, 1928.

Memmi, Albert. *The Colonizer and the Colonized*. Trans. Howard Greenfield. New York: Orion Press, 1965.

Millar, John. *The Origin of the Distinction of Ranks: Or, An Inquiry into the Circumstances which give rise to Influence and Authority, in the Different Members of Society*, 4th ed. Edinburgh: Longman, 1806.

*Monthly Review*. 119 (1783): 492n.

Montrose, Louis. "Professing the Renaissance: The Poetics and Politics of Culture." *The New Historicism*. Ed. H. Aram Veeser. New York: Routledge, 1989.

Moore, Francis. *Travels Into the Inland Parts of Africa*. London: Printed by Edward Cave at St. John's Gate, 1738.

Morrison, Toni. *Playing in the Dark: Whiteness and the Literary Imagination*. New York: Vintage Books, 1990.

———. *Sula*. New York: Knopf, 1973.

Morrison, William, ed. *The American Heritage Dictionary of the English Language*. Boston, MA: Houghton Mifflin, 1981.

Mtubani, Victor. "The Black Voice in Eighteenth-Century Britain: African Writers Against Slavery and the Slave Trade." *Atlanta University Review of Race and Culture* 45 (June 1984): 85.

Nardal, Paulette. *La Revue du Monde Noir*. Paris, 1930.

Nelson, Cary, and Lawrence Grossberg, eds. *Marxism and the Interpretation of Culture*. Urbana: University of Illinois Press, 1988.

Neusner, Jacob. *Confronting Creation: How Judaism Reads Genesis: An Anthology of Genesis Rabbah*. Columbia, SC: University of South Carolina Press, 1991.

Newberry, John, ed. *The World Displayed: Or, A Curious Collection of Voyages and Travels*, 3rd ed. 20 vols. London, 1759–61.

Nezikin, Seder. *The Babylonian Talmud*. Trans. Rabbi Dr. I. Epstein. London: Soncino Press, 1935.

*Notes and Queries*. 3rd series 2 (1 November 1862).

Nussbaum, Felicity. "The Politics of Difference." *Eighteenth-Century Studies* 23 (Summer 1990).

Nutall, A. D. *Pope's 'Essay on Man'*. London: George Allen and Unwin, 1984.

Ogude, S. E. "Facts into Fiction: Equiano's Narrative Revisited." *Research in African Literatures* 13 (Spring 1982): 31–43.

Ovington, John. *A Voyage to Surat in the Year 1689*. Ed. H. G. Rawlinson. London: Oxford University Press, 1929.

Paquet, Sandra Pouchet. "The Heartbeat of a West Indian Slave: The History of Mary Prince." *African American Review* 26 (Spring 1992): 131–46.

Pascoe, C. F. *Two Hundred Years of the S.P.G.: An Historical Account of the Society for the Propagation of the Gospel in Foreign Parts*. London, 1901.

Patterson, David. *Literature and Spirit: Essays on Bakhtin and His Contemporaries*. Lexington: University Press of Kentucky, 1988.

Paulson, Ronald. *Hogarth's Graphic Works*. Vol. 1 of 2. New Haven, CT: Yale University Press, 1965.

Peckard, Peter. *Am I Not A Man? And A Brother? With All Humility Addressed to the British Legislature*. Cambridge, 1788.

Pepys, Samuel. *The Diary of Samuel Pepys*. Ed. Robert C. Latham and William Matthews. Vol. 3. Berkeley: University of California Press, 1970.

Petty, Sir William. *The Petty Papers: Some Unpublished Writings of Sir William Petty*. Ed. Marquis of Lansdowne. Vol. 2 of 2 vols. London: Constable, 1927.

Pinkerton, W. "Cats, Dogs, and Negroes as Articles of Commerce." *Notes and Queries*. 3rd series 2 (1862), 345–46.

Plymley, Katherine. *The Diary of Miss Katherine Plymley*. Folder R 88/74. Cambridgeshire Public Records Office, Cambridge, England.

Poovey, Mary. "My Hideous Progeny: Mary Shelley and the Feminization of Romanticism." *PMLA* 95 (May 1980): 332–47.

Pope, Alexander. *An Essay on Man*. Ed. Maynard Mack. 1950.

———. "An Essay on Man," 1733–1734. *Reproductions of the Manuscripts in the Pierpont Morgan Library and Houghton Library*. Ed. Maynard Mack. Oxford: 1962.

———. *Pastoral Poetry and An Essay on Criticism. The Poems of Alexander Pope*. Vol. 1. Audra and Aubrey Williams, eds. London: Methuen, 1961.

Porter, Dorothy. *Early Negro Writing, 1760–1837*. Boston, MA: Beacon Press, 1971.

Postel, Guillaume. *De Originibus*. Basle: Per Ioannem Oporinum, 1561.

Pratt, Mary Louise. "Conventions of Representation: Where Discourse and Ideology Meet." *Contemporary Perceptions of Language: Interdisciplinary Dimensions*. Ed. Heidi Byrnes. Washington, DC: Georgetown University Press, 139–55.

———. *Imperial Eyes: Travel Writing and Transculturation*. London: Routledge, 1992.

———. "Scratches on the Face of the Country." In *"Race," Writing, and Difference*. Ed. Henry Louis Gates, Jr. Chicago: University of Chicago Press, 1986.

Price, Lawrence M. *Inkle and Yarico Album*. Berkeley, 1937.

Priestley, F.E.L. (Francis Ethelbort Louis). "Pope and the Great Chain of Being." In *Essays in English Literature from the Renaissance to the Victorian Age*. Ed. Millar MacLure and F. W. Watt. Toronto: University of Toronto Press, 1964.

Prince, Mary. *The History of Mary Prince, A West Indian Slave, Related by Herself*, 1831. Ed. Moira Ferguson. Ann Arbor: University of Michigan Press, 1993.

———. *The History of Mary Prince, A West Indian Slave, Related by Herself*, 1831. London: Pandora, Reprint, 1987.

Pringle, Thomas. Supplement by the Original Editor, Thomas Pringle. *The History of Mary Prince: a West Indian Slave, Related by Herself*, 1831. London: Pandora, Reprint, 1987.

Reade, Aleyn Lyell. *Johnsonian Gleanings*. 11 vols. London: Arden Press, 1912.

Reiss, Timothy J. *The Meaning of Literature*. Ithaca: Cornell University Press, 1992.

"Review of *Letters of Ignatius Sancho.*" *European Magazine and London Review* 2 (September 1782): 199.

"Review of *Letters of the Late Ignatius Sancho, an African.*" *The Gentleman's Magazine* 52 (1782): 437.

"Review of *The Life of Olaudah Equiano, or Gustavus Vassa, the African.*" *General Magazine and Impartial Review* (July 1789): 315.

"Review of *The Life of Olaudah Equiano, or Gustavus Vassa, the African.*" *Gentleman's Magazine* 59 (1789): 539.

Rice, C. Duncan. "Literary Sources and the Revolution in British Attitudes to Slavery." In *Anti-Slavery, Religion, and Reform: Essays in Memory of Roger Anstey*. Ed. Christine Bolt and Seymour Drescher. Kent, England: William Dawson and Sons, 1980, 320-21.

Richardson, Samuel. *Pamela*. Vol. 1 of 2 vols. London: J. M. Dent and Sons; New York: E. P. Dutton, 1950, 6. First published 1914, 230.

Robeson, Eslanda Goode. "Black Paris." *New Challenge: A Literary Quarterly* (January and June 1936).

Rogers, J. A. *Sex and Race: Negro-Caucasian Mixing in All Ages and Lands*, 5th ed. Vol. 3 of 3 vols. New York: Helga M. Rogers, 1944.

Rogers, Pat. *Essays on Pope*. Cambridge: Cambridge University Press, 1993.

———. *Literature and Popular Culture in Eighteenth Century England*. Sussex, England: Harvester Press, 1985.

Rogers, Woodes. *A Cruising Voyage Round the World*. London: Printed for A. Bell and B. Lintot, 1712.

Rousseau, G. S., and Pat Rogers. *The Enduring Legacy: Alexander Pope Tercentenary Essays*. Cambridge: Cambridge University Press, 1988.

Rushworth, John. *Historical Collections of Private Passages of State, Weighty Matters in Law, Remarkable Proceedings in Five Parliaments*. 8 vols. London: D. Browne, 1721-22.

Said, Edward W. *Culture and Imperialism*. New York: Knopf, 1993.

———. "Secular Criticism." *Critical Theory Since 1965*. Ed. Adams and Searle. Florida: Florida State University Press, 1986, 605-24.

———. *The World, the Text, and the Critic*. Cambridge: Harvard University Press, 1983.

Sambrook, James. *The Eighteenth Century: The Intellectual and Cultural Context of English Literature, 1700-1789*. London: Longman, 1986.

Samuels, Wilfred D. "The Disguised Voice in *The Interesting Narrative of Olaudah Equiano, or Gustavus Vassa the African.*" *Black American Literature Forum* 19 (Summer, 1985): 64-69.

Sancho, Ignatius. *Letters of the Late Ignatius Sancho: An African, to Which are Prefixed, Memoirs of his Life*, 1st ed. 2 vols. London: J. Nichols, 1782.

———. *Letters of the Late Ignatius Sancho: An African, to Which Are Prefixed, Memoirs of his Life by Joseph Jekyll*, 5th ed. London: Printed for William Sancho, 1803.

——. *Letters of the Late Ignatius Sancho, An African.* The Black Heritage Library Collection. Freeport, NY: Books for Libraries Press, 1971.

Sandiford, Keith A. *Measuring the Moment: Strategies of Protest in Eighteenth-Century Afro-English Writing.* London: Associated University Presses, 1988.

Schiebinger, Londa. "The Anatomy of Difference: Race and Sex in Eighteenth-Century Science." *Eighteenth-Century Studies* 23 (Summer, 1990): 387–405.

——. *The Mind Has No Sex? Women in the Origins of Modern Science.* Cambridge, MA: Harvard University Press, 1989.

Scholes, Robert. "Language, Narrative, and Anti-Narrative." In *On Narrative.* Ed. W.J.T. Mitchell. Chicago: University of Chicago Press, 1981.

Scott, Sarah. *The History of Sir George Ellison.* London: A. Millar, 1766.

——. *The History of Sir George Ellison.* Ed. Betty Rizzo. Lexington: University Press of Kentucky, 1996.

Sekora, John, and Darwin T. Turner, eds. *The Art of Slave Narrative: Original Essays in Criticism and Theory.* Macomb: University of Western Illinois Press, 1982.

Sha, Richard C. "Gray's Political 'Elegy': Poetry as the Burial of History." *Philological Quarterly* 69 (Summer 1990): 337–57.

Shankar, Subramanian. "From Hearts of Darkness to Temples of Doom: The Discursive Economy of the Travel Narrative in the Colonial Context." Ph.D. Dissertation. University of Texas-Austin, 1993.

Sharp, Granville. *Extract of a Letter to a Gentleman in Maryland Wherein is Demonstrated the Wickedness of Tolerating the Slave Trade*, 3rd ed. First published in London, 1793. London: J. Phillips, 1797.

Shaw, Rosalind. "The Invisible Chi in Equiano's *Interesting Narrative.*" *Journal of Religion in Africa* 19 (1989): 164–56.

Sherburn, George, ed. *The Correspondence of Alexander Pope.* 4 vols. Oxford: Clarendon Press, 1956.

Shklovsky, Viktor. "Art as Technique." In *Contemporary Literary Criticism: Modernism Through Poststructuralism.* Ed. Robert Con Davis. New York: Longman, 1986.

Shyllon, Folarin O. *Black People in Britain, 1555–1833.* London: Oxford University Press, 1977.

Sibley, Agnes Marie. *Alexander Pope's Prestige in America, 1725–1835.* New York, 1949.

Smith, Adam. *Theory of Moral Sentiments.* Ed. D. D. Raphael and A. L. Macfie. Vol. 2. Oxford: Clarendon Press, 1956.

Smith, Malvaern Van Wyk. "'The Most Wretched of the Human Race': The Iconography of the Khoikhoin (Hottentots), 1500–1800." *History and Anthropology* 5 (1992): 285.

Smith, Robert. "Rereading *Banjo*: Claude McKay and the French Connection." *CLA* (September 1986): 46–58.

Smith, Samuel Stanhope. *An Essay on the Causes of the Variety of Complexion and Figure in the Human Species.* Ed. Winthrop Jordan. Philadelphia, 1787. Reprint. Cambridge, MA: Harvard University Press, Belknap, 1965.

Smith, William. *A New Voyage to Guinea.* London: John Nourse, 1744.

Solomon, Harry M. *The Rape of the Text: Reading and Misreading Pope's "Essay on Man."* Tuscaloosa: University of Alabama Press, 1993.

——. "Reading Philosophical Poetry: A Hermeneutics of Metaphor for Pope's *Essay on Man.*" In *The Philosopher as Writer: The Eighteenth Century.* Ed. Robert Ginsburg. London: Associated UP, 1987.

Spacks, Patricia Meyer. "Ev'ry Woman is at Heart a Rake." *Eighteenth-Century Studies* 8 (1974): 31.

Spence, Joseph. *Observations, Anecdotes, and Characters of Books and Men.* Ed. James M. Osborn. 2 vols. Oxford: Clarendon Press, 1966.

Sprat, Thomas. *The History of the Royal Society.* London: Printed by T. R. for J. Martyn and J. Allestry, 1667.

Starling, Marion W. *The Slave Narrative.* Washington, DC: Howard University Press, 1988.

Steele, Sir Richard. *The Tatler.* Ed. Donald F. Bond. 3 vols. Oxford: Clarendon Press, 1987.

Stepan, Nancy Leys. "Race and Gender: The Role of Analogy in Science." *Isis* 77 (June 1986): 261-77.

——. "Race and Gender: The Role of Analogy in Science." In *Anatomy of Racism.* Ed. David T. Goldberg. Minneapolis: University of Minnesota Press, 1990.

Sterne, Laurence. *Letters of Laurence Sterne.* Ed. Lewis Perry Curtis. Oxford: Clarendon Press, 1935.

——. *The Life and Opinions of Tristram Shandy.* Ed. Ian Watt. Boston: Houghton Mifflin, 1965.

——. *A Sentimental Journey Through England and France.* London: Oxford University Press, 1960. Rept. of 1928 edition.

——. *Sermons of Mr. Yorick.* From *The Complete Life and Works of Laurence Sterne.* Ed. Wilbur Cross. Vol. 5 of 6 vols. New York: AMS Press, 1970. Rept. of 1904 edition.

Stuart, Charles. *A Memoir of Granville Sharp.* New York: American Anti-Slavery Society, 1836.

Sumner, Charles. *The Life of Granville Sharp. Works,* Vol. 3. Boston: Lee and Sheppard, 1875-83.

Swift, Johanthan. *Gulliver's Travels. The Prose Works of Jonathan Swift.* Ed. Herbert Davis. New York: Oxford University Press, 1977.

——. *Gulliver's Travels and Other Writings by Jonathan Swift.* Ed. Louis A. Landa. Boston: Houghton Mifflin, 1960.

——. *Tale of A Tub.* Ed. A. C. Guthkelch and D. Nichol Smith. Oxford: Clarendon Press, 1920.

Sypher, Wylie. *Guinea's Captive Kings: British Anti-Slavery Literature of the XVIIIth Century.* Chapel Hill: University of North Carolina Press, 1942.

Temple, Sir William. "An Essay upon the Ancient and Modern Learning," 1690. In *Five Miscellaneous Essays,* 3rd ed. Ann Arbor, MI: University of Michigan Press, 1963.

Thackeray, William Makepeace. *Vanity Fair.* New York: Grosset and Dunlap, 1935.

Thomas, Deborah. *Thackeray and Slavery.* Athens: Ohio University Press, 1993.

Thompson, E. P. *Whigs and Hunters.* New York: Pantheon Books, 1975.

Thompson, Thomas. *The African Trade for Negro Slaves, Shewn to be Consistent with Principles of Humanity, and with the Laws of Revealed Religion.* London: Simmons and Kirkby, n.d.

Thomson, James. *The Poetical Works of James Thomson.* Vol. 2 of 2 vols. Boston: Little, Brown, 1866.

Tobin, James. *An Apology for Slavery.* London: Gordon Turnbull, 1786.

Todd, Dennis. "The Hairy Maid at the Harpsichord: Some Speculations on the Meaning of *Gulliver's Travels.*" *Texas Studies in Literature and Language* (Summer 1992): 239–83.

Todd, Janet. *Sensibility: An Introduction.* London: Methuen, 1986.

Tornielli, Agostino. *Annales Sacri and Profani.* Frankfurt: Apud Ioannem Theobaldum Schon Wetterum, 1611.

Vaillant, Janet G. *Black, French, and African: A Life of Leopold Sedar Senghor.* Cambridge, MA: Harvard University Press, 1990.

"Variety of the Human Species: Tartars, Hottentots, Negroes, Americans, etc." *London Magazine* (16 July 1750): 318.

Veeser, H. Aram, ed. *The New Historicism.* New York: Routledge, 1989.

Virgil, *Georgics.* Ed. C. S. Jerram. Oxford: Clarendon Press, 1892.

Voltaire. "On the Antiquity of Nations." In *The Best Known Works of Voltaire.* New York: Blue Ribbon Books, 1940.

Wallerstein, Immanuel. "The Ideological Tensions of Capitalism: Universalism versus Racism and Sexism." In *Race, Nation, Class: Ambiguous Identities.* Ed. Etienne Balibar and Immanuel Wallerstein. London: Verso, 1991.

Walvin, James. *Black and White: The Negro and English Society 1555–1945.* London: Penguin Books, 1973.

Walvin, James, and Paul Edwards. *Black Personalities,* 223–37.

Warren, George. *Histoire Générale des Antilles de l'Amerique.* Lyon: Cesar de Rochefort, 1667.

Werkmeister, W. H. "Kant, Nicolai Hartmann, and the Great Chain of Being." In *The Great Chain of Being and Italian Phenomenology.* Ed. Angela Ales Bello. Vols. 69–97. Boston, MA: D. Reidel, 1981.

West, Cornel. *Keeping Faith: Philosophy and Race in America.* New York: Routledge, 1993.

———. "Marxist Theory and the Specificity of Afro-American Oppression." In *Marxism and the Interpretation of Culture.* Ed. Cary Nelson and Lawrence Grossbert. Urbana: University of Illinois Press, 1988, 17–29.

Wheatley, Phillis. *The Poems of Phillis Wheatley.* Ed. Julian D. Mason. Chapel Hill: University of North Carolina Press, 1966.

White, Charles. *An Account of the Regular Gradation in Man, and in Different Animals and Vegetables; and from the Former to the Latter.* London: C. Dilly, 1799.

White, Hayden. "New Historicism: A Comment." In *The New Historicism.* Ed. H. Aram Veeser. New York: Routledge, 1989.

Whitefield, George. "To the Inhabitants of Maryland, Virginia, North and South Carolina, Concerning Their Negroes." In *Three Letters From the Reverend Mr. G. Whitefield.* Letter 3 of 3 letters. Philadelphia, 1740.

Wilberforce, William. *A Practical View of the Prevailing Religious System of Professed Christians in the Higher and Middle Classes of Society, Contrasted with Real Christianity.* Philadelphia: Printed by John Ormrod, 1798. 1st American edition.

Williams, Eric. *Capitalism and Slavery.* New York: G. P. Putnam's Sons, 1966.

Williams, Gomer. *History of the Liverpool Privateers and Letters of Marque, With an Account of the Liverpool Slave Trade.* Reprint of the 1897 1st ed. New York: A. M. Kelley, 1966.

Williams, Raymond. *Culture.* Cambridge: Fontana Paperbacks, 1981.

———. *Culture and Society: 1780–1950.* New York: Columbia University Press, 1983.

———. *Problems in Materialism and Culture: Selected Essays.* London: Verso, 1980.

Wilson, Thomas, Lord Bishop of Sodor and Man. "An Essay Towards an Instruction for the Indians," 1741. In *The Works of the Right Reverend Father in God, Thomas Wilson.* Oxford: John Henry Parker, 1851.

Winant, Howard. *Racial Conditions: Politics, Theory, Comparisons.* Minneapolis. University of Minnesota Press, 1994.

Wollstonecraft, Mary. *Review of the Interesting Narrative of the Life of Olaudah Equiano, or Gustavus Vassa, Analytical Review* (May 1789).

———. *A Vindication of the Rights of Men, in a Letter To the Honourable Edmund Burke; Occasioned By His Reflections on the Revolution in France,* 2nd ed. London: J. Johnson, 1790.

Wotton, William. *Reflections Upon Ancient and Modern Learning,* 1694.

Wright, Josephine. *Ignatius Sancho (1729–1780): An Early African Composer in England: The Collected Editions of His Music in Facsimile.* New York: Garland, 1981.

Young, Robert J. C. *Colonial Desire: Hybridity in Theory, Culture and Race.* London: Routledge, 1995, 180.

*The Zohar.* Vol. 1. Trans. Harry Sperling and Maurice Simon. London: Soncino Press, 1935.

Zook, George F. *The Company of Royal Adventurers Trading into Africa.* Lancaster, PA: Press of the New Era Printing Co., 1919.

# Index

**About the Author**

HELENA WOODARD is Associate Professor of English at the University of Texas at Austin, where she specializes in eighteenth-century British literature and culture, and in African American literature.

# FAIR FORMS

*Essays in English Literature from Spenser to Jane Austen*

*Transported with celestiall desyre*
*Of those faire formes . . .*

EDMUND SPENSER, 'An Hymne of Heavenly Beautie'

# FAIR FORMS

*Essays in English Literature
from Spenser to Jane Austen*

EDITED BY MAREN-SOFIE RØSTVIG

D. S. BREWER · CAMBRIDGE

Published by D. S. Brewer Ltd
240 Hills Road, Cambridge

First published 1975

ISBN 0 85991 007 5

*This volume has been published with the aid of
a grant from the Norwegian Research Council
(Norges Almenvitenskapelige Forskningsråd)*

Printed by The Anchor Press Ltd
and bound by Wm Brendon & Son Ltd
both of Tiptree, Essex

# Contents

# List of Illustrations

# Preface

Structural analysis is a key that unlocks many doors, and so no
wonder the study of literary theory has been structurally oriented
from its very beginning and at no time more so perhaps than today.
To deplore the lack of proper attention to structure therefore may seem
utterly perverse, if not frivolous. I would nevertheless argue that the
theoretical interest in structure has failed to influence practical criticism to the extent that one would have expected in view of its professed importance. If one considers the sustained energy with which
critics have pursued poetic imagery, for example, or the uses of irony,
it is at once apparent that the concept of structure, vital though it is,
has elicited no comparable massed attempt to unravel its many complexities. Efforts along these lines have been sporadic rather than sustained; they have seldom been taken far enough, nor have they been
worked into some kind of survey or connected argument about the
role of structure in pre-Romantic literature.

It may be futile to call for any such survey; the very nature of the
task may make it impossible to perform. Even Swift's seven sages
shut up close in seven chambers for seven years (with or without
computers) would most likely have had to admit defeat. But what
one may legitimately expect is a keener awareness of the role of structure in individual textual analyses, and a more systematic attention
than one usually finds.

It is possible, however, that this awareness is in the process of becoming more widely shared. The studies collected here, for example,
are sharply focused on structure, not because the editor insisted on
some kind of unifying principle, but quite simply because this was
the direction taken by each contributor. As a consequence this volume
displays a wide range of structural approaches extending from a

classical investigation of narrative structure in a novel by Jane Austen, to the structural complexities (often of a numerological kind) of Spenser's *Fowre Hymnes* and Milton's 'On the Morning of Christ's Nativity'.

Einar Bjorvand's investigation of the complex patterns of cross references within Spenser's *Fowre Hymnes* enables the reader to perceive and interpret the overall thematic movement with far greater precision than has been so far achieved. The analysis was partly carried out by means of Mr Bjorvand's recently published concordance to Spenser's poetic *progressio quaternaria*.

Each essay is, of course, self-contained, but the two studies of Milton's *Nativity Ode* are complementary. These trace various sequential arrangements, sometimes of a balanced or symmetrical character, and sometimes of the kind usually referred to as numerological. As these essays indicate, the two types of arrangement may be so closely connected that it is singularly illogical to admit the one and reject the other in the manner of some American Milton scholars. But in the case of Dryden's *Essay of Dramatick Poesie* and Fielding's *Tom Jones* the structural analyses submitted here contain no references to the now largely forgotten subject of symbolic numbers. They depend, instead, on an analysis of the author's use of structural allusions. While we are thoroughly familiar with the technique of tracing verbal echoes or related image-clusters, we have failed to perceive the point that it was possible for a *structure* to be imitated and consciously echoed not merely as a matter of convenience, but in order to invoke the associations invested in it. As H. Neville Davies shows, this is what Dryden did when he decided on the form for his *Essay of Dramatick Poesie*, and once we grasp the import of the selected form we realise that Dryden's essay is an ambitious defence of London as a cultural centre in the mid-1660s.

Although my own study of *Tom Jones* touches on the topic of structural allusion in its discussion of Samuel Johnson's *Rasselas*, structural analysis is largely a point of departure for the discovery of Fielding's use of various aspects of the myth of Hercules. The action of the central section (Books VII–XII) is seen to constitute an exact narrative version of the theme so popular among Renaissance and neoclassical painters of the Choice of Hercules.

The essay which concludes the volume—Grete Ek's analysis of Jane Austen's *Pride and Prejudice*—argues that the opposition between Darcy and Elizabeth is apparent rather than real. Beneath the antithetical framework we recognise a substructure based on a gradual revelation of facts that contradict the dramatic illusion of the first half of the novel. The resolution, therefore, terminates a process of clarification rather than one of substantial change.

If this volume as a whole carries a message, it must be that the mechanics of literary design, if examined with due care, may afford important new insights into basic thematic concerns. It is implicit in this message that the gap between numerological and more traditional approaches to structure should be bridged, since strictly speaking it does not exist.

*Oslo*                                                                                  M.-S. R.
*22 April 1974*

# I

# *Spenser's defence of poetry*

## SOME STRUCTURAL ASPECTS OF THE *FOWRE HYMNES*

### Einar Bjorvand

In his teaching that 'every one that exalteth himself shall be humbled; but he that humbleth himself shall be exalted', Christ has epitomised the crucial predicament of the devout Christian. The truly righteous man is to be known—not only to God, but also to his fellow Christians —through protestations of sinfulness, and by his confession and repudiation of former errors. 'God, be merciful to me a sinner', prayed the publican, smiting his breast. Yet, plainly this behaviour may become a kind of self-praise: the Pharisee too may adopt the attitude of the repentant publican, but he will remain a Pharisee. 'For faith consists not in a body bending but in a mind believing.'[1]

What then of the penitent sinner who speaks to us through the dedicatory epistle to his *Fowre Hymnes*? Is he a publican or a Pharisee? Has he humbled his mind as well as his body? The question is of interest because the answer may shed light on the structure of the *Hymnes* and help us to decide whether they are arranged in a sequence of steady and gradual ascent, or whether the second pair should be seen as contrasted to the first pair. Spenser certainly takes great care to place his 'lewd layes' well into the past. He has created a myth which associates, very appropriately, passionate love with youth and allows it to be superseded, with growing maturity, by love of God. He promises 'to amend, and by way of retractation to reforme' the product of erring youth.[2] But Spenser's statement that the first pair of the *Hymnes* was written early in his career should not be taken at its face value; for the mass of both external and internal evidence leaves little doubt that the hymns of earthly love and beauty were in fact written, or rewritten, after the publication of the *Amoretti* in 1595.[3] Furthermore, the dedication might seem to invite the conclusion that Spenser, now in his forties and at the end of his poetical career, had come to embrace a religious outlook on life that involved a rejection of sexual love. But such a view would make nonsense of Spenser's praise of the two Countesses as representatives of love and beauty 'both in the one and the other kinde'.[4]

The theories outlined above seem to corroborate the supposition that despite Spenser's tone of high moral seriousness, the 'retractation' should be regarded as a conventional cliché.[5] But the fact that such retractions were in fashion does not deprive the dedication of its claims on our attention. Several considerations may have guided Spenser in his phrasing of the dedicatory epistle. It may be designed to safeguard his hymns from moral censure. But we should also be aware that the preamble functions as a prologue to the hymns and may be intended to play its part in shaping the attitude of the reader. Perhaps its most obvious effect is to put the reader on the alert, watching keenly for implicit as well as explicit contrasts and cross-references within the subtly organised structure of the *Fowre Hymnes*.

It seems a reasonable deduction, at all events, that Spenser's major concern was not merely to render his first pair of hymns harmless by neutralising their moral blemishes, but that he was much more concerned with the artistic unity of his work as a whole. Critics have tried to account for this essential unity, which is perceptible in the *Fowre Hymnes*, either by interpreting the last two hymns as a complement to the first two,[6] or by regarding the account of love and beauty in the first pair as a description of lower steps on the Neoplatonic ladder of love.[7] But both of these tidy assumptions require further inspection. After all, the poet-speaker of the last two hymns can hardly be said to be recommending the experiences recorded in the first two hymns as necessary or even desirable 'steps' on the ladder to heavenly love and beauty. In fact, the transition from the first to the last pair of hymns suggests a Christian conversion rather than a gradual ascent. The first two hymns record a stage in the poet's life, a stage which he eventually outgrew when he 'put away childish things'. It may be argued that we are nearer to the true relationship between the two pairs by saying, with Robert Ellrodt, that 'if a structural unity is discovered in the *Fowre Hymnes*, it will be the unity of a diptych with parallel but contrasted themes on each leaf, not the continuous ascent of a Platonic *scala*'.[8] There are others besides Ellrodt who have glimpsed a system of contrasts and verbal echoes in the *Hymnes*, but the rich complexity of Spenser's scheme seems never to have been investigated.

Spenser was not content simply to state his present attitude to his 'early' hymns and then offer them as a warning to others 'of like age and disposition'. He also had to ensure that the reader would be willing to accompany the poet on his ascent to the vision of heavenly love and beauty. The first pair of hymns was needed both to point a contrast between earthly and heavenly love and also to give the true story of man's journey to harmony with God and his fellow men. Surely, until man realises that he *is* a sinner, until he can pray with the publican, 'God, be merciful to me a sinner', he is denied the divine grace needed for his ascent.

The discussion of the relationship between the two pairs of hymns touches on Spenser's conception of the function of his poetry. Does his poetry have the power not only to 'show the way' but also to 'intice any man to enter into it'?[9] How can Spenser make sure that the reader will not prefer love's 'Paradize' of pleasure in the first hymn to the 'sweete pleasures' of the 'soueraine light' in the last hymn? Spenser must have realised the rhetorical inadequacy of a mere appeal to the reader not to renew his 'passed follies'; a far wiser poetic strategy would be to permit the first pair to be, not simply a record of youthful errors, but part of a design to 'intice' the reader into choosing the right path. Such a design would enable Spenser to defend his poetry in the eyes of both God and man. The first two hymns prepare the way for the second pair and 'the two later hymns are designed to gain strength and meaning from the two former. The method is a complex system of parallels and contrasts'.[10]

Some contrasts and parallels strike the reader immediately: 'two Hymnes of earthly or naturall loue and beautie' are followed by 'two others of heauenly and celestiall'. Furthermore, each hymn praises one guardian deity, Cupid and Venus in the first two hymns, and Christ and Sapience in the 'heavenly' hymns. Thus the masculine love-god, Cupid, who has descended to earth from '*Venus* lap aboue', is paralleled by the loving Christ descending 'out of the bosome of eternall blisse'. Similarly, the maternal queen of beauty, Venus, characteristically remaining 'aboue', is paralleled in the last hymn by the heavenly, feminine figure of Sapience. But the pattern of parallelism and contrast can be seen to be more complex than this. It has been shown that in retrospect the *Fowre Hymnes* may be seen as displaying similar and clearly related patterns of falling and rising, and that there is an intricate interplay of parallel and contrasted verbal elements between the hymns.[11] But so far no attempt has been made to show

how the complex pattern of thematic and verbal contrasts and parallels is underscored by the stanzaic design of the hymns. The two later hymns represent a fresh start rather than a continuous progression from the former two. They may thus be seen to run parallel with the first pair, and the parallelism is brought out, not only in the thematic movement of the hymns, but also by their structure. Such a parallel structure throws new light on related and antithetical aspects of theme, imagery and form, and thus, ultimately, on the relationship between the two pairs.

The detection of a parallel structure in the *Fowre Hymnes* should come as no great surprise since a similar structural arrangement has been demonstrated in the *Epithalamion*.[12] The structure of *Epithalamion* is probably concentric, the first stanza matching the last stanza, the second stanza the penultimate one and so on. In the *Fowre Hymnes*, however, an exactly symmetrical arrangement of stanzas would distort the general thematic movement which clearly indicates that each of the 'earthly' hymns should be paired with its 'heavenly' counterpart.

For Spenser the publican's behaviour was only a part solution. As I hope to show, Spenser was concerned to vindicate his poetry, and he wrote and revised his *Fowre Hymnes* according to a structural pattern that allows even the first two hymns to form by parallelism and contrast, foreshadowing and antithesis, a glorification of God in his Trinity of supreme love, beauty, and wisdom.


II


Many readers, turning from the dedication to the introductory stanzas of *An Hymne in Honour of Love*, seem to have been surprised by the Petrarchan description of love. The Petrarchan elements in the first two hymns have been taken as evidence of the inclusion of older material.[13] But the modern reader sees a contrast between Petrarchism and Neoplatonism which may not have been there for Spenser.[14] And if we assume that Spenser had outgrown Petrarchism by the time he was preparing his hymns for publication, the question arises why he did not leave out the Petrarchan stanzas. However conventional the courtly tradition was, there were other ways open to a poet of his experience and achievement. Spenser must have had some good reason to stress the tyrannical aspects of love. If he wanted his first pair of hymns to fall into a pattern of contrast and parallelism with the second pair, and if he wanted at the same time to make his poems seem to describe his psychological development, the firmly established courtly tradition was well suited to his purpose.

The description of the tormented lover who forgets all other claims on his attention and sees no dangers in the pursuit of love, who invariably overestimates the beauty of his mistress and exaggerates his happiness when well-favoured or his misery when rejected, must have been felt to correspond to at least a traditional psychology of love. The descriptions of the tyrannical Cupid playing with human destinies and of the loving Christ suffering to restore man to his former happiness may be consciously designed to point the contrast between earthly and heavenly love. Spenser may also have brought out this general pattern of contrast between earthly and heavenly love as clearly as he did in order to encourage the reader to pair stanzas or groups of stanzas in his two hymns of love.

One of the problems facing the critic who attempts to uncover the parallel structure of the hymns is what to make of the introductory stanzas. There are six introductory stanzas in *An Hymne in Honour of Love*, but there are only three in *An Hymne of Heavenly Love*. A quick glance through the introductory stanzas of the *Hymne of Love* will, however, reveal that this part of the hymn falls into two parts of three stanzas each; three for the lover's complaint and promise 'to sing the praises' of Cupid's name, and three invoking Cupid, the Muses and Nymphs, and the ladies. In the *Hymne of Heavenly Love* the invocation and repudiation of his 'lewd layes' in the three introductory stanzas, are followed by three stanzas in praise of the three persons of the Trinity. Thus the first three stanzas after the introduction of the *Hymne of Heavenly Love* describing the Father (stanza 4), the Son (stanza 5), and the Holy Spirit (stanza 6), parallel the invocation of Cupid (stanza 4), the Muses and Nymphs (stanza 5), and the young ladies (stanza 6) in the *Hymne of Love*.[15] But stanzas 4 to 6 of the *Hymne of Heavenly Love* also have further significance. Renaissance artists frequently designed their works so as to place particular emphasis on the sovereignty of the centre. 'Almost as a regular practice, they would devote the central place to some principal figure or event, or make it coincide with a structural division of the poem.'[16] If the sixteen introductory stanzas are disregarded, the three stanzas in praise of the Trinity become the three central stanzas of the *Fowre Hymnes*, with the Son in the triumphant mid position. The positioning of the Trinity at the centre of the *Fowre Hymnes* may be seen to be even more telling if the stanzas of the *Hymnes* can be seen to group themselves around this centre in a way which would enhance the formal perfection of the work and also form a key to our understanding of the thematic development of the whole sequence.

Stanza 7 (lines 43–49) in each hymn of love forms an introduction: to the *rule of tyranny* in the *Hymne of Love* and to the *rule of grace* in the *Hymne of Heavenly Love*.[17] Cupid, the great 'god of might', the 'subduer of mankynd', may be seen as the antithesis to the Holy Spirit who is praised as the eternal 'spring of grace and wisedome trew'. The contrast becomes apparent when the poet-speaker of the *Hymne of Love*, impressed and over-awed by the power of Cupid, humbly asks, who 'can expresse the glorie of thy *might*?', while the poet-speaker of the *Hymne of Heavenly Love* hopes to be inspired by the Holy Spirit to 'tell the marueiles by thy *mercie* wrought' (my italics).

Stanzas 8 to 10 (lines 50–70) of the two hymns offer parallel accounts of the birth and early activities of Cupid and the creation and 'eternall blis' of the prelapsarian angels. The ambivalence which surrounds Cupid, born of plenty and want, is contrasted with the 'infinite increase of Angels bright' created by the 'fruitfull loue' of God in his own likeness. While Cupid is stirred to rise from Chaos in 'which his goodly face long hidden was / From heauens view, and in deepe darknesse kept' (*HL* 9), the angels inherit 'the heauens illimitable hight', 'adornd with thousand lamps of burning light' (*HHL* 9). While the angels enjoy 'eternall blis', Cupid wakes up in a sublunary world of time indicated by the presence of Clotho. The 'hardie flight' of winged Cupid (*HL* 10) through the dark waste forms a clumsy imitation of the easy flight and 'nimble wings' of the angels (*HHL* 10) who wait on God and 'behold the glorie of his light'. The contrast is underscored by the selection of rhymewords. 'Bright-light-hight-spright' abound in the *Hymne of Heavenly Love*, while 'light' in stanza 10 of the *Hymne of Love* occurs only to stress the absence of light in Cupid's world ('yet wanting light'). The most frequent rhymewords in the *Hymne of Love* are 'fyre-desyre-flame', but when the poet 'turns to heavenly love, fire and flame [and desire] are conspicuously absent (except for the hellfire in *HHL*, line 89) until the very end of the poem when their meaning is presumably divinised by the identification of Love with Christ'.[18] By the end of stanza 10 the contrast between Cupid and the angels has been established in terms of the contrast between time and eternity, earth and heaven, darkness and light.

The story of the birth of Cupid may also have another significance. The glory and mystery of the 'wondrous cradle' of Cupid's infancy reminds us of Christ's nativity:

> where he encradled was
> In simple cratch, wrapt in a wad of hay,
> Betweene the toylefull Oxe and humble Asse.
>
> (*HHL* lines 225–27)

To grasp this contrast between the exaltation of Cupid and the humility of Christ helps our understanding of their separate roles.

Cupid is said to be older than his own nativity (*HL* line 54), like Christ, who before his birth was coeternal with God the Father. The parallelism is underlined in the structure of the two hymns since the stories of the nativities of Cupid and Christ are both to be found in the second stanza after the introduction. To readers accustomed to interpreting the second Psalm as the allegory *par excellence* of the Son as eternal godhead, direct and oblique reference to the *second* person of the Trinity in the *second* stanza of the hymn proper may have been felt to be appropriate. Furthermore, both Cupid and Christ are born in time, Cupid through Venus and Christ through the Virgin, and 'while Cupid is "begot of Plentie and of Penurie" (*HL, l.* 53), Christ also expresses the paradox of the richness and poverty of Love ("And in what rags, and in how base aray, / The glory of our heavenly riches lay," *HHL, ll.* 228–229)'.[19] Simply to see the similarities, however, is not enough. It is true that the description of Cupid as 'elder then [his] owne natiuitie' and 'the eldest of the heauenly Peares' (*HL* lines 54 and 56) may seem to link him with Christ, but on the other hand the denomination 'eldest' has no meaning in relation to the *eternal* Son. This becomes clear in the *Hymne of Heavenly Beautie* where Sapience is described as 'peerelesse maiesty' (*HHB* line 186). The seeming splendor of Cupid is reduced to earthly vainglory, and he becomes an earthly parody rather than a type of Christ. Spenser frequently uses the technique which Milton brought to perfection in *Paradise Lost*, where, for instance, Satan 'High on a throne of royal state' (II, 1), is implicitly contrasted with God 'High throned above all highth' (III, 58).[20] Dryden takes the same process one stage further by alluding to Milton's description of Satan when, in *MacFlecknoe*, the 'Prince of dulness' appears 'High

on a Throne of his own Labours rear'd' (lines 106–7). 'Satan not
God is the original imitated' and 'the proper wit of the poem is that
Flecknoe can only parody a parody of God'.[21] When used by an
intelligent poet the technique of presenting praise that finally appears
as dispraise is a powerful one.

The Son in the third hymn becomes man to serve man while Cupid
descends only to rule over man. And surely, while dualism is an essential characteristic of earthly love, the poverty of Christ is self-imposed.
Christ is 'derived not from a desire for something lacking nor from a
mixture of contraries but from single Plenty alone'.[22] Spenser stresses
the ambiguous and controversial nature of Cupid. He makes the
reader associate him both with the angels and with Christ, but the
final effect of the cross-references is not to give an exalted impression
of Cupid but to increase awareness of the utter inadequacy of this god
of love.

Stanzas 11 to 14 (lines 71–98) strengthen the impression of Cupid's
role as both type and parody. Stanza 11 starts in much the same vein
as that in which stanza 10 ended. Cupid was surrounded by darkness
until

> *His owne faire mother, for all creatures sake,*
> *Did lend him light from her owne goodly ray:*
>
> > *(HL lines 72–3)*

and his situation is echoed in the description of the angels (*HHL* 11)
who spend their time in the eternal light of God who 'his beames
doth still to them extend'. Stanzas 12 to 14 of the *Hymne of Heavenly
Love* describe the civil war in heaven and relate how order was
restored as God 'blew away / From heauens hight . . . / To deepest
hell' the rebel angels. The parallel stanzas in the *Hymne of Love*
describe the civil war among the elements and relate how Cupid
managed to

> *place them all in order, and compell*
> *To keepe them selues within their sundrie raines,*
> *Together linkt with Adamantine chaines.*
>
> > *(HL lines 87–9)*

It is interesting to note that Cupid in his creative activity uses the
same kind of force that God resorted to in expelling the angels. Milton
seems to have been aware of the connection since he uses the same

phrase in *Paradise Lost* but applies it to Satan who was thrown down from heaven 'to dwell / in adamantine chains' (I, 47–8). The harmoniously ordered elements reappear in the description of order and harmony in the created universe in *An Hymne of Heavenly Beautie* (lines 36–49). There the stress is not on the contrary forces of the elements but on their upward movement. The thematic parallel at this point between the two hymns of love is reinforced by the mutual rhymes: 'fyre-conspyre-fyre-yre' in stanza 12 of the *Hymne of Love* are echoed by 'yre-aspyre-fyre' in stanza 13 of the *Hymne of Heavenly Love*. It is significant that the creative activities of Cupid parallel the activities of God, not as a creator, but as a destroyer.

Stanzas 15 to 17 of the *Hymne of Love* (lines 99–119) declare that man 'breathes a more immortall mynd' than other creatures. And since beauty, 'borne of heauenly race', is the nearest resemblance man can find on earth to 'th' immortall flame / Of heauenly light', beauty will be the object of all his earthly desires. Adding depth to this idea of man's 'immortall mynd' stanzas 15 to 17 of the *Hymne of Heavenly Love* relate how God made man in his likeness according 'to an heauenly patterne' and 'endewd [him] with wisedomes riches, heauenly, rare'. The basic pattern of contrast is emphasised by the rhymes. 'Spright' is a rhymeword in stanza 16 of both hymns, but while God 'breathd a liuing spright' into man, the lover in the first hymn possesses only a 'deducted spright'. 'Aspyre' is another telling rhymeword since its only occurrence in the third hymn is in a reference to the aspiring pride of the rebel angels (*HHL* 13).[23] The seventeenth stanzas of both hymns are linked because both employ the rhymewords 'see-bee' in the couplet. The 'fragile men' of the *Hymne of Love* are, of course, so 'enrauisht' at the sight of the earthly reflection of heavenly beauty that they completely forget its source (*HL* 17). One may be reminded of St Paul's warning about those who 'worshipped and served the creature more than the Creator'.

Man did not know how to make proper use of his 'wisedomes riches', and so he fell

> *Into the mouth of death to sinners dew,*
> *And all his off-spring into thraldome threw.*
> (*HHL* 18, 123–4)

The 'thraldome' of fallen man strongly recalls the sad predicament of Cupid's subjects who 'lye languishing like thrals forlorne' (*HL* 20, 136). And the 'neuer dead, yet euer dying paine' of the sinners (*HHL*

18, 126) may remind the reader of the torment of lovers whose inner flame

> *suckes the blood, and drinketh vp the lyfe*
> *Of carefull wretches with consuming griefe.*
> (*HL* 18, 125–6)

Cupid is the 'tyrant Loue' who makes the lovers' pains his play and who seeks 'their dying to delay' (*HL* 20). The tyranny of Cupid as well as the sufferings of fallen man may be said to last until Christ has identified himself with the sinner-lover in the incarnation when

> *He downe descended, like a most demisse*
> *And abiect thrall, in fleshes fraile attyre.*
> (*HHL* 20)

Again the image of thraldom is evoked, but this time the lover, already identified as fallen man, is released from his thraldom when his role as thrall is taken over by Christ. 'The parallel to the lover's anguish is that of Jesus.'[24] This is clearly brought out by stanzas 21 to 24 (lines 141–68) of the two hymns of love. The lover is Cupid's poor

> *vassall, whose yet bleeding hart,*
> *With thousand wounds thou mangled hast so sore.*
> (*HL* 21)

Yet, if he could raise his head and look at the suffering Christ, his own wounds and 'bleeding hart' would be soon forgotten at that

> *huge and most vnspeakeable impression*
> *Of loues deepe wound, that pierst the piteous hart*
> *Of that deare Lord . . .*
> (*HHL* 23)

Christ wanted to put an end to man's hellish misery, 'for mans deare sake he did a man become'; Cupid, however, has increased the lover's pains, 'enfrosen' the 'disdainefull brest' of the beloved (stanza 21 in both hymns). The lover in the *Hymne of Love* complains of the injustice of Cupid who, in spite of the poet's high praise, does not 'moue ruth in that rebellious Dame' but is content to 'let her liue thus free', and the poet 'to dy'. The poet-speaker in the *Hymne of Heavenly Love* is shocked at the gross crime of those who 'slew the iust, by most vniust decree' (stanza 22 in both hymns). The injustice of Christ's executioners 'doing him die, that neuer it deserued', is paralleled by the injustice of Cupid who does not scruple to 'afflict as well the not deseruer' (stanza 23 in both hymns). And we could hardly wish for a sharper contrast than that between the god who on his 'subiects most doest tyrannize' and Christ who willingly suffered on the cross to 'free his foes, that from his heast had *swerued*' (stanza 23). Cupid, however, wants first of all to make sure 'if they will euer *swerue*' before he restores 'them vnto grace' (my italics). While Christ granted grace freely because man had 'swerued' and could never be in a position to deserve it, Cupid, the feudal lord, wants to make sure that his subjects are deserving and true servants before he restores them to his favour (stanza 24).

While Christ suffers in order to lift man up, Cupid makes man suffer in order to assert his own power. The poet's final explanation of Cupid's harsh treatment of his subjects is that it makes them 'better to deserue' his grace

> *And hauing got it, may it more esteeme,*
> *For things hard gotten, men more dearly deeme.*
> (*HL* 24)

If this is true, Cupid shows greater psychological cunning than Christ, who generously 'our life hath left vnto vs free' (*HHL* 27).

The parallel between the pains of the lover and those of Christ is emphasised even by the choice of rhymewords. We have already seen how words like 'deseruer', and 'swerue—deserue' in the *Hymne of Love* (stanzas 23 and 24), are echoed by 'deserued-swerued' in the *Hymne of Heavenly Love* (stanza 23). Similarly, the set 'hart-part-smart' in stanza 21 of the first hymn is paralleled by 'hart-part-dart' in stanza 23 of the third hymn. (Rhymewords from the set 'hart-part-smart-dart' and their plural equivalents are frequent in descriptions of the relationship between Cupid and the lover, see stanzas 1, 5, 18, and 21 of the *Hymne of Love*). Once we have become aware of this pattern we may also respond to the rhymes 'blame-shame-became' and 'tree-decree' in stanza 22 of the *Hymne of Heavenly Love* as echoes of the similar sets 'name-Dame-flame' and 'thee-me' in stanza 22 of the *Hymne of Love*.

This sequence of stanzas shows how Spenser was able to use the traditional lover's complaint in an exciting new way to epitomise the essential predicament of fallen man. By this point it should have become clear to the reader that the pagan world of the first hymn is identical with the fallen world, and that this intimate relationship between the hymns is signalled by 'the strategic recurrence of words and images'.[25]

The central stanzas of the *Hymne of Love*, stanzas 22 to 23 (central if we include the introductory stanzas), express the lover's complaint about Cupid's tyranny over mankind, and establish a crucial contrast between the two hymns since the central stanza of the *Hymne of Heavenly Love*, stanza 21, relates the story of how for 'mans deare sake' Christ 'did a man become'. In this way the central stanza of the *Fowre Hymnes* (*HHL* 5) describes Christ as the second person of the Trinity, Christ in his heavenly aspect, while the central stanza of the third hymn itself describes Christ as man, Christ in his earthly aspect.

In stanzas 25 to 28 of the *Hymne of Love* (lines 169–196) true love is contrasted to 'loathly sinful lust', and in stanza 28 the true lover in his 'refyned mynd' admires 'the mirrour of . . . heauenly light'. In the corresponding stanzas in the third hymn we are admonished to admire Christ who is the 'glorious Morning starre', the 'lampe of light' and the most 'liuely image' of the face of God. We are exhorted to love Christ who

> *our life hath left vnto vs free,*
> *Free that was thrall, and blessed that was band.*
> (*HHL* 27)

He has saved us from the second death and given us something far more real than a reflection in a mirror:

> *the food of life, which now we haue,*
> *Euen himselfe in his deare sacrament.*
> (*HHL* 28)

While the readers of the *Hymne of Heavenly Love* are urged to prove their love of Christ through love of their fellow human beings and to contemplate the love and mercy of Christ (29–32, 197–224), the lover in the *Hymne of Love* concentrates on the reflection of beauty which he has seen, to the exclusion of its source. On this image printed 'in his deepest wit' he 'feeds his hungrie fantasy' (*HL* lines 197–8). In so doing he seems to lose all power of judgement and to be constantly deceiving himself:

> *Thrise happie man, might he the same possesse;*
> *He faines himselfe, and doth his fortune blesse.*
> (*HL* 30, 209–10)

It has been argued that here 'as in line 240 "faines", i.e. "feigns" probably means imagines rather than pretends. We may compare lines 216–17 where the lover's "fayning eye" is conjuring up a *mental* and perhaps an idealised, but not a wholly false image of his lady's beauty'.[26] But surely, the choice of an ambiguous word like 'faines' may be interpreted as a discreet author's comment anticipating the radical criticism of the earthly lover in the last pair. The word occurs twice in the *Hymne of Heavenly Beautie* (lines 216 and 273), and on both occasions it refers to a false imagination. In fact, the epithet 'thrise happie' is probably an example of prolepsis, the reader of the *Hymne of Heavenly Beautie* knowing better who should be considered 'thrise happie' when he finds the echo:

> *thrise happie man him hold,*
> *Of all on earth, whom God so much doth grace,*
> *And lets his owne Beloued to behold:*
> *For in the view of her celestiall face,*
> *All ioy, all blisse, all happinesse haue place.*
>                                    (*HHB* lines 239–43)

And if this does not suffice to bring out the full measure of the lover's folly, the utter inadequacy of his self-centred, earthbound love and its ill effects on his judgements, here is how he regards his faint, earthly reflection of beauty:

> *His harts enshrined saint, his heauens queene,*
> *Fairer then fairest, in his fayning eye.*
>                                    (*HL* lines 215–16)

It is the discovery of this 'complicated web of recurrent elements' in the hymns which enables the reader to see the happiness and beauty in the transient world of the earthly lover in its true perspective.[27]

The Christian lover is inspired with an unselfish love that reaches out to his fellow men and up to Christ. He knows that his faith and fortune depend on the love and grace of Christ; thus he urges the reader to

> *Lift vp to him thy heauie clouded eyne,*
> *That thou his soueraine bountie mayst behold,*
> *And read through loue his mercies manifold.*
>                                    (*HHL* 32)

But the earthly lover is shut in by his selfish, earthbound love. His 'galley' is 'charged with forgetfulness'. He is concerned only with his own temporary happiness and can trust only himself and his own powers.

> *Then forth he casts in his vnquiet thought,*
> *What he may do, her fauour to obtaine;*
> *What braue exploit, what perill hardly wrought,*
> *What puissant conquest, what aduenturous paine,*
> *May please her best, and grace vnto him gaine.*

> (*HL* 32)

Readers familiar with the third hymn will once more observe the contrast between earthly and heavenly love. 'For the "brave exploits" of the one there is the "humble carriage" of the other' (*HHL* 34).[28]

The traditional, and implicitly critical, review of the lover's psychic development and religious adoration of his beloved in the *Hymne of Love*, is interrupted by the apparently serious praise of Cupid in stanza 33. This is the only stanza in the *Fowre Hymnes* which is one line short. It is difficult to spot this startling irregularity as the fourth line, although metrically regular, exceeds the normal line length by more than one third and is carried over into an indented fifth line, while the fifth line proper is missing. In the Quarto edition (1596) the layout normally adopted is to print four stanzas on each page so that the stanzas on two facing pages will match each other in exact symmetry.[29] The normal procedure with long lines is to print the remaining words or letters at the end of the line immediately above or below it. The obvious effect of carrying the fourth line of stanza 33 over into the next line is to keep an illusion of symmetry in spite of the 'missing' line, thus making the discrepancy less easily detectable at first glance. The effect may, of course, merely be the result of a compositorial error; failing to find enough room to continue the excessively long line at the end of the lines preceding and succeeding it, the compositor has carried the line over, and because of the symmetry thus achieved, may have failed to notice his mistake. Such a theory, however, presumes that the proof-reader would have failed to notice the irregular indentation. (Note that B3r on which *HL* 33 is found, and B2v, the page facing it, were also facing each other in the outer forme of sheet B.) In view of the fact that the *Fowre Hymnes* is more carefully printed than any other of Spenser's works printed in his lifetime, this seems improbable. Some commentators even suppose that Spenser assisted at the printing. That the omission should be accidental is unlikely also because it is repeated in the Folio edition of 1611. There is nothing in the syntax to indicate that a line should be missing: it makes perfectly good sense as it stands. The 'error' therefore would seem to be intentional. Corroborative evidence may be deduced from the division of the long line: 'Through seas, through flames, through thousand / swords and speares'. This division may be seen to produce an additional 'internal' or visual rhyme: 'thousand-withstand-hand'. It may thus be argued that instead of an incomplete rhyme-scheme, ababcc, we are left with a new variation: aba(c)bcc. My belief that this division and its possible effect are the results of conscious design is strengthened by the fact that the long line is divided in exactly the same way in the Folio edition of 1611. This effect is lost in the text of the *Variorum Edition* where the line is divided: 'through thousand swords / and speares'.

These considerations make me conclude that the 'error' is Spenser's own and that he made it deliberately. In so doing he relied on a tradition according to which it was perfectly acceptable for a poet to depart from the established stanzaic form to emphasise his themes. Among the early poems of Sir Thomas More, for example, there is a sequence of nine stanzas designed to accompany nine illustrations on a tapestry. The first seven of these stanzas have seven lines, but the eighth, entitled 'Eternity', has eight lines, no doubt to make the form of the stanza as well as the stanza number accord with its subject matter, the number eight symbolising eternity.[30]

Although I do not wish to attach symbolic significance to the number of lines left in Spenser's stanza, one may observe that the overestimation of the powers of Cupid in the long fourth line results in a stanza which is as inadequate as the god which it praises. We should also note that what may initially seem a failure on Spenser's part to calculate the number of lines in his stanza correctly, agrees with the main fiction of the dedication—that the first two hymns were composed at the beginning of his career when he was young and inexperienced. This technical or poetical failure, however, may also serve as a sign of spiritual failure. The spiritual failure of the poet may be formally expressed through his lack of elementary, technical skill and such a failure is suggested by the excessive praise of Cupid. One may object that Cupid is praised even more excessively elsewhere and particularly in the last stanza of the hymn, and without similar formal indications of error. One possible solution is that it may perhaps be significant that the formal error occurs in this particular stanza. We know from earlier studies of Spenser that his structures were often highly complex and carefully worked out. As I have already noted, this is stanza 33 and thirty-three was, more than any other number, associated with Christ, since Christ was popularly believed to have been thirty-three years old when he died. Since we have seen that the two hymns of love contain several contrasted descriptions of Christ and Cupid, Spenser may have wished to provide this formal indication of the inadequacy of Cupid and the error of his followers by making his 'mistake' in this particular stanza. This interpretation is enforced when we turn to stanza 33 of the *Hymne of Heavenly Love* and find there a description of the birth of Christ. The description of the life and sufferings of Christ in stanzas 33 to 35 is a little puzzling since it seems in many ways to be a mere repetition of what has already been said in stanzas 20 to 23. The popular import of the number thirty-three and the need to establish a contrast to the first hymn are two considerations that may have prompted the repetition. The reader should also note the contrast between the extravagant praise of the power and glory of Cupid and the plain description of the simple and low birth, and the painful and miserable life of Christ. This is a clear example of the contrast between pride and humility.

In stanza 33 Cupid is praised not only as the lover's god, but also as his guide. But, as Spenser takes care to point out, this guide is blind. There were at least two ways of depicting Cupid: either as blind with a bandage over his eyes, or as seeing. Erwin Panofsky informs us that 'the bandage of blindfold Cupid . . . [was introduced] wherever a lower, purely sensual and profane form of love was deliberately contrasted with a higher, more spiritual and sacred one, whether marital, or "Platonic," or Christian'.[31] He also asserts that 'the Renaissance spokesmen of Neoplatonic theories refuted the belief that Love was blind . . . and used the figure of Blind Cupid, if at all, as a contrast to set off their own exalted conception'.[32] This may seem to fit in very nicely with the idea that Cupid is deliberately contrasted with his heavenly and Christian counterparts. To make matters a little more complicated, however, Edgar Wind has pointed out that the 'tradition that saw in the blind Cupid a symbol of unenlightened animal passion, inferior to the intellect' was reversed by people like Marsilio Ficino, Pico della Mirandola, Lorenzo de' Medici and Giordano Bruno.[33] They saw in blind Cupid a symbol of a superior form of love, either for the reason mockingly given in *A Midsummer Night's Dream*:

> *Love looks not with the eyes, but with the mind;*
> *And therefore is wing'd Cupid painted blind.*[34]
>
> (I, i)

or for the reason given by Pico: 'Love is said by Orpheus to be without eyes because he is above the intellect.'[35] It is this last interpretation of Cupid's blindness which is implied in Benivieni's *Canzone d'Amore* in the two last lines of stanza 11:

> *O Love, on my weak wings, bestow*
> *The promised pinions, and the blind way show!*[36]

Thus there are two ways of interpreting Cupid even when he is described as blind, either as blind passion without reason, or as a higher intellectual vision blinding the eyes of the body only to activate the eyes of the mind.

Certainly, the Cupid of *An Hymne of Love* may be interpreted as blind in a bad sense. He is the blind god who guides the lover so that he does not 'see his feares', and his blindness reminds us of Christ's saying that 'if the blind lead the blind, both shall fall into the ditch'. The significance of the reference to Cupid as the lover's *guide* both in stanza 33 and in the last stanza of the *Hymne of Love* is underlined by the reference to man's departure from the ways of God as 'mans misguyde' in the *Hymne of Heavenly Love* (line 144).

It seems likely that Spenser was aware of the Neoplatonic interpretation of the blindness of Love, but he did not choose to invest his Cupid with the kind of mystical blindness with which Benivieni furnished his god of love. But if Spenser knew the tradition Benivieni refers to, and if the two pairs of hymns were composed according to a conscious pattern of parallels and contrasts, we would expect a reference to Benivieni's and Pico's 'blind way' in the last pair. And our expectation is not disappointed. In the *Hymne of Heavenly Love* the poet declares that if the reader gives himself to Christ he will be so inflamed with love that all earthly things will

> *Seeme durt and drosse in thy pure sighted eye,*
> *Compar'd to that celestiall beauties blaze,*
> *Whose glorious beames all fleshly sense doth daze*
> *With admiration of their passing light,*
> Blinding *the eyes and* lumining *the spright.*
>
> (*HHL* 40, 276–80; my roman)

The reader is actually told to renounce earthly love

> *with which the world doth blind*
> *Weake fancies, and stirre vp affections base.*
>
> (*HHL* 38, 262–3)

In the *Hymne of Beautie* we are told that love has such power over man that 'it can rob both sense and reason blynd' (*HB* line 77), and in the *Hymne of Heavenly Beautie* the reader is encouraged to

> *Mount vp aloft through heauenly contemplation,*
> *From this darke world, whose damps the soule do blynd.*
>
> (*HHB* 20, 136–3)

Thus the description of Cupid as blind reinforces the antitheses between earthly and heavenly love, and the contrast is given added emphasis by the formal incompleteness and the significant placing of the stanza in which this description of Cupid is found. At the same time, however, the very ambiguity of Cupid's blindness in the Renaissance suggests that he is presented not only as the negation of the true vision but also as a foreshadowing of that higher, inner vision which is granted to those who seek heavenly love and beauty.

Among those who pursued their love even into Hell itself, Orpheus is the supreme example:

> *And* Orpheus *daring to prouoke the yre*
> *Of damned fiends, to get his loue retyre.*
>
> (*HL* 34)

The corresponding stanza in the *Hymne of Heavenly Love* focuses on the sufferings of Christ to redeem man from Hell:

> *His cancred foes, his fights, his toyle, his strife,*
> *His paines, his pouertie, his sharpe assayes.*
>
> (*HHL* 34)

This contrast and parallelism between Cupid and Orpheus, and Christ may have a further significance. Since they are both mentioned at this crucial point in the *Hymne of Love*, they may serve not only as a contrast but even as a foreshadowing of Christ. Orpheus descending to Hell to free his Eurydice from death, and Cupid making way 'both through heauen and hell' for those who obey him, are both reminiscent of Christ, who descended even to the realm of the dead to redeem fallen man. The fact that there are no classical allusions in the third hymn[37] supports an interpretation of Orpheus and Cupid as types of Christ, since the type must disappear on the arrival of the anti-type. It is supported also by the early Fathers of the Church who argued 'that the pagan legend of Orpheus in some way prefigures the story of Christ's ministry, and that just as the coming of Christ outdates the Old Law, so Christ the new Orpheus replaces the old Orpheus of Helicon and Cithaeron'.[38] We know that 'well into the Middle Ages writers compared the actions of Orpheus and Christ in the underworld, showing that what Orpheus had begun, Christ had finished',[39] and medieval commentaries on Ovid identified Orpheus with Christ, notably the *Ovide Moralisé* where 'the whole legend [of Orpheus] is taken as a figure for Christ's harrowing of hell'.[40]

Whether we choose to interpret Orpheus as a type of Christ or not, it seems safe to say that both in the way he is described and through the significant position he occupies, he seems to remind the reader of Christ and to lead him on to the third hymn. But by the time he gets there he will realise that Orpheus is outdated and outshone by the true God, who alone possesses the power to bring his beloved out of Hell. If Spenser has succeeded in achieving this response in the reader, he has succeeded in vindicating his poetry against the accusations of allegedly bad effects on readers.

In stanza 35 of the *Hymne of Love* (lines 238–44) the lover is approved of by his mistress and experiences feigned 'heauens of ioy' which make him forget his previous pains to such an extent that

> *Had it bene death, yet would he die againe,*
> *To liue thus happie as her grace to gaine.*

When paired with stanza 35 of the *Hymne of Heavenly Love* this looks like a clear travesty of the pains of Christ, who died on the cross 'with bitter wounds through hands, through feet and syde', and who alone can grant man grace and secure him joy in heaven.

The transitory and imaginary nature of the lover's paradise is brought out clearly in stanzas 36 to 39 of the first hymn (lines 245–73), where his illusory paradise is turned into a 'wretches hell' through the fears of rivals that 'torment / His troubled mynd with more then hellish paine!' In stanzas 36 to 39 of the third hymn the self-centred love of the earthly lover is replaced by the self-effacing love of the Christian, who is urged to forget himself and 'melt into teares' at the sight of the suffering Christ. The Christian is told to shun

*All other loues, with which the world doth blind*
*Weake fancies, and stirre vp affections base.*
                                    (38, 262–3)

This is a striking comment on the earthly lover's 'fayning fansie' which gives rise to all kinds of 'affections base': envy, fear, and mistrust (stanza 38).

The contrast between amorous love and Christian love is brought out even in the description of the lover's relationship to his fellow beings, particularly when we recall the description of Christian charity in stanzas 29 to 31 of the *Hymne of Heavenly Love*. To the lover whose only pain is his own possible dissatisfaction and whose only aim is his own happiness, his fellow beings are important only as potential rivals and competitors. Cupid's relationship to the lovers is mirrored in their relationship to their neighbours. The lord-vassal relationship between Cupid and his subjects does not encourage a relationship of mutual love and charity among his subjects. Conversely, Christ's suffering love for man is mirrored in the mutual love among his followers.

The description of the lovers who have to go through a painful Purgatory before they reach Love's paradise and take part in a banquet of sense where 'they doe feede on Nectar heauenly wize' and lay their heads in the 'snowy bosome' of Pleasure, may be compared to the last stanzas of the *Hymne of Heavenly Love*. There is no mention of any Catholic Purgatorium for Christ has gone through all their pains, and 'all the worlds desire' is purged away, not through pains but through love of Christ. The last decisive difference between earthly love aroused by earthly beauty and 'celestiall loue / Kindled through sight of those faire things aboue' (*HHL* 41), is that the one trusts in the senses while the other has had recourse to the 'bright radiant eyes' of the spirit. The 'bright and glorious' sun of Cupid's paradise (*HL* 40) is nothing

> *Compar'd to that celestiall beauties blaʒe,*
> *Whose glorious beames all fleshly sense doth daʒe*
> *With admiration of their passing light,*
> *Blinding the eyes and lumining the spright.*
>                                    (*HHL* 40)

In stanza 42 of the first hymn the lover has come full circle. He has joined with Pleasure in a paradise which seems to be identical with the 'siluer bowres' of Venus.[41] But the sensuous pleasures enjoyed by the lovers are clearly contrasted to the pleasures of the Angels (*HHL* 11) and to the 'sweete pleasures' enjoyed by those who seek heavenly beauty (*HHB* 43).

The last stanza of the *Hymne of Love* reveals to what extent the first hymn is 'lewd' not because there is anything wrong with amorous love *per se*, but because its advocate in this hymn has lost his sense of proportion. He does not seem to be conscious of a wider perspective. He is not aware of the existence of a sun which is even more glorious than the one he can perceive with his eyes, and he allows his spiritual eyes to be blinded by the transitory glory of what can be experienced with the senses. There is no room for Christian love because earthly love has so taken possession of the lover that it has taken the place even of religion. Certainly, any Christian would be expected to react to a poet offering to sing of Cupid's 'immortall praise / An heauenly Hymne, such as the Angels sing' (*HL* 44, 301–302). There must be something seriously wrong when Cupid takes the place properly belonging to God himself. The poet offers to raise Cupid's name

> *Boue all the gods, thee onely honoring,*
> *My guide, my God, my victor, and my king;*[42]

And if this is not enough to alert the reader and make him aware of his folly, the last stanza is paralleled and implicitly negated in the first stanza of the *Hymne of Heavenly Love*.[43] In this stanza the poet asks to be lifted up to 'heauens hight' to see the admirable works of God

> *That I thereof an heauenly Hymne may sing*
> *Vnto the god of Loue, high heauens king.*
> (*HHL* 1, 6–7)

The rhymes 'sing-honoring-king' in the last stanza of the *Hymne of Love* echo not only the rhymes 'sing-king' in the last introductory stanza of that hymn, but are also echoed in the first couplet of the *Hymne of Heavenly Love*. And the lovers who play with Pleasure 'without rebuke or *blame*' and are 'deuoyd of guilty *shame*' (my italics) in the third stanza from the end of the *Hymne of Love* are proved false by the reappearance of the rhymes 'flame-blame-shame' in the retraction of the third stanza of the *Hymne of Heavenly Love*, just as they are contrasted to the suffering Christ (*HHL* 22), who alone was without 'all blemish or reprochfull *blame*' and was treated 'with despightfull *shame*' by man (my italics).

If we accept this parallel reading of the two hymns of love, even the poet's last prayer to Cupid to accept his 'simple song, thus fram'd in praise of thee' may be significant. It is beautifully 'fram'd' for instance in the sense that the rhymes of the last couplet, 'mee-thee', echo the rhymes of the first couplet, 'bee-thee'. It is also interesting to note that stanza 33 of the first hymn, which seems to establish the contrast between Cupid and Christ in such a significant way, is followed by eleven stanzas which bring us to the obvious blasphemy of stanza 44. This seems appropriate since eleven was the number of transgression and hence of sin. Above all, however, we should note the predominance of the number four in the sum total of the forty-four stanzas, since the number four is 'the number *par excellence* of the created universe'.[44]

We have seen how Spenser has turned the pagan world of the first hymn into the world of fallen man. The strange mixture of Neo-platonism and traditional courtly love poetry which has puzzled his critics has enabled Spenser to align his first hymn with the third and thus to show the way from heathen gods to Christ, from fallen man to redeemed man, from the rule of tyranny to the rule of grace. The rule of Cupid is allowed to foreshadow the rule of Christ in a way that enabled contemporary readers to read the hymns in much the same way that they were used to reading the Bible, for 'in the Old Testament the New is concealed, and in the New the Old is revealed'.[45] Before man can smite his breast and cry 'God, be merciful to me a sinner' and receive grace, he must be conscious of sin. We might say that the first hymn seeks to convince the reader of the necessity of grace by showing him the misery of life without grace.


III


According to Plato 'all communion between mortals and gods was established...through the mediation of Love'.[46] Thus the hymn to Cupid has prepared the way for the hymn to Venus, and the hymn to Christ serves as a necessary precursor to the *Hymne of Heavenly Beautie*. For, 'however much anyone is illuminated only by the light of nature and of acquired science, he cannot', Bonaventura teaches us, 'enter into himself that he may delight in the Lord in himself, unless Christ be his mediator'.[47]

The *Hymne of Heavenly Beautie* begins where the *Hymne of*

*Heavenly Love* ends.[48] 'Rapt with the rage of [his] own rauisht thought' the poet-speaker ascends the ladder of increasing beauty until he reaches God's 'mercie seate' and a vision of heavenly Sapience. The poet-speaker of the *Hymne of Beautie* is sufficiently well-informed to know about the heavenly origin of true beauty. He passes from love considered as stemming from beauty to beauty as the cause of love but concentrates on the effects of beauty as immediate cause to the exclusion of beauty as ultimate cause. Thus he remains firmly on earth and is largely content to admire how the heaven-born souls form their 'fleshly bowres'.

The speaker of the *Hymne of Beautie* is also in a sense beside himself not 'with the rage' of his 'rauisht thought' but with 'wontlesse fury' and Cupid's 'raging fyre' (*HB* and *HHB* 1). The lover in the *Hymne of Beautie* entreats Venus to 'vouchsafe' to illuminate his 'dim and dulled eyne' with her 'loue-kindling light' enabling him to inspire 'admiration of that heauenly light' in his readers (*HB* 2–3). The transported speaker in the *Hymne of Heavenly Beautie* petitions the Holy Spirit to 'vouchsafe' to inspire him with 'some sparkling light' of the 'eternall Truth' so that he may teach the 'hearts of men'

> *to loue with ʒealous humble dewty*
> *Th' eternall fountaine of that heauenly beauty.*
>
> (*HHB* 3)

The *third* stanza of the *Hymne of Heavenly Beautie* provides commentary on the *third* stanza of the hymn to Venus. This is emphasised by the choice of identical rhymes: 'Beauty-dewty' and 'delight-sight-light' in the third stanza of the second hymn are echoed by the rhymes 'sight-delight' and 'dewty-beauty' in the third stanza of the last hymn.

The lover wants his hymn to beauty to serve an additional purpose. His hopes are that it will please his lady so 'that she at length will streame / Some deaw of grace, into [his] withered hart' which 'wasted is with woes extreame' (*HB* 4). The speaker of the *Hymne of Beautie* is not really interested in the heavenly origin of beauty, but concentrates on its manifestations in the beauty of the beloved. Thus while 'the movement of the earthly hymn is down,. . . the movement of the heavenly hymn is up'[49] The poet in the *Hymne of Heavenly Beautie* takes as his point of departure the discovery of beauty in the well-ordered universe. Comparing himself to the young falcon he hopes to ascend even to 'contemplation of th' immortall sky' (*HHB* 4).

In stanzas 5 to 9 of the *Hymne of Beautie* (lines 29–63), the poet

describes how the great 'workmaister' made everything according to
the 'goodly Paterne' of perfect beauty. Flowing from the 'bright
starre' of Venus this beauty streams into the *res creatae*. With it
Venus points Cupid's 'poysned arrow, / That wounds the life, and
wastes the inmost marrow' (*HB* lines 62–3). In the corresponding
stanzas of the last hymn the reader is invited to observe the purposeful
and beautiful organisation of the 'endlesse kinds of creatures' which
people the universe, and in an ascending movement he is urged to
admire the well-ordered elements and 'last that mightie shining
christall wall, / Wherewith he hath encompassed this All' (lines 41–2).
The frail mind of mortal man can reach only a partial understanding
of the infinite beauty and wisdom of God, but by reading in the
*liber creaturarum* (lines 127–33), man may form some idea of the
beauty of those heavens 'much higher in degree'.

The structure of parallelism and contrast does not seem to work on
a stanza by stanza pattern in these sections. But the procedures of the
narrators are clearly related in a less complex way. The speaker of the
heavenly hymn ascends to discover perfect, heavenly beauty in God,
and the speaker of the earthly hymn imitates this procedure by peeling
off layers of inessential qualities of beauty to disclose the true nature
of earthly beauty. The speaker of the second hymn is preoccupied
with that beauty which is 'in earth layd vp in secret store' and its
effects on man. He is primarily concerned to establish (in stanzas
10 to 15) that the beauty which can

> *Moue such affection in the inward mynd,*
> *That it can rob both sense and reason blynd,*
>
> (*HB* 11, 76–7)

is not an 'outward shew of things, that onely seeme' (line 91). But
even that beauty which arouses the desire of earthly lovers 'is heauenly
borne and can not die' (line 104). This does not mean that he takes
an interest in its origin, but it helps him to explain the psychological
effects of beauty. The poet-speaker of the *Hymne of Heavenly Beautie,*
however, has to pursue his search through the hierarchy of the
heavens which

> *by degrees redound,*
> *And rise more faire, till they at last ariue*
> *To the most faire, whereto they all do striue.*
>
> (*HHB* 11, 75–7)

In stanzas 16 to 21 of the *Hymne of Beautie* we are told how the soul descended from 'that great immortall Spright' to be 'embodied' in 'fleshy seede' and then framed 'her house' to make it a 'pallace fit for such a virgin Queene' (line 126).

> *For of the soule the bodie form doth take:*
> *For soule is forme, and doth the bodie make.*
> (*HB* 19, 132–3)

Consequently, a fair body is the certain outward sign of a fair soul. But, the poet hurries to inform us,

> *oft it falles, that many a gentle mynd*
> *Dwels in deformed tabernacle drownd.*
> (*HB* 21, 141–2)

While the poet in the second hymn stresses the body as the mirror of the beautiful and immortal soul, the poet of the *Hymne of Heavenly Beautie* sees the acts of God as the true

> *looking glasse, through which he may*
> *Be seene, of all his creatures vile and base,*
> *That are vnable else to see his face.*
> (*HHB* 17, 115–17)

If we can look at the bright beams of the sun only through a mirror,

> *how can we see with feeble eyne,*
> *The glory of that Maiestie diuine.*
> (*HHB* 18, 123–4)

The second hymn recommends that we observe beautiful bodies because 'all that faire is, is by nature good' (*HB* 20). The speaker of the heavenly hymn urges the reader to observe God's works as a means of experiencing His goodness, and he ends on very much the same note as the speaker of the earthly hymn: 'for all thats good, is beautiful and faire.' (*HHB* 19).

The Christian's journey does not end here. By means of 'perfect speculation' and 'through heauenly contemplation' he mounts aloft, and imitating the eagle he fixes his eyes on 'that bright Sunne of glorie' (*HHB,* 20). The comparison between the eyes of the eagle and the speculative mind of the Christian contemplator is found in *The Faerie Queene.*[50] When Mercy accompanies the Red Cross

Knight to the hermitage of Contemplation they find him to be an 'aged Sire' with 'snowy lockes':

> *All were his earthly eyen both blunt and bad,*
> *And through great age had lost their kindly sight,*
> *Yet wondrous quick and persant was his spright,*
> *As Eagles eye, that can behold the Sunne.*
>
> *(I, x, 47)*

The contrast between man's eyes, which can perceive God only in his works, the faint reflection of the divine emanations, and the eagle's eye which has the power of direct vision, is thus directly related to the distinction between the eyes of the body and the eyes of the spirit significant for the discussion of the blindness of Cupid.

It comes as no surprise to find that words like 'eye-eyes-see-sight-behold-look' occur twice as frequently in the hymns of beauty as in the hymns of love.[51] We should be aware, however, that two essentially different types of vision are suggested in the two hymns of beauty. Just as the Red Cross Knight approached heavenly Contemplation guided by Mercy, so the Christian of the fourth hymn can ascend 'through heauenly contemplation' by virtue of grace granted by Christ, leaving behind 'this darke world, whose damps the soule do blynd'. So the lover of heavenly beauty is eventually endued with some of the characteristics of the angelic mind (see *HHB* 34, 232). Rereading the hymns we note that in the *Hymne of Love* Cupid is compared to a young eagle:

> *he gan to mount vp hyre,*
> *And like fresh Eagle, make his hardie flight*
> *Through all that great wide wast, yet wanting light.*
>
> *(HL lines 68–70)*

It is ironical that eagle-like Cupid, imitating the Spirit of God in Genesis, flies through *darkness* where the keen eyesight of the eagle can be of no use.

But we should not forget when we read the *Hymne of Heavenly Beautie* that the eagle has wings. In the Bible the eagle was interpreted as a symbol of regeneration and as a type of Christ who lifts the souls of men to heaven on his strong wings.[52] It is sufficient to remind ourselves of the Psalms, 103.5: 'thy youth is renewed like the eagle' and Isaiah, 40.31: 'but they that wait upon the Lord shall renew their strength; they shall mount up with wings as eagles;' we realise something of the fascination that a symbol like the eagle must have had for Spenser. Carrying the ambiguity of Cupid as both type and parody one step further, eagle-like Cupid may even be seen as a kind of travesty of Christian regeneration 'renewing still [his] yeares' (*HL* 8, 55).

The wings and awkward flight of Cupid have already been contrasted to the 'nimble wings' and easy flight of the Angels. In the *Hymne of Heavenly Beautie* the poet-speaker, regenerated through Christ and lifted up on his eagle's wings, compares himself to a young falcon that begins on earth and promises

> *From thence to mount aloft by order dew,*
> *To contemplation of th' immortall sky,*
> *Of the soare faulcon so I learne to fly,*
> *That flags awhile her fluttering wings beneath,*
> *Till she her selfe for stronger flight can breath.*
>
> (*HHB* 4, 24–8)

When he has completed his ascent he can throw himself down in fear and reverence before 'the footestoole of his Maiestie' (*HHB* 21).

The *Hymne of Heavenly Beautie* seems to be the most beautifully structured of all the hymns. While the central stanza of the *Hymne of Beautie* describes the 'deformed tabernacle' of man, the central stanza of the last hymn, stanza 22, gives us a glimpse of the perfect Tabernacle of God as we are urged to fall down before his 'mercie seate'. It is, of course, extremely appropriate and in keeping with the tradition of 'placement in the middest' that in the middle line of this mid-stanza we see God sitting 'vpon the righteous throne on hy' (*HHB* 22, 151).

While the poet of the heavenly hymn ascends to the vision of the perfection of beauty, the poet of the earthly hymn deplores the grievous corruption of beauty through lust (*HB* 22–5, 148–75). The virtue of those 'faire Dames' is a very pale reflection indeed of that 'heauenly vertue' which breeds the 'immortall light' encircling the throne of God

> *hid in his owne brightnesse from the sight*
> *Of all that looke thereon with eyes vnsound:*
>
> (*HHB* 26)

Compared to that light, 'Loue' which can 'illumine' the 'resplendent ray' of the ladies and 'adde more brightnesse' to their 'goodly hew' is a poor substitute (*HB* 26).

The 'faire Dames' are praised as the 'liuely images of heauens light' (*HB* 24, 163). When this phrase is linked with the 'mirrours' mentioned in stanza 26 and related to the parallel group of stanzas in the heavenly hymn, the contrast is made quite clear: weak reflections and indirect vision on the one hand, and true light and direct vision on the other.

In stanza 27 of the *Hymne of Beautie* the ladies are urged to show forth their 'heauenly riches' so that 'men the more admyre their fountaine may'. In stanza 27 of the *Hymne of Heavenly Beautie* we turn from the weak reflections of beauty in the earthly hymn to the divine beauty of heavenly Sapience, the true 'fountaine' of beauty. She rules both in 'the house of God on hy' and on the earth. Her fairness, in contrast to that of her mortal counterparts, exceeds 'all humane thought'.

The description of Sapience sitting in the bosom of the Father ('There in his bosome Sapience doth sit', *HHB* line 183), can be regarded as an echo of Christ's descent

> Out of the bosome of eternall blisse,
> In which he reigned with his glorious syre.
> (*HHL* lines 134–5)

These closely parallel descriptions of Christ and Sapience can be added to those already suggested by Robert Ellrodt, and to a certain extent they strengthen his theory that Sapience should be interpreted as the second person of the Trinity. There is, however, every probability that 'the ideas of many authors, representative of three traditions, Christian, Platonic, and Kabbalistic' can be 'brought to bear upon Spenser's image of Sapience'.[53] In order to assess the relative importance of these sources, however, we should also know something about how Spenser looked upon the relationship between them. Surely, in the syncretistic philosophy of Spenser it would be wrong to posit any opposition between Christianity and the Neoplatonic philosophy of Ficino and Pico. These authors merely advanced and clarified the dark sayings of Plato which, if unveiled, would be seen to be in accord with the basic truths of the Bible.[54]

Since Sapience is above all the divine person to whom the *Hymne of Heavenly Beautie* is dedicated, we would expect Spenser to make her appearance significant in the manner he has made the appearance of Christ significant. We may note first of all that there are 169 stanzas in the *Fowre Hymnes*, and if 'we subtract the introductory stanzas, the sum total is 153'.[55] This number may refer to the number of fish caught by Simon Peter on Christ's order (John XXI. 11). It was explained by Augustine as the sum of the first seventeen numbers, and 'this was designed to reveal to the initiated the means by which man is to be saved. Man is saved, not by works alone (through obedience to the ten commandments), but by grace (the seven gifts of the Holy Ghost). We must add Grace to the Law, 7 to 10'.[56] It is probable that Spenser made conscious use of the number 153. If we include the introductory stanzas in our count, the description of heavenly Sapience in stanza 27 of the *Hymne of Heavenly Beautie* is stanza 153. Thus in the last hymn Spenser managed to place 'high heauens king' in his appropriate place of majesty, seated on the high throne of his mercy seat in the middle of the heavenly tabernacle, in the middle of the hymn. And yet he was able, by his subtle use of the number 153, which is the triangular number based on 17, to place Sapience at the very pinnacle of his poetical edifice. (It is relevant to note that even the two first hymns contribute in the count and thus form a meaningful base on which the exalted picture of heavenly Sapience may be placed.)

Stanzas 28 to 30 stress the importance of harmony and the incomparable beauty of heavenly Sapience. The contrast between the supreme rule of Sapience, imposing order among all 'lower creatures', and those who 'loosely loue' and reduce love to a 'discordant warre', is pointed out in stanza 28; and in stanza 29 the harmony and heavenly extraction of the 'likely harts' (*HB* 29), are related to the statement about the heavenly origin of all creatures who 'do in state remaine, / As their great Maker did at first ordaine' (*HHB* 29). The idea of adherence to God's original plan is echoed in the next stanza of the earthly hymn, which argues that only those should combine in love 'whom heauen did at first ordaine'; (*HB* 30). The statement (in *HHB* 30) that mortals are unable to describe heavenly beauty, and that it cannot 'on earth compared be to ought,' is an apt comment on the attempt in the earthly hymn to reach heavenly beauty indirectly through earthly beauty. The approach is only made possible through Christ's descent to earth, and through his offer to lift up man on his eagle's wings.

It is highly appropriate that the following two stanzas in the *Hymne of Heavenly Beautie* (lines 211–24), should show Venus dethroned.

She is no more the high goddess and queen of beauty. 'Had she remained still' the poets who had spent their 'plenteous vaine in setting forth her prayse' would certainly regret their former activity. Spenser's disparaging remarks on the 'fabling wits' of the poets who had praised Venus reflects badly on his second hymn. The deposal of Venus in the last hymn can also be taken as a reference to the second hymn (lines 260–6): where the poet expresses his hopes that she will place her throne in men's hearts and spread her 'louely kingdome ouer all'.

The task of picturing heavenly Sapience makes the poet come closer to despair as his muse is much 'too weake and faint' (line 230). The lover in the *Hymne of Beautie*, however, has no such qualms. The sharp eyesight of the lover enables him to discover the hidden pleasures of the exquisite beauty of the beloved (lines 232–8). The description that follows is a true banquet of sense, very properly with an allusion to the gods that feed on 'Nectar in their bankets free' (lines 239–52). A few stanzas earlier the lover insisted on his ability to extract from the sight of the beloved a form which he presented to his mind 'free from fleshes frayle infection' (line 217), of which he would shape a 'heauenly beautie to his fancies will' (line 222). But in stanzas 35 to 38 he seems content to delight in those aspects of her beauty which present themselves to his senses. He has indeed been too bold and has allowed his fancy to run wild; in this deluded state the lover sees 'many wonders' 'that others neuer see' (stanza 36). He adopts an attitude that finds no room in the heavenly hymns for God 'hath scattered the proud in the imagination of their hearts' (Luke I.51). The lovers who '*behold*' and '*vnfold*' the beauty of the beloved in the *Hymne of Beautie* are contrasted to the Angels who '*behold*' the beautiful face of heavenly Sapience

> *And those most sacred mysteries* vnfold,
> *Of that faire loue of mightie heauens king.*
> (*HHB* lines 234–5, my roman)

The contrast between the happiness enjoyed by the earthly lover and that of the lover of heavenly beauty is highlighted in the description of the extreme joy and superlative happiness of those whom Sapience allows into her presence. The close relationship between the two sections is underlined by the appearance of the rhymes 'free-bee' in stanza 36 in both hymns.

The *contemptum mundi* attitude of the last stanzas of the *Hymne of Heavenly Beautie* is perhaps no surprise. The effect on those who are allowed to take part in the heavenly pleasures is, of course, to root out all 'fleshy sense, / Or idle thought of earthly things' (lines 267–8). When they have seen her divine beauty and experienced heavenly bliss 'All other sights but fayned shadowes bee' (line 273). Earthly love and honour 'seem to them basenesse, and all riches drosse' (line 279). From their high vantage point

> *that faire lampe, which vseth to enflame*
> *The hearts of men with self consuming fyre,*
> *Thenceforth seemes fowle, and full of sinfull blame;*
> *(HHB* 40, 274–6)

In contrast to the earthly lover who delights in the beauty he can perceive with his eyes, the heavenly lovers can delight in nothing

> *But in th' aspect of that felicitie,*
> *Which they haue written in their inward ey;*
> *(HHB* 41, 284–5)

Leaving the deceitful shadows of earthly beauty behind and forgetting the time when they were 'with false beauties flattering bait misled' (line 290), they look up to the light of perfect beauty which inspires love of God and

> *which loathing brings*
> *Of this vile world, and these gay seeming things;*
> *(HHB* 43, 299)

Having reached this point their journey is at an end, and the rising movement which started in rapturous, ravished thought has found its supreme end in eternal rest. This circular quality of the last hymn is also underlined by the recurrence of rhymewords. Thus the rhymes 'sight-delight', and 'light-spright' in stanzas 41 and 43 echo the rhymes 'sights-delights-sprights', 'Spright-light', and 'sight-delight' in stanzas 1 to 3. Above all, however, we should note that the *rest* achieved in the last stanza of the *Hymnes* also marks the end of the problems of the lover who started the first hymn by complaining that Cupid had subdued his heart and was 'raging' 'therein with *restlesse* stowre' (*HL* 1). Thus the structural unity of the *Fowre Hymnes* seems to bear out that the problems of the lover-sinner find their solution not through hymns in praise of Cupid and Venus but in the mind's journey to God as described in the last pair of hymns.

Apart from the opening stanzas the tyranny of Cupid and Venus over man which dominated substantial parts of the first hymn, has been largely absent from the second. But in the last three stanzas of the *Hymne of Beautie* the lord-vassal relationship and the lover's prostrate adoration of Cupid and Venus is back in full force. The poet is Venus's vassal and her 'poore liegeman', and he has composed this hymn in praise of Venus in order that she may grant him success in love.

The praise offered to the poet's beloved in the penultimate stanza and particularly in the last stanza is excessive in almost every respect. Her beauty is said to have such power that she 'can restore a damned wight from death'. This could, of course, simply mean that the pains of frustrated love have worked such changes and such sorrows in him that he now seems more dead than alive. If the beloved can be moved to give him grace at last he will once more be able to enjoy life. But if we see this statement as part of the general pattern of conscious contrasts between earthly and heavenly love and beauty, the mock-religious description of the power of the lady is clearly reminiscent of Christ of whom the poet says: 'He gaue vs life, he it restored lost' (*HHL* line 181) and 'vs wretches from the second death did saue' (*HHL* line 193). Similarly, when the poet asks the lady 'n a beautiful line to 'deigne to let fall one drop of dew reliefe', so that there may be an end to his grief and sorrow, this reminds the reader not only of similar statements in the first two hymns but also of the poet's prayer to the Holy Spirit in the *Hymne of Heavenly Love* to

> *Vouchsafe to shed into my barren spright,*
> *Some little drop of thy celestiall dew.*
> (*HHL* lines 45–6)

The lady is also called '*Venus* dearling'. The word *dearling* is used only twice in the hymns, the second time in the crucial stanza 27 of the *Hymne of Heavenly Beautie* where Sapience is introduced and described as the 'soueraine dearling of the *Deity*'. If this is not enough to bring out the ambiguity and blasphemy of the poet's praise of the beloved in the last stanza of the second hymn, consider the poet's praise of his beloved as the 'flowre of grace'. This phrase recurs in the *Hymne of Heavenly Love* where Christ is called 'floure of grace'. He alone deserves the epithet. None of the epithets used about the lady are exceptional in themselves. Spenser had described ladies in like fashion earlier, but the significant way in which these phrases are echoed in later descriptions of Christ and Sapience makes the reader aware of the excessiveness of the poet's praise.

The last stanza of the *Hymne of Beautie* is particularly significant, not simply because of its excessive, mock-Christian praise of the lady, nor merely because it is the last stanza of the first pair, but mainly because it is the central stanza of the whole work. That is to say, that of the 169 stanzas in the *Fowre Hymnes* this is stanza 85. This assertion may seem a little puzzling since I have argued above that stanzas four to six of the *Hymne of Heavenly Love* in praise of the triune Deity are the central stanzas of the *Fowre Hymnes*. It is obvious that in a poem with some stanzas that are more or less clearly marked as introductory the poet may have chosen to include or exclude the introductory stanzas from the total number. It is also clear that if we exclude the introductory stanzas the central stanza of the *Fowre Hymnes* is the second stanza proper of the *Hymne of Heavenly Love*. This seems highly appropriate since that stanza is devoted to the second person of the Trinity. In my discussion of the significance of the number 153 in relation to the *Fowre Hymnes* I have shown that this number is relevant to our understanding of the structure of the *Fowre Hymnes* even when we include the introductory stanzas. It is possible that Spenser has invested his *Hymnes* with a double centre.[57] The triune Deity occupies as it were the affirmative centre and Venus and the beloved the negative centre. It is important that the reader realises that the crucial final stanza of the second hymn is preceded by 84 stanzas in praise of earthly love and beauty, and is succeeded by an equal number of stanzas in praise of heavenly love and beauty. And the central stanza around which they are grouped is seen to refer not only to Venus and the beloved, but also to Christ and Sapience. The two pairs are thus not only opposed but also closely related. The poet-speaker of the *Hymne of Beautie* is perhaps not led on to the search for heavenly beauty, but the author of the *Fowre Hymnes* has seen to it that the reader is.

## IV

Spenser could have turned his back on his first two hymns when they met with criticism and asked forgiveness of God and man. But he chose a more complex, though not necessarily more pharisaical, solution. He was, first of all, a poet, and it was as such that he was criticised. He felt the need to defend his art, and he possessed the genius to be able to do so, not in an elaborate, philosophical treatise, but by proving in practice that poetry is so powerful that it may guide man to virtue even when it apparently takes the form of a paean to the 'snowy bosome' of Pleasure.

On their own the first pair give a distorted picture, but when they are combined with the second pair a true picture is seen to emerge although the first, distorted picture is still a part of it. This is what Spenser has tried to say in the dedicatory epistle, and this is the effect he has achieved. If we read the hymns as two distinct pairs they may seem mutually exclusive, but when we read the four hymns as a whole, as the *Fowre Hymnes*, we discover that Spenser has managed to create harmony in discord—*discordia concors*.

By means of such devices as foreshadowing, contrast, parallelism, verbal echoes, and elaborate structural patterns Spenser has succeeded in making the first two hymns point to the heavenly love and beauty of the last two hymns. In this way even the first pair may be said to glorify the generous love and divine wisdom of Christ and Sapience, not so much through direct statements, as through the subtle interplay with the last pair. In so doing he has utilised the chief asset of poetry: it can move the reader's imagination so that he makes the right choice in spite of his infected will.

# APPENDIX

# *A List of Verbal Echoes in Spenser's* Fowre Hymnes

The list presents verbal echoes of the first pair of hymns found in the second pair. All the instances listed may not constitute verbal echoes in the strictest sense, but the cumulative effect justifies their inclusion. My selection has, of course, been guided by my interpretation of the poem as a whole.

| | | |
|---|---|---|
| Abusd, abused | HB 150, 172 | HHL 242 |
| Admyre | HB 224 | HHB 16 |
| Adornd, adorne | HB 151 | HHB 188 |
| Affection | HB 76 | HHL 11, 157 |
| Against | HL 81 | HHL 84 |
| Aloft | HL 68 | HHB 24, 136 |
| Amiable | HB 131 | HHL 273 |
| Approch | HL 248 | HHB 100 |
| Aray, arayd | HL 285 | HHL 228 |
| Aspect | HL 217 | HHB 284 |
| Aspyre | HL 109 | HHL 88 |
| Assayes | IIB 88 | HHL 235 |
| Assure | HL 297 | HHL 97 |
| Attend | HB 261 | HHL 68, HHB 97 |
| Auengefull | HL 30 | HHB 150 |
| Author | HL 128 | HHL 256 |
| | | |
| Bait | HB 152 | HHB 290 |
| Basenesse | HL 191 | HHB 279 |
| Beauty | HB 15 | HHB 21 |
| Bee | HL 119, HB 250 | HHL 119, HHB 252 |
| Begot | HL 53 | HHL 30 |

| | | |
|---|---|---|
| Beheast | HL 93 | HHB 202 |
| Behold | HB 253 | HHB 232 |
| Behoue, behoues | HB 184 | HHL 178 |
| Being | HL 96 | HHL 191 |
| Bitter | HL 5 | HHL 245 |
| Blame | HL 288, HB 155 | HHL 18, 149, HHB 276 |
| Bleed, bleede | HL 12 | HHL 248 |
| Bleeding | HL 142 | HHL 164 |
| Blemish, blemishment | HB 215 | HHL 149 |
| Blesse, blessed, blest | HL 210, 284 | HHL 184 |
| Blind, blynd, blinding | HL 226, HB 77 | HHL 262, 280, HHB 137 |
| Blisse, blisses | HL 23, 207 | HHL 134, HHB 243 |
| Bosome | HL 289 (see 'lap' HL 24, 62) | HHL 134, HHB 183 |
| Bountie | HL 284 | HHL 223 |
| Bowre, bowres | HL 23, HB 202 | HHB 249 |
| Breast, brest | HL 27, 224, HB 3 | HHL 259, 269 |
| Bright, brighter | HB 56 | HHB 188 |
| Brightnes, brightnesse | HB 11, 178 | HHB 178, 189 |
| Cleare | HB 11 | HHB 189 |
| Commend | HB 263 | HHB 222 |
| Contented, contentment | HL 246 | HHB 287 |
| Cradle, cratch | HL 51 | HHL 226 |
| Crowne, crownd | HL 292 | HHL 243, HHB 190 |
| Cruell | HL 14, 32 | HHL 151 |
| Damned | HB 287 | HHL 89 |
| Darknesse | HL 60 | HHL 73, 90 |
| Dearling | HB 281 | HHB 184 |
| Death | HB 287 | HHL 193 |
| Delight | HL 281, HB 16, 123, 151 | HHL 272, HHB 17, 258 |
| Deserued, deseruer | HL 159 | HHL 160 |
| Desire, desyre | HB 5 | HHL 268 |
| Dew, deaw | HB 27 | HHL 46 |
| Dewty | HB 17 | HHB 20 |

| | | |
|---|---|---|
| Dislike, dislikes | HL 86 | HHL 34 |
| Downe | HB 109 | HHL 136 |
| Drop | HB 277, 284 | HHL 46 |
| | | |
| Eagle, eagles | HL 69 | HHB 138 |
| Earth | HL 111, 214 | HHB 210, 283 |
| Earthly | HL 185 | HHL 5 |
| Eldest | HL 56 | HHL 31 |
| Embrace | HL 111 | HHL 261 |
| Endewd, endewed | HB 135 | HHL 112 |
| Enlarge | HL 105 | HHL 52 |
| Entire, entyre | HB 223 | HHL 271 |
| Exceed, exceede | HB 231 | HHB 209 |
| Excell | HB 41 | HHB 206 |
| Ey, eye | HL 132, 216, HB 226 | HHL 276, HHB 23, 144, 285 |
| Eyes, eyne | HL 118, HB 20, 72, 232–4 | HHL 222, 280, 283, HHB 123, 179 |
| | | |
| Face | HB 41, 168 | HHL 171, HHB 204, 207 |
| Faire | HL 72, HB 139, 281 | HHB 133, 216 |
| Fairenesse | HB 231 | HHB 204 |
| Fairer, fairest | HL 216, HB 230 | HHB 102 |
| False | HL 261 | HHL 240 |
| Fancies, fansie | HL 254, HB 222 | HHB 289 |
| Fashiond | HB 33 | HHL 109 |
| Fayne, fayning | HL 216, 254 | HHB 216, 223 |
| Feare, feares | HL 223, 226 | HHB 141, 146 |
| Feeble | HL 185, HB 3, 24 | HHL 5, 269, HHB 123 |
| Feed, feede | HL 38, HB 248 | HHL 196, HHB 29 |
| Felicitie, felicitye | HL 217 | HHB 284 |
| Fierie | HB 241 | HHB 95 |
| Fixe, fixed, fixeth | HB 228 | HHB 139, 272 |
| Flight | HL 69 | HHB 28 |
| Floure, flowre | HB 282 | HHL 169 |
| Flowing | HB 55 | HHL 100 |
| Foes | HL 263 | HHL 161, 234, HHB 156 |
| Force, forse | HL 8, 229 | HHL 250 |

| Fount, fountaine | HB 186 | HHL 99, HHB 21 |
| Free | HL 154, HB 249 | HHL 183–4, HHB 251 |

| Gazefull | HB 12 | HHB 29 |
| Golden | HL 178 | HHL 1 |
| Grace | HB 27, 277, 282 | HHL 44, 99, 169 |
| Great | HB 5 | HHL 268 |
| Grieue, grieued | HL 129 | HHL 252 |
| Grone | HL 129 | HHL 252 |
| Guilt, guilty | HL 290, HB 157 | HHL 141, 167 |

| Happie | HL 209 | HHB 239 |
| Hart, harts | HL 123, 142 | HHL 156 |
| Heast, heasts | HL 160 | HHL 161 |
| Heauenly | HL 169, 302, HB 119, 185, 222 | HHL 6, 112, 229, HHB 21, 248, 262 |
| Heauens | HL 189, 215, HB 109 | HHL 2, 7, 57, 88, HHB 235 |
| Hell, hellish | HL 253, 265 | HHL 89, 130 |
| Hew | HB 150 | HHB 231 |
| Hid, hidden | HL 59 | HHB 178, 248 |
| Higher, see Hyer, hyre | | |
| Hight | HL 189, HB 109 | HHL 2, 57, 88, HHB 67 |
| Hope | HL 206 | HHL 122 |
| House | HB 117 | HHB 193 |
| Hungrie, hungry | HL 198 | HHL 196, HHB 288 |
| Hyer, hyre | HL 68 | HHB 19 |
| Hymne, hymnes | HL 41, 302, HB 10, 21, 272 | HHL 6, 70 |

| Idle, ydle | HL 66, 256 | HHB 268, 289 |
| Image | HL 132, 197 | HHL 259, HHB 105, 114 |
| Images | HB 163 | HHB 3 |
| Immortall | HB 23 | HHB 13, 169 |
| Increast | HL 96 | HHB 203 |
| Inner | HL 124 | HHL 158 |

| | | |
|---|---|---|
| Please, pleased | HB 54 | HHB 270 |
| Pleasure | HL 287 | HHL 75, HHB 264 |
| Pleasures | HL 275, HB 259 | HHL 220, HHB 256, 300 |
| Plumes | HL 178 | HHB 134 |
| Powre | HL 1, HB 271 | HHB 186, 196 |
| Praise, prayse | HL 301, 307, HB 7–8 | HHL 9, HHB 220, 263 |
| Praises, prayses | HL 10 | HHL 14, HHB 233 |
| Purest | HL 178, HB 105, 109 | HHL 98, HHB 47 |
| | | |
| Quench, quenched | HL 102, 202, HB 175 | HHL 18 |
| | | |
| Rage, raging | HL 117, HB 4, 73 | HHB 1 |
| Rauisht | HB 12 | HHL 268, 281, HHB 1 |
| Remaine, remained | HL 92 | HHL 125 |
| Resplendent | HB 177 | HHB 126 |
| Restore, restored | HL 164, HB 287 | HHL 139, 181 |
| Riches | HB 119, 185 | HHL 112, HHB 248 |
| Rigour | HL 152 | HHB 158 |
| | | |
| Sake | HL 72 | HHL 147 |
| Satietie, satiety | HL 201 | HHB 282 |
| Seat, seate | HL 66 | HHL 82, HHB 148, 159 |
| See | HL 118, 226, HB 38, 234 | HHL 118, 283, HHB 117, 255 |
| Sense | HB 77 | HHL 278 |
| Shadow, shadowes | HB 168 | HHB 291 |
| Shame | HL 290 | HHL 19, 151 |
| Sharp, sharpe | HL 16, 121 | HHL 235 |
| Shew | HB 286 | HHB 114 |
| Shine, shynes, shyning | HB 168, 175 | HHB 169 |
| Sight | HL 119, 195, HB 18, 131, 166, 220 | HHL 5, 287, HHB 15, 178, 281 |
| Sing | HL 10, 21, 302 | HHL 6, 14 |
| Sit | HL 24 | HHB 183 |
| Skie, sky | HL 178 | HHB 25 |
| Sore, sores | HL 143 | HHL 162, 166 |
| Sorrow, sorrowes | HL 16, HB 28 | HHL 251 |

| | | |
|---|---|---|
| Soule, soules | HB 14, 60, 137, 159, 248 | HHL 196, 251, HHB 137, 288 |
| Spright | HL 106 | HHL 110 |
| Stirre | HB 73 | HHL 263 |
| Striue, striueth | HL 247 | HHB 77 |
| Sunne | HB 220 | HHB 139 |
| Sweet, sweete | HL 190, HB 199, 245, 252 | HHL 273, HHB 4, 257, 269, 300 |
| Swerue, swerued | HL 165 | HHL 161 |
| | | |
| Taking | HL 64 | HHL 146 |
| Thinke, thinks | HL 205 | HHB 266 |
| Thought | HB 224 | HHB 223 |
| Thraldome, thrall, thrals | HL 136, HB 278 | HHL 124, 137, 184 |
| Thrise | HL 209 | HHB 239 |
| Throne | HB 265 | HHB 151–2 |
| Time | HL 61 | HHL 36 |
| Tongue | HL 264 | HHB 204 |
| Truth | HL 176 | HHB 11, 159 |
| | | |
| Vnfold | HB 255 | HHB 234 |
| Voide | HB 215 | HHL 32 |
| Vouchsafe | HL 19, HB 19 | HHL 45, HHB 8 |
| | | |
| Wings | HL 64 | HHL 1, 66 |
| Wound, wounds | HL 143, HB 63 | HHL 156, 245 |
| Wretches | HL 265 | HHL 193 |
| | | |
| Yre | HL 84, 234 | HHL 86, HHB 182 |

# 2

# *Elaborate song*

## CONCEPTUAL STRUCTURE IN MILTON'S 'ON THE MORNING OF CHRIST'S NATIVITY'

### Maren-Sofie Røstvig

As Milton explains in his *Animadversions* (1641), the imperfections of man extend to the very words of praise that he offers to the Deity: as a rule his 'thanke-offering' must be a 'plain ungarnish't present' only, but when the glorious acts of God have been fully achieved, he 'may then perhaps take up a Harp, and sing thee an elaborate song...'[1]

The poetic perfection envisaged here is of course unattainable within our fallen world, but it must nevertheless be permissible to characterise Milton's *Nativity Ode*—his ceremonial gift to the infant Christ—as 'elaborate song' rather than a 'plain ungarnish't present' snatched up in a hurry. And if his words of praise should be felt to possess some measure of perfection, this is so partly because they have been made to reflect the very structures by means of which God perfected and accomplished his glorious acts. Augustine would have appreciated the art with which this has been done, and so would poets like Edmund Spenser and Giles Fletcher. The task that I have set myself here is to explain this art, and although I hope to make my argument sufficiently persuasive for acceptance, I shall also feel a major obligation to try to convey the conceptual richness of the structures selected by Milton as appropriate, and their intrinsic aesthetic beauty.

I have seldom come across structures that yield greater aesthetic delight, and it is possible that they are there, in the poem, not so much to persuade as to move. Although they relate to matters of faith they seem designed, to borrow the words of William Whitaker, 'to give pleasure, not to coerce assent',[2] or, to quote a modern scholar, 'to deepen and change the meaning of the narrative from the specific to the general and universal.'[3] It does not necessarily follow that Milton must have believed implicitly in the presence of these structures, in the Bible and the created universe, if he saw fit to use them. As long as they were felt as powerfully evocative images they would do to adorn his song.

The major images of the Christian religion are very complex, and structural images are no exception. Such images, by the way, connect so closely with the traditional kind of verbal image that they cannot be kept absolutely apart. The Tree of Life, for example,—in the Garden of Eden, on Golgotha, and in the Heavenly Jerusalem— acquires added symbolic richness by being seen as a structuring element placed at the beginning, middle, and the end. The semantic complexity of the structures attributed to the glorious acts of God posits a very real problem in literary criticism: if the critic, in his attempt to elucidate a particular poetic structure, were to follow the example set by Biblical exegetes, he might easily be encouraged to range so far afield that the connection with the text may be obscured. I hope I have avoided this hazard, but I have nevertheless on occasion included arguments that some readers perhaps may find objectionable as going beyond the limits set by Milton's text. My defence for so doing is a simple one: it seemed to me that since the structures possess this conceptual complexity, then the point of incorporating them in a poem on the Nativity must be to invoke the nexus of ideas that they embody. If my first critical premiss, therefore, is that the structures are there as the result of conscious planning rather than instinctive artistic tact, my second is that the entire conceptual range may be drawn on in an *explication de texte,* even if this should mean going beyond the strict limits of what I am tempted to refer to as the para- phrasable prose content. But the use of such material for the purpose of literary criticism presupposes sufficient familiarity and sympathy with certain ways of thinking typical of much Renaissance theology, Protestant as well as Roman Catholic, and sufficient critical tact in assessing the degree of relevance.

The analysis presented here will be found to stress the concepts of the circle, the centre, and the 'well-balanced world' hung on 'hinges', my argument being that these images have been worked into the structure of the poem to permit Milton's gift to the child to consti- tute an image of his acts as Creator and Redeemer. My structural units are stanza-length (respectively seven and eight lines), the number of stanzas in each part (4 and 27), and the sum total of lines (28 and 216).[4]

My 'warrant' for considering structure in this manner is taken primarily from traditional interpretations of the Psalms, especially Psalm 119 (Vulgate 118) and the fifteen Psalms of Ascent (Psalms 120–34). My inclusion of the Platonic *lambda*-formula has similar Biblical authority, the appropriate points of reference in this case being comments on the Mosaic account of creation and the creation-passage in *Job* 38:4–8 (echoed by Milton in stanza 12). However, my most important frame of reference for interpreting the structural numbers was provided by theological glosses on the Apocalyptic passages invoked by Milton's vision of Christ as universal King and of the complete perfection that will be ours at the end of Time.

The basic structure in the hymn proper is created by a thematic movement focussed around a triple centre-piece so that the overall pattern may be presented as a sequence of 12—3—12 stanzas. For H. Neville Davies, writing without knowledge of my analysis, the thematic movement seemed to indicate a division into 15—11—1. His thematic analysis of the first fifteen stanzas, however, not only is compatible with my own but supplements it, and the same is true of his analysis of the last twelve stanzas as a sequence of 11 plus 1. Biblical exegesis similarly offers examples of the attribution, to the same work, of different structures. Thus the Psalms could be divided in various ways—into three times fifty, for example, or a sequence of 70 plus 80—and each arrangement carried its own symbolic significance. When Cassiodorus discusses various ways of dividing the books of the Bible into groups (*Institutiones*, I, 14), he recommends them all because a 'careful consideration and inspection' will show that so far from conflicting they tend 'to make one another mutually intelligible'. Statements by the Fathers on this matter 'are not contradictory but varying'; through the divisions they recommend, all of them have created structural expressions of the contents of divine revelation. The actual phrase used by Cassiodorus is that they 'through their divisions have adapted the sacred books to appropriate mysteries'.

When poets like Vaughan and Cowley appropriated structures as well as themes from the works of their predecessors, they reveal that different poets could 'read' a structure in slightly different ways, or put a given structure to a somewhat different use. But similarity need not necessarily indicate borrowing. The presence of fairly similar structures in poems possessed of thematic similarities may quite simply constitute evidence of the extent to which certain themes were associated with certain structures. If Cowley for example wrote his 'Hymn to the Light' without awareness of Milton's use of related themes and structures, one must perforce conclude that Cowley drew on a general tradition which enabled him to achieve the degree of similarity to Milton's ode that I discuss below.

In assessing structural analyses, then, one must take into account the fact that a poem may accommodate more than one structural effect. A structural image, in other words, may possess the same kind of willed ambiguity that we have been accustomed to recognise in verbal imagery. I suppose it is because structures seem so unambiguous —a seven-line stanza is a seven-line stanza—that certainty has been more or less expected. When a poet takes the trouble to explain the meaning invested in a structure, certainty is of course achieved, but such authorial glosses are the exception rather than the rule, and for good reasons: they reduce the 'mystery' of the poem, to use the word so popular among Biblical expositors. As Augustine puts it in his *De doctrina Christiana* (II, vi, 7), things that are easily discovered 'seem frequently to become worthless', while 'what is sought with difficulty is discovered with more pleasure.'[5] But our understanding of the message of salvation does not depend on these more difficult passages; that which is stated obscurely and with great art can always be found elsewhere in phrases easily grasped by all. This argument seems to me to apply to Milton's poem as well; one can enjoy it without perceiving the elaborateness of its art. It conveys its basic message both simply and memorably.

As far as Milton's structural rhetoric is concerned, I wish I could assert with Augustine's supreme confidence that the more obscure the prophetic eloquence, the sweeter it becomes when explained (*De doctrina Christiana*, IV, vii, 15).

## I. *Structural Exegesis*

To begin with the beginning is, I believe, to begin with Psalm 119 (Vulgate 118) and with a summary of the symbolism attributed to its form, since it was this symbolic import which made the form appropriate for Nativity hymns.

Psalm 119 is an acrostic poem, the sequence of initial letters spelling out the 22 letters of the Hebrew alphabet. It consists of 22 groups of 8 verses, each of which begins with the appropriate letter in the alphabet, a technique used in *Lamentations* 1–4, where it may be better known today. As I have explained elsewhere,[6] a prophetic message was attributed to the textual arrangement of this Psalm, partly in terms of its use of the alphabet and partly in terms of its structural numbers (8 and 22). The idea of fullness or completeness was conveyed (so it was argued) by using all the letters in the alphabet, a concept seen as appropriate since the Psalm presents all the precepts required for the achievement of eternal life. A summary of patristic interpretations may be found in the *Commentarium In Librum Psalmorum* (Lugduni, 1611–1613) by the Jesuit Lorinus. Thus Lorinus observes that Cassiodorus followed Augustine in admiring the perfection of this Psalm, a perfection revealed by the Tree in the middle of the Garden of Eden: *sub similitudine arboris, quae in medio paradisi erat, Augustino hunc psalmum reuelatum fuisse.*[7] Why the structure should seem like the Tree which is Christ is explained more fully by Bonaventura in his *Collationes in Hexaemeron* (XVII, 12). Augustine apparently had a vision of a tree with 22 branches each of which had 8 twigs from which issued *guttae dulcissimae*, and he suddenly understood that this tree was the Psalm which begins *Beati immaculati in via* ('Blessed are the undefiled in the way, who walk in the law of the Lord . . .'). To realise this one must follow Augustine in connecting the form of Psalm 119 with the contents of Psalm 1 as Bonaventura explains, conveniently quoting the first few lines to display the similarity in theme and phrasing ('Blessed is the man that walketh not in the counsel of the ungodly . . . But his delight is in the law of the Lord . . . And he shall be like a tree planted by the rivers of water . . .').[8] The tree in Psalm 1 was universally accepted as an allusion to the Tree of Life in the Garden of Eden, both being images (or types) of Christ, and Augustine reveals a visual, almost architectural or spatial approach to textual structure when he has this vision of Psalm 119 as a tree full of the sweetest sap. In Psalm 1 as in *Genesis* this image of Christ is verbal, while it is the literary structure that conveys it in Psalm 119, and the ease with which it was possible to turn from verbal to structural images or the other way round is typical of the tradition extending from Hilarius and Augustine to Lorinus.

Representative comments on the conceptual content of the structural numbers may be fetched from a Renaissance edition of the medieval Bishop Haymo's *Pia, Brevis Ac Dilucida In Omnes Psalmos Explanatio* (Freiburg, 1533). The structure shows that the Law (10) and apostolic doctrine (12) combined (so as to make 22) lead to beatitude (the Octonarius represented by the groups of eight verses). In this manner God rescues man from the confusion which is the consequence of the Fall, to a state of order. Similar remarks are found in the commentary written by a Protestant theologian, Johannes Bugenhagius *(In Librum Psalmorum Interpretatio,* 1524). Bugenhagius felt that the form had been selected to show that this Psalm contains everything stated in the sacred Scriptures concerning the attainment of perfection—a comment bearing on the alphabetical technique of composition. He goes on to explain that the number 8 must refer to the resurrection because Christ rose on the eighth day which signifies the time of grace. This time of grace cannot pertain to the seven days of this world, all of which terminate with a night so that they cease being days. All those will be resurrected who walk with God and *not* according to the elements of this world *(secundum mundi elementa).*

All this, and more, could be adduced as legitimate commentary by exegetes convinced that structure conveyed part of the prophetic message. After reading a fairly wide range of commentaries on selected parts of the Bible, I have formed the conclusion that the truly basic reason for associating the structure of Psalm 119 (or of *Lamentations*) with Nativity hymns must be its highly ordered form, and the connection made between this form and Christ as the creative Logos. The creative Word imposes order on chaos, and hence the words of praise offered to Christ in celebration of his Nativity must themselves be highly ordered. The standard example cited by exegetes is Sedulius' Nativity hymn beginning *A solis ortus cardine,*[9] but I am unable to say how common the practice actually was.[10] Venantius Fortunatus employed an alphabetical structure on one occasion, but not in a Nativity hymn,[11] and when he wrote a poem that might qualify as such thematically, he devised structural patterns of such ingenuity that one can only marvel at the skill with which he manipulated his 33 lines, each consisting of 33 letters, at the centre of which is the letter which itself holds the centre of the alphabet.[12]

Augustine reinforced the association between Christ and a meaningful arrangement of letters and numbers in his comment on the supposed prophecy, by the Sibyls, of the birth of Christ in an acrostic poem consisting of 27 lines. Augustine found the number appropriate because it is a cube ($3^3$), since cubes symbolise the permanence and stability of the divine *(De civitate Dei* XVIII, 23). This use of classical number lore in a purely Christian context illustrates a syncretistic tendency extending through the Middle Ages and into the Renaissance, when it received renewed impetus.[13] The way in which classical myth was interpreted so as to convey the same truths that we find in divine revelation has been explored by Edgar Wind and Don Cameron Allen,[14] and it was of course much easier for classical number lore to be subsumed under a Mosaic revelation than for pagan myth; numbers figure so importantly in so many Biblical passages that it must have seemed eminently logical to assume a Hebrew source for the Pythagorean and Platonic numerical accounts of creation. I have discussed this assumption elsewhere,[15] so suffice it here to quote one or two arguments advanced by Francesco Giorgio in his *Problemata* (1536, 1574, and 1622),[16] a collection of Biblical cruxes. Problem III, i, 26 discusses the reason for the alphabetical composition employed in Psalm 119 and *Lamentations* (and, in so doing, refers to and quotes from Sedulius' Nativity hymn), while V, ii, 176 associates the music of the spheres inferred from *Job* 38 with the inaudible music of the divine numbers used in the work of creation, adding that it is of this divine order that the prophet sings in Psalm 119. This inaudible music was given mathematical expression by Plato and Pythagoras, as theologians with a syncretistic bias took care to remind their readers, adding that the ultimate source for this classical number lore was in Moses and the prophets. Strictly speaking, therefore, one should not refer to this lore as 'pagan' if one wishes to represent the point of view of theologians like Augustine, Aquinas or Cornelius à Lapide.[17] If readers of this essay, therefore, should hesitate to attribute to conscious intent the fact that Milton's ode has three cubes as the chief structural numbers (8, 27, and 216 are the cubes of 2, 3, and 6), and that 8 and 27 represent the inaudible music of the divine numbers used in the work of creation,[18] they must take care to do so for reasons that can be accepted. It would be an historical anachronism to argue that such number lore would be inadmissible in a poem on the Nativity.

Milton may not have read Mantuan's comments on the form of Psalm 119, but his familiarity with the symbolism attributed to its structure can be taken for granted. He would have studied this *lusum poeticum* (to borrow Mantuan's words)[19] with complete awareness of the belief that the formal arrangement of this particular Psalm as of all the Psalms as a whole had been so designed by the Holy Ghost as to convey a message of its own. Distinctly odd as this belief seems to us today, it must nevertheless be classified as being well within the orthodox fold in the age itself. We must remember that the first half of the seventeenth century in England was virtually obsessed

by typological exegesis, and that typology exploits numbers. Typological imagery, therefore, spilled over into the pages of poets as well as
preachers, as all readers of George Herbert and John Donne will
know. This marked interest in typology was in large measure a direct
consequence of that belief in Providence and in England as God's
chosen nation that for a time made the Millennium seem at hand.
And to think typologically is to think in terms of meaningful, carefully balanced patterns imposed by the hand of Providence on the course
of human history, which is one reason why structure assumed such
great significance. The concern with structure, therefore, should be
seen as a direct manifestation of a way of thinking that must be characterised as widespread, and even a poet who may have refused to commit himself fully to it as an article of faith, would have felt its poetic
potentiality—its power to move the minds and hearts of men.

If this belief in the prophetic or conceptual import of structure was
at all widely known, poets other than Milton must have felt the
attraction of imitating patterns attributable to divine inspiration. And
so they did, as we may see from the poetry of Giles and Phineas
Fletcher and most clearly, perhaps, from Giles Fletcher's *Christ's
Victory and Triumph* (Cambridge, 1610). His defence of poetry in the
prefatory epistle to the reader invokes the poetic passages in the Bible
and the example set by 'sedulous Prudentius' and 'prudent Sedulius'
and the 'choicest witts of Christendome'. What Giles Fletcher himself
refers to as 'poetical diuinity' no doubt prompted his choice of an
eight-line stanza in imitation of Psalm 119. This may seem a bold
assertion, but readers may possibly agree on studying the last stanza
of the last part. This concluding stanza deplores man's inability,
caught up as he is in the web of Time, to grasp the vision of Eternity
that the poet has tried to present in the preceding 50 stanzas:

> *Impotent words, weak lines, that strive* in vain
> In vain, *alas! to tell* so heavenly sight,—
> So heavenly sight, *as none greater* feign,
> Feign *what he can, that seems of greatest* might:
>   Might *any yet compare with* Infinite?
>   Infinite *sure those joys, my words but* light;
> Light *is the palace where she dwells—O blessed wight!*[20]

Giles Fletcher has given structural expression to the links in the
chain of Time by means of phrasal repetition as indicated typographi-
cally by romans. But not only have the lines been linked in a circular

pattern, their number has been reduced from 8 to 7. This is the only stanza that has been tampered with in this unusual manner, and the linking of the lines explains why. If the stanzaic structure is to reflect the nature of Time as it revolves around the ever-repeated cycle of weeks, the number of lines must be seven. I consider these structural phenomena as adequate proof of intent, and on the strength of the formal symbolism displayed in this last stanza I conclude that the eight-line stanza should be taken to reflect the eighth 'day' of Eternity in the manner familiar to students of Psalm 119 and of the 15 Psalms of Ascent. The fact that there are 15 such Psalms was interpreted as showing that the ascent takes us from the 7 of Time to the 8 of Eternity.[21] Giles Fletcher may conceivably have trusted some of his readers to realise why he shortened the Spenserian stanza to eight lines in a poem concerned with Christ's victory and triumph, but he underlined his artistic purpose by creating a final stanza whose departure from the established norm explains the reason for the norm.

## II

### *The Structure of Milton's Ode*

I find it inconceivable that Milton, who must have studied Fletcher's poem with considerable care,[22] should have failed to observe how the last stanza underlines the symbolism invested in the stanzaic pattern. I find it more reasonable to suppose that he was inspired by Giles Fletcher and the exegetical tradition Fletcher invokes, to exploit the same polarity between Time and Eternity in the two stanza-patterns he created for his ode. Like Giles Fletcher (and, of course, Spenser before him), Milton encouraged his readers to adopt a structural perspective by providing verbal clues to the conceptual content of the chosen form. 'This is the month,' he proclaims in the first line of the four seven-line stanzas that constitute the introduction, 'and this the happy morn' when the Son 'Forsook the courts of ever-lasting day / And chose with us a darksome house of mortal clay.' A reader accustomed to structural exegesis and to the use of Biblical structures in religious poetry, would have observed the care with which the poet has observed structural decorum and would have enjoyed it as an aspect of his art. The structural numbers of the introduction—4, 7, and 28—enact the weekly and seasonal cycles of Time; in its capacity as the lunar cycle the sum total of lines, 28, aptly represents the mutability of this world of 'mortal clay', but it may also suggest that our earthly existence borrows its light from that Son who is the Sun of our spiritual existence.

The transition to the eight-line stanza of the hymn with its varied rhythmical movement is strongly felt, but a sense of continuity is suggested by the concluding alexandrine. This rhythmical element is shared, thus showing that the worlds of Time and Eternity, although separate, must not be entirely unconnected. The point of the incarnation is to enable man to achieve the ascent.

The introduction provides another important clue when it presents Christ as King, seated 'at heaven's high council-table' 'the midst of trinal unity'. This recalls the greatest Biblical vision of Christ as King as presented in the Book of Revelation. As St John puts it (*Rev.* 4:1–5 and 5:8–14), 'a door was opened in heaven' and he saw 'a throne set in heaven, and one sat on the throne', and 'there was a rainbow round about the throne'. Also there are around the throne 'four and twenty seats: and upon the seats I saw four and twenty elders sitting'. These elders fall down before the Lamb, 'having every one of them harps', and so Christ is worshipped with 'a new song', the voices of 'every creature which is in heaven, and on the earth' being added to praise him 'that sitteth upon the throne'. It is interesting that Milton should begin his introduction by invoking this most familiar and most impressive Apocalyptic vision of Christ as King; he is clearly concerned to fuse the two images—of Christ as eternal King surrounded by the elders and worshipped with 'a new song', and of Christ as the 'heaven-born-child' in the manger hymned by cherubim and seraphim. As the singer of his own hymn, Milton joins his voice to both 'quires'. The importance, to Milton, of the Apocalyptic vision, is brought out again in stanzas 13–15, where we recognise direct verbal echoes. Thus heaven 'as at some festival' is seen to 'open wide the gates of her high palace hall' to provide a glimpse of what the introduction refers to, in a phrase reminiscent of Giles Fletcher, as 'the courts of everlasting day'. These gates are envisaged as opening when the 'ninefold harmony' (13) has been fully achieved so that 'hell itself will pass away' and permit the return to Earth of Truth and Justice, 'Orbed in a rainbow', with Mercy sitting 'between' (15).

When these Apocalyptic echoes are recognised, one perceives that stanzas 13–15 form a triple centre-piece depicting the glory of the Heavenly Jerusalem. The points of transition are easily felt: the passage begins with the joyous command to the spheres to 'ring out' and it is at an end when we reach the emphatic retraction. 'But wisest fate says no.' It must be stressed that the vision invoked in the introduction and in this triple centre-piece is a vision whose meaning was explained almost entirely in terms of its structural symbolism. To think of this vision was to think of its structural import.

But before this import is discussed we must consider the thematic movement through the twelve stanzas that precede the centre, and the twelve that follow. There is a strongly felt contrast between the central section and the rest of the poem, as well as between the two flanking sections of equal length. While the centre-piece presents the perfection of the Heavenly Jerusalem when God's glorious acts will have been fully achieved, the rest of the hymn describes the impact of the incarnation, beginning and concluding with a stanza showing the child in the manger. We observe, however, that in the first stanza it is Nature who pays homage to the incarnate Deity, while it is the angels who do so in the last. And as we read on from the first stanza to the centre-piece, we realise that they form a carefully planned sequence showing the impact of the incarnation on the world of Nature and of man, concluding with a climactic last stanza (12) recalling Christ's work as Creator—his first act within the world of Time. And after we have passed through the three stanzas on the harmony of Eternity (consequent on the completion of his glorious acts), we are made to envisage his last work in the world of Time when the 'trump of doom' announces Judgement Day. The centre-piece, therefore, is surrounded by stanzas devoted to respectively the first and the last day of Time, and to the first and the last work of Christ. Stanza 17, moreover, shows us Christ seated on his throne 'in middle air' sentencing souls, thus indicating that this second major thematic movement (stanzas 16–27) is devoted to a different sphere of life, namely a realm of spiritual powers and principalities to invoke *Ephesians* 6:12. In this sphere, too, the superior power of the Son is manifested. In some ways this overall thematic movement reminds one of the many representations in sacred art of Christ surrounded on the one hand by the orderly ranks of the blessed and, on the other, by a confused array of the damned. Even more appropriate, perhaps, is a comparison with Spenser's use of so-called encyclo-paedic infolded images as explained by Gerald Snare.[23] When pre-sented iconographically the key figure—God, for example, or man—

is placed seated within a circle surrounded by its attributes or acts as circular emanations. But to return to Milton, we observe that the two sequences I have indicated (1–12 and 16–27) are dominated by the concept of reign or rule. In the first earthly kings acknowledge their 'sovran Lord', just as the Sun hides his head to see 'a greater Sun appear', but in the realm of man and Nature Christ is no hostile power. He purifies and fulfils, but does not expel: Nature 'was almost won / To think her part was done, / And that her reign had here its last fulfilling' (10). In the second sequence on the effect of the incarnation within a realm of spiritual powers, the purification is partly by expulsion, partly by replacement: evil powers are overcome and the imperfect foreshadowings replaced by full and final revelation.[24] The idea of kingship is again strongly stressed: Christ evicts from their thrones powers that have usurped his place. Their spurious kingdoms must needs fail the moment they feel the 'dreaded infant's hand'.

Before I consider the two sequences in greater detail, I would like to stress the importance of the chronological structure indicated by stanzas 1/27 and 12/16. The circular effect created by letting the hymn begin and end with the babe in the manger is easily felt, but it is surely an equally striking structural phenomenon that the first sequence concludes with Christ's work of creation (12), while the second begins with Judgment Day (16). Since Christ was born not only *in medio noctis* but also *in medio annorum*, a beautiful temporal scheme is perceived. When we reach the centre of the hymn we are referred back to the beginning of Time (as stated at 14:3) and to its end (16:8)— a chiastic arrangement recalling the fusion of beginning and end in Eternity. Conversely the true mid-point is found at the beginning (1) and at the end (27). Not only is the chronological scheme plainly circular, but the great circle of Time is shown as issuing out of Eternity and returning to it again. Such is the beauty and the theological appropriateness of this structure that it becomes an object of contemplation in its own right. And if one tries to fuse this abstract structural pattern with the poem, one's ability to experience it as a whole is perceptibly increased. It becomes possible to hold the poem in one's mind in an act almost disconnected with the world of Time: sequential reading is supplemented by an almost visual act of instant perception.

But Christ is the beginning, middle, and end in other respects as well. Such is the connotative richness of the structure I have indicated that it may be as well to explain some of the theological concepts involved by referring to Bonaventura, a writer whose epigrammatic style invites quotation. Bonaventura begins his *Collationes in Hexa-emeron*[25] by showing the many ways in which Christ 'holds the middle' at the same time that he circumscribes everything. We are reminded of the well-known rule for epic poetry when Bonaventura writes that we must always begin with the middle, that is Christ (*incipiendum est a medio, quod est Christus*; I, 10), who became our true mid-point through his incarnation (*Hoc medium fuit Christus in incarnatione*; I, 20). The theological appropriateness of letting Christ circumscribe the whole poem (1 and 27) and the centre (12 and 16) is brought out when Bonaventura writes that Christ *habet rationem principii, medii et finis ultimi* (I, 13), or again when he compares Christ as our beginning, middle, and end to the circle and its centre in his most famous work, the *Itinerarium mentis in Deum*:

> Rursus revertentes dicamus: quia igitur esse purissimum et absolutum, quod est simpliciter esse, est primarium et novissi-mum, ideo est omnium origo et finis consummans.—Quia aeternum et praesentissimum, ideo omnes durationes ambit et intrat, quasi simul existens earum centrum et circumferentia.— Quia simplicissimum et maximum, ideo totum intra omnia et totum extra, ac per hoc 'est sphaera intelligibilis, cuius centrum est ubique et circumferentia nusquam' (Alan. ab Insulis, Theolog. Regul. 7).—Quia actualissimum et immutabilissimum, ideo 'stabile manens moveri dat universa' (Boeth., III de Consolat., metr. 9).—Quia perfectissimum et immensum, ideo est intra omnia, non inclusum, extra omnia, non exclusum . . . ideo est omnia in omnibus (I Cor 15, 28) . . .
>
> *(Itinerarium mentis in Deum, V, 8)*

To paraphrase this loosely, as pure being Christ is the first and the last and the end of everything; because he is eternal and most present he circumscribes and enters into everything so that he is as it were both the centre and the circumference of all things. He is at once inside and outside everything because he is highest unity, or most One, and the greatest (both *simplicissimum* and *maximum*). Thus he is 'an intelligible sphere whose centre is everywhere and whose circumference nowhere'. He is in everything without being enclosed by it, and he is outside everything without being excluded. In short, he is all in all despite the fact that 'all' is multiplicity (*omnia sunt multa*) and he is One (*ipsum non sit nisi unum*).[26]

I have quoted so extensively in order to show the wealth of associations connected with a fairly simple structural concept involving beginning, middle and end, or circle and centre. Unless these associations are present as we consider the highly ordered structure of Milton's poem, it will seem but a *lusus poeticus* and a pretty idle one, to quote Mantuan, rather than a device whereby *omnia sunt prophetica*.[27]

The juxtaposition, in stanzas 12 and 16, of Christ as creator and judge, anticipates the similar effect in *Paradise Lost* where the first half concludes with Christ as triumphant victor and judge, while the second half begins by showing Christ as omnipotent creator. In both poems Christ 'holds the middle' as our *sol iustitiae* (*Malachi* 4:2) who expels the powers of darkness.

The fact that stanzas 1 and 27 and again 12 and 16 display strong thematic linking may be an indication of the presence of recessed symmetry around the centre, and this supposition is borne out by an analysis of the thematic movement as indicated in my diagram. I would not insist on a pattern worked out in terms of one to one equivalents; the thematic movement seems based on groups of stanzas. One observes that the most magnificent images have been placed closest to the centre, stanzas 11–12 and 16–17 focussing on Christ. Stanzas 12/16 display the acts of Christ on the first day (as creator) and the last (as judge), while 11/17 describe the homage paid by the angelic hosts to 'heaven's new-born heir' (11) and his appearance as 'dreadful judge in middle air' (17).

Stanzas 2–10 and 18–26 praise the acts of Christ within the world of Time, the first sequence being concerned with the world of man and nature, the second with the world of spiritual powers. The thematic pairing is emphatic in 2/26, where the common denominator is guilt: Nature hides her 'guilty front' (2) just as guilty spirits are seen to vanish into their 'infernal jail' (26). At the other end of the thematic 'chain' the linking is equally clear: in stanza 10 Nature hopes to see her reign fulfilled, while in stanza 18 Satan's 'usurped sway' ceases. In both spheres of life the true ruler has appeared. The stanzas that fall in between are linked through related themes; 'universal peace' is the theme of stanzas 3–5, while the absence of peace is stressed in the stanzas placed equidistant from the centre on the other side (23–5). The next group of stanzas (6–7 and 21–2) magnify the *true ruler* by revealing the inadequacy of the acts performed by man and Nature or by spiritual powers. The next thematic key word is *true revelation* of the divine to men (8–9) and to powers, whether these be false or merely inadequate (19–20). The symmetrical structure also manifests itself in the rising movement of stanzas 2–10 and the corresponding falling movement of stanzas 18–26. Initially one ascends in contemplation from Earth with its elements and societies of men to the stars and the sun (6–7), and from there one moves to the heavenly voices heard by the shepherds (8) and to the theme of the harmonious union between Heaven and Earth (9–10). This rising movement continues in the stanzas that take us into the realm of Christ as related to the world of man and Nature (11–12), the peak being reached in the three stanzas on the heavenly Jerusalem (13–15). After this centre has been passed we begin at the same high level with two stanzas (16–17) presenting Christ in his relationship to a world of spiritual powers. The spatial connotations of the stanzas that follow are realised on remembering that the dragon whose reign ceases (18) falls from Heaven (*Rev.* 20:2), and that the 'straiter limits' imposed on him are on a cosmic scale. The false idols and deities are connected with the stars (22) or the elements (23) and when these are ousted from their 'wonted' seats (21) Satan's sway is indeed reduced. The descent is also a spiritual descent from lesser goods to absolute evil: stanzas 19–21 describe pagan myth and ritual in terms that reveal an awareness of intrinsic beauty, and this beauty must be recognised for the simple reason that pagan myth foreshadows the incarnation. The Pan who is ousted in stanza 20 is a type of the true, or 'mighty Pan' whose coming is announced in stanza 8. Similarly the Sun who hides his head for shame is a natural type of Him who is the source of all light. Without Christ the Sun is as inadequate a ruler as the rites of stanza 21 are inadequate, and for the same reason. The impact of pure evil is strongly felt in the stanzas that follow (22–5), and the thematic movement concludes when we are taken underground with the fettered ghosts that 'Troop to the infernal jail' (26).

As my diagram shows, the overall 12—3—12 pattern modifies into one of three groups of nine, one for each part of the triple world. It is a particularly felicitous arrangement that the sphere of Christ and Eternity should be at the centre (11–17) at the same time that it circumscribes them all in stanzas 1 and 27. To do justice to the structure my diagram ought to have been three-dimensional so as to allow for the spatial effect of ascent and descent. The appropriateness of having three groups of nine is obvious, since this is the traditional pattern of the threefold world. However, Milton has varied this pattern in a manner which recalls Cusanus' Circulus Universorum (*De coniecturis* I, xvi).[28] He has fused the macrocosmic and the microcosmic, inserting a world of spirits and powers between a hierarchically structured heaven and the world of Nature and man. As a consequence one receives a strong impression that man is placed in a world where spiritual powers manifest themselves everywhere and at all times, and the thematic alignment between these two spheres underlines their interconnection. Thus in stanzas 6 and 5 (reading from the centre outwards to each side) Christ commands the stars and the elements, in 22 and 23 idols and powers associated with the stars and the elements. And in 4 and 3 the hand of Peace pacifies the world of men and 'sea and land', while conversely the 'dreaded infant's hand' deprives the powers of evil of all rest in 24 and 25. The thematic alignment between stanzas or groups of stanzas is clearly the result of tracing the impact of the incarnation through spheres of life that are subtly interconnected. One may derive a purely aesthetic pleasure from a contemplation of the beauty of order as manifested in this poem, but there is even greater pleasure in discovering that the order of the poem is the order imposed by him whom the poem celebrates. As a consequence of this discovery a problem has been resolved which has puzzled many readers—why Milton paid such sustained attention to the theme of the cessation of oracles and the expulsion of false gods.

To summarise: the overall structure combines two patterns, a sequence of 12—3—12 and another of 1—9—7—9—1 stanzas. The first resembles that of the created universe (as described in stanza 12), the 27 stanzas being 'hung' on 'well-balanced' stanzaic 'hinges'. The balance of each sequence is equally perfect, as it must be to mirror the perfect unity of the Creator. Symmetry is a matter of *aequalitas*, so that *aequalitas*-structures should be considered as a poetic *mimesis* of the unity which is the supreme attribute of the Deity. No one has brought out the emotional impact of this intellectual argument more strongly than Augustine in his *De vera religione*, the treatise which, together with the *De libero arbitrio*, provides the theoretical basis for the use of conceptual structures in religious poetry. Since our minds suffer the mutability of error, Augustine writes, the standard called truth must be above our own minds in the mind of God, and by this standard we perceive that beauty is harmony. 'In all the arts that which pleases is harmony [*convenientia*], which alone invests the whole with unity and beauty. This harmony requires equality and unity either through the resemblance of symmetrically placed parts, or through the graded arrangement of unequal parts.'[29] We delight in harmony because we delight in absolute equality, which is the similitude of Him who created it; by perceiving this *aequalitas* in the universe or in a work of art, our minds are led back to God. So far Augustine. Milton's ode achieves *aequalitas* in many ways—most strikingly perhaps in the structures indicated here, but also by means of what Augustine calls 'graded arrangement'. This is where the *lambda*-formula becomes relevant, since the key numbers of this formula, 8 and 27, are the key numbers of the hymn.[30] It can be added that each of these numbers illustrates *aequalitas* by being a cubed number, since cubes consist of sides that must needs be of equal size.

So far I have commented on the 12—3—12 sequence largely in terms of its poised symmetry or in terms of its *mimesis* of the great circle of Time which issues out of, and returns to, that Eternity of which it is an image. The two chief metaphors of Christ as *light* and *harmony* are fully realised in the three central stanzas (13–15) on the 'ninefold harmony' of 'heaven's deep organ' and the glorious appearance of Truth, Justice, and Mercy 'Throned in celestial sheen' as an image of the Trinity. Each is also embodied in the structure: the concept of harmony in the *lambda*-numbers and the ninefold arrangement of the three spheres,[31] and that of light in the solar symbolism traditionally invested in the Apocalyptic vision of the Lamb seated amidst the 24 elders. The 12—3—12 sequence may be seen either as a straight sequence of 12 plus a three-in-one centre plus 12, or as a three-in-one centre surrounded by thematically paired stanzas that constitute 12 pairs or circles. The sequence, therefore, enacts both the 24-hour cycle of the sun and the annual cycle of 12 months as the sun passes through the 12 signs of the zodiac. And the image of Christ as our *sol iustitiae* commanding the celestial constellations or again as *lux vera* illuminating the whole earth in its daily and annual cycles, was virtually fused with the image of Christ as the head of the 12 tribes in the Old Testament and of the 12 Apostles in the New. This may be illustrated by a passage in Rabanus Maurus (*Enarrationes in librum numerorum* III, 9) as quoted by Pietro Bongo towards the end of the sixteenth century:

Horis ergo 24 Sol mundanus totem Orbem vndiq. illustrat,

atque noctis tenebras suo ambitu fugat. Qui. n. fidei lumine,
quod per Apostolos atque Prophetas prædicatum est, mentis suæ
oculos illuminat, peccatorum tenebras euitare decertat.[32]

To paraphrase: just as the Sun illuminates the whole Earth in the
course of 24 hours, chasing away the darkness of night, the light of
our true faith revealed by the Prophets and the Apostles illuminates
the eyes of the mind, overcoming the darkness of sin. And as readers
of the Apocalypse will recall, the number 12 prevails also in the structure of the Heavenly Jerusalem with its carefully measured walls
and its numbered doors or gates, and all these occurrences of the
number 12 in the universe, in the history of man, and in Heaven
itself would be summarised in Renaissance expositions of the meaning
of the vision of Christ as King seated amidst the 24 elders.

No wonder, therefore, that the number was applied to the Nativity,
as we see from Cassiodorus' comments on Psalm 13 and again on the
thirteenth Psalm of Ascent (Ps. 131).[33] As he puts it, the ordinal
numbers of these Psalms indicate that Christ was to be born on the
thirteenth day after the winter solstice, thus showing that he was to
be the head of the 12 Apostles (symbolised by the 12 days). Rabanus
Maurus attributed the same symbolism to the literary structure of the
New Testament when he wrote that the account of the acts of the
12 Apostles is followed by the Apocalypse as a thirteenth section the
purpose of which is to reveal Christ in his full glory as their head.[34]
On studying glosses of this kind one sees how easily the transition
is achieved from the *liber creaturarum* to the Scriptures and back again,
the two being all but fused through the analogies traced between
them.

This exposition may seem ingenious, but I hope that I have made
it perfectly clear that the ingenuity is not mine. Neither the selection
of symbolic significances nor even their collocation can be credited
to my account. Once the connection had been made with the structure
of Psalm 119 and with the Apocalyptic vision of Christ in glory, all
that remained was to consult representative theological accounts of
the import attributed to these structures. Bongo's chapter on the
number 24 has the vision of the elders as its point of departure, thus
stressing its importance in Biblical exegesis, and among the sources
drawn on by Bongo are the *Glossa ordinaria*, Augustine, Bede,
Jerome, and Rabanus Maurus—orthodox sources as one would
expect from a handbook authorised by the Roman Catholic church.

As is the practice in numerical exegesis, Bongo resolves the number into various groupings, for example into two twelves or three eights, letting the meaning of the whole number emerge from a consideration of its parts. As the centre-piece in Milton's ode consists of three eight-line stanzas (24 lines), this section, therefore, neatly balances the two twelves provided by the flanking 12-stanza sequences, but I would not stress this particular example of balance or *aequalitas*, nor the point that the three eights of the centre traditionally represent the name of Christ (888). These are, perhaps, unnecessary flourishes more apt to vex the modern reader than to please. What is truly important, however, is the fact that Bongo's summary of received opinion shows quite clearly that the vision of the elders was considered as a clue to a proper understanding of the entire Providential scheme for our redemption, and that this was done on the basis of a numerical argument of the kind that I have used here. What my analysis has shown, therefore, is quite simply that Milton's structure invokes this Providential scheme and on the basis of the same vision. This structure should be seen as a non-verbal, abstract image of this design and of him who realised it through his incarnation and crucifixion. The abstract character of this image is its chief virtue—a strength, not a weakness—since its appeal is to our understanding and not to the world of sense. It moves our minds rather than our passions, but the passions are stirred by the beauty of the intellectual vision.

### III

#### Structural Analogues in Sidney and Cowley

Helen Gardner has observed that in Protestant thought Christ was primarily the Redeemer and the King of Heaven, not the babe in the manger or the crucified Christ. Even when contemplating the crucifixion, in 'The Sacrifice', George Herbert aims at completeness of theological statement: 'As Christ speaks, he reveals not simply the love for man that made him endure a shameful and agonizing death, but the whole economy of salvation . . . He implies the whole scheme that began with Adam's eating of the apple . . . '[35] This is an important observation, and I wonder to what extent this insistence on the whole scheme is indebted to a habit of thinking structurally. This habit was certainly encouraged by typological exegesis with its careful balancing of event against event, so that to think of Christ was to think of certain patterns woven by God through space and time to secure salvation for fallen man. These patterns can be perceived by 'the eye of the mind, only cleared by faith' to quote Sir Philip Sidney, that is, by the man whose mental vision has been purified through regeneration. Just as Augustine put his conversion to the test by submitting his analysis of the Mosaic account of creation in the last three books of his *Confessions*, Milton may be said to indicate the quality of his inner vision by building into his poem on the Nativity those patterns—spatial, chronological or historical—by means of which the creative Word manifests its power. The highly abstract character of these patterns is somewhat softened by their connection with the world of sense. Although these abstract principles may be recognised 'inside ourselves without reference to any material object' as Augustine explains, initially one depends on an act of sense perception (*Confessions* X, 12). Augustine applies this argument to the aesthetic appreciation of works of art in a memorable part of his treatise on Free Will. Through the beauty of his creation God beckons man to consider the beauty of the Creator:

> Wherever you turn, wisdom speaks to you through the imprint it has stamped upon its works.[36] When you begin to slip toward outward things, wisdom calls you back, by means of their very forms, so that when something delights you through the bodily senses, you may see that it has number and may ask whence it comes . . .
>
> (*De libero arbitrio*, II, xvi)

Similarly all artists 'have numbers by which they organize their works' so that when the patterns they see have been transferred to the world of sense in the work of art, 'it delights the inner judge who gazes upward upon numbers'. The artist, like God,'somehow beckons the spectator' to proceed from the 'beauty of the work he has made' to the superior beauty of the 'eternal and immutable Form'. This eternal Form 'is neither contained by nor, as it were, spread out in space, neither prolonged nor changed by time', but through this Form every temporal object receives its form so that it 'can manifest and embody number in space and time'.[37]

The ascent from the visible to the invisible was sufficiently familiar to the Renaissance and sufficiently orthodox by being read into *Romans* 1:20, but the point which requires emphasis today is its connection with the contemplation of numerical form or ordered arrangement as explained by Augustine. As the beauty of the world is a matter of its organisation in terms of number, weight, and measure (*Wisdom* 11:20), the ascent from this beauty to that of God could be achieved through a contemplation of number as the basic aspect of Form. This is why numbers could be used to structure poetic compositions and prose treatises, too: they represent the basic elements of existence. All acts of creation presuppose number, so that if you 'remove measure, number, and order, nothing at all remains' (*De libero arbitrio*, II, xx, 203).

This view of creation (whether artistic or divine) has moved away from the Platonic concept of abstract Form or Idea to structure or pattern,[38] and its popularity in the Renaissance may possibly be connected with the firm belief in the Providential view of history as shaped into a meaningful design by the hand of God. If so, then Plato and Neoplatonic thought may have been less influential, as far as Renaissance poetics is concerned, than the argument advanced by Augustine in his discussion of Free Will and Providence.

It is an unfortunate circumstance that our ignorance of the conceptual use of numbers by thinkers like Augustine and Nicolas Cusanus, and our awareness of the fairly widespread Renaissance fondness for a 'hidden sense' have collaborated to create the impression that all speculations concerned with numbers must be classified as esoteric if not positively occult, and certainly well beyond the limits set by orthodox theology. This is not the place for a refutation of this particular superstition, but I would like to conclude this essay by comparing Milton's use of conceptual structure with that of Sir Philip Sidney and Abraham Cowley. This will widen the perspective somewhat, not merely because it may be wise to indicate the prevalence of the structural approach, but also because the comparison will provide a better perspective on Milton's poem.

Among the eclogues that Sir Philip Sidney inserted between Books III and IV of the *Old Arcadia* is an epithalamion which is one of the first English poems of this kind.[39] Its structure is of unusual interest because of its similarity to Milton's hymn. Its eleven nine-line stanzas fall into a sequence of 6—4—1; the first six stanzas request various good qualities for the two that are to be married, while the four that follow denounce various ills. The eleventh stanza summarises the contents of the ten preceding ones. Although each substructure concludes with a climax, a sense of unity is achieved by letting the last stanza constitute an affirmation: all the good qualities have been fully achieved and the ills expelled, and hence the refrain, too, is changed from the optative to the affirmative mode.

The last stanza in the first, positive movement represents a very real climax. Each of these six stanzas invokes personified powers and deities, the sixth—Virtue—being the most important one:

> *Virtue, if not a god, yet God's chief part,*
> *Be thou the knot of this their open vow:*
> *That still he be her head, she be his heart,*
> *He lean to her, she unto him do bow;*
>    *Each other still allow,*
>    *Like oak and mistletoe,*
>    *Her strength from him, his praise from her do grow.*
>    *In which most lovely train,*
>    *O Hymen long their coupled joys maintain.*

That which the whole poem celebrates is brought into sharp focus here in this apostrophe to Virtue as the 'knot of this their open vow'. It is numerically appropriate that this should be said in the sixth stanza, since 6 is the marriage number fusing 2 (the female principle) and 3 (the masculine one) in the formula $2 \times 3$. The tying of the knot of concord between opposite principles—male and female—is given syntactical expression in the varied arrangements between the personal pronouns (lines three and four present an a-b-b-a pattern and line seven the reversed form b-a-a-b).

But the stanza on Virtue is not only the climax of the positive sequence; it is also the textual centre of the whole poem, five stanzas preceding and five following. That Virtue has been placed where she should be, *in medio*, is true not merely in a numerical sense but rather because the stanza constitutes the centre for a sequence of paired stanzas. The pairing is achieved by pitting positive against negative versions of the same aspect of marriage—honest trust against jealousy, for example, or healthy procreation against disease-ridden sexual license ('foul Cupid'). A table will indicate the thematic links:

| | | | |
|---|---|---|---|
| *Honest open love* image: elm & vine | 2 | 10 | *Distrust* ('vile jealousy, / The ill of ills') image: snake |
| *Purity* ('That they all vice may kill') image: 'lilies pure' | 3 | 9 | *Vice:* pride and sluttishness images: 'peacock pride' and 'sink of filth' |

| | | | |
|---|---|---|---|
| *Union* in life and death | 4 | 8 | *Strife* |
| image: union of 'two | | | image: strife in the house and |
| rivers sweet' | | | with neighbours |
| *Healthy sex, procreation* | 5 | 7 | *Diseased sex* ('foul Cupid') |
| image: younglings of the | | | image: Cupid's golden dart |
| herd | | | 'shall here take rust' |

At the centre of this sequence, then, Virtue holds the middle, thus permitting the structure to express the theme of unity. But symmetry is displayed in other ways as well, as we see on studying the movement within each stanza. Thus a simile is presented in the last four lines of each of the first six stanzas, at the same time that the syntactical movement in the first five lines is so organised as to permit the fifth to constitute the climax. This means that the line which is at the centre, numerically, has been given the key phrase of the whole stanza. The absence of a concluding simile in the negative sequence (stanzas seven to ten) somewhat blurs this image of stanzaic symmetry, but here, too, the fifth line has been awarded the climactic statement ('Avoids thy hurtful art', 'Be hence ay put to flight', 'For ever hence away', and 'Go snake, hide thee in dust'). And in stanza eleven all lines are used to present the summary, except the fifth, which apostrophises bride and groom as 'Happy man, happy wife', thus providing a perfect example of a symmetrically structured stanza. Placed as it is at the stanzaic centre and outside the pattern of affirmative summary, the exclamation helps to create that sense of a final grand climax which is needed to round off the poem as a whole. This need is the greater as the sense of linear movement is so much stronger than the sense of balance around a central stanza. True, we know that Virtue is in the middle in every sense, but the movement through stanzas seven to ten is primarily felt as a linear progression through a catalogue of ills climaxed by the denunciation of jealousy as the 'ill of ills' embodied in the image of the snake. This strongly felt linear movement through ten stanzas may be said to constitute an image of unity through the significance invested in the number 10 as the return to unity. The epithalamion therefore provides an arithmetical image of unity by progressing through a sequence of 10 stanzas concluded with a coda whose function it is to serve as a summary and an affirmative full stop.

Milton's hymn, too, establishes linear progression through two movements combined with balanced symmetry, the symmetry being achieved by letting a positive thematic movement (concluded with a climax) be followed by a negative one concerned with the theme of expulsion. And in both poems the climax of the first movement becomes the centre around which the whole poem is focussed. The central accent is more strongly felt in Milton's poem, partly because he has fused the thematic movement with a chronological pattern showing how Time issues out of, and returns to, Eternity. One's impression that Sidney's structure is more linear while Milton's is decidedly spatial is the result also of that steady rise towards the vision of Eternity (in the triple centre) and the subsequent descent to the level where the hymn began.

On observing this general structural similarity one wonders whether the fairly simple structural formula employed by Sidney[39a] could have been sufficiently well known to have helped Milton to his choice of form. If Milton thought in terms of a progressive sequence of stanzas leading up to a climax, followed by a somewhat shorter regressive sequence so organised that stanzas equidistant from the centre are paired off against each other, then this would help to explain why he saw fit to devote so many stanza units to the theme of expulsion: these constitute the counter-movement required to create the subtle interplay between linear progression and recessed symmetry around a centre.

Abraham Cowley's version of the same basic formula, in his 'Hymn to the Light', indicates that it was not restricted to the epithalamic tradition, but it would have been perfectly appropriate for Milton to invoke this tradition in a poem on the incarnation. The Biblical epithalamion, the *Song of Solomon*, was considered as an Old Testament prophecy, written allegorically, of that final union with Christ in the Heavenly Jerusalem which St John describes in the Apocalypse. At its beginning, middle, and end the Bible was supposed to have not only an image of Christ (as the Tree of Life) but also an image of marriage or union. The marriage between Adam and Eve foreshadowed the union between God and man through the incarnation (and the crucifixion), both pointing forward to the final union in Eternity. Francesco Giorgio is one Renaissance theologian who makes these points, and with unwonted brevity, in his *De harmonia mundi* III, viii, 9. The first three stanzas of Milton's hymn seem to me to invoke epithalamic overtones of the kind associated with Biblical exegesis. Since the incarnation joins Heaven and Earth, this may be why Milton begins by showing an Earth suddenly confronted by that 'greater sun' on whose coming the physical sun must be instantly rejected as inferior. Her feeling of guilt and her desire to hide her 'foul deformities' should perhaps be related to the bride's feeling of unworthiness ('Look not upon me, because I am black . . . ' *Song of Solomon* 1:6), while her 'naked shame' reflects the feeling of our first parents after their fall. As Giorgio puts it in the passage referred to, Christ covers our nudity by regenerating us. His action, in so doing, is like that of the sun: he gives of his riches to all.[40]

Similar epithalamic overtones are felt in Cowley's 'Hymn to the Light' (*Verses Written on Several Occasions*, 1663)[41] which presents the action of Light on the Earth as a marriage union. The thematic and structural similarities to Milton's poem are sufficiently striking to make one suspect that Cowley may have written his lines with an eye on the *Nativity Ode*. What caught Cowley's fancy was the confrontation between light and the powers of darkness, and the stately progress of light from the first day of creation to the last, when it merges with the light of Eternity. An allusion to the incarnate Christ may be felt in the first stanza which presents the creation of Light on the first day as a 'lovely Child' on whose appearance Chaos itself 'put on kind looks and smil'd.' The chronological structure is simple: we move from the first day in stanza 1 to the last day in the last stanza. Although the four-line stanza pattern is equally simple the concluding alexandrine suggests a link with the pattern designed by Milton for his ode. A firmer link is found in Cowley's elaboration of the theme touched on initially by Milton in the hymn—the marriage union between Nature and the Sun, 'her lusty paramour'. Cowley relates 'active Nature' to the Sun as bride to groom: 'Thou the Worlds beauteous Bride, the lusty Bridegroom He!' (stanza 3). Milton's lovely description of the descent of Peace 'softly sliding / Down through the turning sphere', 'With turtle wing the amorous clouds dividing' may have inspired Cowley's passage on the cosmic marriage union:

24

*Through the soft ways of Heav'n and Air, and Sea,*
*Which open all their Pores to Thee;*
*Like a clear River thou do'st glide,*
*And with thy living Stream through the close Channels slide.*

Another theme shared by the two poems is the ousting of ghosts and all kinds of evil spirits and powers. In Milton 'speckled vanity' and 'lep'rpus sin' disappear, leaving their mansions 'to the peering day' (14), while in Cowley 'Night, and her ugly subjects' are 'Asham'd and fearful to appear', just as clusters of 'painted Dreams' vanish 'At the first opening of thine eye' (10 and 11):

### 15
*Ev'n Lust, the Master of a hardned Face,*
*    Blushes, if thou be'st in the place,*
*    To darkness Curtains he retires,*
*In sympathizing Night he rowls his smoaky fires.*

### 16
*When, Goddess, thou lift'st up thy wak'ned head,*
*    Out of the Morning's Purple Bed,*
*    Thy Quire of Birds about thee play,*
*And all the joyful World salutes the rising day.*

### 17
*The Ghosts, and Monster-Spirits, that did presume*
*    A Bodies Priv'ledge to assume,*
*    Vanish again invisibly,*
*And Bodies gain agen their visibility.*

This reads like a revised version of two of Milton's most striking images in his penultimate stanza—first of the Sun 'in bed, / Curtained with cloudy red' but about to rise so that he 'Pillows his chin upon an orient wave' and next of each 'fettered ghost' slipping to 'his several grave'.

Cowley's symmetrical structure is both simpler and more emphatic than Milton's. The fact that the Earth is provided with two sources of light induced him to fashion his hymn around a double centre flanked by twelve four-line stanzas. The central stanzas (13–14) are identified as such formally as well as thematically—formally through carefully balanced parallel phrases ('At thy appearance . . .') and thematically by the apostrophe to the achievement of harmony in the microcosmos of man as grief is balanced by joy, fear by hope. Finally the allusion to reflected light in stanza 13 and to sunshine in stanza 14 serves to link the pivotal centre with the two sources of light in the Sun and the Moon. And as in Milton's hymn the flanking stanzas display recessed symmetry created by tracing similar phenomena in two clearly differentiated spheres of life. My diagram shows that the pairing of individual stanzas around the double centre is sufficiently clear to be easily spotted, but that the pairing nevertheless is seen to function in groups of three stanzas. As we move out from the centre in both directions we encounter first a group of three stanzas concerned with the theme of expulsion, then a similar group where the focus is on the way in which Light adorns everything in the two spheres. The next group of three stanzas stresses the creative action of Light, while images of birth and of marriage union dominate the first three stanzas and the three last ones. The division into two spheres so that stanzas 2–12 are concerned with the air and the sky and the upper spheres while the focus is on the Earth and man in stanzas 15–25, is perhaps the most striking structural similarity between the two hymns. Another similarity is the circular effect created by letting the first stanza present the birth of Light on the first day while the last presents its fusion with the light of Eternity on the last day.

The concepts embedded in Cowley's structural numbers are as simple as they are basic to our human existence. The sequence of 12—2—12 stanzas can be seen to incorporate the chief numbers of Time as created by our two luminaries. Around the double centre are stanzaic 'emanations' in imitation of the 12 unequal hours of the day and night and the 12 solar months, and if we divide the hymn into equal halves of 13 4-line stanzas the structure reflects the annual lunar cycle and the number of weeks in the year through the sum total of lines, 52. As S. K. Heninger has remarked à propos of the absurd notion that structures of this kind should imply esoteric lore, what is reproduced is 'the fairly simple pattern of cosmos. A line count is unlikely to disclose anything more arcane than a calendar, a diapason, a tetrad, or a trinity.'[42]

Since Cowley favoured symmetrical arrangements around a centre he need not have borrowed this particular effect from Milton, but the phrasal and thematic similarities suggest that he actually had Milton's poem in mind. If these similarities should be felt as too imprecise to warrant any firm conclusion, we must needs posit a general tradition of sufficient strength to produce this degree of similarity.

The symmetrical structures I have indicated pose an interesting critical problem. I have observed that my perception of this kind of thematic movement away from a centre towards the beginning and the end induces a habit of reading the poem from the centre outwards. One does this, at first, to test the validity of the feeling that a given poem may be organised symmetrically, and if the theory is confirmed, one finds that the structural analysis enables one to bear the whole poem in mind as one reads it progressively from the beginning in the normal way. As one reads the first stanza of Milton's hymn, for example, one knows, at the back of one's mind, that one will meet the babe in the manger again in the last stanza, that the theme of the second stanza will be repeated, with a variation, in the penultimate stanza, and so on until the centre is reached; after the centre the balance is changed, and that which was remembered becomes the experience of the moment, while that which was experienced regresses and becomes memory.

This interaction between progressive and retrospective form affects our reading in many ways. It invests the structural centre with a uniqueness which turns it into a more powerful climax than could have been achieved by mere terminal heightening. But other aspects are involved as well. If the form that one perceives retrospectively is held in mind with sufficient clarity as one re-reads the poem, a kind of unity is perceived which is difficult to put into words. The best I can do is to repeat what I have already said (p. 65): sequential experience is supplemented by an almost instantaneous vision of the whole poem. It is interesting to discover that Paula Johnson, in grappling with the same problem of the interaction between these two modes of perception, picked on much the same phrase. The retrospective mode, so she puts it, achieves 'increased approximation to simultaneity'. Its function is to provide an aid to the normal way of reading a poem, and this assistance is always provided whether or not we happen to be aware of it.[43]

Since his structures are more obvious, the awareness comes more easily to us as we read Cowley, but once we have grasped the main outlines of Milton's ode it is not at all difficult to keep them in mind as one reads. The patterns indicate a tradition of reading poetry in a way that has been largely lost to us since the Romantic period at least. The fact that symbolic numbers may have been used to create the symmetrical effects need worry no one: the Biblical authority for so doing is too explicit and the habit of reading the Bible with attention to structure too ingrained for the technique to be at all tainted by the unorthodox or the esoteric. I would say, instead, that if one reads Milton's poem with an awareness of its formal structure, one reads it in the manner that Milton's generation would have read the Bible or its supposed summary in the Psalms. That the structures are largely identical makes the comparison even more appropriate.

# Diagram 1: Milton, 'On the Morning of Christ's Nativity'

| | | | | |
|---|---|---|---|---|
| CHRIST (1) | 1 (27) | NATURE pays homage to CHRIST | | |

2 (26) NATURE hides her 'guilty front'

| | | | |
|---|---|---|---|
| | 3 (25) | 'universal | in NATURE |
| | 4 (24) | peace' | in the world of MEN |
| | 5 (23) | | in the ELEMENTS |

**MAN & NATURE (9)**

| | | | |
|---|---|---|---|
| 6 (22) | the true ruler | by the STARS | 12 |
| 7 (21) | recognised | by the SUN | |
| 8 (20) | true revelation of | 'mighty Pan' appears to MEN | |
| 9 (19) | the divine | heavenly voices ravish MEN | |

10 (18) NATURE believes her reign fulfilled

11 (17) CHRIST hymned as King on Earth

12 (16) CHRIST as Creator — the first day

**CHRIST (7)**

| | |
|---|---|
| 13 | Heaven's 'high palace |
| 14 | hall' and its 'ninefold |
| 15 | harmony' |

ETERNITY

16 (12) CHRIST as Redeemer and Creator of a new world — the last day

17 (11) CHRIST as Judge in 'middle air'

| | | | |
|---|---|---|---|
| 18 (10) | The reign of SATAN ceases | | |
| 19 (9) | true revelation of | ousts the false ('words deceiving') | |
| 20 (8) | the divine | replaces shadowy types (Pan) | |

**SPIRITS & POWERS (9)**

| | | | |
|---|---|---|---|
| 21 (7) | the true ruler | various powers leave their seats and false rites cease; idols representing stars are ousted; | 12 |
| 22 (6) | recognised | | |
| 23 (5) | | for powers connected with the elements | |
| 24 (4) | no peace | for false deities | |
| 25 (3) | | for Typhon, son of Earth | |

26 (2) Guilty SPIRITS hide in the 'infernal jail'

| | | |
|---|---|---|
| CHRIST (1) | 27 (1) | ANGELS pay homage to CHRIST |

## Diagram 2
### Abraham Cowley, 'Hymn to the Light'

**Generation**

| Left | Stanzas | | Right |
|------|---------|---|-------|
| Creation of Light the first day | 1 | 26 | Light merges with Eternity the last day |
| Images of union on a cosmic scale (continued) | 2 | 25 | Images of union focussed on the Earth (continued) |
| | 3 | 24 | |

**Action**

| Left | Stanzas | | Right |
|------|---------|---|-------|
| Creative action in the air; arrows are shot from 'Golden Quivers'; the rainbow is created; the movement compared to swiftest 'Post-Angel' | 4 | 23 | Creative action in the Earth; gold is produced (continued) colours are produced; comparison with the goddess Flora |
| | 5 | 22 | |
| | 6 | 21 | |

**Adornment**

| Left | Stanzas | | Right |
|------|---------|---|-------|
| The 'flowry Lights' of the stars form a 'Nocturnal Spring' in a 'bright wood of Stars'; and above the Sun Light moves in regal state attended by 'shining Pageants'; and living stars adorn the Earth | 7 | 20 | On Earth Light creates the flowers of spring |
| | 8 | 19 | and dresses every thing in royal splendour (continued) |
| | 9 | 18 | |

**Expulsion**

| Left | Stanzas | | Right |
|------|---------|---|-------|
| Light ousts the 'ugly Subjects' of the Night | 10 | 17 | Light ousts ghosts and spirits, making real bodies appear; |
| and 'painted Dreams' | 11 | 16 | and a joyful, real world awakes |
| and 'guilty Serpents', 'Ill Omens' and 'ill Sights' | 12 | 15 | and 'Ev'n Lust' is expelled |

**Centre**

| Left | Stanzas | | Right |
|------|---------|---|-------|
| Harmonious balance between Grief and Joy | 13 | 14 | Harmonious balance between Fear and Hope |

Stanzas 1–12 trace the power of Light within the whole cosmic sphere including powers of evil

Stanzas 15–26 trace the power of Light within the sphere of the Earth and of man

84

My comparison between Milton, Sidney and Cowley will have shown that a structure, like all images, may be more or less effective, more or less beautiful, subtle, complex, or appropriate. Like images and themes, structures, too, may be borrowed and, in the process, become elaborated or simplified. Certain structures may be so familiar as to constitute a tradition drawn on by different poets so that a theory of direct indebtedness must be ruled out or at least modified. On the basis of a formal pattern associated with Nativity hymns Milton created a complex structure the perception of which has a profound effect on our response to his poem. Cowley, however, was content with the simplest of structural outlines and with a system of paired stanzas that contributes little or nothing to his main theme. To compare the two hymns is to see a major aesthetic principle in a splendid work of art transferred and transposed to suit the abilities of the lesser poet. The juxtaposition shows up the superior quality of Milton's performance, at the same time that Cowley's proves his familiarity with the tradition drawn on by Milton. Cowley, by the way, documents his familiarity in the footnotes added to his *Pindarique Odes* and his *Davideis*, thus providing the explicit authorial statement so often required by critics as yet unfamiliar with this aspect of Renaissance aesthetics. A footnote appended to the ode on 'The Resurrection' declares quite openly that the Pythagorean doctrine of harmony 'does much better befit *Poetry*, than it did *Philosophy*', while the poem itself announces that it sets the standard for the numbers of Time, which dance to the song 'with smooth and equal measures'. The world, it would seem, is not only God's poem; it is also Cowley's.[44] In this respect, at least, Milton was the more humble poet.

# 3

## *Laid artfully together*

### STANZAIC DESIGN IN MILTON'S
### 'ON THE MORNING OF CHRIST'S NATIVITY'

#### H. NEVILLE DAVIES

FOR thirty years now the apparently lax construction and variety of
imagery in Milton's *Nativity Ode* have been strongly defended.
Although Warton's remark about 'a string of affected conceits' seems
a far cry, it is, after all, not utterly at odds with modern criticism.[1]
'String' and 'affected' are loaded words, but it is precisely the choice
of imagery and plan of construction that much recent criticism of the
poem has attended to. Generally, the modern defence involves dividing the poem into sections, like the movements of a symphony, and
then arguing that these movements contrast with and complement
each other to cohere in a symphonic whole. Appreciation of the unity
of the poem thus depends in part upon perception of the autonomy
of the constituent sections. This is a critical strategy of some flexi-
bility, capable of supporting a wide variety of interpretations, and we
find it—not surprisingly—linked with many different analyses of the
Ode's structure. But on one matter commentators agree: there is a
natural break between the four introductory seven-line stanzas
(hereafter numbered i–iv) and the twenty-seven eight-line stanzas
of the Hymn (hereafter numbered 1–27).

In the Hymn itself different symphonic 'movements' are distinguished by different critics. Comparison of a dozen studies shows it
divided into two, three, or four, but usually three sections, the divisions being made in certain general areas, but by no means in exactly
the same places.[2] A list of stanzas simply marked with the various
divisions suggested in these twelve studies show what degree of
unanimity there is:

1 2 3 4 5 6 7 / 8 / 9 / 10 11 12 13 14 15 / 16 / 17 / 18 / 19 20 21 22 23
24 25 26 / 27.

Most of the critics encompassed by this survey seem to regard their own distinctions between sections as not only right but as natural too. When the conflicting or apparently conflicting suggestions are assembled, however, it becomes evident that what is natural to one reader may not be so to another. The disparity is immediately grasped if the number of stanzas included in each section of the Hymn by the critics that I have referred to is set out in tabular form:

| | | | | |
|---|---|---|---|---|
| Spaeth | 8 | 7 | 12 | |
| Shuster | 8 | 7 | 12 | |
| Barker | 8 | 9 | 9 | 1 |
| Brooks & Hardy | 15 | 12 | (12 = 11+1) | |
| Allen | 7 | 11 | 9 | |
| Røstvig (1963) | 9 | 9 | 9 | (now refined as |
| | 1 | 9 7 9 | 1 | coexisting |
| | with 12 | 3 | 12) | |
| Lawry | 8 | 7 | 11 | 1 |
| Rajan | 8 | 8 | 11 | |
| Carey | 8 | 10 | 9 | |
| Butler | Endorses Røstvig (1963) | | | |
| Swaim | 8 | 7 | 12 | |
| Woodhouse & Bush | 8 | 10 | 8 | 1 |

Such statistical information can easily deceive or mislead, and the chronologically arranged list given here needs to be qualified by two observations: firstly that Barker's fine study enjoys something approaching classic status and probably represents the most orthodox view of the structure, and secondly, that notations that look as divergent as 8 8 11 and 8 7 12, or 7 11 9 and 8 10 9 in fact differ over only a single stanza. But even bearing such qualifications in mind, the list records considerable diversity among a distinguished body of critics.

That the *Nativity Ode* is amenable to a multiplicity of analyses is an aspect of its baroque richness. It is clear that the critics disjointing the poem are, at least in some cases, dividing it according to different principles, and so the variety of their views as evident in the table does not necessarily indicate conflict. The fissures in the texture of the poem that they light upon are not open breaches but rather fractures in different layers, each critic studying a different layer, and the poem's essential continuity arising from the joins being staggered. Rigidly to disallow any critical diversity and insist upon crude conformity would be to commit the folly of those 'irrationall men' ridiculed in *Areopagitica* 'who could not consider there must be many schisms and many dissections made in the quarry and in the timber, ere the house of God can be built'.[3] As an example of a structure unified and diverse, Milton described the Temple, whose divine architecture represents a pattern of perfection:

> And when every stone is laid artfully together, it cannot be united into a continuity, it can but be contiguous in this world; neither can every peece of the building be of one form; nay rather the perfection consists in this, that out of many moderate varieties and brotherly dissimilitudes that are not vastly disproportionall arises the goodly and gracefull symmetry that commends the whole pile and structure.[4]

So it is with Milton's *Nativity Ode*. In its fugal texture (to replace a spatial architectural analogy by a temporal musical one), individual voices or strands of interest are variously drawn out, and the complexity of the counterpoint both enhances the assertion of Milton's recent coming of age and enriches a gift to the infant Christ that vies ambitiously with those of the Magi. But this recognition of complexity does not mean that all ways of dissecting the poem are equally helpful. There is a difference between licence and liberty in literary criticism as there is in other areas of activity.

Underpinning the manifest form of the poem, with its evident division into Proem and Hymn, and its other more subtly overlapping strands, are firm structural foundations. It is with these that the present essay is concerned. My purpose—a deliberately limited one—is merely to suggest, without promoting pedantic demarcation disputes, that the impulse of commentators to split the poem into sections is a right impulse, and to propose that the Ode is structured according to an exact and determinable plan, while an overall pattern of 'linked sweetness' unites the separate parts. The approach adopted here is then, in general, similar to that pursued by Maren-Sofie Røstvig in her 1963 account of Milton's poem and now extended in her contribution to the present volume. But although I have learnt much from both her papers, the scheme that I offer differs somewhat from what she had proposed. I leave it to readers, if they so wish, to judge when 'modest varieties' and 'brotherly dissimilitudes' are or 'are not vastly disproportionall'. It needs only to be remarked by me that the decision is not a simple one.

While my approach is through the symbolism of the stanza numbers,

the consequent analysis of the Ode's structure is in accord with what
has been observed by a fair range of critics who have examined the
poem from quite other points of view. I suggest, therefore, that
the Hymn falls into three clearly defined movements of fifteen,
eleven, and one stanzas respectively, and that the recognition of the
symbolic use of numbers in this scheme reinforces the meaning of the
poem, makes sense of the sudden transitions, and gives significance to
what can be naively mistaken for aesthetic disproportion. There is
reassurance to be found in observing that Spaeth and Shuster long
ago recognised the same broad structural divisions, and that Brooks
and Hardy, Lawry, and Swaim have more recently described such a
structure.

## I

Stanzas 1–15 of the Hymn describe the coming of Christ to reunite
fallen man and God; and for this purpose, as I shall try to show, a
sequence of fifteen stanzas is appropriate. Since the twelfth century
a ladder of fifteen rungs had been commonly associated with ascent
to God, and Christ as mediator expressed by the figure of this ladder.[5]
It was as a type of Christ that Milton's contemporaries frequently
explained Jacob's ladder. Gervase Babbington, for instance, whose
works were sufficiently in demand to be published in folio in 1615,
1622, and 1637, asserts,

> The ladder is Christ. The foot of it in earth noteth his humanitie,
> man of the substance of his mother borne in the world. The top
> reaching vp to heauen, noteth his divinitie, *God of the substance
> of the Father begotten before all worlds, perfit God, and perfit man,*
> by which vnion of natures, he hath ioyned earth and heauen
> together, that is, God and man.[6]

The Master of St Catharine's Hall during Milton's Cambridge career,
Richard Sibbes, relating Jacob's ladder to Christ, writes of Christ as
'a Mediator' who 'brought God and man together'.[7] Such remarks
are commonplace, but they serve well enough to provide a context
for Milton, and they help to illustrate why it was that Milton in his
*De doctrina Christiana*, in which he disposed his material into chapters
according to the significance of the chapter numbers, chose Chapter *15*
of Book I to treat of Christ as mediator.[8] In *Paradise Lost* Milton

uses the same number symbolism. The retractable stairs 'Ascending by degrees magnificent / Up to the wall of heaven' which Satan sees on his cosmic flight are described in a series of fifteen lines (III. 501–15) and compared with Jacob's ladder. Another passage of fifteen lines follows shortly afterwards (III. 540–54) in which Satan sits on the bottom step looking enviously and maliciously down onto the newly created world. The stairs rising behind his back, with their suggestion of ascent to God, are now ignored by Satan, but the structure of fifteen lines speaks to the fit reader, or so I have argued elsewhere, of their significance.[9]

The first of these two fifteen-line passages from Book III of *Paradise Lost* alludes to the gate of heaven in its climactic fifteenth line, quoting Jacob's words as he woke from his vision of a ladder: 'This is the gate of heav'n'. A similar climax comes in the fifteenth line of Satan's second speech to Beelzebub:

> *Fallen cherub, to be weak is miserable*
> *Doing or suffering: but of this be sure,*
> *To do ought good never will be our task,*
> *But ever to do ill our sole delight,*
> *As being the contrary to his high will*
> *Whom we resist. If then his providence*
> *Out of our evil seek to bring forth good,*
> *Our labour must be to pervert that end,*
> *And out of good still to find means of evil;*
> *Which oft-times may succeed, so as perhaps*
> *Shall grieve him, if I fail not, and disturb*
> *His inmost counsels from their destined aim.*
> *But see the angry victor hath recalled*
> *His ministers of vengeance and pursuit*
> *Back to the gates of heaven.*
>
> *(I. 157–71)*

The scrupulous reader will notice the discrepancy, ridiculous or blasphemous, between Satan's incitement to rebellion and the pattern of virtuous ascent implied by the form of the speech, a form principally defined by the reference to the gates of heaven in the fifteenth line. Special point is given by the ladder structure to the title 'Fallen cherub' by which Beelzebub is addressed, and the perversion of Creation advocated in lines 162–5 contrasts with the Christian use of Creation:

> In contemplation of created things
> By steps we may ascend to God.
> (*V. 511–12*)

Such contemplation is the object of Bellarmine's devotional manual *De ascensione mentis in Deum per scalam rerum creaturarum* (1615; English translations 1616 and 1638) with its arrangement in fifteen chapters or rungs.[10] Even while Satan advocates evil, the ordered structure of his speech hints at the alternative, ascent to God.[11] But hints are wasted on the pig-headed. Writing about 'the secret magick of numbers', Sir Thomas Browne noted that

> in this masse of nature there is a set of things that carry in their front, though not in capitall letters, yet in stenography, and short Characters, something of Divinitie, which to wiser reasons serve as Luminaries in the abysse of knowledge, and to judicious beliefes, as scales and roundles to mount the pinnacles and highest pieces of Divinity.[12]

Satan's hell is indeed an 'abysse of knowledge', its new inhabitants intellectually enslaved by a wilfully stupid refusal to recognise the omnipotence of God no matter how strong the evidence to the contrary. Where even capital letters would be ignored, 'the secret magick of numbers' can communicate nothing.

Once the reader has become aware of numerological significance in these fifteen lines, less obviously signalled symbolism becomes apparent. The eleventh line of Satan's speech changes strikingly from the inclusive 'we' form to the assertive first person singular. Both this and the line's reference to grieving and disturbing God are appropriate to its number symbolism, as will become clear later in this paper. (Briefly, eleven is associated with sin and with egotistical transgression.) The futility of Satan's plan is appropriately emphasised in the twelfth line where the ultimate success of God's purpose, his 'destined aim', is admitted. Twelve signifies completion (a piece of number lore which will also be taken up later in this essay). The final three lines of the fifteen-line sequence show God's mercy opposed to Satan's implacable hatred. Another expression of the same divine mercy is the role of Christ as mediator, a role here and elsewhere symbolised by a fifteen-line sequence culminating in a reference to the gates of heaven.[13]

All this material has been adduced only to illuminate Milton's procedure in the *Nativity Ode*. Time is a tedious rehearsal should here have ending and a return be made to the Ode itself where the last line of stanza 15 also refers to the gates of heaven:

> *And heaven as at some festival,*
> *Will open wide the gates of her high palace hall.*

These lines, too, mark the climax of a sequence patterned in a similar way to the fifteen-line passages in *Paradise Lost*. But the association of heaven's gates and the number fifteen is not a private association made only by Milton, like an idiosyncratic Shakespearian image cluster of dogs and sweets. Once again, and unfortunately so since contact with Milton's Ode has only just been renewed, it becomes necessary to digress if the former currency of a now forgotten notion is to be demonstrated.

Giles Fletcher, in the fourth book of *Christ's Victory*, makes the same association in his significantly numbered *fifteenth* stanza with its exuberant reference to Psalm 24:

> *Tosse up your heads ye everlasting gates,*
> *And let the Prince of glorie enter in:*
> *At whose brave voly of sideriall States,*
> *The Sunne to blush, and starres growe pale wear seene,*
> *When, leaping first from earth, he did begin*
> > *To climbe his Angells wings; then open hang*
> > *Your christall doores, so all the chorus sang*
> *Of heav'nly birds, as to the starres they nimbly sprang.*[14]

Writing of Milton's debt to the Fletcher brothers, Joan Grundy characterises the *Nativity Ode* as 'a Christ's victory and triumph in itself'.[15] There can be no doubt that Milton's poem owes more to Giles Fletcher than the single parallel cited in Carey's edition (line 110) might indicate, but it would be quite false to suggest that there is any specific or exclusive indebtedness to Fletcher in Milton's reference to the gates of heaven. Rather, the association seems to be widespread. Bishop Hall, whom Milton also read, has a poem on the death of Dr Whitaker which may equally well have been in Milton's mind as he wrote his *Nativity Ode*.[16] Hall's elegy shows how destruction through death is transcended by eternal life, and Milton would have noticed how the change from the early mournful stanzas to the later triumphant ones is prepared in stanza 14 so that stanza 15 may be the climactic

Open ye golden gates of Paradise,
*Open ye wide vnto a welcome Ghost:*
*Enter, O Soule, into thy* Boure *of* Blisse,
*Through all the throng of* Heauens hoast:
    *Which shall with* Triumph *gard thee as thou go'st*
    *With* Psalmes *of* Conquest *and with crownes of cost.*[17]

Hall's witty use of the word 'ghost' instead of the expected word 'guest' is something Milton would surely have enjoyed, just as Hall would have relished Milton's amusing yet serious interchange of girl friends and sheep in stanza 8 of the Ode.

Milton's sequence of fifteen stanzas is not merely a simple block unit. It is itself internally organised. Stanzas 1–8 set the scene of the Incarnation, stanzas 8–15 recount and elaborate the biblical story. The sequence is, therefore, divided into equal halves, with stanza 8, poised 'e'er the point of dawn', acting as a transitional stanza and having a place in each half. It is a stanza that concludes the expectant scene setting and introduces the biblical shepherds. The obvious structural analogy here is with the double-octave musical scale, a scale of fifteen notes often seen as linking earth and heaven. Such a cosmic *scala* is set out in an eleventh-century manuscript of Boethius's *De institutione musicae*, and the concept was still valid in Milton's day.[18] The lower octave is associated with the created world of time, and the upper, spiritual octave with the supernatural world of eternity. It is a notion that helps to structure the 'steps of gold to heaven gate' in Book III of *Paradise Lost* (501–15) where, in the eighth line, there is a shift from a register of sensual earthly description to a register of increasingly rarefied suggestion.[19] Similarly, stanza 8 of the *Nativity Ode* acts like the central note of a two-octave musical scale, concluding the octave of preparation in the world of nature while simultaneously introducing the upper octave of supernatural involvement. The progression shows an unmistakable rising movement. The Boethius manuscript allocates its lower octave to the sun, moon, and planetary bodies, the upper octave it allocates to the angels and their music. The same division is made by Milton.

Within Milton's upper octave (stanzas 8–15) there is further internal arrangement. The central six of its eight stanzas describe 'the angelic symphony', an arrangement in accord with the significance of six as the number of harmony. It was natural for Milton to arrange it thus, just as it was natural for Marvell to write his *Musicks Empire* in six stanzas. It is appropriate, too, that Milton's stanza 9 should introduce the angels, just as in Chapter 9 of *De doctrina Christiana*, Book I, Milton writes about angels; and that stanza 10 should emphasise the fulfilment of nature and the perfect union of heaven and earth. It is in Chapter 10 of the first book of *De doctrina* that Milton writes of prelapsarian man.[20]

In short, the first fifteen stanzas of the Hymn defined and profiled with the shapes of traditional or, as Rosemond Tuve would have called them, ancient images display by structural reenactment the mediation of Christ that the Nativity initiates. Earthly imperfection and heavenly perfection are here reconciled because Christ comprehends the whole range. But for Milton to have expressed only that would have been unrealistic. The poem is not yet concluded, the work of redemption only begun. Although Christ brings peace, the angels are armed, and there is no reason to suppose that their arms are merely ceremonial: the evil against which they guard is a potent force.

## II

The Incarnation is not the Atonement. We must remember with Traherne that 'the Cross of Christ is the Jacobs ladder by which we Ascend into the Highest Heavens'.[21] The second section of the Hymn comprises eleven stanzas (16–26), the beginning of a new movement being clearly marked by the abrupt termination of the previous line of development:

> *But wisest fate says no,*
> *It must not yet be so.*

These lines form a *volta*, introduced by the typical word 'but' and effectively dividing the hymn, as though it were an enlarged sonnet, into a double octave of stanzas and a double sestet of stanzas. The new section contrasts strongly with the preceding one. The crucifixion in its opening stanza stands out against the nativity scene, and the listing and description of the pagan gods is very different from what has gone before. It is appropriate that eleven, the number of sin, should be chosen for the number of stanzas in this section. In *De doctrina Christiana* Milton devoted the *eleventh* chapter of the first book to the fall of our first parents and to sin. It is, according to the standard handbook of Milton's time, a number 'significans illos qui transgrediuntur Decalogum mandatorum',[22] and is associated also with death. Because of the association with death Milton wrote *Lycidas* in eleven verse paragraphs, and *On the Death of a Fair Infant* in eleven stanzas.[23] Eleven is a number of falling rather than rising and contrasts strongly with fifteen, the number of the ladder:

> Undenarius numerus nullam habet cum divinis, neque cum coelestibus communionem, nec attactum, nec scalam ad supera tendentem.[24]

The opposition between fifteen and eleven which Milton is drawing upon is effectively used by Milton's master, Spenser. Colin's lament for Dido in *The Shepheardes Calender* is appropriately placed in the November eclogue, November being the eleventh month and eleven being associated with death. The lament itself has eleven stanzas with a doleful refrain mourning the death of Dido, followed by four stanzas with joyful refrains celebrating Dido's new life in Elysian fields:

> *There liues she with the blessed Gods in blisse,*
> *There drinks she* Nectar *with* Ambrosia *mixt,*
> *And ioyes enioyes, that mortall men doe misse.*[25]
>
> (194-6)

The four joyful stanzas introduced by a 'but' formula ('But maugre death') make the total up to fifteen, and although there can be no reference to the gates of heaven in a poem adopting non-Christian conventions, there is a ladder-like suggestion that Dido has set up a route between earth and 'heauens hight' that others may follow:

> Dido *is gone afore (whose turne shall be the next?)*
>
> (193)

The change of refrain in the lament is numerologically appropriate in the same way that Kent Hieatt has shown that the change from positive to negative refrain in Spenser's *Epithalamion* significantly marks the change from day to night.[26] Colin's emblem, '*La mort ny mord*', expresses the process of eleven being transformed by fifteen:

> For although by course of nature we be borne to dye . . . yet death is not to be counted for euil, nor . . . as doom of ill desert. For though the trespasse of the first man brought death into

the world, as the guerdon of sinne, yet being ouercome by the
death of one, that dyed for al, it is now made (as Chaucer sayth)
the grene path way to lyfe.

*(Glosse)*

'Death slue not him', says Spenser of Sir Philip Sidney, 'but he made
death his ladder to the skies'.[27]

Spenser's organisation of eleven stanzas within the fifteen stanzas
of the Lay of Dido could have provided Milton with a model for his
juxtaposition of fifteen and eleven stanzas in the Nativity Hymn,
but again there is no need to cite the November eclogue as Milton's
*specific* source. It is sufficient to recognise that Milton was working
within a standard frame of reference. One obvious difference distinguishes Spenser's procedure from Milton's. Spenser's design is
compact, subordinating eleven to fifteen. Milton's looser tandem
structure requires a final resolving section.

# III

Objection is sometimes made to Milton's devoting so many stanzas
to the pagan gods. They account for a surprisingly large proportion
of the poem. Another common objection is to the elaborate imagery
of the penultimate stanza of the Ode, the last stanza of the eleven-
stanza section. But excess is appropriate when it is realised that the
significance of the number eleven lies in its transgressing ten: 'significans illos qui transgrediuntur Decalogum mandatorum'.[28] Sin is
disproportioned, and it is right that stanza 26, the last of the eleven
stanzas, should seem to be running away with the poet. However
delightful this stanza is, it is in danger of deflecting Milton from his
'destined aim'. One of the characteristically baroque features of the
poem is the appearance of exuberant lack of control contained in
the discipline of a securely organised structure. The reassertion of
poetic control comes suddenly in the final stanza which also forms
the final section. The suddenness is itself expressive of God's ultimate
omnipotence, as it is in the last two lines of Herbert's 'The Collar'
or in the last verse paragraph of Dryden's *Absalom and Achitophel*.
Like Spenser's 'But maugre death' and the *Nativity Ode*'s earlier
'But wisest fate' the switch is here also signalled by the word 'but',
and the reader is returned to the nativity scene and the angels of the

upper octave of the fifteen-stanza section, and to 'the virgin blest' not mentioned since the very first stanza of the Ode.

Colin's lament turned eleven into fifteen. Milton began with fifteen and followed it by eleven. He now turns eleven into twelve to resolve the poem, and as he does so announces that 'Time is our tedious song should here have ending' not merely because the baby is asleep, but because the stanza after the eleventh is an appropriate one with which to conclude the poem. The evil number eleven is resolved by the number twelve, the number of completion: 'Plenae, consummatæq; virtutis est Duodenarius'.[29] The disorder and frantic bustle of the previous stanzas suddenly give way to a quiet, ordered and disciplined tableau presented with all the impressive, stylised dignity of an icon. It is here that the 'perpetual peace' of the first stanza is to be found:

> *But see the virgin blest,*
> *Hath laid her babe to rest.*
> *    Time is our tedious song should here have ending:*
> *Heaven's youngest teemed star,*
> *Hath fixed her polished car,*
> *    Her sleeping Lord with handmaid lamp attending:*
> *And all about the courtly stable,*
> *Bright-harnessed angels sit in order serviceable.*

Perhaps we might even observe that the poem ends in a twelfth stanza just as the Christmas festivities end on Twelfth Night. The twelfth day of Christmas is the Feast of the Epiphany, and it is in the final stanza of the poem that 'Heaven's youngest teemed star' guiding the 'star-led wizards' fixes 'her polished car' over the stable.

The twenty-seventh stanza of the Hymn completes the poem in other ways, as Professor Røstvig has shown.[30] The Proem stresses the numbers four and three. Its four stanzas each have 4+3 lines, as is appropriate in a poem about the Incarnation, man being compounded of corporeal four and spiritual three. The final stanza of the whole poem, turning eleven into twelve, expresses the same numbers ($4 \times 3$), and by being the twenty-seventh stanza of the Hymn represents threeness ($3^3$) in opposition to the beginning of the poem where the four-stanza proem represents fourness. It is appropriate, too, that the angels associated with the six musical stanzas (9–14) should reappear in the final line (line 216=$6^3$) in a stanza that harmonises the caco-phonous 'horrid clang', 'hideous hum', and 'loud lament' of the eleven-stanza sequence. The music of the angels cannot now be heard, but its harmonious essence pervades the peaceful scene in the courtly stable. Even Douglas Bush, who so vigorously rejected Professor Røstvig's whole approach, quotes with approval Maynard Mack's remark about 'the number of allusions in this stanza which carry the mind back to earlier symbols' in the poem.[31] It is surely proper to see the number symbolism participating in this resolution.

## IV

The *Nativity Ode* was not the first poem in which Milton used in combination the symbolism of fifteen, eleven, and twelve. These numbers are also significant in the Latin elegy he wrote as an undergraduate on the death of the Bishop of Ely. It may be helpful to pause for a while to consider its structure since the elegy draws, in part, on the same repertoire of ideas as the Ode. At first sight this early poem seems to fall into two sections: the poet's lament, followed by a consolation spoken by the spirit of the dead bishop. Underpinning this simple bipartite structure, however, is a neat symbolic scheme the elements of which were to be incorporated into the design of many later works. If the poem is again divided, this time into *equal* halves each of seventeen distichs, it is evident that the first half is composed of the poet's angry reviling of death and the bishop's surprising refutation of this attack, while in the second half the bishop defends death and declares his delight in heavenly bliss. The division of the poem according to speaker is fundamentally less important than division into a section of abjuration and refutation, and a section of praise. A similar structural strategy supports Milton's companion elegy written on the death of the Bishop of Winchester *(Elegia III)* which also falls into two sets of seventeen distichs. The first set describes the poet's grief, and the second describes a dream in which the poet sees Lancelot Andrewes in heaven. The use, in both poems, of two sets of seventeen distichs probably celebrates the inclusion of the two bishops they honour among the blessed.

Similar significance can be found in *Lycidas,* though there the structure is more complex. Setting aside the eight-line coda, the poem may be divided into two parts, a long first part (lines 1–164) mourning because Lycidas is dead, and a short second part (lines 165–85) roundly asserting that Lycidas is after all not dead, but lives in heaven.

The division is thus similar to the formally well marked distinction, from which it ultimately derives, in Virgil's *Eclogue V* where first Mopsus laments the death of Daphnis and then Menalcus celebrates a triumphant apotheosis. But in *Lycidas,* where a single shepherd, as in Spenser's Lament of Dido, delivers both lament and consolation, the structure cannot be marked by a simple change of speaker.[32] Instead, the new beginning is revealed by the way in which the first line of the second section recalls the first line of the whole poem, as Christopher Ricks has noted.[33] The sudden change of direction at the juncture of the two parts has, of course, been frequently commented upon, but it is possibly Rajan who catches the shift most neatly:

> the poem is manoeuvred with startling authority from the desparation into which it has been deliberately plunged into an almost exultant recovery. 'Weep no more, woful Shepherds, weep no more' is a line alive with both serenity and joyousness; the conviction that sings in it is not merely declared but achieved.[34]

The first seventeen lines of the second part record that Lycidas is now with the saints in heaven. They also form a sequence in which the number of lines expresses symbolically the same idea. Their power to comfort lies partly in the ordered structure of the sequence which modulates so reassuringly from injunction to the shepherds to stop their weeping to the full beatitude of the apocalyptic vision ('And God shall wipe away all tears from their eyes') as the reader is pulled firmly onwards by the conjunctive *so*'s and *and*'s. The hoped for pattern is completed in the seventeenth line as the tear image reappears, though with the word 'weep' metamorphosed into 'wipe', and the limited, backward looking 'no more' replaced by the forward looking, unlimited 'for ever', while securely at the centre of the sequence (the ninth of seventeen lines) is Christ, saviour of those who have faith and himself powerfully immune from forces such as those of the 'perilous flood' that have wrecked Lycidas's 'perfidious bark'. The apocalyptic reference that closes the sequence also puts Christ at the centre, though in a way that accords with pastoral elements of the poem. Through Christ all is resolved:

> For the Lamb which is in the midst of the throne shall feed them, and shall lead them unto living fountains of waters and God shall wipe away all tears from their eyes.
>
> (Rev. VII. 17)

We scarcely notice that in the poem it is not God but 'the saints' who wipe the tears away, for Christ at the centre controls the action and the design by determining the placing of the final line so that beginning and end are equally spaced from the centre:

> *Weep no more, woeful shepherds weep no more,*
> *For Lycidas your sorrow is not dead,*
> *Sunk though he be beneath the watry floor,*
> *So sinks the day-star in the ocean bed,*
> *And yet anon repairs his drooping head,*
> *And tricks his beams, and with new spangled ore,*
> *Flames in the forehead of the morning sky:*
> *So Lycidas sunk low, but mounted high,*
> *Through the dear might of him that walked the waves;*
> *Where other groves, and other streams along,*
> *With nectar pure his oozy locks he laves,*
> *And hears the unexpressive nuptial song,*
> *In the blest kingdoms meek of joy and love.*
> *There entertain him all the saints above,*
> *In solemn troops, and sweet societies*
> *That sing, and singing in their glory move,*
> *And wipe the tears for ever from their eyes.*

(lines 165–81)

The shepherds now dry-eyed, the uncouth swain directly addresses Lycidas himself in a brief, four-line statement that returns us, in preparation for the *commiato*, to the fourfold earth.[35]

In all three elegies the number seventeen is important, and it seems likely that Milton was thinking of Saint Augustine's interpretation of seventeen which makes it the union of the ten of the Old Testament Commandments and the seven of the gifts of the Holy Spirit combining to produce a specially famous piece of number lore associated with a saintly life.[36] The triangular form of the number (i.e. 153) was associated with saints in heaven. This association of saintliness and seventeen lies behind the second book of Milton's *De doctrina Christiana* which devotes its seventeen chapters to consideration of the worship or love of God *(de cultu Dei et charitate)*.

In the poem on the Bishop of Ely the first seventeen distichs may be further divided after line 22. The first eleven distichs are appropriately concerned with the poet's grief as he rails against death. In the twelfth a sudden change is introduced, like the final stanza of the *Nativity*

*Ode* turning eleven into twelve, by the words 'At ecce', and the sequence is concluded by a twelve-line section (lines 23–34) refuting the poet's mournful attitude to death. The Bishop's alternative account is the subject of the second seventeen distichs. Having rejected the idea of death as destroyer, the second half of the poem begins with a sequence of fifteen distichs (lines 35–64) that present death as the means of rising from this world to the next. The sequence culminates, as we might expect, in images describing the entrance to heaven:

> *Donec nitentes ad fores*
> *Ventum est Olympi, et regiam crystallinam, et*
> *Stratum smaragdis atrium,*
>
>                            (lines 62–4)

(until I reached the gleaming gates of Olympus, the palace of crystal and the forecourt paved with emerald.—*Carey's translation*)

Four concluding lines complete the poem bringing the number of distichs in the second half from fifteen to seventeen.

The poem on the Bishop of Ely is, then, similar in structure to Hall's poem on Dr Whitaker. In Hall's elegy there is a single sequence of seventeen stanzas with the entrance to heaven described in stanza 15. Milton's Latin elegy is shorter because the units are distichs not six-line stanzas, but the structure is more elaborate because there are two sequences of seventeen, one of which exploits the eleven to twelve change, and the other the notion of fifteen. It is appropriate that Milton's seventeenth distich (second series) presents Bishop Felton rewarded with eternal felicity just as the seventeenth and final stanza of Hall's elegy asserts that Whitaker now lives in two ways, eternally in heaven and in deathless reputation on earth:

> *Is this to die, to liue for euermore*
> *A double life: that neither liu'd afore?*
>
>                            (lines 101–2)

Analysis of 'In obitum praesulis Eliensis' cannot, of course, in itself prove that Milton made structural use of certain number symbolism in his *Nativity Ode*, and the obvious pressing question must be faced. Quite simply, what external evidence is there that the structural scheme for the *Nativity Ode* proposed in this paper would have been accepted by Milton or could have been recognised by Milton's early readers? Not surprisingly, there is no relevant direct statement, but there is some reason to suppose that half a century later Dryden would not have found the analysis unacceptable in general outline at least. It is well known that Dryden echoes Milton's Ode in his own Ode on Anne Killigrew. Like Milton's poem, Dryden's can be seen as a nativity poem, an ode celebrating the new life in heaven of Anne, the 'Youngest Virgin-Daughter of the Skies'.[37] Can it be by chance that the first fifteen lines of Dryden's poem share with the last stanza of Milton's the words 'youngest', 'virgin', 'heaven's', 'fixed', 'time', 'star', 'blest', and 'song', and that Dryden's 'Seraphims' recall Milton's 'Bright-harnessed angels'? Like Spenser's Dido, Anne has gone 'As Harbinger of Heav'n, the Way to show', and it is not surprising that the first sentence of Dryden's poem is of fifteen lines and is about Anne's 'Promotion' from earth to heaven:

> *Thou Youngest Virgin-Daughter of the Skies,*
> *Made in the last Promotion of the Blest;*
> *Whose Palmes, new pluckt from Paradise,*
> *In spreading Branches more sublimely rise,*
> *Rich with Immortal Green above the rest:*
> *Whether, adopted to some Neighbouring Star,*
> *Thou rol'st above us, in thy wand'ring Race,*
>    *Or, in Procession fixt and regular,*
>    *Mov'd with the Heavens Majestick Pace;*
>    *Or, call'd to more Superior Bliss,*
> *Thou tread'st, with Seraphims, the vast Abyss:*
> *What ever happy Region is thy place,*
> *Cease thy Celestial Song a little space;*
> *(Thou wilt have Time enough for Hymns Divine,*
>    *Since Heav'ns Eternal Year is thine.)*

The witty afterthought completing the sentence refers to the sufficiency of eternity for Anne's celestial song. Dryden in the world of time does not have this leisure, and we are reminded of Milton's reference to the constraints of time and of his numerological form: 'Time is our tedious song should here have ending' (211). Milton in his Hymn, and Dryden too, is bounded by time; Anne in her 'Hymns Divine' is not. The second sentence, completing Dryden's opening stanza, stresses that Dryden's poetry is mortal, its seven lines indicating, as do the seven-line stanzas of Milton's Proem, that the condition of man is 'a darksome house of mortal clay' (14):

> *Hear then a Mortal Muse thy Praise rehearse,*
>   *In no ignoble Verse;*
> *But such as thy own voice did practise here,*
> *When thy first Fruits of Poesie were giv'n;*
> *To make thy self a welcome Inmate there:*
>   *While yet a young Probationer,*
>   *And Candidate of Heav'n.*

$$(16\text{--}22)$$

The first stanza of Dryden's poem, then, juxtaposes a sequence of fifteen lines about Anne's ascent to heaven with a sequence of seven lines about the imperfection of mortal art.

It is the third stanza of Dryden's poem describing Anne's nativity that has previously been particularly associated with Milton's Ode, especially its reference to audibility of the music of the spheres at the time of birth.[38] In Dryden, Milton's six musical stanzas become six musical lines:

> *Thy Brother-Angels at thy Birth*
> *Strung each his Lyre, and tun'd it high,*
> *That all the People of the Skie*
> *Might know a Poetess was born on Earth.*
> *And then, if ever, Mortal Ears*
> *Had heard the Musick of the Spheres!*

$$(44\text{--}9)$$

The process of adaptation is revealing. Dryden's parenthetical 'if ever' allows him to pay an extravagant compliment while simultaneously denying it and implying that there was nothing special about Anne's birth. There is nothing double-edged about Milton's use of the conditional:

> *Ring out, ye crystal spheres,*
> *Once bless our human ears,*
>   *(If ye have power to touch our senses so).*

$$(125\text{--}7)$$

Dryden's last stanza, with its reference to the Last Judgement, has also been associated with the *Nativity Ode* (lines 155–6, 163–4).[39]

It is, however, the structure of Dryden's fourth stanza that I wish to compare most closely with the *Nativity Ode*. The stanza presents Anne as a redeeming Christ figure, at once human and superhuman:

> *Her Wit was more than Man, her Innocence a Child!*
> (70)

As Christ atones for the sin of man, so Anne atones for the sin of the
fallen world of letters. Through her, poets may rise from this 'Second
Fall'. The fifteen lines of the stanza deliberately imply, by numerological means, a connexion between Anne and Christ as ladders of redemption, but the structure only reinforces what the words already
pointedly imply.

I have argued that the *Nativity Ode* is composed of four sections:
a four-stanza Proem, and a Hymn made up of sections of fifteen,
eleven, and one stanzas respectively. The same structure is more
compactly èvident[40] in Dryden's single stanza which may, like Milton's
Hymn, be divided into three sections:

> *O Gracious God! How far have we*
> *Prophan'd thy Heavn'ly Gift of Poesy?*
> *Made prostitute and profligate the Muse,*
> *Debas'd to each obscene and impious use,*
> *Whose Harmony was first ordain'd Above*
> *For Tongues of Angels, and for Hymns of Love?*
> *O wretched We! why were we hurry'd down*
> >  *This lubrique and adul'rate age,*
> >  *(Nay added fat Pollutions of our own)*
> *T'increase the steaming Ordures of the Stage?*
> *What can we say t'excuse our Second Fall?*
> *Let this thy* Vestal, *Heav'n, attone for all!*
> *Her* Arethusian *Stream remains unsoil'd,*
> >  *Unmixt with Forreign Filth, and undefil'd,*
> *Her Wit was more than Man, her Innocence a Child!*

First comes a series of questions expressing the evil into which
literature has fallen, suitably composed of eleven lines—the 'steaming
Ordures of the Stage' appear like a smoking sacrifice in some obscene
rite associated with one of Milton's pagan gods. Dryden's eleven
lines are answered by one line, resolving the evil of eleven by the
virtue of twelve. The twelfth line serves the same function as the
final stanza of Milton's Ode, and in it Anne is seen as both vestal
virgin and atoning redeemer. We may appropriately recall the
opening of Milton's final stanza which refers to both Mary and
Christ:

*But see the virgin blest,*
*Hath laid her babe to rest.*

Dryden's three concluding lines bring the total for the stanza to fifteen. The structure bears further analysis. A double-octave arrangement is superimposed by distinguishing the first, central, and final lines by metrical irregularity. They are the three lines that correspond to the three soundings of the musical tonic. The use of a quatrain in the middle of the stanza instead of the couplets used elsewhere dovetails the rhyme scheme of the first octave into the rhyme scheme of the second octave just as the median tonic common to both octaves unites the musical scale of two octaves. It is a technique later used by Shadwell.[41] Besides all this, Dryden's choice of his fourth stanza to exploit these structural ideas probably refers to the four stanzas of Milton's Proem as well as being appropriate to the grossness which it is hoped Anne's goodness may purge.

Dryden's use of the numbers four, eleven, and one all contained in fifteen (compact in the manner of Spenser's Lay of Dido) make his stanza a witty and moving epitome of the *Nativity Ode*,[42] but there is more to the parallel than similarity in construction. Milton's Ode is a gift of poetry to Christ, Milton's offering to his maker of the talent with which he was endowed. The gift of poetry concerns Dryden also, but *he* writes of the profanation of the 'Heav'nly Gift of Poesy' in a fallen world. Magi that 'haste with odours sweet' (23) have given way to debauched dramatists who hurry down 'T'increase the steaming Ordures' of the London playhouses.

Other poems, none perhaps more than Cowley's elegy 'On the Death of Mr Crashaw', have contributed to Dryden's achievement in the Anne Killigrew Ode, described by Johnson as the noblest ode in the language,[43] but the shaping force of Milton's 'order serviceable' on that achievement has been unjustly neglected. Comparison of the two odes furthers our understanding of Dryden's poem and provides insight into the way that Dryden read Milton.


# V


The *Nativity Ode* is not just a simple accumulation of proem+15 stanzas+11 stanzas+1 stanza. The poem is bound together by an articulating pattern of matching threads appearing and reappearing symmetrically around its centre. This sets up a web of tensions that prevents the accreted units from disintegrating.

The three central stanzas of the poem are clearly marked. The central stanza of the Hymn supposes that

> *if such holy song*
> *Enwrap our fancy long,*
> *Time will run back, and fetch the age of gold.*
> (stanza 14)

The lines suggest a mid-point at which there is a choice between equidistant possibilities: movement forward through history or return to the golden age. 'There are' says Cowley, writing of what he means by 'the *Orb* of *Round Eternity*', 'two sorts of Eternity; from the *Present backwards* to Eternity, and from the *Present forwards*. . . . These two make up the whole *Circle* of *Eternity*.'[44] In the central stanza of Milton's Hymn the poem is poised between movement forward and movement backwards.

The central stanza of the Ode as a whole (i.e. Proem+Hymn; iv+27) is stanza 12 of the Hymn, and it is also marked by a pivotal image: 'the well-balanced world on hinges hung'.[45] These two differently calculated centres frame the magnificent stanza which most readers rightly and instinctively identify as the effective centre of the poem. It is an impressive, splendid, and detachable set piece, grammatically distinguished and heightened by being the only stanza in the Hymn declaimed in the imperative mood. Appropriation of it for downright practical purposes by a nineteenth-century adapter of *Comus* and by a twentieth-century book designer, both relying on the arresting power of the lines to compel attention, is as solid evidence as any of the wide recognition of the stanza's commanding presence and powerful impact. In this way it formed the opening solo and chorus—albeit sadly mutilated—of Macready's 1843 production of *Comus* at Drury Lane,[46] and the opening chorus of the Easter production at the same theatre in 1865.[47] Similarly, it has been exploited graphically on the cover of the Grey Arrow paperback edition of David Daiches's *Milton* (London, 1963). Though such instances may be unimportant in themselves, they are revealing indicators of the way that the lines have been regarded. But to remove the stanza from the poem is to strip it of at least some of its dignity. In its proper context in the Ode Milton gave the stanza pride of place by a setting flanked by two stanzas each a centre in its own right. Like an emperor with kings as attendants, it occupies a position of sovereign honour. In short, placement in the midst enhances the magnificence of the verse while the rhetorical power of the lines distinguishes the place in the poem that they fill. Rhetorical structure and verbal rhetoric combine to reinforce one another.

> *Ring out, ye crystal spheres,*
> *Once bless our human ears,*
> *(If ye have power to touch our senses so)*
> *And let your silver chime*
> *Move in melodious time;*
> *     And let the base of heaven's deep organ blow,*
> *And with your ninefold harmony*
> *Make up full concert to the angelic symphony.*

If numerically allusive expression of the 'ninefold harmony' is to be found in the poem, it is probably in the nine words at the heart of this stanza.

Around this centre, stanzas are disposed in linked pairs. Stanzas 12 and 14, which I have already discussed, form a pair of pivotal stanzas flanking the angelic symphony. Together the three stanzas 12–14 make up the nub of the poem. Prompted by the account of the angelic music that precedes them, they describe or invoke the music of the spheres. As Lawrence Stapleton perceptively argued some twenty years ago in a neglected article that draws attention to the importance of both number and central accent in Milton's poem, it is entirely appropriate that this sublime music comes at the centre.[48] The point now needs to to taken up once more, and thus it may be helpful to revive Stapleton's line of investigation.

Stapleton observed a telling similarity between 'the pattern of ideas' in Clement of Alexandria's *Exhortation to the Greeks* and the thematic structure of Milton's Ode. Whether or not Milton himself knew Clement's writings by 1629 (and Stapleton is careful not to claim that Milton *necessarily* had the *Exhortation* in mind), it is clear that familiarity with 'worthy' Clement's vigorous and memorable treatise usefully equips a modern reader of Milton with a ready understanding of much that is important in the Ode. I have already argued that the structural import of the first fifteen stanzas of Milton's Hymn presents Christ as a saviour who descended to earth so that men may rise to heaven. Turning to the first chapter of Clement's *Exhortation* we find the same concept, but simply stated rather than expressed through structure, and although the actual image of a ladder is not to be found in Clement's treatise, just as it is verbally absent from Milton's poem, the notion of ascent to God through a saviour whose nativity makes that ascent possible is pervasive. Indeed, ascent through Christ is Clement's controlling idea, the very point at which the twin energising forces of the *Exhortation*—Christianity and Platonism —fuse

The first fifteen stanzas of the Hymn and Clement's first chapter also culminate in a similar way. Clement works up to a climactic reference to the gates of heaven opening to disclose a vision of God, an image that can be compared with stanza 15 of Milton's Hymn:

> 'For I am the door,' He says somewhere; which we who wish to perceive God must search out, in order that He may throw open wide for us the gates of heaven. . . . And I know well that He who opens this door, hitherto shut, afterwards unveils what is within, and shows what could not have been discovered before, except we entered through Christ, through whom alone comes the vision of God.[49]

End of chapter. With such a progression in mind, the dramatically truncated version of it found in the Ode, where Milton at the end of his initial fifteen-stanza section cuts straight from the wide open gates of heaven's high palace hall not, like Clement, to a divine vision but instead to the harshly juxtaposed reality of smiling babe and bitter cross, can be seen counterpointed against a pattern that determines the expectations of a properly oriented reader. Only the reader who expects something like Clement's vision can respond fully to the effect gained by Milton's change of direction at stanza 16.

Clement's subsequent chapters describe the pagan gods, and the religious practices and philosophical beliefs of the pre-Christian world. All are either inadequate or evil, and Clement describes them in order to dismiss them just as Milton, in the second section of his Hymn, dismisses types and perversions of Christ. The nativity involves both Milton and Clement in the same sort of rejection of the past.

The general shape of the *Exhortation* as I have here described it is, then, broadly similar to that of Milton's Hymn with its contrasting sections of fifteen and eleven stanzas. Within these similar structures there are many similarities of idea, the most significant being the importance of music in both works. Music accompanies the birth of Christ in the poem and fills its central stanzas; Clement makes Christ himself the musician, a musician far superior even to such wonder-working performers of antiquity as Arion and Orpheus: 'far different is my minstrel', boasts Clement. 'He calls once again to heaven those who have been cast down to earth.'[50] But for Clement, Christ is also the music as well as the musician. He is the new music ousting the old music of pagan shadowy types, though this apparently new music proves after all to be not really new for it is the lost harmony of Creation restored. Clement recalls how 'this pure song, the stay of the universe and the harmony of all things, stretching from the centre to the circumference and from the extremities to the centre, reduced this whole to harmony.'[51] Similarly, Milton gives 'harmonious order' to his poem by arranging it around a musical centre, and while the music is not, for Milton, explicitly identified with Christ, it honours Christ's nativity, as does the whole poem that is centred upon it. Like Clement's music, Milton's too is associated with the music of Creation (stanza 12), and if Clement's syncretistic delight in compiling assertions that God is at the centre of all things is allowed to provide a conceptual basis, it is possible to regard Milton's centralised structure as implicitly identifying the music with Christ.[52] Milton can be seen as suggesting through structure what Clement openly expresses in words.

Milton's distinction between the angelic music attested by the gospels and the unheard music of the spheres is important in the Ode because Milton is careful to distinguish the fabulous or conjectural: 'as 'tis said' (stanza 12), 'If ye have power' (stanza 13), 'For if such holy song' (stanza 14). The distinction also separates the central stanzas from those that precede them. Shape in the triple centre itself is emphasised by surrounding the great call for music to celebrate the Nativity (stanza 13) with framing allusions to the primeval state, unspoiled at the Creation in stanza 12 and regained at the Millenium in stanza 14. It is stanza 13 that celebrates the present time, 'the happy morn' (*Hodie Christus natus est*) while stanza 12 recalls the past and stanza 14 looks to the future. The stanzas that follow this central group are differentiated from it by their non-musical subject matter.

Flanking the triple centre at one remove are stanzas 11 and 15, 'a globe of circular light' (stanza 11) linked with 'orbed in a rainbow' (stanza 15), a link less effectively made, but already present, when, in the first edition, the word 'orbed' was not used. Moving outwards again, we find that the next pair of linked stanzas shows a negative rather than a positive correlation. This is because one of the pair belongs to the fifteen-stanza section of the Hymn (stanza 10) while the other is the first of the eleven contrasting wicked stanzas (stanza 16). The pattern now established continues. The fulfilment of stanza 10 contrasts with the delay of stanza 16, 'This must not yet be so'. Either side of this pair, the 'music sweet' of stanza 9 is set against the 'horrid clang' of stanza 17, and the pastoral eighth stanza contrasts with the 'scaly horror' of the predatory dragon in stanza 18. The sun's respectful response to the 'greater sun' is described in stanza 7, while in stanza 19 the sun god flees. Stanza 6 shows the stars standing still in recognition of the new authority; stanza 20 expresses pagan nature's regret at the passing of the old order. 'Peaceful was the night' in stanza 5 is sharply contrasted with the 'midnight plaint' of stanza 21. Stanza 4 contrasts absence of physical violence, chariots 'Unstained with hostile blood', with the bloody and violent deities of stanza 22, 'wounded Thammuz', Dagon 'the twice battered god', and Baal-Peor for whose sake Cozbi was slain (*Numbers* XXV. 18). Rather similarly, the peace and amity of stanza 3 contrasts with the human sacrifices demanded by Moloch who appears in stanza 23. Stanza 2 describes snow, while in stanza 24 the grass is 'unshowered', and the earlier stanza's reference to a 'saintly veil of maiden white' is contrasted with the later stanza's mention of a shroud (though the primary meaning of 'shroud' may be 'place of shelter or retreat') and of the sable stoles of sorcerers. This pair of stanzas also displays a contrast between 'speeches fair' and 'lowings loud'. 'The heaven-born-child / All meanly wrapped' of stanza 1 becomes in stanza 25 the 'dreaded infant'. The last stanza of the Proem (iv) in which the Magi and the Ode haste *to* Christ is paired by the last stanza of the eleven-stanza section (26) in which shadows, ghosts, and fays flee *from* Christ. The outermost pair of all is composed of stanza iii of the Proem and the final stanza of the whole Ode. In this pair (now that the eleven stanzas have been worked through) Milton reverts to a positive relationship. The 'Bright-harnessed angels sit[ting] in order serviceable' link straightforwardly with 'the spangled host keep[ing] watch in squadrons bright' of the invocation. The two remaining introductory stanzas that precede the invocation lie outside the pattern. They provide a formal statement of the fact and purpose of the Incarnation. It is in response to this statement that the Ode grows, the notion of a gift poem being proposed only in stanza iii.

Bearing in mind how easy it is to make connexions between almost any stanzas in this poem, it is only reasonable to have doubts about whether Milton really did dispose his poem symmetrically around stanza 13.[53] Furthermore, a scheme which seems to ignore two stanzas may seem unsatisfactory, so unsatisfactory perhaps as to be unconvincing. In the face of such doubts, confidence might be strengthened by reflecting that a pattern of positive and negative links between paired stanzas that accords exactly and predictably with the distinction between the eleven stanzas and the stanzas contrasted with them (i.e. the fifteen stanzas that precede them and the single stanza that follows them) indicates that the connexions are unlikely to be fortuitous or casual. The intelligent complexity of the scheme tends to affirm its authenticity. Acceptance of a pattern which excludes two stanzas at the beginning of the poem may be made easier by thinking of a mannerist *trompe l'oeil* painting in which a painted frame forms part of the picture. It is a suggestion that Alastair Fowler has made in relation to the *commiato* of *Lycidas*, but it could be just as helpful in relation to the opening of the *Nativity Ode*.[54] Here the three possible beginnings (the actual beginning of the poem, the invocation of the muse in stanza iii, and the ostensible beginning of the gift-poem inspired by the muse) correspond to three formally denoted points of departure: line 1; the outermost limit of the symmetrical pattern at line 15; the beginning of the Hymn at line 29. The choice of alternatives blurs the distinction between introduction and poem, frame and picture.

The point of the *trompe l'oeil* cleverness lies in Milton's eagerness to race the Magi. 'O run, prevent them' he cries, and we should remember the witty ploy by which Milton later responds to this word 'prevent' in line 8 of the sonnet on his blindness, where he contrives to begin the sestet half a line too early in order to express the haste of patience (the paradoxically active patience of *Hebrews* 12, 1–2, at that). What looks like a blind poet's blunder proves to be a vindication of his undiminished skill:

> *When I consider how my light is spent,*
>   *Ere half my days, in this dark world and wide,*
>   *And that one talent which is death to hide,*
>   *Lodged with me useless, though my soul more bent*
> *To serve therewith my maker, and present*
>   *My true account, lest he returning chide,*

> *Doth God exact day-labour, light denied,*
> *I fondly ask; but Patience to prevent*
> *That murmur, soon replies, God doth not need*
> *Either man's work or his own gifts, who best*
> *Bear his mild yoke, they serve him best, his state*
> *Is kingly. Thousands at his bidding speed*
> *And post o'er land and ocean without rest:*
> *They also serve who only stand and wait.*
> (Sonnet XVI)

In the *Nativity Ode*, too, Milton anticipates the expected starting point.[55] 'The star-led wizards' are already on the road in the stanza that precedes the Hymn, but Milton 'prevents' (i.e. *comes before*) them by beginning his symmetrical structure one stanza before that. It is revealing that even as Milton asks for inspiration, a pattern is already being formed, and it is significant, if we are to read precisely what is said, that Milton seeks to race the Magi not with a hymn but with a 'humble ode', thus confirming that the gift-poem is not the Hymn, but a larger entity that includes the Hymn. It is almost as if Milton were responding wittily to Lancelot Andrewes's complaint in a Christmas Day sermon for 1622. 'Our Epiphanie', lamented Andrewes, wryly comparing the prompt response of the Wise Men with the dilatoriness of most Christians, 'would (sure) have fallen in Easter-weeke at the soonest.'[56] But Milton is no such laggard. He has given himself a head start, and he has got away unobserved as well, for it is only when the pattern is complete that his plan is revealed. The synoptic view of the poem's symmetrical, concentric form that is required to reveal Milton's strategy is available only in retrospect when the race has been won.[57]

Failing absolutely direct and explicit authorial statement in support of a symmetrical pattern centred round stanza 13, the most encouraging evidence would be confirmation by one of the poem's early readers. It was reassuring to see the relationship between the structure of Dryden's Anne Killigrew stanza and the structure of the *Nativity Ode*. It would be equally reassuring to be able to refer to an imitation of Milton's symmetrical arrangement. But while we can be reasonably sure that in the Anne Killigrew Ode Dryden really was adapting Milton, the relationship between Henry Vaughan's 'The Morning Watch' and Milton's Ode is problematical. Milton's 1645 volume appeared at what was for Vaughan an impressionable time, and it is

easy to see why the *Nativity Ode* would have attracted him strongly.
It is tempting to conjecture. There is, moreover, *some* evidence that
encourages one to recognise the form of Vaughan's poem as an
epitome of the symmetry of Milton's Ode. But consideration of this
evidence must be accompanied by the text of the poem.

The Morning-watch.

*O Joyes! Infinite sweetnes! with what flowres,*
*And shoots of glory, my soul breakes, and buds!*
*All the long houres*
*Of night, and Rest*
*Through the still shrouds*      5
*Of sleep, and Clouds,*
*This Dew fell on my Breast;*
*O how it* Blouds,
*And* Spirits *all my Earth! heark! In what Rings,*
*And* Hymning Circulations *the quick world*      10
*Awakes, and sings;*
*The rising winds,*
*And falling springs,*
*Birds, beasts, all things*
*Adore him in their kinds.*      15
*Thus all is hurl'd*
*In sacred* Hymnes, *and* Order, *The great* Chime      17
*And* Symphony *of nature. Prayer is*
*The world in tune,*
*A spirit-voyce,*      20
*And vocall joyes*
*Whose* Eccho *is heav'ns blisse.*
*O let me climbe*
*When I lye down! The Pious soul by night*
*Is like a clouded starre, whose beames though sed*      25
*To shed their light*
*Under some Cloud*
*Yet are above*
*And shine, and move*
*Beyond that mistie showrd.*      30
*So in my Bed*
*That Curtain'd grave, though sleep, like ashes' hide*
*My lamp, and life, both shall in thee abide.*[58]      33

E. C. Pettet has already demonstrated the symmetry of 'The Morning-Watch', but the poem's thirty-three lines (the import of *that* number I pass over) are not paired line by line as the stanzas of Milton's Ode are. Such an exacting correspondence would hardly be workable: a line allows too little scope. Instead, a looser plan was adopted by Vaughan:

> With this compulsive, most lyrical opening goes a memorable and satisfying close, which, besides returning us to the beginning, admirably balances with it—in the two long, five-stress lines (appropriately varied by a conclusive rhyme), in the similar density of metaphor, and, above all, in the fact that it epitomises Vaughan's night sensations, the terror and the assurance, as the opening epitomises his spiritual exhilaration at day break.
>
> For further pleasing structural correspondence we may observe how the opening is followed, and the close preceded, by a description, in short lines, of night. Without being unduly repetitive, the second passage recalls the first by its reference to 'cloud' and 'shroud', though at the cost of a repeated rhyme; while the two sections also match in that each is dominated by a single spiritual metaphor, 'dew' in one instance and 'star' in the other.[59]

I have quoted Pettet at such length because his observations are, in the context of the present argument, unbiassed. Having established, then, that it is possible to regard both the *Nativity Ode* and 'The Morning-Watch' as designed symmetrically, it is appropriate to observe particular similarities that may result from conscious borrowing.

We may notice that the central line of Vaughan's poem (line 17) and its two flanking lines,

> *Thus all is hurl'd*
> *In sacred* Hymns, *and* Order, *The great* Chime
> *And* Symphony *of nature. Prayer is* . . .

recall the 'silver chime' and 'angelic symphony' of the notionally central stanza of the *Nativity Ode*. As in Milton's poem the centre is triple. In association with these echoes attention is drawn to structural concerns by possible allusion to Milton's 'order serviceable' and to the numerically symbolic stanza sequence of the Hymn by Vaughan's 'sacred *Hymnes*, and *Order*'. Vaughan's lines

> *heark! In what Rings,*
> *And* Hymning Circulations *the quick world*
> *Awakes, and sings;*
> *The rising winds,*
> *And falling springs,*
> *Birds, beasts, all things*
> *Adore him in their kinds.*
>
> (lines 9–15)

with their paired images of rising and falling, birds and beasts, and of circles ('Rings' suggests both a circle and the sound invoked in 'Ring out, ye crystal spheres') all implying symmetrical arrangement around a central point, may recall Milton's early morning *(Illa sub auroram lux mihi prima tulit)* song of adoration *ad praesepe* symmetrically arranged around a mid-point. Possibly the nine words at the heart of Milton's central stanza (lines 128–9) are remembered in the 9+9 words of Vaughan's three central lines, but more striking is the coincidence that Vaughan's central line is the seventeenth line while the 'central' stanza of Milton's Ode is the seventeenth stanza (i.e. 4 proem+13 Hymn stanzas).[60] This correspondence does not mean, however, that 'The Morning-Watch' has the same number of lines as the *Nativity Ode* has stanzas. There is good reason for the difference. Because the centre of Milton's poem is a centre between a pair of lesser centres, there are two stanzas at the beginning of the Ode, as has been shown, without corresponding stanzas at the end. Vaughan, untroubled with the complexity of multiple centres, simply added two lines to the end of his poem to balance the two lines at the beginning, thus achieving a symmetrical pattern that comprehends the whole of his poem. In this way, line 17, the notional centre, becomes the arithmetical centre of the poem as well. Vaughan emphasises that his two extra lines are a coda by making them an addendum to the repeating pattern of eight (or in one case seven) lines, and by making them pentameters he matches them with the two opening lines of the poem to give symmetry.

Vaughan's neat adjustment and adaptation of Milton's pattern has been achieved only at the expense of some distortion. There is one piece in the puzzle that will not quite fit without forcing. Vaughan has, appropriately enough, copied the eight-line stanza of Milton's Hymn by adopting a repeating eight-line metrical pattern and rhyme scheme, the units linked syntactically to provide continuity. But strict adherence to this scheme, with a couplet added at the end, would have given thirty-four lines instead of the thirty-three that are required if line 17 is to be central. One of the eight-line units has, therefore, been replaced by a seven-line sequence, or so it seems. It would be typical of Vaughan's art to follow the example of an earlier poem while producing an effect that is all his own, and typical of him to be satisfied with an ambitious scheme that seems not quite to work out; but it may well be better to reserve judgement on the success of Vaughan's manipulations until more is known about numerically determined structures in poetry of the sixteenth and seventeenth centuries, particularly about whether irregularities in form are sometimes actually intended to alert the reader to significant structure. [61]

Milton's poem and Vaughan's have little in common thematically. Both are devotional early morning poems, and there are parallels in imagery and vocabulary. The ladder of mediation set up by Christ's action of becoming man has been turned into its contemplative counterpart, a neoplatonic ascent of meditation:

> *O let me climbe*
> *When I lye down!*

>                   (lines 23–4)

The babe laid to rest in the manger at the end of Milton's poem has been replaced by the poet in his bed at the end of Vaughan's: the bed, like the sun's in Milton's stanza 26, is curtained. All things considered, Vaughan seems to be using Milton's pattern merely because he wants to rather than for any reason significant to the reader. Were it not for the need to account for the curiously irregular seven-line unit beginning at line 17 where an eight-line unit is expected, there would be little reason to take note of a relationship between the two poems. As far as the present essay is concerned the interest lies in what Vaughan's poem may reveal about his awareness of structural pattern in Milton. It seems probable that Vaughan was imitating Milton's concentric symmetry, a probability surely worth entertaining, but like all probabilities it remains no more than just that.

My analysis of the *Nativity Ode* shows three major structural patterns. A manifest structure divides the Ode into proem and Hymn. It is an aspect of the poem's form which this essay largely ignores, not because it is of no importance, but because it has received attention from other commentators and, besides, has been perceived by every reader. Instead the focus here has been on two deeper structures, one aesthetic and one semiotic. The aesthetic structure binds together all but the first two stanzas of the poem in a cohesive and pleasing symmetry of echo and prolepsis. It is a type of arrangement found elsewhere, notably, as Max Wickert has shown, in Spenser's *Epithaamion*,[62] and also in shorter poems like Vaughan's 'The Morning-Watch'. Interlocked with this aesthetic pattern is an agglomerative, semiotic structure composed of numerically significant units, and epitomised in the fourth stanza of Dryden's ode on Anne Killigrew. In his sixth elegy, Milton described for Charles Diodati the composition of the *Nativity Ode* begun early on Christmas morning, 1629:

> I am writing a poem about the king who was born of heavenly seed, and who brought peace to men. I am writing about the blessed ages promised in Holy Scripture, about the infant cries of God, about the stabling under a poor roof of Him who dwells with His Father in the highest heavens, about the sky's giving birth to a new star, about the hosts who sang in the air, and about the pagan gods suddenly shattered in their shrines. These are the gifts I have given for Christ's birthday: the first light of dawn brought them to me.[63]

Such a programme modestly conveys no hint that the poem would be anything other than 'a string of affected conceits'. It alludes to *dona*, 'gifts' for Christ's birthday, not to a single gift. In fact, the 'humble ode' is a magnificent presentation piece constructed with all the art and learning that Milton, newly arrived at his majority, could command. It is the offering of a magus. M.l.on is determined not only to race the Wise Men, but also to produce a gift to rival theirs. The magnificence of the gift honours the recipient, of course, but it also indicates the status of the donor, his allegiance, his taste, his judgement, and the resources at his disposal.

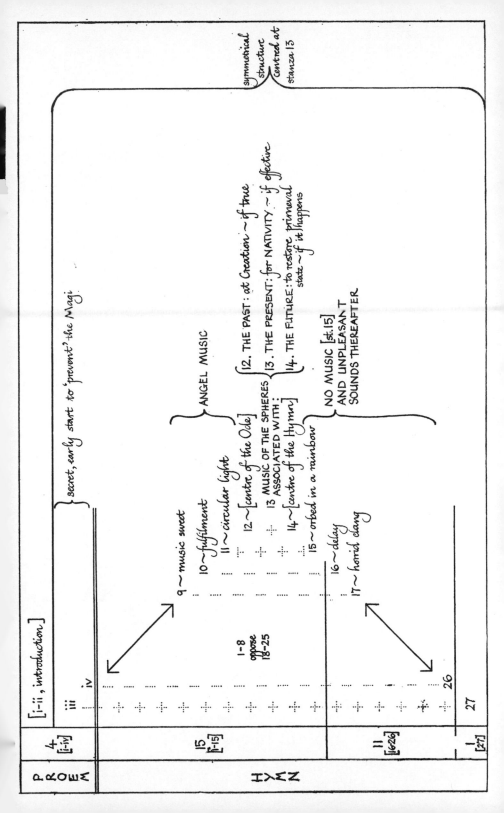

# 4

# *Dryden's Rahmenerzählung:*

## THE FORM OF 'AN ESSAY OF DRAMATICK POESIE'

### H. Neville Davies

DRYDEN'S critical essays, relaxed in style and often engagingly frank in their observations, give every appearance of openness; yet although the style persuades us otherwise, their evasive author was not a directly communicative writer. He was certainly never the man to disclose professional secrets, and his *Essay of Dramatick Poesie,* apparently so rich in circumstantial detail, is a case in point. Such teasing mysteries as the real life identities of the four disputants disguised under the 'borrowed names' Neander, Lisideius, Eugenius, and Crites, and, indeed, the whole question of what in the *Essay* is fiction and what is reportage pose perennial problems for investigation. But some mysteries are more easily penetrated, and it is high time that one of them, the literary form of Dryden's major prose work, was better understood; high time, not only because a better understanding is not hard to come by, but also because such an understanding aids a full response to the *Essay* and helps us to appreciate what Dryden was trying to do in what was, after all, a novel venture. 'To a considerable extent Dryden's dialogue form is an adaptation of the Ciceronian dialogue along both pre-Ciceronian and original lines' assert the latest and most thorough of Dryden's editors.[1] And so it is. Of course the *Essay* has something of the form of a Ciceronian dialogue, and thereby deliberately aligns itself with a great tradition of sceptical inquiry, but to see it simply as a Ciceronian dialogue adapted along 'pre-Ciceronian and original lines' (i.e. like Cicero, only different) is unhelpful. Considering how markedly unlike any classical dialogue, Latin or Greek, the *Essay* is, the notion of adaptation along 'original lines' is patently inadequate, while the glib explanation that 'Dryden returns to Plato in developing the *mise en scène,* especially for the initial dramatic scene, to lengths further than those favored by Cicero'[2] is unlikely to satisfy any reader who stops to compare the *Essay* with the *Phaedo*, the *Symposium*, or the *Republic*.

Where the California editors have gone astray is in insisting that 'Dryden's debts are classical' (p. 351). The following pages attempt to challenge their assumption, and accordingly my first task is to re-examine the form of the *Essay* and to argue that its structural basis is to be found in the framework of an English, late sixteenth-century collection of tales resourcefully transformed, the inset stories replaced by long speeches. The book in question can best be introduced by a short preamble which must begin by recording the death in 1588 of Dick Tarleton. The demise of this great Elizabethan entertainer did not bring to an end the publication of stories and jests associated with him, and in 1590 'Robin Goodfellow' published two editions of *Tarltons Newes Out of Purgatorie. Onelye Such a Jest as his Jigge, Fit for Gentlemen to Laugh at an Houre* . . . which offers yet another set of Tarleton anecdotes, this time posthumous ones. The narrator claims to have been visited, while asleep, by the spirit of the late comedian, and to have reproduced in his book the stories he was then told about the people Tarleton had met in purgatory, 'Eight scurrilous tales, anti-papal and distinctly bawdy', as Muriel Bradbrook describes them.[3] This astutely promoted publication, recently attributed to Robert Armin, was answered by *The Cobler of Caunterburie. Or an Inuectiue against Tarltons Newes Out of Purgatorie. A Merrier Iest than a Clownes Iigge, and Fitter for Gentlemens Humors* . . . (1590), an entertaining collection of six tales set in a carefully engineered and inventive framework. It is a book that amounts to very much more than a mere answer to *Tarltons Newes*, and, to judge from subsequent reprintings, one that seems to have been more popular than fake Tarleton. *Tarltons Newes* was reprinted in 1630, but the *Inuectiue* against it was reissued in 1608, 1614, 1681 (and probably in 1600), as well as being ineptly adapted in 1630 as *The Tinker of Turvey* and imitated in 1620 by *Westward for Smelts*. But despite this seventeenth-century popularity, its use by Dryden, possibly *The Cobler of Caunterburie's* greatest claim to fame, has passed unrecognised.[4]

Described by Margaret Schlauch, and justly so, as 'a minor anonymous masterpiece',[5] *The Cobler of Caunterburie* is regrettably little known today, perhaps because it has not been fully reprinted since Ouvry's edition of 1862. A summary must therefore be offered, and a summary that concentrates on structure will be pertinent to the argument that follows. The volume opens with a vigorous epistle by the

titular Cobbler, in which he introduces himself somewhat in the
style of Nashe's future Jack Wilton, and offers his book as a desirable
alternative to *Tarltons Newes*. A second, shorter epistle follows,
signed 'Yours in choller, *Robin Goodfellow*', in which Tarleton's
pretended amanuensis in the *Newes Out of Purgatorie* angrily complains about a cobbler turning author. Thus a context of rival literary
factions is established by two preliminary documents before we pass
on to the main body of the text. The work itself begins like this with
the Cobbler as narrator:

> Sitting in the Barge at Billinsgate expecting when the tide
> would serue for Graues-end diuerse passengers of all sorts
> resorted thither to go downe: at last it began to ebbe, and then
> they cryed away when I came to ye staires though I was resolued
> to go downe in a Tilt-boat, yet seeing what a crew of mad com-
> panions went in the Barge and perceiuing by the winde, there
> was no feare of raine, I stept into the Barge and tooke vp my
> seate amongst the thickest: with that the Barge-men put from
> the staires, and hauing a strong ebbe, because there had much raine
> water fallen before, they went the more merrily downe and
> scarce had we gotten beyond Saint Katherines, but that a perrye
> of winde blewe something loude, that the watermen hoyst vp
> sailes, and laide by their Oares from labour. Being thus vnder
> Saile going so smugly downe, it made vs all so merry, that we
> fell to chat, some of one thing and some of another, all of mirth,
> many of knauery . . . (p. 5).

These opening sentences deftly set the scene in a barge going down
the Thames, a host of details lending authenticity to the occasion. As
conversation continues, a Gentleman, whom we may suppose preferred to remain aloof, pulls out a book and starts to read. His sociable
fellow passengers are not to be so easily ignored, and the Cobbler
engages him in conversation by asking what book it is that he is
reading. The reply to this tiresome question is predictable: 'mary
quoth he a foolish toy, called *Tarltons newes out of Purgatorie*'.
The information, unenthusiastically given though it is, immediately
prompts a critical discussion about the merits of the book: 'some
commended it highly, and sayd it was good inuention, and fine
tales: tush quoth another, most of them are stolne out of *Boccace
Decameron*: for all that, quoth the third, it is pretie and wittie'. The
Cobbler (now presented in the third person instead of writing as a

first person narrator) magisterially gives *his* considered opinion: 'Maisters, quoth he, I haue read the booke, and tis indifferent, like a cup of bottle ale, halfe one and halfe the other: but tis not merrie enough for *Tarltons* vaine, nor stuffed with his fine conceits: therefore it shall passe for a booke and no more' (p. 6). As his touchstone of excellence this confidently dismissive critic shows commendable taste in naming 'old father *Chaucer*'; and since, as he says, 'wee are going to Graues-end, and so (I thinke) most of vs to *Canterburie*', the Cobbler's own home town, he proposes that they tell tales 'to passe away the time till we come off the water, and we will call them *Caunterburie* tales' (p. 6). The company agrees, and the Cobbler himself puts his plan into operation by telling the first of these stories. His contribution is followed by five others, and then, on arrival at Gravesend, the enterprising initiator of the scheme makes a further proposal: 'I can (quoth the Cobler) remember—all the tales told on the way, 'and very neere verbatim collect and gather them together: which by the Grace of God gentlemen, I meane to do, and then set them out in a pamphlet vnder mine owne name, as an inuective against *Tarltons newes out of Purgatorie:* and then if you please to send to the *Printer*, I will leaue a token, that euery one of you that told a tale, shall haue a booke for his labor' (p. 83).

The debt to Chaucer extends further than this summary so far indicates. In the first place, each of the six tales is prefaced by a character sketch of the teller written in pastiche Chaucerian verse and modelled on the descriptions of the pilgrims in Chaucer's General Prologue. In the second place, the contention between Chaucer's Reeve and Miller is imitated so as to become a major structural feature in the later work. The Cobbler's opening tale tells how a prior of Canterbury cuckolded a smith, but the passengers on the barge happen to include a Smith, and angered by the Cobbler's tale he responds by relating how a jealous cobbler was cuckolded by none other than a smith. The first two tales, therefore, form a pair, both involving cuckoldry. The next two stories also form a pair. First the Gentleman tells a story of treacherous love in which a naïve Cambridge scholar falls in love with a beautiful but wicked girl from the nearby village of Cherry Hinton. The girl makes a fool of her lover by callously leading him on, and by a particularly cruel trick almost brings about his death from pneumonia, but some years later, after her marriage to another man, the scholar, now more experienced in the ways of the world, gains his revenge by cuckolding her husband and exposing her infidelity. The reply to this harsh, indelicate story comes from a Scholar who tells a touching tale of true love, and in an attempt to raise the tone of the narratives relates the only tale in the collection in which adultery does not occur. His story is of two idealised young lovers separated by various cruel misfortunes. Eventually reunited, they find themselves condemned to death, but as they are about to be burnt at the stake a friend of their parents recognises them, they are reprieved, and a happy ending ensues. The high romance and Mediterranean setting of this elevated tale distinguishes it from the other five, and makes it an admirable contrast to the Gentleman's tale about the Cambridge scholar and the heartless girl from Cherry Hinton.

The final two stories also form a pair, with the tellers both recalling Chaucerian figures, and with both of them telling stories that hinge on the use of clever excuses in an adulterous situation. First of all an Old Wife, clearly related to Chaucer's Wife of Bath, tells a triangular story about a husband, a wife, and the wife's lover: the clever wife tricks her wary husband by persuading him that he was drunk at the time when he thought he had discovered her infidelity. A Summoner, the last of the passengers to tell a tale, thinks it appropriate that he should conclude the series since he practises the same profession as one of Chaucer's pilgrims and since *The Canterbury Tales* has, from the outset, furnished a model for their entertainment on the barge. He also tells about a husband, a wife, and the wife's lover, but this time, as befits a male narrator, it is the lover who cleverly dupes the husband. (In accordance with *fabliaux* conventions, husbands are the butts of male and female narrators alike.) And because the series of tales began with one about a prior, the Summoner thinks it suitable to come full circle by telling a story about an abbot, the abbot taking the role of the resourceful lover. But while the clever wife in the previous story persuaded her husband that he was drunk, the abbot in this story goes one stage further and persuades the husband that he was actually dead and has been revived.

The structure within which the six stories are framed is a lively and attractive one articulated with intelligence and skill. Reduced to its simplest outline it can be conveniently represented by a summary diagram

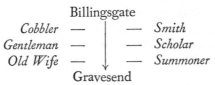

Billingsgate

| Cobbler | — | — | Smith |
| Gentleman | — | — | Scholar |
| Old Wife | — | — | Summoner |

Gravesend

Unity is given by the focus on cuckoldry, with the exceptional Scholar's tale only sharpening the impression by so deliberately diverging from the pattern. And while the river journey suggests progress, a satisfying sense of completion is also conveyed by terminal recapitulation when a story about an abbot at the end of the sequence matches a story about a prior at the beginning, and when the Chaucerian allusions of the last two story-tellers remind us of the model initially proposed by the Cobbler.

With this summary in mind, the structure of Dryden's *Essay of Dramatick Poesie* can be profitably looked at afresh. First of all there is a general similarity in situation linking the Elizabethan story collection and the Restoration dialogue. In both works a small group of people from London is travelling by barge on the Thames, and although both works are largely taken up with recording the words supposed to have been spoken during that journey, each author takes care, in his own way, to establish the occasion in a lively manner.[6] The opening of Dryden's *Essay*, set against the menacing boom of distant gunfire, is too well known for there to be any need to quote from it here; and the opening of *The Cobler of Caunterburie* has only just been quoted. In both books informal conversation at the beginning leads to more formalised discourse in which the speakers speak at length, uninterrupted, and according to a set plan, and in both books it is discussion about bad literature that gives rise to this more formal discourse. In *The Cobler of Caunterburie* bad literature is represented by *Tarltons Newes Out of Purgatorie*, and in Dryden's *Essay* by the 'ill verses' that are sure to be written to celebrate the English naval victory off Lowestoft. The same number of long speeches is found in both works, and, like the author of *The Cobler of Caunterburie*, Dryden organises his in three answering pairs that provide the vehicle for three debates:

*Ancients* v. *Moderns*
*French* v. *English*
*blank verse* v. *rhyme*

Like the Cobbler, Dryden is both participant (Neander) and presenter, but by presenting himself as Neander he avoids the awkward change from first person to third person narration that jolts the reader of *The Cobler of Caunterburie*. The difficulty of combining reportage and participation is a problem never really solved by the author of the earlier book. Dryden not only copes without difficulty in this respect, but even exploits the situation when as author he allows his spokesman Neander to appear slightly ridiculous in the final paragraph. Lastly, both works begin with a conflict, and although there is an enormous difference in scale between the naval battle of the *Essay* and the merely verbal altercation between the Cobbler and 'Robin Goodfellow', I hope to show later that the basic issue is much the same.

For all that the connexion between the two books is a substantial one, Dryden can certainly not be accused of following his source blindly. For instance, he took the setting for his debates from *The Cobler of Caunterburie*, but the chattily inconsequential, dateless information of the Cobbler he excitingly replaced by a superb evocation of a memorable historical occasion. The transformation is as remarkably inventive in its inception as it is in its execution. But the outstanding alteration is, of course, the substitution of debate speeches for stories. The conceptual shift involved in this change, however, was less violent than the modern reader might at first suppose, for the vocabulary of Dryden's time tends to blur the distinction. Dryden refers to his *Essay* as 'discourse' on more than one occasion: 'I confess I find many things in this Discourse which I do not now approve' he warns Lord Buckhurst; the short preface 'To the Reader' begins by referring in a wittily nautical image to 'The *drift of the ensuing Discourse*'; and in the *Essay* itself the conversation of the four men is regularly termed 'discourse'. It is a word that recalls Corneille's 'Discours des trois unités' and 'Discours du poëme dramatique', to which the *Essay* is much indebted. But 'discourse' is also the word used in the 1620 translation of the *Decameron* to refer to the inset *novelle* when the Induction is headed 'The Induction of the Author, to the Following Discourses'. Similarly, in the 1654 translation of the *Heptaméron* we read that Marguerite de Navarre '*hath surpassed* Boccace *in the elegant Discourses which she hath made on every one of her Accounts*'.[7] For Dryden, the word *discourse* applied equally well to either a narration (OED *sb.* 4) or an argument (OED *sb.* 3), or even to a whole treatise (e.g. the *Essay* itself: OED *sb.* 5), and since the one term covered all these forms the switch from paired narrative to debate would have been more easily made then than now.[8]

The noisy, confident, 'merie cobler', 'the quaintest Squire in all Kent', 'iudiciall Censor of other mens writings', is very much the central, cohesive figure in *The Cobler of Caunterburie*, a robust, red-faced, bald-headed man never at a loss for words. It is he who discovers that one of the passengers is reading *Newes Out of Purgatorie*, and it is he who offers the most authoritative judgement on that unfortunate book. It is the Cobbler who proposes the telling of tales, and who tells the first of them ('I myselfe will be ring-leader'). It is the Cobbler again who undertakes to write down the tales and have them printed. As an interloper in the literary world, brash, energetic, and aggressive, he is a new man, a neander, but it is a very different figure from Dryden's Neander that this upstart presents. Adopting a totally different tone, Dryden's dedicatory epistle refers modestly to the *Essay* (a modest title in itself) as 'an amusement', admits its 'rude and indigested manner', apologises for 'many errours', and discloses that the principal object in publishing it is merely to stimulate Lord Buckhurst's literary activities: 'I confess I have no greater reason, in addressing this Essay to your Lordship, then that it might awaken in you the desire of writing something, in whatever kind it be, which might be an honour to our Age and Country' (p. 5). It is the aristocratic Eugenius, probably a portrait of Buckhurst himself, who proposes the debate, and who earlier breaks the 'strict silence' on the barge to congratulate the rest on 'that happy Omen of our Nations Victory' as the sound of gunfire recedes. It is at the invitation of Eugenius that Neander first addresses his three companions. The barge, and the definition of a play, are provided by the francophile Lisideius who thus supplies the indispensable bases for both the journey and the debates. Crites, 'a person of a sharp judgment, and somewhat too delicate a taste in wit', censorious critic of 'ill verses' and objector to Lisideius's definition, is perhaps the most vividly drawn of the four men, and the one most like the Cobbler. He is the first to speak in the formal debate. Neander does not dominate socially in the way that the Cobbler does. We could, for example, never make even a fleeting comparison between Neander and Shakespeare's Bottom, though such a comparison would not be entirely wide of the mark in the case of the Cobbler.

Apart from concurring in general decisions, Neander makes no contribution until the others have all spoken at length and until invited to speak by Eugenius. When he eventually makes his *début*, in answer to Lisideius, he speaks only 'after a little pause', and when he later answers Crites he is careful (unlike Crites himself on other occasions) not to interrupt. We can imagine Neander rather ill at ease in the company of persons whose 'witt and Quality have made known to all the Town', his social awkwardness being amusingly caught at the end of the *Essay* when he pursues his 'Discourse so eagerly, that *Eugenius* had call'd to him twice or thrice ere he took notice that the Barge stood still' (p. 80). But Neander's clumsy failure to fit his discourse elegantly and unaffectedly into the time allotted him, and, worse still, his insensitive lack of awareness that the barge had become stationary, enable Dryden to draw attention unostentatiously to the larger authorial skill in the contrivance of the framework.[9] As Dryden mentions Eugenius's unavailing attempts to attract Neander's attention, attempts which Dryden would not have known about were he at this point entirely identified with Neander, there is a useful separation between reporter and participant. The readily apparent social failure is deliberately achieved by Dryden's less immediately obvious yet all-embracing artistic control, and serves to make palatable the overriding point that it is Neander who had won the last two debates. Furthermore, the absurdity of Neander's speech overrunning while he is actually recommending rhyme as a means of circumscribing the over-luxuriant fancy, renders pleasantly acceptable his smart observation, which might otherwise have seemed too self congratulatory, that second thoughts are usually best 'as receiving the maturest digestion from judgment' (p. 80), a general proposition of some significance since Neander has spoken second in both of the last two debates. The Cobbler dominated by thrusting himself forward, but Dryden, in his own person and through his spokesman, Neander, establishes himself by more subtle means. Neander's victory in the war of opinions reflects something of the Cobbler's vindication of himself from the disparaging onslaught of 'Robin Goodfellow', and mirrors the English victory in the naval engagement that 'had allarm'd the Town' on that July afternoon; but the Cobbler's unsophisticated assertiveness is dispensed with. 'Their wit', wrote Dryden of the Elizabethans, 'was not that of gentlemen; there was ever somewhat that was ill-bred and clownish in it.'[10] His own age he sees as an age of 'gallantry and civility', though he well knew how often it fell short of its ideals. 'Dryden intends to show that literary debates can be conducted with candour and civility' explains Donald Davie, echoing Dryden's own words. I do not agree with Davie that 'It cannot be said that he succeeds.'[11] As early as 1661, Robert Boyle had, in his dialogue *The Sceptical Chymist, or, Chymico-Physical Doubts and Paradoxes*, employed 'a style more fashionable than that of mere scholars is wont to be', and deliberately provided 'an example how to manage even disputes with civility; whence perhaps some readers will be assisted to discern a difference betwixt bluntness of speech and strength of reason, and to find that a man may be a champion for truth without being an enemy to civility; and may confute an opinion without railing at them that hold it'.[12] Dryden attempts to set before literary critics an example like that which Boyle provided for natural scientists. And, like *The Sceptical Chymist*, Dryden's *Essay* is 'a book written by a gentleman, and wherein only gentlemen are introduced as speakers', neither ill-bred nor clownish.

It will have been noticed that Crites and Neander speak twice in the debates, Lisideius and Eugenius only once, and this disparity shows up another modification that Dryden made to the structure that he found in *The Cobler of Caunterburie*. Because the six narrators are replaced by only four debaters, two of Dryden's cast have to speak twice. The arrangement that he arrives at is plausible enough, with the two more urbane characters speaking only once, and the two others showing less restraint. In each of the debates the second speaker has the advantage, and thus it is Neander-Dryden and Eugenius-Buckhurst who occupy the three winning positions:

*Crites* v. *Eugenius*
*Lisideius* v. *Neander*
*Crites* v. *Neander*

Dryden's use of a smaller body of speakers than is to be found in his source has the effect of pulling the *Essay* more tightly together than it would be were the simple and obviously schematised debate structure not cross grained with an apparently more natural interplay between characters.

One last difference that calls for comment is the distinction between a single and a return journey. The Cobbler and his 'mad companions' go down river from Billingsgate to Gravesend; the four men of Dryden's *Essay* make a journey down river and then return to Somerset Stairs. Both books are shaped by having endings that hark back to the beginning, and both have a progressive element. In *The Cobler of Caunterburie* it is the final inset stories that recall the opening, while the movement of the barge indicates progress, an arrangement that gives importance to the journey and pattern to the story-telling. But while the journey is important to the travellers, it is of no consequence to the reader, and the patterning of the stories though pleasing is ultimately pointless. In the *Essay* the functions are rightly reversed, so that the river journey neatly rounds off the book by concluding where it began, while the truly important inset debates supply the progressive element as one subject leads to another and the debates shift from broader to narrower discriminations: the *Ancients* v. *Moderns* debate followed by a debate discriminating among the *Moderns,* and the *French* v. *English* debate followed by a debate about just one aspect of dramatic composition. Dryden happily put the logical momentum into the discourses and relegated the formal patterning to the underlying river journey, a journey that gets nowhere but serves a literary function by providing a context for the discussion on board the barge.

A return journey (as opposed to a single journey) has three significant moments: the beginning, the end, and the turning point. The importance of London, the city threatened by the Dutch fleet, is emphasised in the *Essay* by its being the beginning and end of the journey. The turning point divides both the journey and the *Essay* into two parts. The down river trip is largely silent, the atmosphere on the barge tense. But eventually, after it is realised that the Dutch fleet is retreating, conversation flows, at first unrestrained, in the now relaxed atmosphere. Gradually the talk becomes less miscellaneous, and an issue arises when Crites and Eugenius disagree about the respective merits of ancient and modern literature. For the purposes of argument they agree to 'limit their Dispute to *Dramatique Poesie*', and Lisideius provides further discipline by supplying a definition of a play. It is at this signal moment that the order is given 'to the Water-men to turn their Barge', and the sequence of six long speeches that occupy the return journey begins (p. 15). Thus three stages are represented on the excursion: 1. silence while the men are apprehensive and the fate of England is uncertain; 2. lively but initially undisciplined conversation prompted by the removal of fear and expressing relief and elation ('the Muses . . . ever follow peace'), this gradually leading to . . . 3. an artful, settled, structured series of debates dependent upon agreed limitations and the acceptance of the authority of a workable even if 'not altogether perfect' definition, and dependent also upon the confidence that stems from the naval victory and a consequent sense of national security.[13] Cultural activity depends upon peace, but it is only when the first adolescent excitement is organised in artful discipline that full cultural maturity is achieved. The turning point on the journey draws attention to the change between the third stage of development and the earlier immature phases, and on the return trip the frightening noise of cannon fire is replaced by its civilised counterpart, verbal contest between friends. Like the naval battle, the war of opinions also leads to an English victory, so that Neander brings back to London another victory to complement the one that is already being celebrated there, while Dryden as author of the whole *Essay*, supplies an example of cultural behaviour to set before his fellow writers.[14] The claim that Dryden had 'no greater reason, in addressing this Essay to your Lordship, then that it might awaken in you the desire of writing something, in whatever kind it be, which might be an honour to our Age and Country' (p. 5) is not false. It flatters Lord Buckhurst in its suggestion of exclusiveness, but Dryden's wish to promote writing that 'might be an honour to our Age and Country' is genuine.

Almost thirty years ago, George Williamson showed that Dryden's *Essay* undertook, among other things, to defend England against the slighting strictures of Samuel Sorbière.[15] The honour of his 'Age and Country' is one of Dryden's main preoccupations in the *Essay*. In 1663 Sorbière, Louis XIV's historiographer, had been courteously received by the newly incorporated Royal Society, and generally entertained by English intellectuals. On his return to France he published an arrogant and ill-informed account of what he had observed of English life, and this *Relation d'un voyage en Angleterre où sont touchées plusieurs choses qui regardent l'état des sciences, et de la religion, et autres matières curieuses* (Paris 1664) angered his late hosts so much that Thomas Sprat interrupted his writing of a history of the Royal Society, a project that was in itself a celebration and commendation of the new life of Restoration London as expressed in the aims and methods of the Society, to reply to Sorbière's ungracious publication with some *Observations on Monsieur de Sorbier's Voyage into England. Written to Dr Wren, Professor of Astronomy in Oxford* (1665). Wren, who happened to be visiting Paris in 1665, is addressed not only because he was the most impressive representative of contemporary English intellectual life, a Restoration complete man prodigiously successful in many spheres, frequently praised for his modesty, but also, presumably, because he was the unofficial title-holder in what amounted to an Anglo-French mathematical contest. In 1658 Pascal had challenged English geometers to solve a problem, and it was Wren who had met the challenge by proposing constructions from which the solution could be derived. He then counterchallenged with a problem originally formulated by Kepler, and to which the French savants had no reply, so it was indeed suitable that 'Thomas Sprat, Fellow of the Royal Society', as he proudly styles himself on the title-page, should address his *Observations* to his colleague Christopher Wren.[16] Among the wide range of issues that Sprat took up, Sorbière's disparaging remarks about English drama are vigorously refuted. Dryden, too, responds to Sorbière's disparagement of English drama in the second of the *Essay*'s three debates, but it is not only when Neander replies to Lisideius that Dryden answers Sorbière. As a riposte to the complaint that the English are 'very much united amongst themselves against Strangers'[17] the final paragraph of the *Essay* shows the French community in London enthusiastically celebrating the victory of their adopted country by dancing in the streets. There can be no doubt about the French *émigrés'* wholehearted identification with English aspirations. In *Annus Mirabilis* Dryden had already contrasted Louis and Charles,

> Lewis *had chas'd the* English *from his shore;*
> *But* Charles *the* French *as Subjects does invite*
>
> (stanza 43)

and boasted that

> *Were Subjects so but onely by their choice,*
> *And not from Birth did forc'd Dominion take,*
> *Our Prince alone would have the publique voice;*
> *And all his Neighbours Realms would desarts make.*
>
> (stanza 44)

In the *Essay* Dryden neatly shows this to be so by his inclusion of the description of a 'crowd of *French* people' dancing outside the Savoy where Charles had granted them regular use of the chapel.[18]

In other ways, too, the *Essay* replies to Sorbière's *Relation*. In response to his observation of an aggressive attitude in England towards the Dutch, we see a telling example of Dutch aggression, the naval battle itself; and as a comment on Sorbière's claim that English naval power had declined, Dryden gives us an English naval victory.[19] Sorbière's criticism that the English are lacking in eloquence is magnificently refuted by the eloquence of the speeches that Dryden professes to be recording in the *Essay*, while the serious nature of the subject matter of that eloquence makes nonsense of the contention that the learned men of England are not communicative.[20] Perhaps Dryden claims more for England than Sprat had. Sprat confessed that 'we yield to the *French* in the Beauty of their *Cities*, and *Palaces*'[21] and while Dryden attempts no defence of London's architecture—a

city devastated by fire when the *Essay* was published, but with ambitious plans for rebuilding ('New deifi'd she from her fires does
rise', *Annus Mirabilis*, line 1178)—his references to Somerset Stairs
and to 'the *Piazze*' at Covent Garden, which even Sorbière compared
favourably with the *Place-Royale* (*la place des Vosges*), modestly
indicate that London is not without architectural interest.²² It is as a
whole, then, that the *Essay* parries the verbal onslaught from France,
and it does this as determinedly as the navy is shown to have re-
pulsed the Dutch attack by sea, and as adroitly as an executioner
'who separates the head from the body, and leaves it standing in its
place' or as a satirist who makes 'a man appear a fool, a blockhead,
or a knave, without using any of those opprobrious terms'.²³ Dryden,
well able to follow Boyle's advice and 'confute an opinion without
railing at them that hold it', exposes Sorbière's conceited book as the
maladroit impertinence of a slow witted ignoramus, without demeaning
himself by so much as a single allusion to its author. We cannot help
observing that Sprat's straightforward, angry rejoinder to Sorbière is,
in comparison, 'a plain piece of work, a bare hanging'.²⁴ Dryden's
response is oblique, just as Wren's response was to Pascal's problem.

Writing of the structure of English plays, Sorbière offensively
explained that the English 'do not matter tho' it be a Hodch Potch,
for they say, they mind only the Parts as they come on one after
another, and have no regard to the whole composition'.²⁵ Sorbière's
English readers must have found the arrogance of this remark even
more offensive in view of the rambling, formless nature of the book
in which it appeared. With nonchalant suavity Louis's historiographer had presumed that his reader would 'take some pleasure in the
Irregularity of my Stile, and be glad to hear my Notions and Adven-
tures: I desire therefore that you would not expect any Method or
Ornament in my Writing, but be pleased with the Freedom of my
Thoughts upon some very Important Subjects which fall in among
the Trifles I shall recount unto you'.²⁶ Despite an apology for the
'rude and indigested manner' of his *Essay*, for Dryden, too, can display modest *politesse*, Dryden's work is the very opposite of formless.

There is wit in Dryden's choice of the dialogue, a quasi dramatic
form, for an enquiry into dramatic poesy, and there is even greater
wit in the use of that form to respond to Sorbière's specific criticism
of English plays. Sorbière had complained about the neglect of the
unities;²⁷ Neander points out that English dramatists prefer liveliness

to the statuesque perfection that servile observation of the unities can give. But that English writers are quite capable of observing the unities when they think it appropriate to do so is brilliantly demonstrated by the achievement of the *Essay* itself which triumphantly mocks the rules by simultaneously observing and flouting them, leaving legalistic pedants bewildered whether to scold or applaud. Thus unity of place is provided by the barge, but because the barge is a moving vehicle there is continuous *variety* of place, though by beginning and ending in London the moving barge can be described, in one sense, as having made no progress. Furthermore, Dryden's choice of place, and the decision to adapt the river journey of *The Cobler of Caunterburie*, wittily cocks a snook at Sorbière's complaint that English authors 'frequently never cite the Books from whence they Borrow, and so their Copies are taken for Originals'.[28] Sorbière had sailed from Calais to Dover, and then, instead of proceeding by coach directly to London, as he could have done, went to Canterbury. From there he travelled overland to Gravesend, 'where for the greater Expedition, I took the Boat, and the Opportunity of the Tide', to London.[29] Dryden has, therefore, found in *The Cobler of Caunterburie*, where the travellers go by boat to Gravesend and then on by road to Canterbury, a 'voyage' complementary to Sorbière's to supply the formal basis for his reply, and then by citing Plato and Cicero has teasingly planted promising looking clues that source hunters three centuries later are still pursuing down the false trail of the classical dialogue.

Unity of time is strictly observed in the *Essay* in so far as the action is continuous and confined to a few hours; but although the excursion is composed of two parts of equal distance (the journey there and the journey back), the turning point is very obviously not placed so as to come half way through the *Essay*. The first tenth, approximately, of the *Essay* describes a largely silent journey down the river, while the remaining nine tenths reproduce the words spoken on the way back. The two halves are grossly disproportionate, but as Lisideius, who admires French observance of the unities, explains, 'some parts of the action [of a play may be] more fit to be represented, some to be related' (p. 40). Dryden's transition from a foreshortened time scale to something like real time in no way disconcerts the reader, especially since a down-river journey, with the current, may plausibly be rapid ('made haste to shoot the Bridge', page 8), while a leisurely progress up stream, against the current, will be slower. In a finely paced sentence that by its syntactical movement gently establishes a leisurely stroke, the watermen are asked to 'row softly' so that their passengers 'might take the cool of the Evening in their return' (p. 15). Once again, the pedant who seeks to determine whether unity is or is not observed according to the rules finds himself confounded by a nicely balanced instance of Dryden having it both ways. Dryden's treatment of unity of action similarly mocks the rules. The naval battle and victory celebrations can be thought of as a sub-plot, or 'under-plot' to use Lisideius's term, related thematically to a main plot in which the participants are Lisideius himself and the three men with whom he shares a barge; thematically linked because in both plots England successfully strives to vindicate her honour. Furthermore, sub-plot decorously mirrors main plot in its nautical setting. Like the vigorous, upstart cobbler seeking to set up as author in spite of the professional disapproval of the literary establishment as represented by 'Robin Goodfellow', the English fleet in Dryden's *Essay* defies European naval power, Neander defies French rules, and Dryden himself debunks Sorbière. But is it, after all, appropriate to distinguish between a sub-plot and a main plot when one grows out of the other, and when it is difficult to say which grows out of which? Is the naval engagement not perhaps better thought of as the main plot? Or perhaps, after all, the action is single? Certainly Lisideius would have found Dryden's presentation of the battle 'both convenient and beautiful':

> But there is another sort of Relations, that is, of things hapning in the Action of the Play, and suppos'd to be done behind the Scenes: and this is many times both convenient and beautiful: for, by it, the *French* avoid the tumult, to which we are subject in *England*, by representing Duells, Battells, and the like; which renders our Stage too like the Theaters where they fight Prizes.
>
> (p. 39)

That Dryden knows how to 'avoid the tumult' the *Essay* itself demonstrates, though the word 'avoid', with its suggestion of manifestly deliberate strategy, fails to do justice to the grace of Dryden's art. The delight of the *Essay* lies not in arresting contrivance, but in *sprezzatura*.

## II

So far I have described a structure in which a sequence of three debates is contained within a private river excursion, and in which the river excursion is itself framed, in turn, in the context of the public events of 'that memorable day'. I have tried to show too that the *Essay* is not, in essence, a series of debates, attractively packaged in wrappings that must eventually be discarded before we engage with what is really important—some supposed core of meaning stated in the debates themselves; but that, like an onion, the *Essay* is composed of layers that are themselves the necessary substance of the whole. Even this comparison is a dangerous one, however. To strip away the layers of an onion is to be left with a smaller and smaller onion; to reduce Dryden's *Essay* by a similar process is to destroy it instantly, for the *Essay* depends upon the exhilaratingly patterned interplay between constituent parts which coalesce in an organic whole. Peeling an onion reduces its bulk, not its complexity or flavour.

These are suitable remarks to make before reminding the reader that the outermost frame of the *Essay* is not provided by the account of the events of 3 June, 1665. Dryden's dedicatory letter, which precedes the relation of those events in the physical make up of the book, presents his work as the product of an enforced retreat into the country in time of plague, and as a communication to Lord Buckhurst prompted by a serious patriotic purpose. Both the account of the circumstances of composition, and the decision to address Lord Buckhurst personally are important features, and it is to them that we should now turn. Once again the relationship between frame and inset is significant, a significance that is by no means limited to the obvious connexion between the framing figures of author and dedicatee and the two successful debaters of the inset who represent them, Eugenius and Neander.

The years 1665 and 1666 revealed the new and exciting life of Restoration London to be a precarious affair, subject, despite all its energy and brilliance, to the onslaught of plague, fire, and foreign foe. A frightening alternative from the recent past heightened the sense of alarm, while feelings of guilt, whether for present ungodliness or previous regicide, fostered a sense of insecurity whenever confidence faltered. When Dryden wrote his *Essay*, London society had been forced to disperse, and the theatres, which symbolised the

new spirit more strikingly than any other aspect of Restoration life,
were closed. The time was not a reassuring one. Dryden took advantage of his retirement to take stock, and the *Essay* is, in part, a nostalgic
evocation of all that was best in those years immediately following
the re-establishment of the monarchy. But the nostalgia is not just
wistful languishing among purling brooks. The *Essay* is both an
energetic recreation that provides a lively memorial to the achievement of half a decade, and, at the same time, an original creation that
resourcefully provided an imaginative substitute for the way of
life frustrated by 'the violence of the last Plague'. The 'violence'of
the plague had 'driven' Dryden from London, but Dryden in rural
exile, as determined as the English fleet when attacked by the Dutch,
builds with the triumphant permanence of art a lovingly realised
London of the mind. Even more challengingly, the *Essay* seems to
have been a deliberate attempt to raise morale by depicting England
at a moment of cultural and military victory; and in its incitement of
Buckhurst to write, and its pretense that the ideal discourse on the
barge is faithful to the actuality of London life, looks to an even more
glorious future when men will proudly serve their country through
the practice of writing, and when the art of civilised discourse will be
such that what was once a courtly ideal will have become an accepted
norm.

It was in the summer of 1667, the summer when Dryden published the *Essay*, that the Treaty of Breda brought the Second Dutch
War to an inglorious end after a series of naval disasters. The battle
off Lowestoft, it is true, had been a handsome English victory, but
by noting only the first 'happy Omen of our Nations Victory', the
sound of retreating gun fire, Dryden avoids any reference to the
failure to consolidate the defeat of the Dutch by destroying their
entire fleet in a vigorous pursuit. A month after Lowestoft an attack
on Dutch ships sheltering in Bergen failed wretchedly, while the
two following summers each produced further naval disasters for
England: in 1666 the resounding defeat of the Four Days' Battle in the
Channel, and in 1667 the final humiliation of a successful Dutch raid
on Chatham harbour when ships of the line were burnt at their
moorings, the flagship captured and towed away, and the Thames
shown to be patently open so that London itself could have been
bombarded. During the autumn of 1667 and the spring of 1668 the
mismanagement of the war was to be debated in the Commons, and
it was in this context that Dryden published his account of the events

of 'that memorable day' when England triumphed at sea and in debate. It seems likely that the publication of the *Essay* so that it would be read in the late summer and autumn of 1667 was calculated to boost national morale.

Dryden's reference to the disastrous epidemic of bubonic plague which raged in London in 1665 is usually taken to be a purely topical allusion opening up no wider significance. But the habitual mode of Dryden's poetry and prose is one of suggestive allusiveness, and, as Achsah Guibbory has observed in a study of Dryden's views of history, Dryden likes to locate 'his subjects within a historical framework through allusions which are, in fact, historical parallels'.[30] Just such a historical parallel is provided by the plague reference, and the allusion is one, I suggest, that expands the *Essay*'s meaning in the mode characteristic of Dryden's writings. The 'last Plague' finds its parallel in the notorious outbreak that occurred in Florence in 1348, and which Boccaccio described so horrifyingly in the Induction to his *Decameron*. Like Boccaccio's 'seven honourable ladies, and three noble gentlemen' who left plague-stricken Florence for the wholesome countryside, Dryden left London; and like *The Cobler of Caunterburie*, from which Dryden derived the form of his Thames debates, the *Decameron* is a framework collection of tales or 'discourses'. The link between the *Essay* and the *Decameron* is both direct and indirect for *The Cobler of Caunterburie*, which constitutes an indirect link, is itself considerably indebted to Boccaccio's collection, notwithstanding the objection raised to *Tarltons Newes* by one of the Cobbler's fellow passengers that most of its stories 'are stolne out of *Boccace Decameron*'.[31] In fact, *The Cobler of Caunterburie* is open to just that charge.[32] There are, however, two closely connected motives not found in the Elizabethan collection which Dryden has taken over directly from Boccaccio, and disconnected from each other. Flight from a plague-stricken city to a country retreat is one, and associated by Dryden with the story of how he came to write the *Essay*, while a series of framed 'discourses' spoken by supposedly real people, their identities deliberately hidden by pseudonyms,[33] is the other, and a model, in combination with *The Cobler of Caunterburie*, for the ordering of the primary events which the *Essay* apparently recalls. The conflicting claims of two framework collections, the *Decameron* and *The Cobler of Caunterburie*, are cleverly resolved in the *Essay* by the use of a double frame, but because *The Cobler of Caunterburie* is itself derived from the *Decameron*, the conflict is a temporary difficulty and affects only Dryden's opening. The combination of war and plague, and, indeed, of reported speeches as well, may suggest yet another literary parallel, but if Dryden remembered Thucydides's vivid description of plague-stricken Athens in the second year of the Peloponnesian War he does not encourage readers of the *Essay* to pursue the parallel.

At the end of his *Essay* where an allusion to the end of the *Decameron* provides a suitable conclusion, Dryden contrives a neat fusion by transferring the Boccaccio allusion to the inset account of the events of 3 June. In this way, the *Decameron* frame is completed without any harking back to the circumstances attending the writing of the *Essay*. One implication following from this is that any notion that Dryden wrote the *Essay* with its present ending and then, at a later stage, added a dedicatory letter not previously envisaged must be rejected out of hand, no matter how well supported by Dryden's hoary old bluff about finding the *Essay* while looking through his 'loose Papers'. The 'loose Papers' topos is a stock formula included for reasons of decorous modesty. Clearly, the final paragraph and the dedicatory letter were written with each other in mind.

Dryden's terminal allusion to the *Decameron* might easily pass unnoticed were it not that expectations arising from a symmetrical structure alert the reader to its presence. Boccaccio, it will be remembered, records that his story-tellers returned 'to Florence, where the three Gentlemen left the seven Ladies at the Church of Santa Maria Novella, from whence they went with them at the first. And having parted with kinde salutations, the Gentlemen went whether themselves best pleased, and the Ladies repaired home to their houses' (vol. iv, p. 312). Dryden's final sentence is a witty variation of this. His company returns to the city from which it set out, and lands at Somerset Stairs. 'Walking thence together to the *Piazze* they parted there; *Eugenius* and *Lisideius* to some pleasant appointment they had made, and *Crites* and *Neander* to their several Lodgings' (p. 81). Rather as Boccaccio's ladies go dutifully home, while the men went freely 'whether themselves best pleased', Dryden's two less courtly characters (the two who had spoken twice in the debates) return to their lodgings while the more aristocratic pair proceed 'to some pleasant appointment', Boccaccio's innuendo becoming slightly broader in Dryden's version. Dryden's choice of the fashionable *Piazza* at Covent Garden as the point of dispersal combines a reference to Italy with a convincing piece of social realism. In conjunction with this allusion it may also be that the *al fresco* dancing of the French people which Dryden's four men witness on their moonlit walk from the barge is intended to recall the songs and dances with which Boccaccio's Florentines concluded each day as described, for instance, in the passage immediately preceding the account of the return to Florence.

The framing allusions to the *Decameron* provide a delicate means for Dryden to make certain large claims. In the first place, they help to project the exemplary character of the *Essay*, as becomes apparent if we recall the title of the 1620 English translation of the *Decameron*, a title that styles it *The Modell of Wit, Mirth, Eloquence and Conversation*. Just such a model is afforded by the *Essay*. But more important even than the presentation of the *Essay* as a new *Decameron*, is the alignment of Renaissance Florence and Restoration London.

Before Dryden's time, Englishmen looking towards the cities of Italy were dazzled above all by the lustre of Venice, while after Dryden's time it was increasingly the civilisation of Florence that they admired. According to J. R. Hale, the shift in emphasis can be seen for the first time in James Howell's *A German Diet* (1653), an ingeniously structured collection of debates written by Dryden's predecessor in the office of Historiographer Royal.[34] But whatever the truth of Hale's precise assertion, the esteem of Florence as the city where preeminently the new learning had flourished had always been recognised.[35] Its cultural achievements were to endure with a permanence denied the transitory political success of any other Italian city. Florence was also distinguished as the seminal city from which Renaissance thinking spread through Italy, to France, and to England. It is the names of three Florentines, Dante, Petrarch, and Boccaccio, that we, like Dryden, associate most immediately with the new impetus, and in many respects it is Boccaccio, biographer of Dante and scholar of his works, close friend of Petrarch, who is the most representative early Renaissance figure. The *Decameron* is, of course, Boccaccio's most considerable work.

The preeminence of Florence is intimately connected with its role in the establishment of the Italian language. It was the writers of Florence who refined the Tuscan dialect to produce a literary language; and the reputation of the *Decameron* rests, as much as upon anything, on its linguistic elegance. Boccaccio's concern for this aspect of his work is a concern he shares with Dryden, for, like Boccaccio, Dryden saw the refinement of the language as being the particular responsibility of his own time. Both men had the advantage of being able to build on the work of an earlier generation, so that just as 'Dante had begun to file their language, at least in verse', and I use Dryden's own words, so had the poets Waller and Denham initiated a process of linguistic refinement in England. 'The reformation of their prose was wholly owing to Boccace himself, which is yet the standard of purity in the Italian language', recorded Dryden at the end of his life, and the *Essay* may surely be seen as an attempt to set up a similar 'standard of purity' for English prose.[36] Such an approach explains why Dryden went to the uncharacteristic trouble of correcting points of language when he revised the text for the edition of 1684. But to present the *Essay* as a model comparable in mid-seventeenth-century England with that provided by the *Decameron* in *trecento* Italy is to make a very considerable claim, one better made, as Dryden seems to have realised, by suggestive implication than by crudely categorical assertion. In the Preface to the *Fables* Dryden chooses to compare Boccaccio and Chaucer, but this should not blind us to a possible comparison between Boccaccio and Dryden himself.

   The state of the English language was inextricably bound up, for Dryden, with the defence of England from French sneers, Dutch naval power, natural calamity, and bad writing. His sense of patriotism is very much in the spirit of Renaissance humanism, and he would certainly have agreed, for instance, with what Milton had to say in a letter (10 September 1638) to the Florentine philologist, Benedetto Bonmatthei:

> Nor is it to be considered of small consequence what language, pure or corrupt, a people has, or what is their customary degree of propriety in speaking it. . . . For, let the words of a country be in part debased by wear and wrongly uttered, and what do they declare, but, by no light indication, that the inhabitants of that country are an indolent, idly-yawning race, with minds already long prepared for any amount of servility? On the other hand, we have never heard that any empire, any state did not flourish moderately at least as long as liking and care for its language lasted.

Milton even suggests that the fall of Athens 'and its low and obscure condition followed on the general vitiation of its usage in the matter of speech'.[37]

Boccaccio's celebration of Florentine life and Dryden's celebration of London life afford another point of comparison. Just as the *Decameron* is suffused with the new spirit of Boccaccio's Florence, even while the Black Death brings about its near collapse, so Dryden's *Essay* celebrates the new and threatened life of 'The Metropolis of Great Britain, the Most Renowned And Late Flourishing City of London', to quote the dedication of *Annus Mirabilis*, a poem prompted by thoughts similar to those which lie behind the *Essay*. Dryden's use of local colour evokes not only London, however, but reaches out towards Italy also. The references to Somerset Stairs and Covent Garden at the end of the *Essay* seem particularly well calculated to display the London of the mid 1660s as the possible inheritor of the Italian Renaissance tradition. The splendid, monumental portico of Corinthian columns which Inigo Jones had built onto the west end of St Paul's Cathedral, begun in 1635, was the most imposing example of building in the Italian manner in London, but the destruction of the body of the cathedral by fire in 1666 made any reference to it unsuitable, given that Dryden's object was to raise morale. The unhappy regicide associations of the Banqueting House at Whitehall rendered yet another important building unsuitable for mention; but both Somerset Stairs and Covent Garden were without taint, and lay west of the area destroyed by the Fire. Both are remarkable examples of Inigo Jones's use of classical forms, and fit without strain in the slight narrative thread of the *Essay*.

Covent Garden, built during the 1630s, was the first geometrically laid out urban space to be designed in England. Thirty years later, in the 1660s, it was still unique. St Paul's Church, on the west side of the square, was a particularly important building, the first post-Reformation church to be erected in London on a new site. Inigo Jones had responded vigorously to the Earl of Bedford's commission to provide a parish church as cheaply as possible ('I would not have it better than a barn') for the new residents of Covent Garden by undertaking to build 'the handsomest barn in England'. Sir John Summerson has explained the rationale of the building:

> A church which was to be of the simplest, cheapest kind could not inappropriately be a temple structure incorporating the Tuscan order. As such it would have classical dignity at the vernacular level: it would be the 'handsomest barn' of the anecdote.[38]

Hence it became the first building in England to have a classical portico with detached columns, and in a London not yet equipped with Wren's fifty-two churches, St Paul's Covent Garden must have presented a forcefully Italianate impression. At a time when the rebuilding of the City churches destroyed in the Fire was a matter of major public interest, the style that Jones chose for the Earl of Bedford's church at Covent Garden must have attracted a great deal of careful attention. According to Sir John Summerson, it was not merely the church that exploited the Tuscan order. He sees the whole development as having a unified design. The houses on the north and east sides of the square, raised over arcades known by Londoners as 'piazzas', were, he argues, part of 'a continuous exercise in the Tuscan':

> Covent Garden therefore was Tuscan from beginning to end, a comprehensive essay in the Tuscan mood—Tuscan all the way from the high sophistication of the portico to the vernacular of the houses—a new vernacular, the first statement of what we naturally think of today as the Georgian house.[39]

Evelyn's diary and a biographical note on Inigo Jones published in 1725 seem to indicate that Covent Garden was thought, by some, to be based on the piazza in the *Tuscan* city of Leghorn, and Dryden too may have imagined the British Vitruvius to have been remembering an Italian original.[40] The 'Tuscan' architecture and the particular association with Leghorn all tend to link Covent Garden with Tuscany, and so with Florence, its chief city. But even if Dryden saw no specifically Tuscan connexion, or did not associate the Tuscan architectural style with the geographical area of Tuscany, the more general Italian association remains.[41] It is, I suppose, even possible that in some way Dryden may have actually associated Jones's portico at Covent Garden directly with the famous façade which the Florentine Vitruvius, Alberti, had built onto the medieval structure of the *Decameron*'s S. Maria Novella in the second half of the fifteenth century. If so, Dryden would have been thinking of the Florentine church as it was a century or more after Boccaccio's time, but such anachronistic associations are easily made, and, in an age less well supplied with handy reference books than our own, easily accepted.

It is difficult to be quite sure what the water stairs at Somerset House, built by Inigo Jones between 1628 and 1631, looked like in the 1660s, but both John Webb's drawing of the gateway (possibly an unexecuted design) and early eighteenth-century views of Somerset House and the river show neo-classical structures of considerable distinction.[42] Like Covent Garden, they recall the architecture of Renaissance Italy. The stairs also bring to mind Somerset House itself where Jones carried out a great deal of work for Queen Henrietta Maria during the 1630s.

If, then, by literary and architectural allusion Dryden is drawing a parallel, or even merely hinting at a parallel between Renaissance Italy and Restoration England, in the way that I have suggested, he is not doing so for the first time. In a commendatory poem addressed 'To My Honored Friend, Dr Charleton' and prefacing Charleton's *Chorea Gigantum* (1662) Dryden had already associated the restoration of the monarchy and the restoration of learning. Earl Wasserman has shown, in a fine elucidation of the poem, how Dryden made use of the notion that 'Scholasticism was to the history of European thought as the Interregnum was to English political history' and assumed a close relationship between recent political changes and cultural developments.[43] The Restoration was, for Dryden, not just the restoration of Charles to his throne, but a full restoration of the liberal spirit in all possible manifestations, indeed a renaissance comparable with the Italian Renaissance. The advancement of scientific learning in England and the coronation of Charles II came to represent for Dryden the overthrow of tyranny, intellectual and political, and in the new age that was dawning literature could be expected to flourish.

> And though the fury of a Civil War, and Power, for twenty years together, abandon'd to a barbarous race of men, Enemies of all good Learning, had buried the Muses under the ruines of Monarchy; yet with the restoration of our happiness, we see reviv'd Poesie lifting up its head, & already shaking off the rubbish which lay so heavy on it.

> *(Essay,* p. 63)

While the verses to Dr Charleton announce this new Renaissance, the *Essay* elaborately attempts to substantiate the claim. Even the choice of the dialogue form, with its generic allusion to the classical past, recalls at the same time the academies of Renaissance Italy. But the form adopted by Dryden also allows him to make the *Essay* massively comprehensive. Crites and Eugenius debate the merits of

Ancients and Moderns, while the *Essay* itself draws richly on both; Ancients Greek and Latin, Plato and Cicero, and Moderns from Boccaccio to Buckhurst. French and English literature are compared in debate, but Dryden as essayist draws with equal assurance on Corneille's *discours* and on the Elizabethan *The Cobler of Caunterburie.* Above all, a strenuous debate between the conflicting claims of rhyme and blank verse is conducted through the medium of an ambitious and impressively well achieved new model for prose composition.

In his reply to Sorbière, Sprat had complained that England was unjustly slighted by arrogant Europeans:

> The *Italians* did at first indeavour to have it thought, that all matters of Elegance, had never yet pass'd the *Alps:* but being soon overwhelm'd by Number, they were content to admit the *French*, and the *Spaniards*, into some share of the honour. But they all three still maintain this united opinion, that all wit is to be sought for no where but amongst themselves: It is their established Rule, that good sense has alwayes kept neer the warm Sun, and scarce ever yet dar'd to come farther then the forty ninth degree Northward.[44]

Dryden does not complain, he acts, and the *Essay* shows that at fifty-one degrees north lies a city that the world would do well to take seriously.

Restoration prose has been well described by J. R. Sutherland. It is, in the main, he tells us,

> a slightly formalised variation of the conversation of gentlemen. The gentleman converses with ease, and with an absence of emphasis which may at times become a conscious and studied underemphasis, but which is more often a natural expression of his poise and detachment. He is imperturbable; nothing puts him out, or leads him to quicken his pace; indeed, a certain nonchalance and a casual way of making the most devastating observations are characteristic of him, for if he is always polite he is never mealy-mouthed, and has no middle-class inhibitions. He will never betray too great eagerness, or ride his ideas too hard, or insist too absolutely, for that is to be a bore; he will not consciously exploit his personality, or indulge in eccentricity or whimsies, for that is to be selfish, to think too much about

himself. On all occasions, like a good host, he will consult the convenience and the pleasure of those he is entertaining; and he will therefore try to express himself clearly and politely and unpedantically, and, if he can manage it, with a witty turn of thought and phrase. He will not dogmatize, or proselytize, or appeal exclusively to the emotions; to do that is the mark of the ignorant zealot and the godly fanatic, of whom no Restoration gentleman wished to be reminded.[45]

As a neat description of what I have been trying to show about Dryden's *Essay* Professor Sutherland's words could hardly be bettered. The way in which Dryden adapted *The Cobler of Caunterburie*, the unassertive delicacy of the framing references to the *Decameron*, the nonchalance of the devastating response to Sorbière, the lack of dogmatism inherent in the debate form, the entertaining nature of the setting for the debates, and the nimble wit all reveal Dryden as a gentleman. So does the prose style, and Dryden's achievement in this respect is partly the result, as Sutherland has also pointed out, of casting a large part of the *Essay* as a formalised conversation between gentlemen.[46] But the debates are not straightforwardly presented in a simple dialogue form, for the whole piece is a communication to Lord Buckhurst which the general reader just happens to be able to share. The familiar style of the letter provides Dryden with an intermediate mode of discourse lying between conversation and impersonal prose:

> we should write [letters] as we speak; and that's a true familiar Letter which expresseth one's Mind, as if he were discoursing with the Party to whom he writes,

says James Howell, in the first of his familiar letters.[47]

Dryden encloses the dialogue in a report or letter to Lord Buckhurst because in this way he ensures that he writes in the appropriate style: 'This, my Lord, was the substance of what was then spoke on that occasion; and *Lisideius*, I think was going to reply, when he was prevented thus by *Crites*' (p. 64 with Q1 reading). But however effective the device of personal address might have been to Dryden as a compositional aid, especially in his earliest prose pieces, it need have no relevance to the reader, and when Dryden revised the *Essay* for a second edition he removed the explicit reference to 'my Lord' in the passage just quoted. The framework provided by direct address to Buckingham is mere scaffolding. The framework provided by *The Cobler of Caunterburie* and the *Decameron*, on the other hand, is the essential and elegant structure of the whole edifice. Our delight in the texture of the *Essay* should be combined with delight in its significant and splendidly vigorous design.

# 5

# Tom Jones
## and the Choice of Hercules

MAREN-SOFIE RØSTVIG

PICO DELLA MIRANDOLA'S *Oration on the Dignity of Man* is perhaps the best known expression of the humanist belief in man as a being whose freedom is such that he may turn himself into what he pleases, angel or beast,[1] and if one looks for a similar theme in Renaissance art, nothing can be more appropriate than the Choice of Hercules.[2] The many Renaissance versions of this theme present the situation of the young man who has to choose between two contrasting modes of existence and the values they embody. At its simplest the choice is between Virtue and Vice; a more philosophical variant posits a choice between an active and a contemplative life, while the subtlest version contrasts mere sensual pleasure with the supreme beauty which reconciles Pleasure to Virtue. Milton's companion poems may be said to confront the reader with a choice between an active and a contemplative life, while *Comus* shows a protagonist already irrevocably committed to the path of virtue and deaf to all the seductive speeches of her opponent. *Paradise Lost*, however, invites us to analyse the various steps involved in the process of choosing. But Adam's choice, although fatal is not final; when the epic reaches the concluding lines infinite vistas of choice are opened up: 'The world was all before them, where to choose / Their place of rest, and providence their guide'.

This is the passage Henry Fielding invokes as Tom Jones, after his expulsion from Paradise Hall, ponders the nature of *his* choice; as Fielding puts it, his problem is 'what course of life to pursue'.[3] And if we turn to another eighteenth-century writer fascinated by the theme of choice, Samuel Johnson, we find him invoking the same Miltonic passage when he lets Rasselas exclaim, after his escape from the Happy Valley, 'I have here the world before me; . . . surely happiness is somewhere to be found.'[4]

As I hope to show, the story of *Tom Jones* is an eighteenth-century dramatisation of the Choice of Hercules, but before I can present my argument a context has to be established. By way of introduction, therefore, I want to show, first, that Fielding may have fetched from the Earl of Shaftesbury not only his moral philosophy but also his application of the principle of harmony to literary composition. Once this has been discussed, a study of narrative structure in *Tom Jones* will reveal the thematic importance of the concept of choice, and at this point it will finally be possible to compare Fielding's story with some literary and iconographical versions of the myth of Hercules, and particularly that of the choice as transmitted by the Earl of Shaftesbury and by an artist like William Hogarth.

## I

Moral and religious pessimists are content to associate the choice of Virtue with eternal bliss in a Heavenly Jerusalem; as far as this life is concerned the fate of the virtuous will be thorns and brambles rather than roses and raptures. It is a measure of their optimism that Renaissance humanists could envisage a choice of Virtue reconciled to Pleasure,[5] but although Dr Johnson shared the typically humanist belief in Free Will, he would have nothing to do with any facile belief in virtue rewarded. To his disillusioned eye Virtue and Pleasure were irreconcilable powers joined in a desperate struggle 'which will always be continued while the present system of nature shall subsist'. The records of poetry and history can exhibit nothing more than 'pleasure triumphing over virtue, and virtue subjugating pleasure'.[6]

Since his best known moral thesis concerns the keenness of the pleasure derived from virtuous action, the Earl of Shaftesbury may perhaps be said to present an early eighteenth-century version of the humanist theme of Pleasure reconciled to Virtue. This pleasure is largely a matter of observing the supreme beauty of moral action. The pleasure and the delight which we take in contemplating order, proportion, and symmetry in the external world, superior though it is to the pleasures of mere sense experience, nevertheless is itself 'far surpassed' by observing 'a *beautiful, proportion'd,* and *becoming* Action.'[7] The primacy of this experience of moral beauty is clearly indicated when Shaftesbury derives the artist's ability to imitate the order of nature from his experience of the beauty of moral order in the microcosmos of man. His *Advice to an Author* puts this quite succinctly: an artist is capable of imposing order on his work only to the extent that he perceives 'the inward Form and Structure of his Fellow-Creature' and of himself; it is this which enables him to 'imitate the Creator' and become 'a just PROMETHEUS, under Jove'.[8]

Shaftesbury is equally explicit when it comes to explaining exactly what he understands by the imposition of order on a work of art—a part of his argument that has tended to be overshadowed by his discussion of moral harmony. We must take care not to read into his comments on literary structure merely an Aristotelian insistence on a beginning, middle, and end; his views concerning artistic unity should be related to the fusion between Platonic and Christian theories of creation associated with Augustine and with Renaissance syncretists.[9] Like these Shaftesbury posits two steps in the creative procedure: (1) a pre-conceived pattern, and (2) the disposition of the subject-matter according to this pattern so that unity may be achieved. The artist's purpose is to form 'a *Whole*, coherent and proportion'd in it-self, with due Subjection and Subordinacy of constituent Parts'. Before a piece of writing may be considered as 'legitimate', therefore, it must possess '*exterior Proportion* and *Symmetry* of Composition' and this means devising 'a Pattern or Plan of Workmanship.'[10]

Shaftesbury presents the same ideas in a playful manner in his *Miscellaneous Reflections*, his point of departure being the deplorable absence, among modern writers, of a sense of form. They are content to scatter their ideas abroad without any plan or pattern, while a competent writer must behave like 'an able Traveller' who knows how important it is to plan the stages of his journey ahead of time. He measures the distance 'exactly' and 'premeditates his Stages, and Intervals of Relaxation and Intention, to the very Conclusion of his Undertaking'. He knows, too, how to vary his pace: 'He is not presently *upon the Spur*, or in his full *Career*; but walks his Steed *leisurely* out of his Stable, settles himself in his Stirrups, and when fair Road and Station offer, puts on perhaps to *a round Trot*; thence into *a Gallop*, and after a while *takes up*'. He suits his pace to the condition of the road to save his horse so as not to 'bring him puffing, and in a heat, into his last Inn.'[11]

Fielding repeatedly exploits the same metaphor, first in *Joseph*

*Andrews* II, 1 and then in *Tom Jones* II, 1 and XVIII, 1. True, Fielding varies the metaphor—in *Joseph Andrews* II, 1 it is the reader who travels through the book, looking for entertainment and suitable resting-places—but the context is the same. Like Shaftesbury, Fielding's concern is with the disposition of his material into books and chapters, or as stated in the chapter heading, with 'divisions in authors'. *Tom Jones* II, 1 takes up the issue of varied pace; his own writing, so Fielding argues, is totally unlike that of newspapers which always have the same number of words 'whether there be any news in it or not'. Newspapers are in this respect to be 'compared to a stage-coach, which performs constantly the same course, empty as well as full'. A journalist keeps 'even pace with time, whose amanuensis he is', but not so Fielding whose readers will find 'some chapters very short, and others altogether as long'. They must not be surprised, therefore, 'if my history sometimes seems to stand still, and sometimes to fly'.

Shaftesbury's metaphor is directly echoed in a passage towards the end of *Tom Jones* XI, 9 when Fielding, after having conducted Sophia Western safely to London, pauses to compare his 'history' to 'the travellers who are its subject'. 'Good writers will indeed do well to imitate the ingenious traveller' who knows to 'retard his pace' when confronted by scenes worthy of his attention, 'which delay he afterwards compensates by swiftly scouring over the gloomy heath of Bagshot' or over uneventful, open plains where one spots little more than a single tree in the course of sixteen miles. 'Not so travels the money-meditating tradesman' or the 'offspring of wealth and dulness. On they jogg, with equal pace, through the verdant meadows, or over the barren heath . . . ' Fielding leaves it to his sagacious reader to apply his metaphor to 'the Boeotian writers' renowned for their dullness and 'to those authors who are their opposites'. If we take this advice at all to heart, we are compelled to observe that Fielding has just retarded his own pace from weeks and days to two twelve-hour spans in the two books prior to Book XI, so that these must presumably contain matter well worth perusing with particular care. And sagacity is apparently required to unravel the author's meaning; the lazy reader will miss as much as the lazy traveller:

> Bestir thyself therefore on this occasion; for tho' we will always lend thee proper assistance in difficult places, as we do not, like some others, expect thee to use the arts of divination to discover our meaning, yet we shall not indulge thy laziness where nothing

but thy own attention is required; for thou art highly mistaken if thou dost imagine that we intended, when we begun this great work, to leave thy sagacity nothing to do, or that, without sometimes exercising this talent, thou wilt be able to travel through our pages with any pleasure or profit to thyself.

Fielding was not content to adapt a popular Renaissance theme; to alert his reader he also adopts the Renaissance stance of the author who challenges his public to discover the meaning of the 'dark conceits' scattered through his work. And I agree with Fielding that the 'arts of divination' are superfluous; the clues are there in the text.

The last of Fielding's prefatory chapters (XVIII, 1) reverts to the stage-coach metaphor as the author bids farewell to his fellow-travellers, all of whom must certainly agree that the tour has been extremely well planned from beginning to end. But this is what we would expect from an author who commands his readers to trust his ability as a planner in the following frequently-quoted passage from chapter X, 1:

> . . . we warn thee not too hastily to condemn any of the incidents in this our history, as impertinent and foreign to our main design, because thou dost not immediately conceive in what manner such incidents may conduce to that design. This work may, indeed, be considered as a great creation of our own; and for a little reptile of a critic to find fault with any of its parts, without knowing the manner in which the whole is connected . . . is a most presumptuous absurdity.

Fielding, then, is completely at one with Shaftesbury in his insistence on unity of design; his work is an ordered cosmos, a creation of his own.

When Shaftesbury later on in his *Miscellaneous Reflections* returns to the issue of the necessity of using 'a *Model* or a *Plan*', he adds a three-page footnote by way of comment[12] and in the course of this footnote the reader is referred back to the passage on the 'able Traveller' who premeditates the stages of his journey. The footnote is interesting in itself as a discussion of purely literary topics, but its interest is increased on noticing how closely Fielding follows Shaftesbury's lead in some of his own observations on the art of writing. Thus when Shaftesbury states that if a poet's fiction is to convince, he must take as his guide 'not *the Possible,* but *the Probable* and *Likely*', this is of course what Fielding says when he discusses the marvellous

in *Tom Jones* VIII, 1. The two are in complete agreement also with
regard to character portrayal: patterns of angelic perfection or diabolical depravity fail to interest readers, let alone to influence their
moral behaviour. But when a good character suffers the evil effects
of his vices, 'we are not only taught to shun them for their own sake,
but to hate them for the mischiefs they have already brought on those
we love' (*Tom Jones* X, 1). Shaftesbury had already advanced the same
argument, but somewhat more philosophically. After having analysed
the vices and virtues of various Homeric heroes, he concludes that this
is how the poet imparts his moral lesson. His fable shows how 'the
*Excesses* of every Character' are redressed:

> And the Misfortunes naturally attending such Excesses, being
> justly apply'd; our Passions, whilst in the strongest manner
> engag'd and mov'd, are in the wholesomest and most effectual
> manner corrected and *purg'd*.

In short, 'in *a Poem* (whether *Epick* or *Dramatick*) a compleat and
*perfect Character* is the greatest *Monster*, and of all Poetick Fictions
not only the least *engaging*, but the least *moral* and *improving*.'

Shaftesbury's footnote is at its most interesting when it touches
on unity of design. Shaftesbury is not content with a general sense of
unity; the principle of unity entails placing episodes with such exact-
ness that they cannot be fitted in anywhere else without disastrous
consequences:

> 'Tis an infallible proof of the want of just *Integrity* in every
> Writing, from the *Epopee* or *Heroick* Poem, down to the familiar
> Epistle . . . if every several Part or Portion fits not its proper
> place so exactly, that the least Transposition wou'd be im-
> practicable. Whatever is *Episodick,* tho perhaps it be *a Whole*,
> and in it-self *intire*, yet being inserted, as a *Part*, in a Work of
> greater length, it must appear only in its *due Place*. And that
> Place alone can be call'd its *due*-one, which alone befits it. If
> there be any Passage in the Middle or End, which might have
> stood in the Beginning; or any in the Beginning which might
> have stood as well in the Middle or End; there is properly in
> such a Piece neither Beginning, Middle, or End. 'Tis a mere
> *Rhapsody*; not a Work . . .

If *Tom Jones* is a 'great creation' in the sense defined here by Shaftesbury, this would entail a careful placing of the digressions and not

only of the various episodes that constitute the plot that Ronald S. Crane has taught us to appreciate.[13] While we recognise and honour the kind of unity which emerges from a successful fusion of incidents that at first seem very loosely related, an easily perceived symmetrical disposition of parts is apt to strike us as a mechanical device of doubtful aesthetic value. No particular admiration has been stirred by observing Fielding's neat division of his story into three equal parts: six books on Allworthy's estate, six on the road, and six in London. The division has been recognised but not explored. It is important, however, to realise that this tripartite arrangement is combined with a central accent on Books IX and X as indicated by the chronological scheme; as we approach the textual centre the narrative pace slows down from years and months to weeks and days and, finally, to the two twelve-hour spans of Books IX and X. After we have passed through this centre with its setting in the inn at Upton, the speed is again increased, but only in terms of days. Since the plot indicates the central role of the events that take place in the inn at Upton, the chronological pin-pointing of Books IX and X as the textual centre merely confirms what we already know, but since it is these books that present Fielding's version of the Choice of Hercules, the structural clue is far from superfluous. It compels the reader to 'bestir himself on this occasion' to discover the author's meaning.

If Fielding took Shaftesbury's advice concerning unity of design at all seriously, it must be possible to show that the notorious digression on the Man of the Hill not only belongs in the pattern, but that it could have been placed nowhere else. It occurs just prior to Books IX–X, in the last six chapters of Book VIII. And on the other side of the textual centre we find that chapters 2–7 of Book XI present the story of Mrs Fitzpatrick as told to Sophia Western. This symmetrical disposition around the centre suggests that the digressions have a bearing on important thematic issues, and that they have been placed where these issues had to be underlined. If this were not so, then the symmetrical structure would be nothing but a mere stylistic flourish. It is hard to believe this, the more so since Douglas Brooks has shown how closely the interpolated tales in *Joseph Andrews* are related to their immediate context in the story.[14]

Since the Man of the Hill, unlike Mrs Fitzpatrick, has no function in the plot, his story can possess thematic relevance only. Critics, however, have found little to interest them in this story of a misspent life apart from the warning which it contains to beware of bad company in London. But if this were its chief thematic relevance, its proper placing would have been just prior to Tom's arrival in London in Book XIII, and not before the events in the inn at Upton. Since the story of the Man of the Hill leads up to these events, its purpose must be to point the reader's attention in the right direction.

It will be remembered that the story falls into two parts. The first phase in the life of the Man of the Hill shows him in eager pursuit of the pleasures of sense and the gifts of fickle Fortune: drinking, gambling, and loving constitute the sum of his achievement—his love being for a woman of easy virtue and a friend so enslaved by the spirit of gambling that everything is sacrificed to it. These characters are exactly what they seem; they never pose as other than what they are— slaves of sensual delights and of Fortune—and so their behaviour is entirely predictable. The disastrous issue of events, therefore, is the consequence of poor judgement and self-deception. The pleasures so eagerly pursued are mere phantoms of the imagination. When the Man of the Hill finally turns his back on the world in disgust, the basic bias of his character remains unchanged. Although he has forsworn drink and all human company, he persists in his pursuit of pleasure—so much so that an initial capital letter is distinctly in order. The only difference is that his quest is now for the pleasures of the mind alone. Both phases in his career, therefore, illustrate the conscious choice of Pleasure. His life is so designed as to illustrate, not vice abandoned in favour of virtue, but the pursuit of two contrary kinds of pleasure, each taken to an excess. That the second phase should be condemned as thoroughly as the first appears from two considerations: despite the fact that he has a gun he remains a mere spectator as Mrs Waters is attacked, and his solitary existence is depicted in such a manner as to constitute a conscious caricature of the Epicurean ideal of the happiness of complete solitude. In its wealth of clearly visualised, significant details Fielding's caricature of this ideal comes fairly close in spirit to Hogarth's paintings, and I would suggest that this is how we ought to view a number of the episodes in Fielding's novel—as a series of satirical pictures conveying a specific moral lesson.[15] The last 'painting' in this particular series shows the hermit on the brow of his hill, watching Mrs Waters in the hands of her cruel assailant 'with great patience and unconcern'. To recognise the caricature one must of course know the original, in this case the Epicurean ideal of happiness current during the last few decades of the seventeenth century, partly in a plainly hedonistic version and partly in a more elevated philosophical alternative capable of appealing to the more serious-minded. As I have shown elsewhere,[16] many Restoration poets favoured Lucretius' picture of the Happy Man as a detached and unconcerned spectator of the follies of men, placed on top of a hill from which he may contemplate the spectacle of the mad pursuit of Fortune. Because this man has taught himself to limit his desires to the pleasures of the mind as enjoyed in solitude, his invulnerability was supposed to be absolute. The basic concept in poems concerned with this type of *beatus vir* is that of conscious choice, a word sometimes found in the title itself, and 'The Choice' would be an entirely appropriate heading for Fielding's interpolated tale. As Tom Jones himself points out, the man's misfortunes were due to his 'want of proper caution in the choice of friends and acquaintance'. But it is a choice of life which is entailed and not merely a choice of friends, and the narrative itself comments ironically on the second choice of complete solitude by underlining its hazards. No retreat from the world can remove a man from the reach of Fortune; the only power capable of providing some measure of protection is divine Providence. But Providence can do no more than place Tom Jones in a position where he may serve as the rescuer; it is Tom's prompt response that saves the life first of the Man of the Hill and next of Mrs Waters.

The life-story of the Man of the Hill invites analysis in terms of an Aristotelian contrast between defect and excess; the pleasures of the body illustrated in the first phase exclude those of the mind, and the other way round. One could also say that the Man of the Hill begins by bestowing his love too freely and on unworthy objects, while he concludes by entirely withdrawing his love from men and bestowing it on the Deity instead. The relevant argument has in fact already been presented by Mr Allworthy in his discussion of charity in Book II, ch. 3. The whole drift of the New Testament proves that charity must entail moral action to relieve the distressed, such actions being their own reward as they engender such exquisite sensations of delight in those who perform them that they become 'in some degree epicures'. This, then, is one way in which pleasure and virtue may be reconciled. Allworthy goes on to add that a man can harden his heart to the distresses of others only if he should become convinced that all men are depraved: '. . . this persuasion must lead him, I think, either into atheism or enthusiasm; but surely it is unfair to argue such universal depravity from a few vicious individuals . . . ' This persuasion is dramatised in the career of the Man of the Hill, the first part of which is marked by an atheistic hedonism of the grossest kind, while he ends his life as a religious enthusiast. As he passes from the one extreme to the other, the Man of the Hill enjoys a brief period of harmony which comes to an end with the death of his father. Fielding had already pursued a similar Aristotelian pattern of defect, a Golden Mean, and excess in *Joseph Andrews,* where the structure is just as obvious if not more so. A sequence of three chapters is so arranged as to take the reader through three scenes illustrating, first the complete lack of charity in Parson Trulliber (II, 14), then the unexpected generosity of the pedlar (II, 15), and finally the fine gentleman's profuse, but false, verbal professions (II, 16). Once one has spotted the Aristotelian structure one can virtually predict the nature of the third episode on the strength of the first two.

To revert to *Tom Jones,* the two extremes dramatised in the life of the Man of the Hill have been refuted in advance by Mr Allworthy, the gist of whose argument (II, 5) is repeated by Tom Jones in his rejection of the view that human nature is 'necessarily and universally evil' (VIII, 15). The enthusiastic phase may also be refuted in terms fetched from Shaftesbury: an appreciation of the beauty of the universe is perfectly useless unless related to the higher beauty of just harmony and proportion in the world of moral action, and it is this superior beauty that Tom Jones displays as he rescues Mrs Waters. The contrast between the two men, therefore, is a contrast between false and true virtue (or moral beauty) and false and true pleasure.

A similar contrast is established between Mrs Fitzpatrick and Sophia Western, each of whom has made her choice, and it is a reflection of their status as women that it turns on a choice of husband. The story of Mrs Fitzpatrick's marriage shows that she, too, has erred grossly in her choice, but in contrast to the Man of the Hill she has been deceived by a pleasing appearance in the man she married. Yet she has erred just as grossly in her second choice: elopement with the Irish peer. The contrast between the two women is strongly underlined: Mrs Fitzpatrick's air of virtue is mere hypocrisy, while Sophia has 'a heart as good and innocent, as her face was beautiful' (X, 5).

Both digressions, then, turn on the theme of *choice*—the choice of pleasures subsequently revealed as false or deceptive, and as opposed to virtue. We can now examine the intervening books in order to assess the possible relevance of this theme.

## II

No sooner has Tom Jones proved the superior beauty of moral action as he rescues Mrs Waters with 'his trusty oaken stick', than his attention is riveted on her exposed breasts so that 'for a few moments they stood silent, and gazing at each other' (IX, 2). No reader is likely to forget how, during their progress to Upton, Mrs Waters succeeds in keeping her female attributes in view, and in the inn Mr Jones must again use his 'cudgel' to defend the honour of the lady. Once this honour has been vindicated the hero proceeds to satisfy his hunger, and no sooner has this been done than he falls a victim to the amorous warfare conducted by Mrs Waters. But before this is permitted to happen Fielding pauses, strangely enough, to describe the man with whom we ought to be perfectly familiar: he is a veritable Adonis with regard to beauty and a Hercules with regard to strength. The author also pauses to characterise the kind of love involved in this episode as mere appetite. The ensuing description of the amorous warfare is a particularly delightful example of Fielding's mock epic style: it is conducted throughout in complete silence by means of looks and sighs, the hero's best protection being his tremendous appetite:

> First, from two lovely blue eyes, whose bright orbs flashed lightning at their discharge, flew forth two pointed ogles. But happily for our heroe, hit only a vast piece of beef which he was then conveying into his plate, and harmless spent their force. The fair warrior perceived their miscarriage, and immediately from her fair bosom drew forth a deadly sigh . . . so soft, so sweet, so tender, that the insinuating air must have found its subtle way to the heart of our heroe, had it not luckily been driven from his ears by the coarse bubbling of some bottled ale, which at that time he was pouring forth.

But when the cloth is removed, so are his defences, and 'without duly weighing his allegiance to the fair Sophia', he surrenders.

This episode alone might have sufficed to inform contemporary readers that this is a mock epic version of the Choice of Hercules, one of the most popular of themes among painters since the Renaissance. It was Ronald Paulson's study of *Hogarth, His Life, Art, and Times* (1971) that drew my attention to the frequency with which the theme of a choice between Virtue and Vice (or Pleasure) informs Hogarth's work, and a particularly good example is presented by the popular print called *The Lottery* (1724).[17] In his comments on Hogarth's various versions of this basic theme Paulson draws on Shaftesbury's brief treatise entitled *A Notion of the Historical Draught or Tablature of the Judgment of Hercules* (1713) included in the third volume of the *Characteristics*.[18] To read Shaftesbury's account is to realise the use that Fielding has made of this tradition; this use is so obvious that it is virtually unnecessary to re-read *Tom Jones*, IX–X, to spot the parallels. This is particularly true of the temptation scene in IX, 5. When Fielding prefaces his mock epic passage on the amorous warfare with the remark that this is 'a description hitherto unessayed either in prose or verse', he is, in fact, quite right; the theme of the Choice of Hercules had been the peculiar province of painters. As Erwin Panofsky has shown, the iconographical tradition of the choice does not extend back in time beyond the middle of the fifteenth century,[19] but literary versions of various aspects of the Heracles myth are of course another matter. Although Fielding draws on literary traditions, too, and not only on iconographical versions of the Choice, for the moment I want to focus on Fielding's adaptation of the latter as summarised by Shaftesbury.

This can best be done by listing the main points that serve to identify the mid-section in Fielding's narrative as a mock epic version of the Choice of Hercules. As we have seen, Fielding pauses to describe Tom Jones as a Hercules at the very moment when Mrs Waters (as Pleasure/Vice) reaches the climax of her persuasive efforts, and the hero has been given the prime Herculean attribute of a stick or cudgel which he wields to good effect. But even more significant is Mrs Waters' free display of her bosom together with her rhetoric of silent persuasion, while the last, decisive link in the chain is the fact that Fielding places his hero at a cross-road to make his choice. As for Sophia, Fielding uses descriptive terms indicating beyond doubt that he presents her as the kind of superior Beauty where Virtue and Pleasure are reconciled.

If my argument holds, then Tom Jones should be seen not as merely having yet another illicit amour in the inn at Upton, but as Hercules at the crossroads confronted by the contrary persuasions of Pleasure and Virtue. And if this is indeed so, then the story told by the Man of the Hill concerning his choice of life leads directly on to this decisive event in Tom's life, and no 'reptile of a critic' must 'presume to find fault' either with the contents of this digression or its placing. And as far as Fielding's art is concerned, this interpretation, if accepted, would show that the use of mock epic mythology extends from the descriptive terms into the action itself. While *Joseph Andrews* provides the male protagonists with an added dimension by invoking the Biblical Joseph and Abraham, classical myth performs much the same service in *Tom Jones*. Fielding's narratives, like Hogarth's modern history painting, score important points by placing the contemporary world, as Ronald Paulson has put it, 'in relation to conventions of biblical or mythological resonance . . .'[20]

My theory that Fielding drew on Shaftesbury's discussion of the Choice of Hercules is supported by the many instances that *Tom Jones* affords of Shaftesbury's pervasive influence. It is possible, of course, that Fielding may have turned to William Shenstone's early poem on *The Judgment of Hercules* (1740),[21] a work clearly inspired by Shaftesbury's treatise, or that he knew the iconographical tradition even better than the noble Earl, but a comparison between Shaftesbury's *Judgment of Hercules* and *Tom Jones* IX–X nevertheless shows several distinct points of similarity that are more easily accounted for by positing a conscious use, by Fielding, of Shaftesbury's argument.

Thus Shaftesbury stipulates that the setting should be 'in the Country, and in a place of Retirement, near some Wood or Forest' to suggest 'Solitude, Thoughtfulness, and premeditated Retreat'. This is certainly true of Fielding's narrative, where the encounter with the Man of the Hill is the preface to his meeting with Mrs Waters in X, 2. The hero has indeed had his moment of philosophical reflection in a place whose sole function is to serve as a setting for complete retirement from the world. To revert to Shaftesbury, he observes that during the first phase when Hercules is accosted by Pleasure and persuaded by her, the 'Reign of Silence must be absolute'. Hercules must be silent to preserve his dignity, Pleasure because her appeal is to the senses. Her language, Shaftesbury remarks, must be that of the eyes, the persuasive power of rational speech being the attribute of Virtue. Pleasure should be associated with objects suggesting 'the Debauches of the Table-kind', while other 'indulgences' may be suggested by 'certain Draperys thrown carelessly on the ground, and hung upon a neighbouring Tree, forming a kind of Bower and Couch for this luxurious Dame . . .' Shaftesbury does not say that Pleasure should expose her bosom to view, but this is true of most pictorial

representations of this 'luxurious Dame', including the picture which
adorns the title-page of Shaftesbury's treatise—a plate by S. Gribelin
of a painting by Paolo de Matteis.[22] Hogarth's version of the Choice
of Hercules in *The Lottery* in the same manner shows a half naked
figure surrounded by objects of a similar kind, as Ronald Paulson has
remarked.[23]

My enjoyment of Fielding's narrative is distinctly enhanced by
observing the use that he makes of a theme made familiar by a host
of painters and sometimes in a satirical vein as in the case of Dürer[24]
and Hogarth. The character of the amorous Mrs Waters epitomises
the seductiveness of sensual pleasure: as such she seems to me curiously at variance with the homely and grammatically inclined Jenny
Jones whom we met in the first part, so that it is difficult to avoid the
conclusion that at this point Fielding sacrificed consistency of character
to the needs of this important occasion. Perhaps consistency of
character is not to be expected in such a minor character, or can it be
that we are to suppose that the intervening years have achieved this
striking metamorphosis? However this may be, Mrs Waters is certainly as delightful as the occasion requires; Shaftesbury's rule that
every action in a history-painting must display *'Probability,* or
*seeming Truth'*[25] has been fully realised.

It is interesting that Fielding should present as the alternative choice
to Vice/Pleasure the kind of Virtue that represents the highest kind
of Beauty, the enjoyment of which creates the highest pleasure that
mortal man is capable of. The iconographical tradition usually stresses
the contrast between Vice and Virtue rather than more subtle philosophical concepts, and in some emblems Vice is an old hag hiding
behind a beautiful mask, while Virtue has been so totally deprived
of sex as to appear in the shape of an old man with a book.[26] The
painters, however, usually present Virtue as a beautiful woman, her
beauty being combined with a lofty serenity that is positively awe-
inspiring. Beauty is of course Sophia Western's primary characteristic, and when she is introduced in X, 3 as the foil to Mrs Waters
this is the aspect which is given reiterated emphasis. As Fielding
remarks, there is 'in perfect beauty a power which none almost can
withstand' (X, 3), and certainly not Tom Jones. Her second attribute
would have seemed strange in any other context than the Choice of
Hercules, and this is the sweetness of her voice, a quality associated
with penetration in musical thought.[26a] As Shaftesbury explains,
it is the privilege of Virtue to persuade through rational speech, and

To dirtie droſſe, no higher dare aſpyre,
Ne can his feeble earthly eyes endure
The flaming light of that celeſtiall fyre,
Which kindleth loue in generous defyre,
And makes him mount aboue the natiue might
Of heauie earth, vp to the heauens hight.

Such is the powre of that ſweet paſſion,
That it all ſordid baſeneſſe doth expell,
And the refyned mynd doth newly faſhion
Vnto a fairer forme, which now doth dwell
In his high thought, that would it ſelfe excell;
Which he beholding ſtill with conſtant fight,
Admires the mirrour of ſo heauenly light.

VVhoſe image printing in his deepeſt wit,
He thereon feeds his hungrie fantaſy,
Still full, yet neuer ſatisfyde with it,
Like *Tantale*, that in ſtore doth ſterued ly:
So doth he pine in moſt ſatiety,
For nought may quench his infinite defyre,
Once kindled through that firſt conceiued fyre.

Thereon his mynd affixed wholly is,
Ne thinks on ought, but how it to attaine;
His care, his ioy, his hope is all on this,
That ſeemes in all bliſſes to containe,
In fight whereof, all other bliſſe ſeemes vaine.
Thriſe happie man, might he the ſame poſſeſſe;
He faines himſelfe, and doth his fortune bleſſe.
And

And though he do not win his wiſh to end,
Yet thus farre happie he him ſelfe doth weene,
That heauens ſuch happie grace did to him lend,
As thing on earth ſo heauenly, to haue ſeene,
His harts enſhrined ſaint, his heauens quene,
Fairer then faireſt, in his fayning eye,
Whoſe ſole aſpect he counts felicitye.

Then forth he caſts in his vnquiet thought,
What he may do, her fauour to obtaine;
What braue exploit, what perill hardly wrought,
What puiſſant conqueſt, what aduenturous paine,
May pleaſe her beſt, and grace vnto him gaine:
He dreads no danger, nor misfortune feares,
His faith, his fortune, in his breaſt he beares.

Thou art his god, thou art his mightie guyde,
Thou being blind, leſt him not ſee his feares,
But carieſt him to that which he hath eyde,
Through ſeas, through flames, through thouſand
    ſwords and ſpeares:
Ne ought ſo ſtrong that may his force withſtand,
With which thou armeſt his refiſtleſſe hand.

Witneſſe *Leander*, in the Euxine waues,
And ſtout *AEneas* in the Troiane fyre,
*Achilles* preaſſing through the Phrygian glaiues,
And *Orpheus* daring to prouoke the yre
Of damned fends, to get his loue retyre:
For both through heauen & hell thou makeſt way,
To win them worſhip which to thee obay.

B iij

1. Pages 8–9 of the first edition of Spenser's *Fowre Hymnes*. (John Rylands University Library, Manchester.)

2. Hercules between Pleasure and Virtue. Engraving by Sim. Gribelin of a painting by Paulo de Matthaeis reproduced from the fourth edition of Shaftesbury's *Characteristicks* (1727) III, 345.

3. Hercules at the crossroads between Virtue and Vice. From Geoffrey Whitney, *A Choice of Emblemes* (Leyden, 1586). *(Bodleian Library.)*

this is surely why Fielding goes out of his way, again and again, to stress this attribute. Sophia is said to possess 'a voice much fuller of honey than was ever that of Plato, though his voice is supposed to have been a bee-hive' (X, 9). Not only does her beauty eclipse that of Mrs Fitzpatrick as the sun and moon do the stars, but her voice ravishes landladies and beasts as well as men (XI, 3 and X, 9). The climactic assertion occurs just after the comparison to the voice of Plato:

> Reader, I am not superstitious, nor any great believer in modern miracles. I do not, therefore, deliver the following as a certain truth; for, indeed, I can scarce credit it myself: but the fidelity of an historian obliges me to relate what hath been confidently asserted. The horse, then, on which the guide rode, is reported to have been so charmed by Sophia's voice, that he made a full stop, and exprest an unwillingness to proceed any farther. (X, 9)

The real reason is that the guide has stopped using his 'armed right heel', but the point has been made and in a manner appropriate to mock epic. The sweet voice of reason charms that archetypal image of the unruly passions, the horse. Shaftesbury makes the same point when he states that Virtue may be shown as having a bit or bridle to indicate her ability to restrain. However, in the very next chapter— XI, 2—Sophia neglects 'the management of her horse' and so sustains a fall which is an affront to her modesty, and a second fall of the same kind which is witnessed by a number of bystanders. Fortune 'seems to have resolved to put Sophia to the blush that day', and one wonders why; one possible reason is a desire, on the part of Fielding, to stress the modesty of Virtue as contrasted with the patent immodesty of Vice. Just after Mrs Waters has displayed her tempting female attributes, then, Sophia Western is shown as experiencing 'a violent shock' to her modesty. This experience occurs when Sophia is in the company of false Virtue (Mrs Fitzpatrick), when they have found 'a wide and well-beaten road' leading to 'a very fair promising inn' (compare *Matthew* 7:13–14). Fielding's descriptive terms—a 'wide and well-beaten road' and 'very fair promising inn'—places the fall from the horse in a context that is easily identified. This is the kind of prospect which in emblematic representations of the Choice is associated with Vice. In this 'fair promising inn' Sophia Western is in bad company indeed; Mrs Fitzpatrick's true character is perceived readily enough, her appearance of virtue being a mere mask put on to deceive the world. Conversely Sophia herself is taken for Jenny Cameron, a common whore albeit a royal one, and her reputation suffers even more from the intemperate behaviour of Mrs Honour. Book XI concludes with 'a Hint or two concerning Virtue' and with the parting of the two cousins.

The portrayal of Mrs Waters and of Sophia Western, then, is entirely in keeping with the tradition of the Choice of Hercules as explained by Shaftesbury, but so far I have discussed only the first phase in the process of the Choice: the momentary leaning, by Tom Jones/Hercules, in the direction of Pleasure/Vice in Book IX. The second phase begins when Tom Jones discovers Sophia's muff—an event which causes what the chapter-heading (X, 6) refers to as 'the Madness of Jones'—and when he resolves 'never more to abandon the pursuit' of Sophia (X, 7); it concludes with the last Book in this division, XII. Once Sophia has been brought safely to London at the end of Book XI, the narrative returns to Tom Jones and to the theme of his Choice. After leaving the inn at Upton, Tom Jones and Partridge reach the cross-roads where Tom has a second fit of madness at the end of which he chooses to follow the paths of Glory in a truly Herculean spirit (XII, 3). By 'mere chance' he happens to pursue the very road taken by Sophia, and the next chapter confronts him with yet another cross-roads where he meets a lame fellow in rags who has found Sophia's pocket-book. This makes up Tom's mind for him: he grabs occasion by the forelock and with passionate intensity he proceeds to pursue Sophia and Sophia alone.

But at this point the narrative insists on slowness: Tom wants to push on as quickly as possible to the place where the book was found, but the lameness of his guide compels him to moderate his pace to one mile an hour, the distance being more than three miles. Afterwards, however, his speed is such that Partridge must beg him 'a little to slacken his pace' (XII, 5). 'Our heroe' forgoes food and sleep and carries on through darkness and rainy weather 'with the utmost eagerness' (XII, 8), and in the end he rides post. During all this time Fortune favours him with as much grace as before she had vented her malice on his unfortunate person; indeed, the very chapter-heading proclaims that Fortune seems in a better mood with Jones. This benignant aspect carries over into the last third when Tom, as soon as he has arrived in London, sets out 'in pursuit of Sophia'. He succeeds in finding the place he is looking for, 'whether it was that Fortune relented, or whether it was no longer in her power to disappoint him'. After he has begun his eager pursuit of Sophia the absolute power of Fortune, so it would seem, has become abrogated. The introduction of reflections on state lotteries at this point (XIII, 2) shows how much the issue of Fortune occupies the author's mind, and one understands why on recalling one or two points in connection with emblematic representations of Fortune in relation to Virtue. As Rudolf Wittkower explains in an essay on 'Chance, Time, and Virtue'[27] man grasping Occasio-Fortuna by the forelock may be interpreted as Virtue overcoming Chance, Virtue often being represented as Hercules. This theme may be found in literature as well; a play performed before Lucrezia Borgia in 1502 shows Hercules as the champion of Virtue in her battle with Vice. And if we are to judge from what happens to Sophia in Book XI, she certainly needs a champion. But the curious episode of Tom's limping progress still remains to be explained. It fits very neatly into the context I have suggested so far, when seen as an emblematic representation, in a manner appropriate to mock epic, of the proverb quoted by Partridge on first meeting Tom Jones: *festina lente* (VIII,4). The posture that Shaftesbury recommends for Virtue (in a representation of the Choice of Hercules) is one foot planted on the ground and the other lifted on a piece of rock to suggest respectively firmness of purpose and aspiration. This is a posture also associated with emblematic representations of *festina lente*,[28] the lifted foot often being shown as winged to indicate speed. Geoffrey Whitney uses a juxtaposition of crab and butterfly to convey the same point in an emblem of this kind,[29] and I take it, therefore, that the picture of Tom 'hurrying slowly' in the company of a lame man is Fielding's narrative version of this emblem, which exhorts us to combine speed with patience, daring with prudence. It is the role of Fortune to admonish to speed, while Wisdom imposes firmness, and whoever reconciles the two is bound to succeed. Fortune must favour men guided by Virtue, as we learn from one of George Wither's emblems[30] or from one cf Erasmus' *adagia* incorporating a quotation from Cicero: *Duce virtute comite Fortuna*.[31] To be led by Virtue and accompanied by Fortune is indeed an enviable position, and it is pleasant to see Tom Jones enjoying it as he hurries towards the 'Elysian fields' of London with its ample quota of Cerberus-like porters guarding the entrance to his Sophia. The attempted rape of Sophia in this underworld is yet another narrative link with the myth of Hercules.

Fielding's allusion to the emblematic representation of *festina lente* serves very neatly to link Tom Jones with the other mythical character whom he resembles, Adonis. As Edgar Wind informs us,[32] the extremely popular Renaissance story of the chastising of Adonis (unchaste love), the *Hypnerotomachia Poliphili*,[33] contained more than eighty woodcuts on the theme of *festina lente*. Tom is described as an Adonis by Fielding himself (IX, 5) and by Lady Bellaston (XV, 7), and it is just after Partridge has quoted the proverb to Tom (VIII, 4) that the very first comparison occurs. The myth of Adonis, then, combines with that of Hercules to provide the penumbra of associations that Fielding desired. It may be my ignorance of the former that makes me load the scales in favour of Hercules, but the myth of Hercules seems to me to provide the basic groundwork for Fielding's story. Before I consider some further uses of this myth, however, I would like to compare Fielding's version of the Choice with Hogarth's as presented in his print of *The Lottery*.[34]

Hogarth's drawing is dominated by two gigantic wheels, one governed by Fortune and the other by Wantonness. Two wheels are required since the one draws a number and the other a paper indicating whether it is a blank or a prize. On the bottom left is an unfortunate wretch who has drawn a blank, while Good Luck forms the central figure in a tableau on the right. Good Luck is shown as a Hercules importuned by a half naked personification of Pleasure on the one hand and, on the other, by Fame who persuades him to raise fallen Virtue. This overall composition recalls the central section of *Tom Jones*, where the beginning of Tom's peregrinations is heralded by his singular misfortune in losing his banknotes, just as his retrieval of Sophia's note marks their end in Book XII. Hogarth's Herculean Good Luck is placed between Pleasure and Virtue—the latter in a fallen position on the ground—and the figure of Glory is encouraging him to raise sinking Virtue. Fielding's narrative equivalents are located in Books XI–XII, where Sophia Western sustains her fall from her horse in XI, 2 and where the hero, in the opening chapters of Book XII, briskly opts for an active life devoted to the pursuit of Glory. Partridge does very nicely as Fielding's version of Folly (drawn by Hogarth in a cap and bells).

I do not want to press this parallel between Fielding and Hogarth too far; for one thing, Hogarth's print is far from unique in combining the concept of Fortune with the Choice of Hercules. Thus the title-page of George Wither's *Emblemes* (1635) shows Fortune with her sail at the centre where the choice is being made, together with a cauldron from which lots are being drawn. That this drawing is based on the Pythagorean Y may not be immediately apparent, but the composition is nevertheless sufficiently clear once it is realised that the bottom part represents childhood. The letter Y was taken to represent the Herculean choice by virtue of its shape, the first, undivided part symbolising the period of childhood prior to the moment of choice. The arms of the letter may be seen in the two towering hills, one embodying the open road to Pleasure and per-dition, the other the arduous path to Virtue and eternal life.[35] One sees how the children (dressed like adults) emerge from the sub-terranean fountain to wander up the path of life to the place where the choice has to be made.

Wither's emblematic title-page underlines the Christian import of the choice, an import usually documented by referring to *Matthew* 7:13–14 on the choice between the two gates and the two roads. However, *Proverbs* 16 will be found to provide an interesting nexus of apt quotations. Thus verses 17 and 25 tell us that 'the highway of the upright is to depart from evil: he that keepeth his way preserveth his soul', while conversely 'there is a way that seemeth right unto a man, but the end thereof are the ways of death'. And as for Dame Fortune, the lot may be cast into the lap, 'but the whole disposing thereof is of the Lord' (verse 33), just as a man's heart may devise his way, 'but the Lord directeth his steps' (verse 9). The sweet voice of Wisdom is equally proverbial: 'The wise in heart shall be called prudent: and the sweetness of the lips increaseth learning.' 'Pleasant words are as an honey-comb, sweet to the soul, and health to the bones' (verses 21 and 24).

## III

As we have seen, the entire mid-section (Books VII–XII) is influenced by the theme of the Choice of Hercules to a greater or lesser extent, beginning with the expulsion from Paradise Hall. But the material adduced so far cannot explain all the details, nor can it account for the overall thematic movement of the whole novel. A better per-spective will be achieved by enlarging the scope to include other aspects of the Hercules myth. The literary tradition includes both comic and serious versions as we may learn from G. Karl Galinsky's recent book on *The Herakles Theme. The Adaptations of the Hero in*

*Literature from Homer to the Twentieth Century* (Oxford, 1972).
Fielding himself glances in the direction of Theocritus (*Idyll* 13)
when he says of Squire Western that he called for the missing Sophia
'in as hoarse a voice, as whileom did Hercules that of Hylas' (X, 8).
This is a poem which presents Hercules as the lover struck with
madness when he loses the handsome boy. The madness of Hercules
is given serious treatment in Greek tragedy, but in Aristophanes'
*Frogs* this well-known theme is parodied in a manner which distinctly resembles Tom Jones's two fits of madness (X, 6 and
XII, 3).

There is, then, ample literary precedent for Fielding's comic
version of the Heracles theme, and particularly for the scenes showing
the hero's deplorable drunkenness (towards the end of Book V)
and his obvious gluttony (IX, 5), a gluttony which prevents him from
even noticing the seductive behaviour of his female companion. The
situation is exactly parallel to the scene in Alexis' *Hesione* when the
girl whom Hercules rescues from a sea monster is similarly ignored
the moment that food is served:

> *When he saw two serving-men bring in the tray*
> *With motley side-dishes abounding gay,*
> *He had no eyes for me.*[36]

The comic Hercules was immoderately addicted to wine, food, and
women in that order,[37] and if one re-reads the chapters describing
Jones's drunkenness and his amorous encounter with Molly Seagrim,
one observes how strongly Fielding brings out the passionate nature
of his hero—his 'naturally violent animal spirits' (V, 9). His wrath
is as powerful as his mirth, but both are outdone by his amorous
propensities. Just as the drunken Hercules, in Propertius' version
(*Elegy* IV, 9), hears the giggle of girls from a shady shrine which
fires his sexual passion, Tom Jones is suddenly confronted by a
giggling Molly in a shady grove characterised as the 'temple of *Venus
Ferina*'. Galinsky calls Propertius' burlesque version 'the most
comical and witty treatment of Herakles in Latin literature',[38] but
there is little reason to suspect an immediate source, the figure of the
comic Hercules being far too popular with poets and playwrights
alike for any one source to be at all likely. Rubens, for example,
painted a picture of the drunken Hercules reproduced by Galinsky,
who also includes Dürer's satirical version of the Choice among his
plates. Then, too, various French operas from the second half of the

seventeenth century present Hercules as a Don Juan, and the same is true of Handel's *Admeto* (1727) and his oratorio *Hercules* (1744).[39]

Many readers will have felt that the comic episodes are more frequent and more uproarious in the first twelve books than in the last six. Tom Jones discovering Mr Square squatting behind the arras in Molly Seagrim's attic, or Tom Jones defending the honour of Molly Seagrim, or 'fondly overcome with female charm' in the inn at Upton—this is what springs to mind the moment we consider the novel in terms of its greatest comic scenes. The reason for the uneven distribution is not difficult to fathom: towards the end the hero must be shown to have acquired enough wisdom to be worthy of the lovely Sophia. And for this purpose, too, Fielding could draw on the myth of Hercules for his most telling effects, the myth in this case being that of the Gallic Hercules—a dignified humanist version closely connected with the theme of the Choice. This means that it was actually possible for Fielding to suggest the ambiguous moral character of his hero by drawing on various traditions associated with Hercules. He could use Xenophon's account of the Choice in the *Memorabilia* (2.1.21–34) as his point of departure, since it presents the young Hercules as a simple lad possessed of a high degree of good nature. This must be improved by a knowledge of virtue which will enable him to deliberate before acting. By adducing just enough of the legend of the drunken Hercules Fielding suggests how vulnerable his hero is to the persuasive powers of Pleasure, while later on he may invoke the dignified image of the Gallic Hercules to show the mental powers of his hero—powers enabling him to become that benefactor of his friends whom Xenophon praises in his fable of the Choice. It is entirely in keeping with this progress that the hero's exploits initially are largely on the level of physical action, while towards the end he must depend on the powers of his mind. No oaken stick, however trusty, can perform the labour of uniting Nancy Miller to the man whose child she carries; for this particular purpose Tom Jones calls upon, and commands, all the powers of rhetoric associated with the Gallic Hercules.

The Gallic Hercules is the male embodiment of wisdom and especially of the irresistible powers of eloquence. Renaissance emblems show this power by letting the words issuing out of the mouth of Hercules, form a golden chain which keeps the audience captive in the most literal manner.[40] It was widely held that the French kings were descended from this prototype of the good orator and the good

ruler, and this belief was still sacrosanct in the early eighteenth century
so that Nicolas Fréret was imprisoned in the Bastille for four months
in 1715 for having cast doubts on it in a memorandum addressed to
the Academy.[41]

It is in Book XIV, chs. 6–8 that Tom Jones makes his decisive
appearance as the Gallic Hercules. His pursuit of Sophia, in complete
disregard of physical discomforts, has proved his total commitment
to his choice; the episode of Nancy Miller will prove his ability to
assist fallen Virtue. On learning the facts of Nancy Miller's case, he
at once promises to persuade young Nightingale to marry the girl
he has betrayed, adding that 'I think the picture which I shall lay
before him, will affect him.' And the 'picture' is a classical example of
persuasive rhetoric at the end of which Nightingale exclaims: 'I
wanted not your eloquence to rouse me.' The tempering of anger,
greed, and the taste for pleasure is the role usually assigned to the
Gallic Hercules, as explained for example by Ripa in his *Iconologia,*
and the subduing of Avarice is the motif on a medal reproduced by
Rudolf Wittkower in his essay on 'Chance, Time and Virtue.'[42]
Avarice is, of course, the besetting sin of old Mr Nightingale, and in
tackling him Tom Jones is undertaking 'an impossibility' as his
friend points out (XIV, 7). In describing this episode Fielding uses
the word 'labour' in a fairly obtrusive manner; thus he writes that
'Mr Jones was acting the most virtuous part imaginable in labouring
to preserve his fellow-creatures from destruction' (XV, 1), and as
Tom Jones presents himself to old Mr Nightingale, the latter twice exclaims that 'he would lose his labour' (XIV, 8). And so he does, since
'neither history nor fable have ever yet ventured to record an instance
of anyone, who by force of argument and reason hath triumphed over
habitual avarice' (XIV, 8). But the labour of securing Nancy Miller's
marriage is fully achieved, and Tom's reward is to feel the highest
form of pleasure on seeing a whole family raised from a state of
misery—'more perhaps than worldly men often purchase to themselves by undergoing the most severe labour, and often by wading
through the deepest iniquity' (XV, 8).

It was only to be expected that once our hero has entered into the
'Elysian fields' of London he should again be assaulted by the votaries
of mere sensual Pleasure. And Pleasure (personified by Lady Bellaston) pursues him appropriately enough in the 'temple' presided
over by 'the great high-priest of pleasure' during a fashionable masquerade (XIII, 7). Ronald Paulson has drawn attention to the many

occasions on which Hogarth includes the various appurtenances of a masquerade as emblems of licentious pleasure, but similar iconographical details are typical of Renaissance versions of the Choice of Hercules. One sees this on leafing through the plates included by Erwin Panofsky in his *Hercules am Scheidewege* (1930). Masks are displayed next to the figure of Pleasure/Vice in Annibale Caracci's famous painting of the Choice (Plate 44), and in versions painted by Sebastiano Ricci, Jan Lyss, and Michel Corneille le Jeune (Plates 50–2). The masks suggest the falseness of the pleasures offered by Vice, and Lady Bellaston is drawn so as to resemble the figure of vicious Pleasure as seen for example in George Wither's emblem on the Choice (number I, 22). The emblem shows her as possessed of devilish attributes hidden from view partly because they are placed at the back, partly by the interposition of a mask held in front of the leering face. As Wither's poem puts it, 'her Face / Was but a painted *Vizard*, which did hide / The foul'st Deformity that ever was.' The identification is reinforced by so shaping the scene when Lady Bellaston enters Tom's bedroom (XV,7) as to repeat some of the features of the scene with Mrs Waters in the inn at Upton. Tom is again compared to Adonis ('you might at this instant sit for the picture of Adonis'), and the attack is again mounted in silence by means of looks ('a look, in which the lady conveyed more soft ideas than it was possible to express with her tongue'). But as far as Tom Jones is concerned the illicit relationship entails no pleasure, and it is surely this point that Fielding is concerned to make. He wanted to show how firmly the hero resists the combined allure of wealth, high social rank, and pleasure, and he could not have foreseen that later generations would take such a serious view of the sexual relationship that this would overshadow the stout refusal to be caught in the snares of Pleasure. Circumstances conspire against Tom Jones to compel him against his will to engage in an affair for which he has no relish. (This richly comic situation prevents Tom Jones from sharing the fate of Joseph Andrews vis-à-vis Lady Booby.) The fact that Tom Jones, despite the intensity with which he pursues his Sophia, goes out of his way to be a true benefactor of his friends and acquaintances, proves his moral mettle. The role played by rhetoric in this part of the novel is underscored when Lady Bellaston persuades Lord Fellamar to undertake the rape of Sophia. As the chapter-heading explains, 'she applies her Eloquence to an ill Purpose' (XV,4). She acts, to use Fielding's words, 'like a true orator' and is only too successful. Her words 'sunk deeper into his lordship than anything which Demosthenes or Cicero could have said on the occasion'. Her power to corrupt is proved in the case of Lord Fellamar, just as Tom Jones's persuasion of young Nightingale proves his ability to advance the cause of Virtue.

It is sufficiently plain that Tom Jones is no paragon of sexual virtue even in the third part, but we must not permit the immorality of his affair with Lady Bellaston to obscure the features that identify him as the Hercules who has made his choice. And with Sophia herself as the pledge of his constancy (as the hero craftily argues in the penultimate chapter) the reader is willing to believe that he will persist. One may perhaps feel that Fielding has loaded the scales too heavily in favour of the lovely Sophia so that the choice was only too easy, if not downright tempting. Who would not be pleased to make a similar choice if lucky enough to be presented with it? The answer must be that Tom Jones obtains his Sophia only after he has proved his ability to act like the Gallic Hercules. He has learnt to add the powers of his mind to his instinctive good nature, progressing from a comic Hercules addicted to the life of the senses to the dignified Hercules who may rightly be the consort of the female personification of wisdom.

But if Sophia Western serves as a virtually irresistible image of perfection, must not Fielding be said to have violated the principle that characters of angelic goodness or diabolical depravity must be avoided? Sophia's perfection, however, is sufficiently modified by the comic mode to be fully acceptable; she has as it were two faces in the manner attributed by Shaftesbury to the 'philosophical HERO' of the dramatic dialogues of Antiquity. As he explains in his *Advice to an Author,* this hero

> was in himself *a perfect Character*: yet, in some respects, so veil'd, and in a Cloud, that to the unattentive Surveyor he seem'd often to be very different from what he really was: and this chiefly by reason of a certain exquisite and refin'd Raillery which belong'd to his Manner, and by virtue of which he cou'd treat the highest Subjects, and those of the commonest Capacity both together, and render 'em explanatory of each other.

In this manner the '*heroick* and *the simple, the tragick,* and *the comick Vein*' were fused, yet in such a fashion that despite the 'Mysteriousness of the principal Character, the *Under-parts* or *second Characters* shew'd human Nature more distinctly, and to the Life.' This sort of writing, therefore, constitutes a pocket-mirror in which we may see two faces: the 'commanding Genius' and 'that rude, undisciplin'd and head-strong Creature, whom we our-selves in our natural Capacity most exactly resembled'.[43]

Fielding fully exploits the ambiguity inherent in this joco-serious approach, and Sophia, too, is exposed to that 'exquisite and refin'd Raillery' which permitted him to treat the highest subjects together with the most common ones so that they illuminate each other. But in the case of Fielding's use of various aspects of the Hercules myth the comic mode has so obscured the pattern which it modifies that it has been virtually ignored. Yet it is by playing the two against each other that we perceive what Shaftesbury calls the two faces: the myth embodying the abstract concepts of Beauty, Wisdom, and Virtue in all their dignity, and the actual events that are their manifestation in the world we all know. If we are blind to the former, the latter will lose much of their resonance.

The vision of ideal beauty afforded by the lovely Sophia has its formal counterpart in the highly ordered structure of the work. Fielding may have been inspired by the Earl of Shaftesbury to achieve this juxtaposition of the beauty of ordered structure with the beauty of moral harmony in the world within, but the presence in his library of several editions of Plato indicates an interest in the Platonic tradition and so does his copy of Ralph Cudworth's *True intellectual System of the Universe* (1678).[44] It is nevertheless convenient to draw on Shaftesbury for comments explaining this interesting collaboration between form and content, or external and internal harmony. The platonic vision of ideal beauty may be glimpsed in a character such as Sophia or in the formal organisation of the work itself, the two being interdependent. Shaftesbury links the two in the following passage taken from his *Advice to an Author*:

> HOWEVER difficult or desperate it may appear in any Artist to endeavour to bring *Perfection* into his Work; if he has not at least the *Idea* of PERFECTION to give him Aim, he will be found very defective and mean in his Performance. Tho his Intention be to please the World, he must nevertheless be, in a manner, *above it*; and fix his Eye upon that consummate *Grace*, that Beauty of *Nature*, and that *Perfection* of Numbers, which the rest of Mankind, feeling only by the Effect . . . suppose to be

a kind of *Charm,* or *Inchantment,* of which the Artist himself can give no account.[45]

It is impossible to tell whether Shaftesbury here uses his key phrases ('consummate *Grace*', 'Beauty of *Nature*' and *Perfection* of Numbers') to refer to external or internal harmony, to structural organisation or to character portrayal, but this is exactly the point: the two cannot be kept separate. It seems both possible and probable that Fielding similarly related his theme of moral harmony to the structural harmony imposed upon the text by various kinds of symmetrical arrangements. The undoubted presence of these structural features lends strong support to an interpretation along the lines suggested here: behind all the comedy we should perceive the 'highest Subjects' and the most 'consummate *Grace*' to use Shaftesbury's phrases, and it is particularly important to do this as we consider Tom Jones himself in his role as a richly comic eighteenth-century Hercules. We should do him an injustice if we fail to perceive how he first enacts the famous Choice and then achieves the higher level represented by the Gallic Hercules. Fielding must have invented the Nancy Miller/Nightingale subplot primarily to enable his hero to engage in actions that may underline his new role; we already know that he possesses an instinctive good nature, but we need to discover that he is perfectly capable of other than merely physical exploits. Since the sweetness of rational discourse is the attribute given to Sophia in her role as Virtue, Tom Jones becomes a proper mate for her when he, too, is seen to possess it.

## IV

Readers who find it difficult to accept this favourable reading of Tom Jones's character will find a strong ally in Dr Johnson, whose reaction to the story was entirely predictable. He condemned it because it shows a morally ambiguous hero (as explained in *Rambler* 4), and because it links the idea of lasting happiness with the idea of conscious choice. That Samuel Johnson read *Tom Jones* as a story based on the theme of choice may, I think, be inferred from the pages of *Rasselas.* Johnson rejects out of hand the notion that choices can be made so as to ensure a lasting state of happiness; only a God can survey the whole of existence so that a valid choice can be made, and only a God can ensure the duration of the state ultimately chosen. Johnson's annoyance with Fielding's analysis of human existence must have been just as great as Fielding's with Richardson's. *Rasselas* is an analysis and a refutation of all pleasing visions of lasting happiness, and it is distinctly interesting that the narrative should pursue a tripartite, symmetrical structure consisting of three groups of sixteen chapters and a conclusion.[46] Could Johnson have arranged his material in this manner to permit the structural similarity to *Tom Jones* to underline the thematic antithesis? This seems a possibility on observing how the later writer almost parodies the thematic movement through the three parts of *Tom Jones*. While Tom Jones is expelled from a Paradise Hall whose owner is an eighteenth-century *imago Dei*, in Johnson's story the hero laboriously makes his escape from a valley which at first seems a perfect paradise of pleasure. At the point of exodus (as the first third moves into the second) each hero is intent on choosing his future way of life, but *Rasselas* contains no major confrontation scene issuing in a final choice—only a sequence of choices paraded in front of readers and travellers alike, each of which is eventually rejected as false. Johnson is intent on letting his travellers experience what has been called a pattern of comic disillusion,[47] and the choices examined in the mid-section (chapters 17–32) constitute closed systems of unhappiness of the kind associated with Pope's couplet rhetoric.[48] The same evils prevail whether a man's state be private or public, high or low, and grief and joy are equally transient whatever the circumstances under which one lives. In the last third the rescue of the mad astronomer may serve as Johnson's counterpoint to Tom Jones's rescue of Nancy Miller, the power of rhetoric, or persuasion, being replaced by normal human fellowship. The astronomer is saved quite simply by being introduced to human society at its best; good conversation plus the diversions of every-day life restore his sanity. The undramatic character of this episode is remarkable; in comparison Tom Jones's persuasion of his friend seems virtually melodramatic.

The comment that Johnson's *Rasselas* offers on Fielding's vision of life is conveyed as much structurally as through the turn of the narrative, and nowhere more so than in the last chapter, the 'conclusion, in which nothing is concluded'. This is a chapter which presents a sequence of four choices, all of them different. These choices are so arranged and described that readers familiar with Renaissance thought (or with classical philosophy) will observe that they constitute a complete circle or quaternion in the manner of the four

elements and the four qualities.[49] This is one reason why the conclusion is inconclusive: through these four choices it presents a complete 'wheel of life'.

Pekuah's choice comes first. She is 'weary of expectation and disgust' and 'would gladly be fixed in some unvariable state'. And the
state she prefers is one of complete seclusion from the world. The last
choice—that of Imlac and the astronomer—represents the exact
opposite: a willing acceptance of a state of flux. The two are 'con-
tented to be driven along the stream of life without directing their
course to any particular place'. Two choices are entailed in each case:
one of a state of mind, another of environment. Despite the complete
contrast with regard to environment (Pekuah seeing herself as totally
apart from the world or out of it, Imlac and the astronomer being
completely immersed), the two states have one element in common:
the absence of desire. Both display *stasis* of mind.

In between these extremes (the first choice and the last) fall the
choices of the brother and sister, both of whom are said to *desire*:
'She desired first . . . ' and 'The prince desired . . . ' Both are prompted
by desire to act, rejecting the state of mental passivity, the difference
between them being one of chosen environment. She chooses a private
sphere ('a college of learned women'), he one which is completely
public. His kingdom, however, is to be a small one so that he himself
as head of state may 'administer justice in his own person'. What
they have in common is commitment to an active life.

The pattern traditionally attributed to the four elements and the
four qualities is exactly analogous. Although the elements of earth
and fire are completely contrary in that the one is hot and the other
cold, they share the quality of dryness, and if one presents the sequence
in tabular form, one perceives that a link is always provided between
each element and the next, the last connecting with the first so that
the circle is closed:

| earth | water | air | fire |
|---|---|---|---|
| dry & cold | cold & moist | moist & hot | hot & dry |

This is why Augustine and Milton can say that the 'quaternions'
of the elements and of the seasons 'run / Perpetual circle'.[50]

The four choices listed in the last chapter of *Rasselas* are similarly
connected by links into an all-encompassing circle or cycle. Two of
the qualities attributed to the elements were supposed to be active

(hot and cold), the other two passive, and Johnson, too, posits two active and two passive qualities or aspects. The mental attitude to life may be active or passive, just as one's physical environment may be private or public. One may be out of the stream of life (apart) or immersed in it, as indicated in the following table:

| Pekuah: | Nekayah: | Rasselas: | Imlac/ |
|---|---|---|---|
| | | | astronomer: |
| passive & apart | apart & active | active & immersed | immersed & passive |

The sequence of choices begins with double *stasis* or complete withdrawal from life, mentally as well as physically; the second choice carries on the theme of retirement from the public sphere, but posits intense mental activity ('to learn all sciences' and to 'divide her time between the acquisition and communication of wisdom'). The prince, however, boldly commits himself to an active life in a public sphere, and this progression reaches its climax with total immersion in the flux of life by Imlac and the astronomer. But since they have no desire to direct 'their course to any particular port', they achieve the mental *stasis* characteristic of Pekuah's choice, so that in this respect the last choice connects with the first, and the circle is closed.

These four choices are aligned with the textual division into three parts, Pekuah's choice connecting with the Happy Valley, Nekayah's and Rasselas's with the mid-section, and that of Imlac and the astronomer with the events of the last third.

The first choice recalls the Happy Valley because of its complete seclusion, and because life in the valley imposes complete quiescence (on the basis of the false assumption that all desires are satisfied). But the *stasis* envisaged by Pekuah is voluntary, not imposed, and it stipulates a *rejection* of the quest for pleasure, and not a total commitment to it. Just as Pekuah's choice constitutes a comment on, and rejection of, the first third of Johnson's story, the last choice mirrors the experience of the last third when the travellers are at the mercy of all the hazards of life. The flux, which they experience very much against their will, is willingly embraced by Imlac and the astronomer, while they reject the state of mental flux (the eternal transition from expectation to disgust and back again to expectation). They are content to be carried along by the stream of life. The prince and the princess, too, similarly modify their choices so as to incorporate their experiences of life in the mid-section, where the prince investigates the public sphere and the princess the private.

All this shows how carefully Samuel Johnson plotted the structure of his tale, and how logically thought out his conclusion is. Although the conclusion has always been felt as open-ended, it is now possible to see somewhat more clearly how its inconclusiveness functions. Each traveller has learnt an important lesson enabling him or her so to modify his choice as to avoid the more obvious hazards and perversions. Pekuah's choice avoids the hedonism of the Happy Valley and the see-saw pattern of the hermit, whose life is a never-ending cycle of ascetic solitude and convivial pleasures. The princess on her part tempers her fondness for learning by company, thus avoiding the fate of the astronomer and also the evils that accompany the restriction to mere family life. The prince modifies the size of his kingdom and the scope of his public activities, while Imlac and the astronomer have learnt that we cannot hope to direct our course to a chosen port; life plays with us and we must be content to accept life on these terms.

The four choices, then, represent ideal states modified by experience, but they also represent all possible choices. Between them they cover all the combinations of mentally and physically active or passive states. However, the most important lesson taught by experience is that none of these wishes can be obtained.

Never has a refutation been more complete. Not only does this story about a 'choice of life' conclude by presenting a complete cycle of choices, but no sooner has the cycle been presented than it is withdrawn. 'Of these wishes that they had formed they well knew that none could be obtained. They deliberated a while what was to be done, and resolved, when the inundation should cease, to return to Abissinia.'

Although one may relish Johnson's psychological realism, it is difficult not to prefer Fielding's vision of life. If the choice between Fielding and Johnson is a test of the reader's sense of moral values, I suspect that he who chooses Fielding does so because he believes in the higher beauty represented by Sophia. It is his sincere love of this higher beauty which guarantees the hero's faithful adherence to the path of virtue, and whoever separates virtue from pleasure in this life does so because the humanist version of the Choice of Hercules has ceased to carry conviction. Fielding seems to me to have grasped the true inwardness of this choice and to have succeeded

4. Hercules between Vice and Virtue. From George Wither, *A Collection of Emblemes* (London, 1635). The plates are taken from Gabriel Rollenhagen's *Nucleus Emblematum,* 1611–13. *(Bodleian Library.)*

5. The Gallic Hercules. From Andreas Alciatus, *Emblematum libellus* (1535), p. 490. *(Bodleian Library.)*

6. The Gallic Hercules.
From Vincenzo Cartari, *Le imagini degli dei degli antichi* (Padua, 1608),
p. 314 (actual size.)
*(The Shakespeare Institute, University of Birmingham.)*

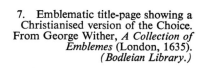

7. Emblematic title-page showing a Christianised version of the Choice.
From George Wither, *A Collection of Emblemes* (London, 1635).
*(Bodleian Library.)*

in conveying it to his readers through a mode of writing indebted to the joco-serious tradition so popular in the Renaissance. His 'exquisite and refin'd Raillery', to use Shaftesbury's phrase, permitted a presentation of absolute beauty which strikes one the more strongly because it must perforce be oblique.

# 6

# *Mistaken conduct and proper 'feeling':*
# *A study of Jane Austen's*
# Pride and Prejudice

Grete Ek

> Seldom, very seldom, does complete truth belong to any human disclosure; seldom can it happen that something is not a little disguised, or a little mistaken; but where, as in this case, though the conduct is mistaken, the feelings are not, it may not be very material.       Jane Austen, *Emma* (Ch. XIII)

In a recent study of Jane Austen's novels, *Pride and Prejudice* is described as 'the greatest example of the novel of antitheses'.[1] With few exceptions, critics seem to favour the general concept that the protagonists represent largely opposing attitudes that need to be modified and then finally reconciled within the framework of the comic resolution. Thus Elizabeth is at first proudly independent and contemptuous of convention, whereas Darcy is an equally proud exponent of social stratification. Before being united in mutual affection and mutual allegiance to social and ethical norms, the initial, basic assumptions of both must be transcended and 'improved'.[2]

The reading submitted here presents a different interpretation of the relationship between conflict and resolution. It is possible to argue that the initial conflict is in itself ironic: the very situations and the very response which create antagonism also reveal a basic affinity between hero and heroine. The resolution, then, eventually terminates a process of clarification rather than one of substantial change, and serves to affirm attitudes that are at all times the common property of Darcy and Elizabeth. The 'contrived' conflict necessarily conceals attraction between them, which the reader is nonetheless allowed to suspect while enjoying the inevitable movement towards a climax of misunderstanding. Beneath the antithetical framework we may recognise a substructure based on a gradual and consistent disclosure of facts that invariably contradict the dramatic illusion in the novel's first half.[3]

This is not to say that Jane Austen has found a new way of proclaiming 'whatever IS, is right', or that the conflict is more or less literally a storm in a teacup. Clearly her conception of 'reality' informs the artistic medium—as Lionel Trilling observes when contending that her irony 'is only secondarily a matter of tone. Primarily it is a method of comprehension. It perceives the world through an awareness of its contradictions, paradoxes, and anomalies.'[4] A conflict based on contrasts that are not what they seem is quite proper in a world that makes it possible—nay, highly probable—that people should be led to misunderstand one another. In *Pride and Prejudice* not only immature conduct on the part of the protagonists but also fictional 'alliances' encouraged by the social structure reinforce that lack of knowledge about the self and about others which creates disorder. The discovery of true partnership—which to my mind remains the novel's central issue—accompanies the removal of misconceptions. Darcy and Elizabeth dramatise the issue, seconded by a number of minor characters whose own interrelationships and whose interaction with hero and heroine serve to clarify events on centre stage.

The novel may conveniently be called a mystery story, where the reader accompanies an engaging heroine in her search for the truth about a man she at first comes to despise, and then finally learns to love. It so happens that she discovers herself in the process. The first half is designed so as to baffle and mislead Elizabeth—and to some extent the reader—while at the same time providing adequate preparation for a dénouement gradually effected after the proposal scene. Darcy's conduct must be such as to make Elizabeth's increasing antagonism possible and acceptable and yet anticipate the eventual revelation of his true character. The presentation of Elizabeth caters to even more diverse requirements: she must invite allegiance so that we may share in the suspense, display limitations that will help us to partake of the author's superior understanding, *and* reveal characteristics that make her final union with Darcy highly plausible. What we need to recognise, then, is the extent to which Jane Austen balances the construction of a credible conflict with a concomitant affirmation of certain underlying 'truths' that can only be fully developed and clarified in the second half of the novel. Our awareness of these 'truths' will not only prepare us for the resolution, but increase our sense of dramatic irony, in so far as our knowledge is constantly superior to that of the protagonists. As I have suggested, 'knowledge' in *Pride and Prejudice* is practically synonymous with knowledge of *character*, as character defines itself both in a social and in a more purely personal context.

At the Meryton Assembly, Darcy's refusal to play 'eligible' produces a delightfully absurd response. The norm by which his conduct is judged is set by that paragon of folly, Mrs Bennet, and presumably by a great number of match-making parents and marriageable daughters with an equal claim to 'understanding' and 'judgment'. Dorothy van Ghent observes that Jane Austen turns the novel's opening paragraph inside-out by showing that it is an unmarried woman who is in want of a wealthy husband. Thus the Mrs Bennets are acting in accordance with the realities of an acquisitive society, 'febrile with social and economic rivalry'.[5] Their behaviour is nonetheless silly enough to provide Mr Bennet with constant entertainment, and is activated by a notion of 'prudence' that bears faint relation to the cardinal virtue. Direct authorial comment, informing us that Mrs Bennet 'was a woman of mean understanding, little information, and uncertain temper' (p. 5)[6] combines with ironic exposure in the initial domestic scenes at Longbourn to define both a certain type of woman and her 'code', which invariably conditions our reactions to events in the Assembly room:

> . . . Mr. Darcy soon drew the attention of the room by his fine, tall person, handsome features, noble mien; and the report which was in general circulation within five minutes after his entrance, of his having ten thousand a year. The gentlemen pronounced him to be a fine figure of a man, the ladies declared he was much handsomer than Mr. Bingley, and he was looked at with great admiration for about half the evening, till his manners gave a disgust which turned the tide of his popularity; for he was discovered to be proud, to be above his company, and above being pleased; and not all his large estate in Derbyshire could then save him from having a most forbidding, disagreeable countenance, and being unworthy to be compared with his friend (p. 10).

Darcy commits the sin of not dancing with young ladies he does not know. Public opinion is fickle indeed. 'His character was decided.

He was the proudest, most disagreeable man in the world, and every body hoped that he would never come there again' (p. 11). Mrs Bennet's later vacillation between abuse and approval of Mr Collins —according to his 'usefulness'—effectively parallels that of Meryton in general upon their first meeting with Darcy. At this point, readers might be inclined to make a favourite of Darcy, if only because he manages to mortify his public.

The author, however, balances this impression by including Elizabeth among the characters affronted by Darcy's pride. Whereas his behaviour seems perfectly justified when seen in relation to the expectations of female Meryton, it becomes offensive the minute it narrows down to a concrete act of rudeness directed against the heroine. The insult is repeatedly referred to in subsequent sequences: ' "She is tolerable; but not handsome enough to tempt *me*; and I am in no humour at present to give consequence to young ladies who are slighted by other men . . . " ' (p. 12). As it provides sufficient motivation for Elizabeth's hostility, the episode has considerable dramatic value. Furthermore, it pinpoints her weaknesses as well as his: if Darcy is haughty, Elizabeth certainly has her share of vanity and pride. Even so, any feeble attempt to pronounce moral judgement comes to nought. Elizabeth joyfully concedes to her own short-comings (' " . . . I could easily forgive *his* pride, if he had not morti-fied *mine*" '; p. 20), and Mary Bennet's homiletic speech on vanity and pride does not encourage further edifying reflections in the reader. It is obvious, also, that Elizabeth is too quick in condemning Darcy: in jumping to conclusions on the basis of appearances, she is acting in the best of Meryton traditions. Nor does this take us very far, as everyone, including Darcy, seems to partake of a general inclination to pronounce hasty judgement: 'Darcy . . . had seen a collection of people in whom there was little beauty and no fashion, for none of whom he had felt the smallest interest, and from none received either attention or pleasure' (p. 16). On the surface, then, moral dis-tinctions are blurred, but the conduct of hero and heroine respectively establishes an effective—if morally neutral—contrast between rigidity on the one hand, and resentment of that quality on the other.

As the response of both is largely determined by environmental incompatibility, this contrast is clearly deceptive. Elizabeth is part of a setting unacceptable to Darcy, and for one moment she has become the object of his scorn, unjustly, but understandably so. By the same token, Darcy's haughtiness is reinforced by his association with Mrs

Hurst and Miss Bingley, of whom Elizabeth—very wisely and perceptively—cannot 'approve'. The reader, on the other hand, is invited to join with the author in her assessment of the reality behind the façade: 'In understanding Darcy was the superior', says the reliable commentator in one of her rare direct appearances. 'Bingley was by no means deficient, but Darcy was clever. He was at the same time haughty, reserved, and fastidious, and his manners, though well bred, were not inviting' (p. 16). At the earliest possible stage Jane Austen states outright that her hero's conduct leaves something to be desired, yet he is superior in *understanding*—a compliment of the highest order, given to those whose basic principles are above reproach. Mrs Hurst and Miss Bingley are 'proud and conceited', for no even faintly acceptable reason, and their pride, though related to the quality associated with Darcy, is unaccompanied by any positive virtue. The factual information conveyed is naturally far less significant than the author's reasoning, implying above all that we need to distinguish between characters who display a superficial similarity of manner, and that conduct in a narrow sense is not necessarily an adequate expression of the mind.[7]

The splendid irony of the initial 'conflict' is brought out only when seen in a larger context: the hero and the heroine have in fact—quite plausibly—fallen out over a social code which they both despise. Elizabeth is no more looking for a matrimonial 'prize' than Darcy is willing to be one. Various minor episodes serve to illustrate this affinity. While Elizabeth cannot imitate her father's abuse of Mrs Bennet, she obviously shares his keen sense of the ridiculous and futile in matrimonial machinations. She can only witness the addresses of Mr Collins with numb incredulity—and then emphatically reject both his 'reasoning' and that of her mother. Similarly, Darcy sees fit to rebuff the amorous Miss Bingley: ' "Undoubtedly . . . there is meanness in *all* the arts which ladies sometimes condescend to employ for captivation. Whatever bears affinity to cunning is despicable" ' (p. 40). If there is 'individualism' in *Pride and Prejudice*, Darcy and Elizabeth have an equal share in it, in that they are both defending themselves against unions that are based on an absurdly narrow definition of 'prudence', and that disregard 'essentials'.[8] The juxtaposition of Elizabeth and Charlotte, both single women of no fortune and little consequence, both wooed by a comic monster who offers security, establishes a strong contrast between idealism and its antithesis—which is not to say that Charlotte is condemned. Her position is pitiful in that she surrenders to a one-dimensional existence. It is easy to see this as the darkest aspect of the novel, and perhaps the most troubling, because Charlotte's options are so severely limited. The celebration of integrity clashes somewhat uncomfortably with the obvious need for security, and Elizabeth is conveniently saved from ever having to bear the consequences of her idealism. We must concede that the admirable principles of Elizabeth and Darcy both may not be uniformly applicable within a world 'haunted' by the 'specter of the shabby-genteel spinster'.[9]

It is the most wonderful paradox that the ultimate proclamation of independence comes through Elizabeth's refusal of Darcy himself —a Darcy who clearly resents having been 'captivated'. At that moment, *her* open disregard of social and pecuniary advantage confronts *his* unpleasant but understandable assumption that any woman will accept a man of his consequence. It seems to me indisputable that her idealism and his arrogant defensiveness spring from the same contempt for that universally acknowledged truth.

The question of 'prudent' marriages relates closely to that of social pride, which more than any other element serves to maintain a sense of contrast between the main characters. No one would deny that Darcy betrays a strong feeling of social superiority, or that Elizabeth resents his attitude. The problem is complex, and the presentation deliberately confusing. Thus the one episode which supposedly testifies to a wholly inexcusable awareness of social distinctions on his part, namely his interference to prevent Bingley from marrying Jane, is shown to have far more diverse origins than Elizabeth is at first capable of comprehending. Similarly, Wickham's denunciation of Darcy—which involves accusations of excessive pride—proves to be founded on pure fiction. In both instances, the reader may be inclined to withhold judgement from the beginning, as we receive information second-hand, and our ability to perceive Elizabeth's limitations may prevent us from putting infinite trust in her subsequent interpretations. Such neutrality, however, is counteracted by certain exchanges with the Bingleys that Elizabeth does not witness as well as by momentary glimpses of Darcy's mind: in spirit these revelations seem to correspond with Elizabeth's evaluation of him. He maintains that Jane's and Elizabeth's uncles in Cheapside 'must very materially lessen their chance of marrying men of any consideration in the world' (p. 37), and is even afraid that his conduct may have raised false hopes in Elizabeth:

He wisely resolved to be particularly careful that no sign of admiration should *now* escape him, nothing that could elevate her with the hope of influencing his felicity; sensible that if such an idea had been suggested, his behaviour during the last day must have material weight in confirming or crushing it. Steady to his purpose, he scarcely spoke ten words to her through the whole of Saturday, and though they were at one time left by themselves for half an hour, he adhered most conscientiously to his book, and would not even look at her (p. 60).

His 'wisdom' is at best a partial virtue: as has been shown by Kenneth Moler in particular, Darcy is certainly related to the class-conscious heroes of Richardson and Fanny Burney.[10]

Whereas the conflict is perfectly plausible, it is not necessarily founded on factual disagreement. Elizabeth and Darcy both provide correctives to a superficial assessment of their attitudes. Thus it would be wrong to conceive of a Darcy solidly entrenched behind aristocratic principles: his association with the Bingleys, who have acquired their money 'in trade', in itself defeats such a supposition. This relationship is indeed proper in a society which always allowed a certain amount of interchange between classes. Nor do we have adequate reason to see Elizabeth as an advocate of 'instinct' and 'feeling', as opposed to Darcy's consideration for his social place. It will be remembered that Elizabeth recognises Darcy's right to be proud —a significant remark, in itself untouched by irony, which is 'lost' in the facetious context in which it occurs. Her reactions to his first proposal also testify to her own acceptance of his social superiority: '. . . she could not be insensible to the compliment of such a man's affection, and though her intentions did not vary for an instant, she was at first sorry for the pain he was to receive . . .' (p. 189). While Darcy's pride is somewhat excessive, it is fairly clear that class consciousness as such carries no negative connotation, and we may assume, with Dr Chapman, that a seemingly impassable gulf 'yawned between [Fitzwilliam Darcy] and Mrs Bennet's daughter.'[11] Darcy's own acknowledgement of Elizabeth's and Jane's moral superiority suggests a possible bridging of the gulf: the question of good breeding, predominantly moral in its conception, helps to define alliances that cut across traditional class barriers.

The display of ill breeding by characters whom the social structure aligns with hero and heroine respectively furthers the movement towards a climax of antagonism; yet the response of Darcy and Elizabeth offers supreme proof of their affinity. The vulgarity of Elizabeth's connections at first cements Darcy's feeling of superiority, and Elizabeth is affronted and humiliated because she must remain loyal to a family whose follies never cease to amaze her. Paradoxically, her awareness of his attitude towards indecorous behaviour—an attitude which she obviously shares—cannot but increase her hostility. When Mrs Bennet visits Netherfield during Jane's illness, her conduct shocks everyone, including the tolerant Bingley. As is the case at the Netherfield ball later on, Darcy does no more than faintly echo Elizabeth's own reactions: 'Darcy only smiled; and the general pause which ensued made Elizabeth tremble lest her mother should be exposing herself again' (p. 45). The author emphasises the similarity of situation and psychological response by rendering Elizabeth's mortification at the ball in the very same terms: 'It vexed her to see [Mr Collins] expose himself to such a man' (p. 98). 'To Elizabeth it appeared, that had her family made an agreement to expose themselves as much as they could during the evening, it would have been impossible for them to play their parts with more spirit, or finer success' (pp. 101–2). What Elizabeth fears is *exposure*, an unmasking of a reality that involves a violation of propriety, sense, decorum. Her acute discomfort reveals her own concern for such essential ethical norms. The absurdity of Mr Collins has always been obvious to Elizabeth. Darcy is 'eyeing him with unrestrained wonder' (p. 98). In *Emma*, a similar effect is obtained when Emma and Mr Knightley display an all but identical attitude to the conduct of Emma's relatives, preparing us for their ultimate union.[12]

By the same token, Elizabeth resents the offensive snobbery and ill breeding displayed by Darcy's own acquaintances and relations, and as her perceptions are far from unbiased, she identifies Darcy with his environment. There is no reason for the reader to be unaware of her mistake. Darcy is obviously amused by Miss Bingley's stupidity and embarrassed by her incivility to Elizabeth: ' . . . Elizabeth had been at Netherfield long enough. She attracted him more than he liked—and Miss Bingley was uncivil to *her*, and more teazing than usual to himself' (pp. 59–60). At Rosings we are explicitly informed that he disapproves of Lady Catherine's behaviour: 'Mr. Darcy looked a little ashamed of his aunt's ill breeding, and made no answer' (p. 173). The author is in fact subjecting Darcy to a process of humiliation that parallels Elizabeth's own, the only difference being that

Elizabeth's mind is always at the centre of our attention, whereas Darcy's reactions are merely hinted at. In both instances, their mortification denotes the soundness of their principles.

We have seen that Darcy and Elizabeth both reject a certain type of social 'code', and that this naturally does not imply a questioning of contemporary values in general. They resent the *parody* of an established virtue, not the virtue itself. Furthermore, their common allegiance to propriety, along with an acceptance of a stratified—if partly flexible—social structure, makes neither protagonist particularly 'individualistic' vis-à-vis inherited norms. On the other hand, moral allegiance obviously crosses the barriers that initially seem to estrange them. A discovery of such allegiance enables the reader—and eventually the maturing protagonists—to see that just as they belong together, people like Lady Catherine, Mrs Bennet, Lydia, and Miss Bingley—to name a few—are of a piece: Lady Catherine and Mrs Bennet both try to pawn off their daughters, and Miss Bingley and Lydia pawn *themselves* off to the best of their ability. All four ladies betray a total lack of true breeding in their relationship with others. The 'exaggerated figures of fun' are not, then, outside the moral scheme because they are caricatures and frequently productive of pure comedy. The unhappy critic might perhaps be made to sound like Mary Bennet if he were to subject each individual to grave moral evaluation, but we may agree that they represent *attitudes* that are potentially subversive, and that Darcy and Elizabeth both detest.[13] It is possible to say, I believe, that the underlying conflict is not between Darcy and Elizabeth at all, but between sound—if faulty— characters on the one hand, and foolishness and indecency on the other. The moral education of the main characters involves no modification of their basic principles, but an awakening to awareness of their own place in the moral scheme. As the *conduct* of both is in some respects immature during the first phase of their relationship, their humiliation is a prerequisite to full awareness of how conduct should be guided by principles. Thus a discovery of moral allegiance involves a recognition of failings and virtues alike.

A total identification with Elizabeth would clearly blur these essential issues. If the author's main problem in *Emma* is one of maintaining sympathy for the heroine despite her 'almost crippling faults', we may surely say that Jane Austen faces the inverse problem in *Pride and Prejudice* when she needs to expose the heroine's weaknesses despite her almost totally disarming charm and delightful good sense.[14] A recognition of Elizabeth's limitations, however, takes us only part of the way. We might easily assume that some of her shortcomings testify to her being different from Darcy in 'essentials', which would not deduct from her attractiveness. We have to take still another look behind appearances. Elizabeth, it is generally agreed, is admirable enough to give reliable commentary at times, and we may frequently recognise the author's ironic voice in that of her heroine. If we go one step further, however, we see that Elizabeth is unwittingly judging herself. She is allowed the privilege of having very sound principles indeed, her conduct being sometimes at splendid variance with her own assumptions. A minor episode will bear this out. Jane has met Bingley, and is expressing her admiration for his sense, good humour, and happy manners: ' "He is also handsome," replied Elizabeth, "which a young man ought likewise to be, if he possibly can. His character is thereby complete" ' (p. 14). Elizabeth's irony is obviously directed against superficial assessments. In a later exchange with Charlotte she states her belief that partnership must be based on a thorough knowledge of the other person's *character*. There is little doubt that in this respect Elizabeth expresses the ideal norm of the novel, as contrasted with the maxims of Charlotte, and with the unhappy reality of the Bennet household, where 'the experience of three and twenty years had been insufficient to make his wife understand [Mr Bennet's] character' (p. 5). Significantly, Darcy subscribes to Elizabeth's own theory when he warns her not to judge him on the basis of report: ' " . . . I could wish, Miss Bennet, that you were not to sketch my character at the present moment, as there is reason to fear that the performance would reflect no credit on either" ' (p. 94). Anyone who is not blind to Elizabeth's faults will appreciate the complex irony of her remark to Jane, as it comments on her own reactions to Darcy at the Meryton Assembly, and later on backfires with a vengeance, mocking her stubborn persistence in a dislike for Darcy based on 'first impressions', as well as her infatuation with a man who recommends himself chiefly through a handsome exterior and agreeable manners.[15] May we not say that the conduct is mistaken, though the feelings are not?

To be sure, a battalion of admirable precepts will by no means fully account for Elizabeth's excellence, or make her future lover one whit more palatable than Edmund Bertram. Robert Louis Stevenson once remarked that when Elizabeth opened her mouth he wanted to go down on his knees; male infatuation aside, his statement pretty

nearly defines the general response to the heroine.[16] Darcy's performance is at all times less immediately appealing. It is therefore
important to appreciate those significant correctives to Elizabeth's
prejudice—and ours—that the author does provide. If Darcy were
in fact rigid and stationary—however morally sound the basis of his
posture—he would hardly inspire affection either in the reader or in
Elizabeth. But he does inspire affection, and our awareness of attraction between hero and heroine should be complemented by our
recognition of a shared system of values. Darcy's growing attachment to Elizabeth possibly 'redeems' him more completely than any
other element that may modify our initial conceptions and produce
true sympathy for him. Everyone will notice how Jane Austen
occasionally dips into his mind to tell us in no uncertain terms that
he is falling in love:

> . . . no sooner had he made it clear to himself and his friends
> that she had hardly a good feature in her face, than he began
> to find it was rendered uncommonly intelligent by the beautiful
> expression in her dark eyes. To this discovery succeeded some
> others equally mortifying. Though he had detected with a critical
> eye more than one failure of perfect symmetry in her form, he
> was forced to acknowledge her figure to be light and pleasing;
> and in spite of his asserting that her manners were not those of
> the fashionable world, he was caught by their easy playfulness
> (p. 23).

The examples might be multiplied: ' . . . Darcy had never been so
bewitched by any woman as he was by her' (p. 52). 'He began to
feel the danger of paying Elizabeth too much attention' (p. 58).
The disclosure of such delightful sentiment frequently occurs in a
troublesome context: as often as not it coincides with his fear of
attracting a socially inferior woman. Thus response to his reflections
on social inequality will necessarily condition the effect of his more
'tender' emotions. In the light of such privileged information, however—further provided by exchanges between Darcy and Miss
Bingley—incidents that naturally seem insignificant to Elizabeth
become evidence of Darcy's infatuation. When 'Mr. Darcy drew his
chair a little towards her' (p. 179), when he puts off his departure
from Rosings, when he is so often silent, we suspect reasons that
Elizabeth cannot divine. I cannot agree, then, that the effect of his
first proposal is one of 'overwhelming surprise'.[17] If we accept also

that the social gap between them is a real obstacle to their union, Darcy's struggle with himself becomes understandable and meaningful.

Naturally Elizabeth is stunned when Darcy asks her to marry him. She has misinterpreted every one of his actions, and she despises him to the best of her ability. Yet she is clearly fascinated by him. His presence never fails to provoke an emotional response in her, and because the author suggests—however subtly—that her resentment is not factually justified, we are made to feel that 'fascinated but clear dislike' may become an equally strong positive emotion once the reasons for dislike have been removed.[18] Surely the intensity of her resentment is an indication of emotional involvement from a very early stage: she may despise him, but she is never indifferent to him. Significantly, Elizabeth's interest in Wickham springs from her preoccupation with Darcy himself: '. . . she was very willing to hear him, though what she chiefly wished to hear she could not hope to be told, the history of his acquaintance with Darcy' (p. 77). We shall miss an essential ingredient in Elizabeth's response to Darcy unless we grasp the splendour of the man as our bewitching heroine must have done—or she would never have cared for his reactions. G. B. Stern's observations may well be a bit facetious, but I believe they are true to the spirit of the novel:

> I seem to have caught this insistence that he is tall. Obviously glamour heroes have to be tall. He has authority and a certain lordliness . . . His bearing is symbolical; he steps down from the heights as from Mount Olympus—or from the hills of Hollywood. The remote legends of his wealth and great estates in Derbyshire are also in the true hero and Prince Charming tradition. . . . Yes, he is remote, lordly, exclusive. And so *very* tall.[19]

We smile at the effusion, perhaps, and yet we should be thankful that the fascination Darcy held for Elizabeth should not have been lost completely in twentieth-century dissertations on social inequality.

Although Darcy frequently does not appear to his advantage in his verbal encounters with the glorious, slightly impertinent Elizabeth, his exchanges with Miss Bingley reveal his ability to be both witty and resourceful—qualities that Elizabeth possesses to a far higher degree. Furthermore, analyses by Reuben Brower and Howard Babb go to prove that the dialogues between Elizabeth and Darcy carry more than surface meaning. 'It is important', says Brower, ' . . . that in these ironic dialogues no comment is included that makes us take

Darcy's behaviour in only an unpleasant sense.'[20] He points to the dramatic function of these dialogues: they serve to maintain a contrast between the characters so that their estrangement seems logical, while suggesting a different interpretation which may account for the opposite line of development in the second part of the novel. Quite naturally, the illusion of incompatibility will carry over from the social situation to the simple confrontation between two personalities; by the same token, our awareness of their basic attitudes to a total social and moral context will enable us to see to what extent the apparent contrast is real or imaginary. An appreciation of the largely fictitious basis of their disagreement is nowhere more vital than during the first proposal scene, when the mistaken conduct of both reaches an absolute climax and more strongly than ever reinforces whatever sense of contrast our enjoyment of the dramatic illusion may have brought about. Darcy's addresses are couched in language that is uncomfortably wooden, the Richardsonian echoes being no happy addition to his idiom.[21] His reflections on social inequality seem almost preposterously rude: ' " . . . Could you expect me to rejoice in the inferiority of your connections? To congratulate myself on the hope of relations, whose condition in life is so decidedly beneath my own?" ' (p. 192). His arrogance is matched only by her supreme disregard for anything beyond her biased perceptions, which effectively blurs their affinity. At that moment the opposing positions are seemingly so rigidly defined that all subsequent development would appear totally implausible if we did not already possess adequate information to invalidate a substantial part of their disagreement.

After the proposal scene, a predominantly scenic presentation gives way to 'internalised' drama: the mystery has been presented, complete with genuine and misleading clues, and the resulting conflict—aided by the immaturity of both protagonists—has moved to its inevitable climax. It remains for Elizabeth to come to terms with a reality which has been implicit only, and which the reader has been allowed to suspect. The change in narrative technique reflects the author's concern with Elizabeth's development to maturity; the parallel with *Emma* leaps to the eye, though in that novel the 'reported thought process' is even more pronounced.[22] Darcy's explanatory letter is little short of a dramatic device designed to turn the course of the action. It seems a convenient enough means of removing certain factual misconceptions, Elizabeth's reaction being far more important than the information conveyed. Apart from the specific circumstances surrounding Wickham, the letter tells us little that we should not have suspected already. The conclusions Elizabeth reaches between the receipt of the letter and her visit to Pemberley may be regarded as a stepping-stone between the first and the second phase of progression, equally vital to the consistency of both: while providing 'correct' interpretations to the ambiguous statements and actions of the first cycle, they logically introduce the evolution that brings Darcy and Elizabeth together.

Much praise has been bestowed upon the internal dialogue that presents Elizabeth's reassessment of the other characters and of her own past conduct. Reuben Brower calls her thought-pattern 'legalistic': the evidence is submitted to a thorough examination, and judgement is passed on the basis of this evidence alone.[23] The sympathetic reader will delight in the heroine's ability to free herself of that prejudice which has thwarted her judgement, which decreases distance between character and observer:

> . . . every line [of the letter] proved more clearly that the affair, which she had believed it impossible that any contrivance could so represent, as to render Mr. Darcy's conduct in it less than infamous, *was capable of a turn which must make him entirely blameless throughout the whole* (p. 205).[24]

Elizabeth has never been greater than in the recognition of her own folly: she proves to be a truly *rational* person, fully capable of acting upon the extent of her knowledge:

> She grew absolutely ashamed of herself.—Of neither Darcy nor Wickham could she think, without feeling that she had been blind, partial, prejudiced, absurd.
> 'How despicably have I acted!' she cried.—'I, who have prided myself on my discernment! . . . Had I been in love, I could not have been more wretchedly blind. But vanity, not love, has been my folly.—Pleased with the preference of one, and offended by the neglect of the other, on the very beginning of our acquaintance, I have courted prepossession and ignorance, and driven reason away, where either were concerned. *Till this moment, I never knew myself*' (p. 208).[25]

If we accept Elizabeth at this point, we must necessarily accept the woman who falls in love with Fitzwilliam Darcy. If we accept her reading of his past behaviour—and we do only to the extent that the 'truth' is in part known to us already—we will not be surprised to find that he is a man worthy of her love:

> . . . proud and repulsive as were his manners, she had never, in the whole course of their acquaintance, an acquaintance which had latterly brought them much together, and given her a sort of intimacy with his ways, seen any thing that betrayed him to be unprincipled or unjust—any thing that spoke him of irreligious or immoral habits (p. 207).

Like Emma, Elizabeth has to 'understand, thoroughly understand her own heart' before committing herself to another person.[26] Emma and Elizabeth both gain wisdom from their association with the men they eventually marry. And here the parallel ends. Reuben Brower contends that a drama of irony should end once the ambiguities have been removed; consequently, the latter part of *Emma* is more success-ful than that of *Pride and Prejudice*.[27] I am not convinced that the comparison is a happy one. The moment Emma understands her own heart, her knowledge is complete, for conflict has arisen solely as a result of her own shortcomings. Mr Knightley is an invariable quality, an ever-present, ever-known residuary of wisdom and virtue, who is waiting to receive her the moment she perceives her own folly. In *Pride and Prejudice* knowledge pertains to others as well as to the self, and Darcy is an *unknown* quality, whose own conduct has contributed to the misunderstandings that are the basis of the plot. Darcy must be unmasked, not only to the extent that reasons for dis-like no longer apply, but to the extent that he unambiguously displays those qualities that have been implicit only. Mid-way through the novel, Elizabeth merely realises that her reasons for disliking him have been illusory, and that he is a fundamentally upright person: 'His attachment excited gratitude, his general character respect; but she could not approve him; nor could she for a moment repent her refusal, or feel the slightest inclination ever to see him again' (p. 212). In very simple terms: Emma has always known and always needed Mr Knightley. Elizabeth must learn to know Darcy and then to need him before she can become his wife.

The episodes following Elizabeth's return from Rosings serve to consolidate the conclusions so painfully arrived at during the scene of re-evaluation, each episode being a dramatisation of the points Darcy advanced in his defence: 'She felt anew the justice of Mr. Darcy's objections; and never had she before been so much disposed to pardon his interference in the views of his friend' (p. 229). Clearly her response to the general conduct of her family—and to Lydia's indecorous behaviour in particular—recalls her previous disapproval; there is a difference in degree, not in kind, her gravity betraying a stronger awareness of the consequences of immoral habits: ' ". . . Our importance, our respectability in the world, must be affected by the wild volatility, the assurance and disdain of all restraint which mark Lydia's character . . ." ' (p. 231). Her turning away from Wickham is a near-symbolic act. A rejection of him is a rejection of the novel's 'essential' negatives: a serious character, he combines impropriety and false prudence. As we have seen, Elizabeth's basic principles are constant, but the ability to distinguish between mask and reality, and the wisdom to act according to one's basic assumptions, belong to the mature individual. As Elizabeth prepares to go on that journey which will take her to Pemberley, we are shown what she leaves behind and indirectly what she will some day seek. By virtue of a humiliation that has in fact elevated her, Elizabeth's fate will never be that of her father:

> . . . captivated by youth and beauty, and that appearance of good humour, which youth and beauty generally give, [he] had married a woman whose weak understanding and illiberal mind, had very early in their marriage put an end to all real affection for her. Respect, esteem, and confidence, had vanished for ever; and all his views of domestic happiness were overthrown (p. 236).

Having once herself set the ideal norm for compatibility, the mature Elizabeth cannot but base her affection on respect, esteem, and confidence.

Elizabeth's visit to Pemberley falls into two distinct parts, the first providing basic information about Darcy, the second portraying the actual meeting. The Pemberley episode relates closely to all the episodes in the first cycle that reveal both characters' concern for decorum, the half-hidden truths having anticipated a subsequent unambiguous presentation of a residuary of common values. Just as Sir Thomas Bertram's estate may be called the moral centre of *Mansfield Park*, Pemberley is at once the thematic and dramatic centre of gravity in *Pride and Prejudice*: the union of Darcy and Elizabeth—the end-all of the novel's movement—is effected at and through Pemberley, which incorporates the 'essentials' of both.

Mansfield Park receives Fanny, and Pemberley receives Elizabeth; for all their differences, both heroines find a moral home to which they have always aspired by virtue of their sense and sanity.

A seemingly minor episode anticipates both Darcy's position in regard to the estate he has inherited and Elizabeth's reaction to it:

> 'I am astonished,' said Miss Bingley, 'that my father should have left so small a collection of books.—What a delightful library you have at Pemberley, Mr. Darcy!'
>
> 'It ought to be good,' he replied, 'it has been the work of many generations.'
>
> 'And then you have added so much to it yourself, you are always buying books.'
>
> 'I cannot comprehend the neglect of a family library in such days as these.'
>
> 'Neglect! I am sure you neglect nothing that can add to the beauties of that noble place. Charles, when you build *your* house, I wish it may be half as delightful as Pemberley.'
>
> . . .
>
> Elizabeth was so much caught by what passed, as to leave her very little attention for her book . . . (p. 38).

Pemberley, then, represents a living tradition guarded and improved by Darcy, and Elizabeth's interest in the conversation betrays her awareness of the connection between the man and his estate.[28]

The amount of detail in the description of Pemberley is surprising and hence highly significant. By contrast, Rosings is never clearly visualised, beyond very general statements. Our introduction to the estate reads more or less like an inventory of neo-classical aesthetic concepts: there is not only grandeur, but order and harmony tempered by variety; the morally edifying open prospect is not neglected (it will be remembered that Sotherton, that breeding-ground of indecorous conduct, has high walls that impede the view), and the proprietor further betrays his commendable principles by following nature, not distorting it. Elizabeth is rapturous: 'She had never seen a place for which nature had done more, or where natural beauty had been so little counteracted by an awkward taste' (p. 245). Clearly Pemberley commands such close attention on account of its emblematic significance.[29] It is a complex emblem: we note how the word 'taste' relates not only to the proprietor, but indirectly also to the beholder, Elizabeth. We need divine no direct Shaftesburian influence to perceive its ethical connotations. A true child of an age which insisted on the interaction between ethics and aesthetics, Jane Austen not surprisingly sees taste as one of the essential elements of human character. Thus Anne Elliot is said to have been 'an extremely pretty girl, with gentleness, modesty, taste, and feeling',[30] while Edmund Bertram 'encouraged [Fanny's] taste, and corrected her judgment'.[31] Through her later reactions to the union of Jane and Bingley, Elizabeth stresses the importance of having a similarity of taste; in this context, it seems to me equally obvious that the word carries all its ethical implications: '. . . Elizabeth really believed all [Bingley's] expectations of felicity, to be rationally founded, because they had for basis . . . a general similarity of feeling and taste between her and himself' (pp. 347–8).

By the same token, Elizabeth realizes that the master of Pemberley must command not only respect, but also admiration. The Age of Pope is not far removed: Pemberley might well have belonged to Burlington, Darcy might well have been praised in an epistle in-cluded among the poet's *Moral Essays*. In her description of Pember-ley, Jane Austen includes a direct reference to Lady Catherine's estate, which establishes a contrast between good taste and what Pope termed 'a false Taste of Magnificence':

> The rooms were lofty and handsome, and their furniture suitable to the fortune of their proprietor; but Elizabeth saw, with ad-miration of his taste, that it was neither gaudy nor uselessly fine; with less of splendour, and more real elegance, than the furniture of Rosings. (p. 246).

The 'grandeur' of Rosings represents a distortion of true magnificence, just as Lady Catherine's ridiculous pride is a distortion of a proper feeling. As in Pope, the gaudy and preposterous (very properly extolled by none other than Mr Collins) sets off what is 'suitable', harmonious, and consequently proof of true virtue.

The subsequent insistence on Darcy's benevolence, as revealed by his housekeeper, naturally accompanies his responsible and tasteful care of the estate. The personal morality of the landowner invariably takes on social implications: his is the responsibility to 'ease, or emulate the care of Heav'n'. Nor is the disclosure of his benevolence acceptable and logical merely within the framework of the Pemberley episode as such. Ironically, it is Wickham's portrayal that provides the most complete preparation for a total vision of Darcy: he places the master of Pemberley in his total context, as someone whose duty and privilege it is to judge and dispose. Even in Wickham's terminology, Darcy is often 'liberal and generous', and he is known to 'give his money freely, to display hospitality, to assist his tenants, and relieve the poor' (p. 81). Wickham's presentation of facts is such as to impute Darcy's benevolence to pride, and all positive virtue is negated by his supposedly uncharitable treatment of Wickham himself. Once fact has been extracted from Wickham's fiction it is easy to see that Darcy has not 'saved up a formidable change to deliver as one lump in the scene at Pemberley',[32] but that the total presentation of him has been carefully prepared for. Similarly, Elizabeth's one-time abhorrence of his alleged unkindness to Wickham clearly demonstrates her own appreciation of the virtue of benevolence.

Towards the end of the novel, Jane asks her sister how long she has loved Darcy. Elizabeth's answer is obviously ironic, and yet there is a grain of truth behind the playful façade: ' "It has been coming on so gradually, that I hardly know when it began. But I believe I must date it from my first seeing his beautiful grounds at Pemberley" ' (p. 373). Following Sir Walter Scott's remark that the heroine 'does not perceive that she has done a foolish thing until she accidentally visits a very handsome seat and grounds belonging to her admirer',[33] a number of critics have chosen to interpret Elizabeth's response to Pemberley as an indication of acquisitiveness. Far from making Elizabeth less attractive, this 'worldliness' supposedly renders her even more 'warmly human'.[34] It is obvious that such a reading of the text would be inconsistent with her previous idealism, and I also find it totally incompatible with the actual events at Pemberley. It is Darcy's *character* that fascinates Elizabeth, as was indeed the case in the days when she despised him, and nothing short of the gradual discovery of his true nature can warm her heart towards him:

> The commendation bestowed on him by Mrs. Reynolds was of no trifling nature. What praise is more valuable than the praise of an intelligent servant? As a brother, a landlord, a master, she considered how may people's happiness were in his guardianship!—How much of pleasure or pain it was in his power to bestow!—How much of good or evil must be done by him! *Every idea that had been brought forward by the housekeeper was favourable to his character* . . . (pp. 250–1).[35]

Mrs Reynolds explains that her master is affable to the poor. 'Elizabeth listened, wondered, doubted, and was impatient for more. Mrs. Reynolds could interest her on no other point. She related the subject of the pictures, the dimensions of the rooms, and the price of the furniture, in vain' (p. 249). It amazes me how anyone should manage to extract a 'sense of property' from such a response.

At one time Elizabeth disliked Darcy so intensely that she went out of her way to have her ill opinion of him confirmed. During that first extensive interview with Wickham, she was also impatient for more information about Darcy: she was 'unwilling to let the subject drop' (p. 77), she 'found the interest of the subject increase, and listened with all her heart' (p. 78). At Pemberley the pattern repeats itself. Again Elizabeth searches for Darcy through another person. The similarity of psychological situation and subject-matter along with the structural parallelism of the two scenes—with their widely different outcomes—serve to emphasise the nature of the progression Elizabeth has gone through; also, our recollection of the earlier scene reminds us of the constant interest she displays for him.

The Pemberley episode is far more than a plot device vital to the disclosure of Darcy's true character and to Elizabeth's parallel change of sentiment towards him. A social and moral code invested in Pemberley suffuses the novel: its traditions 'demand' commitment to propriety and decency, and a responsible interaction with the social and human environment. The various characters in *Pride and Prejudice* invariably define themselves in relation to the ideal, which is not static in its conception: a new generation will always have to be 'buying books' for the 'family library'. The eventual meeting of Darcy and Elizabeth is a meeting between characters whose moral allegiance has been made clear through their response to the claims of Pemberley, implicitly in the novel's first half, explicitly when juxtaposed in face of the estate itself.

Beginning with that unexpected meeting between the two in the woods of Pemberley, the final scenes of *Pride and Prejudice* turn what might have been little more than plausible theory into an immediate experience for the heroine: Elizabeth is not to love the image of a good and decent man, but rather the full personification of that image, as presented to her through actions that apply to her own situation. It is the pattern of the letter episode repeated: what has been suggested already—only this time unambiguously—is emphatically confirmed, the facts themselves being secondary in importance to

Elizabeth's response to them. Artistic unity is achieved as the author brings the 'correct' reading of each initial episode to its logical conclusion. The scenes that finally bring Darcy and Elizabeth together quite naturally echo those that estranged them, showing how greater maturity on the part of both leads to unification rather than estrangement. The prelude to Darcy's easy acceptance of the Gardiners is, of course, his previous acceptance of Elizabeth and Jane: like the Bennet sisters, their uncle recommends himself by intelligence, taste, and good manners. Thus Darcy's 'reformation' is in fact far less fundamental than the dramatic illusion might lead us—and Elizabeth— to believe. That his conduct should finally reflect his finer principles is entirely appropriate and indeed satisfying, in that it recalls Elizabeth's own evolution to maturity. In both instances, a very proper process of humiliation helps to modify a pride that prevented the full realisation of a largely admirable social and moral code: ' "... As a child I was taught what was *right*, but I was not taught to correct my temper. I was given good principles, but left to follow them in pride and conceit. ... By you, I was properly humbled ..." ' (p. 369). Darcy's words might apply to both. It is perhaps easier to accept Elizabeth's development because we are allowed to witness every progressive step of that process, whereas we merely observe the *effects* of Darcy's parallel struggle with himself. This does not make his conduct inconsistent, merely less immediately predictable—and herein lies the suspense of the action.

The world at large has not changed, and because their essential principles are unaltered, their response to it remains very much the same. Darcy continues to rebuff Miss Bingley—as he always did— and just as he was once ashamed of his aunt's ill breeding he now appreciates Elizabeth's firmness and dignity in face of Lady Catherine's foolish snobbery. Similarly, he will never learn to condone Mrs Bennet's vulgarity, nor is he expected to. Elizabeth will never cease to be vexed at the conduct of her family. The concluding scenes at Longbourn re-emphasise that common concern for decorum which we observed in Darcy and Elizabeth both from the beginning.

When Lydia and Wickham run away together, they carry impropriety to its logical extreme, and Wickham dramatises the marriage-ability issue by becoming Lydia's husband upon the receipt of money. The obvious thematic relevance being thus established, it is impossible to dismiss the episode as merely conventional and productive of 'irrelevantly directed moral judgment'.[36] The fact that contemporary sentimental fiction abounds with elopements does not make Jane Austen's use of the convention any less effective. Lydia is naturally no fully realised individual, but neither are a number of other 'simple' characters, who remain safely within the novel's moral scheme. Nor do I find it correct to say that neither the conduct of the imprudent couple nor the reactions of Darcy and Elizabeth have been adequately prepared for. Wickham certainly presents a full dress rehearsal in his attempt to elope with Georgiana Darcy, and Lydia has always been second to none in her brainless vulgarity. It is precisely Lydia's behaviour that appals Elizabeth when she returns from Rosings. Darcy's own conduct betrays the intimate connection between concern for propriety and the virtue of benevolence. It is the promise of Pemberley fulfilled: through his treatment of Lydia and Wickham, Darcy reasserts his sense of decorum and his goodness—to Elizabeth most of all. Darrell Mansell—who certainly would not agree with the above attempt to explain the episode in 'realistic' terms—makes the fine point that the elopement epitomises Elizabeth's final, necessary 'humiliation', forcing her to admit that she cannot escape from being a Bennet. Darcy undergoes a parallel process in that Lydia's actions recall those of his own sister: 'Thus Lydia's elopement has the effect of uniting these two in a common shame for a common "family" frailty in their blood.'[37] Even so, I find that the episode primarily serves to set the protagonists apart from foolishness and impropriety, in whatever social class these attitudes might appear. Its dramatic effectiveness cannot be denied: it brings about Elizabeth's ultimate realisation of her love for Darcy.

For *Pride and Prejudice* is above all a story of love—a love that blurs the identity of neither, however similar those principles without which their union would be impossible. From the beginning to the end, Darcy is sometimes silent, sometimes grave, often awesome— as when he asks Elizabeth's hand in marriage—and he has yet to learn to be laughed at by a woman who never loses her sprightliness. Yet every event subsequent to the Meryton assembly goes to prove that difference in temperament is no barrier to intensity of feeling, be it hatred or love: what began as a confrontation between two strong personalities terminates in a union where both retain their individuality. For that we should be grateful. Darcy and Elizabeth are not 'complying' or 'easy', like Jane and Bingley, nor would we wish them ever to become so. For all his good qualities, Darcy is not perfect, merely 'exactly the man, who, in disposition and talents, would most suit

[Elizabeth]' (p. 312)—the man for whom she has nourished every possible feeling—except indifference.

It is all too easy for the post-Romantic reader to underrate the intensity of Elizabeth's affection for Darcy and conclude that his love for her is somehow stronger because more intuitive. As a young girl, I was informed that Elizabeth's mind is 'firmly in control of her emotions; and notwithstanding that she is "in love" with Darcy we cannot imagine that she will be a passionate or adoring wife to him.'[38] This is the kind of response that Jane Austen must have anticipated as she mockingly addressed her public:

> If gratitude and esteem are good foundations of affection, Elizabeth's change of sentiment will be neither improbable nor faulty. But if otherwise, if the regard springing from such sources is unreasonable or unnatural, in comparison of what is so often described as arising on a first interview with its object, and even before two words have been exchanged, nothing can be said in her defence, except that she had given somewhat of a trial to the latter method, in her partiality for Wickham, and that its ill-success might perhaps authorize her to seek the other less interesting mode of attachment (p. 279).

The 'less interesting mode of attachment' is not, of course, incompatible with depth of feeling, which does but gain in plausibility from being 'reasonable and just' (p. 334). Elizabeth's gradual awakening to a full realisation of her attachment is described with shrewd psychological insight, through those subtle touches that are far more revelatory than any number of emotional outbursts. The elopement episode serves to clarify her feelings: the events at Pemberley told her that he cared for her still and that she had every reason to value such a man's affection; at the moment when she believes he is gone forever, she sees that she cannot afford the loss:

> She became jealous of his esteem, when she could no longer hope to be benefited by it. She wanted to hear of him when there seemed the least chance of gaining intelligence. She was convinced that she could have been happy with him; when it was no longer likely they should meet (p. 311).

There is nothing very sensible about staying awake at night because you suspect that a man may never come back.

When Darcy does come, we recognise in the description of Elizabeth the hand that was to create Anne Elliot. A small gesture may betray emotion, silence may speak more eloquently than words: '... Elizabeth, to satisfy her mother, went to the window—she looked,—*she saw Mr. Darcy with [Bingley], and sat down again by her sister*' (p. 333).[39] The visit is entirely unexpected, and all Elizabeth does is sit down. All we hear is a silly conversation between Kitty and her mother. Elizabeth's lively mind has been an open book to us—suddenly there is nothing but silence and inactivity. Her numbness is as real as Anne's, when she 'descried, most decidedly and distinctly, Captain Wentworth walking down the street. . . . For a few minutes she saw nothing before her. It was all confusion.'[40] Again as in *Persuasion* a story can be told by the expression on a person's face: 'The colour which had been driven from [Elizabeth's] face, returned for half a minute with an additional glow, and a smile of delight added lustre to her eyes . . . ' (p. 334).[41] And as in the later novel, the closed rooms with a crowd of people, where only glances and polite phrases can be exchanged, create almost a feeling of claustrophobia which intensifies the uncertainty of the woman, whose reactions fluctuate between hope and resignation. Only Elizabeth is younger, more impetuous, less chastened than Anne: 'She followed him with her eyes, envied every one to whom he spoke, had scarcely patience enough to help anybody to coffee; and then was enraged against herself for being so silly!' (p. 341). She has all the energy of a Mary Crawford, and so she can form a 'desperate resolution' (p. 365) and approach Darcy on the delicate subject of his generosity to Lydia and Wickham. The author does, in fact, dispense with an unusual amount of reticence when allowing Elizabeth to have tears in her eyes and tell her father how much she loves Darcy. 'I am happier even than Jane;' she writes to Mrs Gardiner, 'she only smiles, I laugh' (p. 383). And this is as far as Jane Austen will ever take her reader. Like all her lovers, Darcy and Elizabeth ' "walk off the stage into a cloud"—where it would be indecent to attempt to follow them.'[42] To be sure, *Persuasion* presents a fuller and far more moving picture of human emotion, because it is all about a mature woman's love. Elizabeth had to learn what Anne already knew.

There is nothing unfinished, however, about the image of love that *Pride and Prejudice* ultimately projects. The search for a partner becomes a moral act, which is reflected in the novel's structure. It is a movement from conflict based in part on ignorance to order grounded in awareness. In recognising both their mistaken conduct and their essential affinity the protagonists are made to overcome elements that created chaos and to realise those possibilities for harmony that were implicit even in that initial state of disorder—implicit in their common value system and in their capacity for emotional commitment.

# Notes

## 1. Spenser's defence of poetry:
## some structural aspects of the *Fowre Hymnes*

### EINAR BJORVAND

[1]'Fides enim non res est salutantis corporis, sed credentis animi.' St Augustine, *De Catechizandis Rvdibvs: Liber Vnvs*, translated by J. P. Christopher (Washington, D.C., 1926), pp. 30 and 31.

[2]All references to Spenser's *Hymnes* are to *The Works of Edmund Spenser: A Variorum Edition*, Volume VII, *The Minor Poems*, Volume 1, edited by C. G. Osgood and H. G. Lotspeich (Baltimore, 1943).

[3]See Josephine Waters Bennett, 'The Theme of Spenser's *Fowre Hymnes*', *Studies in Philology*, 28 (1931), 49–57; and Robert Ellrodt, *Neoplatonism in the Poetry of Spenser* (Geneva, 1960), pp. 13–24.

[4]See F. M. Padelford, 'Spenser's *Fowre Hymnes*: A Resurvey', *Studies in Philology*, 29 (1932), 216.

[5]See J. W. Bennett, *Studies in Philology*, 28, 49–52; and Ellrodt, p. 14.

[6]J. B. Fletcher, 'A Study in Renaissance Mysticism: Spenser's "Fowre Hymnes"', *PMLA*, 26 (1911), 452–75. Fletcher is refuted by Padelford, 'Spenser's *Fowre Hymnes*', *JEGP*, 13 (1914), 418–33.

[7]J. B. Fletcher, 'Benivieni's Ode of Love and Spenser's *Fowre Hymnes*', *Modern Philology*, 8 (1911), 545–60; R. W. Lee, 'Castiglione's Influence on Spenser's Early Hymns', *Philological Quarterly*, 7 (1928), 65–77; W. L. Renwick, *Daphnaida and Other Poems* (London, 1929), pp. 210–11; the best arguments in favour of this view still seem to be those presented by Joan Waters Bennett in *Studies in Philology*, 28, 18–27, and in 'Spenser's *Fowre Hymnes*: Addenda', *Studies in Philology*, 32 (1935), 131–57. Ellrodt undertakes a refutation of their interpretations, pp. 130–40.

[8]Ellrodt, p. 117.

[9]Sir Philip Sidney, *Defence of Poesie*. The quotation is taken from a stimulating article by Andrew D. Weiner, 'Moving and Teaching: Sidney's *Defence of Poesie* as a Protestant Poetic', *The Journal of Medieval and Renaissance Studies*, 2 (1972), 259–78 (p. 270).

[10]William Nelson, *The Poetry of Edmund Spenser: A Study* (New York and London, 1963), p. 99.

[11]See Paula Johnson, *Form and Transformation in Music and Poetry of*

the *English Renaissance* (New Haven and London, 1972), pp. 125–31 and 152–3, and William Nelson, pp. 97–115.

[12]The first attempt at a full structural analysis of the *Epithalamion* was by A. Kent Hieatt in *Short Time's Endless Monument: the Symbolism of the Numbers in Edmund Spenser's 'Epithalamion'* (New York, 1960), later discussed and refined by among others Max A. Wickert in 'Structure and Ceremony in Spenser's *Epithalamion*', *ELH*, 35 (1968), 135–57, and by Alastair Fowler in *Triumphal Forms: Structural Patterns in Elizabethan Poetry* (Cambridge, 1970), pp. 103–07 and 161–73. Much of Hieatt's analysis still holds good, but Wicker's more recent analysis of the strictly symmetrical structure seems more convincing than the pairing suggested by Hieatt.

[13]See J. W. Bennett, *Studies in Philology*, 28, 54–6, and volume 32, 152; and Sears Jayne, 'Attending to Genre: Spenser's *Hymnes*', abstract in the *Spenser Newsletter*, 3 (1972), 6.

[14]See Ellrodt, pp. 20–21; 123–24.

[15]Hereafter the hymns will be referred to as *HL, HB, HHL,* and *HHB*, and stanza and line references are given in numerals, e.g. (*HL* 14, 114–16). When reference is made to lines only, this is indicated, e.g. (*HL* lines 114–16).

[16]Alastair Fowler, *Triumphal Forms*, p. 62.

[17]The contrast between 'Love the tyrant and Love the redeemer' has also been pointed out by Paula Johnson, *Form and Transformation*, p. 130.

[18]Paula Johnson, p. 129.

[19]John Mulryan, 'Spenser as Mythologist: A Study of the Nativities of Cupid and Christ in the *Fowre Hymnes*', *Modern Language Studies*, 1 (1971), 13–16 (p. 15).

[20]See Maren-Sofie Røstvig, 'Milton and the Science of Numbers', *English Studies Today*, Fourth Series (Rome, 1966), 283–84.

[21]Michael Wilding, 'Allusion and Innuendo in *MacFlecknoe*', *Essays in Criticism*, 19 (1969), 359–60.

[22]William Nelson, p. 100.

[23]The word 'aspyre' occurs only once more in the heavenly hymns, in stanza 40 of the *Hymne of Heavenly Beautie*, which describes the essential 'basenesse' of 'that pompe, to which proud minds aspyre'. The same set of rhymewords, 'aspyre-fyre-desyre', recurs in stanza 27 of the first hymn, where it is used to underline the lack of these qualities in the lover who succumbs to lust. For this and similar information, see my *A Concordance to Spenser's 'Fowre Hymnes'* (Oslo, 1973).

[24]William Nelson, p. 101. See also Paula Johnson, p. 129.

[25]Paula Johnson, p. 128.

[26]Enid Welsford, *Spenser, 'Fowre Hymnes', 'Epithalamion': A Study of Edmund Spenser's Doctrine of Love* (Oxford, 1967), p. 152.

[27]Paula Johnson, p. 128.

[28]William Nelson, p. 102.

[29]See illustration, facing p. 160.

[30]See *The English Works of Sir Thomas More*, edited by W. E. Campbell, 2 vols (London and New York, 1931), I, 332–35.

[31]Erwin Panofsky, *Studies in Iconology: Humanistic Themes in the Art of the Renaissance* (New York, 1939), pp. 125–26.

[32]Ibid., p. 125.

[33]*Pagan Mysteries in the Renaissance*, revised and enlarged edition (Harmondsworth, 1967), p. 52.

[34]Quoted by Wind, p. 58.

[35]From the *Conclusiones*, quoted by Wind, p. 51. Wind's views have been reaffirmed by C. D. Gilbert in 'Blind Cupid', *JWCI*, 33 (1970), 304–05: 'For Ficino and Pico, Love was not blind because it was irrational but because it was above reason' (p. 305).

[36]Translated by J. B. Fletcher in *Modern Philology*, 8 (1911), 545–60 (p. 549).

[37]See Philip B. Rollinson, 'A Generic View of Spenser's *Four Hymns*', *Studies in Philology*, 68 (1971), 298.

[38]John Block Friedman, *Orpheus in the Middle Ages* (Cambridge, Mass., 1970), p. 57.

[39]Ibid.

[40]Friedman, p. 125.

[41]See Enid Welsford, p. 145.

[42]I take the use of a capital 'G' in God in this line to be significant.

[43]See J. W. Bennett, *Studies in Philology*, 28, 36.

[44]See M.-S. Røstvig's comments on the *Fowre Hymnes* in 'The Hidden Sense: Milton and the Neoplatonic Method of Numerical Composition', in *The Hidden Sense and Other Essays*, edited by M.-S. Røstvig et al. (Oslo, 1963), p. 90.

[45]'in veteri testamento est occultatio novi, in novo testamento est manifestatio veteris.' Augustine, *De Catechizandis Rvdibvs*, pp. 28 and 29.

[46]Edgar Wind, p. 38.

[47]St Bonaventura, *The Mind's Road to God*, translated by George Boas (Indianapolis, 1953), p. 28.

[48]See Paula Johnson, pp. 130–31.

[49]William Nelson, p. 102.

[50]This parallel is not noted in the *Variorum Edition*. Robert Ellrodt cites a parallel in Leone Ebreo's *Dialoghi d'Amore*, but it seems unlikely that any particular source can be pinned down since the simile was, in all probability, a commonplace. See Ellrodt p. 186.

[51]See my *Concordance*, 'Appendix I: A Word-frequency Index'.

[52]See John Block Friedman, pp. 50–2.

[53]See Jon A. Quitslund, 'Spenser's Image of Sapience', *Studies in the Renaissance*, 16 (New York, 1969), 181–213 (p. 212).

[54]See also William Nelson, pp. 114–15.

[55]M.-S. Røstvig, *The Hidden Sense*, p. 90.

[56]Ibid.

[57]See Alastair Fowler, *Triumphal Forms*, pp. 62–124. See also Davies's discussion of the double centre in Milton's 'On the Morning of Christ's Nativity' below, pp. 105–106.

## 2. Elaborate song: conceptual structure in Milton's 'On the Morning of Christ's Nativity'

### M.–S. RØSTVIG

[1]'O perfect, and accomplish thy glorious acts; for men may leave their works unfinish't, but thou art a God, thy nature is perfection ... When thou hast settl'd peace in the Church, and righteous judgement in the Kingdome, then shall all thy Saints address their voyces of joy, and triumph to thee ... And he that now for haste snatches up a plain ungarnish't present as a thanke-offering to thee, . . . may then perhaps take up a Harp, and sing thee an elaborate song to Generations.' Quoted from *Complete Prose Works of John Milton*, ed. Don. M. Wolfe (New Haven and London, 1953), I, 706 by Jason P. Rosenblatt, 'The War in Heaven in *Paradise Lost*,' *PMLA*, 87 (1972), 38.

[2]William Whitaker, *A Disputation on Holy Scripture, Against the Papists* (1588) as quoted by Andrew D. Weiner, 'Moving and Teaching: Sidney's *Defence of Poesie* as a Protestant Poetic,' *The Journal of Medieval and Renaissance Studies*, 2 (1972), 273.

[3]Weiner, p. 276. Mr Weiner rightly insists on the importance of contemporary habits of reading the Bible: 'Through their reading of the scriptures and their attendance at sermons, the Elizabethans . . . must have developed the habit of reading slowly and painstakingly, and Sidney clearly expects his readers to bring the same reading habits to poetry . . . We must, in short, read very carefully, paying attention not only to the surface of the narrative but also to the signs which may be embedded in it.' (276 f.) Weiner does not include numbers among such 'signs', although these are specifically discussed as such by Augustine in his *De doctrina Christiana*. The numbers used to create conceptual structures were classified by a Renaissance poet like Guy le Fevre de La Boderie as allegorical; see

his preface to his translation of Francesco Giorgio's *L'Harmonie du Monde* (Paris, 1578 and 1579).

⁴ have excluded the microstructure of each stanza (the number of feet or syllables, for example) as too conjectural. It may be noted here, though, that the abstract metrical pattern in the hymn posits 36 syllables, the square of 6, which is a circular number. (A circular number is a number which returns to itself in the last digit when multiplied with itself.) The sum total of lines, 216, is the cube of 6 which means that it represents a perfect sphere or globe, since 6 is circular. Many theologians observed that the Hebrew letters in the name of God are circular numbers (5, 6 and 10) so that the name describes the nature of the Deity—his all-encompassing aspect and his eternal existence.

⁴ᵃCassiodorus, *Divine and Human Readings,* tr. Leslie Webber Jones (New York, 1966), p. 102.

⁵My quotations are from Saint Augustine, *On Christian Doctrine,* tr. D. W. Robertson Jr (The Library of Liberal Arts: New York, 1958).

⁶See my monograph on 'Structure as Prophecy' in *Silent Poetry: Essays in Numerological Analysis,* ed. Alastair Fowler (London, 1970), 32–72, and especially pp. 50–53.

⁷*Commentarium in librum Psalmorum* (1611–16), III, 479.

⁸Bonaventura, *Collationes in Hexaemeron. Das Sechstagewerk. Lateinisch und Deutsch* (Darmstadt, 1964), pp. 536 f. It must be borne in mind that the structure of the 150 Psalms was believed to constitute a summary and abridgement of the whole Bible, beginning with the Garden of Eden and the tree in Psalm 1 and concluding with the hymns in honour of Christ in the Heavenly Jerusalem as described in the Book of Revelation.

⁹Migne, *Patrologia latina,* 19 (Paris, 1846), columns 765–70.

¹⁰See Francesco Giorgio, *Problemata* (Venice, 1536 and Paris, 1574 and 1622), III, i, 26 and Gasparius Sanctius, *In Ieremiam Prophetam Commentarii* (1618). Both make the point that the alphabetical technique of composition was adopted in Nativity hymns, and both quote the opening lines of Sedulius' hymn. Cornelius à Lapide, *Commentaria In Ieremiam* (1621), like Sanctius, associates the technique with the classical art of memory, the letters serving instead of images. This is a technique which permits one to keep the whole poem in mind at once—an argument which applies to all kinds of conceptual structure, whether alphabetical, numerical, or symmetrical.

Giles Fletcher refers to Sedulius and Prudentius in his preface to *Christ's Victory and Triumph* (1610).

¹¹'Hymnus de Leontio episcopo,' Migne PL 19; see also M. Nisard, ed., *Collection des Auteurs Latins, avec la traduction en français. Ausone, Sidoine Apollinaire, Venance Fortunat* (Paris, 1887), pp. 55–57. The poem is numbered I, 16 in all collected editions.

[12]'Ad Syagrium episcopum Augustidunensem,' pp. 138–41 and 146–48 in Nisard's edition.

Fortunatus himself explains the significance of the chosen structure in an accompanying letter. Since he wrote the poem to serve as a gift or ransom to secure the liberty of a prisoner of war, its subject had to be the ransom offered by Christ to redeem fallen man. And in order to celebrate Christ the poem had to consist of 33 lines of 33 letters each, thus creating a perfect square. At its centre meet five acrostic lines traced through the square formed by the letters, the unifying centre being the letter which is *permedia* of the 23 letters in the Latin alphabet. (This letter, because of its position, clearly symbolises Christ.)

The structure, therefore, presents an image of Christ as our unifying centre, and the firmness of the form reflects the firmness of the providential scheme for our redemption. Thematically the poem falls into two equal parts: lines 1–16 describing the creation of man, his fall and expulsion, a centre-line affirming our eternal damnation under the Law (modified by the presence of the centrally placed letter representing Christ), and a counter-movement (lines 18–33) of redemption through the incarnation and the crucifixion.

[13]For the Middle Ages, see Robert M. Jordan, *Chaucer and the Shape of Creation* (Cambridge, Mass., 1967) and Wolfgang Haubrichs, *Ordo als Form. Strukturstudien zur Zahlenkomposition bei Otfrid von Weissenburg und in karolingischer Literatur* (Tübingen, 1969). D. P. Walker's useful studies in the *prisca theologia* are now available in book form: *The Ancient Theology. Studies in Christian Platonism from the Fifteenth to the Eighteenth Century* (London, 1972).

[14]Edgar Wind's *Pagan Mysteries in the Renaissance* needs no recommendation: to it may be added D. C. Allen's *Mysteriously Meant. The Rediscovery of Pagan Symbolism and Allegorical Interpretation in the Renaissance* (Baltimore and London, 1970).

[15]See note 6 and my essay entitled 'Ars Aeterna: Renaissance Poetics and Theories of Divine Creation,' *Mosaic*, 3 (1970), 40–61. This essay can also be found in *Chaos and Form*, ed. Kenneth McRobbie (Winnipeg, 1972), 101–19.

[16]Giorgio's importance in his own age and his usefulness as a source is being increasingly recognised today. The large extent to which he draws on orthodox theology requires emphasis, as he is too often associated with esoteric traditions. Frances Yates does this persistently, but references to and quotations from Augustine are frequent throughout the pages of his *De harmonia mundi* (Venice, 1525 and Paris, 1545, 1546, and 1564 and, in French translation, 1578 and 1579). For a brief account of his life and works see J.-F. Maillard, 'Le "De harmonia mundi" de Georges de Venise,' *Revue de l'Histoire des Religions*, 179 (1971), 181–203.

[17]Cornelius à Lapide published a number of commentaries on parts of

the Bible during the first few decades of the seventeenth century, and these draw extensively on patristic interpretations. Cornelius à Lapide must be the last major exegete to pursue a fourfold method of interpretation.

For Aquinas' comments on *Job* 38 see his *Opera*, vol. 13 (Antverpiae, 1612). Aquinas, too, refers the harmony of creation to the Pythagorean theory of the music of the spheres and to the 'musical' arrangement of the angelic hierarchies. The 'music' of both is a matter of an order embodying the crucial mathematical ratios.

[18]The fact that harmony is a matter of mathematical ratios (as explained in commentaries on Plato's *Timæus*) scarcely requires documentation today. In the study referred to in note 6, 'Structure as Prophecy,' I have shown that Platonic and Pythagorean number lore can be found in Biblical exegesis so that it cannot be considered as at all remarkable that Christian poets could exploit this tradition. The analysis submitted here, in terms of Biblical concepts, should be taken to supplement and modify, but not replace, the analysis offered primarily in terms of classical concepts in my study of 'The Hidden Sense: Milton and the Neoplatonic Method of Numerical Composition' published in *The Hidden Sense and Other Essays* by M.-S. Røstvig et al. (Oslo, 1963), pp. 1–112. The absorption of classical number lore into Christian theology is a topic I shall discuss more fully in a forthcoming publication.

[19]I have picked these words from Mantuan's comments on Psalm 119; see Baptista Spagnuolus Mantuanus, *In omnes Davidicos Psalmos . . . commentaria* (Rome, 1585).

[20]The romans are my own. I have used the edition published in the Ancient and Modern Library of Theological Literature, London, no date.

[21]The same argument applies to the sum total of Psalms, 150, their division into a sequence of 70 plus 80 being taken to convey the same message. The progression from 7 to 8 is one of Augustine's favourite numerical arguments; see for example his sermon on Psalm 150. The number 7 was associated with the Old Testament, 8 with the New.

[22]To read *Christ's Victory and Triumph* is to be reminded again and again of themes and phrases in Milton's poem. See for example IV, 13 and IV, 19–21. Fletcher's twice-repeated line, 'So Him they lead along into the courts of day' (IV, 19 and 20), may have prompted Milton's 'the courts of everlasting day' in the introduction. Milton's 'globe of circular light' (stanza 11) is usually compared to Fletcher's 'A globe of wingèd angels' (IV, 13), where *globe* means *troop*.

[23]'Spenser's Fourth Grace,' *JWCI*, 34 (1971), 354: 'The picture of a great figure seated within a circle while its attributes are in a circle about it certainly is not original with Spenser. The traditional iconography of the microcosm often pictures man or God within a circle while their attributes

or acts were personified around them. Ficino had pictured the emanations of God in such a way.'

²⁴In an essay on 'Christ's Nativity and the Pagan Deities', *Milton Studies*, 2 (1970), 103–12, Lawrence W. Hyman argues that Milton's attitude to the pagan past was one of regret; a conflict must necessarily inhere 'in any action which banishes a world which we also find beautiful.' But this is to ignore the typological approach to human history as a gradual revelation of the truth, first through 'veils and shadows' (*per vela et umbra*) and at last fully and quite clearly through the incarnation. The world of Nature and the world of pagan myth contained their types as well as the Biblical narrative, and these types must necessarily be beautiful since otherwise they would not point to Him who is the source of beauty and truth. His incarnation is that which they prophesy, however obscurely, and like the mere shadows they are, they must flee the moment that the true Sun of Justice appears. When, in the penultimate stanza, the 'yellow-skirted fays' and the 'moon-loved maze' are seen as beautiful, this is so, not because Milton was the victim of an unresolved inner conflict, but because the 'flocking shadows pale' belong in a typological context.

²⁵See note 8 for the edition used.

²⁶*Itinerarium mentis in Deum* (München, 1961), p. 134. See also VI, 7 pp. 144–47.

²⁷See note 19.

²⁸Nikolaus von Kues, *Philosophisch-Theologische Schriften*, Vol. II (Wien, 1966), p. 74. Cusanus' diagram figures prominently, but without acknowledgement or reference, in the preface written by Nicholas le Fevre de La Boderie to the one-volume edition of Pico's *Heptaplus* and Giorgio's *De harmonia mundi* published in French translation by himself and his brother Guy at Paris in 1578 and 1579. I reproduce this diagram in 'The Hidden Sense' (see note 18). In their prefaces the brothers Guy and Nicholas le Fevre de La Boderie refer quite frequently to 'le docte Cusanus' and so do Pico and Giorgio.

²⁹*De vera religione*, xxx, 55. For the Latin text and a reliable translation into French, see *Oeuvres*, vol. 8 (Paris, 1951), p. 103. The translation into English is my own. See my discussion of this passage in 'Ars Aeterna,' *Mosaic*, 3 (1970), 49 f.

³⁰For comments on the symbolism invested in this formula readers are referred to 'The Hidden Sense' or to Christopher Butler's *Number Symbolism* (London, 1970).

In his *De Trinitate* IV Augustine stressed the importance of the ratio 2:1 (the octave or diapason) in the work of creation and the scheme of redemption. This ratio conveys the idea of return or the closing of the circle, and so does the *lambda*-formula as a whole. The last number in this formula, 27, may represent them all as constituting the sum of the other numbers. These are the numbers that organise the perpetual descent from and ascent to the Deity, and this is true also of the shorter *tetractys*-formula associated with Pythagoras. In Christian thought both formulas were associated with Jacob's Ladder, and with the idea of Christ as the Ladder joining Heaven and Earth.

[31]See my diagram.

[32]Pietro Bongo, *De Numerorum Mysteria* (Bergomi, 1591), p. 448. Bongo's chapter on the number 24 begins by connecting it with the vision of the 24 elders in *Rev.* 4.

[33]For a modern edition of the *Expositio Psalmorum* see the *Corpus Christianorum* vols. 97–98 (Turnholti, 1958).

[34]Wolfgang Haubrichs, *Ordo als Form* (Tübingen, 1969), pp. 64–70, summarises patristic and early medieval expositions of the number 13.

[35]Helen Gardner, *Religion and Literature* (London, 1971), p. 179.

[36]Compare *Wisdom* 8:1; the imprint is the 'sweet order' imposed by Wisdom on 'all things' *(disponit omnia suaviter)*.

[37]Saint Augustine, *On Free Choice of the Will*, tr. Anna S. Benjamin and L. H. Hackstaff (Library of Liberal Arts: New York, 1964), pp. 73–75.

[38]The two are fused in Tasso's *Discorsi del Poema Eroico;* see Annabel M. Patterson, 'Tasso's Epic Neoplatonism,' *Studies in the Renaissance,* 18 (1971), 108 f.: Tasso accepted the fusion, 'achieved by Augustine and Aquinas . . . of two radically different meanings of the term "Idea". The original transcendental absolutes . . . have become confused with any preconception or design in the mind of an artist or craftsman of what he is about to make.'

[39]*The Countess of Pembroke's Arcadia,* ed. Jean Robertson (Oxford, 1973), pp. 245–48.

[39a]It is well known that Sidney's poem is indebted to an epithalamion in Gil Polo's continuation of Montemayor's *Diana*: see Jean Robertson's comment in her introduction to the edition of *The Countess of Pembroke's Arcadia*, p. xx. For the text of Bartholomew Yong's translation of Gil Polo, see Judith M. Kennedy's *A Critical Edition of Yong's Translation of George of Montemayor's Diana and Gil Polo's Enamoured Diana* (Oxford, 1968), pp. 378 f. Yong's translation of Gil Polo's epithalamion was included in *England's Helicon* (1600, 1614); see Hyder Rollins' ed. (Cambridge, Mass., 1935), I, 133 f.

On comparing Sidney's poem with Yong's translation the indebtedness is obvious, but so are the differences. The earlier poem is much shorter; its seven nine-line stanzas move towards a clear terminal climax in the sixth stanza, the seventh forming a coda. Central accent is established, however, by placing a direct apostrophe to the bride and groom in the fourth stanza, and there is some evidence indicating a symmetrical grouping around the centre. The structure of Sidney's epithalamion is much firmer and bolder. Sidney's revision therefore indicates that he desired a more complex structural effect and one which could be sustained through eleven stanzas, thus affording more opportunities for thematic pairing.

For a later example of structural reorganisation of a borrowed theme, see Abraham Cowley's version of Casimire Sarbiewski's ode 'E Rebus Humanis Excessus' in the Pindaric ode entitled 'The Ecstasy'. What Cowley did was to use the last stanza as a pivotal centre, adding an appropriate number of stanzas on an original theme in such a manner that the second thematic movement balances the first through thematic pairing. See my essay on 'Structural Images in Cowley and Herbert: A Comparison', *English Studies*, 54 (1973), pp. 4 f.

I am grateful to H. Neville Davies for drawing my attention to B. Yong's version of Gil Polo's poem.

[40] *L'Harmonie du Monde* (Paris, 1579), pp. 777–79.

[41] I have used the folio edition of Cowley's works published in 1700.

[42] S. K. Heninger Jr in *Renaissance Quarterly*, 25:3 (1972), 335 (in a review of Christopher Butler's book on *Number Symbolism*).

[43] Paula Johnson, *Form and Transformation in Music and Poetry of the English Renaissance* (New Haven and London, 1972), pp. 14 f. See also p. 72, where the point is made that we usually fail to recognise how important a perception of retrospective form is for our understanding of a work. Finally see p. 94 for comments on our attitude to the concept of artistic unity.

[44] Augustine's characterisation of the world as God's poem was well known to the Renaissance, and Cowley refers to it at length in a footnote on the *Davideis*, Book I: 'I have seen an excellent saying of St. *Augustines*, cited to this purpose, *Ordinem sæculorum tanquam pulcherrimum Carmen ex quibusdam quasi antithetis honestavit Deus—sicut contraria contrariis opposita sermonis pulchritudinem reddunt, ita quadam non verborum sed rerum eloquentia contrariorum oppositione sæculi pulchritudo componitur.* And the *Scripture* witnesses, that the World was made in *Number, Weight,* and *Measure;* which are all qualities of a good *Poem.* This order and proportion of things is the true *Musick* of the World . . .' Cowley's Scriptural reference is to *Wisdom* 11:20 *(omnia in mensura, et numero, et pondere disposuisti).*

3. Laid artfully together: stanzaic design in Milton's
'On the Morning of Christ's Nativity'

H. NEVILLE DAVIES

[1]*Poems upon Several Occasions . . . by John Milton*, edited by Thomas
Warton (London, 1785), p. 267.
[2]Sigmund Spaeth, *Milton's Knowledge of Music* (Princeton, 1913),
reprinted (Ann Arbor, Mich., 1963), pp. 90–92; George N. Shuster, *The
English Ode from Milton to Keats* (New York, 1940), pp. 67–70; A. E.
Barker, 'The Pattern of Milton's "Nativity Ode" ', *UTQ*, 10 (1941),
167–81, reprinted in *Milton: Modern Judgements*, edited by A. Rudrum
(London, 1968), pp. 44–57; *Poems of John Milton. The 1645 Edition*,
edited by Cleanth Brooks and J. E. Hardy (New York, 1951), pp. 95–104;
D. C. Allen, *The Harmonious Vision* (Baltimore, Md, 1954), chapter II;
Maren-Sofie Røstvig, 'The Hidden Sense' in *The Hidden Sense and Other
Essays*, by Røstvig et al. (Oslo and London, 1963), pp. 44–58; Jon S.
Lawry, *The Shadow of Heaven: Matter and Stance in Milton's Poetry*
(Ithaca, N.Y., 1968), pp. 27–41; Balachandra Rajan, 'In Order Serviceable',
*MLR*, 63 (1968), 13–22, reprinted as chapter II in Rajan's *The Lofty
Rhyme* (London, 1970); John Carey, *Milton* (London, 1969), chapter II;
Christopher Butler, *Number Symbolism* (London, 1970), pp. 140–43
(although Butler takes issue with Røstvig, he accepts a basis of 9+9+9);
K. M. Swaim, ' "Mighty Pan": Tradition and Image in Milton's *Nativity
Hymn*', *Stud. in Philol.*, 68 (1971), 484–95; *A Variorum Commentary on
the Poems of John Milton*, Volume II, edited by A. S. P. Woodhouse and
Douglas Bush (London, 1972), part 1, pp. 69, 81, 94–95, 109. Bush specifically rejects (p. 48) any division between stanzas 15 and 16 for reasons
strangely at odds with the text of the poem.
[3]Edited by William Haller in *The Works of John Milton*, edited by
F. A. Patterson, 20 vols (New York, 1931–40), IV (1931), p. 342
[4]*Areopagitica*, p. 342. See also James R. McAdams, 'The Pattern of
Temptation in *Paradise Regained*', *Milton Studies*, 4 (1972), 177–93
(p. 177).
[5]See H. N. Davies, 'The Structure of Shadwell's *A Song for St Cecilia's
Day, 1690*', in *Silent Poetry. Essays in Numerological Analysis*, edited by
Alastair Fowler (London, 1970), pp. 205–20. Reference should have been
made in that essay to Hugh Hare, Lord Colarane's translation of Loredano,
*The Ascents of the Soul* (Wing L3065) and his own *La scala sancta* (Wing
L3069) both edited by his wife, Lucy, and published in 1681. Even in the
twelfth century the concept was widely disseminated as chapters IV and V

of the Old Norse Maríu saga demonstrate: see O. Widding and H. Bekker-Nielsen, 'The Fifteen Steps of the Temple. A Problem in the Maríu Saga', *Bibliotheca Arnamagnæana*, 25 (1961), 80–91.

For William Hazlitt, Poussin 'was among painters (more than anyone else) what Milton was among poets' (*Complete Works*, edited by P. P. Howe, 21 vols (London, 1930–34), VIII (1931), p. 169), and this affinity has been recognised by others, too, especially by Mario Praz ('Milton and Poussin' in his *On Neoclassicism*, translated by A. Davidson, 2nd edn (London, 1969), 11–39). Poussin's 'The Holy Family on the Steps,' completed in 1648, depicts the Holy Family positioned on a flight of steps, possibly steps to the Temple, and it has been suggested that these steps allude to Mary as the *scala coelestis* by which the Son of God descended into the world and through which we can ascend to heaven. But the allusion is not numerological since the steps continue outside the picture. See Howard Hibbard's monograph, *Poussin: The Holy Family on the Steps* (London, 1974), chapter IV.

⁶This and other passages are quoted in C. A. Patrides, 'Renaissance Interpretations of Jacob's Ladder', *Theologische Zeitschrift*, 18 (1962), 411–18 (p. 413).

⁷Quoted by Patrides, p. 413.

⁸The numerological plan of *De doctrina* is discussed by M.-S. Røstvig in *The Hidden Sense*, pp. 39–41.

⁹For a fuller discussion of *Paradise Lost*, III, 501–15 and 540–54 see H. N. Davies, 'The Structure of Shadwell's *A Song for St Cecilia's Day, 1690*', pp. 209–215. Milton's poems are quoted from John Carey and Alastair Fowler's Longmans Annotated English Poets edition (London, 1968).

¹⁰See H. N. Davies, 'The First English Translations of Bellarmine's *De ascensione mentis*', *The Library*, 25 (1970), 49–52.

¹¹If God is a joker taunting Satan with the dangling stairs at III. 523–25, as Michael Wilding has it (*Milton's 'Paradise Lost'* (Sydney, 1969), p. 29), then the fifteen-line structure of I. 157–71 may afford a similar cruel joke whereby Satan is made to taunt himself ('my self am hell)'. Alternatively, the structure of Satan's speech may, by dramatic irony, distance the alert reader from the speaker who can be supposed to blunder inadvertently into a symbolic pattern antithetically opposed to what he is saying. In either case, we observe that the newly fallen angel, like a fallen autumn leaf discoloured but not yet decayed, still retains in his mind and instinctively uses patterns associated with his former life, if, that is, the concept of ascent would have had any meaning in a sinless state. But the main point is, of course, that the pattern jars horribly with the sentiment.

¹²*Religio medici* (I.12), edited by L. C. Martin (Oxford, 1964), p. 12.

¹³For Christ as the number fifteen see François Secret, *L'ésoterisme de*

*Guy Le Fèvre de La Boderie,* études de philologie et d'histoire 10 (Geneva, 1969), p. 94. Secret quotes La Boderie's *La Galliade* (1578), fol. 91: 'Mais l'homme. Dieu Jesus, le Christ, l'Oint, le David/Qui de David l'esprit par son esprit ravit, / Du systeme formel est la quinziesme chorde / Et le dixieme neuf du divin Decachorde . . . ' I am grateful to Professor Røstvig for this reference.

14Giles and Phineas Fletcher, *Poetical Works,* edited by F. S. Boas (Cambridge, 1908), I, 78.

15*The Spenserian Poets* (London, 1969), p. 207. See also M. M. Mahood, *Poetry and Humanism* (London, 1950), pp. 171–75.

16Cf., for instance, Hall's stanza 4 and Milton's line 125. The similarity between the two poems was brought to my notice by Mrs E. E. Duncan-Jones but it is interesting that her perception of the relationship was without any reference to number symbolism. My numerological connexion is, therefore, an additional link between poems already recognised as related.

17*Poems of Joseph Hall,* edited by A. Davenport (Liverpool, 1949), p. 4.

18See Kathi Meyer-Baer, *Music of the Spheres and the Dance of Death* (Princeton, N.J., 1970), pp. 80–82, and P. J. Ammann, 'The Musical Theory and Philosophy of Robert Fludd', *JWI,* 30 (1967), 202. In a much less exact form, the scale of music and a ladder linking earth and heaven are still sometimes associated. See, for example, Karen Blixen's story 'The Deluge at Norderney' in Isak Dinesen, *Seven Gothic Tales* (London, 1934), p. 211.

19H. N. Davies, 'The Structure of Shadwell's *A Song for St Cecilia's Day, 1690*', p. 210.

20The symbolism of the numbers alluded to in this paragraph is too common to need careful documentation. Such documentation can be readily found in Vincent F. Hopper, *Medieval Number Symbolism* (New York, 1938; reprinted New York, 1969); Alastair Fowler's two books, *Spenser and the Numbers of Time* (London, 1964) and *Triumphal Forms* (Cambridge, 1970), and a volume of essays collected by Fowler, *Silent Poetry* (London, 1970); and Christopher Butler, *Number Symbolism* (London, 1970).

21Cent. I, med. 60. *Centuries, Poems, and Thanksgivings,* edited by H. M. Margoliouth (Oxford, 1958), I, 31. Cf. Tilley, *Proverbs,* C840.

22(Signifying those who transgress—*literally* 'step beyond'—the decalogue of the Commandments.) Pietro Bongo, *De numerorum mysteria* (Basel, 1618), p. 377. This book is an expansion of Bongo's *Mysticae numerorum significationis* (Bergamo, 1585).

23D. Brooks, 'Symbolic Numbers in Fielding's *Joseph Andrews*' in *Silent Poetry,* p. 259, n. 61, and A. Fowler, ' "To Shepherd's Ear": The Form of Milton's *Lycidas*', *Silent Poetry,* p. 171.

24(The number eleven has no connexion with the divine, or with the heavenly, nor has it any contact, nor is it a ladder pointing to those things that are above.) Bongo (1618), p. 377.

[25]Spenser is quoted from *The Works . . . A Variorum Edition,* edited by E. Greenlaw et al., 9 vols (Baltimore, Md, 1932–57).

[26]See M.-S. Røstvig, '*The Shepheardes Calender*—A Structural Analysis', *Renaissance and Modern Studies,* 13 (1969), 69–71. Cf. Spenser's *Doleful Lay of Clorinda* which also has an 11 +4 structure, though there then follow three more stanzas which return to the mourners. A line from stanza 15, 'There liveth he in euerlasting blis' makes the same point as stanza 15 of Dido's lament (line 194). Hieatt's book about Spenser's *Epithalamion* is *Short Time's Endless Monument* (New York, 1960).

[27]Spenser's 'An Epitaph vpon the right Honourable sir Phillip Sidney knight' has fifteen stanzas. The words quoted are from 'Another of the same' (line 20), a poem of ten stanzas.

[28]Bongo (1618), p. 377.

[29]Bongo (1618), p. 386. Different numbers may, of course, have similar significance, and here the significance of twelve rather resembles that of ten. Douglas Brooks in his *Number and Pattern in the Eighteenth-Century Novel* (London and Boston, Mass., 1973) discusses the change from *eleven* to *twelve.*

[30]*The Hidden Sense,* p. 58.

[31]*A Variorum Commentary on the Poems of John Milton,* Vol. II, edited by A. S. P. Woodhouse and Douglas Bush (London, 1972), part 1, p. 109.

[32]It could be so marked, as has just been observed, in *In obitum praesulis Eliensis;* but in that poem two structural principles are at work: a narrative surface structure indicated by a change of speaker, and a deeper structure recording basic thematic layout. The former is presumably generated from the latter, while the delight given by the poem lies partly in the delicate balance in the narrative between wayward neglect of and boring subservience to the controlling thematic structure.

[33]*English Poetry and Prose, 1540–1674,* edited by Christopher Ricks, Sphere History of Literature in the English Language, vol. II (London, 1970), p. 262.

[34]Balachandra Rajan, *The Lofty Rhyme. A Study of Milton's Major Poetry* (London, 1970), p. 52.

[35]The significance of lines 165–85 forming the *tenth* paragraph of the poem is discussed in J. A. Wittreich, Jr, 'Milton's "Destin'd Urn": The Art of *Lycidas*', *PMLA,* 84 (1969), 60–70 (p. 67). See also Fowler's "To Shepherd's Ear": The Form of Milton's *Lycidas*' in *Silent Poetry,* pp. 171–72.

[36]The symbolism of seventeen as explained by Saint Augustine has been frequently outlined. See, for example, Butler, *Number Symbolism,* p. 27.

[37]Dryden's poem is quoted from *The Works of John Dryden*, III, edited by Earl Miner and V. A. Dearing (Berkeley and Los Angeles, Calif., 1969), pp. 109–15.

[38]John Heath-Stubbs, 'Baroque Ceremony. A Study of Dryden's "Ode to the Memory of Mistress Anne Killigrew" (1686)', *Cairo Studies in English* (1959), p. 80; Arthur W. Hoffman, *John Dryden's Imagery* (Gainesville, Florida, 1962), pp. 105–06.

[39]Hoffman, p. 116.

[40]Cf. the relationship between Spenser's *Epithalamion* and Cowley's 'The Long Life' as described in Alastair Fowler's *Triumphal Forms*, pp. 13–15.

[41]Davies, 'The Structure of Shadwell's *A Song for St Cecilia's Day, 1690*', p. 222. Lines 39–53 of Shadwell's poem employ a rhyme scheme similar to Milton's, and for a similar reason. They differ slightly in that Shadwell ends with a couplet preceded by a triplet while Milton has the couplet before the triplet.

[42]Other aspects of the numerological form of the poem are treated in Fowler's *Triumphal Forms*, pp. 113–15. Fowler rightly rejects the analysis attempted by John T. Shawcross in *Hartford Studies in Literature*, I (1969).

[43]*Lives of the English Poets*, edited by L. A. Hind, Everyman Library, 2 vols (London, 1925), I, 244.

[44]D. B. Morris, 'Drama and Stasis in Milton's "Ode on the Morning of Christ's Nativity" ', *Stud. in Philol.*, 68 (1971), 210–11.

[45]The central stanza of the Ode as a whole is miscalculated as stanza 16 in Fowler's *Triumphal Forms*, pp. 115–16, n. 3.

[46]Quoted from the prompt-book in C. H. Shattuck, 'Milton's *Comus*: A Prompt-Book Study', *JEGP*, 60 (1961), 736.

[47]The printed text (D. H. Stevens, *Reference Guide to Milton*, Chicago, Ill., 1930, item 420), apparently adapted from Macready by Edmund Falconer, is ignored by Shattuck and by the article that Shattuck is supplementing, A. Thaler, 'Milton in the Theatre', *Studies in Philol.*, 17 (1920), 269–308.

[48]'Milton and the New Music', *UTQ*, 23 (1954), 217–26.

[49]*Exhortation to the Greeks*, with an English translation by G. W. Butterworth, Loeb Classics (London, 1919), p. 27.

[50]*Exhortation*, p. 9.

[51]*Exhortation*, p. 13.

[52]See especially pp. 157–63.

[53]The ease of making connexions is particularly evident in Lawrence W. Kingsley, 'Mythic Dialectic in *The Nativity Ode*', *Milton Studies*, 4 (1972) 163–76.

[54]' "To Shepherd's Ear": the Form of Milton's *Lycidas*', in Fowler's *Silent Poetry*, p. 174.

[55]In both poems a poetic gift is important, and the angels in the Ode provide a ready example of those who serve being in attendance. Perhaps, as he looked back over his poetic career when writing this sonnet, Milton remembered his first major poem. The way in which Milton as gift bearer shows his eagerness by beginning the symmetrical pattern of his *Nativity Ode* two stanzas before the expected starting point, is similar to the way in which Jonson demonstrates the officious eagerness of the pikes to present themselves as tribute in *To Penshurst*. Alastair Fowler divides Jonson's poem into three 'draughts', each of seventeen couplets. Violating this formal division, the pikes scrape into the last line of the first draught 'As loth, the second draught, or cast to stay' ('The "Better Marks" of Jonson's *To Penshurst*', *RES*, n.s. 24 (1973), 276). Fowler might also have noted the speed of the 'Fat, aged carps' that enmesh themselves in just one line, and before the end of the first 'draught'.

[56]Lancelot Andrewes, *Seventeen Sermons on the Nativity. A New Edition,* "The Ancient and Modern Library of Theological Literature' (London, n.d.), pp. 253–54.

[57]For a discussion of retrospective form, see Barbara Herrnstein Smith, *Poetic Closure. A Study of How Poems End* (Chicago, Ill., and London, 1968), pp. 11–13, 36–37, and Paula Johnson, *Forms and Transformations in Music and Poetry of the English Renaissance* (New Haven, Mass., and London, 1972), pp. 14–15, 71–74, *et passim*. A retrospective summary of Milton's Ode in the form of a diagram follows this essay.

[58]*The Works of Henry Vaughan*, edited by L. C. Martin (Oxford, 1914), II, 424–25.

[59]*Of Paradise and Light* (Cambridge, 1960), p. 126.

[60]Henry Vaughan may well have been interested in numbers through association with his brother. See *The Works Of Thomas Vaughan*, edited by Arthur E. Waite (London, 1919), pp. 302–06.

[61]See Bjorvand's discussion of the shortened six-line stanza in Spenser's *Hymne of Love*, pp. 26–28, and Røstvig's comments on Giles Fletcher's similar use of a shortened stanza in *Christ's Victory and Triumph*, p. 62.

[62]M. A. Wickert, 'Structure and Ceremony in Spenser's *Epithalamion*', *ELH*, 35 (1968), 135–37. See also Røstvig's analysis of Sidney's epithalamium, pp. 74–77. Three recent books studying this type of structure are A. Fowler, *Triumphal Forms: Structural Patterns in Elizabethan Poetry* (Cambridge, 1970), M. Rose, *Shakespearean Design* (Cambridge, Mass., 1972), and D. Brooks, *Number and Pattern in the Eighteenth-Century Novel* (London and Boston, Mass., 1973). Rose's Chapter 4 should be read in conjunction with K. Brown, ' "Form and Cause Conjoin'd", *Hamlet* and Shakespeare's Workshop', *Shakespeare Survey* 26 (1973), 11–20. It is becoming common to notice structural patterns of this sort, and to refer to them as patterns of 'recessed symmetry'. It is not only in Renaissance

literature that they are to be discovered. What seems like free-flowing association in Molly's monologue at the end of Joyce's *Ulysses* has recently been shown to be organised in eight paragraphs forming an *a b c d d c b a* sequence. See D. Tolomeo, 'The Final Octagon of *Ulysses*', *James Joyce Quarterly* 10 (1973), 439–454.

[63]Carey's translation, p. 119.

4. Dryden's Rahmenerzählung: the form of
*An Essay of Dramatick Poesie*

H. Neville Davies

[1]*The Works of John Dryden*, XVII, edited by S. H. Monk et al. (Berkeley and Los Angeles, Calif., 1971), p. 351. All quotations from the *Essay* are from this edition.

[2]California edition, p. 351.

[3]M. C. Bradbrook, *The Rise of the Common Player. A Study of Actor and Society in Shakespeare's England* (London, 1962), p. 169.

[4]The books mentioned in the foregoing paragraph are most conveniently available as follows: *Tarlton's Newes* in *Tarlton's Jests,* The Shakespeare Society, (London, 1844), a volume that reprints extensive extracts from *The Cobler* in an appendix, *The Tinker of Turvey* (London, 1859), and *Westward for Smelts,* The Percy Society, volume 22 (London, 1848); all three edited by J. O. Halliwell[-Phillipps]. *The Tinker of Turvey* is also to be found in Charles C. Mish's *Short Fiction of the Seventeenth Century* (New York, 1963), and *Tarltons Newes* in facsimile in *The Collected Works of Robert Armin,* edited by J. P. Feather, 2 vols (New York and London, 1972), vol. I. The complete text of *The Cobler,* collating the editions of 1590 and 1608, was edited by Frederic Ouvry (London, 1862): references here are to this edition. Walter R. Davis thinks *The Tinker* 'an interesting revision' subtly structured *(Idea and Act in Elizabethan Fiction,* Princeton, N.J., 1969, p. 240), but I incline to Mish's view that 'Whoever made the alteration was not very well advised' ('English Short Fiction in the Seventeenth Century', *Studies in Short Fiction,* 6, 1969, 265). It is a pity that the title of his anthology led Mish to reprint the inferior adaptation. The possibility that Dryden's *Essay* was based on a derivative of *The Cobler* can be reasonably discounted since the structure of *The Cobler* is more like that of the *Essay* than are those of either *The Tinker* or *Westward for Smelts.* Possibly the adaptations encouraged Dryden to attempt a more radical adaptation. Malone, who possessed a slightly imperfect copy of the first

edition of *The Cobler*, does not seem to have connected the book with Dryden's *Essay*.

[5]*Antecedents of the English Novel 1400–1600 (from Chaucer to Deloney)* (Warsaw and London, 1963), p. 157.

[6]The California editors note that Cicero's *De legibus* 'boasts a river scene' (p. 356, n. 74), but Cicero's location is a rural one on the *banks* of a river, and on an island, and seems to me to be quite unlike Dryden's river setting. There are rivers in Macedon and Monmouth, too.

[7]*Heptameron, or the History of the Fortunate Lovers . . . Now made English by Robert Codrington* (London, 1654), A4 ᵛ.

[8]See also H. James Jensen, *A Glossary of John Dryden's Critical Terms* (Minneapolis, Minn., 1969), p. 41.

[9]'Any comparison with the dialogues of Plato . . . is wildly out of place' asserts George Watson (*Of Dramatic Poesy and Other Critical Essays*, 2 vols, Everyman's Library, edited by G. Watson (London, 1962), I, 12). But perhaps Dryden intends us to draw a parallel between Neander and Socrates as he is presented in the *Symposium*, late for the feast because lost in a fit of abstraction, and, at the end, still talking (about drama) when nearly everyone has gone, two of his last three listeners, the comic dramatist Aristophanes and his host, the tragic dramatist Agathon falling asleep before he has finished, the third listener only half awake. Incidentally, the speakers in the *Symposium* and in Dryden's *Essay* are celebrating victories.

[10]'Defence of the Epilogue' (1672). *Dryden: Of Dramatic Poesy and Other Critical Essays*, edited by G. Watson, Everyman's Library, 2 vols (London, 1962), I, 180.

[11]'Dramatic Poetry: Dryden's Conversation Piece', *Cambridge Journal*, 5 (1952), 553–61 (554).

[12]*The Sceptical Chymist*, edited by M. M. Pattison Muir, Everyman's Library (London, 1937), p. 7.

[13]Cf. Paul Ramsey, *Explicator*, 13 (1955), 46.

[14]The relationship between English naval victory in the battle and English literary victory in the debates was pointed out by Charles Kaplan in *Explicator*, 8 (1950), 36.

[15]George Williamson, 'The Occasion of *An Essay of Dramatic Poesy*', *Mod. Philol.*, 44 (1946), 1–9, rptd in Williamson's *Seventeenth Century Contexts* (London, 1960), pp. 272–88, and *Essential Articles for the Study of John Dryden*, edited by H. T. Swedenberg (London, 1966), pp. 65–82.

[16]John Summerson, *Sir Christopher Wren* (London, 1953), p. 59, gives a short account of the 'contest'.

[17]*A Voyage to England . . . Done into English from the French Original* (London, 1709), p. 5. See also p. 46, and cf. *Observations* (1665), p. 77.

[18]Norman G. Brett-James, *The Growth of Stuart London* (London, 1935), ·d 489.

[19]*Observations*, pp. 167–69. Sorbière's observation of an aggressive attitude was probably not mistaken, though it is a fact that Obdam, the Dutch admiral, had orders to seek his enemy even into the Thames.

[20]*A Voyage*, p. 70. *Observations*, pp. 174, 256–57.

[21]*Observations*, p. 45.

[22]*A Voyage*, pp. 13–14. For current developments in Paris see Michael Greenhalgh, 'Bernini in France, 1665', *History Today*, 23 (1973),398–406.

[23]'A Discourse Concerning the Original and Progress of Satire' (1693). *Dryden: Of Dramatic Poesy and Other Critical Essays*, II, 136–37.

[24]'A Discourse', p. 137.

[25]*A Voyage*, p. 70.

[26]*A Voyage*, p. 5.

[27]*A Voyage*, p. 69.

[28]*A Voyage*, p. 70.

[29]*A Voyage*, p. 3.

[30]A. Guibbory, 'Dryden's View of History', *Philol. Quart.*, 52 (1973), 187–204 (190).

[31]Ouvry's edition, p. 6.

[32]*Decameron* viii, 7; v, 6 and v, 2; vii, 1 and vii, 8; and iii, 8 underlie the last four of *The Cobler of Caunterburie's* six tales.

[33]Cf. *The Decameron . . . Translated into English Anno 1620*, edited by E. Hutton, The Tudor Translations, 4 vols (London, 1909), I, 26–27. All references are to this edition.

[34]J. R. Hale, *England and the Italian Renaissance* (London, 1954), pp. 35–36. The structure of *A German Diet* is somewhat more complex than Hale allows.

[35]See Herbert Weisinger, 'Who Began the Revival of Learning? The Renaissance Point of View', *Papers of the Michigan Academy of Science, Arts, and Letters*, 30 (1944), 625–38 (630).

[36]Preface to *Fables Ancient and Modern* (1700). *Dryden: Of Dramatic Poesy and Other Critical Essays*, II, 271–72. The title-page of the 1620 translation of the *Decameron* calls Boccaccio 'The First Refiner of Italian Prose'.

[37]Masson's translation of letter 8, reprinted in *The Works of John Milton*, edited by F. A. Patterson, 20 vols (New York, 1931–40), vol. XII (1936), p. 33.

[38]John Summerson, *Inigo Jones* (Harmondsworth, 1966), p. 88.

[39]*Inigo Jones*, p. 93.

[40]*The Diary of John Evelyn*, edited by E. S. de Beer, 6 vols (Oxford, 1955), II, 184 (21 October 1644). Inigo Jones, *Stone-Heng*, 2nd. edition [*with related works by Charlton and Webb*] (London, 1725), 'Memoirs', sig. a1ᵛ.

[41]For further description of Covent Garden see James Lees-Milne, *The Age of Inigo Jones* (London, 1953), pp. 84–86. A painting of Covent Garden,

*c.* 1649, is reproduced in the catalogue by John Harris, Stephen Orgel, and Roy Strong of the Jones quatercentenary exhibition held at the Banqueting House, Whitehall, *The King's Arcadia: Inigo Jones and the Stuart Court* (London, 1973), p. 185. Wenceslaus Hollar's etching of St Paul's Covent Garden, *c.* 1640, is reproduced in Margaret Whinney, *Wren* (London, 1971), p. 15, and M. Whinney and Oliver Millar, *English Art 1625–1714,* Oxford History of English Art (Oxford, 1957), pl. 4b.

⁴²Summerson, *Inigo Jones,* p. 75. Webb's drawing is reproduced in *The King's Arcadia,* p. 152. An eighteenth-century engraving of Somerset House, including the water stairs, is reproduced from *Nouveau Théâtre de la Grande Bretagne* (1724) in the California edition of Dryden's *Essay,* facing p. 8. The likely route taken by the four men from the river to Covent Garden, passing Somerset House with its well planned grounds and the Savoy, can be followed in Philippa Glanville's *London in Maps* (London, 1972). Plate X shows a large scale map by Wenceslaus Hollar, *c.* 1658, which gives a vivid three-dimensional effect by representing buildings in isometric projection. The contrast between the layout of Covent Garden and the older, unplanned areas is particularly striking.

⁴³Earl Wasserman, *The Subtler Language* (Baltimore, Md., 1959), pp. 15–33, rptd in *Dryden. A Collection of Critical Essays,* edited by B. N. Schilling (Englewood Cliffs, N.J., 1963), pp. 71–85.

⁴⁴*Observations,* pp. 226–63.

⁴⁵*Restoration and Augustan Prose,* papers delivered by James R. Sutherland and Ian Watt at the Clark Library Seminar, 14 July, 1956, (Los Angeles, Calif., 1956), pp. 5–6. Cf. Sutherland, *On English Prose,* The Alexander Lectures, 1956–57 (Toronto, 1957), pp. 67–68.

⁴⁶*Restoration and Augustan Prose,* p. 16; *On English Prose,* pp. 69–70.

⁴⁷*Epistolæ Ho-Elianæ. The Familiar Letters of James Howell Historiographer Royal to Charles II,* edited by Joseph Jacobs, 2 vols (London, 1892), I, 17.

## 5. Tom Jones and the Choice of Hercules

### M.-S. Røstvig

¹'O great liberality of God the Father! O great and wonderful happiness of man! It is given him to have that which he chooses and to be that which he wills ... At man's birth the Father placed in him every sort of seed and sprouts of every kind of life. The seeds that each man cultivates will grow and bear their fruit in him. If he cultivates vegetable seeds, he will become a

plant. If the seeds of sensation, he will grow into brute. If rational, he will come out a heavenly animal. If intellectual, he will be an angel, and a son of God . . . it is not the rind which makes the plant, but a dull and non-sentient nature; not the hide which makes a beast of burden, but a brutal and sensual soul; not the spherical body which makes the heavens, but right reason; and not a separateness from the body, but a spiritual intelligence which makes an angel.' Pico della Mirandola, *On the Dignity of Man, On Being and the One, Heptaplus* (New York, 1965), pp. 5 f.

²The classical study of this theme in Renaissance art is Erwin Panofsky's *Hercules am Scheidewege* (Leipzig, 1930) published as vol. 18 in the Studien der Bibliothek Warburg. See also note 40.

³*Tom Jones* VII, 2. All quotations are from the Penguin ed. published in 1966.

⁴*Rasselas* ed. J. P. Hardy (Oxford, 1968), ch. 16.

⁵See, for example, Ben Jonson's masque, *Pleasure Reconciled to Virtue* in *Works*, ed. C. H. Herford and Percy and Evelyn Simpson (Oxford, 1925–52), VII, 473–91. For a discussion of the theme, see Edgar Wind, *Pagan Mysteries in the Renaissance* (Harmondsworth, 1967), pp. 81–96.

⁶James Boswell, *The Life of Samuel Johnson, LL.D.* (London: Everyman's Library, 1946), I, 254 f.

⁷Anthony Ashley Cooper, Earl of Shaftesbury, *Characteristicks Of Men, Manners, Opinions, Times* (London, 1727), II, 104 f. All quotations are from this edition.

⁸Shaftesbury, I, 207.

⁹See my study 'Ars Aeterna: Renaissance Poetics and Theories of Divine Creation,' *Mosaic* 3 (1970), 40–61; reprinted in *Chaos and Form*, ed. Kenneth McRobbie (Winnipeg, 1972) pp. 101–19.

¹⁰Shaftesbury, I, 336.

¹¹Shaftesbury, III, 25 f.

¹²Shaftesbury, III, 259–63.

¹³R. S. Crane, 'The Plot of *Tom Jones*,' *Twentieth-Century Interpretations of Tom Jones*, ed. Martin C. Battestin (Englewood Cliffs, New Jersey, 1968), pp. 68–93.

¹⁴Douglas Brooks, 'The Interpolated Tales in *Joseph Andrews* again,' *MP*, 65 (1967–68), 208–13. The tales of 'The Unfortunate Jilt' and 'The History of Two Friends' are seen by Mr Brooks to 'answer each other across the novel. They are linked not only by being based on a common model but also by the similarity of events in each . . . the vain Leonora abandons the worthy Horatio . . . the vain Leonard abandons the innocent and perplexed Paul.' Each tale is interrupted by a scene of frantic activity as when Adams defends Joseph (II, 5) or Joseph Fanny (IV, 11). (This is true of *Tom Jones* as well, where the tales told by the Man of the Hill and by Mrs Fitzpatrick are followed by acts of violence.)

[15]This has been suggested by Douglas Brooks in relation to *Joseph Andrews;* see his essay on 'Abraham Adams and Parson Trulliber: the Meaning of "Joseph Andrews", Book II, Chapter 14,' *MLR*, 63 (1968), 794–801. Brooks sees Parson Trulliber as an incarnation of Gluttony as depicted for example by Cesare Ripa or Spenser (*FQ* I, iv, 21–23).

[16]*The Happy Man, Studies in the Metamorphoses of a Classical Ideal,* Vol. I: 1600–1700 (2nd ed., Oslo, 1962), pp. 227–310. See also Vol. II: 1700–1760 (2nd ed., Oslo and New York, 1971), pp. 184 f.

[17]Reproduced by Ronald Paulson, *Hogarth. His Life, Art, and Times* (New York, 1971), I, 122 (plate 30).

[18]Not included in the modern edition of Shaftesbury's *Characteristics,* ed. J. M. Robertson (London, 1900). As always, my references are to the fourth edition of 1727.

[19]Panofsky, *Hercules am Scheidewege,* p. 155.

[20]Paulson, I, 276.

[21]William Shenstone, *Poetical Works,* ed. George Gilfillan (Edinburgh, 1854), pp. 186–201. Shenstone makes the point usually observed by painters that the breasts of Pleasure are exposed ('Exposed her breast . . . ' line 111).

[22]Reproduced by Panofsky, plate 77.

[23]Paulson, I, 274.

[24]Edgar Wind, ' "Hercules" and "Orpheus": Two Mock-Heroic Designs by Dürer,' *JWI,* 2 (1938–39), 206–18.

[25]Shaftesbury, III, 349.

[26]See George Wither, *A Collection of Emblemes 1635* (Menston, 1968), p. 22 (Emblem I, 22), or the collection to which he is indebted, Gabriel Rollenhagen's *Nucleus Emblematum.*

[26a]See H. Neville Davies, 'Sweet Music in Herbert's "Easter", '*Notes & Queries,* 213 (1968), 95 f. and G. L. Finney, *Musical Backgrounds for English Literature: 1580–1650* (New Brunswick, n.d.), pp. 76–101. Sweet music could pierce the mind and make it receptive to love.

[27]Rudolf Wittkower, 'Chance, Time, and Virtue,' *JWI,* I (1937–38), 313–21.

[28]Wind, *Pagan Mysteries,* p. 103 and plate 54.

[29]Geoffrey Whitney, *A Choice of Emblemes* (1585), p. 121. This device adorns the coins of the Emperor Augustus, as Wind informs us *(Pagan Mysteries,* p. 107).

[30]Wither, *Emblemes,* p. 139 (Emblem III, 5): *'Good* Fortune *will with him abide, | That hath true* Vertue, *for his guide.'*

[31]Wittkower, pp. 316 f. The device is found in Alciati's emblems.

[32]Wind, *Pagan Mysteries,* p. 103.

[33]For an account of this work see Anthony Blunt, 'The Hypnerotomachia Poliphili in 17th Century France,' *JWI,* I (1937–38), 117–37. Passages

from the *Hypnerotomachia* are incorporated verbatim in the fifth book of Rabelais' *Gargantua*. A new translation of the *Hypnerotomachia* into French appeared as late as 1703.

³⁴See note 17.

³⁵Christian versions of the Choice of Hercules would invoke Matthew 7:13–14. An iconographical half-way stage between the mere letter Y and the two hills is represented by emblems showing various objects hanging from each arm of the letter. See Zacharias Heyn, *Emblemata. Emblemes Chrestienes et Morales* (1625), discussed by Purvis E. Boyette, 'Milton's Abstracted Sublimities: The Structure of Meaning in *A Mask*,' *Tulane Studies in English*, 18 (1970), 45.

³⁶G. Karl Galinski, *The Herakles Theme* (Oxford, 1972), p. 93.

³⁷P. 96.

³⁸P. 156.

³⁹P. 234. Handel 'took pains to dissociate his hero from any trace of crudely selfish love' and saw to it that the story was given a happy end. Themes connected with Hercules were popular during the 1740s; to Shenstone's *Judgment of Hercules* (1740) and Handel's oratorio from 1744 must be added Joseph Spence's *Polymetis* (1747) which includes a poem in twenty-seven stanzas on the Choice.

Fielding's own library contained many classical texts concerned with the Hercules myth; see the library catalogue reproduced by Ethel Margaret Thornbury, *Henry Fielding's Theory of the Comic Prose Epic* (Madison, 1931), pp. 168–89. Item 621 is *Xenophontis Opera* (Paris, 1625) where we find the fable of the Choice in Xenophon's *Memorabilia*. Fielding's shelves were stocked with all the important Greek and Latin playwrights including Aristophanes.

⁴⁰See Edgar Wind, ' "Hercules" and "Orpheus",' and Robert E. Hallowell, 'Ronsard and the Gallic Hercules Myth,' *Studies in the Renaissance*, 9 (1962), 242–55.

⁴¹Hallowell, p. 255.

⁴²See note 27.

⁴³Shaftesbury, I, 194–96.

⁴⁴See note 39 for the reference to the catalogue of Fielding's library.

⁴⁵Shaftesbury, I, 332.

⁴⁶Emrys L. Jones, 'The Artistic Form of *Rasselas*,' *RES*, 18 (1967), 387–401.

⁴⁷Paul Fussell, *The Rhetorical World of Augustan Humanism* (Oxford, 1969), pp. 276 f.

⁴⁸C. Rawson, 'Order and Cruelty,' *Essays in Criticism*, 20 (1970), 36.

⁴⁹E. M. W. Tillyard, *The Elizabethan World Picture* (London, 1950), p. 65 aligns the elements and the qualities with the four humours. For a

popular Renaissance survey, see Pierre de La Primaudaye, *The French Academie* (London, 1618), pp. 726–28.

[50]Milton, *Paradise Lost*, V, 181 f. and Augustine, *De doctrina Christiana*, II, xvi, 25. See my discussion of Milton's use of quaternions in 'Images of Perfection,' *Seventeenth-Century Imagery* ed. Earl Miner (Los Angeles, 1971), p. 11.

# 6. Mistaken conduct and proper 'feeling': a study of Jane Austen's *Pride and Prejudice*

## GRETE EK

[1]Alistair M. Duckworth, *The Improvement of the Estate: A Study of Jane Austen's Novels* (Baltimore and London, 1971), p. x.

[2]Besides Duckworth's valuable study, other recent works offering interpretations along such lines are for example A. Walton Litz, *Jane Austen: A Study of Her Artistic Development* (London, 1965), and Kenneth L. Moler, *Jane Austen's Art of Allusion* (Lincoln, Nebraska, 1968). These works reflect the welcome tendency of later years to consider how a social, ethical, and intellectual context finds expression in Jane Austen's novels. The first overt application of the 'art-nature dichotomy' to *Pride and Prejudice* is found in Samuel Kliger, 'Jane Austen's *Pride and Prejudice* in the Eighteenth-Century Mode', *University of Toronto Quarterly*, XVI (1947), 357–70. For a predominantly socio-economic approach, see especially Dorothy van Ghent, *The English Novel: Form and Function* (New York, 1961), David Daiches, 'Jane Austen, Karl Marx, and the Aristocratic Dance', *The American Scholar*, XVII (1948), 289–96, and Mark Schorer, 'Pride Unprejudiced', *Kenyon Review*, XVIII (1956), 72–91. The argument of largely opposing attitudes moving towards synthesis permits a view of Darcy as a character in his own right, not merely as a 'function' subordinated to Elizabeth's development. The approach of Marvin Mudrick, for example, reduces Darcy to a 'choice' for Elizabeth (*Jane Austen: Irony as Defense and Discovery* (Princeton, 1952)). The most recent study that focuses squarely on the heroine's psychology is Darrel Mansell, *The Novels of Jane Austen: An Interpretation* (London, 1973).

[3]Howard S. Babb, who offers an exhaustive analysis of the dramatic function of dialogue in *Pride and Prejudice*, contends that Darcy renounces none of his essential values in the course of the novel, and that Elizabeth comes to endorse his assumptions. See *Jane Austen: The Fabric of Dialogue* (Columbus, Ohio, 1962).

<sup>4</sup>'Mansfield Park', *The Opposing Self* (New York, 1955), pp. 206–7.

<sup>5</sup>*The English Novel*, p. 101. See Ronald Paulson, *Satire and the Novel in Eighteenth-Century England* (New Haven and London, 1967), p. 296, for an excellent analysis of the matchmakers' society.

<sup>6</sup>All citations of Jane Austen's fiction are based on the edition of R. W. Chapman (5 vols., 3rd ed., Oxford, 1933). Page references to *Pride and Prejudice* are inserted directly into the text.

<sup>7</sup>In the first part of his article 'Jane Austen and the Moralists', *The Oxford Review*, 1 (1966), 5–18, Gilbert Ryle discusses Jane Austen's 'wine-taster's technique of comparative character-delineation', involving a differentiation between degrees of the same quality. He pays particular attention to the concept of pride in *Pride and Prejudice*.

<sup>8</sup>Paulson makes this point (see especially pp. 298–301). The tenor of his argument, however, differs from mine in that he sees the basic conflict as one between 'a conventional and limiting system of values and the freedom and integrity of the individual' (p. 301), the ending being partly pessimistic because 'one can never get rid of the Collinses and Wickhams, let alone the Mrs Bennets and Lydias' (p. 304). For a similar interpretation, see D. W. Harding, 'Regulated Hatred: An Aspect of the Work of Jane Austen', *Scrutiny*, VIII (1940), 346–62. I believe that we need to distinguish between a parody of convention—which fools and knaves invariably embrace—and positive norms grounded in sense. See p. 186.

<sup>9</sup>The quotation is from Daiches, 289.

<sup>10</sup>Moler sees the portrait of Darcy as basically inconsistent, ascribing the 'flaw' to remnants of a parody figure in the first version of the novel. Darcy's possible 'ancestors' are also discussed in Q. D. Leavis, 'A Critical Theory of Jane Austen's Writings', *Scrutiny*, X (1941), 61–87, in Henrietta Ten Harmsel, *Jane Austen: A Study in Fictional Conventions* (London, The Hague, and Paris, 1964), and in Frank W. Bradbrook, *Jane Austen and Her Predecessors* (Cambridge, 1966). The charges of inconsistency levelled at Darcy recur with considerable frequency, Mudrick being one of his most prominent detractors. See *Irony as Defense and Discovery*, especially pp. 116–17. For a different view, see Babb.

<sup>11</sup>*Jane Austen: Facts and Problems* (the Clark lectures, 1948; rpt. Oxford, 1967), p. 192.

<sup>12</sup>*Emma*, pp. 98–107.

<sup>13</sup>Mudrick insists that the 'simple' characters are beneath moral judgement. His conception of 'morality' in *Pride and Prejudice* is one that excludes the application of 'conventional' norms: ' . . . the power of choice is all that distinguishes [the individual] as a being who acts and who may be judged' (p. 124). The caricatures cannot choose and thus cannot be judged.

<sup>14</sup>See Wayne C. Booth, *The Rhetoric of Fiction* (Chicago and London, 1961), pp. 243–66.

[15]See Babb for a full treatment of Elizabeth's limitations.

[16]Robert Louis Stevenson's remark is referred to in Elizabeth Jenkins, *Jane Austen: A Biography* (1938; rpt. London, 1948), p. 160.

[17]Babb, p. 114.

[18]The quotation is from Everett Zimmermann, 'Pride and Prejudice in *Pride and Prejudice*', *Nineteenth-Century Fiction*, XXIII (1968), 68. Zimmermann argues against an 'antithetical' interpretation of the novel.

[19]Sheila Kaye-Smith and G. B. Stern, *Talking of Jane Austen* (London, 1943), pp. 56–57.

[20]'Light and Bright and Sparkling: Irony and Fiction in 'Pride and Prejudice', *The Fields of Light: An Experiment in Critical Reading* (1951; rpt. London, Oxford, and New York, 1968), p. 175.

[21]E. E. Duncan-Jones notes that Darcy's opening 'address' (' "In vain have I struggled . . . " ') may be a direct echo of Mr B—'s letter to Pamela announcing his honourable intentions. ' "In vain my Pamela, do I struggle against my affection for you . . . " ' ('Proposals of Marriage in *Pride and Prejudice* and *Pamela*', *Notes and Queries*, CCII (1957), 76). See my note 10.

[22]See W. A. Craik, *Jane Austen: The Six Novels* (London, 1965), p. 79.

[23]Brower, p. 176.

[24]Italics added.

[25]Italics added.

[26]*Emma*, p. 412.

[27]Brower, pp. 180–81.

[28]The most detailed treatment of the Pemberley episode is given by Duckworth. His excellent analysis is too comprehensive to be fully summarised here; let me note briefly that he sees Pemberley as the meeting-point of two attitudes that are partly admirable, partly in need of modification. Darcy's commitment to tradition needs the addition of 'individual energy'; it is Elizabeth who eventually supplies this vitality, after having herself realised that 'individual energy must be generated within social contexts, for, lacking social direction and control, it turns too easily to withdrawal from society, or to irresponsibility and anarchy' (p. 132). I see this antithesis as apparent only.

[29]The tradition of the country house poem is naturally pertinent in this context. G. R. Hibbard in his survey of the genre points out that the country house is expressive of an attitude to life. See 'The Country House Poem of the Seventeenth Century', *Journal of the Warburg and Courtauld Institutes*, XIX (1956), 159–74. C. Molesworth sees this 'attitude' as the poet's ideal conception of the cause-and-effect relationship between virtue and property, pitted against a rising tendency to regard money as the basis of property. See his 'Property and Virtue: The Genre of the Country-House Poem in the Seventeenth Century', *Genre*, I (1968), 141–57. For a discussion of Jonson's *To Penshurst* which focuses on the timeless moral and

even religious significance of the description, see Alastair Fowler, 'The "Better Marks" of Jonson's *To Penshurst*', *The Review of English Studies*, n. ser., XXIV (1973), 266–82. However 'virtue' be defined, the general view remains that 'in every country house poem the structure and the people who inhabit it are the same. Their virtue creates their environment; their environment, their property, is a perfect expression of their virtue.' (Molesworth, 153–54.)—A useful, if necessarily sketchy, review of the emblematic use of the country house in poetry and fiction has been recently provided in Richard Gill, *Happy Rural Seat: The English Country House and the Literary Imagination* (New Haven and London, 1972), pp. 227–52. See especially pp. 243–46, where Gill discusses Jane Austen's place within this tradition: he pays particular attention to *Mansfield Park*, where 'individual characters are portrayed in terms of their contrasting and changing relationships with Mansfield Park and its mode of life' (p. 244). Similarly, 'the good taste manifest at Pemberley deepens Elizabeth Bennet's appreciation of Darcy's qualities' (p. 243). See also Litz, pp. 103–04, for the idea that the Pemberley episode should be interpreted in the light of eighteenth-century conceptions of taste.

[30] *Persuasion*, p. 26.

[31] *Mansfield Park*, p. 22. See also Ann Banfield, 'The Moral Landscape of *Mansfield Park*', *Nineteenth-Century Fiction*, XXVI (1971), 1–24.

[32] Mansell, p. 100.

[33] Review of *Emma*, in B. C. Southam, *Jane Austen: The Critical Heritage* (London and New York, 1968), p. 65.

[34] The quotation is from Van Ghent, p. 108. In *Jane Austen's Literary Manuscripts* (London, 1964), B. C. Southam contends that it is the 'sense of property which warms her heart towards Darcy' (p. 60).

[35] Italics added.

[36] Mudrick, p. 119. Generally speaking, the elopement episode invites scant enthusiasm on the part of critics. Brower, for example, feels that it belongs 'to a simpler world where outright judgments of good and bad or of happy and unhappy are in place' (p. 180).

[37] *Jane Austen: An Interpretation*, p. 101.

[38] A. C. Ward, 'Introduction' to *Pride and Prejudice*, Longmans edition (London, 1958), p. xviii.

[39] Italics added.

[40] *Persuasion*, p. 175.

[41] Cp. *Persuasion*, p. 245. Anne is described as 'Glowing and lovely in sensibility and happiness', which is all the more striking because we have been told that 'her bloom had vanished early' (p. 6).

[42] Chapman, *Facts and Problems*, p. 193. The idea is that of Mary Lascelles (*Jane Austen and Her Art* (London, 1939) ); I have been unable to trace the exact passage.

# Textual appendix

### 'On the Morning of Christ's Nativity'

## I

This is the month, and this the happy morn
Wherein the Son of heaven's eternal King,
Of wedded maid, and virgin mother born,
Our great redemption from above did bring;
5   For so the holy sages once did sing,
  That he our deadly forefeit should release,
And with his Father work us a perpetual peace.

## II

That glorious form, that light unsufferable,
And that far-beaming blaze of majesty,
10  Wherewith he wont at heaven's high council-table,
To sit the midst of trinal unity,
He laid aside; and here with us to be,
  Forsook the courts of everlasting day,
And chose with us a darksome house of mortal clay.

## III

15  Say heavenly Muse, shall not thy sacred vein
Afford a present to the infant God?
Hast thou no verse, no hymn, or solemn strain,
To welcome him to this his new abode,
Now while the heaven by the sun's team untrod,
20   Hath took no print of the approaching light,
  And all the spangled host keep watch in squadrons
     bright?

## IV

See how from far upon the eastern road
The star-led wizards haste with odours sweet,
O run, prevent them with thy humble ode,
25    And lay it lowly at his blessed feet;
Have thou the honour first, thy Lord to greet,
    And join thy voice unto the angel quire,
From out his sècret altar touched with hallowed fire.

## The Hymn

### 1

It was the winter wild,
30    While the heaven-born-child
    All meanly wrapped in the rude manger lies;
Nature in awe to him
Had doffed her gaudy trim,
    With her great master so to sympathize:
35    It was no season then for her
To wanton with the sun her lusty paramour.

### 2

Only with speeches fair
She woos the gentle air
    To hide her guilty front with innocent snow,
40    And on her naked shame,
Pollute with sinful blame,
    The saintly veil of maiden white to throw,
Confounded, that her maker's eyes
Should look so near upon her foul deformities.

### 3

45    But he her fears to cease,
Sent down the meek-eyed Peace,
    She crowned with olive green, came softly sliding
Down through the turning sphere
His ready harbinger,
50        With turtle wing the amorous clouds dividing,

And waving wide her myrtle wand,
She strikes a universal peace through sea and land.


### 4

No war, or battle's sound
Was heard the world around
55    The idle spear and shield were high up hung,
The hooked chariot stood
Unstained with hostile blood,
   The trumpet spake not to the armed throng,
And kings sat still with awful eye,
60 As if they surely knew their sovran Lord was by.


### 5

But peaceful was the night
Wherein the Prince of Light
   His reign of peace upon the earth began:
The winds with wonder whist,
65 Smoothly the waters kissed,
   Whispering new joys to the mild ocean,
Who now hath quite forgot to rave,
While birds of calm sit brooding on the charmed wave.


### 6

The stars with deep amaze
70 Stand fixed in steadfast gaze,
   Bending one way their precious influence,
And will not take their flight,
For all the morning light,
   Or Lucifer that often warned them thence;
75 But in their glimmering orbs did glow,
Until their Lord himself bespake, and bid them go.


### 7

And though the shady gloom
Had given day her room,

The sun himself withheld his wonted speed,
80  And hid his head for shame,
As his inferior flame,
The new enlightened world no more should need;
He saw a greater sun appear
Than his bright throne, or burning axle-tree could bear.


8

85  The shepherds on the lawn,
Or ere the point of dawn,
Sat simply chatting in a rustic row;
Full little thought they then,
That the mighty Pan
90  Was kindly come to live with them below;
Perhaps their loves, or else their sheep,
Was all that did their silly thoughts so busy keep.


9

When such music sweet
Their hearts and ears did greet,
95  As never was by mortal finger strook,
Divinely-warbled voice
Answering the stringed noise,
As all their souls in blissful rapture took:
The air such pleasure loth to lose,
100  With thousand echoes still prolongs each heavenly close.


10

Nature that heard such sound
Beneath the hollow round
Of Cynthia's seat, the airy region thrilling,
Now was almost won
105  To think her part was done,
And that her reign had here its last fulfilling;
She knew such harmony alone
Could hold all heaven and earth in happier union.

### 11

At last surrounds their sight
*110* A globe of circular light,
    That with long beams the shame-faced night arrayed,
The helmed cherubim
And sworded seraphim,
    Are seen in glittering ranks with wings displayed,
*115* Harping in loud and solemn quire,
With unexpressive notes to heaven's new-born heir.

### 12

Such music (as 'tis said)
Before was never made,
    But when of old the sons of morning sung,
*120* While the creator great
His constellations set,
    And the well-balanced world on hinges hung,
And cast the dark foundations deep,
And bid the welt'ring waves their oozy channel keep.

### 13

*125* Ring out, ye crystal spheres,
Once bless our human ears,
    (If ye have power to touch our senses so)
And let your silver chime
Move in melodious time;
*130*    And let the base of heaven's deep organ blow,
And with your ninefold harmony
Make up full consort to the angelic symphony.

### 14

For if such holy song
Enwrap our fancy long,
*135*    Time will run back, and fetch the age of gold,
And speckled vanity
Will sicken soon and die,
    And lep'rous sin will melt from earthly mould,

And hell itself will pass away,
140  And leave her dolorous mansions to the peering day.


### 15

Yea Truth, and Justice then
Will down return to men,
 Orbed in a rainbow; and like glories wearing
Mercy will sit between,
145  Throned in celestial sheen,
 With radiant feet the tissued clouds down steering,
And heaven as at some festival,
Will open wide the gates of her high palace hall.


### 16

But wisest fate says no,
150  This must not yet be so,
 The babe lies yet in smiling infancy,
That on the bitter cross
Must redeem our loss;
 So both himself and us to glorify:
155  Yet first to those ychained in sleep,
The wakeful trump of doom must thunder through
  the deep.


### 17

With such a horrid clang
As on Mount Sinai rang
 While the red fire, and smould'ring clouds out brake:
160  The aged earth aghast
With terror of that blast,
 Shall from the surface to the centre shake;
When at the world's last session,
The dreadful judge in middle air shall spread his
  throne.

### 18

165 And then at last our bliss
Full and perfect is,
    But now begins; for from this happy day
The old dragon under ground
In straiter limits bound,
170    Not half so far casts his usurped sway,
And wroth to see his kingdom fail,
Swinges the scaly horror of his folded tail.


### 19

The oracles are dumb,
No voice or hideous hum
175    Runs through the arched roof in words deceiving.
Apollo from his shrine
Can no more divine,
    With hollow shriek the steep of Delphos leaving.
No nightly trance, or breathed spell,
180 Inspires the pale-eyed priest from the prophetic cell.


### 20

The lonely mountains o'er,
And the resounding shore,
    A voice of weeping heard, and loud lament;
From haunted spring, and dale
185 Edged with poplar pale,
    The parting genius is with sighing sent,
With flower-inwoven tresses torn
The nymphs in twilight shade of tangled thickets mourn.


### 21

In consecrated earth,
190 And on the holy hearth,
    The lars, and lemures moan with midnight plaint,
In urns, and altars round,
A drear and dying sound
    Affrights the flamens at their service quaint;

*195*  And the chill marble seems to sweat,
    While each peculiar power forgoes his wonted seat.


### 22

    Peor, and Baalim,
    Forsake their temples dim,
        With that twice battered god of Palestine,
*200*  And mooned Ashtaroth,
    Heaven's queen and mother both,
        Now sits not girt with tapers' holy shine,
    The Libyc Hammon shrinks his horn,
    In vain the Tyrian maids their wounded Thammuz
        mourn.


### 23

*205*  And sullen Moloch fled,
    Hath left in shadows dread,
        His burning idol all of blackest hue;
    In vain with cymbals' ring,
    They call the grisly king,
*210*      In dismal dance about the furnace blue;
    The brutish gods of Nile as fast,
    Isis and Orus, and the dog Anubis haste.


### 24

    Nor is Osiris seen
    In Memphian grove, or green,
*215*      Trampling the unshowered grass with lowings loud:
    Nor can he be at rest
    Within his sacred chest,
        Nought but profoundest hell can be his shroud,
    In vain with timbrelled anthems dark
*220*  The sable-stoled sorcerers bear his worshipped ark.


### 25

    He feels from Juda's land
    The dreaded infant's hand,

The rays of Bethlehem blind his dusky eyn;
Nor all the gods beside,
225 Longer dare abide,
    Not Typhon huge ending in snaky twine:
Our babe to show his Godhead true,
Can in his swaddling bands control the damned crew.

### 26

So when the sun in bed,
230 Curtained with cloudy red,
    Pillows his chin upon an orient wave,
The flocking shadows pale,
Troop to the infernal jail,
    Each fettered ghost slips to his several grave,
235 And the yellow-skirted fays,
Fly after the night-steeds, leaving their moon-loved maze.

### 27

But see the virgin blest,
Hath laid her babe to rest.
    Time is our tedious song should here have ending:
240 Heaven's youngest teemed star,
Hath fixed her polished car,
    Her sleeping Lord with handmaid lamp attending:
And all about the courtly stable,
Bright-harnessed angels sit in order serviceable.

# Index

# INDEX OF FICTIONAL CHARACTERS

# INDEX OF CRITICS CITED IN TEXT

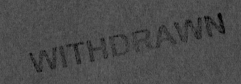